Joseph Smith's POLYGAMY

Joseph Smith's Polygamy

Volume 1: History

Brian C. Hales

with the assistance of Don Bradley

Salt Lake City, 2013
Greg Kofford Books

Copyright © 2013 Brian C. Hales
Cover design copyright © 2013 Greg Kofford Books, Inc.
Cover design by Loyd Ericson

European printing, 2015
Paperback ISBN 978-1-58958-685-7
Hardcover ISBN 978-1-58958-189-0

Photographs designated "Courtesy LDS Church History Library" are courtesy of the Church History Library, the Church of Jesus Christ of Latter-day Saints, Salt Lake City, Utah.

Published in the USA.
All rights reserved. No part of this volume may be reproduced in any form without written permission from the publisher, Greg Kofford Books. The views expressed herein are the responsibility of the author and do not necessarily represent the position of Greg Kofford Books.

Greg Kofford Books
P.O. Box 1362
Draper, UT 84020
www.gregkofford.com
facebook.com/gkbooks

Library of Congress Cataloging-in-Publication Data

Hales, Brian C., 1957- author.
 Joseph Smith's polygamy / Brian C. Hales, with the assistance of Don Bradley.
    volumes cm
 Includes bibliographical references and index.
  ISBN 978-1-58958-189-0 (v. 1) — ISBN 978-1-58958-548-5 (v. 2) — ISBN 978-1-58958-190-6 (v. 3)
 1. Smith, Joseph, Jr., 1805-1844—Family. 2. Polygamy—Religious aspects—Church of Jesus Christ of Latter-day Saints—History—19th century. 3. Polygamy—Illinois—Nauvoo—History—19th century. 4. Church of Jesus Christ of Latter-day Saints—Doctrines. I. Bradley, Don, author. II. Title.
  BX8643.P63H35 2012
  289.3092—dc23
                    2012040061

To Jolie, Christy, James, and Dallin.
3 John 1:4.

CONTENTS

Volume 1: History

1	Joseph Smith's Polygamy: An Introduction	1
2	Joseph Smith's Morality, 1820s to 1835	31
3	Charges of Immoral Conduct against Joseph Smith, 1836-1842	55
4	Fanny Alger and the Beginnings of Mormon Polygamy	85
5	The Joseph Smith-Fanny Alger Relationship: Plural Marriage or Adultery?	107
6	Oliver Cowdery and the Aftermath of the Alger-Smith Relationship	127
7	Oliver Cowdery's Article on "Marriage"	153
8	Pre-Nauvoo Preparations for Plural Marriage	183
9	Eternal Plural Sealings Begin	219
10	October 1841 to June 1842: Ten Additional Sealings	253
11	Sexuality in Joseph Smith's Plural Marriages	277
12	The Puzzle of "Polyandry"	303
13	Joseph Smith and Sylvia Sessions Lyon: Polyandry or Polygyny?	349
14	Sexual Polyandry: Examining the Contradictory Evidence	377
15	Sealings for "Time and Eternity" and for "Eternity Only"	413
16	The Fourteen "Polyandrous" Wives	443
17	Nauvoo Plural Marriage Slowly Expands	475
18	Joseph Smith Marries Additional Plural Wives	497
19	John C. Bennett Impacts Plural Marriage in 1842	515
20	John C. Bennett: Polygamy Confidant or Sexual Opportunist?	547
21	John C. Bennett, Sarah Pratt, and Orson Pratt	575
22	Post-Bennett Resurgence	595

Volume 2 contains a full bibliography and index for Volumes 1–2. See Volume 2 table of contents for the list of appendices.

Tables and Figures

Table 1.1	Plural Marriages, 1841-47	3
Table 1.2	Nauvoo Men Who Entered Polygamy before June 27, 1844	22
Table 1.3	Plural Wives of Joseph Smith	24
Table 2.1	Joseph Smith's Travels through Erie County, Pennsylvania	41
Figure 2.1	Analysis of the Time of Proximity between Emma Smith, Vienna Jacques, Polly Beswick, and Nancy Alexander	51

Table 2.2	Vienna Jacques Timeline	52
Table 3.1	Fawn Brodie's List of Alleged Joseph Smith Plural Wives after Fanny Alger	58
Table 3.2	Twelve Women Alleged to Have Been Sexually Involved with Joseph Smith before 1841	82
Table 4.1	Historical Accounts Referring to a Relationship between Joseph Smith and Fanny Alger	94
Table 4.2	Historical Accounts that Include a Date for the Beginning of the Relationship (Marriage) and/or Aftermath of the Joseph Smith and Fanny Alger Marriage	98
Table 5.1	Joseph Smith and Fanny Alger: Plural Marriage or Adultery?	125
Table 6.1	Timeline of Oliver Cowdery's Possible Plural Marriage/Adultery	133
Table 8.1	Reports of "Angel with a Drawn Sword"	188
Table 10.1	Joseph Smith's Plural Wives, 1841–42	259
Table 11.1	Children Attributed to Joseph Smith	298
Table 12.1	Twelve Statements about Possible Polyandrous Wives	311
Table 12.2	Witness Credibility of Polygynous (Non-Polyandrous) Sexual Relations Compared to Witnesses of Polyandrous Sexual Relations	345
Figure 13.1	Childbearing Chronology of Sylvia Sessions adjacent to Prominent Historical Events	373
Table 14.1	Polyandrous Husbands Identified by Compton: Known Attitudes	394
Table 14.2	Plural Wives as Candidates for Temple Lot Depositions in 1892	407
Table 15.1	Plural Sealings and Proposals in Nauvoo	428
Figure 16.1	Marinda Johnson's Childbearing Chronology and Other Historical Events	453
Figure 16.2	Zina Huntington's Childbearing Chronology and Other Historical Events	461
Table 16.1	Possible Dynamics of Polyandrous Unions	474
Table 19.1	John C. Bennett Letters	534
Table 19.2	Chronology of John C. Bennett's Mormon-Related Life	544
Table 20.1	John C. Bennett's Description of Nauvoo Polygamy	563
Table 20.2	Differences between Joseph Smith's Plural Marriage and John C. Bennett's Spiritual Wifery	565
Table 22.1	Individuals Tried by the Nauvoo High Council, 1841-44, for Sexual Indiscretions	606

Introduction

People commonly ask me why I have become so interested in plural marriage as taught by Joseph Smith and other early LDS leaders. My personal focus began in 1989 when I learned that a close family member had joined the Allred polygamy group. She has since left that lifestyle completely, but her brief involvement is what prompted my own historical inquiry. Through years of study I have become convinced that modern polygamists have no genuine authority to seal marriages and that their plural unions are "not valid" in the eyes of God (D&C 132:18). With the help of J. Max Anderson, author of *Polygamy Story: Fiction and Fact* (Salt Lake City: Publishers Press, 1979), we published *The Priesthood of Modern Polygamy: An LDS Perspective* (Salt Lake City: NPI, 1992).

Years later it became apparent to me that the history of these polygamists, who style themselves as "Mormon fundamentalists," had not been adequately documented and that a historical analysis of their religious movement might be useful. With the help of publisher Greg Kofford and editor Lavina Fielding Anderson, I wrote *Modern Polygamy and Mormon Fundamentalism: The Generations after the Manifesto* (Salt Lake City: Greg Kofford Books, 2006). A three-year research project, it makes more accessible useful information regarding the movement, based on the documents and treating the development of fundamentalism in a way that I hope is even-handed for both polygamists and LDS Church members. It received the "Best Book of 2007 Award" from the John Whitmer Historical Association. Two years later I authored a paperback, *Setting the Record Straight: Mormon Fundamentalism* (Salt Lake City: Millennial Press, 2008) providing an abbreviated view of the movement.

In talking to people about modern polygamous groups, I noticed that about half of the questions posed were about Joseph Smith's polygamy, many of which I could not answer. Eventually I considered tackling another research and writing project. I was aware that delving into such a controversial topic could generate misunderstandings. Yet I was encouraged by Elder Marlin K. Jensen, then Church Historian and Recorder. When an interviewer asked him, "Are there projects that the Brethren would prefer that religious educators or teachers not work on? Are there topics other than the sacred, private, and confidential that we should avoid?" he answered, "I can respond only for myself, but I know of no prohibitions that have been issued. It seems to me if the

Brethren have authorized a 'no holds barred' examination of the Mountain Meadows Massacre,[1] any legitimate project not involving sacred, private, or confidential material might be considered."[2] It appeared to me that a new look at Joseph Smith's polygamy might be useful to scholars, Church members, media specialists, and others attempting to reconstruct Mormonism's early years.

These three volumes represent the culmination of five years of work. Early in the project I enlisted the aid of Don Bradley as my research assistant. He has contributed to this project in innumerable ways; without his help, it could not have been completed. He has sifted painstakingly through the archives of the various repositories throughout the state of Utah and beyond, verifying reference materials cited by other authors, as well as discovering new manuscripts heretofore unknown and unpublished. Significantly, Don appears to have been the first investigator to conduct research in the specific folders in the Andrew Jenson Papers held at the LDS Church History Library that deal with Joseph Smith's polygamy. Jenson used these notes to write his oft-quoted "Plural Marriage" article published in the 1887 *Historical Record*. A landmark article, it acquires even more significance by stepping behind the published version to examine the treasure trove of information regarding Joseph Smith's plurality.[3] For example, Jenson's research notes discuss the Prophet's first plural marriage to Fanny Alger, "eternity only" sealings, issues dealing with sexuality in his plural marriages, the number and identity of the Prophet's polygamous wives, and other topics.[4]

At one point it became apparent that, if we continued searching, it might be possible to acquire copies or transcripts of essentially all of the known documents dealing with Joseph Smith's polygamy and/or sexuality, and to include them in one publication. It would be a large book but could constitute a valuable contribution to understanding the Prophet's plural marriage teachings and practices. Furthermore, by presenting the documents themselves with due attention to the context in which they were created (as opposed to constructing a chronological narrative from the information they contained), significant

---

1. Earlier in the same interview Elder Jensen had mentioned: "A trio of historians—Richard E. Turley Jr., Ronald W. Walker, and Glen M. Leonard—working with Historical Department staff assistance, are finishing a landmark volume on the Mountain Meadows Massacre. . . . [The] publication of the book sometime during this year by Oxford University Press will be a significant event." Elder Marlin K. Jensen and David F. Boone, "A Historian by Yearning: A Conversation with Elder Marlin K. Jensen," *The Religious Educator* 8, no. 3 (2007): 6–7. That work was published in 2008 under the title of *Massacre at Mountain Meadows: An American Tragedy*.

2. Jensen and Boone, "A Historian by Yearning," 13.

3. Andrew Jenson, "Plural Marriage," *Historical Record* 6 (July 1887): 219–40.

4. Andrew Jenson Papers, MS 17956, Box 49, fd. 16, LDS Church History Library.

questions of plausibility, accuracy, generalizability, motives of authors, and authorship of pseudonymous documents could be answered.

In pursuit of that goal, we have consulted hundreds of manuscripts, documents, and books. From the outset, I have maintained a firm commitment not to categorically reject any source of information. Antagonistic, apologetic, and neutral documents have all been given equal consideration and scrutiny. Attempting to evaluate each document in its respective context to determine credibility and potential usefulness, I have included both contemporary sources and those written three and even four generations later. It is my sincere hope that I have overlooked no relevant document. Accordingly, I have attempted to track down and examine every document about which I have learned or which has been cited elsewhere that makes claims about Joseph Smith's polygamy. If in ten years, researchers appraise these three volumes as containing perhaps 90 percent of available evidence, then, as the author, I will be pleased.[5]

My attempt to include all known pertinent evidences dealing with Joseph Smith's polygamy has, of necessity, created a large publication, with the history portion split into two volumes and a third dedicated to an examination of the accompanying theological principles. I alert readers to the fact that at times I have become more of an editor than author as I reproduce lengthy accounts dealing with the founding and flourishing of plural marriage in Nauvoo. In several places, multiple recollections appear as sequential block quotations, even though the different accounts contain redundant information. As a consequence, parts of this text allow participants to tell their own story—and to tell it over and over if multiple narratives are available. Benjamin F. Johnson and Mary Elizabeth Rollins are two examples of participants who left multiple accounts, allowing the reader to see how different accounts focus on different aspects of the experience, adding some details and omitting others. Not all readers will be interested in such close textual work; but it is required to meet my goal for completeness. I have retained original spelling and punctuation unless otherwise noted.

One consequence of this approach is the emergence of a new story about Joseph Smith's polygamy. The most popular view—preached from many American pulpits and editorial desks through the nineteenth century, canonized by Fawn Brodie in the twentieth, and repeated over and over in many subsequent publications—is that the primary drive behind the establishment of plural marriage in Nauvoo, Illinois, in the early 1840s was Joseph Smith's

---

5. Potential sources of future new discoveries of pertinent evidences and manuscripts include (1) documents that are currently available but that I have missed, and (2) still-uncatalogued sources located at various repositories, especially the LDS Church History Library.

desire to expand his sexual opportunities. However, the surviving records from the 115 Mormon men and women who entered polygamy before Joseph's death in June 1844, and others who were taught by him, tell a different story, a story they continued to tell, most of them until their deaths. It is a story of skepticism, sincerity, inspiration, suffering, and blessing.

Volumes 1–2, *Joseph Smith's Polygamy: History*, primarily contains historical evidences, reconstructions, and analysis. Some theological elements, including the practice of polyandry, are also unavoidably explored to provide context for historical events. Wherever possible, however, I extracted theological discussions from the chronological unfolding of the practice of plural marriage for a close-grained examination in Volume 3, *Joseph Smith's Polygamy: Theology*.

I list Don Bradley as my assistant in the authorship of Volumes 1–2, acknowledging his invaluable research, his dogged determination to track down every available source, and his insightful readings of the documents, resulting in suggestions about the implications of both what writers said and how they said it that continually pushed the manuscript toward more careful and more consistent interpretations. He maintained this enthusiasm from the manuscript's inception to its completion. Were it not for his input, the analysis of the historical development of polygamy in Nauvoo would have been much weaker. I also express sincere appreciation to Todd M. Compton and H. Michael Marquardt, who reviewed early drafts of Volumes 1–2 and provided many helpful comments. We do not always agree about the interpretation of a particular document, but the manuscript is much stronger for their candid discussions and interpretations. I am also grateful to Ronald O. Barney, Alexander L. Baugh, Gary J. Bergera, W. Randall Dixon, Jill Mulvay Derr, W. Lawrence Foster, D. Michael Quinn, Alex Smith, and Gregory L. Smith. Likewise, they may not always agree with my interpretations, but they have offered important criticism, suggestions, and encouragement. Ronald E. Romig, Lachlan Mackay, and Mark A. Scherer of Community of Christ have been consistently gracious, helpful, and encouraging in providing indispensable information and interpretation based on their career-long study of Nauvoo sources.

I extend special thanks to R. Jean Addams, Bryon Andreason, Danel W. Bachman, Phillip L. Barlow, Alexander L. Baugh, Christopher Bench, David L. Bigler, Peter J. Blodgett, Drew Briney, Martha Sonntag Bradley, Newell G. Bringhurst, Lisle G Brown, Samuel Morris Brown, Richard Lyman Bushman, LaJean Purcell Carruth, Thomas K. Checketts, Lyndon Cook, Rex E. Cooper, Katrina Denman, Linda Wilcox DeSimone, Ronald K. Esplin, Roberta Fairburn, Jayne Winters Fife, Robert Fillerup, Boyd Fisher, Marcus Flansburg, Craig L. Foster, Kenneth Godfrey, John Hajicek, Van Hale, John Christian Hamer, Erin Jennings, Richard L. Jensen, Robin Scott Jensen,

Dean C. Jessee, Jeffery O. Johnson, Steven L. Johnson, David Keller, Tom Kimball, Larry King, Michael Landon, Stan Larson, Clark Layton, Carol Cornwall Madsen, Gordon A. Madsen, Joshua Mariano, S. Reed Murdock, Carol Holindrake Nielson, Linda King Newell, Connell O'Donovan, Steven L. Olsen, Ugo Perego, Michael Preece, Bobbie Reynolds, Shirley Ricks, Glenn N. Rowe, Robin Russell, William D. Russell, William Shepard, William W. Slaughter, Jonathan A. Stapley, Donna Toland Smart, Mark Lyman Staker, Dan Vogel, Jeffrey Walker, Stan Watt, John W. Welch, David Whittaker, April Williamsen, and Allen Wyatt.

I am also grateful for Greg Kofford, my publisher, for his willingness to produce such a large project without demanding edits that would diminish its completeness. Also I appreciate the personal attention offered by Loyd Ericson who provided editing and typesetting for the volumes. In addition, I thank Lavina Fielding Anderson for her helpful insights, numerous suggestions, expert editing, and friendship.

Chapter 1

Joseph Smith's Polygamy: An Introduction

As a personality of the nineteenth century, Joseph Smith stands out as extraordinary. While many writers have been critical of him and his teachings, most historians are impressed with at least some of his accomplishments, even those who believe he was a charlatan. He published a 500-page book of scripture, organized a new religion, dictated more than a hundred revelations, founded at least three cities, built one temple and began three more, and produced a remarkable theological framework that both expanded and contradicted Christian thinking of the era.[1]

Non-Mormon Harold Bloom, Sterling Professor of Humanities at Yale University, considers Joseph Smith

> an authentic religious genius, unique in our national history. . . . Smith's genius for restoration exceeded that of Muhammad, and the religious necessity and sincerity of Smith's vision are beyond doubt.
>
> There have been many other religion-making imaginations in America before, contemporary with, and since Joseph Smith's, but not one of them came near his in courage, vitality, or comprehensiveness, or in so honest a realization of the consequences of a charismatic endowment. . . . Joseph Smith [was] the most gifted and authentic of all American prophets. . . .
> There is no other figure remotely like him in our entire national history, and it is unlikely that anyone like him ever can come again.[2]

Of all of Joseph Smith teachings and practices, none has been more controversial than plural marriage. Historian Jessie L. Embry postulated why: "Polygamy has an enduring hold on the American imagination for a number of reasons. Its linkage of spiritual claims and sexuality combine two of the strongest human motivations. It has the association of exotic cultures and

---

1. John L. Brooke, *The Refiner's Fire: The Making of Mormon Cosmology, 1644–1844*, xvi.
2. Harold Bloom, *The American Religion: The Emergence of the Post-Christian Nation*, 82, 104, 109–10, 126. Bloom's 1992 complimentary assessment may have evolved over the last twenty years. In a November 12, 2011, *New York Times* article, he referred to Joseph Smith as a "superb trickster and protean personality." Quoted in David Ward, "Scholar Employs Hatchet Opportunism in Mormon Critique," *Deseret News*, November 27, 2011, G7.

bizarre practices."³ The historical record plainly indicates that the Prophet married women polygamously and encouraged other men to do likewise.

Joseph Smith's Polygamy: An Overview

Joseph Smith organized the Church of Christ (now the Church of Jesus Christ of Latter-day Saints) on April 6, 1830. Historical documents indicate that, by the end of the following year, he had concluded that polygamy could be acceptable to God, but he also taught that he was not then permitted to practice it. Evidence supports that, in Kirtland, Ohio, in the 1830s—probably 1835 or early 1836—he experienced his first plural relationship with a domestic in the Smith household named Fanny Alger. That union ended in 1836; and the following year, Church members left Ohio to live in western Missouri, which they were expelled from by 1839.

Settling in a small Illinois hamlet on the Mississippi River which he renamed Nauvoo, the Prophet slowly introduced plural marriage to selected Church members beginning in late 1840. Called a "sealing," Joseph Smith's first polygamous marriage in Nauvoo (and second overall) occurred on April 5, 1841. During the next seventeen months, he was sealed to more than a dozen plural wives. A few other men and women were also invited to participate in the practice, although he never openly taught the principle, so far as records indicate.

By the end of August 1842, Joseph Smith discontinued plural marriages for a period of five months, undoubtedly due to the influences of dissenter John C. Bennett. The Prophet resumed polygamous matrimony in February of 1843, being sealed to more than another dozen plural spouses during the next ten months, bringing the total to more than thirty. Current evidence supports that, after November 2, 1843, during the last eight months of his life, Joseph contracted no new polygamous unions. By the time of Prophet's death on June 27, 1844, an additional twenty-nine other Nauvoo men had married a total of fifty plural wives.⁴

Several different forces combined to create the environment in which Joseph Smith was martyred, but none was more important than his ill-kept secret of plural marriage. (See Table 1.1.)

Controversies in Joseph Smith's Polygamy

Any reconstruction of Joseph Smith's polygamy will encounter multiple controversies and differences of interpretations of the historical record. One involves

---

3. Jessie L. Embry, "Ultimate Taboos: Incest and Mormon Polygamy," 93.
4. See George D. Smith, *Nauvoo Polygamy: "... but we called it celestial marriage,"* 574–656. George D. Smith identifies thirty-two plural husbands and fifty-four plural wives, but data for three of the marriages appear inconclusive.

TABLE 1.1
PLURAL MARRIAGES, 1841–47

Time Period	Joseph Smith	Prior to Joseph Smith's Death (June 1844)	Joseph Smith's Death to the Opening of Nauvoo Temple (Dec. 1845)	Sealed in the Nauvoo Temple (Dec. 1845 to Feb. 1846)	Iowa (March 1846 to July 1847)	Totals
New Male Polygamists	1	29	51	108	7	196
New Plural Wives	35	50	135	263	34	521

contrasting opinions concerning his general reputation during the 1830s and even before. Did it or did it not include licentiousness?

A second area includes Joseph Smith's relationship with Fanny Alger in the mid-1830s. Did it constitute his first plural marriage or was it an adulterous union?

A third issue concerns the types of "sealings" that the Prophet contracted. Were they all for "time and eternity"—that is, for this life and the next, or were some of them for "eternity" only, meaning only after death?

Fourth, debates exist regarding the presence or absence of sexual relations in Joseph Smith's polygamous marriages. What does the evidence indicate concerning his conjugal relations? Was he sexually involved with any, with most, or with all of the women sealed to him?

Fifth, if sexuality was included in his plural unions, were any children born to polygamous wives? What has recent DNA evidence demonstrated concerning the Prophet's possible offspring?

The sixth controversy involves the observation that a number of the Prophet's sealed wives were legally married to other men. Did Joseph Smith practice sexual polyandry (one wife with two husbands)?

A seventh disputed area is the role of John C. Bennett, the mayor of Nauvoo in 1841, who was excommunicated for adultery in 1842. Many authors assume he was a polygamy insider who simply perverted Joseph Smith's teachings. Do available historical data support this position?

The eighth contested topic involves the purported number of Joseph Smith's plural wives. Authors' estimates range from a couple of dozen to perhaps over a hundred. How many women were sealed to the Prophet during his lifetime and what was the nature of those sealings?

A ninth concern exists regarding two of the Joseph's plural wives who were fourteen when they were sealed to him. Was he engaged in sexual ephebophilia (the attraction of older individuals to adolescents)?

The tenth problematic topic stems from two dozen or so allegations that Joseph Smith was sexually involved with non-wives—women to whom he was not married. By his own teachings, such relationships would have constituted adultery. Did Joseph Smith ever have sexual relations with a woman to whom he was not married?

An additional concern involves Joseph Smith's public denials that indicated that he was not practicing polygamy although privately he was married to several plural wives. What were the circumstances and the nature of his disclaimers? If deception was involved, was it isolated to this single issue or is there documentation that it spread to other areas of his life? Does the evidence support that he was a charismatic hypocrite who taught one standard and obeyed another?

Lastly, what were the reaction and involvement of Joseph Smith's legal wife, Emma Hale Smith? Did she ever accept plural marriage? How would we characterize her relationships with her husband's plural wives? Is there evidence that she ever doubted the Prophet's true motivations in establishing polygamy among the Latter-day Saints?

This book will address each of these controversies specifically, with a thorough discussion of all known historical documents pertaining to each issue. Through this process, I hope that the most reliable interpretation of Joseph Smith's plural marriage behaviors will become clearer.

Plural Marriage after Joseph Smith's Death

After Joseph Smith's martyrdom, plural marriage continued as a well-known secret among many Church members, expanding under the direction of the presiding Quorum of the Twelve Apostles. Brigham Young controlled all new sealings, using this critical Joseph Smith teaching as a means of emphasizing continuity in leadership, building internal unity, and linking the practice indissolubly with the more visible public symbol of the temple. In February 1846, the Latter-day Saints exodus west had begun. Pausing for another year on the Iowa frontier, they bade the United States good-bye in 1847 and were soon in an area where plural marriage could be openly practiced and eastern citizens' public opinions could not be enforced.

It was not until August 1852 that the Saints publicly acknowledged the practice and doctrine, following up with energetic public defenses, both by missionaries and in publications.[5] Ten years thereafter came the first federal legis-

---

5. See Davis Bitton, "Polygamy Defended: One Side of a Nineteenth-Century Polemic," in his "The Ritualization of Mormon History," 34–53; and his "The

lation against polygamy, with more to follow. The government stepped up its anti-polygamy campaign until 1890, when the U.S. Supreme Court upheld laws that disfranchised the Church and confiscated much of its property. With missionary work and temple work hindered, Church President Wilford Woodruff issued an inspired Manifesto removing the mandate to continue contracting new plural marriages from the Latter-day Saints. Church leaders continued to grant secret permission for new polygamous unions to a few Church members each year until 1904 when Wilford Woodruff's successor, Joseph F. Smith, issued a Second Manifesto, thereby withdrawing permission for any new polygamous marriages.[6] After repeated warnings, Church leaders began in 1909 taking action against the membership of those who continued to enter new plural unions.

Over about twenty years, scattered individuals in and out of the Church attempted to practice plural marriage without permission from the Church president. Between 1904 and the 1920s, no organization existed among these maverick pluralists, nor did they assert the possession of special priesthood keys that transcended Church authority. However, starting in 1921, Lorin C. Woolley claimed ordination to a previously unheard-of priesthood office as a member of an unknown authoritative council that ostensibly could authorize new plural marriages. In 1935, Elden Kingston asserted his own unique authority to practice polygamy. Twenty years later, the LeBaron brothers arrived with their own distinctive offices and authorities. During these years and afterwards, dozens of other "Mormon fundamentalist" polygamists entered the scene with their novel interpretations and priesthood claims.[7]

Today the Church of Jesus Christ of Latter-day Saints excommunicates anyone preaching or practicing plural marriage, confirms that officiators in such marriages possess no genuine priesthood authority to perform them, and denies any validity to such unions. Yet upwards of 38,000 individuals, most of them in the Mountain West claim a tie to Joseph Smith's polygamy and have chosen that lifestyle.

Latter-day Saints believe that between 1830 and April 1904, God directed the process through which its theologically distinctive marital relations came full circle. The early 1830s standard of strict *monogamy* expanded to *permit* polygamy. Then in 1852 plural marriage was officially considered a *com-*

Ritualization of Mormon History," *Utah Historical Quarterly* 43 (Winter 1975): 67–85.

6. On January 11, 1900, at a meeting of the First Presidency and the Quorum of the Twelve: "Elder John Henry Smith asked President Snow if he thought it was wise for the brethren to speak from the public stand on the principle of plural marriage. President Snow answered that the subject should be let alone and that there was too much being said about it already." *Minutes of the Apostles of the Church of Jesus Christ of Latter-day Saints, 1900–1909*, 5.

7. See Brian C. Hales, *Modern Polygamy and Mormon Fundamentalism: The Generations After the Manifesto*. See also Brian C. Hales, *Setting the Record Straight: Mormon Fundamentalism*.

mandment to all Church members. Thirty-eight years later, the directive was removed through the issuance of the 1890 Manifesto, but plural unions were still secretly *permitted* for fourteen more years. Joseph F. Smith's 1904 declaration blocked all new authorizations for plural marriage reinstating *monogamy* as the only acceptable marital form.

Echoes and shadows of polygamy persist among splinter groups today, but comparing their efforts to Joseph Smith's polygamy demonstrates overwhelming dissimilarities, which lie outside the scope of this study.

A Brief Historiography of Joseph Smith's Polygamy

Over the century and a half since the Prophet's death, very few publications have addressed Joseph Smith's polygamy in any depth. The only recorded public statements made by him and his associates were carefully worded denials that the Saints were engaged in its practice. No authorized publications discussing the practice were printed during his lifetime. In the five decades immediately following Joseph Smith's death, no Latter-day Saint attempted to reconstruct the process through which plural marriage unfolded in the Prophet's life and among early Church members.

One series of events helped to preserve the memories of Nauvoo polygamists. Ironically, it arose from the scattered visits of missionaries from the Reorganized Church of Jesus Christ of Latter Day Saints (RLDS Church, now Community of Christ) to Utah.[8] On several occasions in the 1860s and

---

8. Roger D. Launius, *Joseph Smith III: Pragmatic Prophet*, 233, provided this view of the interaction between Joseph Smith III, president of the Reorganized Church of Jesus Christ of Latter Day Saints and his cousin, LDS apostle Joseph F. Smith: "One relative in the Great Basin, however, seemed to avoid Joseph [Smith III] during his first weeks in Salt Lake City. Joseph F. Smith, an apostle in the movement and the member of the family with the most authority in the Mormon hierarchy, was antagonistic toward the Reorganization and had taken a lead in defending plural marriage from its attack. He had begun in 1869 collecting evidence of Joseph Smith, Jr.'s involvement in the institution, and eventually compiled several hundred affidavits [sic] of witnesses and other documents demonstrating his complicity. Considerable animosity apparently existed between Joseph Smith [III] and this Utah cousin. Joseph F. Smith may also have shunned Joseph Smith III because of comments attributed to the Reorganized Church president in the *Tribune*. In discussing the succession question of the Utah Mormon church, Smith had told a *Tribune* reporter that he thought that when Brigham Young died several men could assert claims to the prophetic office. Smith believed that Brigham Young, Jr., known derogatorily as 'the fat boy'; John Taylor, the able president of the Twelve Apostles; and Joseph F. Smith would each try to attain the office. But [Joseph] Smith [III] accused his cousin of hungering for power, for he 'will claim the leadership, as the most faithful one nearest of kin to the original prophet.' Joseph F. may well have been upset by this obvious defamation" (internal references omitted). Launius's estimate of "hundreds" of affidavits is excessive. See also Roger D.

1870s, the sons of Joseph and Emma visited the West, preaching, among other gospel principles, their firm beliefs that that their father had nothing to do with polygamy and that it was a post-Nauvoo creation of Brigham Young.[9] The first was an 1866 visit from Alexander Hale Smith, who was en route to his mission field in California. He preached in Salt Lake City and had a sharp exchange of views with his cousin, LDS Apostle Joseph F. Smith. Alexander's relationship with his other cousins, Patriarch John Smith and Samuel H. B. Smith, were pleasant and cordial, though he was disappointed that they sidestepped a full discussion of polygamy.[10]

Alexander returned three years later accompanied by his youngest brother, David Hyrum. Joseph F. Smith wrote on July 13 to Martha Smith Harris, the daughter of Samuel Harrison Smith and, hence, first cousin not only to Joseph F. but also to Alex and David: "Alexander and David Smith are expected in town daily—they are coming full of bitterness & hatred toward polygamy and Utah Mormons."[11] A San Francisco paper reported that "David Smith preached against the errors which he says have been grafted on the doctrines of Joseph Smith since his death" and that the LDS Church was "determined to hold a series of meetings to answer the statements of David Smith."[12]

In preparation for his cousins' visit in the summer of 1869, Joseph F. Smith sought to record the testimonies of Nauvoo polygamists still living. Unfortunately, he did not keep a journal for this period, so his thinking and internal commentary on this project cannot be known. By August 1, he had contacted many of them obtaining fourteen affidavits from twelve of Joseph Smith's plural wives, along with attestations from seven other men and women who had been sealed in plural marriages during the Prophet's lifetime, and nine additional testimonies to Joseph's personal involvement, which together could refute Alexander and David Smith's claims.[13] Five of the testimonials were on separate sheets,

---

Launius, "Politicking against Polygamy: Joseph Smith III, the Reorganized Church, and the Politics of the Antipolygamy Crusade, 1860–1890," 35–44.

9. Valeen Tippetts Avery, "Irreconcilable Differences: David H. Smith's Relationship with the Muse of Mormon History," 3–13.

10. Alexander Hale Smith, "Account," 349–51; Alexander Hale Smith, quoted in Richard and Pamela Price, "LDS Leaders Accused Oliver Cowdery of Polygamy," 25–26.

11. Joseph F. Smith, Letter to Martha Smith Harris, July 13, 1869.

12. Our Own Correspondent, "The Mormon Church War," *Daily Evening Bulletin* (San Francisco), September 1, 1869. I have rearranged the sentence order.

13. William Clayton, Letter to Madison M. Scott, November 11, 1871, lamented the claims of "sons of the Prophet": "As to young Joseph Smith saying that the church here have apostatized; that *we* have introduced polygamy, denying bitterly that his father ever had a revelation on the subject, that is all mere bosh! *I believe* he knows better, and I have often felt sorry to learn that the sons of the prophet should spend their time in contending against a pure and holy principle which their father had his blood shed to

In 1869–70, Joseph F. Smith accumulated dozens of affidavits in four composition books, all documenting Nauvoo plural marriage. Courtesy of the LDS Church History Library.

while the remaining twenty-five were compiled into composition books. Apostle Joseph F. Smith had generated an impressive arsenal to defend the Utah Church's stance. Even after the visit of the RLDS missionaries, Elder Smith continued his accumulation until April 23, 1870. By that time he had forty-four recorded in his affidavit books and thirteen on separate sheets for a total of fifty-eight separate affirmations.[14]

An article in a San Francisco paper quoted Joseph F. Smith as saying that to show that his uncle, the Prophet, was a polygamist, "he would present the affidavits of twelve women now living that they were the spiritual wives of Joseph Smith, and so continued to the time of his death; that he had the evidence of hundreds of men who had been taught the doctrine by Joseph and Hyrum."[15] While Joseph F. Smith may have overstated his case, he did indeed possess twelve signed affidavits from the Prophet's plural wives and eighteen other affidavits. Perhaps as many as two and three hundred men and women had been involved in Nauvoo polygamy; but by 1869, many of them had died. Joseph Smith III and his brothers were apparently aware of their cousin's claims. On August 3 from Salt Lake City, Alexander Smith wrote to his older brother, RLDS President Joseph Smith III, in Illinois, before they had met with Joseph F., "Joseph F. has armed himself with the affidavits of some twenty-five or thirty (so I am told) women in the Territory, who declared they belonged to our father, etc., and these are the weapons they expect to use against us."[16] In the subsequent confrontation, Joseph F. Smith did refer to the affidavits and may have quoted from them, but

---

establish. They will have a heavy atonement to make when they meet their father in the next world. They are in the hands of God, and my respect for their father will not permit me to say much about the wicked course of his sons" (emphasis his).

14. Affidavit Book 2 also contain an additional testimony from Bathsheba Smith dated November 19, 1903. Whether this was solicited personally by Joseph F. Smith or simply added by a Church historian is unknown.

15. Our Own Correspondent, "The Mormon Church War."

16. Alexander H. Smith, Letter to Joseph Smith III, August 3, 1869, in *The RLDS Church History Set*," DVD (Independence, Mo.: Christian Technologies, 2006).

they were not published until ten years later.[17] Despite the bitter feelings between the two branches of the Smith family, the resistance of Joseph and Emma's sons to the claims that Joseph Jr. had introduced polygamy was actually important in producing first-hand witness statement that might never otherwise have existed.

Ultimately, Joseph F. Smith compiled two books of affidavits and two nearly identical duplicate books, all bearing original signatures. He kept two in his own possession (labeled Books 1 and 2) and two were stored at the Church Historian's Office (later labeled Books 3 and 4). All four are now housed in the LDS Church History Library.[18]

Several years afterwards Joseph F. Smith wrote to Orson Pratt, an apostle senior to him in the Twelve, referring to the process through which his affidavit books were produced:

> A few years ago [May 1869 to April 1870] I obtained the affidavits of as many as I knew of, with a few exceptions, who received personal instructions or commandment from The Prophet respecting the Subject of celestial marriage [,] all of which are filed away in the H.O. [Historian's Office]. . . . When the subject first came before my mind I must say I was astonished at the scarcity of evidence, I might say almost total absence of direct evidence upon the Subject. as connected with the Prophet Joseph himself. There was nothing written and but few living who were personally knowing to the fact that Joseph Taught the principle. True much had been written in support of the Doctrine, bearing upon scriptural—and rational evidences, but not a word. except the Revelation itself. Showing that The Prophet was the Author—under God. . . . Such testimonies may not appear very important just now. Perhaps not while personal witnesses are living. And perhaps I might not live to witness their true value but my children may. I am in favor of leaving no vacancies in the foundation walls, but want to see them laid solid, at least so far as the record of facts, may be truthfully and consistently made.[19]

Considering the voluminous and energetic defenses of the principle of plural marriage that Mormons had mounted since the public announcement in 1852 that were almost exclusively doctrinal in their approaches, it is understandable that Elder Joseph F. Smith "was astonished at the scarcity of evidence, I might say almost total absence of direct evidence upon the Subject" regarding

---

17. "Joseph the Seer's Plural Marriages," *Deseret News*, October 22, 1879, 604–5. The publication of some of the affidavits was undoubtedly designed to refute Emma Smith's denial on February 5, 1879, that Joseph practiced polygamy. She died weeks later on April 30, but the interview was not published until October. "Last Testimony of Sister Emma," *Saints' Herald*, October 1, 1879, 289–90.

18. All four are catalogued as MS 3423.

19. Joseph F. Smith, Letter to Orson Pratt Sr., July 19, 1875.

its historical unfolding and the Prophet's personal involvement.[20] Accordingly, Joseph F. Smith's collection of manuscripts and documents has become a major cache of information and is housed at the LDS Church History Library.[21] Seven of the affidavits were printed in the *Deseret News* in 1879,[22] but no one apparently used the collection to synthesize a history of polygamy at that time or for decades afterwards.

The first LDS author to seriously tackle Joseph Smith's involvement with plural marriage was Andrew Jenson, publisher of the *Historical Record: A Monthly Periodical Devoted Exclusively to Historical, Biographical, Chronological, and Statistical Matters*, printed between 1882 and 1890. Although Jenson is best known as an assistant Church historian, he was an independent researcher during these eight years. He was not set apart as a "historian in Zion" until April 16, 1891.[23] Even more interesting there is no evidence that he had access to the Joseph F. Smith affidavit books until at least the 1890s.

However, Jenson contacted a few of Joseph Smith's plural wives, but his notes do not list the women he attempted to interview. Ten of Joseph's wives were still alive at that point.[24] Available documents show that he asked at least Eliza R. Snow Smith Young, Zina Diantha Huntington Jacobs Smith Young, and Malissa Lott Smith Bernhisel Willes for dates, locations, sealers, and witnesses to Nauvoo plural marriages. He also wrote letters to members of their families requesting information and enlisted the assistance of *Woman's Exponent* editor, Emmeline B. Wells.[25] On March 12, 1887, Emmeline wrote to Mary Elizabeth Rollins Lightner Smith: "I write to ask you to prepare a careful sketch of your life for publication in the *Historical Record* along with others of the wives of Joseph Smith the Prophet. . . . Aunt Eliza [Snow] asked me to write you and

---

20. Ibid.

21. Joseph F. Smith, Affidavits, Ms 3423, Affidavit Books 1–4. See Vol. 2, Appendix C, which summarizes the affidavit books and their contents, and discussion in Chapter 13.

22. "Joseph the Seer's Plural marriages," *Deseret News*, October 22, 1879, 604–5.

23. For Jenson's setting apart date of April 16, 1891, see Andrew Jenson, *Autobiography of Andrew Jenson: Assistant Historian of the Church of Jesus Christ of Latter-day Saints*, 193.

24. Included were Eliza R. Snow (d. 1887), Zina Diantha Huntington Jacobs (d. 1901), Presendia Huntington Buell (d. 1892), Mary Elizabeth Rollins Lightner (d. 1913), Patty Bartlett Sessions (d. 1892), Martha McBride Knight (1901), Emily Dow Partridge (d. 1899), Almera Johnson (d. 1896), Lucy Walker (d. 1910), Helen Mar Kimball (d. 1896), and Malissa Lott (d. 1898). To simplify references to these women, some of whom were many times married, I usually refer to them by their birth names only; however, the bibliography includes "see" references under all of their married names.

25. See, for example, Marietta Holmes Welling June 30, 1887 letter to Andrew Jenson concerning her mother, Elvira Ann Cowles Holmes, and her plural marriage to Joseph Smith. Document 6, Andrew Jenson Collection, MS 17956, Box 49, fd. 16. As of this writing, this collection has not been fully catalogued.

ask you to prepare this and sent her love."[26] On June 22, Zina D. H. Young also wrote Lightner: "Brother Andrew Jenson, the historian was in yesterday. He is making quite a success in getting up the \brief record of/ the wives of President Joseph Smith."[27]

In July 1887, Jenson published a twenty-seven page article, "Plural Marriage," in his monthly *Historical Record*. It identified by name twenty-seven plural wives of Joseph Smith.[28] He also reprinted all seven of the Joseph F. Smith affidavits that the *Deseret News* had printed in 1879 and added several more new attestations.[29] Jenson's historical outline was not greeted with enthusiasm by all Church leaders at the time. President John Taylor died in hiding in July 1887; and, on August 6, his successor, Wilford

Andrew Jenson. Brian C. Hales Collection.

Woodruff, wrote Jenson: "The attention of the Twelve has been called to your number of the 'Historical Record' for July 1887, in which you publish a list of names of women who were sealed to the Prophet Joseph. We do not question your good desires in making these names public, but we are led to question the propriety of giving this publicity to them at the present time. . . . Advantage may be taken of their publication and, in some instances, to the injury, perhaps, of families or relatives of those whose names are mentioned."[30] Woodruff had reasons for his misgivings. Harsh federal legislation had been passed recently: the Edmunds Act in 1882 and the Edmunds-Tucker Act just five months earlier in 1887. Church leaders made a sixth desperate attempt to achieve statehood, holding a constitutional convention in late June that the voters "almost unanimously approved . . . in August." (After two years of negotiations, it failed to pass in Congress.) As historians James B. Allen and Glen M. Leonard note: "Church leaders deemed it prudent to remain silent on the issue of plural marriage. Beginning in 1887, they rarely if ever discussed the principle in public discourse. They counseled Church publications to refrain from bringing it up at

---

26. Emmeline B. Wells, Letter to Mary Elizabeth Rollins Lightner, March 12, 1887.

27. Zina Diantha Huntington Young, Letter to Mary Elizabeth Rollins Lightner, June 22, 1887, 2.

28. Andrew Jenson, "Plural Marriage," *Historical Record* 6 (July 1887): 233–34.

29. Several of these affidavits were originally recorded in the Joseph F. Smith, Affidavit Books. See Appendix C.

30. Wilford Woodruff, Letter to Andrew Jenson, August 6, 1887.

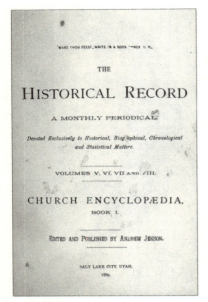

Title page of the bound version of the *Historical Record* and first page of Jenson's article on plural marriage. Brian C. Hales Collection.

that particularly crucial time."[31] Clearly, Jenson was out of step with his leaders by launching his documentation project at this point.

In September 1890 when Wilford Woodruff's Manifesto withdrew official support for new plural marriages, the time seemed even less propitious for a public discussion of Nauvoo polygamy. But one year later in 1891, documenting polygamy received concentrated and historically valuable attention. The RLDS Church led by Joseph Smith III sued the Church of Christ (Temple Lot),[32] disputing its claim to own the temple lot in Independence, Missouri, that Edward Partridge, acting for the Church, had purchased in 1831 and which his widow, Lydia, had sold in 1848 to finance her family's trek west.[33] The Church of Christ (Temple Lot) held physical possession, and the RLDS Church took the official position that, since it was the true successor

---

31. James B. Allen and Glen M. Leonard, *The Story of the Latter-day Saints*, 2d ed., rev. and enl., 413.

32. Known colloquially as "Hedrickites" after Granville Hedrick, who was ordained the church's first leader in 1863. They prefer the title of "Church of Christ (Temple Lot)."

33. B. C. Flint, *An Outline History of the Church of Christ (Temple Lot)*, 112. The term "Temple Lot" is not an official part of this church's name but is frequently added parenthetically to differentiate it from many other churches with similar names.

of the church originally founded by Joseph Smith, it owned the property outright.[34] Although the LDS Church was not a party to the suit, it provided support to the Church of Christ (Temple Lot). The issue was parsed this way: If the Church of Christ (Temple Lot) could prove that plural marriage was part of the original Church, then the RLDS Church was obviously not the true successor since it failed to practice such a key doctrine. The trial court for the Western District of Missouri ruled in favor of the Reorganized Church, but the United States Court Eighth Circuit Court of Appeals reversed the ruling, and the Church of Christ (Temple Lot) retained the property. Ironically, it was staunchly opposed to plural marriage and seemed to have pursued polygamy as a line of inquiry only for strategic purposes.[35]

During the proceedings, the RLDS complainants called numerous witnesses to establish the absence of plural marriage in Nauvoo during Joseph Smith's lifetime.[36] Depositions were taken in Salt Lake City where the respondents (Church of Christ) summoned their witnesses, primarily members of the Utah Church, to affirm polygamy as both a teaching and practice during the Nauvoo period. They included three plural wives of Joseph Smith (Lucy Walker, Emily Partridge, and Malissa Lott). The Temple Lot case transcript, as it is popularly known, comprises more than 1,700 pages.[37] Although the testimonies are all late recollections, the details provided are a rich and informative body of publicly available information.[38]

The next significant publication devoted to polygamy was written by Joseph Fielding Smith, son of then-President of the Church, Joseph F. Smith, entitled: *Blood Atonement and the Origin of Plural Marriage* (Salt Lake City: Deseret News, 1905). It contained transcripts of eleven of the fifty-eight affidavits that his father had compiled in 1869–70. Joseph Fielding Smith also included the first publication of nine additional testimonials recorded between 1871 and 1903 affirming Joseph Smith's personal involvement in Nauvoo polygamy.[39]

---

34. S. Patrick Baggette II, "The Temple Lot Case: Fraud in God's Vineyard," 136.

35. See R. Jean Addams, "The Church of Christ (Temple Lot) and the Reorganized Church of Latter Day Saints: 130 Years of Crossroads and Controversies," 29–53.

36. Those quoted in later chapters attesting to the practice of Nauvoo polygamy are Mary Eaton, John H. Carter, John Taylor (not the apostle), Williard Griffith, John Hawley, and James Whitehead.

37. A 507-page edited version has been published and distributed by several booksellers including Herald House and Price Publishing Company; however, the heavy editing makes it of little use to polygamy researchers.

38. The originals are housed at the Eighth District Court in Kansas City, Kansas, with a carbon copy at the Community of Christ Archives and both a microfilm and digitized microfilm at the LDS Church History Library.

39. The nine testimonials were from Lucy Walker (1902), Catherine Phillips Smith (1903), Almira W. Johnson Smith Barton (1883), William Clayton (1871), Howard

Fawn Brodie, taken about 1945 when she published *No Man Knows My History*. Courtesy of Newell Bringhurst.

Nine years later came the first in-depth treatise from an antagonistic writer. In 1914, Charles A. Shook, who was raised in an RLDS family but later apostatized, wrote *The True Origin of Mormon Polygamy*, which focused extensively on the RLDS position and provided an analysis of historical data that excelled previous polygamy works in breadth and comprehension.[40] Lawrence Foster praises Shook for "reproduc[ing] and skillfully analyz[ing] most of the early evidence."[41] Additional documentation has emerged to supersede some of Shook's conclusions, but his effort was remarkable for the time.

Decades later in 1945, Fawn Brodie, niece of Church President David O. McKay, wrestled with polygamy in her landmark biography of Joseph Smith, *No Man Knows My History*. Brodie wrote to Claire Noall in 1943: "I think polygamy was disguised whoredom. But the disguise was so good that it metamorphosed the system into something quite different. After all the difference between fornication and sacred matrimony is merely a few mumblings from any mangy justice of the peace."[42] This view is reflected throughout her book as she spins her interpretation of Joseph Smith's polygamy. In spite of its cynical outlook, psychologist Charles L. Cohen correctly acknowledged: "Over the years *No Man Knows My History* has more powerfully influenced how both professional historians and the wider public view Joseph Smith than has any other single text."[43]

In the 1940s and 1950s, sociologist Kimball Young conducted oral interviews of members of "about seventy-five families" whose ancestors partici-

---

Coray (1882), Leonard Soby (1886), John W. Rigdon (1905), Orange L. Wight (1905), and Bathsheba W. Smith (1903). See Joseph Fielding Smith, *Blood Atonement and the Origin of Plural Marriage*, 67–88.

40. Shook was also the first to print an important 1885 affidavit from William Law. Charles A. Shook, *The True Origin of Mormon Polygamy*, 124–28.

41. Lawrence Foster, *Religion and Sexuality: Three American Communal Experiments of the Nineteenth Century*, 291.

42. Fawn M. Brodie to Claire Noall, December 31, 1943; quoted in Newell G. Bringhurst, *Fawn McKay Brodie: A Biographer's Life*, 89.

43. Charles. L. Cohen, "No Man Knows My Psychology: Fawn Brodie, Joseph Smith, and Psychoanalysis," 55.

pated in plural marriage.⁴⁴ Using that data, he published *Isn't One Wife Enough?: The Story of Mormon Polygamy* in 1954. Despite its lack of footnotes and his use of pseudonyms, Young's data and interpretation made it a standard reference on Mormon polygamy for many years.⁴⁵

At about this same time, Stanley S. Ivins, son of Apostle Anthony W. Ivins, conducted research and statistical analyses elucidating a more reliable view of the actual incidence of plural marriage at its peak in Utah. He worked as a college professor teaching animal husbandry at the University of Nebraska but made numerous trips during the 1940s and 1950s to historical repositories throughout the country researching plural marriage. Arguably the most experienced of all investigators of Mormon polygamy before or since, he compiled lists of women who he believed were sealed to the Prophet both while living and after his death.⁴⁶ Unfortunately, none of his data dealing with Joseph Smith was published during his lifetime or under his supervision, which severely limited the circulation of his impressive contribution to Mormon polygamy research.⁴⁷

Stanley Ivins. Used by permission, Utah State Historical Society. All rights reserved.

In his 1975 master's thesis, LDS educator Danel Bachman produced an exhaustive reference on the subject.⁴⁸ His "A Study of the Mormon Practice of Plural Marriage before the Death of Joseph Smith" became the most detailed academic work to that point to address Joseph Smith's polygamy.⁴⁹ Bachman accumulated essentially all research then available and sleuthed out many previously unknown sources. Unfortunately, the thesis has never been published and has had limited private circulation.

---

44. Kimball Young, *Isn't One Wife Enough*, ix.

45. Some of Kimball Young's research notes are available at the Huntington Library.

46. See Stanley S. Ivins Collection, Utah State Historical Society. This list is accurately transcribed in Jerald Tanner and Sandra Tanner, *Joseph Smith and Polygamy*, 41–47.

47. Stanley S. Ivins, "Notes on Mormon Polygamy," 309–21.

48. Danel W. Bachman, "A Study of the Mormon Practice of Plural Marriage before the Death of Joseph Smith."

49. In 1986, Andrew Ehat termed Lawrence Foster's 1976 dissertation "Between Two Worlds: The Origins of Shaker Celibacy, Oneida Community Complex Marriage, and Mormon Polygamy" "still . . . the best available analysis of early Mormon plural marriage." Ehat, "Pseudo-Polyandry: Explaining Mormon Polygyny's Paradoxical Companion."

One year later, William Lawrence Foster, finished his doctoral dissertation entitled: "Between Two Worlds: The Origins of Shaker Celibacy, Onedia Community Complex Marriage, and Mormon Polygamy" (University of Chicago, 1976). A pioneering work that provided significant research into Joseph Smith's teachings and practice of plural marriage, it formed the basis for his 1981 *Religion and Sexuality: Three American Communal Experiments of the Nineteenth Century*. Although Foster's focus was the practice of three contrasting marital systems in the nineteenth century, his solid research and writing skills further expanded the knowledge base of Joseph Smith's polygamy.

The first book-length treatise to deal with plural marriage chronologically was Richard S. Van Wagoner's 1986 volume, *Mormon Polygamy: A History*. Six of nineteen chapters dealt with polygamy before Joseph Smith's martyrdom. Its chronological comprehensiveness is a contribution to the literature, but Van Wagoner relied heavily on published sources without consistently addressing their accuracy, touched only briefly on polygamy's associated theological considerations, and provided minimal analysis to accompany his brisk narration.

The most in-depth discussion of the lives of the Prophet's plural wives was published ten years later by historian Todd Compton. His 1997 award-winning history, *In Sacred Loneliness: The Plural Wives of Joseph Smith*,[50] contains chapter-length histories of the thirty-three most probable wives married during Joseph Smith's lifetime and provides more biographical details than any previous publication.[51] His work represents a significant milestone in the landscape of documenting Joseph Smith's polygamy.[52] While his referencing system is sometimes challenging, his sources are voluminous, reflecting a great deal of original research.

In 1994, author George D. Smith published an article discussing 153 Nauvoo polygamists (both husbands and wives), beginning with Joseph Smith and including those who entered polygamy in Nauvoo before the city's evacua-

---

50. Todd Compton, *In Sacred Loneliness: The Plural Wives of Joseph Smith*, received the "best book" award of the year from both the Mormon History Association and the John Whitmer Historical Association.

51. Ibid., 4–8. See also Todd Compton, "A Trajectory of Plurality: An Overview of Joseph Smith's Thirty-Three Plural Wives," 1–38.

52. Critiques include Richard Lloyd Anderson and Scott H. Faulring, "Review of *In Sacred Loneliness: The Plural Wives of Joseph Smith*, by Todd M. Compton," 75–77; Danel W. Bachman, "Prologue to the Study of Joseph Smith's Marital Theology: Review of *In Sacred Loneliness: The Plural Wives of Joseph Smith*." *FARMS Review of Books* 10, no. 2 (1998): 105–37; Alma Allred, "Review of Todd Compton's *In Sacred Loneliness*," December 6, 1999, updated version of paper presented at Mormon History Association meeting, Ogden Utah, 1999. http://www.shields-research.org/Reviews/Rvw-Sacred_Loneliness_Allred.htm; Danel W. Bachman, "'Let No One… Set On My Servant Joseph:' Religious Historians Missing the Lessons of Religious History," May 17, 1999.

tion in 1846.⁵³ In 2008, he expanded this earlier research into the book-length *Nauvoo Polygamy: "... but we called it celestial marriage,"* which provides remarkably detailed statistics of all known Nauvoo polygamists in its Appendix B. His revisionist narrative, however, takes the naturalistic approach beyond the Brodie extreme. George D. Smith describes plural marriages as "adventuresome marital arrangements," "communal relationships," "extracurricular romances," "theological philanderings," and simply, "entanglements."⁵⁴ No attempt is made to see polygamy through the eyes of Nauvoo participants, all of whom would probably have disagreed with George D. Smith's descriptions, viewing it instead as a sacred principle and spiritual mandate. Throughout *Nauvoo Polygamy*, George D. Smith portrays Joseph Smith's plural marriages as a device providing him (and other men) with sexual access to women beyond their legal wives. Perhaps its greatest weakness is a lack of adequate documentation.⁵⁵

Joseph Smith's Teachings on Plural Marriage

Authors who approach Joseph Smith's polygamy are forced to confront important limitations in the availability and reliability of pertinent historical documents. The best source of information would be Joseph Smith. As for his private teachings, it is regrettable that, with two or three exceptions, none of his scribes recorded them at the time. (See discussion below.) Doubtless these occasions of private teaching were far more numerous than the documentary record would suggest. Wilford Woodruff commented, "I heard Joseph Smith teach a great many things that never were written down."⁵⁶ Historian Dean Jessee observed: "More than two dozen persons are known to have assisted the Prophet in a secretarial capacity during the final fourteen years of his life, the years of his intensive record-keeping activity."⁵⁷ Almost no information

---

53. George D. Smith, "Nauvoo Roots of Mormon Polygamy, 1841–46: A Preliminary Demographic Report," 9, see also chart #122 [unpaginated 60–61]. Since Smith's work begins in the Nauvoo period, he does not include Fanny Alger, whom most other authors have included.

54. George D. Smith, *Nauvoo Polygamy*, 225, 237, 242, 247, 261, 334.

55. For reviews of *Nauvoo Polygamy*, see Brian C. Hales, "The Latest Word," Review of George D. Smith, *Nauvoo Polygamy: "... but we called it celestial marriage,"* 213–35; Gregory L. Smith, "George D. Smith's *Nauvoo Polygamy*," 37–123; Robert B. White, "A Review of the Dust Jacket and the First Two Pages: Review of George D. Smith, *Nauvoo Polygamy: "... but we called it celestial marriage,"* 125–29.

56. Wilford Woodruff, Deposition, Temple Lot Transcript, Respondent's Testimony, Part 3, p. 54, question 516.

57. Dean C. Jessee, "The Reliability of Joseph Smith's History," 29. Jessee added: "There was very little in the life of Joseph Smith and the movements of the Saints

regarding plural marriage is found among all their recordings. No letters were written explaining the topic; no journal entries explicate the practice.

Research shows that the Prophet left only one document specifically discussing the subject: his revelation recorded on July 12, 1843, on celestial marriage, now LDS Doctrine and Covenants 132. Joseph dictated two other documents in conjunction with the expansion of polygamy, but neither actually mentions plural marriage. The first is a letter from Joseph to Nancy Rigdon written in the spring of 1842 and first published by John C. Bennett on August 19, 1842; the second is a revelation that Joseph Smith received on behalf of Newel K. Whitney, July 27, 1842.[58]

During the Prophet's life, the revelation on celestial marriage received limited private circulation, but it was not printed or made available to Church members generally. Hence it does not qualify as a "public" manuscript for that period. However, it was published by Brigham Young in 1852 and was canonized as part of the LDS Doctrine and Covenants in 1876. (See Appendix A.) Even though Section 132 is lengthy (sixty-six verses, 3,271 words) and provides important insights and information, it still does not answer many of the questions that inevitably arise regarding plural marriage. William Clayton, who recorded the revelation from Joseph Smith's dictation, reported that, after concluding, he "remarked that there was much more that he could write on the subject, but what was written was sufficient for the present."[59]

Accordingly, we must acknowledge that the only individual who knew personally about Joseph Smith's motives, intentions, and practice of polygamy left no record about these central matters. Those of us now living a century and a half later know almost nothing about his thoughts and feelings on the subject. LDS historian Ronald O. Barney observed: "Everything we say about Joseph Smith and polygamy, regardless of our personal biases and beliefs, must be qualified by the basic premise that we cannot know some of the most important things that we would like to know, because all we have are fragments, shards, crumbs, etc. . . . We don't know what he was thinking; we don't know how he came to consider the principle; and we don't know any of the whys that are so salient to this topic."[60]

---

during the first half of the nineteenth century that contributed to continuity in the writing of church history. At almost every point where the effort to keep records and write history can be observed, the picture is one of adversity" (30).

58. For the letter to Nancy Rigdon, see John C. Bennett, "Sixth letter from John C. Bennett," *Sangamo Journal* (Springfield, Illinois), August 19, 1842; rpt., John C. Bennett, *The History of the Saints: Or an Exposé of Joe Smith and Mormonism*, 243–44. The revelation for Newel K. Whitney, July 27, 1842, is quoted in H. Michael Marquardt, ed., *The Joseph Smith Revelations: Text and Commentary*, 315–16. See discussion in Chapters 17 and 18.

59. William Clayton, Affidavit, February 16, 1874, quoted in Jenson, "Plural Marriage," 226.

60. Ronald O. Barney, email to Brian Hales, July 10, 2007. Used by permission.

Scholar Andrew Ehat acknowledged in 1986 that only a "slim amount of data" was available: "Joseph Smith never lived to see a sufficient period of peace so he could in public sermon, by further written revelation, or, perhaps, by way of treatise, detail his rationale for the complex story of polygamy. Thus scholars, apologists and detractors alike have all been left to pick and choose from a very slim amount of available data concerning this controversial topic."[61]

Historical Sources Contemporaneous with Joseph Smith

Beyond Joseph Smith himself, the next potential source of useful information is individuals who may have heard the Prophet teach on the subject. For example, Nathan Tanner recalled in 1869 that "he heard President Joseph Smith, while in conversation with himself . . . and others, teach the doctrine of Celestial Marriage or plurality of wives."[62] Sarah Perry Peak Kimball similarly remembered that "President Joseph Smith personally taught her the doctrine of a plurality of wives" prior to her being sealed to Heber C. Kimball.[63] Regrettably, no contemporary records have been found from such listeners. The only journal keeper friendly to the Prophet who mentions plural marriage with any regularity was William Clayton.

It also appears that many key documents written at the time have been lost. For example, plural wife Mary Elizabeth Rollins Lightner recalled in 1905: "My journal got burned up, so [I] cannot remember dates. . . . I could tell you many things that I cannot write. I remember every word he [Joseph Smith] ever said to me of importance."[64] In fact, Mary's recollections are a very important source of information but are far from complete. Another polygamous spouse of the Prophet, Patty Bartlett Sessions, kept a Nauvoo diary that was quoted in publications as late as 1884 but which is currently unavailable despite intense searching by multiple researchers.[65]

Several dissenters recorded contemporary accounts. Oliver Olney and William Law left journal entries for the Nauvoo period. Olney began his diary shortly after being cut off from the Church in 1842.[66] William Law was called as a counselor in the First Presidency on January 19, 1841 (D&C 124:126) and was personally familiar with the revelation on celestial marriage (now D&C 132). However, he did not begin his journal until January 1, 1844, just weeks

---

61. Ehat, "Pseudo-Polyandry," 16.
62. Joseph F. Smith, Affidavit Book 1:76.
63. Ibid., 1:80.
64. Mary Elizabeth Rollins Lightner, Letter to Emmeline B. Wells, summer 1905, 4–6.
65. Donna Toland Smart, Carol Cornwall Madsen, Don Bradley, and LDS Church archivists have searched unsuccessfully for these diaries. Carol Cornwall Madsen, telephone conversation with Brian Hales, October 5, 2008.
66. Oliver Olney Papers, Beinecke Library, Yale University.

before his own excommunication.[67] Both men remained in Nauvoo and were thus geographically positioned to record contemporary events occurring in the city. Several other detractors of the period published books and pamphlets. The first was *History of the Saints* written by John C. Bennett in November of 1842, based on six letters published earlier that year.[68] A second was printed four months later by Oliver H. Olney: *The Absurdities of Mormonism Portrayed: A Brief Sketch*. William Law helped compose the *Nauvoo Expositor* published in June of 1844. Shortly thereafter, Joseph H. Jackson printed: *A Narrative of the Adventures and Experiences of Joseph H. Jackson in Nauvoo, Exposing the Depths of Mormon Villainy*.[69] These six men, Joseph Smith, William Clayton, John C. Bennett, Oliver Olney, William Law, and Joseph H. Jackson, provide the only contemporary documents that could possibly describe Nauvoo polygamy accurately. As discussed in several subsequent chapters, sensationalizing and reliability issues plague the Bennett, Law, Olney, and Jackson accounts.

Late Recollections

Beyond contemporary authors, our only source of information concerning Joseph Smith's polygamy comes from later recollections written by Nauvooans who were personally involved, besides those who recorded affidavits in 1869–70. Some are brief references to polygamy found in longer autobiographical sketches, while others constitute reminiscences of distinct plural marriage events from the 1840s. Unfortunately, not all early polygamists were willing in later years to share their knowledge and experiences. Todd Compton observed: "Joseph's plural wives were remarkably reticent throughout their lives, often telling the stories of their marriages to Joseph only to their children, and often only at the end of their lives."[70]

In addition, even individuals taught by the Prophet may not have fully understood the doctrines associated with plural marriage. Compton notes: "It should . . . be borne in mind that the men and women involved in Nauvoo polygamy and polyandry did not understand it thoroughly; it was new doctrine;

---

67. Lyndon W. Cook, *William Law: Biographical Essay—Nauvoo Diary—Correspondence—Interview*, 37.

68. Current research supports that John C. Bennett was the very first writer to accuse Joseph Smith of polygamy, in letters to the *Sangamo Journal* printed in July of 1842. Most of those letters were republished in his *History of the Saints* issued in September of that year.

69. Much of his material in *A Narrative of the Adventures and Experiences of Joseph H. Jackson in Nauvoo, Exposing the Depths of Mormon Villainy*, came from letters Jackson wrote to the *New York Herald*, September 5 and 7, 1844, and to the *Weekly Herald* (New York City) September 7, 1844.

70. Compton, *In Sacred Loneliness*, 644.

it was not preached openly; and though Joseph taught polygamy to his inner circle, practical experience often differed from didactic religious doctrine."[71]

Later recollections are far less desirable than contemporary accounts for many reasons. Historian Maureen Ursenbach Beecher provided this depressing view of late reminiscences: "Personal texts . . . are the fictions we create in order to make our lives acceptable to ourselves and our imagined readers. Our memories are often flawed and distorted, as people discover when they share their version of a particular event with that of a sibling or a spouse. In addition, by omissions, by evasions, or by outright untruths we reshape events to our liking."[72]

Problems with late recollections hamper every historical reconstruction. Sadly, perhaps 98 percent of the available evidence dealing with Joseph Smith's polygamy falls into this latter category. While compiling accounts for the six-volume *History of the Church* only twelve years after Joseph Smith's death, Wilford Woodruff lamented: "We almost daily get new statements from men who were directly or indirectly connected with the scenes of the last four days of the lives of the Prophet and Patriarch." Importantly he added, "Many of these accounts are in direct opposition to each other."[73]

My research identifies thirty men who were involved with plural marriage in Nauvoo prior to June 27, 1844. [74] Only a few appear to have recorded their experiences in Nauvoo. (See Table 1.2.)

A review of Joseph Smith's plural wives also fails to identify the volume and type of documents that would be the most useful. Six left brief references[75] and eight more provided longer accounts.[76] Historian Janiece Lyn Johnson acknowledged the difficulties inherent in record keeping in the Nauvoo period: "Their [Mormon women's] continual transitory mode made writing more difficult, and they often lacked the time and resources to commit their experiences to paper. . . . Pen, ink, and paper were precious."[77] (See Table 1.3.)

---

71. Compton, "A Trajectory of Plurality," 31.

72. Maureen Ursenbach Beecher, ed., *The Personal Writings of Eliza Roxcy Snow*, xviii.

73. Wilford Woodruff, Letters to John Bernhisel, June 30, 1856, and to George A. Smith, June 30, 1856; quoted in Jessee, "The Reliability of Joseph Smith's History," 36.

74. See Chapter 28 and Gary James Bergera, "Identifying the Earliest Mormon Polygamists, 1841–44," 1–74; George D. Smith, *Nauvoo Polygamy*, 574–656.

75. Included are Presendia Huntington Buell, Sylvia Sessions Lyons, Patty Bartlett Sessions, Eliza Partridge, Almera Johnson, and Desdemona Johnson Wadsworth.

76. Longer more detailed accounts were provided by Zina Huntington Jacob Smith Young, Mary Elizabeth Rollins Lightner, Eliza R. Snow, Sarah Ann Whitney, Lucy Walker, Helen Mar Kimball, and Malissa Lott.

77. Janiece Lyn Johnson, "'Give It All Up and Follow Your Lord': Mormon Female Religiosity, 1831–1843," 9.

TABLE 1.2
NAUVOO MEN WHO ENTERED POLYGAMY BEFORE JUNE 27, 1844

Pre-June 27 Nauvoo Polygamous Men	1840–44 Writings that Discuss Joseph Smith and Polygamy	Later Recollections that Discuss Joseph Smith and Polygamy
Joseph Smith	D&C 132	
William Clayton	YES	YES
James Adams	NONE	
Ezra Taft Benson		
Reynolds Cahoon		
Joseph W. Coolidge		
Howard Egan		
William Felshaw		
William D. Huntington		
Orson Hyde		YES
Benjamin F. Johnson		YES
Joseph A. Kelting		
Heber C. Kimball		YES
Vinson Knight		
Isaac Morley		
Joseph B. Noble		YES
John E. Page		
Parley P. Pratt		YES
Willard Richards		YES
William Sagers		
Hyrum Smith		
John Smith		
William Smith		
Erastus Snow		YES
John Taylor		YES
Theodore Turley		
Lyman Wight		
Edwin D. Woolley		
Brigham Young		YES
Lorenzo Dow Young		

Other Nauvooans		
George F. Adams		
Thomas Bullock		
John D. Lee		YES
Amasa M. Lyman		
Ebenezer Robinson		YES
David Fullmer		YES
Thomas Grover	NONE	YES
John Benbow		YES
James Allred		YES
Joseph C. Kingsbury		YES
Lorenzo Snow		YES
Joseph Fielding		YES
Alexander Neibaur		YES

Common Non-LDS View: Joseph Smith the Womanizer

Beginning in the summer of 1842, as the knowledge of Joseph Smith's plural marriage teachings expanded to outsiders, publications began to appear purporting to expose the truth about Mormon polygamy. Virtually all of them reflected the idea that Joseph Smith was a womanizer who used polygamy to expand his sexual opportunities. As startling stories of plural marriage spread to the East, anti-polygamy sentiment crescendoed. Soon clergy and journalists were denouncing the evils of polygamy, their censorious tone giving them license to address a subject so titillating. Anti-Mormon articles, books, and pamphlets poured from the presses. The Church's missionaries did not mention the practice, but their very association with the scandal-blackened Church exacerbated the already offended sensibilities of the Christian populace.

Research shows that after 1842, throughout the rest of the nineteenth century, hundreds of publications were written condemning the Mormons, their prophet, and the practice of plural marriage. (See Appendix G.) Fictional accounts from the period also hindered understanding. Leonard J. Arrington and Jon Haupt observed: "Because anti-Mormon propaganda frequently borrowed from fiction . . . a journey over these century-old literary landscapes leaves the historian with a feeling that he is visiting a nightmare world of unreality."[78]

The earliest charges of licentiousness against Joseph Smith and the Mormons came from the four dissenters mentioned above who left the Church

---

78. Leonard J. Arrington and Jon Haupt, "The Missouri and Illinois Mormons in Antebellum Fiction," 38.

TABLE 1.3
PLURAL WIVES OF JOSEPH SMITH

Woman's Name	1840–44 Diaries that Discuss Joseph Smith and Polygamy	Recollections that Discuss Joseph Smith and Polygamy
Fanny Alger (Smith Custer)		
Louisa Beaman (Smith)		
Zina Diantha Huntington (Jacobs Smith Young)		YES
Presendia Huntington (Buell Smith Kimball)		
Lucinda Pendleton (Morgan Harris Smith)		
Agnes Moulton Coolbrith Smith (Smith)		
Sylvia Sessions (Lyon Smith Kimball Clark)		YES
Mary Elizabeth Rollins (Lightner Smith Young)		YES
Patty Bartlett (Sessions Smith Parry)		
Marinda Nancy Johnson (Hyde Smith)		
Elizabeth Davis (Goldsmith Brackenbury Durfee Smith Lott)		
Sarah Kingsley (Howe Cleveland Smith Smith)		
Delcena Diadamia Johnson (Sherman Smith Babbitt)	NONE	
Eliza R. Snow (Smith Young)		YES
Sarah Ann Whitney (Smith [Kingsbury] Kimball)		YES
Martha McBride (Knight Smith Kimball)		
Ruth Vose (Sayers Smith)		
Flora Ann Woodworth (Smith Gove)		
Emily Dow Partridge (Smith Young)		YES
Eliza Maria Partridge (Smith Lyman)		
Almera Woodward Johnson (Smith Barton)		
Lucy Walker (Smith Kimball)		YES
Sarah Lawrence (Smith Kimball Mount)		
Maria Lawrence (Smith [Young] Babbitt)		
Helen Mar Kimball (Smith Whitney)		YES
Hannah S. Ells (Smith)		
Elivira Cowles (Holmes Smith)		
Rhoda Richards (Smith Young)		

Desdemona Catlin Wadsworth Fullmer (Smith Benson Mclane)	NONE	
Olive Gray Frost (Smith Young)		
Malissa Lott (Smith Bernhisel Willes)		YES
Nancy M. Winchester (Smith Kimball Arnold)		
Fanny Young (Carr Murray Smith)		
Esther Dutcher		
Mary Heron		
Other Polygamous Women		
Bathsheba Smith		YES
Mercy R. Thompson	NONE	YES
Mary Ann West		YES

Note: None of these women kept an 1840–44 diary that mentions polygamy or Joseph Smith in the context of polygamy.

in Nauvoo. Their sensationalized charges set the standard that would expand in printed works throughout the next century. For example, John C. Bennett claimed his account was "faithful and unexaggerated" and alleged that Joseph Smith and the Latter-day Saints were guilty of "debauchery, lasciviousness, bestiality . . . fornication, adultery, rape [and] incest."[79] Oliver Olney criticized: "Hundreds are convinced of the fact that fornication and adultery [are] common in the Nauvoo. . . . Many at this time are suffering under the stigma of being seduced."[80] William Law claimed that "whordoms [sic] and all manner of abominations are practiced under the cloak of religion" in Nauvoo.[81] Joseph H. Jackson wrote: "Joe Smith boasted to me that he . . . from the commencement of his career had seduced 400 women. . . . From my knowledge of the spiritual wife system I should think that the number of secret women in Nauvoo cannot be much less than six hundred."[82] These astounding charges were accompanied by no documentation, but many authors repeated them and readers accepted them.

These four authors, especially John C. Bennett, would be quoted over and over in subsequent books dealing with Mormonism. They are still quoted today as authoritative sources of information regarding Joseph Smith's polygamy by authors who are less concerned about credibility. Danel Bachman characterized the early publications:

---

79. Bennett, *The History of the Saints*, 225, 257.
80. Oliver H. Olney, *The Absurdities of Mormonism Portrayed: A Brief Sketch*, 16.
81. *Nauvoo Expositor*, June 7, 1844, 1–4.
82. Joseph H. Jackson, *A Narrative of the Adventures and Experiences of Joseph H. Jackson in Nauvoo, Exposing the Depths of Mormon Villainy*, 13, 25.

> The earliest writings on the subject [of Mormon polygamy] were exposés. These were characterized by vindictive, hypercritical, and moralistic judgments of the Mormons and their beliefs. Offended sensibilities burst forth in righteous indignation at the Mormon affront to American morals and the underpinnings of society. Critics felt that Americans should be warned of the dangers inherent in this cancer upon the body politic through "true" accounts of the corruption and licentiousness of Joseph Smith's followers. . . . Occasionally such works were published by disaffected or expelled Mormons. At best, these materials distorted the facts, and, at worst, they completely departed from the truth.[83]

The common outsider's view of Joseph Smith characterizing him as a womanizer is not surprising. The Christian morals of nineteenth-century America reserved no space for a restoration of Old Testament plural marriage.[84] To ascribe a religious justification to Joseph Smith's polygamy was essentially unthinkable, unless a person first embraced him as a prophet. This principle may still apply to many observers today. Richard L. Bushman observed: "Polygamy is an interesting thing because it serves as a Rorschach test. People project onto Joseph Smith and polygamists their own sense about human nature."[85]

LDS View: Joseph Smith as Prophet-Restorer

In contrast to the common non-LDS view that Joseph Smith was licentious, the beliefs of Church members during the same period generally reflected the conviction that he established plural marriage acting as a prophet-restorer. That is, in a prophetic role, Joseph was performing part of the "restitution of all things" prophesied in Acts 3:20–21: "And he shall send Jesus Christ, which before was preached unto you: Whom the heaven must receive until the times of restitution of all things, which God hath spoken by the mouth of all his holy prophets since the world began."[86]

In the eyes of most Latter-day Saints, plural marriage was a commandment of God, a strict practice that was tightly regulated. Helen Mar Kimball Whitney, plural wife of Joseph Smith, writing to a correspondent in her later years, argued that the very difficulties it would inevitably bring actually constituted proof of its divine origin:

> The Prophet said . . . that it [plural marriage] would damn more than it would have because \so many/ unprincipled men would take advantage of it,

---

83. Bachman, "A Study of the Mormon Practice of Plural Marriage," 1–2.
84. For a discussion of pre-nineteenth-century polygamy, see John Cairncross, *After Polygamy Was Made a Sin: The Social History of Christian Polygamy*, 1–183.
85. Richard L. Bushman, "Mormonism and Democratic Politics: Are They Compatible?"
86. See Jan Shipps, *Mormonism: The Story of a New Religious Tradition*, 61–62.

but that did not prove that it was not a pure principle. If Joseph had had any impure desires he could have gratified them in the style of the world with less danger of his life or his character, than to do as he did. The Lord commanded him to teach & to practice that principle.[87]

Nauvoo polygamist Joseph Kelting recalled his first discussion with Joseph Smith regarding polygamy, which probably occurred in the fall of 1843: "He [Joseph Smith] then began a defense of the doctrine by referring to the Old Testament. I told him I did not want to hear that as I could read it for my self. . . . He then informed me that he had received a revelation from God which taught the correctness of the doctrine of a plurality of wives, and command[ed] him to obey it. He then acknowledged to having married several wives."[88]

Many of the original pluralists in Nauvoo also proclaimed that forces beyond the Prophet's charisma and persuasiveness convinced them to accept the principle. They described their own spiritual experiences as pivotal in their decisions to participate. Their convictions of the restoration of plural marriage by a genuine prophet were affirmed by what scholars today would classify as "charismatic" experiences. For example, Nauvoo High Council member James Allred remembered that "he did not believe it at first, it was so contrary to his feelings, but he said he knew Joseph was a prophet of God so he made a covenant that he would not eat, drink or sleep until he knew for himself, that he had got a testimony that it was true, that he had even heard the voice of God concerning it."[89]

Published Views Versus Unpublished Views

While other nineteenth-century assessments of Joseph Smith and polygamy beyond the extreme labels of "womanizer" or "prophet-restorer" could probably have been found, those two dominated the views of Americans and Europeans during the nineteenth century and beyond. A significant difference also existed between the two characterizations in that the womanizer portrayal was widely published while the prophet-restorer opinion was seldom voiced in print except by the Saints themselves.

The historical record demonstrates that leaders of the Church of Jesus Christ of Latter-day Saints did not publicly acknowledge the practice of plural marriage until 1852.[90] This means that Church writers printed no defenses

---

87. Helen [Mar Kimball Whitney], Letter to Mary Bond, n.d., 3–9.
88. Joseph A. Kelting, "Statement."
89. James Allred, "Statement," October 15, 1854.
90. In 1848 Catherine Lewis, *Narrative of Some of the Proceedings of the Mormons; Giving an Account of their Iniquities*, 12, acknowledged: "I know not of any letters being written by any of the Apostles on this subject [of polygamy]." Missionaries in their respective areas would sometime print defenses of the practice of polygamy. Orson Pratt was perhaps the only

of the practice before 1852. Thereafter, a few Church publications by Apostles Orson Pratt[91] and Parley P. Pratt, and by Elders Orson Spencer, Benjamin F. Johnson, and others, provided doctrinal defenses, including the affirmation that Joseph Smith was restoring biblical plural marriage.[92] However, the number of apologetic publications was puny compared to those condemning the practice, leaving the skeptics and detractors with no opposition in the realm of publications for a crucial decade and vastly unequal publications afterward.

Sometimes in response to public criticism, Church leaders sought to discredit the accusers. However, none of the written defenses included historical reconstructions of how plural marriage was introduced to Church members by Joseph Smith in Nauvoo, despite the fact that disclosing such details might have more effectively contradicted some of the allegations made. After 1852, LDS pamphlets were issued to refute antagonistic claims, but little was said about its historical unfolding in Illinois until Andrew Jenson's 1887 article.

The discrepancy between the unpublished views of participants and the published views of antagonists created challenges for readers throughout the nineteenth century. Inquirers seeking to accurately understand the LDS practice of polygamy were confronted with aggressive allegations from published anti-Mormon sources that Joseph Smith was a womanizer. However, the private view held by thousands of Latter-day Saint polygamists, that Joseph Smith was a prophet-restorer, was largely unknown and unavailable.

Nineteenth-century authors seeking to portray a balanced approach to Mormon polygamy generally had to travel to the Rocky Mountains to meet the Latter-day Saints and interview them personally. A surprising number of writers actually engaged in that level of field research.[93] But many more

---

voice that attempted to explain and actively promote the principle of plural marriage. See Orson Pratt, August 29, 1852, *Journal of Discourses*, 1:53–66; see also the twenty issues of *The Seer* that Pratt published in Washington, D.C. and reprinted in London in 1853–54.

91. David J. Whittaker explained: "This series [of articles found in *The Seer*] constituted the most extensive defense of plural marriage to appear in early Mormon literature. Although [Orson] Pratt later returned to discuss polygamy in several discourses, he did not add any new arguments to *The Seer* series, nor did other Mormon authors in the nineteenth century." David J. Whittaker, "The Bone in the Throat: Orson Pratt and the Public Announcement of Plural Marriage," 308.

92. Parley P. Pratt, *"Mormonism!" "Plurality of wives!"*, San Francisco: P. P. Pratt, 1852; Orson Spencer, *Patriarchal Order or Plurality of Wives!*, Liverpool, 1853; Benjamin F. Johnson, *Why the "LATTER DAY SAINTS" Marry a Plurality of Wives: A Glance at Scripture and Reason...*, San Francisco: Excelsior Printing Office, 1854; see also Franklin D. Richards, *A Compendium of the Faith and Doctrines of the Church of Jesus Christ of Latter-day Saints* (Liverpool: Orson Pratt, 1857). For a review article, see David J. Whittaker, "Early Mormon Polygamy Defenses," 43–63.

93. See, for example, Horace Greeley, "Overland Journey, [Part] 21: Two Hours

simply quoted Bennett, Law, and other printed sources, adding their own interpretations and offering their compositions to the public as accurate history.

Even today, researchers writing about Joseph Smith's polygamy must resist the temptation to preferentially cite published documents because of the comparative ease and accessibility. The message of the published and unpublished caches of documents is generally very different. Writers who rely on printed publications to the exclusion of unpublished documents will undoubtedly struggle to maintain balance and objectivity, if that is their goal. A goal of these three volumes is to allow the reader to see Joseph Smith's polygamy as the Nauvoo polygamists viewed it and gain a perspective that arguably has not be made fully available before.

Summary

Research demonstrates that Joseph Smith introduced and practiced polygamy during his lifetime. Plural marriage spread after his death and was established in Utah as an important doctrinal principle. Very few contemporary accounts discussing early plural marriage have been discovered in the historical record. The vast majority of sources are late recollections penned by participants who offered important observations but which are susceptible to the weaknesses of memory and personal biases.

A notable discrepancy exists in the messages and quantities of publications produced by non-Mormon writers and Latter-day Saint authors in the nineteenth century. Non-LDS writers published hundreds of narratives from 1842 onward, virtually all describing Joseph Smith as a womanizer. To combat this gossipy and scandal-mongering perspective, LDS defenders issued a few apologetic pamphlets after 1852, but they concentrated on building a doctrinal defense rather than providing a history, and they constituted only a small fraction of the total number of publications talking about Mormon polygamy in the remainder of the nineteenth century and first decades of the twentieth. Unpublished recollections penned by Nauvoo polygamists during this period were generally unavailable to anyone but trusted family members. Over the decades, however, these private reminiscences have been compiled in various repositories and many are now available for review. They provide an indispensable view to any researcher seeking a more complete understanding of Nauvoo polygamy.

---

with Brigham Young," *New-York Daily Tribune*, August 20, 1859, 718; also quoted in Greeley, *An Overland Journey from New York to San Francisco in the Summer of 1859*, 138. This interview was reprinted in the *Millennial Star* as "Two Hours with Brigham Young," 21 (September 17, 1859): 608–11, with the following qualification: "Although the wording of the conversation might not be exactly as spoken, on the whole, we have no hesitation in endorsing it by republication" (605).

Chapter 2
Joseph Smith's Morality, 1820s to 1835

By 1842, Joseph Smith had secretly established the practice of plural marriage for himself and a few other Church members in Nauvoo, Illinois. However, his involvement with polygamy prior to that time has been poorly documented in previous historical reconstructions. Sociologist Kimball Young wrote: "With regard to the plural marriage system the mystery of its origin is peculiarly tantalizing. Certainly the precise steps in its emergence are almost impossible to trace."[1] Lawrence Foster agreed: "Probably our knowledge of the development of polygamy before Nauvoo will always remain rather conjectural. . . . [T]he intellectual and practical development of Mormon polygamy before Nauvoo cannot be reconstructed with any degree of certainty."[2]

Despite these challenges, a limited amount of evidence concerning Joseph Smith's pre-1841 marital practices can be identified in the historical record. Important questions to guide that exploration are: Whom was he reportedly involved with? How many women were implicated? What evidence is there about the nature of his associations with the women who later became his plural wives? Were any of these relationships more likely to be sexual trysts rather than bona fide plural marriages? How reliable are these reports and narratives? Answers to these inquiries have not yet been adequately described in available publications. Accordingly, every allegation of sexual involvement with a woman must be investigated to determine the credibility of the person making the account as well as the reliability of the account itself. Analysis of the described relationship is also of immense importance.

My research into the period between 1830 and 1835 identifies six reports of sexual activity with women other than Joseph Smith's legal wife, Emma Hale Smith.[3] Three were made contemporaneously and three were directed at the

---

1. Kimball Young, *Isn't One Wife Enough?* 82.
2. Lawrence Foster, *Religion and Sexuality: Three American Communal Experiments of the Nineteenth Century*, 134.
3. I exclude from this list of six two allegations as not being credible. The first is an anonymous article, "One of the Priesthood," in *Saintly Falsity* (Salt Lake: Salt Lake Tribune Office, 1885), 1, 2, which claims: "In a meeting of a Female Relief Society, in 1853, in this city, Mrs. Whitney told the sisters present that she had been sealed to Joseph four years before

Prophet many years after the relationship reportedly occurred. One of the six involves Fanny Alger, a claim that I investigate separately in Chapters 4–8.

Before looking at the remaining five narratives, a related allegation about Joseph Smith's marriage to Emma Hale on January 18, 1827, should be addressed. Some writers have suggested that, in fact, the nuptial was deceitful.[4] Emma's father, Isaac Hale, claimed: "While I was absent from home, he [Joseph Smith] carried off my daughter, into the state of New York, where they were married."[5] However, in Emma's interview with her son Joseph Smith III in 1879, she specifically denied any compulsion or underhandedness: "I had no intention of marrying when I left home; but, during my visit at Mr. Stowell's [a friend of Joseph's], your father visited me there. My folks were bitterly opposed to him; and, being importuned by your father, aided by Mr. Stowell, who urged me to marry him, and preferring to marry him to any other man I knew, I consented. We went to Squire Tarbell's and were married."[6] Both of these sources reflect

---

the date of the revelation as given [1839]; Mrs. J_____ [Zina Huntington Jacobs?] said she was sealed to him six years before that [1837]; Mrs. B_____ [Presendia Huntington Buell?] said she was sealed to him nine years before that [1834]; and Eliza R. Snow Smith Young arose and declared that she was sealed to him long before any of them [pre-1834]." A second is from an even later publication by A. Theodore Schroeder, *Some Facts Concerning Polygamy* (Salt Lake City: n.p., 1898), 3, 9, which repeats some of the faulty information from *Saintly Falsity*: "At or prior to 1835, the Prophet had taken into his household Eliza R. Snow who admits herself to have been a polygamous wife of the Prophet. . . . She goes out of her way to justify her presence in the Smith household by saying that she 'Was teaching the Prophet's family school'. . . . The real truth doubtless is that she was even in 1835, a plural wife of the Prophet. According to apostates, Eliza R. Snow stated in 1853, before a meeting of the 'Female Relief Society,' that she was sealed to Joseph Smith nine years before the date of the revelation [D&C 132, written July 12, 1843], making it 1834. . . . As early as 1833 [the conduct of the Saints] was such as to make their neighbors believe that they were practically polygamists, and although Rigdon as early as 1835 took a plural wife, which must have been known to the prophet, and notwithstanding that[,] probably Smith had already entered the polygamic state with Eliza R. Snow." The historical inaccuracies in these two documents are too numerous to justify serious consideration, beginning with the fact that the Relief Society had not been reconstituted in 1853. However, these types of statements are not uncommon in the historical record and were apparently believed by many.

4. See W. Wyl [pseud. for Wilhelm Ritter von Wymetal]. *Mormon Portraits, or the Truth about Mormon Leaders from 1830 to 1886*, 74–75; James H. Kennedy, *Early Days of Mormonism: Palmyra, Kirtland, and Nauvoo*, 38–44; Anon. *Appalling Disclosures! Mormon Revelations, Being the History of Fourteen Females*, 4.

5. Isaac Hale, Statement, *Susquehanna Register* (Montrose, Penn.) May 1, 1834, quoted in Eber D. Howe, *Mormonism Unvailed*, 263, see also 234, 244; also John C. Bennett, The History of the Saints: Or an Exposé of Joe Smith and Mormonism, 81; Danel Bachman, "A Study of the Mormon Practice of Plural Marriage before the Death of Joseph Smith," 51.

6. Emma Hale Smith, "The Last Testimony of Sister Emma," *Saints Herald* (Plano, Illinois), October 1, 1879; typescript reprinted in Vogel, *Early Mormon Documents*, 1:540.

important biases; but beyond Isaac Hale's, I have found no evidence suggesting indecency in their elopement.

The Case of Eliza Winters

According to my research, the earliest allegation of sexual impropriety committed by Joseph Smith reportedly occurred between October of 1825 and June of 1829, involving a woman named Eliza Winters. Testimony of the described incident was not recorded until 1834 and came, not from Eliza, but from Emma Hale Smith's cousin, Levi Lewis. Apparently Lewis swore an affidavit prior to March 20, 1834.[7] A few weeks later on May 1, 1834, portions of his statement were published in the *Susquehanna Register and Northern Pennsylvanian*: "Levi Lewis states, that he has 'been acquainted with Joseph Smith Jr. and Martin Harris, and that he has heard them both say, adultery was no crime. Harris said he did not blame Smith for his (Smith's) attempt to seduce Eliza Winters &c.;' . . . 'With regard to the plates, Smith said God had deceived him – which was the reason he (Smith) did not show them.'"[8]

Although Lewis's recollection is not an account of illicit sexual activity but a second-hand report of an "attempted" seduction, I include it here. This statement is sometimes misquoted as saying that Levi Lewis accused Joseph Smith of trying to seduce Eliza Winters, rather than Lewis allegedly quoting Martin Harris concerning Joseph's assumed behavior.[9] Unfortunately, the original Levi Lewis affidavit has not been found; but the portion of the quotation stating that Joseph "did not show" the golden plates to others, is false and therefore obviously raises suspicions regarding the accuracy of the remaining charges.[10]

Regrettably, we know nothing more of Levi Lewis's alleged interactions with Joseph and Martin during which the two men rather improbably confided in him about Joseph's shocking misconduct and made a statement that they later contradicted on numerous other occasions throughout their lives. Nor does it seem probable that Martin might have heard about Joseph Smith's alleged immoral behavior with Eliza, either from Joseph himself or from an even more

---

7. Vogel, *Early Mormon Documents*, 4:296.

8. "Mormonism," *Susquehanna Register and Northern Pennsylvanian*, May 1, 1834 quoted in Eber D. Howe, *Mormonism Unvailed*, 268–69; and Dan Vogel, *Early Mormon Documents*, 4:296–97.

9. See for example, Richard S. Van Wagoner, *Mormon Polygamy: A History*, 4; George D. Smith, *Nauvoo Polygamy: "... but we called it celestial marriage,"* 29; Vogel, *Early Mormon Documents*, 4:296; Dan Vogel, *Joseph Smith: The Making of a Prophet*, 178; Grant H. Palmer, "Sexual Allegations against Joseph Smith, 1829–1835," 1.

10. See the "Testimony of the Three Witnesses" and "Testimony of the Eight Witnesses" in the front matter of current editions of the Book of Mormon. In the 1830 first version, the testimonies were printed at the end of the book, on pages corresponding to 589–590.

unlikely third party. Martin was known for loose talk and a lack of discretion. LDS scripture condemned him as a man who "depended upon his own judgment and boasted in his own wisdom" (D&C 3:13). An 1844 account by someone who was not a defender of Mormonism commented, "Few men can talk faster and say less than Martin."[11] Ezra Booth, Harris's contemporary in Ohio and briefly a member of the Church, claimed disparagingly: "Martin Harris is what may be called a great talker, an extravagant boaster; so much so, that he renders himself disagreeable to many of his society."[12] Both of these men had motives to impeach Martin in his testimony as one of the Book of Mormon Three Witnesses, but they were apparently not alone in their views.

Levi's recollection might have disappeared from history altogether had publisher E. D. Howe not repeated the statement from the *Susquehanna Register* in his 1834 book, *Mormonism Unvailed*. Howe's antagonistic book can be seen as the first anti-Mormon publication. Certainly it was influential. David J. Whittaker acknowledged: "Howe's naturalistic explanation of Joseph Smith and the Book of Mormon became the cornerstone of anti-Mormon writing."[13]

Levi Lewis, who made the affidavit in question, was the son of Emma's maternal uncle Nathaniel Lewis, a Methodist minister. He was generally friendly to Joseph Smith, unlike the attitude of Levi's brothers. According to historian Mark Nelson, "In 1828 Joseph and Emma placed their names on the rolls of the local Methodist congregation. When Levi's brothers discovered this addition to the congregation they insisted that Joseph either remove his name from the rolls or publicly denounce all of his super-natural claims. Joseph would eventually remove his name."[14]

As a further problem with Levi Lewis's affidavit, it is difficult to identify a logical time and place when Joseph could have made an attempt at seducing Eliza. Joseph Smith first visited the area to work for Josiah Stowell for two months—October and November of 1825. A year later, he returned to the vicinity for three months—from November 1826 until January 18, 1827. He and Emma wed on this date, then left immediately for the Smith home in Manchester, New York, where they stayed for eleven months, except for a brief visit to Harmony in August 1827 when they were reconciled with Emma's family. In December of 1828, the young couple moved back to Harmony to be close to the Hale family. This stay lasted until June of 1829, which represents the last month when the seduction "attempt" could have taken place.

---

11. James H. Hunt, *Mormonism: Embracing the Origin, Rise, and Progress of the Sect with an Examination of the Book of Mormon*, 9.

12. Howe, *Mormonism Unvailed*, 183.

13. David J. Whitaker, "East of Nauvoo: Benjamin Winchester and the Early Mormon Church," *Journal of Mormon History* 21 (Fall 1995) 2:43.

14. Email correspondence from Mark Nelson to the author dated October 17, 2007.

Born in Delaware in 1812, Eliza Winters apparently moved to Harmony prior to 1829. I have found no evidence that she interacted with Joseph Smith or his family in Pennsylvania, although one late recollection states that she was Emma's friend in Harmony.[15] Her exact location—even whether she was living in Harmony itself—during this period is unknown. Mark B. Nelson provides this history:

Martin Harris later in life. Courtesy of the LDS Church History Library.

> Eliza Winters was born in Delaware in 1812 and was married in 1837 in Susquehanna County. I have found no evidence when her family moved to the area but her older sister was married in Harmony in 1829 so it was obviously before then. I have found no evidence that Joseph and Eliza ever interacted although it is probable that they knew each other. Eliza would have been 13 when Joseph first came to Harmony (assuming she lived there in 1825) and 18 when Joseph and Emma moved. Her name first shows up with her encounter with Martin [Harris] . . . in late 1832.[16]

Concerning the Martin Harris interaction, Mark B. Nelson and Steven C. Harper wrote:

> On November 1, 1832, he [Martin Harris] preached to a group of townsfolk, including a single woman named Eliza Ann Winters. She later told the court that Martin loudly denounced her. Picking Winters out of the crowd, Martin allegedly said: "She has had a bastard child." Whatever the truth of the matter, Winters sued Martin Harris for slander. In her complaint to the court she testified that Martin's claim of fornication was intended to "render her infamous and scandalous," soiling her "good name." She sued for restoration of her reputation and punitive damages of a thousand dollars. . . . Martin left an affidavit with the court. Apparently his absence did not hinder his defense. Judgment was "entered against the plaintiff." Winters, it appears, was either "infamous and scandalous" before Martin denounced her, or could not convince the court that his words were legally slanderous.[17]

---

15. Rhamanthus M. Stocker, *Centennial History of Susquehanna County, Pennsylvania*, 557, quoted in Vogel, *Early Mormon Documents*, 4:346.

16. Mark Nelson, email to Brian Hales, October 17, 2007.

17. Mark B. Nelson and Steven C. Harper, "The Imprisonment of Martin Harris in 1833," 114–15.

Steven Harper acknowledges that in 1832 "Harris charged Eliza Winters with adultery"—or, more likely, fornication and two years later "Joseph was accused of misconduct with Eliza Winters" that had occurred years before. But Harper concludes: "Given subsequent events and the anti-Mormonism of the area, it seems likely to me that anything substantive with which Joseph could have been branded as adulterous would have been shouted from the housetops. The fact that there is only the Lewis statement suggests to me that there is nothing there. It's very common . . . for them to claim knowledge beyond what they themselves know."[18] Mark Nelson similarly assessed:

> I have concluded that Levi mixed his rumors. Eager to find some pejorative information about Joseph, Levi grabbed onto this mixed rumor and ran with it. Noteworthy is that no other person made this same claim, including Levi's wife, although they all lived in the same neighborhood and were subject to the same slanderous innuendo. Clearly those Harmony individuals quoted by Howe wanted to distance themselves from Joseph and demonstrated their disdain for the prophet, yet none other asserted the claim that Joseph tried to seduce young Eliza Winters. Likewise, neither Eliza nor Benjamin Comfort [her representative in the above-mentioned lawsuit], or any of their family were asked to provide affidavits or statements. If one's goal is to slander Mormonism and its prophet, surely Eliza's testimony of impropriety would have been valuable. Significantly, no statements were gathered from her or any of her family.[19]

Importantly, nearly fifty years later, the seventy-year-old Eliza Winters was interviewed by newspaperman Frederick G. Mather who visited Susquehanna County, Pennsylvania, to gather information from Joseph Smith's former acquaintances. His primary purpose was to obtain derogatory statements regarding the Smith family for publication in an article that was printed weeks later in the *Binghamton Republican*.[20]

In the interview, Mather recorded Eliza saying "Joe Smith never made a convert at Susquehanna, and also that his father-in-law became so incensed by his conduct that he threatened to shoot him if he ever returned."[21] Yet notwithstanding these negative recollections, she failed to make any accusations regarding Joseph Smith's improper conduct toward her. Mather had created the perfect opportunity for Winters to share any scandal she might have remembered, but she was silent about an attempted seduction. Her apparent

---

18. Steven Harper, email to Brian Hales, October 15, 2007.
19. Mark Nelson, email to Brian Hales, October 22, 2007.
20. Vogel, *Early Mormon Documents*, 4:345.
21. Frederick G. Mather, "The Early Mormons, Joe Smith Operates at Susquehanna," *Binghamton Republican*, July 29, 1880, in Vogel, *Early Mormon Documents*, 4:358, see also 314, 297 note 3.

reticence to incriminate the Prophet on that occasion is puzzling if the Lewis allegation was true.[22] Later in the meeting, another interviewee, a Mr. Bush, was quoted saying, "Joe Smith was a good, kind neighbor; and that is the testimony of Mrs. McKune, Mrs. Squires and Mr. Skinner."[23] "Mrs. Squires" was Eliza Winters Squires.

Eliza Winters's prompt, though unsuccessful, counterattack when Martin Harris accused her of having given birth to an illegitimate child shows that she did not easily tolerate abuse. Notwithstanding, she apparently had nothing to say aside from the well-known friction between Joseph and his father-in-law. In short, she failed to corroborate the Levi Lewis accusation in the 1820s, in 1832, or even more importantly, in 1880 during an interview designed specifically to air such grievances.

Furthermore, even though Levi Lewis's report was printed in 1834, other periodicals and books published during the next decade, whether unbiased or anti-Mormon, seldom repeated it as evidence against Joseph Smith's moral character.[24] These two sentences, which appeared near the end of Howe's book, were generally neglected for many years by dozens of writers, even though their obvious goal was to belittle the Prophet.[25] Nor have I found any record that Levi Lewis repeated this accusation, even though his brothers recalled his statement in 1879.[26]

Regarding the charge that Joseph Smith tried to seduce Eliza fifty years earlier, Dan Vogel characterized her apparent silence on the topic as "an accusation she neither confirmed nor denied."[27] However, if Winters had denied Lewis's report, Mather probably would not have included her comments in his article, as they did not suit his purpose of disparaging Joseph Smith. I see as a more likely scenario that Mather knew about the topic from its publication and

---

22. Dan Vogel treats Lewis's report as somewhat credible. See Vogel, *Joseph Smith: The Making of a Prophet*, 178, 619; Vogel, *Early Mormon Documents*, 4:296–97.

23. Mather, "The Early Mormons, Joe Smith Operates at Susquehanna," in Vogel, *Early Mormon Documents*, 4:360.

24. The only reprint I have found is in Daniel P. Kidder's 1842, *Mormonism and the Mormons: A Historical View of the Rise and Progress of the Sect Self-Styled Latter-Day Saints*, 34–35; however, it is Kidder's only allegation in his 342-page book that Joseph Smith committed any sexual sin.

25. Even John C. Bennett in his 1842 *History of the Saints*, which reproduced whole pages of Howe's affidavits, did not repeat the Lewis statement. See John C. Bennett, *The History of the Saints: Or an Exposé of Joe Smith and Mormonism*, 61–84, 115–22.

26. In 1879 a series of letters between Joseph and Hiel Lewis, Levi's brothers, was published in the *Amboy Journal*. They mention the alleged seduction attempt only after two long exchanges. Evidently, it was not then viewed as a significant issue. Vogel, *Early Mormon Documents*, 4: 14–16.

27. Vogel, *Early Mormon Documents*, 4:346.

reprinting, raised the point with Eliza, and then simply dropped the issue when Eliza refused to validate Levi Lewis's version of what Martin Harris had said.

Richard L. Bushman summarized the episode briefly and with obvious skepticism: "One of Emma's cousins . . . Levi Lewis, said Martin Harris spoke of Joseph's attempt to seduce Elizabeth Winters, a friend of Emma's in Harmony. But the reports are tenuous. Harris said nothing of the event in his many descriptions of Joseph, nor did Winters herself when interviewed much later."[28]

1830 "Testimony" of Improper Conduct

A second allegation against the Prophet came from researcher Dan Vogel in 2002 in his *Early Mormon Documents* series. Although the event occurred in 1830, Vogel is, to my knowledge, the first to report an actual accusation of sexual impropriety during the trial. Vogel writes: "His [Joseph Smith's] July 1830 trial in South Bainbridge included testimony accusing him of improper conduct with two of Josiah Stowell's daughters, Miriam and Rhoda."[29] No trial records are extant, and I have been unable to identify any record matching Vogel's description of "testimony accusing him [Joseph Smith] of improper conduct." In his 2004 biography, *Joseph Smith: The Making of a Prophet*, Vogel speculates about why the Broome County prosecutor might have asked the two women to testify but does not refer to or quote any actual testimony.[30] Rather, the foundation for this episode comes from Joseph Smith himself, who recalled in his personal history in 1842: "The court was detained for a time, in order that two young women (daughters to Mr. Stoal) with whom I had at times kept company; might be sent for, in order, if possible to elicit something from them which might be made a pretext against me. The young women arrived and were severally examined, touching my character, and conduct in general but particularly as to my behavior towards them both in public and private, when they both bore such testimony in my favor, as left my enemies without a pretext on their account."[31]

In addition, on February 17, 1843, Josiah Stowell Jr. (b. 1809), the younger brother of Rhoda (b. 1805) and Miriam (b. 1807) Stowell, responded to inquiries made by Mormon missionary John S. Fullmer regarding Joseph

---

28. Richard Lyman Bushman, *Joseph Smith: Rough Stone Rolling*, 323.

29. Vogel, *Early Mormon Documents*, 4:206 note 9. Vogel names the daughters. I have found no records naming them as participants although they are the most likely candidates. See Dean C. Jessee, ed. *The Papers of Joseph Smith: Volume 1, Autobiographical and Historical Writings*, 254, note 2.

30. Vogel, *Joseph Smith: The Making of a Prophet*, 512–14.

31. "History of Joseph Smith," *Times and Seasons* 4, no. 3 (December 15, 1842): 41. See also Vogel, *Early Mormon Documents*, 1:118.

Smith's 1820s reputation. Josiah Jr. had not converted to Mormonism and therefore had no apparent religious biases. Concerning the Prophet he wrote:

> I have bin Intemetely acquainted with him about 2 years[.] he then was about 20 years old or there about I also when to school with him on winter[.] he was a fine likely young man & at that time did not Profess religion he was not a Profain man although I did onc[e] in a while hear him swair he never gambled to my knowledge I do not believe he ever did[.] I well know he was no Hoars Jocky for he was no Judge of Hoarses I sold him one[.] that is all I ever knowd he dealt in the kind[.] I never new him to git drunk I believe he would now and then take a glass he never Pretend=ed to Play the Slight of hand nor Black leg.[32]

It seems probable that, if Joseph Smith had behaved improperly with either of Josiah Jr.'s sisters, he would have mentioned it and given a less favorable report to Fullmer.

The following year in 1844, Joseph Smith's non-Mormon attorney in Broome County, John S. Reed, visited Nauvoo and, in the convention that nominated Joseph for U.S. president, commented about that trial: "Let me say to you that not one blemish nor spot was found against his character; he came from that trial, notwithstanding the mighty efforts that were made to convict him of crime by his vigilant persecutors, with his character unstained by even the appearance of guilt."[33]

Richard L. Bushman observed: "Considering how eager the Palmyra neighbors were to besmirch Joseph's character, their minimal mention of moral lapses suggest [that] libertinism was not part of his New York reputation."[34] Marvin Hill concurred: "[It is a] fact that none of the earliest anti-Mormon writers, neither Dogberry or E. D. Howe, charge Smith with sexual immorality."[35] Thus, Vogel seems to have referred to "testimony" based on his assumption that asking the two women to testify could have occurred only if prior "testimony" existed concern-

---

32. Mark Ashurst-McGee, "The Josiah Stowell Jr.– John S. Fullmer Correspondence," 113.

33. John S. Reed, "Some of the Remarks of John S. Reed, Esq., as Delivered before the State Convention," *Times and Seasons* 5, no. 11 (June 1, 1844): 550–51.

34. Bushman, *Joseph Smith: Rough Stone Rolling*, 323. See also Rodger I. Anderson, *Joseph Smith's New York Reputation Reexamined*, 149–50, for the only allegation of sexual misconduct (Howe's third-hand report) in his review of all of the available derogatory statements concerning Joseph Smith during the New York period. See also John L. Brooke, *The Refiner's Fire: The Making of Mormon Cosmology, 1644–1844*, 181.

35. Marvin S. Hill, "Secular or Sectarian History? A Critique of *No Man Knows My History*," in Newell G. Bringhurst, ed., *Reconsidering* No Man Knows My History: *Fawn M. Brodie and Joseph Smith in Retrospect*, 80. Similarly Reverend William Harris in his 1841 *Mormonism Portrayed; Its Errors and Absurdities Exposed, and the Spirit and Designs of Its Authors Made Manifest*, accuses Joseph Smith of setting up his religion, "for the gratification of his own vanity and selfishness," but makes no accusation of sexual misconduct in its sixty-four pages.

ing Joseph's improper conduct. The possibility that the prosecutor was on a fishing expedition is a more likely possibility, especially in light of later recollections. Regardless, available historical evidence indicates Joseph Smith was completely exonerated of wrong-doing where the Stowell sisters were concerned.

William Bond's Narrative

The third episode was recounted only after a lengthy lapse of time—in 1890. William Bond of Erie County, Pennsylvania, repeated a story charging Joseph Smith with "improper intimacy" that reportedly occurred in 1829–30:

> In about the year 1829–30, Joseph Smith visited Erie County, Pennsylvania, often as he was passing from Ohio into western New York, and held meetings to gain proselytes in the Mormon faith. . . . Some of the old and more substantial citizens, Henry Teller, Ranson Bromley, Henry Slator, and others, noticed an improper intimacy between Joseph Smith and a certain woman, which led to a further investigation of Smith's character, and finally exposure of his improper conduct before one of these assemblies. Smith, however, having friends, still declared his innocence. The next evening a wooden horse was found before the inn where Smith was lodging, and on the horse was written: "Assistance will be given by twelve gentlemen to mount this horse (he being high), and if the seat is hard a quantity of feathers and tar shall not be withheld to make the journey pleasant, as he is a fast rider.["] I need not inform you Smith was seen no more in that vicinity.[36]

This very late account is problematic in several respects. It is true that Joseph traversed the area several times, but the chronology of Joseph Smith's travels contradicts the allegations. Joseph's first trip through Erie County was with Emma, westbound from Fayette, New York, in 1831. Erie, Pennsylvania, is located about eighty miles east of Kirtland, Ohio. In 1833, accompanied by Sidney Rigdon and Freeman Nickerson, Joseph visited Springville, in Erie County, for two days. On the first day, "a large and attentive congregation assembled at Brother Rudd's in the evening, to whom we bore our testimony."[37] The next day, he continued his journey, arriving in Elk Creek on the other side of the county.[38] Available records fail to suggest that anything untoward occurred or that Joseph was threatened by locals whose memories prompted retaliation for some previous indiscretion.

---

36. William Bond, *The Early History of Mormonism, and the True Source Where the Aborigines of This Continent Came From*, 18–19.

37. "History of Joseph Smith," *Times and Seasons* 6, no. 1 (April 15, 1845): 864; see also *History of the Church*, 1:416.

38. J. Christopher Conkling, *A Joseph Smith Chronology*, 36, 53–54, 92.

TABLE 2.1
JOSEPH SMITH'S TRAVELS THROUGH ERIE COUNTY, PENNSYLVANIA

Date	Traveling Companion(s)	Purpose
1829–1830	——— No visits to the area ———	
1831 – January	Emma and family	Migration to Kirtland, Ohio, from Fayette, New York
1832 – October	Newel K. Whitney	To acquire goods for store in Kirtland
1833 – October	Sidney Rigdon, Freeman Nickerson	Preaching mission
1834 – February	Parley P. Pratt	To assemble volunteers for Zion's Camp
1836 – August	Hyrum Smith, Sidney Rigdon, Oliver Cowdery	To seek financial relief for the Kirtland Safety Society

In a 1993 article, Cheryl Harmon Bean researched the LDS baptisms in Erie County between 1831 and 1833. She identifies at least 122 new members coming from that county alone but mentions no record suggesting that Joseph Smith had earlier been accused of improprieties in the area.[39]

In addition, if Bond's allegations were true, it is surprising that such an intriguing and public scandal remained secret for more than fifty years. Erie was geographically close to Kirtland; it seems unlikely that the Mormon prophet's "intimacies" would have gone unnoticed by Joseph's enemies like Philastus Hurlburt, E. D. Howe, or Grandison Newell. Furthermore, "substantial citizens, Henry Teller, Ranson, Bromley Slator, and others" apparently headed up this impromptu committee on public decency. These men were indeed in the area during 1829–30, but no other negative records, either personal or public, concerning Joseph Smith have been located.

According to Bond's recollection, even more men than these leading citizens were involved, since an "assembly" appraised Joseph's improper conduct and resolved to expel him under threat of administering "tar and feathers." If this assembly occurred, it seems highly unlikely that nobody referred to the event until many decades later, that it was told by only a single individual, and that he does not explain how he happened to know of this story. He provides no historical source for his report.

---

39. Cheryl Harmon Bean, "LDS Baptisms in Erie County, Pennsylvania 1831–1833," 59–102.

An 1832 Romance with Marinda Johnson?

One often-repeated allegation suggests that the Prophet was intimately involved with Marinda Nancy Johnson in Hiram, Ohio, in 1832, which resulted in the Prophet's being mobbed and beaten. Marinda's brother Luke, who was not personally involved in the proceedings but who was acquainted with the perpetrators and the specific circumstances, wrote:

> In the fall of [1832], while Joseph was yet at my father's [John Johnson's home], a mob of forty or fifty came to his house, a few entered his room in the middle of the night, and Carnot Mason dragged Joseph out of bed by the hair of his head; he was then seized by as many as could get hold of him, and taken about forty rods from the house, stretched on a board, and tantalized in the most insulting and brutal manner; they tore off the few night clothes that he had on, for the purpose of emasculating him, and had Dr. Dennison there to perform the operation; but when the Dr. saw the Prophet stripped and stretched on the plank, his heart failed him, and he refused to operate.[40]

Besides Joseph Smith, the mob also attacked Sidney Rigdon at the same time. Sidney and Phoebe Rigdon's son, John, left this account:

> Not long after he [Sidney Rigdon] had moved to Hyrum [Hiram, Ohio], Joseph Smith came there to live and sometime during the winter or early spring of the year J. Smith and Sidney Rigdon were one morning before daylight taken out of bed and tarred and feathered by a mob. The mob came and got Rigdon first. He was a man weighing about 225. As they dragged him some distance over the frozen ground by his heels bumping the back of his head so that when they got him to the place where they were to put the tar and feathers on him he was insensible. They covered him with tar and feathers and pounded him till they thought he was dead and then went to get Joseph Smith. He fought them but they got hold of him at last and carried him out and they took him where Rigdon lay and Joseph thought he was dead. The mob covered him with tar and feathers and pounded him till they got tired and left them both on the ground. Joseph Smith soon after the mob left got up and went home not very badly hurt. He was bruised some about the head.
>
> My father must have lain on the ground when the mob left him for some time. At last he got up in a dazed condition did not know where he was nor where to go but at last got his face turned toward his home more by accident than design and went reeling along the road not knowing where he was and would have passed his house but my mother was out the door watching for him and went out as he came along and got him in the house. She got the tar and feathers off from him as best she could and got him to

---

40. "History of Luke Johnson," *Millennial Star* 26 (December 31, 1864): 834; see also continuation in 27 (January 7, 1865): 5–7.

Drawing by unknown artist, published in Charles Mackay, ed., The Mormons, or Latter-day Saints; with Memoirs of the Life and Death of Joseph Smith, the American Mahomet, *4th ed. (London: Office of the National Illustrated Library, 1851), 55; 1851 edition in my possession.*

bed. In the morning Joseph Smith came over to see him but he was crazy. He wanted him to get him his razor. Joseph Smith wanted to know what he wanted it for he said he wanted to kill his wife. Joseph Smith soothed him as best he could and left him. In a few days my father regained his mind.[41]

In 1895, LDS Bishop Frederick Kesler recalled additional details reportedly obtained from the Prophet himself: "On one occasion, at a meeting held near the Temple in Nauvoo, Joseph arose to make a few remarks, and he related the incident of the mob knocking one of his front teeth out in their successful effort to pour acquifortis down his throat. His spirit, he said, left

---

41. John Wickliffe Rigdon, "The Life and Testimony of Sidney Rigdon," in Karl Keller, ed., "'I Never Knew a Time When I Did Not Know Joseph Smith': A Son's Record of the Life and Testimony of Sidney Rigdon," 25–26; original holograph in LDS Church History Library. See also "Lecture Written by John M. [sic] Rigdon on the Early History of the Mormon Church" available on *New Mormon Studies: A Comprehensive Resource Library.*

John Johnson Home, July 2007. Brian C. Hales Collection.

his body, and hovered over it in the air, and returned after it was over. They supposed they had killed him, but he had to come back and take his body."[42]

Concerning this event, Fawn Brodie wrote: "It is said that Eli Johnson demanded that the prophet be castrated, for he suspected Joseph of being too intimate with his sister, Marinda Nancy."[43] In fact Brodie was quoting Clark Braden, a Church of Christ minister,[44] who debated future RLDS Presiding Bishop E. L. Kelley in 1884. Braden's version of this episode is: "In March, 1832, Smith was stopping at Mr. Johnson's in Hiram, Ohio, and was mobbed.

---

42. Frederick Kesler, quoted in "Joseph, the Prophet, His Life and Mission as Viewed by Intimate Acquaintances," *Salt Lake Herald Church and Farm Supplement*, January 12, 1895, 212.

43. Fawn M. Brodie, *No Man Knows My History: The Life of Joseph Smith, the Mormon Prophet*, 119. This view is repeated in Donna Hill, *Joseph Smith: The First Mormon*, 146 and Linda King Newell and Valeen Tippetts Avery, *Mormon Enigma: Emma Hale Smith*, 65.

44. Throughout his life, Braden seemed determined to refute the RLDS Church's position. See his "Did Joseph Smith Teach and Practice Polygamy?" *Christian Oracle*, April 30, 1891, 4, which stated: "There was published in the *Oracle* in May, 1889, a letter written by William Marks, a member of the First Presidency of the Josephite Mormon Church, in which Marks clearly stated that he *knew* that Smith taught and practiced polygamy. It created quite a stir among the Josephites. They attempt to evade it by saying that it was written long after Smith's death. We give below an article written by Marks and published in the Mormon paper in St. Louis in 1853 (*Zion's Harbinger and Baneemy's Organ* [St. Louis] 3, no. 7 [July 1853]: 52–54), just nine years after Smith's death."

The mob was led by Eli Johnson, who blamed Smith with being too intimate with his sister Marinda, who afterwards married Orson Hyde."[45]

It appears that Braden was the very first person to assert a motive for the mob attack that involved inappropriate sexual conduct. Current research supports that the allegation was not included in any publication printed during the fifty-two years prior to the 1884 debate.[46] In fact, a review of books written between 1832 and 1844 about Mormonism shows that no author mentioned the mobbing until after the *Times and Seasons* published an account in August 1844, two months after the Prophet's death.[47]

Even after that point, sexual impropriety does not appear as a motive for the mobbing. For example, in 1853 Reverend W. Sparrow Simpson, author of *Mormonism: Its History, Doctrines, and Practices*, comments on Joseph Smith's exposure "to the American process of tarring and feathering" and attributes this hostile action "on account of his [Joseph Smith's] strange and pernicious doctrines" without any specific reference to licentious behavior as a motivator.[48] Similarly, in 1861, Jules Remy and Julius Brenchley's *A Journey to Great Salt Lake City* discusses the 1832 mobbing as an attack provoked simply by the Prophet's doctrines, revelations, and missionary successes in the area.[49] Antagonistic author John H. Beadle in his 1870 exposé, *Polygamy; or Mysteries and Crimes of Mormonism*, listed three reasons: "for attempting to establish communism, for forgery and dishonorable dealing."[50]

At the funeral of Symonds Ryder in 1870, preacher B. A. Hinsdale observed: "It may seem strange that a man of Father Ryder's strong mind and honest heart, could even temporarily have fallen into the Mormon delusion.

---

45. E. L. Kelley and Clark Braden, *Public Discussion of the Issues between the Reorganized Church of Jesus Christ of Latter Day Saints and the Church of Christ (Disciples) Held in Kirtland, Ohio, Beginning February 12, and Closing March 8, 1884 between E. L. Kelley, of the Reorganized Church of Jesus Christ of Latter Day Saints and Clark Braden, of the Church of Christ*, 202. See Wayne A. Ham, "Truth Affirmed, Error Denied: The Great Debates of the Early Reorganization," 8.

46. For one example, see *History of the Mormons* (1853), 16.

47. "History of Joseph Smith," *Times and Seasons* 5, no. 15 (August 15, 1844): 611.

48. W. Sparrow Simpson, *Mormonism: Its History, Doctrines, and Practices*, 14.

49. Jules Remy and Julius Brenchley, *A Journey to Great Salt Lake City*, 1:282.

50. John H. Beadle, *Polygamy; or Mysteries and Crimes of Mormonism*, 37. Accusations of sexual improprieties also do not appear in James H. Kennedy, *Early Days of Mormonism: Palmyra, Kirtland, and Nauvoo* (1888), 105; William Alexander Linn, *The Story of the Mormons from the Date of Their Origin to the Year 1901* (1923). 135–37. An 1888 account from another antagonist, Reverend Samuel F. Whitney, Newel K. Whitney's brother, also includes a report of the ordeal, noting that castration was intended, but without any allegation of sexual misconduct as a motivating factor. Quoted in Arthur B. Deming, *Naked Truths about Mormonism* 1 (January 1888): 4, column 1.

Let us not fail to remember, however, that Mormonism in northern Ohio, in 1831, was a very different thing from Mormonism in Utah, in 1870. It then gave no sign of the moral abomination which is now its most prominent characteristic."[51] The "moral abomination" referred to was polygamy, which was widely criticized in 1870, but apparently unknown to Ryder in 1832. Five years later in 1875, Amos S. Hayden's *Early History of the Disciples in the Western Reserve* attributes the attack to the mob members' belief that Joseph Smith had concocted "a plot . . . to take their property from them."[52]

Three years prior to the Braden-Kelley debate, the link between the mobbing and sexual misconduct, specifically polygamy, seemed even more plausible. In April 1881 an unidentified writer using the penname "Historicus" published an article in the *Anti-Polygamy Standard*, a Salt Lake newspaper, in which he stated: "Joseph told Lyman E. Johnson confidentially that polygamy was a true principle. . . . In addition to Lyman, three others, Eli, Edward and John Jr., joined the new church but apostatized in the winter of 1831–32. When the fact is known that these brothers assisted in the tarring and feathering of the prophet, it is not a very far-fetched conclusion to arrive at that they knew of what Smith had told their brother Lyman about polygamy."[53] The author "Historicus" freely admitted that the conclusion was based upon speculation, not evidence. He obviously was unaware of any documentation that Clark Braden would quote three years later supporting the claim, if any such evidence actually existed. Braden was in the Midwest but was connected with antagonist factions in the Utah Territory and may have read "Historicus's" report. In fact, this account might have been the basis for Braden's accusations. Interestingly, Braden repeats an error found in the original *Times and Seasons* account, which incorrectly identified Edward Johnson as a participant. John and Elsa Johnson's son, Edwin, had died before the 1830 census.[54] In addition, Braden asserts that one of Marinda's brothers, "Eli Johnson," was also involved, but she had no such sibling. Historian Mark Staker has verified that John Johnson's brother, Eli, Marinda's uncle, was living at the Johnson home at the time.[55]

---

51. Amos Sutton Hayden, *Early History of the Disciples in the Western Reserve*, 252.

52. Ibid., 220–21.

53. Historicus (pseud.), "Sketches from the History of Polygamy: Joseph Smith's Especial Revelations," 1.

54. Mark Lyman Staker, *Hearken O Ye People: The Historical Setting for Joseph Smith's Ohio Revelations*, 367 note 41.

55. Ibid., 336–37, 346–52. Bill Shepard wrote: "There is an Eli Johnson who married in Portage Co. and executed deeds but I've not attached him to a family. John's younger brother Eliphaz may have visited Ohio but I've not found evidence that he ever lived there. But I can't say that for sure so it would probably be best not to speculate." Bill Shepard, email to Michael Marquardt, March 22, 2005.

Except for this hypothesized connection between Historicus and Braden, what might Braden's source have been? Braden was born in 1831, and it seems improbable that he would have discovered documentation that had remained unknown for more than fifty-two years. Most likely, he simply read the account of the mobbing, which was available in both LDS and RLDS publications, even repeating an error in that document. Then he assumed that, since emasculation was mentioned, at least some of Joseph Smith's offenses were sexual in nature. If Braden had any evidence beyond his own assumptions, he left no record of what it was, nor have I found any documentation that suggests a historical record.

Mark Staker quotes an account by historian Harriet Taylor Upton, who visited Hiram soon after the Braden-Kelley debate, interviewed local residents, and then published in her 1910 history of the Western Reserve: "Several stories have been told as to why this [mobbing] was done. The truth is that they received this treatment because they were Mormons, because they had interested the people of that vicinity in their belief, and because some of these converts had decided them to be frauds. This was before the days of polygamy. It was largely a quarrel among different religions in the beginning, later because it was believed the new followers were to be deceived."[56]

Importantly, pre-1884 accounts strongly suggest that the mob members were primarily concerned with attempts to live the law of consecration, which they interpreted as attempts by Sidney Rigdon and Joseph Smith to confiscate their property.[57] The brutal assault was equally directed at Rigdon, whom they left for dead. Richard S. Van Wagoner theorizes in *Sidney Rigdon: A Portrait of Religious Excess* that Rigdon was, in fact, the primary target.[58] Some indication of how widespread the concern about property ownership was appears in Orson Hyde's accusations, during his brief 1838 apostasy, that Rigdon had tried to usurp control over the Johnson farm.[59] Symonds Ryder, one of the mob leaders later wrote:

> When they [Joseph Smith and other leaders] went to Missouri to lay the foundation of the splendid city of Zion, and also of the temple, they left their papers behind [in Hiram, Ohio]. This gave their new converts an opportunity

---

56. Staker, *Hearken O Ye People*, 337; quoting Harriet Taylor Upton, *History of the Western Reserve*, 699.

57. Max H Parkin, "Joseph Smith and the United Firm: The Growth and Decline of the Church's First Master Plan of Business and Finance, Ohio and Missouri, 1832–1834," 4–66.

58. Richard S. Van Wagoner, *Sidney Rigdon: A Portrait of Religious Excess*, 108–18. See also Mario S. De Pillis, "The Development of Mormon Communitarianism, 1826–1846," 19–20.

59. Orson Hyde, quoted by John Wickliffe Rigdon, in Keller, "'I Never Knew a Time When I Did not Know Joseph Smith,'" 25–26.

to become acquainted with the internal arrangement of their church, which revealed to them the horrid fact that a plot was laid to take their property from them and place it under the control of Joseph Smith the prophet [through the law of consecration]. This was too much for the Hiramites. . . . Determined not to let it pass with impunity; . . . accordingly, a company was formed of citizens . . . in March, 1832, and proceeded to headquarters in the darkness of night, and took Smith and Rigdon from their beds, and tarred and feathered them both, and let them go. This had the desired effect, which was to get rid of them. They soon left for Kirtland.[60]

It appears that Brodie's willingness to believe Braden's claims without significant scrutiny is another manifestation of her underlying assumption that Joseph Smith's libido was actively seeking sexual opportunities throughout his life, including as early as 1832. Todd Compton disagrees with Brodie: "There is no good evidence supporting the position (found in Brodie, *No Man Knows My History*, 119, 462) that Joseph Smith was married to Marinda Johnson . . . or had an affair with her, in 1831, and was mobbed by 'her brother Eli' and others as a result."[61] Nor is there any documentation to suggest that Braden's version of the mob's motives was known to anyone during Joseph Smith's lifetime. Marinda herself recalled in 1877: "I feel like bearing my testimony that during the whole year that Joseph was an inmate of my father's house I never saw aught in his daily life or conversation to make me doubt his divine mission."[62]

Vienna Jacques: An 1833 Plural Wife?

A late report of impropriety apparently made decades after the alleged incident, involved a woman named Vienna Jacques (apparently pronounced "jack-ways"[63]). At some point, perhaps during the 1880s, a woman whom some historians call "Mrs. Warner Alexander," allegedly quoted Polly Beswick as quoting Emma Smith regarding an illicit relationship between Joseph Smith and Vienna Jacques. "Mrs. Warner Alexander's" statement reads:

> My father, William Smith and mother Became Mormons in Bolton, N.Y, and moved to Kirtland O. in \left/ 1836. After Jo Smith, the Mormon

---

60. Symonds Ryder, "Letter to A. S. Hayden," February 1, 1868, quoted in Amos Sutton Hayden, *Early History of the Disciples in the Western Reserve, Ohio*, 220–21. See also Max H Parkin, "The Nature and Cause of Internal and External Conflict of the Mormons in Ohio between 1830 and 1838," 254.

61. Todd Compton, *In Sacred Loneliness: The Plural Wives of Joseph Smith*, 642.

62. Edward W. Tullidge, *The Women of Mormondom*, 404.

63. This pronunciation is based on Samuel Harrison Smith, Diary, July 18, 1832, who was serving a mission in the Boston area: "Went about five miles to Wm. Angel's, who[se] wife was a sister to Sister Viena *Jacways*" (emphasis mine). Modern pronunciation is sometimes "jakes."

The signature located at the bottom of the account concerning Vienna Jacques could be Nancy Alexander's signature or the writing of the transcriber. Subsequent reviewers may have mistaken "Mrs Nancy Alexander" as "Mrs Warner Alexander."

Prophet robbed us, I worked out at housework at 25 cents a week. My sister received 50 cents a week, we gave our wages to our parents.

Father had broken his arm six weeks before leaving N. Y., and could not work, Mother had to work very hard, she had 14 children. Polly Beswick, who weighed about 200 pounds, made her home with her sister Mrs. John Tanner,[64] who lived next house to ours and often called on us. She was of good disposition, very agreeable in conversation and everybo\d/y liked her. She worked much of the time in Prophet Jo Smith's family. It was commonly reported, Jo Smith said he had a revelation to lie \with/ Vienna Jaques, who lived in his family, Polly told me, that Emma, Joseph's wife, told her that Joseph would get up in the night and go to Vienna's bed. Polly said Emma would get out of humor, ~~shrea~~ \fret/ and s~~ch~~old and flounce in the harness. Jo would shut himself up in a room and pray for a revelation, when he came out he would claim he had received one and state it to her, and bring her around all right. Polly said emma was a very fine woman.[65]

The earliest copy of this document I have been able to locate is an undated typescript, made from an unknown source, whether from a dictation or as a transcription from a currently unidentified holograph. One source places the year of its origin as 1886.[66] Research indicates that "Mrs. Warner

---

64. John Tanner, the father of Nathan and John Joshua Tanner, was a forty-seven-year-old widower in 1825 when he married Polly Beswick's twenty-two-year-old sister, Elizabeth. Ancestral File.

65. Mrs. Nancy Alexander, "Statement," [1886?]. Unfortunately, the "original" is an newspaper clipping from an unidentified and undated newspaper in the Stanley B. Kimball Collection. See bibliography.

66. The first (1984) edition of Linda King Newell and Valeen Tippetts Avery's *Mormon Enigma: Emma Hale Smith*, lists this document's location as "LDS Archives" on p. 319 note 46. However, according to archivist Ronald G. Watt conversation with Brian Hales (November 12, 2007), this location is incorrect. The second edition of the biography identifies the location as the Stanley B. Kimball Collection (319 note 46), Southern Illinois University. Typescript copy, Linda King Newell Collection, Marriott Library, University of Utah, MS 447, Box 11, fd. 3. This error has been perpetuated by Todd Compton, "A Trajectory of Plurality: An Overview of Joseph Smith's Thirty-Three Plural Wives," 36.

Alexander" was Nancy Maria Smith, born December 1, 1822, to William Smith and Lydia Calkins Smith (no relation to the Prophet's brother William B. Smith). She married Justin Alexander on September 4, 1850, at Kirtland, Ohio, making her "Mrs. Justin Alexander" or "Mrs. Nancy Alexander." It is probable that the transcriber copying the original hand-written statement misread "Nancy" as "Warner."

Other information provided in the document further corroborates Nancy as the author.[67] She and her family gathered to Kirtland only to apostatize, blaming Joseph Smith for robbing them. Nevertheless, Nancy Maria and her husband stayed in the area, and were counted in the 1880 census.[68]

Vienna Jacques. Photo courtesy of the International Society of the Daughters of Utah Pioneers.

The historical record shows that the Joseph Smith family lived in the Kirtland (or Hiram) vicinity from 1831 to 1838. Vienna Jacques visited Kirtland for a few weeks in 1831 and again for a few months in 1833;.[69] During the latter visit, she consecrated approximately $1400 to the Church, a small fortune that she reportedly obtained "in her self reliant way, by patient toil and strict economy."[70] Subsequently she was mentioned in a revelation (D&C 90:28–29) and received a compassionate letter from the Prophet.[71]

A review of this story's chronological and geographical features highlights several concerns. First, there is no evidence Vienna ever lived with the Smith family. During 1833 the Smiths were living in the N. K. Whitney Store compliments of the Whitney family.[72] Joseph and Emma's ability to invite

---

67. Alexander, "Statement."
68. U.S. Census, 1880, Newbury, Geauga County, Ohio.
69. Tullidge, *The Women of Mormondom*, 441. Joseph Smith, Kirtland, Ohio, Letter to W. W. Phelps, Independence, Missouri, November 27, 1832, notes: "Vienna Jaqis had not r[e]ceived her Papers pleas inform her sister \Hariet/ that Shee is well and give my respects to her." Whether Vienna had arrived in Kirtland by that time or was communicating by letter from Boston, is unclear.
70. Jerri W. Hurd, "Vienna Jacques: The Other Woman in the Doctrine and Covenants," 1.
71. Jessee, *The Personal Writings of Joseph Smith*, 293–96; *History of the Church*, 1:407–9.
72. Mark Lyman Staker, email to Brian Hales, December 3, 2010.

Joseph Smith's Morality, 1820s to 1835 51

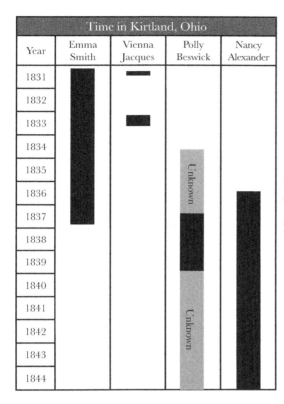

Figure 2.1. Analysis of the Time of Proximity between Emma Smith, Vienna Jacques, Polly Beswick, and Nancy Alexander.

guests to board with them in their own home did not begin until the following year. Mark Staker wrote: "After a long, careful study, we've finally concluded that Joseph Smith moved into his new home on the hill in mid-1834. That home had a large added section on the rear when it was built that was suitable for large gatherings (a wedding, priesthood leadership meetings, a school for Joseph and Emma's children). That part of the home had room for an additional person to stay."[73]

Second, even though Polly Beswick is depicted as being a firsthand witness, this episode occurred years before her arrival in Kirtland. Since she could have learned about these events only secondhand, the level of detail she provides is also curious. Furthermore, making the credibility of the story and the minute details even less likely, this account depends on another, later, "telling" from Polly to Nancy Alexander or even through a third intermediary.

Third, the described behavior of all of the participants, Joseph, Emma, and Vienna, seems implausible. If Alexander's account is true, Joseph Smith would have needed to accomplish one of two difficult tasks during the short

---

73. Mark Lyman Staker, email to Brian Hales, September 9, 2008.

Table 2.2
Vienna Jacques Timeline

Year	Month	Incident
1787		Vienna Jacques is born in Beverly, Massachusetts.
1831		Vienna Jacques reads the Book of Mormon.
1831	Feb	Joseph and Emma Smith arrive in Kirtland from New York.
1831		Vienna Jacques visits Kirtland, is baptized, and stays for six weeks.
1831–1833		Vienna Jacques returns to Boston.
1832	July	Samuel H. Smith visits Vienna in Boston.
1833	Early	Vienna Jacques moves to Kirtland with $1400. She is baptized and donates the money to the Church. She may have stayed with the Smith family.
1833	March	Two verses of a lengthy revelation given to Joseph Smith instruct her to go to Missouri (D&C 90:28–29).
	end April	Vienna's migration to Jackson County is delayed by a Church conference.
	May–June	Vienna Jacques leaves Kirtland, Ohio for Missouri.
1833	July 2	Joseph Smith receives word of Vienna's safe arrival in Zion (Missouri).
	Sept	Joseph Smith writes a letter to Vienna.
1834	Summer	The Smith family move into their new home on the hill.
1835	After May	Polly Beswick moves to Kirtland.
1836		The William Smith family (not Joseph Smith's brother), including William's daughter Nancy Maria Smith (the future "Mrs. Warner Alexander"), moves to Kirtland.
1838	Jan	Joseph Smith leaves Kirtland, Ohio.
		Vienna Jacques marries Daniel Shearer.
1840		Daniel and Vienna Shearer are established in Nauvoo.
1840–1844		Vienna Jacques is *possibly* sealed to Joseph Smith in an "eternity only" marriage.
1844	March	Vienna receives a patriarchal blessing as Vienna Shearer.
1845	July	Vienna receives a second patriarchal blessing as Vienna Shearer.
1846	Jan	Vienna receives her endowment in the Nauvoo Temple.
	Feb	Daniel Shearer receives his endowment.
1869		Vienna refuses to sign an affidavit that she was a plural wife of Joseph Smith

Tracking Polly Beswick between 1835 and 1837 is challenging because it is unclear when she left Kirtland. Nancy Alexander's family did not settle in Kirtland until 1836.

time Vienna was in Kirtland. He would have needed to either convince Vienna Jacques of the appropriateness of polygamy and immediately marry her, while at the same time convincing Emma, not only of the validity of polygamy, but also to let a plural wife live with them in their own home. Or Joseph would have needed to persuade Emma Smith to allow him to engage in sexual intimacy with Vienna (without a plural marriage ceremony) under Emma's very roof. Neither proposal seems very likely.

As a woman possessing conservative moral values, there is little indication that Emma would have ever approved of her husband having sexual relations with a woman to whom he was not married. Emma struggled mightily in 1843 to accept plural marriage even minimally and for brief periods. All records from the Kirtland period demonstrate that she did not then believe that God-approved plural marriage had then been restored. (See my argument in Chapters 4–8; that evidence does not support the presence of polygamy at Kirtland beyond a single secret plural marriage of the Prophet to Fanny Alger.) Accordingly, she would have considered any polygamous intimacy as adultery and certainly would not have been easily persuaded that God approved of it.

Fourth, if Joseph had married Vienna and was able to use revelations or argument to keep Emma compliant, it seems strange that he would almost immediately send Jacques to Missouri. Joseph's behavior in Nauvoo suggests that he attempted to keep his plural wives geographically close to him. Some researchers have suggested that he was planning to move to Missouri soon. However, a revelation on September 11, 1831, designated Kirtland as a "strong hold" for the next five years (D&C 64:21). Importantly, the Lord had promised a great endowment to be given in Ohio (D&C 38:32) and had commissioned the building of a temple in a December 27, 1832, revelation (D&C 88:119).

Summary

The known historical documents at this point contain six reports of alleged sexual impropriety on Joseph Smith's part between the late 1820s and early 1830s. One involves Fanny Alger and will be discussed in Chapters 4–8. Of the remaining five narratives, only one was published during Joseph's lifetime, and it essentially received no attention at the time. Significantly, an investigation of those narratives raises numerous questions about their plausibility, suggesting that none rises above the credibility of sensationalized gossip. I conclude that no credible evidence based on these five narratives supports allegations that Joseph Smith engaged in sexual misbehavior, including polygamy, through the mid-1830s and that no serious challenge to his reputation for personal morality exists for that period.[74]

---

74. William Hepworth Dixon, *Spiritual Wives*, 86, opined in 1868: "My impression

is that [polygamy's] origin might be traced to reports and scandals coming in from Palmyra, Wagnelo, [sic] N.Y., where Joe Smith, since about 1829, had been developing Mormonism." Compton, *In Sacred Loneliness*, 26, similarly reported: "A number of sources, both contemporary and recollected, provide evidence that polygamy was developed and practiced in the New York and Kirtland period." On the contrary, I have found no credible evidence to support the practice of plural marriage by Joseph Smith or other Church members in the New York period. For its practice during the Kirtland period, see Chapters 4–8.

Chapter 3

Charges of Immoral Conduct against Joseph Smith, 1836–1842

Between the late 1830s and the Prophet's first plural sealing in Nauvoo in 1841, a few authors have asserted that Joseph Smith was sexually involved (with or without wedding ceremonies) with several different women.[1] Klaus Hansen wrote: "There is . . . considerable evidence that the prophet had taken several wives even before [April 5, 1841]"; however, he does not provide any details or documentation.[2] Fawn Brodie posited at least four such associations, and my research has uncovered two additional allegations.

Sidney Rigdon's Daughters, Nancy and Athalia

In his biography *Sidney Rigdon: A Portrait of Religious Excess*, Richard S. Van Wagoner writes: "Gossip in Ohio's Western Reserve linked Smith to Athalia and Nancy Rigdon, Sidney's sixteen- and fifteen-year-old daughters."[3] Born in 1821, Athalia would have been sixteen in 1837. Van Wagoner doesn't explain the specific nature of the described "link," but the implication is that it was sexual or romantic. To support the presence of a "link," Van Wagoner refers to an 1884 testimony from a man named William S. Smith (not the Prophet's brother) that was recorded during the debate between Clark Braden and future RLDS Presiding Bishop E. L. Kelley (ordained in 1890):

> Q. Is it your recollection or your impression, Mr. Smith, that you have heard of the sealing of women to men here in Kirtland, and the sealing of Nancy Rigdon to Joseph Smith?

---

1. For example, antagonistic author Harry M. Beardsley, *Joseph Smith and His Mormon Empire*, 388, claimed in 1931 that Joseph Smith had "women of Kirtland and Nauvoo who might be considered as common-law wives." Beardsley provides no evidence to support his assertion.

2. Klaus J. Hansen, *Quest for Empire: The Political Kingdom of God and the Council of Fifty in Mormon History*, 53.

3. Richard S. Van Wagoner, *Sidney Rigdon: A Portrait of Religious Excess*, 291; see also Todd Compton, *In Sacred Loneliness: The Plural Wives of Joseph Smith*, 634.

A. My impression is I have . . .

Q. Did you ever hear it talked of while the Saints lived here?

A. I say I have heard it talked of. My impression is that I have heard it talked of here in Kirtland, and that the story obtained that the difficulty between Joseph Smith and Sydney Rigdon was in consequence of the wish or the manifestation on the part of Joseph Smith that Rigdon's daughter Nancy should be sealed to him.

Q. Will you say that was between Joseph Smith and Rigdon, and that it was a difficulty occurred here in Kirtland. Who did you hear talk about their having trouble here in Kirtland?

A. I cannot tell.

Q. Was it any of the Saints?

A. I can not tell you that.

Q. Do you not know, Mr. Smith, that there was not any report of any such thing as that as of Nancy Rigdon being sealed to Joseph Smith while the Saints were here in Kirtland?

A. My impression is that that report was here in Kirtland. I went to school with Athalia Rigdon, and there was talk among the boys about sealing. I think there was difficulty between Joseph Smith and Rigdon with reference to having Rigdon's daughter sealed to Smith. I would not positively say it was so; that is my impression.

Q. How old was Nancy Rigdon at that time?

A. I do not know; I went to school with Athalia Rigdon.

Q. How old was she?

A. I cannot tell. Nor can I tell how old I was. Nancy Rigdon was the oldest. I do not know how much older than Athalia.

Q. Did you ever hear any of them talk about sealing?

A. Yes, I am positive that I heard that language used among the boys.

Q. Did they not talk about the sealing of the Holy Spirit. Is not that what you heard them talk about?

A. No, the sealing was in some way or other with the women. My impression is that I have heard that story of the quarrel between Rigdon and Smith talked of here in Kirtland.

Q. Is it not probable that they were talking those things after they went to Nauvoo. You got it mixed.

A. It may be, but I give you my best recollection.[4]

It appears from the transcript that Athalia Rigdon's name came up simply because the witness, William S. Smith, had attended school with her.

---

4. E. L. Kelley and Clark Braden, *Public Discussion of the Issues between the Reorganized Church of Jesus Christ of Latter Day Saints and The Church of Christ (Disciples) Held in Kirtland, Ohio, Beginning February 12, and Closing March 8, 1884 Between E. L. Kelley, of the Reorganized Church of Jesus Christ of Latter Day Saints and Clark Braden, of the Church of Christ*, 391.

Accordingly, it seems that inferring a "link" (sexual or otherwise) between Joseph and Athalia would be an extreme interpretation of William Smith's confessedly shaky memory. Connecting Nancy Rigdon with Joseph is somewhat more understandable because, in Nauvoo in early 1842, Joseph Smith did propose a plural sealing to her. However, Nancy Rigdon recalled in 1884: "I never heard of such a thing in Kirtland as sealing. . . . I heard about this first about the year 1842."[5] Accordingly, it is more probable that William S. Smith was simply confused, a possibility he freely admits. In any case, it appears that Van Wagoner was the first to imply a "link" between Joseph and Athalia Rigdon in his 1994 biography of Sidney Rigdon, a link that is unpersuasive without additional evidence.

Fawn Brodie's Claims of Pre-1842 Plurality

In *No Man Knows My History*, Fawn Brodie postulated that Joseph may have married four women prior to his first Nauvoo plural sealing, with two of the marriages occurring in Missouri.[6]

Although I discuss the evidence for and against a sealing to each of the four separately, in more general terms, I find three problems with Brodie's approach to Joseph's plural sealings. First, as the inclusion of question marks next to the marriage dates shows, documentation is lacking for those dates, requiring an extra burden of proof that such sealings actually occurred.

Second, throughout *No Man Knows My History*, Brodie portrays the Prophet as unconcerned with the suffering he experienced in consequence of his 1832 mobbing or the difficulties that resulted from his first venture into plural marriage with Fanny Alger. (For an analysis of the relationship with Alger, see Chapters 4–8.) My research, in contrast, indicates that he was profoundly affected by those events, consistently manifesting concern that confidants would turn traitor. Max Parkin wrote: "[The] ominous threat of mobs was a constant terror to the Mormon Prophet and an expectation of a recurrence of the Hiram outrage undoubtedly was indelibly impressed into his memory."[7] Reportedly, on July 29, 1838, Joseph gave a brief and vivid summary of the persecution he had endured: "I have been beaten, abused, stoned, persecuted, and have had

---

5. Joseph Smith III and Heman C. Smith, *The History of the Reorganized Church of Jesus Christ of Latter Day Saints, Vols. 1–4, 1805–1890*, 4:452.

6. Fawn M. Brodie, No *Man Knows My History: The Life of Joseph Smith, the Mormon Prophet*, 335. See also John L. Brooke, *The Refiner's Fire: The Making of Mormon Cosmology, 1644–1844*, 262–63.

7. Max H Parkin, "Conflict at Kirtland: The Nature and Cause of Internal and External Conflict of the Mormons in Ohio between 1830 and 1838," 261.

TABLE 3.1
FAWN BRODIE'S LIST OF ALLEGED JOSEPH SMITH PLURAL WIVES
AFTER FANNY ALGER

Name of Alleged Wife	Date of Alleged Marriage	Location
Lucinda Pendleton Morgan Harris	1838?	Missouri
Presendia Huntington Buell	1839?	Missouri
Marinda Nancy Johnson Hyde	1839?	Illinois
Clarissa Reed Hancock	1840?	Illinois

Source: Brodie, *No Man Knows My History,* 335–36.

to escape by day and by night. I have been sued at law and have always proved myself innocent. I have had twenty one lawsuits."[8]

Third, Fawn Brodie's approach also seems disconnected from Joseph Smith's reality as recovered from the historical record. She assumes that, unhampered by conscience or other constraints, Joseph Smith jumped from one sexual escapade or polygamous marriage to the next. Brodie seems sure he was deeply engaged in repeated and varied sexual trysts and illicit relationships with numerous women, but experienced no emotional or spiritual consequences. It is true that he frequently expressed fears of betrayal, but there is no evidence of a "conquest" mentality based on rapid, shallow seductions in his documented attitude toward women. Brodie's historical reconstruction of Joseph Smith's activities and personality as virtually consequence-free strikes me as unconvincing and as disconnected from the reality portrayed in contemporary documents.

Lucinda Pendleton Harris

Of the four women included on Brodie's list, Lucinda Pendleton Morgan Harris is unique in that Todd Compton agrees with the probable date of a sealing to Joseph Smith in 1838 but designates it as "[1838?]."[9] Only Compton and Brodie date the relationship to 1838. In his 1973 master's thesis, D. Michael Quinn positioned the marriage in 1841–44;[10] but by 1994, he had broadened

---

8. William Swartzell, *Mormonism Exposed, Being a Journal of a Residence in Missouri from the 28th of May to the 20th of August, 1838,* 27. Swartzell had been a member of the Church.

9. Compton, *In Sacred Loneliness,* 4. See also Harry M. Beardsley, *Joseph Smith and His Mormon Empire,* 229. H. Michael Marquardt, *The Rise of Mormonism: 1816–1844,* 561, is unique in not including Lucinda Pendleton Morgan Harris on his table: "Married Women Sealed to Joseph Smith."

10. D. Michael Quinn, "Organizational Development and Social Origins of the Mormon Hierarchy, 1832–1932: A Prosopographical Study," 278.

the window of that sealing to "1838–1842."[11] Compton and Quinn identify Lucinda as the only other marriage that Joseph contracted between Fanny Alger in Kirtland and Louisa Beaman in Nauvoo.

Lucinda was born September 27, 1801, and married renowned anti-Mason William Morgan in 1819. Morgan was apparently murdered (his body was never found) seven years later, and Lucinda married George Washington Harris in 1830. The Harrises were baptized in 1834 and, by March 1838, were living in Far West, Missouri, where George served on the stake high council.

Proponents of Lucinda's 1838 relationship with Joseph Smith usually cite five pieces of evidence. The first is her proxy sealing to Joseph Smith performed in the Nauvoo Temple on January 22, 1846, which was repeated in the Salt Lake Temple in 1899.[12] However, current evidence indicates that several women who were sealed to Joseph by proxy in the Nauvoo Temple were not married to him while he was living. For example, Cordelia Calista Morley Cox, a daughter of Isaac Morley, refused a sealing proposal from the Prophet during his lifetime but was sealed to him vicariously in the Nauvoo Temple on January 27, 1846.[13]

The second piece of corroborating evidence is considered to be a May 24, 1839, letter from Joseph to George W. Harris.[14] In it, the Prophet wrote: "I have selected a town lot for you just across the street from my own."[15] Todd Compton, sees this invitation to reside close to the Smiths as "immediate evidence of a close bond"—which is probably true.[16] However, on the same day, Joseph Smith wrote a second letter to Judge John Cleveland and his wife, Sarah, residents of Quincy, Illinois. Joseph had never met them, but they had given shelter to Emma Smith and her children after they escaped from Missouri and while Joseph was incarcerated in Liberty Jail. It read similarly: "We have selected a lot for you, just across the street from our own, beside Mr. Harris."[17] The obvious similarity between the two letters lessens the likelihood that Joseph's letter to the Harrises corroborates a plural marriage between him and Lucinda Pendleton Harris.[18]

---

11. D. Michael Quinn, *The Mormon Hierarchy: Origins of Power*, 587.

12. Salt Lake Temple Sealing Records, Book D, 243, April 4, 1899; qtd. in Thomas Milton Tinney, *The Royal Family of the Prophet Joseph Smith, Jr.*, 41; Lisle G Brown, *Nauvoo Sealings, Adoptions, and Anointings: A Comprehensive Register of Persons Receiving LDS Temple Ordinances, 1841–1846*, 282.

13. Cordelia Morley Cox, Autobiography, 4; Brown, *Nauvoo Sealings, Adoptions, and Anointings*, 284.

14. The letter is reprinted in *History of the Church*, 3:362, but erroneously lists the recipient as "E. W. Harris."

15. Journal History, May 24, 1839; *History of the Church*, 3:362.

16. Compton, *In Sacred Loneliness*, 50.

17. Journal History, May 24, 1839; *History of the Church*, 3:362.

18. Joseph Smith married Sarah Cleveland in an "eternity only" sealing, probably in

The locations of the Cleveland and Harris homes in relation to the Smith residence in Nauvoo. Used by permission, Utah State Historical Society. All rights reserved.

Further, property records in Nauvoo show that the Clevelands were, in fact, next-door neighbors, sharing an east-west property line with the Smiths, while the Harris family was located three small blocks to the north. That the Clevelands would be settled closer than the Harrises is counterintuitive, given Brodie's hypothesis that Lucinda was married to Joseph in 1838 while Sarah Cleveland was not sealed to him until 1842.

The third evidence of sealing usually cited is that Lucinda appears third on Andrew Jenson's 1887 list of twenty-seven plural wives of the Prophet.[19] Despite her inclusion, however, an examination of Jenson's notes suggests that his documentation for Lucinda was the weakest of the twenty-seven, and he may have vacillated in his decision to incorporate her. (See discussion in Chapter 33).[20] One of his handwritten notes reads: "better leave her out perhaps."[21]

1842, but his 1839 letter to her and her husband could not have realistically anticipated that eventual sealing. When the letter was written, the Prophet had yet to meet the Clevelands.

19. Andrew Jenson, "Plural Marriage," 233–34. Tinney, *The Royal Family of the Prophet Joseph Smith Jr.*, 41, 136, also lists Lucinda as a plural wife of the Prophet. However, Tinney may have simply been repeating Jenson's claim.

20. Documents 1–2, Andrew Jenson Papers (ca. 1871–1942), MS 17956, Box 49, fd. 16. See also Don Bradley and Brian C. Hales, "LDS Joseph vs. RLDS Joseph: Records of Nauvoo Polygamy and the Conflict that Forged Them."

21. "Lucinda Harris biographical information sheet," Document 2, Andrew Jenson Papers, MS 17956, Box 49, fd. 16. These words are crossed out. The interviewee providing him information about Lucinda at the time Jenson penned this note is unknown but was likely Eliza R. Snow.

Charges of Immoral Conduct against Joseph Smith

Harriet Cook Young. Courtesy of the LDS Church

The fourth and strongest piece of primary evidence for Lucinda's inclusion on Jenson's published list appears to have been the testimony of Brigham Young's plural wife, Harriet Cook Young. Jenson wrote: "Harriet Cook Young is positive that she [Lucinda] was married to Joseph in Missouri."[22] Harriet was a member of the polygamy inner circle in both Nauvoo and Utah, however, born November 7, 1824, and baptized at age seventeen on May 1, 1842, she was not a member of the Church during the Missouri period. A year after her baptism, on November 2, 1843, Joseph sealed her to Brigham Young. Harriet's assertion is significant evidence, but other important witnesses seem to disagree, including Eliza R. Snow and/or Malissa Lott. (See Chapter 33.) Regardless, Jenson ultimately included her name on his list saying she was "one of the first women sealed to the Prophet."[23]

A fifth document, cited by both Brodie and Compton, is a statement attributed to Sarah Bates Pratt, the divorced wife of Orson Pratt. In 1885, years after she had left the Church, controversial journalist Wilhelm Wyl interviewed her. Reportedly, Sarah remembered a conversation with Lucinda forty-three years earlier that she quoted verbatim: "Mrs. Harris was a married lady, a very great friend of mine. When Joseph had made his dastardly attempt on me, I went to Mrs. Harris to unbosom my grief to her. To my utter astonishment she said, laughing heartily: 'How foolish you are! I don't see anything so horrible in it. Why I AM HIS MISTRESS SINCE FOUR YEARS!'" (emphasis in original).[24] If this quotation is actually from Lucinda and if Sarah is recalling the exact words correctly, it would constitute the only known statement from her in the historical record regarding any topic.

Michael Quinn appraises this statement as inconclusive, observing: "If Sarah Pratt had wanted to malign Joseph Smith by inventing a statement and

---

22. Ibid. Harriet was sealed to Brigham Young on November 2, 1843, at age nineteen. Harriet Cook Young, Affidavit, March 4, 1870, in Joseph F. Smith, Affidavit Book, 2:12, 3:12, MS 3423, fd. 5.

23. Jenson, "Plural Marriage," 233.

24. Wilhelm Wyl, *Mormon Portraits, or the Truth about Mormon Leaders from 1830 to 1886, Joseph Smith the Prophet, His Family and His Friends: A Study Based on Fact and Documents*, 60.

attributing it to Lucinda Pendleton Harris, then Sarah Pratt would have used the word 'paramour' which had ONLY the meaning of adulterous mistress, rather than the wifely definitions Webster's first gave for 'mistress.' In view of Sarah Pratt's obvious bitterness toward Mormonism and Joseph Smith, I think her lack of using the WORST POSSIBLE WORD gives credence to her effort to accurately remember what Mrs. Harris told her in 1842."[25]

Modern parlance commonly defines a "mistress" as an adulterous companion. However, Noah Webster's 1830 dictionary lists nine definitions:

> 1. A woman who governs. 2. The female head of a family. 3. That which governs; a sovereign. 4. One that commands, or has possession and sovereignty. 5. A female who is well skilled in any thing. 6. A woman teacher; an instructress of a school. 7. A woman beloved and courted. *8. A woman in keeping for lewd purposes.* 9. A term of contemptuous address.[26]

None of these meanings seems consistent with the documented interactions between Joseph and Lucinda during the four years prior to the statement Sarah Pratt attributed to her. During that time the Prophet had little leisure for a sustained ("four year") interaction. He was engaged in city founding, heightened social tensions with Missouri neighbors, the Mormon War (fall of 1838), incarceration (November 1838–April 1839), purchasing land in and around Nauvoo, rallying his followers, traveling to Washington, D.C., and surrounding areas (November 1839–February 1840), and then settling Nauvoo with his family (April 1839), and establishing the Church there.

In addition, if Lucinda had been a secret willing "mistress" of a charismatic and glamorous man, having spent clandestine intimate moments with him during the years prior to the alleged statement, the apparent nonchalance of her reaction to the knowledge that he had attempted to create a new relationship with another women, even " laughing heartily," seems implausible. A psychologically more reasonable reaction would be disappointment, if not betrayal. The whole scenario seems unrealistic.

Todd Compton does not quote Sarah's exact statement, but paraphrases it as: "Lucinda told her [Sarah Pratt] in 1842 that she started her relationship with Joseph four years previously."[27] At the very least, his reserve communi-

---

25. D. Michael Quinn, email to Brian Hales, January 23, 2011; emphasis his.

26. Noah Webster, *An American Dictionary of the English Language; exhibiting the Origin, Orthography, Pronunciation, and Definitions of Words*, 536, s.v. "mistress"; emphasis mine.

27. Compton, *In Sacred Loneliness*, 650. He might have quoted it verbatim on pp. 43, 49, or 650, which are points of relevant discussion. When I inquired why he had not used Sarah's quotation, Compton explained, "Throughout my book, I always preferred to emphasize evidence that was sympathetic (and obviously first-hand and early, when possible). So as evidence that was 'antagonistic, third-hand and late,' it was worth mentioning, but not worth reproducing at length." Compton, email to Brian C. Hales, July 9, 2011; used by permission.

cates some caution about Sarah's recollection, which he insightfully characterizes as "antagonistic, third-hand, and late."[28]

Sarah Pratt's recollection of Lucinda Harris's alleged statement has other problems in addition to the chronology. In an 1842 publication, Sarah claimed that Joseph Smith proposed plural marriage to her (later she called it a "dastardly attempt" upon her virtue) prior to her husband's return from his mission to England.[29] Orson Pratt arrived in Nauvoo on July 19, 1841.[30] Hence, Sarah's alleged conversation with "Mrs. Harris" must have occurred prior to that date. Counting back four years pinpoints the beginning of the alleged affair as the first half of 1837.

However, Joseph Smith did not meet Lucinda until 1838, when the Smith family moved permanently from Ohio to Missouri. Joseph Smith's diary records: "On the 14th of March [1838], as we were about entering Far West, many of the brethren came out to meet us, who also with open arms welcomed us to their bosoms. We were immediately received under the hospitable roof of Brother George W. Harris, who treated us with all possible kindness, and we refreshed ourselves with much satisfaction, after our long and tedious journey."[31] While it may be seen as a minor point, an affair that began in 1837 was a geographic impossibility.

Other questions concerning the alleged timeline can be identified. The Smiths stayed with the Harris family a little over two months which represents the mostly likely time where a relationship between Joseph and Lucinda might have formed. However, it was not a period where Joseph was situated comfortably in a citadel of power and unquestioned authority. Four months previously, on November 2, 1837, the Prophet was absent when a special council of Church members and leaders convened in Far West to transact Church business. Left unresolved was "a matter between Oliver Cowdery, Thomas B. Marsh" and the Prophet.[32] That issue was likely Oliver's perspective of Joseph's relationship with Fanny Alger because Oliver was aware of the association and considered it adulterous. (See Chapters 4–8.)

Nineteen weeks later when Joseph Smith arrived in Far West on March 14, 1838, the problem was still not resolved. On April 12, less than one month afterwards and right in the middle of Joseph and Emma's stay with the Harris

---

28. Compton, *In Sacred Loneliness*, 650.
29. John C. Bennett, *The History of the Saints: Or an Exposé of Joe Smith and Mormonism*, 230–31.
30. Journal History, July 19, 1841; *History of the Church*, 4:389.
31. Dean C. Jessee, ed., *The Papers of Joseph Smith: Vol. 2, Journal, 1832–1842*, 213; *History of the Church*, 2:8–9. See also Scott H. Faulring, ed., *An American Prophet's Record: The Diaries and Journals of Joseph Smith*, 160.
32. Donald Q. Cannon and Lyndon W. Cook, eds., *Far West Record: Minutes of the Church of Jesus Christ of Latter-day Saints, 1830–1844*, 120; *History of the Church*, 2:521; emphasis mine.

family, Oliver was excommunicated by the Far West High Council, in part for accusing Joseph Smith of adultery. Oliver's accusation that Joseph had committed adultery required Joseph to give "a history respecting the girl business" to the high councilors, who undoubtedly wondered about the actions of their Prophet-leader.[33] (See Chapter 6.) In addition, the *Elders' Journal*, then being edited by Joseph Smith, published articles mentioning polygamy in November of 1837 and again in July 1838.[34]

In summary, historical records indicate that, during the two months, the Smiths boarded with the Harrises family, Joseph was already aggressively deflecting allegations of adultery originating with Oliver Cowdery. As a consequence, he must have been hypersensitive on the topics of polygamy or adultery. In these circumstances, it seems unlikely that Joseph Smith would propose a plural marriage (as asserted by Harriet Cook) or launch an extramarital affair with Lucinda (as alleged by Sarah Pratt) during this period.

Another set of problems involves the plausibility of such a relationship. It seems improbable that Lucinda would have made such a candid, even mocking, statement to Sarah about extramarital sexual relations, no matter how close their friendship. Sharing details of intimate connections was rare due to reserved attitudes about such topics. Importantly, "lewd" relationships merited Church discipline, whether in 1838 or 1842, regardless of the status of the practice of plural marriage. Such a statement would be a plain admission of adultery, a sin designated as next to murder in the Book of Mormon (Alma 39:5). In addition, Lucinda's reported flippancy contradicts the general secrecy that was maintained by individuals who were practicing plural marriage in Nauvoo. For example, Emily Partridge testified that she was unaware of her own sister's sealing to Joseph Smith, even though they were both plural wives and living in the Smith home during the very same time period.[35] One might assume that an illicit relationship would be concealed even more carefully.

As witnesses, Sarah Pratt and Wilhelm Wyl are known to have made allegations that were later shown to contradict other, more reliable evidences. For example, Wyl asked Sarah Pratt about the report that "Joseph had eighty wives at the time of his death." Sarah replied: "He had many more, my dear sir; at least he had seduced many more, and those with whom he had lived without their being sealed to him, were sealed to him after his death."[36] Even

---

33. Donald Q. Cannon and Lyndon W. Cook, eds., *Far West Record: Minutes of the Church of Jesus Christ of Latter-day Saints, 1830–1844*, 168.

34. Editorial, *Elders' Journal* 1, no. 2 (November 1837): 28–29, 43.

35. Emily Partridge, Deposition, in Temple Lot Transcript, Respondent's Testimony, Part 3, p. 371, questions 476–79.

36. W. Wyl (pseud.), [Wilhelm Ritter von Wymetal], *Mormon Portraits, or the Truth about Mormon Leaders from 1830 to 1886*, 54.

the most liberal estimates of Joseph Smith's sealings to women during his lifetime stop in the forties range. (See Chapter 33.) Furthermore, no record has been found from any woman claiming that she had been "seduced" by Joseph Smith. In 1880 Pratt recalled: "An elder once said to me: 'Sister Sarah, you are a regular Satan,' I had been giving my views in regard to polygamy and polygamists. I answered him, there are only two classes of women in Utah, devils or fools."[37] Such harshness and dichotomized thinking, while understandable given the pain of her own divorce and estrangement from the Church, cast reasonable doubts on her ability to be fair and objective late in life.

Wyl's book is replete with stories and accusations that defy historical validation, either due to sketchy details or because of flatly contradictory evidence. For example, he quotes a story about "the beautiful and attractive young wife of Elder Edward Blossom, a high councilor of Zion, (afterwards exalted to the apostleship by Brigham Young)" who was allegedly sexually involved with Joseph Smith.[38] Wyl could have easily determined that no Nauvoo high councilor was named Blossom and that the only high councilor to become an apostle in Utah was Charles Rich who does not resemble this description of Blossom in any way.

Concerning Wyl's accuracy, non-Mormon writer Thomas Gregg wrote: "The statements of the interviews [in his book] must be taken for what they are worth. While many of them are corroborated elsewhere and [corroborated] in many ways, there are others that need verification, and some that probably exist only in the mind of the narrator."[39] Biographer Richard L. Bushman provided this assessment: "He [Wyl] introduced a lot of hearsay into his account of Joseph. Personally I found all the assertions about the Prophet's promiscuity pretty feeble. Nothing there [was] worth contending with."[40] Both Wyl and Sarah Pratt seemed willing to repeat any rumor so long as it was derogatory to Joseph Smith. (See Chapter 21.)

As for dating Lucinda's sealing to Joseph Smith, while acknowledging the inconclusiveness of the available documentation, Compton sees 1838 as a "good possibility" for a marriage[41] and hypothesizes that the relationship continued in Nauvoo. He notes that "in mid-July 1840 George [Lucinda's legal husband] was sent on a mission to travel eastward collecting funds and materials for church publications. He left soon after July 25, labored for a year in the eastern states, especially New York, then returned home in September

---

37. Athena [pseud.], "The Women of Utah," 18.
38. Wyl, *Mormon Portraits*, 65–66.
39. Thomas Gregg, *The Prophet of Palmyra: Mormonism Reviewed and Examined in the Life, Character, and Career of Its Founder*, 504.
40. Richard L. Bushman, email to Brian Hales, August 23, 2007.
41. Compton, *In Sacred Loneliness*, 49.

1841."⁴² He then writes: "Though one can only speculate, this period of his [George's] absence may have been a time when Joseph and Lucinda enjoyed a special closeness."⁴³

Not all historians agree that the Prophet and Lucinda had a plural marriage. Richard Lloyd Anderson and Scott H. Faulring, after reviewing the evidence available to them, conclude: "The claim that Lucinda was sealed to Joseph Smith is not based on impressive evidence."⁴⁴

In summary, the scanty documents available are insufficient to either decisively rule out or conclusively confirm a sealing between Joseph Smith and Lucinda Pendleton. The questionable allegation from Sarah Pratt supports an illicit romance in 1838, while Harriet Cook's assertion (reported by Andrew Jenson) affirms a plural marriage in Missouri during that same period. Accompanying evidence, however, cast doubt on the timeline and the reported relationships.⁴⁵

In presenting his list of "confirmed," "probable," and "possible" plural wives, Compton candidly concedes: "No piece of evidence is perfect."⁴⁶ He includes some women, even though he himself finds the evidence less conclusive than he would have preferred. A gray zone exists, requiring each researcher to draw his or her own line about what constitutes acceptable evidence. With respect to Lucinda Pendleton, I have not removed her from my list; but I believe that, of all of the thirty-five plural wives I have identified (see Chapter 33), the documentation for her plural marriage to the Prophet is perhaps the least

---

42. Ibid., 50–51.

43. Ibid., 51. This comment is highly conjectural and suggests that Joseph Smith was involved with sexual polyandry when there is no reliable evidence to support it. Larry Foster, "Plural Marriage, Singular Lives," 186, in his review of *In Sacred Loneliness*, commented: "[One] reservation that I have about this study is Compton's tendency to state as matters of fact what are, at best, only his own suppositions." The statement is general but follows a paragraph discussing Compton's treatment of sexual polyandry.

44. Richard Lloyd Anderson and Scott H. Faulring, "Review of *In Sacred Loneliness: The Plural Wives of Joseph Smith*, by Todd M. Compton," 75.

45. Supporting the existence of a sexual relationship between Joseph Smith and Lucinda is a family tradition that he fathered a son, Don Alonzo Smith, born August 29, 1840. The child was raised by Lucinda's daughter, Lucinda W. Morgan (daughter of Lucinda Pendleton and her first husband, William Morgan) and her legal husband, David Bates Smith. However, chronological and geographical limitations make Joseph Smith's paternity an impossibility. If Don Alonzo Smith was full term at birth, he would have been conceived approximately December 4, 1839. At that time Lucinda Pendleton Morgan Harris was living in Nauvoo, but Joseph Smith had left Illinois for Washington, D.C., on October 29, not returning until March 4, 1840. In addition, unpublished DNA data by Ugo Perego has demonstrated that Joseph Smith was not the father of Don Alonzo Smith. Ugo A. Perego, email to Brian Hales, December 6, 2011.

46. Compton, "Truth, Honesty and Moderation in Mormon History," section headed "Sexuality in the Polyandrous Marriages."

convincing. Furthermore, I find Missouri in 1838 highly unlikely as the setting for such a plural marriage, despite Sarah Pratt's and Harriet Cook's recollections. If a plural marriage occurred, I think it would have been in Nauvoo.

Presendia Huntington Buell:
No Relationship or Conception On-the-Run?

Fawn Brodie suggests that Joseph Smith fathered a child in 1839 (with or without a prior marriage ceremony) with Presendia Huntington Buell,[47] who was already married to Norman Buell. Brodie seems certain that Oliver Buell, born January 31, 1840, to Presendia, was Joseph's son. She finds in this scenario evidence of Joseph's impulsiveness—almost compulsiveness—for entering into a sexual liaison with a fortuitously available woman despite circumstances in which he was essentially on the run. Brodie wrote: "The extreme informality attending Joseph's earliest marriages (at least as it appears in the available records) is even more evident in the story of the prophet's relationship with Presendia Huntington Buell. During the Missouri troubles of 1838–39 her husband, Norman Buell, temporarily left the church. About this time [sic – Oliver Norman Buell was born January 31, 1840] Presendia bore a son. She admitted later that she did not know whether Norman Buell or the prophet was the father. But the physiognomy revealed in a rare photograph of Oliver Buell seems to weight the balance overwhelmingly on the side of Joseph's paternity."[48]

It is true that the photographs provided by Brodie show a resemblance between Oliver Norman Buell and David Hyrum or Joseph Smith III, two of the sons of Joseph and Emma Smith, but the resemblance is much less striking compared to their two other sons, Alexander and Frederick.[49] Confident that Joseph was Oliver's biological father, Brodie enthused to Dale Morgan: "If Oliver Buell isn't a Smith, then I'm no Brimhall [Brodie's mother's maiden name]."[50] However, as Todd Compton observes: "It would help to have pic-

---

47. Martha Sonntag Bradley and Mary Brown Firmage Woodward, *Four Zinas: A Story of Mothers and Daughters on the Mormon Frontier,* xxiii, explain: "The spelling of Presendia appears in a variety of forms in both legal and personal documents—Presenda, Presendia, Precindia among others." In 1869 Presendia signed her affidavit in Joseph F. Smith, Affidavit Book 1:7 apparently as "Presenda" but a second signature in Joseph F. Smith. Affidavit Book 4:7 is plainly "Presendia," the spelling I use here.

48. Fawn M. Brodie, *No Man Knows My History: The Life of Joseph Smith, the Mormon Prophet,* 301–2.

49. Ibid.; two photos immediately preceding p. 299.

50. Fawn Brodie, Letter to Dale Morgan, March 24, 1945, quoted in Newell G. Bringhurst, *Fawn McKay Brodie: A Biographer's Life,* 97. Morgan in response wrote: "Your chain of reasoning looks logical, but it is attended by a string of ifs all along the line . . . and the probability of error increases as the chain of reasoning lengthens." Ibid.

tures of Norman Buell and George Buell to see if there were family resemblances there."⁵¹ Also, Brodie falters by ignoring the fact, which she may not have known, that the Huntington, Smith, and Buell families had lived in New England for up to six generations and had largely come from the same area of England in the seventeenth century; hence, the genetic stock of this limited population would be expected to share a significant number of resemblances. She also fails to compare photographs of Oliver to either of his two brothers or their sons.

As a second problem, the "admission" that Brodie cites comes from a late and problematic source, Mary Ettie V. Coray Smith. Mary Ettie wrote a memoir of her Mormon years with the assistance of an editor who is actually listed as the author. This book, published in 1860, asserts: "I heard the latter woman [Presendia] say afterwards in Utah, that she did not know whether Mr. Buel [sic] or the Prophet was the father of her son."⁵² Such candor would be surprising for the times. Compton points out: "One wonders if Presendia would have said such a thing. Talk of sexuality was avoided by the Victorian, puritanical Mormons; in diaries, the word 'pregnant' or 'expecting' is never or rarely used."⁵³ While such a discussion might occur in circumstances of great privacy with the closest of friends or to one's female relatives, there is little evidence that Mary Ettie had such an intimate relationship with Presendia. She herself makes no claim to closeness to Presendia, nor does she imply that Presendia was making such statements more publicly.

Another significant problem is the date. Assuming that Oliver was a full-term baby at his birth in late January 1840, he would have been conceived about May 10, 1839. In Brodie's scenario, Joseph would have had conjugal relations with Presendia two and a half years before their documented sealing date in Nauvoo of December 11, 1841. Thus, as Compton observes: "Brodie, in insisting on Joseph as Oliver Buell's parent, is positing an affair, a sexual liaison, not a marriage."⁵⁴ Continuing her thesis that Joseph Smith was a philanderer who seduced respectably married women, Brodie theorizes: "Norman Buell apostatized in the spring of 1839, and if Oliver was born at that time, it is at least conjectural that he left the church because he suspected the paternity of his son."⁵⁵ Oliver Boardman Huntington, Presendia's brother

---

See also Compton, "Fawn Brodie on Joseph Smith's Plural Wives and Polygamy," 166.

51. Todd Compton, "Fawn Brodie on Joseph Smith's Plural Wives and Polygamy," 167

52. Nelson Winch Green, *Fifteen Years among the Mormons: Being the Narrative of Mrs. Mary Ettie V. Smith*, 35. Green is listed as the author but, from the internal evidence, was actually Smith's editor. Brodie quotes her in *No Man Knows My History*, 301.

53. Compton, "Fawn Brodie on Joseph Smith's Plural Wives and Polygamy," 166.

54. Ibid., 167.

55. Brodie, *No Man Knows My History*, 461.

for whom his nephew was named, attributes Buell's apostasy to greed and a lack of faith: "During all this time Norman Buell was in Clay Co. saying good Lord and kind devil, for a time; but the time finally came that he must choose a side, so he chose the Master that would give him the most money then, and in whos hands he thought he would be the safest. He even got to the pitch that he would not let his wife say a word in favor of her brethren, and would say all manner of evil of them himself. He was once an Elder in the church of Jesus Christ."[56] Brodie's suggestion that Buell would quietly apostatize upon learning that his wife was sexually involved with the leader of a church he had despised seems naïve. A more violent reaction seems more plausible.

The chronology of firmly dated events reveals other flaws in Brodie's reconstruction. Brodie posits that Norman Buell's apostasy in the spring of 1839 was provoked by the knowledge that Joseph Smith was sexually involved with Presendia. To compensate for obvious chronological problems, she implies that Oliver's birth date, January 31, 1840, might have been in error.[57] There is no evidence to support such an error. And significantly, assuming a full-term pregnancy, at the time of Oliver's conception (about May 10, 1839), Joseph and Hyrum Smith and their three companions were not lingering in Missouri. They had escaped on April 16 while being transferred to another county. Hyrum made a detailed affidavit about that episode:

> There we bought a jug of whisky, with which we treated the company, and while there the sheriff showed us the mittimus before referred to, without date or signature, and said that Judge Birch told him never to carry us to Boone county, and never to show the mittimus; and, said he, I shall take a good drink of grog, and go to bed, and you may do as you have a mind to. Three others of the guards drank pretty freely of the whisky, sweetened with honey. They also went to bed, and were soon asleep and the other guard went along with us, and helped to saddle the horses.[58]

The location of the escape was about twenty-five miles southeast of Adam-ondi-Ahman, traveling toward Boone County in central Missouri. Brodie incorrectly states: "Joseph's journal entries make it clear that after his escape he was mingling with the last Mormon group to leave Far West, which included the Huntington family."[59] In fact, Joseph Smith's journals contain no entries of any kind for the April 16-21 period.[60] (See map, p. 70.)

---

56. Oliver B. Huntington, Diary (and autobiographical sketch), 1835–1900, 2:45.
57. Brodie, *No Man Knows My History*, 461.
58. Hyrum Smith, Affidavit sworn at the Nauvoo Municipal Court, July 1, 1843, qtd. in *History of the Church*, 3:321 unnumbered note.
59. Brodie, *No Man Knows My History*, 461–62.
60. Dean C. Jessee, Mark Ashurst-McGee, and Richard L. Jensen, eds., *Journals: Vol. 1: 1832–1839*, 336; Dean C. Jessee., ed., *The Papers of Joseph Smith: Vol. 2, Journal,*

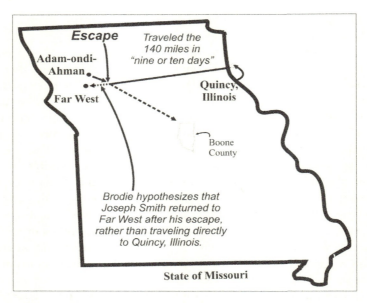

Brodie assumes, also inaccurately, that immediately after gaining his freedom, Joseph went west (not east to Illinois) through the Missouri countryside passing near Haun's Mill, where on October 30, 1838, at least seventeen Latter-day Saints were killed and thirteen wounded by a unit of Missouri "regulators." Then he reached Far West, twelve miles farther west where nearly all of the Mormons had left the state by February 1839, in obedience to the terms imposed at the surrender of Far West the preceding October. Brodie hypothesizes the continued presence of a core group Church members at that time that included the Huntingtons. While there, the Prophet allegedly impregnated Presendia (with or without a marriage ceremony). Then he turned east, arriving in Quincy on April 22. Brodie does not give adequate weight to the fact that Joseph was an escaped prisoner, liable to be arrested on sight, and, not improbably, killed since the governor's order that the Saints must leave the state or be exterminated was still in force from the preceding October. Furthermore, Brodie does not mention the presence of Hyrum, who accompanied Joseph throughout this journey. Brodie's timetable also assumes that Oliver was two to three weeks overdue at birth.

The activities of the group after the escape are described in the *History of the Church*. An entry for April 17, 1839, reads "We prosecuted our journey towards Illinois, keeping off from the main road as much as possible, which impeded our progress."[61] Hyrum Smith also recalled that upon escaping:

1832–1842, 2:307–8, 318; Faulring, *An American Prophet's Record*, 229, 234.

61. Journal History, April 17, 1839; *History of the Church*, 3:322; see also 319–20.

Charges of Immoral Conduct against Joseph Smith 71

"Two of us mounted the horses, and the other three started on foot, and we took our change of venue for the State of Illinois; and in the course of nine or ten days arrived safely at Quincy, Adams county, where we found our families in a state of poverty, although in good health."[62] The account indicates that their escape occurred approximately twenty-five or thirty miles from their starting point of Gallatin, or 140 miles from Quincy, Illinois. Thus, they would have traveled approximately fifteen miles a day to reach Quincy in nine or ten days. Although Hyrum's account has him and Joseph riding horseback, according to Lucy Mack Smith, they had one horse between the two of them. A man on foot can typically cover three to four miles an hour, while a man on horseback can typically cover four to ten. (Certainly the previous six months of incarceration with no exercise and a poor diet would have enfeebled the Smith brothers.) A sidetrip to Far West would have added approximately fifty or fifty-five miles (coming and going) to this total distance. Thus, Joseph and Hyrum could not have gone to Far West within the time frame Hyrum reports, let alone allowed time for a romantic dalliance.

Adding to the improbability of Brodie's scenario is the fact that the Buells did not live in Far West but about twenty-five miles due south at Fishing River, Ray County, Missouri. While it seems likely that Joseph's presence at Far West would have motivated the Buells (or at least the faithful Presendia) to travel there to see him, there is no indication that they did. And although records about Far West are very sketchy after the city was evacuated, clearly, most of the Mormons were gone from the county by the end of February 1839. An important record of events in Far West during the late winter and spring of 1839 appears in Ronald E. Romig's biography of John Whitmer, one of the Eight Witnesses of the Book of Mormon. He had been excommunicated in June 1838 by the Far West High Council with other dissidents and expelled from the city. John did not keep a diary, but he kept a detailed account book in which he also made brief notations of important events. On February 10, 1839, he recorded carefully: "Arrived [in Far West] with my family from Richmond." Over the next several months, he reoccupied the property he still owned in Far West. His entries for April and May record purchases and sale, taking in boarders at his large house that doubled as a hotel, and hiring help for both the farm and the hotel.[63] It does not mention an event as significant as a visit from Joseph and Hyrum Smith. Also still in Far West was W. W. Phelps, who had also been classed with the dissenters in the disciplinary actions of the Far West High Council the previous year. He wrote to his wife, Sally, who

---

62. Hyrum Smith, Affidavit, in *History of the Church*, 3:321 footnote.
63. John Whitmer, Account Book, February 10 and 24, March 11, 1839, p. 36. This information is drawn from Ronald E. Romig, *John Whitmer: Eighth Witness*, chap. 25; used by permission.

was in Illinois, reporting the visit of the Twelve to the temple site on April 26 to ordain new apostles to fill the quorum, lay the cornerstone, and depart for their missions in England to fulfill a revelation Joseph Smith had received a year earlier.[64] Surely Phelps would have mentioned a visit from Joseph and Hyrum Smith earlier that month if one had occurred.

In short, there is no documentary evidence that Joseph Smith was in Far West in April 1839. Presendia and Norman lived at Fishing River in Ray County, Missouri, more than a hundred miles from Quincy. Norman, who had disaffiliated from the Church in 1838, stayed clear of the main body of Saints and operated a mill in Ray County until the fall of 1840.[65] The Buells moved closer to Nauvoo, settling in Lima, Illinois, in the fall of 1840. Though not actively hostile during the early 1840s, Norman continued to remain aloof from the Church, and Presendia left him to accompany the Saints who followed Brigham Young.

Stanley S. Ivins, who arguably conducted the most copious research on Mormon polygamy of any investigator, dismissed Mary Ettie V. Smith's report as "inaccurate and of no value."[66] Fanny Stenhouse, who became disillusioned about polygamy and wrote two popular books about her experience, described Ettie Smith in 1875 as "a lady who wrote very many years ago and in her writings, so mixed up fiction with what was true, that it was difficult to determine where the one ended and the other began."[67] Sir Richard Burton, author of the 1862 publication, *The City of the Saints, and across the Rocky Mountains to California*, judged the Smith/Green publication harshly: "This work, whose exceedingly clap-trap title is a key to the 'popular' nature of the contents, is, *par excellence, the most offensive publication of the kind, and bears within it marks of an exceeding untruthfulness*. . . . Nothing will excuse the reckless accusations with which Mrs. Smith takes away the characters of the Mormon sisters, and the abominations with which she charges the wives of the highest dignitaries."[68]

Mary Ettie herself supplies just such an example by making it clear only ten pages later that the "son" referred to could not have been Oliver but could only have been his younger brother, John Hiram. She states that Presendia Buell became pregnant with Joseph Smith's child while she was living "at

---

64. W. W. Phelps, Letter to Sally Phelps, Far West, Missouri, May 4, 1839. Romig, *John Whitmer*, Chap. 25, specifically notes that, according to Kenney, *Wilford Woodruff's Journal*, 1:327, "an additional eighteen Latter Day Saints were also present [at the meeting on the temple site], apparently all of those still residing in the area:" Woodruff lists them, but the list does not include the Buells.

65. Compton, *In Sacred Loneliness*, 119–20.

66. Stanley S. Ivins, Notebook 4, p. 63.

67. Fanny Stenhouse, *"Tell It All": The Story of a Life's Experiences in Mormonism*, 618.

68. Richard F. Burton, *The City of the Saints, and across the Rocky Mountains to California*, 207–8; emphasis his. Burton also lists eleven specific inaccuracies in Mary Ettie Smith's account.

Lima, Illinois."[69] Oliver was born three and a half years earlier in Missouri, and John Hiram was born on July 13, 1843, after the family had moved to Lima, Illinois. (See Chapter 11.)

After critiquing Fawn Brodie's assessment of Oliver Norman Buell as Joseph's son, Todd Compton concludes: "Every link in Brodie's position that Oliver Buell was Joseph Smith's son is implausible, improbable, or impossible. There is no good evidence that Oliver Buell was the son of Joseph Smith, and thus there is no good evidence that Joseph had an affair with Presendia Buell before he married her in 1841."[70]

Most conclusively, in 2007, geneticist Ugo Perego performed DNA testing on descendents of Oliver Norman Buell, demonstrating a 57.5% disparity between the DNA loci of Joseph Smith and Oliver's male descendants on the Y-chromosome. This lack of correlation shows conclusively that Joseph Smith could not have been Oliver's father.[71] Taken together, the conclusion is inescapable that Brodie is mistaken in asserting that Joseph Smith was sexually involved with Presendia in 1838.

Marinda Nancy Johnson (Again)

Fawn Brodie also listed one other woman as possibly being married to Joseph Smith in 1839, the already-mentioned Marinda Nancy Johnson Hyde. Marinda was purportedly involved with the Prophet in Hiram, Ohio, in 1832, thus prompting her "brother" (actually her uncle) Eli to initiate the Joseph's tar and feathering episode. Marinda married future apostle Orson Hyde civilly on September 4, 1834. Notwithstanding, Brodie pairs Joseph Smith with Marinda again in 1839 by quoting William Hall, author of the tellingly titled *The Abominations of Mormonism Exposed; Containing Many Facts and Doctrines Concerning That Singular People during Seven Years' Membership with Them, from 1840 to 1847* (1852). Non-Mormon historian Hubert Howe Bancroft described Hall:

> William Hall was an old gentleman of simple mind and manners when he wrote his book; he appears to be earnest and truthful. As he says of the saints, so I should say of him: he meant well, but he should beware of bad leaders. Hall was not a great man in the church, like Bennett; nevertheless, like Bennett he wrote a book, but unlike Bennett's, his book reads like that of an honest man, although it is full of bitter accusations against the Mormons. All such works should be taken with some degrees of allowance; for when a

---

69. Green, *Fifteen Years among the Mormons*, 45.
70. Compton, "Fawn Brodie on Joseph Smith's Plural Wives and Polygamy," 171.
71. Ugo A. Perego, Jayne E. Ekins, and Scott R. Woodward, "Resolving the Paternities of Oliver N. Buell and Mosiah L. Hancock through DNA," 128–36.

person begins to rail against any people or individual, he is apt to be carried away and misrepresent, intentionally or unintentionally.[72]

Hall described a colorful scene between Orson Hyde and the Prophet:

> Before I came into the Church, Orson Hyde had become dissatisfied with the doctrine, and had left the Mormons in consequence of it. Being a man of slender means, he was obliged to betake himself to cutting cordwood for a support. This business was not agreeable—he soon found his hands blistered and himself wearied, and began to long for the fleshpots of Egypt. He returned and desired Joe Smith to reinstate him, in his former office, as one of the Twelve Apostles. The conditions imposed by Joe Smith, some of us would consider a little tough. They were these: All the money he had so hardly earned had to be given up to Joe, and, also his wife, as a ransom for his transgression, to obtain his former standing. Many jokes were cracked at his expense, and he was despised throughout the camp.[73]

This extravagant narrative with its plethora of gossipy details comes from an unreliable anti-Mormon source and is the sole support for Brodie's 1839 dating of a plural marriage between Joseph Smith and Marinda Nancy Johnson Hyde. Larry Foster assessed: "William Hall's account [is] of extremely dubious accuracy and must be evaluated with the caution used in evaluating any malicious gossip."[74] Regardless, Brodie writes: "Hall's account, if true, would indicate that Marinda Nancy Hyde became Joseph Smith's plural wife in April 1839, when Hyde was reinstated as an apostle."[75]

Unfortunately for Brodie's reconstruction, Hall's details are not consistent with historical evidence. It is true that, in Missouri in October 1838, Orson Hyde and Thomas B. Marsh, then apostle and president of the Quorum of the Twelve respectively, became disillusioned with the rapid changes that Joseph Smith had introduced into the Church since his arrival in Missouri in the spring of 1838. The high council excommunicated Marsh in March 1839 and sanctioned Hyde two months later. The two apostles left Far West, Missouri, and headed east. At Richmond in Ray County, they were befriended by other dissenters (including David Whitmer and Oliver Cowdery) and were asked to write an affidavit about Joseph Smith's alleged crimes. On October 24, Marsh did so and Hyde, who was ill, appended a short statement of his own attesting that he believed Marsh's de-

---

72. Hubert Howe Bancroft, *History of Utah. 1540–1887*, 152 note.

73. William Hall, *The Abominations of Mormonism Exposed; Containing Many Facts and Doctrines Concerning That Singular People during Seven Years' Membership with Them, from 1840 to 1847*, 113.

74. Lawrence Foster, *Religion and Sexuality: Three American Communal Experiments of the Nineteenth Century*, 308 note 93.

75. Brodie, *No Man Knows My History*, 463. Brodie admits: "It may be, however, that she was not taught polygamy until December 1841, when Hyde was on a mission to Palestine."

scriptions to be factual. This document was sent to Missouri's Governor Lilburn W. Boggs, who used it to justify the militia raids against the Mormons and his own Extermination Order, signed on October 27.

Hyde later claimed that his illness had clouded his judgment and that, after the Mormons left the state, he regretted his decision.[76] On March 30, 1839, he wrote to Brigham Young, who had become president of the Quorum of the Twelve after Marsh's disaffection, asking for reinstatement: "As to the terms upon which I can be received back into my place I shall not be particular: for to live in this way I cannot: and to join any other Society, I have no more disposition." Then he appealed: "Brigham, will you forgive me? Will the church forgive me? If so, God will forgive me."[77] Orson F. Whitney, grandson of Heber C. Kimball, described Orson Hyde's interactions with his grandfather:

> "About this time" [April 1839], says Heber, "Orson Hyde came to me feeling very sorrowful for the course he had pursued the past few months; he said it was because of fear . . . and now lamented his folly and asked me what he should do. I told him to give up his school, remove his family and gather with the Church. He wanted to know if I thought the brethren would forgive him. I said, 'Yes.' He then asked, 'Will you defend my case?' And I promised him I would."
>
> Heber enlisted as his fellow champion of the cause of Brother Hyde, President Hyrum Smith . . . when at the next conference of the Church [May 4], Joseph presented the name of Orson Hyde to the congregation for their [disciplinary] action, Hyrum and Heber pleaded for him so earnestly that the Prophet said: "If my brother Hyrum and Heber C. Kimball will defend Orson Hyde, I will withdraw my motion."[78]

In fact, Hyde reported to Allen Stout, whom he encountered while traveling to Liberty, Missouri (date not specified), that he had received a "vision in which it was made known to him that if he did not make immediate restitution to the Quorum of the Twelve, he would be cut off and all his posterity, and that the curse of Cain would be upon him. I invited him to ride with me, which he was very thankful for as he was very much fatigued."[79] Stout observed that although he (meaning himself) "was not much in love with apostates so soon after

---

76. Another of Hyde's biographers wrote that, after his estrangement, Orson remained "near the Saints and began teaching school [and] repented quickly." Howard H. Barron, *Orson Hyde: Missionary, Apostle, Colonizer*, 105.

77. Orson Hyde, Letter to Brigham Young, March 30, 1839, quoted in Myrtle Stevens Hyde, *Orson Hyde: The Olive Branch of Israel*, 106–7.

78. Orson F. Whitney, *Life of Heber C. Kimball, An Apostle; The Father and Founder of the British Mission*, 244–45.

79. Allen Stout, Journal, 12–13.

my exit from prison . . . I saw that Brother Hyde was on the stool of repentance, and he did repent good and got back to his place in the Twelve."[80]

Except for the fact of Hyde's disaffection, Hall's story is inconsistent in every detail with these documents, which appear to be much more plausible and were created closer to the events themselves. There is nothing to substantiate Hyde's making a small fortune "cutting cord-wood for a support," giving money to the Prophet, or bartering Marinda in exchange for Orson's return to the quorum. Additionally, Hall's reference to a "camp" of Latter-day Saints during this period seems anachronistic—too late for Zion's Camp and too early for the companies of Mormons traveling to Utah. In short, Brodie's inclusion of Marinda Johnson as an 1839 sexual partner of Joseph Smith is based upon a single report, the authenticity of which will not withstand even the most basic fact-checking, which Brodie apparently failed to do.

Clarissa Reed Hancock

Brodie names Clarissa Reed Hancock as one of Joseph Smith's plural wives in 1840: "There is a tradition among some of the descendants of Levi Hancock that Mrs. [Clarissa Reed] Hancock was sealed to Joseph Smith in Nauvoo and that one of her sons may have been his child. Since there seems to be no printed or manuscript evidence to support this story, however, it must be taken with considerable reserve."[81] A few authors concurred with the suggestion of a sealing,[82] while others have concurred with the recommendation of "considerable reserve."[83]

Brodie further asserts: "Legend among the descendants of Levi W. Hancock points to another son of the prophet. If the legend is true, the child was probably John Reed Hancock. . . . Oddly, the next Hancock child, born considerably after Joseph Smith's death, was named Levison, as if to satisfy any doubt that Levi Hancock was in truth the father."[84]

The child in question, John Reed Hancock, was born April 19, 1841, in Nauvoo, meaning that, if the pregnancy went full term, conception would have occurred around July 28, 1840. However, Brodie is correct that there is no support for a relationship between Joseph Smith and Clarissa except the family legend and the fact that both parties were in Nauvoo. The question was

---

80. Ibid.

81. Brodie, No Man Knows My History, 464.

82. See for example, Martha Sonntag Bradley and Mary Brown Firmage Woodward, "Plurality, Patriarchy, and the Priestess: Zina D. H. Young's Nauvoo Marriages," 96.

83. Jenson, "Plural Marriage," 233–34; Quinn, *The Mormon Hierarchy: Origins of Power*, 587–88, and Compton, *In Sacred Loneliness*, 4–8.

84. Brodie, No *Man Knows My History*, 345.

Charges of Immoral Conduct against Joseph Smith

put to rest in 2011 as geneticist Ugo Perego compared Joseph Smith's DNA to that of a descendant of John Reed Hancock. "It is not a match at all to Joseph Smith," declared Perego. "It is a perfect match to all the Hancock males in my database. . . . Case solved."[85]

Brodie's conjecture that "Levison" constituted documentation that Levi was the father, while interesting, loses considerable credibility in the larger context of family history. Levison died at age three. Levi Hancock married plural wife Anna Tew in 1857 who gave birth to a son the next year who received the name "Levison," apparently for reasons other than to clarify paternity questions.

Stanley Ivins lists Clarissa as a plural wife, but adds: "There appears to be no documentary evidence of this."[86] In fact, Andrew Jenson, D. Michael Quinn, H. Michael Marquardt, Todd Compton, and George D. Smith do not include Clarissa as one of the Prophet's plural wives at any time.[87] Compton comments: "Brodie posits a union between Joseph and Clarissa; however, I am aware of no evidence for any such relationship."[88]

Benjamin Winchester's Allegation Regarding a "Miss Smith"

In an 1900 interview, Benjamin Winchester, who had joined the Church in 1832 but disaffiliated and became a Rigdonite after Joseph's death, claimed: "Before the revelation came out on polygamy [July 12, 1843], he [Joseph Smith] had a child to a Miss Smith of Philadelphia. She had two children before he sealed her as his wife. She was a fine looking woman, and traveled for months with Smith, about nine or ten months before her child was born. It could not have been any other man's child. Smith got Philo Dibble to marry her so as to avoid scandal."[89]

Curiously, in a newspaper article published eleven years earlier, Winchester mentioned a "Mrs. Smith" without claiming the Prophet was sexually involved with her:

---

85. Ugo Perego quoted in Michael De Groote, "DNA Solves Joseph Smith Mystery," *Deseret News*, July 10, 2011, B1–B4.

86. Stanley S. Ivins, "Wives of Joseph Smith," in Jerald Tanner and Sandra Tanner, *Joseph Smith and Polygamy*, 46.

87. Jenson, "Plural Marriage," 233–34; Quinn, *The Mormon Hierarchy: Origins of Power*, 587–88; Marquardt, *The Rise of Mormonism: 1816–1844*, 561; Compton, *In Sacred Loneliness*, 4–8.

88. Todd Compton, "Fanny Alger Smith Custer: Mormonism's First Plural Wife?" 189 note 50.

89. W. L. Crowe, Interview of Benjamin Winchester, December 13, 1900.

During the time of Smith's sojourn with me in Philadelphia we visited quite a number of members of the Church there. Among them was a Mrs. Smith, foreman or forewoman of a glove factory, and some eight or ten girls were working in that factory who were, like Mrs. Smith, members of the Church. [Joseph] Smith, after several silly flirtations with the girls which I witnessed and which created a good deal of scandal and caused me some trouble, finally became enamored with Mrs. Smith and induced her and two girls to leave there and go to Nauvoo. I subsequently met Mrs. Smith at Nauvoo, when she told me that she had lent Joseph all of her money and he had gotten her married to a man by the name of Debble — that through the "prophet" she had lost her all and was reduced to a condition of abject poverty.[90]

Apparently, Winchester's memory (he turned seventy-two in the year of the newspaper interview), was not completely reliable. Both "Miss Smith" and "Mrs. Smith" were Hannah Ann Dubois Smith, who married John F. Smith and gave birth to Peter A. Smith in 1835.[91]

Winchester was a member of the branch in the Philadelphia area when Joseph Smith stayed there between December 21 and 30, 1839, with a second visit occurring January 9–30, 1840.[92] That four-week window represents the only time the Prophet traveled to Philadelphia after the Church left Kirtland in the late 1830s. Winchester accused the Prophet and Hannah of conceiving a child during that visit but immediately arranging a marriage to Philo Dibble to avoid the scandal of an illegitimate birth, which assumes that Hannah would have known she was pregnant in less than a month, an unlikely supposition.

Furthermore, Hannah and Philo did marry, but not during the period Winchester specifies. Their nuptials occurred over a year later on February 11, 1841, far too late to cover up the birth of a child conceived in December 1839 or January 1840. The Prophet himself performed the marriage ceremony in Nauvoo.[93] Philo recalled: "On the 11th of February, 1841, I married a second wife—a Widow Smith of Philadelphia, who was living in the family of the Prophet. He performed the ceremony at his house, and Sister Emma Smith insisted upon getting up a wedding supper for us. It was a splen-

---

90. "Primitive Mormonism: Personal Narrative of It by Mr. Benjamin Winchester," *Salt Lake Tribune*, September 22, 1889, 2.

91. Research into Hannah's history has uncovered a family tradition that asserts that John F. Smith was actually Joseph Smith. However, chronology and geography demonstrate that the Prophet could not have been involved with Hannah at this early date. Family rumors, especially those that connect a genealogical line to Joseph Smith, are sometimes actively perpetuated by descendants, despite a lack of credible evidence to support the tradition.

92. For a brief history of the Prophet's visit, see H. Michael Marquardt, "Joseph Smith's Visit to Philadelphia, Pennsylvania," 6–7.

93. "The Dead," *Deseret News*, November 25, 1893, 32.

Hannah Ann Dubois Smith Dibble. Courtesy of the International Society of the Daughters of Utah Pioneers.

did affair, and quite a large party of our friends were assembled."[94] It is true that some of Joseph's plural wives married other men (for example, Sarah Ann Whitney entered a "pretend" marriage with Joseph C. Kingsbury after being sealed to Joseph—see Chapter 16); however, Joseph did not perform any of the weddings. In fact, after first agreeing to perform Henry Jacobs and Zina Huntington's wedding, at the last minute he withdrew and John C. Bennett officiated. Thus, the Prophet's willingness to perform the marriage for Philo Dibble and Hannah Smith argues against Hannah's being one of Joseph's secret plural wives.[95]

Concerning Hannah's offspring after Joseph Smith's visit to Philadelphia, available records corroborate that her first child, Hannah Ann Dibble, was born on January 7, 1842, eleven months following her marriage to Philo. The daughter's conception would have occurred approximately April 16, 1841, well over a year after Joseph had returned to Nauvoo.

I have also explored the possibility that Hannah conceived a child during Joseph's visits to Philadelphia who died in infancy. Such a child would have been born between July and November 1840 but would have been illegitimate, prior to Hannah and Philo's marriage. The available records show no evidence of such a child. The 1842 Nauvoo census contains only the entry of daughter Hannah Ann, but no other offspring for Philo and Hannah. That census also contained a category entitled: "Names of members that had died within three years." The only relevant name included there is "Celia Dibble," Philo's first wife. Had a child been born in 1840 and subsequently died, its name should have been included, although it is true that children who died at or shortly after birth were not always named and/or listed in official or even family records.[96]

Winchester himself, due to his stormy history with Church leaders, may have had personal reasons for easily remembering rumors that would have

---

94. Philo Dibble, "Philo Dibble's Narrative," 92–93.

95. Compton, "A Trajectory of Plurality," 37.

96. Nauvoo Ward Census, February 7, 1842, Fourth Ward, fd. 4, pp. 42–43, frame 641, LDS Church History Library.

tarnished Joseph Smith's memory.[97] Born August 6, 1817, he with his parents, Stephen Winchester and Nancy Case Winchester, and his siblings were baptized in 1833 and immediately moved to Kirtland, Ohio.[98] Serving as a missionary in 1837–39, he proselytized in New Jersey and Pennsylvania, visited Nauvoo for a few months, and moved to Philadelphia in August 1839, where he became a prominent local leader. He attended the conference in Philadelphia on December 23, 1839, during Joseph's first visit when the Prophet organized the Philadelphia Branch. Three months later, Benjamin was installed as the presiding elder.

Serving as the Philadelphia Branch president, Winchester experienced problems. He eventually clashed with Apostle John E. Page, who wrote a letter to Joseph Smith on September 1, 1841:

> Suffer me here to say, that it would be well for some efficient Elder or High Priest to be sent to Philadelphia branch—such an one as would sustain the confidence of the branch to preside over that branch; for the present time there is a feeling existing in the hearts of some concerning Elder Benjamin Winchester that I think cannot be removed better than by changing the President . . . My humble opinion is that Elder Winchester has not been wise in all things as he might have been. . . . Elder Winchester is very sanguine and unyielding in his course of economy concerning matters and things in the Church. I think that all that is strictly necessary to be done is that the Branch have a new President.[99]

Within weeks, Winchester was summoned to Nauvoo where he attended a council meeting with the Twelve Apostles on October 31. Joseph Smith recorded:

> Attended a council with the Twelve Apostles. Benjamin Winchester being present, complained that he had been neglected and misrepresented by the Elders, and manifested a contentious spirit. I gave him a severe reproof, telling him of his folly and vanity, and showing him that the principles which he suffered to control him would lead him to destruction. I counseled him to change his course, govern his disposition, and quit his tale-bearing and slandering his brethren.[100]

Winchester did not receive this rebuke humbly and did not mend his ways. In January of 1842, "Benjamin Winchester was suspended by the Quorum of the Twelve until he made satisfaction for disobedience to the First

---

97. "Minutes of the Church of Jesus Christ of Latter Day Saints in Philadelphia," original at Community of Christ Archives. Typescript excerpts by Michael Quinn, "Philadelphia Branch Records (1840–1854)," in D. Michael Quinn Papers.

98. David J. Whittaker, "East of Nauvoo: Benjamin Winchester and the Early Mormon Church," 32–34.

99. Journal History, September 1, 1841.

100. Journal History, October 31, 1841; see also *History of the Church*, 4:443.

Presidency."[101] Apostle John E. Page presided in Philadelphia and wrote on January 30, 1842, "B. Winchester is my Enemy."[102] Three months later in April, he verbally complained about Page and his leadership and was censured by the Twelve in May "for not following counsel."[103]

Winchester's rebellion continued, and in April 1843 Joseph Smith lamented: "You can never make anything out of Benjamin Winchester, if you take him out of the channel he wants to be in."[104] William Clayton recorded on May 22 that Joseph had "received a letter from Sister [Sybella] Armstrong of Philadelphia complaining of slanderous conduct in B[enjamin] Winchester. The President handed the letter to Dr. [Willard] Richards saying the Twelve ought to silence Winchester."[105]

The Twelve summoned Winchester to Nauvoo again. When he arrived at the end of May, a council was immediately convened to deal with his insubordination, which by now included accusations that the Prophet was guilty of "improper conduct" with "Miss Smith." Joseph flatly denied the allegations, calling them "damnable lies." Minutes from a meeting of the Twelve on May 27, 1843, read: "Prest J. Smith, [said] it has been the character of B[enjamin] Winchester from the beginning to contradict every body & every thing. and I have been under the ire of his tongue." Joseph then explained that he experienced "contention with him [Winchester] at evry house" and so the Prophet, "disgraced him before the conference & to be revenged he told one of the most damnable lies about me visited Sister Smith and Sister Dibbler small hat shop told her to come to Nauvoo with me and I would protect her[.] B. Winchester set up a devil of a howl that I was guilty of improper conduct."[106]

At the meeting Brigham Young added: "Benjemin [sic] Winchester has never for the first time received our council but has gone contrary to it. No one is safe in his hands. He calls Hiram [Hyrum Smith] an old granny & slanders evrybody."[107] Wilford Woodruff summarizes: "Then President Joseph Smith Arose & rebuked Elder Winchester in the sharpest manner. Said he had a lying spirit & had lied about him & told him of many of his errors."[108] That same

---

101. Journal History, January 12, 1842; *History of the Church*, 4:494.

102. John E. Page to "Brethren," January 30, 1842, in Richard E. Turley Jr., ed., *Selected Collections from the Archives of the Church of Jesus Christ of Latter-day Saints*, Vol. 1, DVD #20.

103. Journal History, May 14, 1842, in Turley, *Selected Collections*, Vol. 2, DVD # 1; *History of the Church*, 5:8–9.

104. Journal History, April 19, 1843, in Turley, *Selected Collections*, Vol. 2, DVD # 1; see also *History of the Church*, 5:367.

105. George D. Smith, ed., *An Intimate Chronicle: The Journals of William Clayton*, 105.

106. *Minutes of the Apostles of the Church of Jesus Christ of Latter-day Saints, 1835–1893*, 25, see also 27.

107. Scott G. Kenney, ed., *Wilford Woodruff's Journal, 1833–1898*, 2:235.

108. Ibid.; see also *History of the Church*, 5:410–11.

TABLE 3.2
TWELVE WOMEN ALLEGED TO HAVE BEEN SEXUALLY INVOLVED
WITH JOSEPH SMITH BEFORE 1841

	Women Reportedly Involved	Year of Alleged Incident	Year Allegation Was First Published
1	Eliza Winters	1827–1829	1834
2	Josiah Stowell's daughters	1830	2002
3	"a certain woman"	1829–30	1890
4	Marinda Nancy Johnson	1832	1884
5	Vienna Jacques	1833	1886?
6	Fanny Alger	1833–1835	1842–1881[a]
7	Athalia and Nancy Rigdon	1837	1994[b]
8	Lucinda Pendleton Harris	1838	1885[c]
9	Presendia Huntington Buell	1839	1860[d]
10	Marinda Nancy Johnson (again)	1839	1852
11	Clarissa Reed Hancock	1840	1945
12	"Miss Smith"	1839–1840	1900

---

a. General references to Joseph Smith's involvement with an unidentified young woman in Kirtland were published as early as 1842. Oliver Cowdery referred to Fanny Alger by name in a private letter in 1838, but the earliest published mention of her name that I have found occurred decades later in the 1881 *Anti-Polygamy Standard*. This was by "Historicus," "Sketches from the History of Polygamy: Joseph Smith's Especial Revelations," 1, who called her "Fanny Olger or Alger." Five years later, her correct name was published in Wilhelm Wyl, *Mormon Portraits*, 57, quoting Chauncy Webb: "He [Joseph Smith] was sealed there [in Kirtland, Ohio] secretly to Fanny Alger." Most Church members' first encounter with Fanny Alger's name occurred in 1887 in Andrew Jenson's "Plural Marriage," 233.

b. It could be argued that the 1884 debate was public; however, nothing in the 1884 transcript supports a "link" between Athalia and Joseph Smith as Van Wagoner, *Sidney Rigdon*, 291, implies. Therefore, I believe that, rather than being 1884 testimony, the allegation is more Van Wagoner's interpretation of historical data as presented in *Sidney Rigdon*.

c. Sarah Pratt, quoted in Wyl, *Mormon Portraits*, 60.

d. Green, *Fifteen Years among the Mormons*, 35. The statement is actually Mary Ettie V. Smith's.

day the Prophet recorded in his journal: "Winchester was silenced."[109] Meaning "Elder Winchester should give up his licence & cease Preaching untill he should reform."[110] Apparently this severe action humbled Winchester. He immediately returned to Philadelphia and prepared to move his family to Nauvoo, settling there by November.[111] Winchester evidently made satisfactory restitution; when Joseph Smith declared his candidacy for the presidency of the United States in February 1844, Winchester was called along with over three hundred other missionaries to campaign on Joseph's behalf.[112] Mercurial in his devotion, after the Prophet's death, he aligned himself with Sidney Rigdon's group in Pittsburgh.[113] In the 1850s he moved to Iowa and embraced "spiritualism." He visited Utah in 1871 and, in 1889 at age seventy-two, wrote a recollection entitled "Primitive Mormonism," for the *Salt Lake Tribune*, an article highly critical of Joseph Smith in which he vented long-simmering frustrations.

Whatever Winchester's reasons for accusing the Prophet of sexual misconduct, the historical record demonstrates that Joseph Smith directly denied his charges, and no one else apparently took him seriously at that time. Years later in his 1889 *Salt Lake Tribune* article, Winchester refrained from repeating the accusation, although it resurfaced eleven years afterward in an interview now recorded in the Community of Christ archives.[114]

Summary

Available evidence identifies twelve charges of polygamy or sexual misconduct against Joseph Smith that reportedly occurred prior to his first plural sealing—to Louisa Beaman in Nauvoo in April 1841. Eleven of them have been reviewed above and have been found to be lacking in persuasive evidence. The most complex case, that of Fanny Alger, is discussed in Chapters 4–8.

Several important observations can be made. First, according to available documents, only one of the twelve charges against Joseph Smith (the second-hand accusation from Levi Lewis regarding Eliza Winters) was published during the Prophet's lifetime. The allegation was printed in the *Susquehanna Register and Northern Pennsylvanian* and republished in E. D. Howe's *Mormonism Unvailed* in 1834; but I have found no other mentions in print before 1842. For example, in his 1838 *Exposure of Mormonism*, Richard Livesey wrote a summary of Howe's

---

109. Faulring, *An American Prophet's Record*, 381.
110. Kenney, *Wilford Woodruff's Journal, 1833–1898*, 2:236.
111. Whittaker, "East of Nauvoo," 62.
112. Ibid.
113. Stephen J. Fleming, "Discord in the City of Brotherly Love: The Story of Early Mormonism in Philadelphia," 3–21.
114. W. L. Crowe, Interview of Benjamin Winchester, December 13, 1900. Although this interview is catalogued under Crowe's name, it is not clear whether he was asking the questions.

allegations, identifying eight separate faults of Joseph Smith and his followers, but none of his criticisms deals with any form of sexual impropriety.[115]

As discussed in Chapters 4–8, some reports surfaced in 1837–38 about Joseph Smith's relationship with Fanny Alger; but otherwise, there is little evidence that, in the 1830s, the Prophet was accused, either privately or publicly, of sexual misbehavior. During that decade, his critics openly reprimanded him for many things, but not for unchaste behavior. In the 1970s, anti-Mormon writers Jerald and Sandra Tanner charged: "The charge of sexual immorality was probably one of the most frequent charges made against Joseph Smith."[116] Contemporaneous evidence does not support this statement—at least not before July 1842.

Second, and more importantly, when examined individually for believability, each of the eleven charges reveals significant inaccuracies and internal inconsistencies. Brodie is perhaps the best-known, but also the most guilty, of numerous authors who have arranged these poorly documented allegations into a flowing narrative to depict Joseph Smith's pre-Nauvoo "polygamy history."[117]

---

115. Richard Livesey, *Exposure of Mormonism*, 3–8.
116. Tanner and Tanner, *Joseph Smith and Polygamy*, 76
117. For example, Van Wagoner, *Mormon Polygamy*, 4, lines up the allegations of Eliza Winters, Nancy Marinda Johnson, Benjamin F. [sic] Winchester, and Vienna Jacques, one after the other, citing biased historical sources without any analysis of their reliability. The unsuspecting reader is left with the impression that the storyline is supported by documented history rather than unexamined propaganda.

Chapter 4

Fanny Alger and the Beginnings of Mormon Polygamy

At some point prior to 1837, Joseph Smith entered into a relationship with a young woman named Fanny Alger; this association has been characterized as his first plural marriage. If so, what events led up to this drastic alteration in his marital practices? LDS scholar Danel Bachman wrote that, shortly after the organization of the Church, the Prophet learned concerning the correctness of plural marriage: "Much of the ideological framework of Mormon polygyny had emerged in Joseph Smith's thinking before the end of 1831."[1] He also added: "The overwhelming impression coming from a study of the pre-Nauvoo years is that, like the rest of Mormon theology, the tenet of plural marriage emerged from a primarily religious context."[2]

The four incidents that have been suggested as the catalyst prompting the Prophet to inquire of the Lord specifically concerning polygamy will be discussed below. One occurrence is an 1831 missionary journey to Missouri to preach to the "Lamanites" or the American Indians. A second hypothesis is that the topic arose while Joseph Smith "translated" or revised the Old Testament and, in the narratives about Abraham and Jacob, encountered ancient prophets who practiced plural marriage. (See Vol. 3, Chapter 3.) Less credible influences may be translating the Book of Mormon (in 1829) or bringing forth the Book of Abraham (published March 1, 1842).[3]

1831 Revelation:
"Ye Should Take Unto You Wives of the Lamanites"

The Church of Jesus Christ was organized on April 6, 1830, in Fayette, New York. Months later in October, four missionaries, Parley P. Pratt, Ziba Peterson, Oliver Cowdery, and Peter Whitmer, were commissioned by revelation to journey "into the wilderness among the Lamanites" (D&C 32:2).

---

1. Danel Bachman, "A Study of the Mormon Practice of Plural Marriage before the Death of Joseph Smith," 50.
2. Ibid., 102.
3. See "A Fac-simile from the Book of Abraham," *Times and Seasons* 3, no. 9 (March 1, 1842): 1.

They baptized dozens of converts in the Kirtland, Ohio area and completed the fifteen-hundred-mile journey to the borders of Missouri in January of 1831. On February 1, the Prophet and Emma moved to Kirtland, bringing the center of the Church with them. Five months passed and on June 19, 1831, Joseph Smith, W. W. Phelps, Martin Harris, Sidney Rigdon, and several others traveled to Jackson County, Missouri, on a missionary journey arriving there a few weeks later. On February 27, 1845, "Phelps sd 6 or 8. went over the boundaries of the U.S. to preach—Jos. went to prayer [sic]—he then commenced a revelation that Martin was to marry among the Laminites—& that I was to preach that day—&c &c it was a long revelation. . . ."[4]

The contents of the described revelation are important. In 1861, thirty years after the revelation was reportedly dictated, W. W. Phelps wrote a letter to President Young clarifying that experience. He then recited the "substance" of the revelation identifying it as from "Joseph Smith Jun. given over the boundary, west of Jackson Co. Missouri, on Sunday morning, July 17, 1831":

> Verily, verily, saith the Lord your Redeemer, even Jesus Christ, the light and the life of the world, ye can not discerne [sic] with your natural eyes, the design and the purpose of your Lord and your God, in bringing you thus far into the wilderness for a trial of your faith, and to be especial witnesses, to bear testimony of this land, upon which the zion of God shall be built up in the last days, when it is redeemed.
>
> Verily, inasmuch as ye are united in calling upon my name to know my will concerning who shall preach to the inhabitants that shall assemble this day to learn what new doctrine you have to teach them, you have done wisely, for so did the prophets anciently, even Enoch, and Abraham, and others: and therefore, it is my will that my servant Oliver Cowdery should open the meeting with prayer; that my servant W. W. Phelps should preach the discourse; and that my servants Joseph Coe and Ziba Peterson should bear testimony as they shall be moved by the Holy Spirit. This will be pleasing in the sight of your Lord.
>
> Verily I say unto you, ye are laying the foundation of a great work for the salvation of as many as will believe and repent, and obey the ordinances of the gospel, and continue faithful to the end: For, as I live, saith the Lord, so shall they live.
>
> Verily I say unto you that the wisdom of man in his fallen state, knoweth not the purposes and the privileges of my holy priesthood. but ye shall know when ye receive a fulness by reason of the anointing: *For it is my will, that in*

---

4. See W. W. Phelps, Letter to Brigham Young, August 21, 1861, in "General Church Minutes," See also "Council Meeting Minutes," January 10 to March 24, 1845, p. 5 and *Minutes of the Apostles of The Church of Jesus Christ of Latter-day Saints, 1835–1893*, 39. Phelps's letter, as quoted in the "General Church Minutes" continued: "we have a living Constitution—there is enough for every day—if we die let us all die together, & there will be a jolly lot of spirits dancing into the next world—it wont be to hell, for there is no fiddles there."

time, ye should take unto you wives of the Lamanites and Nephites [emphasis mine], that their posterity may become white, delightsome and Just, for even now their females are more virtuous than the gentiles.[5]

The details found in the revelation raise questions whether Phelps was actually recalling its content or was working from contemporaneous notes or from some other source. His statement that he was providing only the "substance" of the revelation is confusing because the text seems complete. Regardless, Phelps's introduction generates concerns regarding the revelation's overall accuracy. Phelps concluded his letter to President Young:

> About three years after this was given, I asked brother Joseph [Smith, Jr.] privately, how "we," that were mentioned in the revelation could take wives from the "natives"—as we were all married men? He replied instantly "In th[e] same manner that Abraham took Hagar and Katurah [Keturah]; and Jacob took Rachel Bilhah and Zilpah: by revelation—the saints of the Lord are always directed by revelation."[6]

Corroborating Phelps's recollection is a contemporaneous letter from Ezra Booth who wrote to Ira Eddy, editor of the *Ohio Star*, published in Ravenna, on December 6, 1831: "It has been made known by revelation, that it will be pleasing to the Lord, should they form a matrimonial alliance with the natives. . . . It has been made known to one, who has left his wife in the State of New York, that he is entirely free from his wife, and he is at pleasure to take him a wife from among the Lamanites."[7]

Despite Joseph Smith's apparent 1831 introduction to plural marriage and the reported revelation acknowledging it as a correct principle, no polygamous unions were then formed. The revelation states: "For it is my will, that *in time*, ye should take unto you wives of the Lamanites and Nephites" (emphasis mine). Apparently the time was not right in 1831. Additional reports state that when the Prophet first learned of the appropriateness of plural marriage, he was not then allowed to begin its practice (discussed below).

Other Evidence Corroborating the Early 1830s

Ten other witnesses affirmed that they knew the Prophet learned in the early 1830s that plural marriage was a correct principle. Two plural wives whom he married in Nauvoo recalled that the knowledge came in 1831. In 1884, Helen Mar Whitney Kimball, wrote: "The Lord revealed it [plural marriage] to His

---

5. W. W. Phelps, Letter to Brigham Young, August 12, 1861. See also H. Michael Marquardt, *The Joseph Smith Revelations: Text and Commentary*, 374.

6. Phelps to Young, August 12, 1861. See also, Brent Herridge, *Sally Young*.

7. Ezra Booth, Letter to Ira Eddy, December 6, 1831, *Ohio Star* 2 (December 8, 1831) 3. See also Eber D. Howe, *Mormonism Unvailed*, 220.

prophet, Joseph Smith, as early as the year 1831."[8] Lucy Walker testified in 1892 that plural marriage "was revealed to the prophet in '31, but he did not teach it then. . . . He received a revelation on polygamy in 1831."[9] Neither woman explains how or from whom she learned about an 1831 revelation, although Joseph himself is the most likely source. In addition, Emily Partridge affirmed in 1884: "I know he [Joseph Smith] was a prophet of God and I know that he received the revelation on celestial marriage years before it was written [1843]."[10]

According to Orson Pratt, Lyman E. Johnson who was a member of the first Quorum of the Twelve Apostles, recalled that "Joseph had made known to him as early as 1831 that plural marriage was a correct principle."[11] In 1869, Apostle Pratt stated that, when the Prophet first learned about the truthfulness of plural marriage, he was not allowed to practice it:

> In the fore part of the year 1832, Joseph told individuals, then in the Church, that he had inquired of the Lord concerning the principle of plurality of wives, and he received for answer that the principle of taking more wives than one is a true principle, but the time had not yet come for it to be practiced. That was before the Church was two years old. The Lord has His own time to do all things pertaining to His purposes in the last dispensation; His own time for restoring all things that have been predicted by the ancient prophets. . . . Now supposing the members of this Church had undertaken to vary from that law given in 1831, to love their one wife with all their hearts and to cleave to none other, they would have come under the curse and condemnation of God's holy law.[12]

In 1892 Wilford Woodruff explained that the Prophet received an "early" revelation on the subject of plural marriage but that it was kept secret: "Joseph Smith received a revelation from God at a very age [sic] of the church, which never was revealed to the church during his life,—never revealed either openly or privately to the church as a body, but were revealed to individual members of the Church. . . . The whole thing was kept a secret excepting as far as it was revealed to individuals of the church."[13]

---

8. Helen Mar Kimball Whitney, *Why We Practice Plural Marriage*, 53.

9. Lucy Walker, Deposition, in Temple Lot Transcript, Respondent's Testimony, Part 3, pp. 450–51, questions 27, 53. It is unclear whether Lucy is restating information she learned from Joseph Smith directly or if she is merely repeating assertions she heard from others.

10. Emily D. Partridge, "Testimony That Cannot Be Refuted," 165.

11. Lyman E. Johnson, quoted in "Report of Elders Orson Pratt and Joseph F. Smith," *Millennial Star* 40 (December 16, 1878): 788. Pratt was Johnson's missionary companion. Also in Andrew Jenson, "Plural Marriage," 230. The only mission to which Elders Pratt and Johnson were called together commenced January 25, 1832, and ended in September, 1832 (D&C 75:14). *History of the Church*, 1:244, 286.

12. Orson Pratt, October 7, 1869, *Journal of Discourses*, 13:193.

13. Wilford Woodruff, Deposition, in Temple Lot Transcript, Respondent's

Fanny Alger and the Beginnings of Mormon Polygamy

According to a late memoir from Mosiah Hancock, the Prophet taught Mosiah's father, Levi Ward Hancock, concerning polygamy in 1832:

> As early as the Spring of 1832 Bro Joseph said "Brother Levi, The Lord has revealed to me that it is his will that righteous men shall take Righteous women even a plurality of Wives that a Righteous race may be sent forth Uppon the Earth preparatory to the ushering in of the Millennial Reign of our Redeemer For the Lord has such a high respect for the nobles of his kingdom that he is not willing for them to come through the Loins of a careles [sic] People—Therefore; it behoves those who embrace that Principle to pay strict attention to even the least requirement of our Heavenly Father."[14]

Lyman O. Littlefield, who knew the Prophet in Nauvoo, recalled in 1883: "I have the best reasons for believing it [celestial and plural marriage] was understood and believed by him (Joseph Smith, the Prophet) away back in the days when he lived in Kirtland. . . . He was instructed of the Lord respecting the sacred ordinance of plural marriage; but he was not required to reveal it to the Church until sometime during the residence of the Saints in Nauvoo."[15]

Nauvoo polygamist Joseph B. Noble, speaking at a stake quarterly conference at Centerville, Davis County, Utah, on June 11, 1883, recalled "that the Prophet Joseph told him that the doctrine of celestial marriage was revealed to him while he was engaged on the work of translation of the scriptures [Joseph Smith's revision of the Bible], but when the communication was first made the Lord stated that the time for the practice of that principle had not arrived."[16] Records show that the Prophet was working with Genesis in February and March of 1831.[17] There he would have encountered the accounts of polygamous patriarchs like Abraham (Gen. 16:1–6) and Jacob (Gen. 29:30). Three months later, he and his companions departed on their missionary journey to the Lamanites.

A third-hand account states that it was the translation of the Book of Mormon, not the Bible, that prompted Joseph's questions resulting in the revelation. Charles Lowell Walker recorded that he heard Brigham Young preach:

Testimony, Part 3, p. 54, question 513.

14. Levi Ward Hancock, "Autobiography of Levi Ward Hancock with additions [in 1896] by His Son Mosiah Hancock," 61–62. The quotation is from the portion written by Mosiah.

15. Lyman O. Littlefield, "An Open Letter Addressed to President Joseph Smith, jun., of the Re-organized Church of Jesus Christ of Latter-day Saints," 387. See also "Lyman O. Littlefield's Testimony," in Jenson, "Plural Marriage," 230.

16. Joseph B. Noble speaking at a quarterly stake conference held at Centerville, Davis County, Utah, June 11, 1883, quoted in Jenson, "Plural Marriage," 232–33. See Brigham H. Roberts, editor's introduction, *History of the Church*, 5:xxix; see also Hubert Howe Bancroft, *History of Utah*, 161–62.

17. Mark Lyman Staker, *Hearken O Ye People: The Historical Setting for Joseph Smith's Ohio Revelations*, 117 note 22.

"While Joseph And Oliver were translating the Book of Mormon, they had a revelation that the order of Patriarchal Marriag and Sealing was right."[18] Since the Book of Mormon generally condemns the practice of polygamy (see Mosiah 11:2), this seems less likely. Another third-hand even more unlikely possibility was recorded by excommunicated Mormon T.B.H. Stenhouse: "Elder W.W. Phelps said in Salt Lake Tabernacle, in 1862, that while Joseph was translating the Book of Abraham, in Kirtland, Ohio, in 1835, from the papyrus found with Egyptian mummies, the Prophet became impressed with the idea that polygamy would yet become an institution of the Mormon Church."[19]

In an 1886 article published in the *Deseret News*, Joseph F. Smith, then a member of the First Presidency, commented: "The great and glorious principle of plural marriage was first revealed to Joseph Smith in 1831, but being forbidden to make it public, or to teach it as a doctrine of the Gospel at that time, he confided the facts to only a very few of his intimate associates."[20]

Regardless of the precise process through which Joseph comprehended that plural marriage was a correct principle, it appears that he cautiously taught a few of his followers concerning its doctrinal appropriateness several years before he attempted to practice it. George Q. Cannon described what happened:

> The Lord revealed to the Prophet Joseph in an early day, some points connected with the doctrine of celestial marriage. He was told that it was to obey God's will that His ancient servants had taken more wives than one; and he probably learned, also, that His servants in those days would be commanded to carry out this principle. The Prophet Joseph, however, took no license from this. He was content to await the pleasure and command of the

---

18. Andrew Karl Larson and Katharine Miles Larson, eds., *The Diary of Charles Lowell Walker*, July 26, 1872, 1:349. See discussion in Bachman, "A Study of the Mormon Practice of Plural Marriage before the Death of Joseph Smith," 63–66, and Max H Parkin, "Conflict at Kirtland: A Study of the Nature and Causes of External and Internal Conflict of the Mormons in Ohio between 1830 and 1838," 169–72.

19. T. B. H. Stenhouse, *Rocky Mountain Saints*, 182 note. The entire reference reads: "Elder W. W. Phelps said in Salt Lake Tabernacle, in 1862, that while Joseph was translating the Book of Abraham, in Kirtland, Ohio, in 1835, from the papyrus found with the Egyptian mummies, the Prophet became impressed with the idea that polygamy would yet become an institution of the Mormon Church. Brigham Young was present, and was much annoyed at the statement made by Phelps, but it is highly probable that it was the real secret which the latter then divulged. The Conscientious Mormon who calmly considers what is here written on the introduction of polygamy into the Mormon Church will readily see that its origin is probably much more correctly traceable to those Egyptian mummies, than to a revelation from heaven. The first paragraph of the Revelation has all the musty odour of the catacombs about it, and that Joseph went into polygamy at a venture there cannot be the slightest doubt."

20. Joseph F. Smith, *Deseret News*, May 20, 1886; quoted in Jenson, "Plural Marriage," 219.

Lord, knowing that it was . . . sinful to enter upon the practice of a principle like this before being commanded to do so.[21]

Despite these repeated affirmations that Joseph Smith learned of the correctness of plural marriage in the early 1830s, it should be noted that no contemporary evidence exists to confirm such a date. These multiple reminiscences with sometimes conflicting details seem to tell the same general story. However, they were all recalled in an era of where expressing faith in plural marriage was tantamount to affirming faith in Joseph Smith and the Church and could reflect such biases.

Polygamy in Other Religious Sects in the 1830s

In addition to Joseph Smith's private teachings concerning plural marriage in the early 1830s, LDS missionaries encountered polygamy among various religious groups as they proselytized. Samuel Harrison Smith, Joseph's brother, recorded in his diary on July 1, 1832: "Held a meeting at Fanny Bruer's, in the forenoon, preaching, and in the afternoon partook of the Sacrament. Prayer meeting in the evening. Somewhat interrupted this day in the meeting by a man and woman that taught the doctrine of the devil, such as abstaining from meat and having spiritual wives and so forth. They came to our meeting."[22]

Orson Hyde encountered a separate group of "spiritual wife" proponents on October 11, 1832, in Gunkits, Maine (a location that appears nowhere in Maine but which may have been close to Saco): "Went down to Gunkits about 3 miles and again preached to a congregation of Cochranites who gave liberty; told them again to repent and go up to Zion, and we lifted our cry in the Spirit, and I hope some of them will go; but they had a wonderful lustful spirit, because they believe in a 'Plurality of wives' which they call spiritual wives, knowing them not after the flesh but after the spirit, but by the *appearance they know one another after the flesh.*"[23]

Jacob Cochran, who founded "The Society of Free Brethren and Sisters" in 1817 in Saco, Maine, included in his teachings a form of "spiritual wifery" that violated local laws against sexual immorality; and in 1819, he was prosecuted for adultery. The *National Intelligencer*, published in Washington, D.C., reported on November 19, 1819: "*Jacob Cochrane*, the notorious preacher and leader of a new party of religious zealots in this country, has been sentenced by the Supreme Court now sitting at Alfred, to 13 days solitary imprisonment, and four years hard labor in the state's prison, for the crime of adultery. . . . On the

---

21. George Q. Cannon, "History of the Church," 206.
22. Samuel Harrison Smith, Diary, July 1, 1832.
23. Orson Hyde, 1832 Mission Journal, October 11, 1832, typescript; emphasis mine.

> **FROM THE BOSTON PATRIOT, NOV. 6.**
>
> *Jacob Cochrane*, the notorious preacher and leader of a new party of religious zealots in this country, has been sentenced, by the Supreme Court now sitting at Alfred, to 13 days solitary imprisonment, and four years hard labor in the state's prison, for the crime of adultery, of which he was convicted before the Supreme Court at York, in May last, and absconded before the passing of the sentence. On the other three indictments, for lewdness, fornication, and adultery, he has not yet been tried.

National Intelligencer article, November 13, 1819, outlining Jacob Cochran's adultery conviction

other three indictments, for lewdness, fornication, and adultery, he has not yet been tried."[24]

Richard and Pamela Price, RLDS Restorationists who take the position that Joseph Smith was never a polygamist, believe that, through the Cochranite connection, plural marriage entered the Church:

> Latter-day Saint missionaries arrived in southern Maine in 1832, only three years after Jacob Cochran moved from Maine to New York State. The Church missionaries visited the Cochranite communities, stayed in their homes, taught them the gospel, baptized some, and urged them to gather to Zion. As a result, many of his followers joined the Church and moved to Kirtland and Nauvoo. Some took their polygamous beliefs with them. . . . "On August 21, 1835, nine of the Twelve [apostles] met in conference at Saco, Maine."[25] With nine of the twelve apostles making their appearance

---

24. "From the Boston Patriot," *National Intelligencer*, November 13, 1819.

25. Orson Hyde and William McLellin, Letter to J. Whitmer, Kirtland, Ohio, October 1835, *Messenger and Advocate* 2 (October 1835): 206.

Fanny Alger and the Beginnings of Mormon Polygamy

in Saco, there is no doubt that each one of them became well acquainted with the doctrines of Cochranism, for at that time it was a popular secular and religious news topic.[26]

Researcher Richard K. Behrens seems to agree, hypothesizing that plural marriage was brought to the Church in 1835 by Parley P. Pratt, who derived the concept from the teachings of Jacob Cochran who had begun preaching on spiritual wives in 1817. Behrens theorizes that, eighteen years later, "Parley P. Pratt encountered Cochranites in Saco Valley in August 1835. For weeks he and other apostles labored in Maine before returning to Kirtland in September. In September the School of the Elders began discussing polygamy."[27] This view is problematic because there is no contemporary evidence to support it. It seems likely that, if polygamy had been mentioned in Kirtland meetings, Church members would have been alarmed and would have condemned the practice. Pratt's autobiography does not mention any interaction with the Cochranites but states that he first learned of the restoration of the ancient practice of plural marriage from Joseph Smith personally after his return from England in 1843.[28]

Evidence Supporting a Relationship between Joseph Smith and Fanny Alger

Despite a date possibly as early as 1831 for learning that polygamy was a correct principle, multiple pieces of evidence depict the passage of several years before Joseph Smith implemented the practice. It appears his first plural marriage occurred with a young woman named Fanny Alger. Born in September 20, 1816, Fanny became one of what would be ten children in the family of Samuel Alger and Clarissa Hancock Alger. Current research identifies nineteen documents that appear to mention the event in some way. Appendix D also contains the quotations listed in Table 4.1.

An analysis of the nineteen narratives shows that none was written before 1838. In other words, no contemporaneous records exist concerning the relationship. Fifteen of the accounts were composed at least thirty-seven years after the events occurred; thirteen of the narratives are secondhand.[29]

---

26. Richard and Pamela Price, *Joseph Smith Fought Polygamy*, Vol. 1, 18, 29.

27. Richard K. Behrens, "Parley P. Pratt and the Polygamy of Jacob Cochran," handout.

28. Parley learned of eternal marriage in 1840 and plural marriage in 1843. *Autobiography of Parley Parker Pratt: One of the Twelve Apostles of the Church of Jesus Christ of Latter-day Saints*, 1972 printing, 297–98. See also Vilate Kimball, Letter to Heber C. Kimball, June 27–29, 1843.

29. See Todd Compton, section titled "The Date of Fanny Alger's Marriage," in "Truth, Honesty and Moderation in Mormon History: A Response to Anderson,

TABLE 4.1
HISTORICAL ACCOUNTS REFERRING TO A RELATIONSHIP
BETWEEN JOSEPH SMITH AND FANNY ALGER

Date Written	Source	Reference	Discussion
Jan. 21, 1838	Oliver Cowdery	Letter to Warren A. Cowdery, January 21, 1838, copied by Warren F. Cowdery into Oliver Cowdery Letterbook, Huntington Library, San Marino, California.	Oliver did not believe the Joseph-Fanny relationship to be a God-sanctioned plural marriage, referring to it rather as "a dirty, nasty, filthy scrape."
Apr. 12 1838	Ebenezer Robinson, clerk	*Far West Record: Minutes of The Church of Jesus Christ of Latter-day Saints, 1830–1844*, 167–68	No mention of polygamy in the minutes. High council members were apparently satisfied with Joseph Smith's explanation regarding the "girl business," which, I hypothesize, was a simple denial of adultery.
July 1838	Several	*Elder's Journal* 1, no. 3 (July 1838): 45.	Article includes several statements designed to rebut rumors of adultery. No mention of polygamy.
1842	Fanny Brewer	Published in John C. Bennett, *The History of the Saints; or, an Exposé of Joe Smith and Mormonism*, 85.	Her statement has become a standard reference on polygamy at Kirtland; ironically, it mentions, not polygamy, but alleged adultery.
Thirty Year Delay			
1872	William McLellin	Letter to Joseph Smith III, July 1872, Community of Christ Archives	McLellin quotes both Frederick G. Williams and Emma Smith. His letter reports that Joseph was involved with "a hired girl" named "Miss Hill" and with Fanny Alger "in a barn." According to one interpretation, he was describing two relationships; according to another, he described only one but misidentified Fanny's surname.
1875		Quoted by J. H. Beadle, "Jackson County," *Salt Lake Tribune*, October 6, 1875, 4.	McLellin mentions only one relationship where Joseph Smith was "sealed to a hired girl . . in a barn."
1875	Martin Harris	Anthony Metcalf, *Ten Years before the Mast*, 72.	Metcalf quotes Martin as mentioning "improper proposals" (not polygamy or adultery) being made by Joseph to "a servant girl."
1875	Ann Eliza Webb Young	*Wife No. 19, or, the Story of a Life in Bondage, being a Complete Exposé of Mormonism, and Revealing the Sorrows, Sacrifices, and Sufferings of Women in Polygamy*, 66–67.	Born in 1844, Ann Eliza Webb was undoubtedly quoting her parents (Chauncy and Eliza Jane Webb). Refers to "sealing," not adultery.

1876	Eliza Jane Churchill Webb	Eliza J. Webb [Eliza Jane Churchill Webb], Lockport, New York, to Mary Bond, April 24, 1876.	Reportedly Fanny Alger went to live with Webb family for a few weeks after leaving the Smith home. Eliza and Chauncy referred to the relationship as a "sealing" in all their references, with no mention of adultery.
		Eliza J. Webb, Lockport, to Mary Bond, May 4, 1876.	
1881	Historicus [pseud.]	"Sketches from the History of Polygamy: Joseph Smith's Especial Revelations," *Anti-Polygamy Standard* [Salt Lake City] 2, no 1 (April 1881) 1.	The primary source of information may have been William McLellin who died in 1883. This is the first published mention of Fanny Alger by name.
1884	Clark Braden	E. L. Kelley and Clark Braden, *Public Discussion of the Issues between The Reorganized Church of Jesus Christ of Latter Day Saints and the Church of Christ (Disciples)*, 202.	Braden (born in 1831) could not have had first-hand knowledge. He was known for extreme views and sensationalism in interpreting historical evidence.
1885	John Hawley	John Hawley, Autobiography, January 1885, Community of Christ Archives, excerpts typed March 1982 by Lyndon Cook.	Second-hand and late source; Hawley refers to the relationship as a "sealing."
	Alfred Hollbrook	*Reminiscences of the Happy Life of a Teacher*, 223–24	Alfred Hollbrook (b. 1816), an accomplished educator, apparently visited Kirtland, Ohio, in 1837 and included his recollections in his autobiography.
1886	Chauncy Webb	Wilhelm Ritter Von Wymetal (pseud. W. Wyl), *Mormon Portraits or Joseph Smith the Prophet, His Family and His Friends: a Study Based on Facts and Documents*, 57.	Chauncy spoke of a "sealing" that may have resulted in Fanny's becoming pregnant.
1887	Eliza R. Snow	Document 10, in Andrew Jenson Papers (ca. 1871–1942), MS 17956, Box 49, fd. 16.	Eliza wrote Fanny Alger's name with her own hand on a list of Joseph Smith's plural wives and provided other information to Jenson.
1887	Andrew Jenson	"Plural Marriage," *Historical Record* 6 (July 1887): 233.	Although Fanny Alger's name was published six years earlier by a writer called "Historicus," this is probably the first time many Church members heard of her relationship with Joseph. Jenson did not date the marriage, so few members may have known it occurred in the Kirtland period.
1896	Mosiah Hancock	Mosiah Hancock, Autobiography, 1896	Mosiah provides details that a marriage ceremony was performed. He would have to be quoting his father, since he was born in 1834.
1903	Benjamin F. Johnson	Dean R. Zimmerman, ed., *I Knew the Prophets: An Analysis of the Letter of Benjamin F. Johnson to George F. Gibbs, Reporting Doctrinal Views of Joseph Smith and Brigham Young*, 38–39.	Johnson's late recollection depicts the Joseph Smith-Fanny Alger relationship as the first plural marriage in the Church.

Some historians have observed that dating and other details are not entirely consistent within these accounts, suggesting that Joseph Smith was involved with two women (or more) in Kirtland, Ohio.[30] The alleged second woman, a "Miss Hill," was mentioned in an 1872 letter from William McLellin to Joseph Smith III, Joseph and Emma's oldest son, recalling a disclosure that Emma had made to him twenty-five years earlier in 1847 in her Nauvoo home. Joseph III would have been fifteen at the time and living in the Nauvoo home with his mother, brothers, and stepfather at the time of McLellin's visit:

> You will probably remember that I visited your Mother and family in 1847, and held a lengthy conversation with her, retired in the Mansion House in Nauvoo. I did not ask her to tell, but I told her some stories I had heard. And she told me whether I was properly informed. Dr. F. G. Williams practiced with me in Clay Co. Mo. during the latter part of 1838. And he told me that at your birth your father committed an act with a Miss Hill—a hired girl. Emma saw him, and spoke to him. He desisted, [sic] but Mrs. Smith refused to be satisfied. He called in Dr. Williams, O. Cowdery, and S. Rigdon to reconcile Emma. But she told them just as the circumstances took place. He found he was caught. He confessed humbly, and begged forgiveness. Emma and all forgave him. She told me this story was true!! Again I told her I heard that one night she missed Joseph and Fanny Alger. [S]he went to the barn and saw him and Fanny in the barn together alone. She looked through a crack and saw the transaction!!! She told me this story too was verily true.[31]

Several researchers interpret this letter as recounting two separate stories, one about Joseph Smith's involvement with "a Miss Hill" and a second regarding a relationship with Fanny Alger.[32] Four observations indicate that McLellin was telling only one story and simply became confused. First, there is no additional evidence that Joseph Smith had a relationship with a woman named "Hill" at Kirtland or at any time in his life. Richard L. Anderson concurs: "I cannot find a possible 'Miss Hill' in Kirtland, nor is there any verification of the story."[33]

Faulring and Bachman's Reviews of *In Sacred Loneliness*."

30. See, for example, Todd Compton, *In Sacred Loneliness: The Plural Wives of Joseph Smith*, 664; H. Michael Marquardt, *The Rise of Mormonism: 1816–1844*, 450–55; Kathryn M. Daynes, "Plural Wives and the Nineteenth-Century Mormon Marriage System: Manti, Utah 1849–1910," 41–42.

31. William E. McLellin, Letter to President Joseph Smith III, July 1872. The letter is published in Stan Larson and Samuel J. Passey, eds., *The William E. McLellin Papers, 1854–1880*, 488–89. See also Robert D. Hutchins, "Joseph Smith III: Moderate Mormon," 79–81.

32. See, for example, Marquardt, *The Rise of Mormonism*, 450–51; Compton, *In Sacred Loneliness*, 646.

33. Richard L. Anderson, Letter to Dawn Comfort, May 9–15, 1998.

Second, the first part of the paragraph specifies that Emma saw an interaction between Joseph and "a hired girl" identified as "Miss Hill." In the second half of the same paragraph, McLellin states that Emma "saw him [Joseph] and Fanny in the barn together." If there were two separate encounters, Emma apparently witnessed them both. McLellin related that when Emma learned of the relationship she "refused to be satisfied" requiring immense efforts from Joseph to assuage her distress. That he would thereafter engage in the same behavior with a second woman under circumstances that made it possible for Emma to witness it seems highly improbable.

Third, an interview in 1875 between McLellin, who was then sixty-nine, and anti-Mormon journalist and sensational writer J. H. Beadle, who had authored *Mysteries and Crimes of Mormonism* (1870),[34] further supports only one relationship. Beadle visited Independence, Missouri, in 1875 and reported:

> My first call was on Dr. William E. McLellin, whose name you will find in every number of the old *Millennial Star*, and in many of Smith's revelations. I found the old gentleman in pleasant quarters . . .
>
> He also informed me of the spot where the first well authenticated case of polygamy took place,[35] in which Joseph Smith was "sealed" to *the hired girl*. The "sealing" took place *in a barn* on the hay mow, and was witnessed by Mrs. Smith through a crack in the door![36]

McLellin's 1875 story spoke only of one young woman and one relationship. Specifically, he called her "a hired girl" (like "Miss Hill" in the 1872 letter) who was involved with the Prophet "in a barn" (like Fanny Alger in the 1872 letter).[37] And the single interaction was witnessed by Emma. Linda King Newell and Valeen Tippetts Avery hypothesize regarding the confusion surrounding the identity of "Miss Hill": "Perhaps, in his old age, William McLellin confused the hired girl, Fanny Alger, with Fanny Hill of John Cleland's 1749 lewd novel and came up with the hired girl, Miss Hill."[38]

Fourth, McLellin had, by the 1870s, been disaffected from Mormonism for about forty years. If he possessed information on more than one alleged sexual impropriety, it is probable that he would have shared it in other venues than the single confusing reference in his 1872 letter. J. H. Beadle would likely have been elated to include two allegations of Kirtland "sealings" in his published article recounting his interview with McLellin.

---

34. John Hanson Beadle, *Life in Utah: Or, the Mysteries and Crimes of Mormonism*.
35. McLellin and Beadle were then in Missouri. McLellin would have been describing the location hundreds of miles away in Kirtland, Ohio, not guiding Beadle to the actual geographic "spot" where Joseph and Fanny were spied upon.
36. J. H. Beadle, "Jackson County," *Salt Lake Tribune*, October 6, 1875, 4; emphasis mine.
37. Ibid.
38. Linda King Newell and Valeen Tippetts Avery, *Mormon Enigma: Emma Hale Smith*, 66.

TABLE 4.2
HISTORICAL ACCOUNTS THAT INCLUDE A DATE FOR THE BEGINNING OF THE RELATIONSHIP (MARRIAGE) AND/OR AFTERMATH OF THE JOSEPH SMITH AND FANNY ALGER MARRIAGE

Author	Date	Marriage or Aftermath?	Quotation
Levi Hancock via Mosiah Hancock (1832–33)	"Early in the spring of 1832…"	Marriage	[Circumstantial evidence] Levi Hancock married Clarissa Reed in 1832 and presumably the two unions were connected chronologically.
Historicus [pseudo.] (1832–33)	When "Joseph Smith [III] was an infant" [1832–33]	Aftermath	"She [Emma Smith] discovered that Joseph had been celestializing with this maiden, Fanny, who acknowledged the truth, but Joseph denied in toto and stigmatized the statement of the girl as a base fabrication. Emma, of course, believed the girl, as she was very well aware that no confidence could be placed in her husband, and she became terribly worked up about it. She was like a mad woman, and acted so violently that Oliver Cowdery and some of the elders were called in to minister to her and 'cast the devil out of sister Emma.'"
William McLellin	"Joseph [III]… at your birth [November 1832]"	Aftermath	"Your father [Joseph Smith Jr.] committed an act with a Miss Hill—a hired girl. Emma saw him, and spoke to him. He desisted [sic], but Mrs. Smith refused to be satisfied. He called in Dr. Williams, O. Cowdery, and S. Rigdon to reconcile Emma. But she told them just as the circumstances took place. He found he was caught. He confessed humbly, and begged forgiveness. Emma and all forgave him."
Martin Harris	"In or about the year 1833"	Aftermath	"The servant girl of Joe Smith stated that the prophet had made improper proposals to her, which created quite a talk amongst the people."
Benjamin F. Johnson (1835–36)	"In 1835"	Aftermath	"And there was some trouble with Oliver Cowdery, and whisper said it was relating to a girl then living in his (the Prophet's) family; and I was afterwards told by Warren Parish, that he himself and Oliver Cowdery did know that Joseph and Fannie Alger was wife, for they were spied upon and found together."
Eliza Jane Churchill Webb	"in 1835-or 6"	Marriage and Aftermath	"Fanny Alger's mother says Fanny was sealed to Joseph by Oliver Cowdery in Kirtland in 1835-or 6. … Fanny Alger had lived in Joseph's family several years, and when she left there she came and lived with me a few weeks. I suppose your mother will remember what a talk the whole affair made."
Eliza R. Snow	[spring of 1836]	Aftermath	"Alger, Fanny, Joseph Smith's wife. One of the first wives Joseph married. Emma made such a fuss about. Sister E. R. Snow was well acquainted with her as she lived with the Prophet at the time."
Fanny Brewer	"In the spring of 1837"	Aftermath	"There was much excitement against the Prophet, on another account, likewise,— an unlawful intercourse between himself and a young orphan girl residing in his family; and under his protection!!!"

Fanny Alger and the Beginnings of Mormon Polygamy   99

In evaluating this evidence, it appears that the accounts consistently refer to one affiliation between Joseph Smith and Fanny Alger in Kirtland in the mid-1830s. The minor variations in the documents are not unexpected in light of the inherent limitations of the historical record.

Dating the Joseph Smith-Fanny Alger Relationship

Identifying the exact year of the plural marriage or relationship between Joseph Smith and Fanny Alger is challenging. Eight of the nineteen accounts in Table 4.1 provide dates that range between 1832 and 1836.[39] (See Table 4.2.)

Three different scenarios are generally presented in these documents. One positions the marriage/relationship beginning in 1832–33, with the disclosure and backlash occurring shortly thereafter. A second version hypothesizes that the marriage/relationship began in 1832–33 but was not discovered until 1835–37. The third interpretation sees both the commencement and the aftermath as occurring in the 1835–37 period. Reputable polygamy scholars D. Michael Quinn and George D. Smith have suggested 1832–33 for both the beginning and exposure.[40] Smith wrote in *Nauvoo Polygamy*: "Joseph's own retrospective writings begun in 1832, the same year he became head of the church in Kirtland. Yet, that same year, he had famously become involved with a sixteen-year-old carpenter's daughter named Fanny Alger."[41]

Four documents support the first 1832–33 time period.[42] First, Martin Harris appears to be referring to the Alger marriage in a second-hand account from 1875 in which he reportedly told an interviewer: "In or about the year 1833, the servant girl of Joe Smith stated that the prophet had made improper proposals to her, which created quite a talk amongst the people."[43]

---

39. Richard Van Wagoner, "Joseph and Marriage," 32–33. See also Compton, "The Date of Fanny Alger's Marriage," in "Truth, Honesty, and Moderation in Mormon History."

40. D. Michael Quinn, *The Mormon Hierarchy: Origins of Power*, 45, 587.

41. George D. Smith, *Nauvoo Polygamy: "... but we called it celestial marriage"*, 22. Later Smith clarifies: "Before long, talk about Joseph echoed Fanny's name, maybe as early as 1832 but certainly from 1833 to 1835" (38). It appears that George Smith's views on this topic have evolved, perhaps in conjunction with his continued research. In his 1994 "Nauvoo Roots of Mormon Polygamy, 1841–46: A Preliminary Demographic Report," 5, he used 1835. However in his 2002 Sunstone Symposium presentation, "How Joseph Smith Found Thirty Women to Marry Him and How This Changed His Life," he dated the Alger relationship to 1833.

42. Richard Lyman Bushman, *Joseph Smith: Rough Stone Rolling*, 323, suggested that Joseph's involvement with Fanny Alger might have been "as early as 1831" but does not supply any documentation to explain such an early date nor does any appear to be available.

43. Anthony Metcalf, *Ten Years Before the Mast*, 72.

Second and third, William McLellin, as quoted above, and an author using the pseudonym "Historicus" dated the incident to the birth of Joseph Smith, III, which occurred on November 6, 1832.[44] It is possible that "Historicus's" informant was William McLellin (or was McLelllin himself),[45] which would make this a single source.

Fourth, probably the strongest evidence for an 1832–33 marriage is circumstantial. Mosiah Hancock's journal reports that, sometime in the early 1830s, Joseph told Mosiah's father Levi: "I want to make a bargain with you. If you will get Fanny Alger for me for a wife you may have Clarissa Reed."[46] The Levi Hancock-Clarissa Reed marriage occurred March 29, 1833. Todd Compton concludes that the two marriages probably occurred close to each other chronologically: "Joseph probably married Fanny in February or March 1833."[47]

A closer look at the four manuscripts, however, discloses that the fourth is comprised of circumstantial evidence and the first three refer strictly to the discovery of the relationships and repercussions that followed, rather than the beginning of the secret marriage/relationship.

Believing that Joseph Smith became involved with Fanny Alger in 1832–33 *and* that the relationship was soon exposed is problematic. Current evidence indicates that the association was first divulged no earlier than 1836, sometime after the March–April dedication of the Kirtland Temple. Eliza R. Snow declared that she was living with the Smith family at the time the "fuss" about Fanny occurred.[48] Eliza did not move into the Smith home until the spring of 1836.[49] According to Mosiah Hancock, who was born on April 9, 1834, Joseph asked his father, Levi Hancock, in 1836 to rescue Fanny before

---

44. McLellin, to Joseph Smith III, July 1872. A pseudonymous writer, "Historicus," perhaps McLellin himself, similarly dated the Alger marriage/relationship to "the time the present Joseph Smith [III] was an infant." Historicus, "Sketches from the History of Polygamy: Joseph Smith's Especial Revelations," 1.

45. McLellin died in 1883, so he was available in 1881 to reporters who wished to visit him in Independence, Missouri. He had previously reminisced with J. H. Beadle in 1875 and Apostles Orson Pratt and Joseph F. Smith in 1878. Several specific details related by "Historicus" parallel McLellin's comments in his letters to Joseph Smith III, including references to the chronology ("at the time the present Joseph was an infant"), Emma's personal involvement, the appeal to Oliver Cowdery to help reconcile, and the ability to accurately relate Fanny's first name without definite knowledge of her surname.

46. Hancock, Autobiography with additions, 61–62.

47. Compton, *In Sacred Loneliness*, 33; see also Todd Compton, "Fanny Alger Smith Custer: Mormonism's First Plural Wife?" 178, 195. Compton does not assume that the aftermath began in 1833, only that a secret marriage occurred in that year.

48. Document 10, Andrew Jenson Papers, Box 49, fd. 16.

49. Eliza R. Snow, "Sketch of My Life," 7. Her narrative reads, "In the Spring of 1836, I taught a select school for young ladies and boarded with the Prophet's family."

gathering apostates could capture her in the summer of 1836.[50] However, the Alger family, including Fanny, left Kirtland for Missouri in September 1836.[51] Fanny Brewer, who visited Kirtland in 1837 recalled in 1842 that the relationship had created "excitement" there five years earlier.[52] Complaints regarding Joseph Smith's relationship with Fanny Alger were first mentioned in contemporary documents in 1838 (discussed below).

Ten of the narratives provide the names of individuals who were involved with the detection and aftermath of the Smith-Alger relationship: Emma Smith, Oliver Cowdery, Sidney Rigdon, Martin Harris, and Frederick G. Williams. (See Table 4.2.) If they learned of the union in 1832 or 1833, no contemporaneous evidence exists showing that any of them reacted to that knowledge for at least three to four years, with Cowdery being the first. The period between 1832 and the summer of 1836 was filled with activities such as the expulsion of the Saints from Jackson County in the summer of 1833, Zion's Camp in the summer of 1834, and the dedication of the Kirtland Temple in the spring of 1836. It is difficult to believe that Emma Smith and other influential Church members would have kept completely silent concerning a relationship that they apparently considered to be adulterous. (Certainly, none of them would have discussed it publicly except, perhaps, during a period of disaffection from Joseph Smith and disaffiliation from the Church; but it seems improbable that they would have remained individually and collectively silent, not even discussing such a shocking event among themselves.) Joseph Smith, though President of the Church, was by his own revelations subject to Church disciplinary councils (see D&C 107:81–84), but no inquiries were initiated until 1837–38. Even more implausible is the idea that after years had passed, only one, Oliver Cowdery, would suddenly break his silence to accuse Joseph Smith concerning what he saw as immoral behavior (discussed below),

---

50. Mosiah Hancock wrote, in his additions to the Autobiography of his father, Levi Ward Hancock, 64: "As time progressed the Apostates thought they had a good hold on Joseph because of Fanny and some of the smart ones confined her in an upper room of the [Kirtland] Temple determined that the Prophet should be settled according to their notions Brother Joseph came to Father and said "Brother Levi what can be done"?— There being a wagon and a dry goods Box close by and Joseph being strong and Father active Father soon gained the window Sill and Fanny was soon on the ground Father mounts his horse with Fanny behind him and although dark they were in New Lyme forty five miles distant." This account in improbable. The windows of the Kirtland Temple are too high to allow Fanny to execute the safe, stealthy exit as described. In addition, Oliver Cowdery, who appeared to be a primary source of complaint, would not have been classified with any "apostate" group in mid-1836.

51. "Died," Obituary of Samuel Alger, *Deseret News*, October 14, 1874, 7.

52. Fanny Brewer, quoted in John C. Bennett, *The History of the Saints: Or an Exposé of Joe Smith and Mormonism*, 85–86.

although it is true that Cowdery was disaffected from Joseph personally and disillusioned temporarily with Mormonism. An examination of all of the contemporary accounts describing the 1832 to 1836 period reveals no concerns arising from the Prophet's relationship with Fanny Alger or alleged immoral behavior. In fact, concern for Cowdery's behavior arose in 1832 and 1834, but no similar allegations regarding the Prophet's actions (including complaints from Cowdery) are documented during that period. (See Chapter 6.)

In an October 19, 1995, letter to Gary J. Bergera, Michael Marquardt observed: "Concerning Fanny Alger, I have compiled some material relating to what has been said concerning her and Joseph Smith. . . . It appears that whatever occurred with Fanny Alger probably happened in the year 1836 with Fanny leaving Kirtland, Ohio. This year is closer to the events relating to Oliver Cowdery as Cowdery had discussed the matter with Joseph Smith and others in the summer and fall of 1837."[53]

In summary, no contemporary evidence has been found to support even a limited disclosure of the Fanny Alger-Joseph Smith union prior to mid-1836; therefore dating the aftermath to 1832 or 1833 is otherwise unsupported.

The second scenario posits an 1832–33 plural marriage or relationship that was not divulged until 1835–36.[54] This reconstruction, according to Todd Compton, hypothesizes that Joseph Smith married Fanny in conjunction with the marriage of Levi Hancock to Clarissa Reed. Indeed, it might be argued that one cannot accept Mosiah's account that describes how a marriage ceremony was performed, without also accepting the 1833 date associated with the Levi-Clarissa wedding. However, in his narrative, Mosiah also explained:

> When my Father had started on his first mission to preach this Gospel He felt that perhaps he had done wrong in not telling the Prophet that he had made arrangements to marry Temperance Jane Miller of New Lyme— When Father returned from his mission he spoke to the Prophet concerning the matter The Prophet said—"Never mind Brother Levi about that for the Lord has one prepared for you that will be a Blessing to you forever!"

At that time Clarissa Reed was working as a hired girl at the Prophet's home. Mosiah's narrative continues:

> She told the Prophet She loved brother Levi Hancock. . . .
> Therefore Brother Joseph said "Brother Levi I want to make a bargain with you—If you will get Fanny Alger for me for a wife you may have Clarissa Reed."[55]

---

53. H. Michael Marquardt, Letter to Gary J. Bergera, October 19, 1995; used by permission.

54. Todd Compton, email to Brian Hales, September 9, 2008.

55. Hancock, "Autobiography . . . with additions," 62–63.

Fanny Alger and the Beginnings of Mormon Polygamy   103

While Mosiah failed to mention the process through which Joseph introduced Levi to the need to restore Old Testament polygamy, doubtless some conversations on that point would have occurred, as they always did in Nauvoo years later, prior to plural marriages. Regardless, at the time of the discussion between Levi and Joseph, Clarissa was already attracted to Levi, so the marriage may have proceeded quickly, much more rapidly than such an unconventional union as a plural marriage would have been between the Prophet and Fanny Alger. This interpretation also assumes that Fanny and Joseph Smith were able to keep their marriage secret from Emma Smith for several years and that Fanny was the Prophet's plural wife longer than any other woman, including those he married in Nauvoo, although their personal association ended abruptly and permanently in 1836 when she married Solomon Custer.[56] While possible, this scenario seems less likely.

The third timeline specifies that the marriage/relationship commenced in 1835–36 and the detection and repercussions occurred soon thereafter, probably May–June of 1836. As noted above, Michael Marquardt has concluded that it occurred "prior to the fall of 1836."[57] Six other authors have also put this interpretation in print.[58]

Three modern historians and three individuals who lived during Joseph's lifetime have provided information supporting an 1835–36 framework. Richard Van Wagoner, in his history of polygamy, writes that Fanny became a live-in helper in the Smith household in 1835.[59] However, he provides no documentation for this date. Mark Lyman Staker reconstructs the Smith household for this period:

> Mary Johnson [daughter of John and Alice Johnson born in 1818] lived in the Smith home (Whitney Store) to provide assistance to Emma. She died March 30, 1833. Her death was unexpected and shook up the family.

---

56. Joseph was sealed to his first plural wife, Louisa Beaman, in Nauvoo in April 1841 and was killed in June 1844, thirty-nine months later. A late 1832 or early 1833 plural marriage extending to mid-1836 would have surpassed that duration. I believe that evidence for a marriage or relationship between Joseph Smith and any other woman besides Fanny Alger, between 1830 and 1841, including Lucinda Pendleton (Morgan Harris) in 1838, is not persuasive. See Chapter 8.

57. Marquardt, *The Rise of Mormonism*, 451.

58. See Donna Hill, *Joseph Smith: The First Mormon*, 188–89; Lawrence Foster, *Religion and Sexuality: The Shakers, The Mormons, and The Oneida Community*, 137–38; Newell and Avery, *Mormon Enigma*, 66; Kimball Young, *Isn't One Wife Enough?* 91. See also Don Bradley, "Mormon Polygamy before Nauvoo? The Relationships of Joseph Smith and Fanny Alger," 14–58.

59. Richard S. Van Wagoner, *Mormon Polygamy: A History*, 14, states that Fanny "Alger did not live in Smith's home until 1835." See also Newell and Avery, *Mormon Enigma*, 66; Richard Lloyd Anderson and Scott H. Faulring, "Review of *In Sacred Loneliness: The Plural Wives of Joseph Smith*, by Todd M. Compton," 78–79.

I believe Fanny Alger replaced Mary as household help for Emma. If that's the case it is unlikely Fanny lived with the family while they were living at the store and it is unlikely she assisted them before mid-1833. She most likely assisted between 1834 and 1836, in their home up near the temple. After that Eliza R. Snow moved into the house on the hill and taught school for Joseph's children in the rear portion of the home.[60]

The three individuals who may have had first-hand knowledge are Benjamin F. Johnson, Fanny's mother, and Joseph's plural wife Mary Elizabeth Rollins Lightner. Johnson's reminiscence appears in a 1903 letter, written when he was eighty-five. In it, he mentions Fanny Alger and says:

> In 1835, at Kirtland, I learned from my sister's husband, Lyman R. Sherman, who was close to the Prophet, and received it from him, "that the ancient order of Plural Marriage was again to be practiced by the Church." This, at the time did not impress my mind deeply, although there lived then with his family (the Prophet's) a neighbor's daughter, Fannie Alger, a very nice and comely young woman about my own age, toward whom not only myself, but every one, seemed partial, for the amiability for her character; and it was whispered even then that Joseph loved her.[61]

Eliza Jane Churchill Webb, with whom Fanny boarded after being cast out of the Smith home, quoted Fanny's mother, Clarissa Hancock Alger (Levi's sister), saying: "Fanny Alger's mother says Fanny was sealed to Joseph by Oliver Cowdery [sic] in Kirtland in 1835-or 6. . . . Fanny Alger had lived in Joseph's family several years, and when she left there she came and lived with me a few weeks."[62]

Mary Elizabeth Rollins Lightner, after keeping silent for more than fifty years, provided fourteen letters, statements, affidavits, public addresses, and detailed narratives in which she explained her plural sealing to Joseph Smith in 1842. A frequent feature in these documents was the detail that Joseph entered the practice of plural marriage reluctantly and only after repeated visits from an angel who commanded his obedience. For example, in a 1904 letter Mary Elizabeth, reported: "Joseph the Seer . . . said God gave him a commandment in 1834, to take other wives besides Emma, and I was the one he was commanded to take, though I was a thousand miles from him."[63] In early 1834, the Prophet resided in Kirtland, Ohio, while the Rollins fam-

---

60. Mark Lyman Staker, email to Brian Hales, September 9, 2008.
61. Dean R. Zimmerman, ed., *I Knew the Prophets: An Analysis of the Letter of Benjamin F. Johnson to George F. Gibbs, Reporting Doctrinal Views of Joseph Smith and Brigham Young*, 38–39.
62. Eliza J. Webb [Eliza Jane Churchill Webb], Lockport, New York, Letter to Mary Bond, April 24, 1876.
63. Mary E. [Rollins] Lightner, Letter to A. M. Chase, April 20, 1904, quoted in J. D. Stead, *Doctrines and Dogmas of Brighamism Exposed*, 218–19. See also her daughter's "Record Book of Mary Rollins Lightner Carter," *The Life and Testimony of Mary Lightner*, 10.

ily was in Missouri, just over eight hundred miles away. (The Rollins family joined the Church in Kirtland, then later moved to Missouri.) Apparently the angel's first visit occurred before Joseph went to Missouri with Zion's Camp, whose journey began May 5, 1834.[64] Mary also wrote: "When Zions Camp went to Missouri, he received a Commandment to take me for a wife—But was afraid—and I was not sealed to him as a wife, until 1841 [1842]."[65] These statements suggest that the Prophet received the commandment to marry Mary Elizabeth sometime during the first four months of 1834, even though they were geographically separated. Then, in company with Zion's Camp, Joseph visited Clay County, Missouri, near Fishing River, his first visit to that location since 1831 when he received the revelation about the temple site at Independence. Sixteen-year-old Mary Elizabeth was staying there with the family of Algernon Sidney Gilbert (her widowed mother and Gilbert's wife were sisters), but Joseph "was afraid" and did not mention the commandment to her at that time. Eight years passed before he first broached the topic to her.[66] In the meantime, Mary Elizabeth, who had married Adam Lightner, on August 11, 1835, a year after Joseph's visit, related that, during that period, "I had been dreaming for a number of years I was his wife. I thought I was a great sinner. I prayed to God to take it from me for I felt it was a sin."[67]

On other occasions, Mary Elizabeth Rollins affirmed that the angel made three separate appearances to Joseph Smith, the first in 1834 and the last in February of 1842:

> An angel came to him [Joseph Smith] and the last time he came with a drawn sword in his hand and told Joseph if he did not go into that principle, he would slay him. . . . [He said] the angel came to me three times between the years of 1834 and 1842 and said I was to obey that principle or he would slay me.[68]
>
> I was the first woman God Commanded him to take me as a plural wife, \in 1834/.[69] He was very much frightened about [it] until the Angel appeared

---

64. From February 26 to March 28, Joseph traveled almost four hundred miles east to obtain volunteers for Zion's Camp. It is possible that the angel appeared during this journey, which would have made the distance between the Prophet and Mary Elizabeth as much as 1,200 miles.

65. Mary Elizabeth Rollins Lightner, Letter to President Woodruff, October 7 1887.

66. Mary Elizabeth Rollins Lightner, *The Life and Testimony of Mary Lightner*, 14–15.

67. Mary Elizabeth Rollins Lightner, "Remarks" at BYU, April 14, 1905, 2.

68. Ibid., 2–3. Mary Elizabeth also recalled: "Joseph told me that he was afraid when the angel appeared to him and told him to take other wives. He hesitated, and the angel appeared to him the third time with a drawn sword in his hand and threatened his life if he did not fulfill the commandment." Mary E. Lightner, Letter to A. M. Chase, April 20, 1904, 218–19.

69. The words "in 1834" represent an interlineal addition. However, the last number in the "1834" is not as easily discerned as the other three. It possesses a clear up-and-

to him three times. it was in the early part of Feb, 1842 ~~before~~ \that/ he was compelled to reveal it to me personally, by the Angel threatening him.[70]

In 1834 he [Joseph Smith] was commanded to take me for a wife. I was a thousand miles from him. He got afraid. The angel came to him three times, the last time with a drawn sword and threatened his life.[71]

While twenty accounts[72] reporting Joseph Smith's visits from a sword-bearing angel who commanded his participation in polygamy have been identified, only three, all from Mary Elizabeth Rollins Lightner, include dates. Hence, Mary Elizabeth's multiple recollections recounted when she was eighty-four or older, constitute a solo witness to the chronology. (See Chapter 8.) If accurate, her reminiscences may provide an additional element to the emerging timeline. Joseph Smith taught that plural marriage was acceptable to God as early as 1831 but did not then initiate its practice. If an angel appeared in 1834 to demand compliance, then his first plural union would probably have not occurred before 1834.

Summary

Records from varying time periods provide evidence that Joseph Smith had received an assurance as early as 1831 that plural marriage was a correct principle and could be acceptable to God under the proper circumstances. Nothing in the historical records suggests that he personally desired the controversial marital standard or was anxious to enter into it. Multiple accounts report that he entered into a relationship with Fanny Alger sometime in the 1830s. Conflicting evidence exists concerning the time it began, but most sources agree that the union became known to a limited circle with serious repercussions in 1836.

---

down stroke and a limited left-to-right stroke as well. It is different from a number "4" written elsewhere on the page. That it should be a "4," completing the year 1834, is corroborated by the other two quotations included. The slash marks represent interlinear insertions.

70. Mary Elizabeth Rollins Lightner, Letter to Emmeline B. Wells, Summer 1905. See also Mary Elizabeth Rollins Lightner, Statement, February 8, 1902.

71. Mary Elizabeth Rollins Lightner, Statement February 8, 1902.

72. Brian C. Hales, "Encouraging Joseph Smith to Practice Plural Marriage: The Accounts of the Angel with a Drawn Sword," 23–39. Since publishing this article, I have found a twenty-second account in Andrew H. Hedges and Richard Neitzel Holzapfel, eds., *Within These Prison Walls: Lorenzo Snow's Record Book, 1886*, 18.

Chapter 5

The Joseph Smith-Fanny Alger Relationship: Plural Marriage or Adultery?

As I conclude in Chapter 4, I take the position that Joseph Smith's relationship with Fanny Alger began in late 1835 or early 1836 and was not discovered until after the April 1836 dedication of the Kirtland Temple. Precisely why Joseph Smith approached Fanny Alger for a relationship or plural marriage, rather than some other woman in Kirtland, is unclear. It may have been proximity. She was boarding with the Smith family, working as a domestic, and reportedly was an attractive young woman. However, Joseph may have considered other candidates as well. Benjamin F. Johnson, a close friend of the Prophet, remembered: "In talking with my mother . . . he [Joseph Smith] told her that when the Lord required him to move in plural marriage, that his first thought was to come and ask her for some of her daughters; and I can now understand that the period alluded to was at Kirtland, where she had three unmarried daughters at home."[1]

Evidences of a Marriage between Joseph Smith and Fanny Alger

The question of whether a plural marriage ceremony was performed between Joseph Smith and Fanny Alger has been debated for decades and doubtless will continue indefinitely unless further documentation is forthcoming.[2] Five accounts distinctly label the association as the Prophet's first plural marriage: Benjamin F. Johnson, Mosiah Hancock, Eliza R. Snow, sources in the Webb family, and sources in the Alger family.

---

1. Benjamin F. Johnson, *My Life's Review*, 94. According to Andrew Jenson, "Biographical Sketch of Benjamin F. Johnson": "Johnson was one of the first to whom Joseph [taught] a knowledge of plural marriage."

2. Don Bradley, "Mormon Polygamy before Nauvoo? The Relationship of Joseph Smith and Fanny Alger," 14–58.

Benjamin F. Johnson

Benjamin F. Johnson, a close friend of Joseph's, recalled in 1903:

> And now as To your question, "How early did \the Prophet/ Joseph Practice Poligamy?"—I hardly know how to wisely to Reply—For the <u>Truth</u> at times may be better withheld But as what I am writing is to be published only under Strict <u>Scrutiny</u> of the <u>wisest</u> I will Say That the Revilation to the Church at Nauvoo July 12th 1843 on the eternity of the Marriage Covenant and Law of plural Marriage was not the first Rivilation on that Law Received & Practiced by the Prophet—In <u>1835</u> at Kirtland I learned from my Sisters Husband, Lyman R. Shirman,[3] who was close to the Prophet, and Received it from him. "That the ancient order of plural marriage was again to be practiced by the Church This, at the time did not impress my mind deeply. Altho there lived then with his [Joseph Smith's] Family a Neighbors daughter Fannie Alger. A varry nice & Comly young woman about my own age [Benjamin was born in 1818]. towards \whoom/ not only mySelf, but every one Seemed <u>partial</u> for \the/ ameability for her character and \it/ was whispered eaven \then/ that Joseph Loved her.[4]

Mosiah Hancock

Second, according to the only known account of the circumstances—a second-hand report by Mosiah Hancock written in 1896—Joseph did not approach Fanny directly to discuss a polygamous union. Rather, he enlisted the assistance of a friend, Levi Ward Hancock, Mosiah's father, to serve as an intermediary:[5]

> Father goes to the Father Samuel Alger—his Father's Brother in Law and [said] "Samuel the Prophet Joseph loves your Daughter Fanny and wishes her for a wife what say you"—Uncle Sam Says—"Go and talk to the old woman about it twi'll be as She says" Father goes to his Sister and said "Clarissy, Brother Joseph the Prophet of the most high God loves Fanny and wishes her

---

3. Lyman Sherman was a close friend and devout follower of Joseph Smith. He was called as an apostle but died before learning of the appointment. Lyndon W. Cook, "Lyman Sherman—Man of God, Would-Be Apostle," 121–24.

4. Dean R. Zimmerman, *I Knew the Prophets: An Analysis of the Letter of Benjamin F. Johnson to George F. Gibbs*, 37–38. The \ / marks in Johnson's narrative indicate where words are inserted interlineally. Joseph H. Jackson referred to three Nauvoo women who served as intermediaries as "Mothers in Israel." Jackson, *A Narrative of the Adventures and Experiences of Joseph H. Jackson in Nauvoo, Exposing the Depths of Mormon Villainy*, 13.

5. In 1884, Mosiah Hancock, "Correspondence: The Prophet Joseph—Some of His Sayings," 15, commented: "Concerning the doctrine of celestial marriage the Prophet told my father [Levi] in the days of Kirtland, that it was the will of the Lord for His servants who were faithful to step forth in that order. But said Brother Joseph, 'Brother Levi, if I should make known to my brethren what God has made known to me they would seek my life.'"

Levi Ward Hancock. Courtesy of LDS Church History Library.

for a wife what say you" Said She "go and talk to Fanny it will be all right with me"—Father goes to Fanny and said "Fanny Brother Joseph the Prophet loves you and wishes you for a wife will you be his wife"? "I will Levi" Said She. Father takes Fanny to Joseph and said "Brother Joseph I have been successful in my mission"—Father gave her to Joseph repeating the Ceremony as Joseph repeated to him.[6]

Several authors have written that there was no marriage ceremony, thus dismissing Mosiah's narrative as apocryphal.[7] Historian Janet Ellingson considers the Mosiah Hancock account to be "a bit much to swallow."[8] She seems to believe that Joseph and Fanny's relationship was nothing more than a sexual liaison, writing: "There is no contemporary evidence, in either

---

6. Levi Ward Hancock, Autobiography with additions in 1896 by Mosiah Hancock, 63; the portion cited in the text is from Mosiah's addition. Levi's writing of his autobiography is not dated. See also Todd Compton, *In Sacred Loneliness: The Plural Wives of Joseph Smith*, 32. Polygamy scholars are indebted to Compton who discovered that both published versions of the journal (Mosiah Hancock, ed., *The Mosiah Hancock Journal*, and Mosiah Hancock, ed., *The Levi Hancock Journal*, 58 pp.) are incomplete, having had all references to the Fanny Alger marriage removed. See also Todd Compton, "Fanny Alger Smith Custer: Mormonism's First Plural Wife?" 175 note 3.

7. Fawn M. Brodie, *No Man Knows My History: The Life of Joseph Smith, the Mormon Prophet*, 181–82; Richard S. Van Wagoner, *Mormon Polygamy: A History*, 5–6, 14; John L. Brooke, *The Refiner's Fire: The Making of Mormon Cosmology, 1644–1844*, 217; H. Michael Marquardt, *The Rise of Mormonism: 1816–1844*, 453; O. Kendall White Jr. and Daryl White, "Polygamy and Mormon Identity," 166; Gregory A. Prince, *Power from On High: The Development of Mormon Priesthood*, 165. Interestingly, Van Wagoner provided this commentary: "If one views Joseph Smith's introduction of polygamy as a reversion to Old Testament practice rather than an expansion of Christianity, then it is not so shocking to consider the possibility of no formal ceremony being performed for the women prior to Louisa Beeman. Nowhere in the Old Testament is a marriage ceremony mentioned. The custom seemed to be that after an initial contract between the two parties, the husband-to-be, merely 'took her according to the Law of Moses and of Israel.'" Richard Van Wagoner, Letter to Linda King Newell, n.d. The interior quotation does not occur in this form anywhere in the Old Testament. I argue that there was only one plural marriage prior to Louisa Beeman—that of Fanny Alger's and that a plural marriage ceremony was performed.

8. Janet Ellingson, "Alger Marriage Questioned," vi.

Smith's words or actions, that he thought of it as a marriage."⁹ Technically this is true, because no "contemporary evidence" of any kind exists "in either Smith's words or actions" concerning the incident. Nothing is recorded referring to the relationship until three years later in 1838. (See the Oliver Cowdery account, Chapter 6.) However, the lack of contemporary evidence from Joseph Smith does not support either the adultery or plural marriage interpretation.

The Mosiah Hancock narrative is not without its problems. He was born in 1834 and consequently could not have been an eyewitness or participant; furthermore, he recounted the story six decades later in 1896. Other parts of Mosiah's reminiscences raise questions regarding his overall credibility. For example, four pages later in his autobiographical narrative, Mosiah relates:

> My Father brought me a white handled Pocket knife with three blades—I thought I saw the Lord above the corner of our house smiling so sweetly on me I wished to make him a present for I felt that I wanted him to have it[.] I said Lord if you want my knife you can have it and and [sic] I threw it up towards him and I always thought he took it[.] I told Father and he and the rest of the folk sought for the knife but could not find it—Father bought me another knife and I threw it up and it never could be found to my knowledge.¹⁰

Todd Compton provides this useful assessment: "Mosiah's first-hand reminiscences are admittedly subject to the strengths and weaknesses generally found in Mormon and other autobiographies: inaccuracies in dates, misremembered events, an easy willingness to accept the miraculous, and a tendency to over-idealize oneself or a hero such as Joseph Smith. Nevertheless, I accept it as generally reliable, providing accurate information about his own life, his family's life, and Mormonism in Kirtland, Nauvoo and Salt Lake City."¹¹

Despite these cautions, Mosiah's account is consistent with some of Joseph Smith's later plural marriages, in which an intermediary taught the principle of plural marriage and ascertained the willingness of the prospective bride.¹² The narrative also recounts how a marriage ceremony did indeed occur, even providing the name of his father as the officiator and showing that Fanny was willing to enter the relationship.¹³ Furthermore, whatever Levi's involvement, it

---

9. Ibid., vii

10. Levi Ward Hancock Autobiography with additions in 1896 by Mosiah Hancock, 66; quoted portion written by Mosiah.

11. Compton, *In Sacred Loneliness*, 29.

12. Examples include Joseph Bates Noble with Louisa Beaman, Dimick Huntington with his sister Zina, and Benjamin F. Johnson with his sister Almera. Elizabeth Durfee, Patty Sessions, and Marinda Johnson also seem to have performed this role. Compton, *In Sacred Loneliness*, 41–42, views these arrangements as an "exchange of women" between Joseph Smith and Levi Hancock. Yet the assertion is weakened because Levi and Clarissa were already in love.

13. Ellingson, "Alger Marriage Questioned," vi, doubts that "Levi Hancock, a man

does not appear to have affected his beliefs in the Prophet. In an October 23, 1859, meeting with members of the First Presidency and the Twelve, he "bore testimony of the fa[i]thfulness and upright ness of Joseph Smith."[14]

In further support of Mosiah's account, John Hawley, writing his autobiography in 1885, reported information from Fanny Alger's brother John: "What I heard [from] John Olger one of the first (or among the first) members of the Church toald me his Sister was Seald to Joseph in Curtlin [Kirtland], this he Said to me in 1868."[15]

Eliza R. Snow

Recent research by Don Bradley has uncovered a new voice confirming that the relationship between Joseph Smith and Fanny Alger was a plural marriage. Through the latest efforts of several historians researching the Mountain Meadows Massacre and working on the Joseph Smith Papers Project, a large collection of previously uncatalogued documents at the LDS Church History Library has been made available for investigation. Among them was a folder containing Andrew Jenson's research notes used to write "Plural Marriage," his article published in the July 1887 issue of the *Historical Record*.[16]

While collecting data for his article, Andrew Jenson asked Eliza R. Snow, then age eighty-three, to provide information regarding all of Joseph Smith's plural wives. Apparently during his interview, Andrew turned the list he had constructed to that point over to the delicate octogenarian, and she added thirteen names to the list. Most interesting because it was a hitherto unknown confirmation was the name of Fanny Alger, which Eliza wrote in her own hand on Jenson's list. Don Bradley was the first to piece together the handwriting clues.

Importantly, upon Document 1, Eliza wrote Fanny Alger's name, including her among the additional thirteen names penned:

---

who had no civil authority, willingly and quickly accepted Smith's demand that he perform a 'a marriage.'" Compton, "Response to Janet Ellingson," xviii, disagrees: "Ellingson finds it unbelievable that Levi Hancock would consent to perform a marriage without civil authority. Personally, I find it very believable—both that Smith would place his religious authority above civil authority and that one of Smith's disciples would give him unquestioning obedience." Importantly, several men in Nauvoo, including Brigham Young, Heber C. Kimball, Hyrum Smith, and William Clayton, performed plural marriages using only the authority they received from Joseph Smith.

14. *Minutes of the Apostles of the Church of Jesus Christ of Latter-day Saints, 1835–1893*, 234.

15. John Hawley, Autobiography, January 1885, 97; I consulted excerpts typed March 1982 by Lyndon Cook.

16. Andrew Jenson, Documents 1–18, Andrew Jenson Papers (ca. 1871–1942), MS 17956, Box 49, fd. 16. Jenson drafted his article from these notes: "Plural Marriage," 219–40.

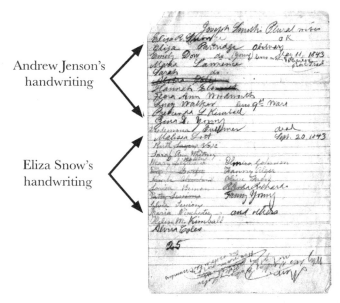

Document 1, Andrew Jenson, Research Notes. This document contains the main list in Jenson's handwriting, followed by that of Eliza R. Snow, listing Fanny Alger's name. Courtesy of the LDS Church History Library.

Eliza's autobiographical sketch verifies that she was closely associated with the Prophet's family during the relevant time period and hence in a position to know Fanny personally: "In the Spring of 1836, I taught a select school for young ladies, and boarded with the Prophet's family: at the close of the term I returned to my parental home."[17] Her *Woman's Exponent* biographer wrote: "Reaching Kirtland she took up her abode in the family of the prophet, and became governess to his children and was companion for Emma during a number of years."[18] Document 10 in Andrew Jenson's files is a biographical sketch of Fanny Alger that was almost certainly written from information that Eliza provided.

From this document, several observations can be made. First, Eliza R. Snow was "well acquainted" with Fanny. Eliza lived in Kirtland in the "spring of 1836," thus identifying the time period. Eliza's familiarity with Fanny was likely due to her physical proximity as both women were boarding with the Smith family at the time.

---

17. Eliza R. Snow, "Sketch of My Life," 7.
18. "Pen Sketch of an Illustrious Woman: Eliza R. Snow Smith," 50. No author is identified but presumably it was Emmeline B. Wells, the editor.

The Joseph Smith-Fanny Alger Relationship

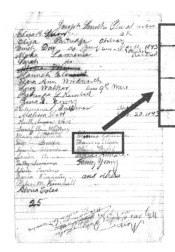

Close-up of Fanny Alger's name, written by Eliza R. Snow on Document 1, Andrew Jenson's list of Joseph Smith's plural wives. Courtesy of the LDS Church History Library.

Alger, Fanny   Used
    Joseph Smiths wife

one of the first wives Joseph married, ~~Emma made such a fuss about in~~
  Sister \E R./ Snow was well acquainted with her \as she/ and lived with the
  Prophet at the time
She afterwards married in Indiana where she became the Mother of a large family
    A brother Alger lives in
      St. Georg
        Write to Pres. McAllister

Andrew Jenson's handwritten notes (Document 10) and typed transcription regarding Fanny Alger. His informant was almost certainly Eliza R. Snow. Photo courtesy of the LDS Church History Library. Jenson makes a note to himself to request more information from "Pres. McAllister." J. D. T. McAllister was president of the St. George Temple.

Second, although the phrase is marked out, Eliza apparently reported that "Emma made such a fuss" about Fanny and her relationship with Joseph. It is probable, but not conclusive, that Eliza was an eyewitness to this "fuss." Another possibility is that Eliza later, after the "fuss," learned about it from Fanny, or from Emma (less likely), or from another source. The actual wording seems to support that Eliza's acquaintance with Fanny and the "fuss" occurred while she "lived with the Prophet at the time" but Jenson does not explicitly say so.

Third, since Eliza personally wrote Fanny Alger's name on Andrew Jenson's list (Document 1), it is apparent that she believed Fanny was a genuine plural wife of Joseph Smith. Eliza's information concerning an actual marriage could have come from Fanny herself, since Eliza was "well acquainted" with her. However, an alternate view suggests that Eliza learned of the "fuss" in Kirtland secondhand or that her knowledge came years later in Nauvoo from the Prophet himself. A third possibility is that Eliza was simply speculating. This seems less likely as Eliza was generally not inclined to promote gossip and less so on the topic of plural marriage.

Eliza's willingness in 1887 to pen Fanny Alger's name on a list of Joseph Smith's plural wives adds a new witness affirming the relationship was a marriage. It could be argued that, if she had believed it was adultery, she would not have mentioned Fanny out of protectiveness for the Prophet's reputation. Interestingly, it appears that she did not suggest to Andrew Jenson (born in 1850) that the marriage occurred in Ohio. Nowhere in Andrew Jenson's article or known files are there any hints of pre-Nauvoo polygamy, and it seems that Eliza did not desire to broach the topic with him.

Importantly, in 1887, most Church members were unaware of Joseph Smith's relationship with Fanny Alger in Kirtland, Ohio. It does not appear that Eliza's inclusion of Fanny's name was a defensive maneuver designed to combat rumors of an illegitimate relationship because the vast majority did not know about her. The earliest publication of Fanny's name had occurred six years earlier in 1881, when an anti-Mormon writer, "Historicus," stated in an article published in the *Anti-Polygamy Standard*: "Emma Smith, Joseph's wife, had a young girl in her employment by the name of Fanny Olger or Alger."[19] Five years later in 1886, another anti-Mormon writer, Wilhelm Wyl, stated that he had learned from a "Mr. W." (likely Chauncy Webb) that "Joseph's dissolute life began already in the first times of the church in Kirtland. He was sealed there secretly to Fanny Alger. Emma was furious, and drove the girl, who was unable to conceal the consequences of her celestial relation with the prophet, out of her house."[20]

---

19. "Historicus," "Sketches from the History of Polygamy: Joseph Smith's Especial Revelations," 1.

20. Wilhelm Wyl reportedly quoting Chauncy Webb, *Mormon Portraits*, 57.

The *Anti-Polygamy Standard* was published between April 1880 and March 1883 as an organ of the Woman's National Anti-Polygamy Society.

Neither of these publications received wide circulation among the Latter-day Saints. Thus, it seems probable that, if Eliza R. Snow had not mentioned Fanny Alger, her name might have continued to be essentially unknown within the LDS community for many decades. Jenson included Fanny Alger in his published article, no doubt based on Eliza Snow's information, but to him, Fanny was just another plural wife and not even the first since he listed Louisa Beaman first and Fanny second in his July 1886 article. It is improbable to me that Eliza Snow would have included Fanny's name if she believed other than that Fanny was a bona fide plural wife.

It might be argued that Eliza R. Snow contradicted herself when recounting her personal experience with plural marriage. She wrote: "In Nauvoo I first understood that the practice of plurality of wives was to be introduced into the church. The subject was very repugnant to my feelings."[21] Some have interpreted this statement as an admission that she first learned of polygamy in Nauvoo, not in Kirtland in 1836. However, she does not say that she "first understood" about plural marriage in Nauvoo. Rather, it was "in Nauvoo" when Eliza "first understood that the practice of plurality of wives *was to be introduced into the church*." The

---

21. Snow, "Sketch of My Life," 13. See also Maureen Ursenbach Beecher, ed., *The Personal Writings of Eliza Roxcy Snow*, 16–17.

wording used is consistent with a possible attempt to be strictly accurate but still not divulge that she learned of plural marriage years before.

Sources in the Webb Family

Perhaps equally useful in determining whether a plural marriage ceremony was performed is to observe the behavior of devout Latter-day Saints who were privy to the Alger-Smith relationship. In all of Joseph Smith's teachings, a marriage ceremony was always required prior to engaging in sexual relations. In February of 1831, Joseph Smith dictated a revelation in the presence of twelve elders addressing the strict sexual behavioral code that would exist in the Church:

> He that looketh upon a woman to lust after her shall deny the faith, and shall not have the Spirit; and if he repents not he shall be cast out.
>
> Thou shalt not commit adultery; and he that committeth adultery, and repenteth not, shall be cast out. (D&C 42:23-24)

The Prophet consistently taught this moral code, both publicly and privately throughout his life. (See Vol. 3, Chapter 5.) In 1848, Heber C. Kimball remembered that Joseph issued clear instructions on the need for an authorized ceremony: "No woman can covenant with a man & on that covenant live then as man & wife[,] this always true, & I heard it from Joseph himself."[22] This was the doctrinal standard Joseph Smith had established in the Church before and after the Saints' stay in Kirtland, Ohio. It seems probable that any deviation from that code of conduct would have revealed the Prophet to be a hypocrite, creating a crisis of faith in the minds of most who understood what was happening. Chauncy and Eliza Jane Webb and their daughter, Ann Eliza Webb (a plural wife of Brigham Young) were such a family and left accounts specifically about the Joseph Smith-Fanny Alger relationship, which they termed a marriage.

A second-hand account from Chauncy Webb states that they were "intimately acquainted with Joseph Smith and his family for eleven years"[23] and "offered to take her [Fanny] until she could be sent to her relatives" after Emma expelled her from the Smith home.[24] Eliza Jane, Chauncy's wife, recalled: "Fanny Alger had lived in Joseph's family several years, and when she left there she came and lived with me a few weeks."[25] Throughout their recollections, they (and their

---

22. "Minutes of First Presidency Meetings with Quorum of the Twelve Apostles, 1847-1861," January 8, 1848.

23. Chauncy Webb, quoted in Wyl, *Mormon Portraits*, 7.

24. Ann Eliza Webb Young, *Wife Number 19; or, The Story of a Life in Bondage, Being a Complete Exposé of Mormonism, and Revealing the Sorrows, Sacrifices, and Sufferings of Women in Polygamy*, 67.

25. Eliza J. Webb [Eliza Jane Churchill Webb], Lockport, New York, Letter to Mary E. Bond, April 24, 1876. Eliza was friends with Charlotte Wilcox Bond (1803-1882) in Kirtland. Mary was Charlotte's daughter (b. 1828). The letters indicate a friendship

The Joseph Smith-Fanny Alger Relationship

Chauncy Webb. Courtesy of the International Society of the Daughters of Utah Pioneers.

daughter Ann Eliza, born in 1844) consistently maintained that a marriage ceremony of some kind was performed, referring to it as a "sealing."[26] Eliza Jane wrote: "I do not know that the 'sealing' commenced in Kirtland but I am perfectly satisfied that something similar commenced, and my judgment is principally formed from what Fanny Alger told me herself concerning her reasons for leaving 'Sister Emma'."[27]

It seems that the Webbs were Alger family confidants, having discussed the relationship with both Fanny and with Fanny's mother.[28] Importantly, it appears that their privileged knowledge did not compromise their faith in Joseph Smith. Chauncy and Eliza Jane followed the Church to Daviess County, Missouri, by 1838 and then to Nauvoo, settling in a home on Granger Street by 1842, where their daughter, Ann Eliza, was born a few months after the Prophet's death, on September 13, 1844.[29] Later they were sealed as a couple in the Nauvoo Temple, where Chauncy served as a temple worker.[30] They also traversed the plains to settle in the Tooele area of Utah.[31] Chauncy served a mission in 1852.[32] It appears the Webbs had an inside view of the proceedings, and their reaction to Joseph Smith's relationship with

---

and inquiries from Mary regarding the topics addressed in Eliza's replies.

26. Ann Eliza Webb Young, *Wife No. 19*, 66–67; Eliza J. Webb, Letter to Mary Bond, April 24, 1876; Wyl, quoting Chauncy Webb, *Mormon Portraits*, 57.

27. Eliza J. Webb, Letter to Mary Bond, May 4, 1876.

28. Eliza J. Webb, Letter to Mary Bond, April 24, 1876.

29. Richard Neitzel Holzapfel and T. Jeffery Cottle, "The City of Joseph in Focus: The Use and Abuse of Historic Photographs," 255.

30. On March 31, 1841, Chauncy Webb officiated at the marriage of John Harvey and Eliza Everett. Lisle G Brown, *Nauvoo Sealings, Adoptions, and Anointings: A Comprehensive Register of Persons Receiving LDS Temple Ordinances, 1841–1846*, 326, citing *Times and Seasons*, 2:405.

31. "QUINCY BRANCH, Tooele Stake, Tooele Co., Utah, consisted of a few families of Latter-day Saints residing in Skull Valley, including the Quincy Ranch. Skull Valley was used as a herd ground for cattle as early as 1857, when a man named Box located there and built a herd-house. Two years later Chauncy Webb also settled in what was then known locally as 'The Dell.'" Andrew Jenson, *Encyclopedic History of the Church of Jesus Christ of Latter-day Saints*, 688. For his mission, see Stanley S. Ivins, Notebook 13, 163.

32. Ibid.

Fanny Alger did not apparently affect their faith in the Prophet and his church. Had they seen the relationship as adultery or hypocrisy, they might have been less willing to follow Joseph Smith and later Brigham Young. Decades later in Utah, both Chauncy and Eliza Jane became estranged from the Church and each other. However, the trajectory of their lives between Kirtland and the Utah Territory indicates that their early experiences with Joseph Smith and Fanny Alger did not undermine their faith in the Prophet.

Sources in the Alger Family

Fanny's parents and brother, John, also suggest that a marriage occurred and that they accepted the relationship as legitimate.[33] Researcher Thomas Milton Tinney observed: "The fact that the parents [of Fanny Alger] came to Utah seriously questions the suggested immoral behavior of the Prophet Joseph Smith, Jr."[34] John Alger, Fanny's brother, stayed with the Church, eventually settling in St. George, Utah. At one point Apostle Heber C Kimball reportedly introduced him as a "Brother of the Prophet Josephs first Plural Wife."[35] John was excommunicated shortly after the issuance of the 1890 Manifesto because he could not accept the discontinuation of plural marriage, a position of perhaps excessive devotion to the principle.[36] It seems less likely that he would have remained faithful up to that point if he felt that his sister had experienced a hypocritical conjugal relationship with Joseph Smith.

According to Ann Eliza Webb Young, Fanny's parents considered "it the highest honor to have their daughter adopted into the Prophet's family, and her mother has always claimed that she was sealed to Joseph."[37] Janet Ellingson viewed this statement skeptically: "In later nineteenth-century Utah, the Hancock and Alger families had everything to gain by remembering and promoting Fanny's relationship with Smith as a celestial polygamous marriage."[38] Again, this is probably true during the Utah period. But if there was no plural marriage in Ohio, it seems unlikely that Fanny's parents, Samuel and Clarissa, who apparently understood what was happening, would have continued to follow the Prophet in view of what must have been viewed, ab-

---

33. "Died" [Samuel Alger obituary], *Deseret News Weekly*, October 14, 1874, 7.

34. Thomas Milton Tinney, "Fanny Alger, the First Plural Wife of the Prophet Joseph Smith Jr.: A Preliminary Genealogical Report," 10.

35. Zimmerman, *I Knew the Prophets*, 45. Johnson's memory is faulty in that the introduction reportedly occurred "in the Saint George Temple." Kimball died before this temple was completed. It seems likely that the conversation occurred, but in another setting.

36. John Alger, Record of Excommunication.

37. Ann Eliza Webb Young, *Wife Number 19*, 67.

38. Ellingson, "Alger Marriage Questioned," vii.

The Joseph Smith-Fanny Alger Relationship

John Alger. Courtesy of the LDS Church History Library.

sent a valid marriage, as hypocritical and exploitive behavior.[39] On the contrary, the Alger parents stayed close to Joseph Smith, moving to Illinois with the rest of the Saints in 1839. They also joined the migration west in 1846, settling in southern Utah and dying there in the 1870s.[40]

Authority to Perform a Plural Marriage?

Returning to one facet of Mosiah Hancock's account, he asserted that his father performed the sealing between Joseph and Fanny. The question arises regarding Levi's authority to perform a plural marriage as described. Obviously civil law would not ratify a bigamous marriage. Nor would the sealing keys be restored until the dedication of the Kirtland Temple in April 1836 (D&C 110:13–16). Therefore, in Kirtland Levi could not have been commissioned with the same authority by which Nauvoo plural marriages would be sealed a half decade later.[41]

The term "sealing" appears in Ohio-period documents, but it appears to have been a "sealing up to everlasting life." Mary Elizabeth Rollins Lightner wrote in 1902: "I was sealed to Joseph Smith, the Prophet by commandment. In the spring of 1831, the Savior appeared and commanded him to seal me up to everlasting life."[42] Her statement has been misunderstood as a marriage proposal.[43] A November 1831 revelation given at Hiram, Ohio, promised several Church missionaries: "And of as many as the Father shall bear record, to you shall be given power to seal them up unto eternal life" (D&C 68:12).[44]

---

39. Eliza Jane Churchill Webb quoted Fanny's mother as saying: "Fanny was sealed to Joseph." Eliza J. Webb, Letter to Mary Bond, April 24, 1876.

40. Compton, *In Sacred Loneliness*, 37, 40.

41. Specifically, Eliza Jane Churchill Webb wrote: "Fanny Alger's mother says Fanny was sealed to Joseph by Oliver Cowdery in Kirtland in 1835-or 6." Eliza J. Webb, Letter to Mary Bond, April 24, 1876. Webb was apparently in error, since all other evidence indicates that Oliver was not involved with Joseph Smith's union with Fanny Alger and later regarded it as adulterous union.

42. Mary Elizabeth Rollins Lightner, "Statement," February 8, 1902.

43. See for example, D. Michael Quinn, *The Mormon Hierarchy: Origins of Power*, 89.

44. Named earlier in the revelation were Orson Hyde, Luke Johnson, and Lyman Johnson (v. 7). See also D&C 1:8–9; 77:8–9. Even after the keys of Elijah were restored,

When Joseph first began performing wedding ceremonies in Ohio, he claimed: "I have done it by the authority of the holy Priesthood," clarifying that "the Gentile law has no power to call me to an account for it. It is my religious privilege."[45] Most likely he invoked his general priesthood authority, rather than specific keys for a sealing ceremony, to unite believing couples in a way not allowed by "Gentile law."[46] Joseph Smith's Melchizedek Priesthood ordination by Peter, James, and John (D&C 27:12; Matt. 16:18–19) would have provided him with authority to confer upon Levi Hancock to perform the marriage.[47]

Immediate Consequences of the Fanny Alger Plural Marriage

A review of the historical record indicates that Joseph Smith's first venture into plurality could not have turned out worse. The immediate consequences seem to have emotionally traumatized Emma and Fanny, while alienating Oliver Cowdery. In addition, later consequences and reports of "adultery" required specific damage control efforts by the Prophet himself to blunt a growing crisis in the Church.

It is doubtful that Emma was initially aware of the polygamous union. Regardless, at some point, she became apprised of the relationship; and her negative reaction makes it plain that she did not consider it a genuine marriage. There is no record that Fanny had a child, but Chauncy Webb intimated that Emma became aware of the union because of Fanny's pregnancy. According to a second-hand report, Chauncy told an interviewer: "In Kirtland, he [Joseph] was sealed there secretly to Fanny Alger. Emma was

---

which permit the sealing of husbands to wives and parents to children, the Prophet acknowledged on May 17, 1843: "The more sure word of prophecy means a man's knowing that he is sealed up unto eternal life, by revelation and the spirit of prophecy, through the power of the Holy Priesthood" (D&C 131:5).

45. Newel Knight, "Sketch of the Life of Newel Knight," 5.

46. There was a belief in Nauvoo that all eternal sealing ceremonies performed outside of a temple, whether monogamous or polygamist, would need to be repeated within temple walls (with the same individuals or by proxy) at some point. By this logic, the Joseph Smith-Fanny Alger plural marriage would also have needed to be reperformed within a temple to have become an eternal marriage.

47. This pattern of Joseph Smith authorizing a man to perform a plural marriage with priesthood authority was also repeated years later in Nauvoo utilizing the sealing authority he had received in 1836 (D&C 110:13–16). In 1892, when asked about the authority he used to seal Louisa Beaman to Joseph Smith, Noble stated: "I know this, that the law giver [Joseph Smith] authorized it. . . . I got it all right—right from the Prophet himself. That is where I got it." Joseph Bates Noble, 1892 Deposition, in Temple Lot Transcript, Part 3, pp. 432, 436, questions 793, 799, 861; sentence order reversed.

furious, and drove the girl, who was unable to conceal the consequences of her celestial relation with the prophet, out of her house."[48]

Ann Eliza Webb Young (b. 1844) described Oliver Cowdery's role in the episode: "Angered at finding the two persons whom most she [Emma] loved playing such a treacherous part towards her, she by no means spared her reproaches, and, finally, the storm became so furious, that Joseph was obliged to send, at midnight, for Oliver Cowdery, his scribe, to come and endeavor to settle matters between them."[49] Precisely what role Oliver played, if any, in trying to calm the emotional turmoil is unclear. (See Chapter 6.) From later developments, it is clear that Oliver did not consider the relationship a marriage.

If Martin Harris is reported correctly in an 1875 interview, neither did he. He does not name Fanny Alger, identifying her only as a "servant girl." The skeptical interviewer, Anthony Metcalf, reported:

> The servant girl of Joe Smith stated that the prophet had made improper proposals to her, which created quite a talk amongst the people. Joe Smith went to Martin Harris to counsel with him concerning the girl's talk. Harris, supposing that Joe was innocent, told him to take no notice of the girl, that she was full of the devil and wanted to destroy the prophet of God; but Joe Smith acknowledged that there was more truth than poetry in what the girl said. Harris then said he would have nothing to do in the matter, Smith could get out of the trouble the best way he knew how.[50]

Martin, therefore, did not consider the relationship to be a valid marriage although, interestingly, in this version Joseph's alleged transgression stopped with making "improper proposals."

Whether through Fanny's alleged pregnancy, viewing a "transaction" through a barn door crack, or through other means, Emma learned of the relationship and apparently reacted dramatically. In 1886, Ann Eliza Webb provided this second-hand account, presumably based on information from her parents:

> Mrs. Smith had an adopted daughter,[51] a very pretty, pleasing young girl, about seventeen years old. She was extremely fond of her; no own

---

48. Wyl, *Mormon Portraits*, 57. Wyl identifies the speaker as "Mr. W." The use of the term "sealed" is anachronistic if referring to the sealing keys mentioned in D&C 110:13–16, 132:7, 18, 19. That sealing authority had not yet been restored in 1835 and could not have been used to perform the marriage.

49. Ann Eliza Webb Young, *Wife Number 19*, 66. In 1838 David W. Patten testified that "Oliver Cowdery . . . said that Joseph told him, he had confessed to Emma." Quoted in Donald Q. Cannon and Lyndon W. Cook, eds., *Far West Record: Minutes of the Church of Jesus Christ of Latter-day Saints, 1830–1844*, 167.

50. Anthony Metcalf, *Ten Years before the Mast*, 72.

51. Ann Eliza Webb Young mistakenly believed that Fanny had been adopted by the Smiths.

mother could be more devoted, and their affection for each other was a constant object of remark, so absorbing and genuine did it seem. Consequently it was with a shocked surprise that the people heard that sister Emma had turned Fanny out of the house.[52]

This sudden movement was incomprehensible, since Emma was known to be a just woman, not given to freaks or caprices, and it was felt that she certainly must have had some very good reason for her action. By degrees it became whispered about that Joseph's love for his adopted daughter was by no means a paternal affection, and his wife, discovering the fact, at once took measures to place the girl beyond his reach.[53]

William McLellin, who was briefly an apostle during the Kirtland period, in a late report stated that Joseph "confessed humbly, and begged forgiveness," adding: "Emma and all forgave him."[54] Additional details of Emma's reaction to her husband's first plural marriage are unavailable. However, two letters that she wrote to Joseph in 1837 contain references that might have referred to the Alger incident, which she apparently considered to be an improper relationship.[55] While he was in hiding on April 25, she closed her letter with: "I pray that God will keep you in *purity* and safety till we all meet again."[56] A week later, she similarly signed a second letter: "I hope that we shall be so humble and *pure* before God that he will set us at liberty to be our own masters."[57]

Fanny's personal feelings are unavailable, but Eliza Jane Churchill Webb recalled speaking with her about "her reasons for leaving 'Sister Emma'."[58] Other evidence suggests that Emma's reaction may have been the primary cause Alger left the area. In 1843 in Nauvoo, Emma would consent to the polygamous sealings of two plural wives to Joseph, the Partridge sisters, only

---

52. Ann Eliza's mother, Eliza Jane Churchill Webb echoed: "I only know that Emma Smith turned Fanny out of her house because of Joseph's intimacy with her." Eliza J. Webb, Letter to Mary Bond, April 24, 1876.

53. Ann Eliza Webb Young, *Wife Number 19*, 66.

54. William McLellin, Letter to Joseph Smith III, July 1872.

55. Richard Lloyd Anderson, "The Religious Dimension of Emma's Letters to Joseph," 119, argues for an alternative view: "Contrary to one suggestion that Emma hinted at concern over her husband's sexual loyalty, her 1837 letters show deep respect for her husband, the opposite of distrust. These and her early Illinois notes reflect her reliance on the Prophet's consistency as a parent and husband. In her 3 May 1837 letter Emma uses 'anxiety' [to describe her feelings] for missing Joseph, and again requests that Joseph return in time to help with the children because they have been exposed to measles, which earlier had robbed them of a child."

56. Emma Smith, Letter to Joseph Smith, April 25, 1837; emphasis mine. Also quoted in Linda King Newell, "Emma Hale Smith and the Polygamy Question," 4.

57. Emma Smith, Letter to Joseph Smith, May 3, 1837; emphasis mine.

58. Eliza J. Webb, Letter to Mary Bond, May 4, 1876.

to cast them out of her home months later and even try to force them to leave the city. (See Chapters 23, 26.) Perhaps her Nauvoo behavior was but a repetition of possible first acceptance, then rejection, of Joseph's first plural wife in Kirtland in 1836.

The Alger family stayed in the Kirtland area until September of 1836, when they left for Missouri. They must have stopped two months later in Wayne County, Indiana, because on November 16, Fanny was civilly married to Solomon Custer there.[59] Her willingness to enter into a legal marriage in late 1836 soon after the dissolution of her plural marriage can be read several different ways.[60] Some analysts believe Fanny's actions indicate that her relationship with the Prophet was nothing more than a sexual tryst. They contend that a marriage, even an interrupted one, would have prevented Fanny from entering into another marriage, unless she had come to believe that a marriage not recognized by civil law was not valid. However, a marriage performed by Joseph's priesthood authority could be dissolved by that same power. Possibly she sought a separation to distance herself from Emma's persecution. It is impossible to know what Fanny was thinking. Todd Compton wrote: "One can only speculate on Fanny's motives for marrying a non-Mormon, after a courtship that could have only been a matter of weeks. Perhaps she felt that Smith had abandoned her after Emma ejected her from the household. It is also possible that she simply fell in love with Solomon, who, unlike Smith, was her own age—nineteen."[61]

Benjamin Johnson recalled: "Soon after the Prophet['s] flight in winter of 37 x 8 [1837–38] The Alger Family left for the west and Stoping in Indianna for a time Fanny Soon Married to one of the Citizens there."[62] Despite this geographic estrangement from the Saints, Johnson insisted: "Altho she never

---

59. Marriage record of Solomon Custer and Fanny Alger, November 16, 1836, Dublin, Wayne County, Indiana. The record reads: "Dublin November 16th, 1836 This day married by me Levi Eastridge a Justice of the Peace for Wayne County and State of Indiana Mr Solomon Custer and Miss Fanny Alger both of this town."

60. Jo Kester, email to Allan Alger, March 4, 2003, reports an Alger family tradition: "Brigham Young, accompanied by Fanny's brother, John Alger, did come to Indiana, before Fanny married Solomon Custer [sic; this would have been after the martyrdom], to ask her to marry him. She answered him by saying, 'You are a fine young man but I want to be an only wife.'" It seems that the only reason Brigham would have visited Fanny, if any of the traditions are true, would be to follow through with his commission to offer himself as a possible husband, for "time" to Joseph Smith's plural wives, thereby reinforcing the contemporary understanding that Fanny was indeed married to the Prophet.

61. Compton, *In Sacred Loneliness*, 37.

62. Zimmerman, *I Knew the Prophets*, 39. See also "Died" [Samuel Alger obituary], 7.

left the State She did \not/ turn from the Church nor from her friendship for the Prophet while She lived."[63] She died in late 1889. Her obituary reads:

> She [Fanny Alger] joined the Universalist church on the evening of the 10th of October, 1874, and until her last, held to that belief. She passed away peacefully and resignedly, with an abiding faith in the justice and love of an All Powerful and Supreme Being, and with joy in the full belief that she would meet with dear ones gone before.
>
> Having fulfilled the duties of life, with a conscientious regard for the welfare and happiness of those who were compelled to lean on her in her middle and early life, she passed away, fully trusting that the welcome applaudit summons, "well done thou good and faithful servant, enter thou into the joy of the Lord," would greet her on the other side. Funeral services were held at the Universalist church in Dublin, on Sabbath morning, Dec. 1, 1889, Rev. P.S. Cook and C.T. Swain, officiating.[64]

Benjamin Johnson also reported, although not explaining how he had this information: "Fanny A. when asked by her Brother & others. Eaven after the prophets death Regarding her Relation to him Replied 'That is all a matter of my—own. And I have nothing to Communicate.'"[65]

Joseph Smith and Fanny Alger: Charting the Evidence

Available references to the Joseph Smith-Fanny Alger relationship can be interpreted differently as either a plural marriage, a friendship, or an adulterous union.[66] (See Table 5.1.) Some of this evidence is discussed in the next chapter.

---

63. Zimmerman, *I Knew the Prophets*, 39. The Lima Illinois Branch, organized October 23, 1842, lists Fanny Custer as a member but whether she was physically present there is not known. See Emer Harris, Book of Patriarchal Blessings, no. 210.

64. Fanny Alger Obituary. There is no record of when or where the obituary was published and I have not been able to locate it. The quotation is from a webite that includes other useful information on Fanny. The obituary has this introductory sentence: "The following obituary was found in the Adolphus Barnes Family Bible." http://www.algerclan.org/getperson.php?personID=I135&tree=alger (accessed September 6, 2008); spelling and punctuation as per original.

65. Zimmerman, *I Knew the Prophets*, 45.

66. A middle-of the-road perspective is promoted by LDS historian Jeffery O. Johnson who believes that available historical sources do not provide evidence that "Joseph Smith had any kind of relationship with Fanny Alger." Jeff Johnson, email to Brian Hales, September 24, 2007. Despite the nineteen sources identified that refer to the incident (see Appendix D), it is true that none of them is without individual credibility problems and that skeptical historians might be unimpressed with the whole.

TABLE 5.1
JOSEPH SMITH AND FANNY ALGER: PLURAL MARRIAGE OR ADULTERY?

Plural Marriage		Ambiguous		Adultery	
Eliza R. Snow in 1887	Eliza was "well acquainted" with Fanny Alger and wrote that Fanny was a plural wife of Joseph Smith.	William McLellin Statements	Wrote that Joseph "committed an act" with Fanny. He also referred to it as a "case of polygamy" and a "sealing."	Oliver Cowdery Statement	Considered the relationship a "dirty, nasty, filthy scrape."
Mosiah Hancock Statement	Provides plausible details of a marriage ceremony performed by his father, but his account is second-hand and late.	Far West High Council	The high councilors were satisfied with Joseph Smith's explanation of the "girl business." Apparently the topic of plural marriage was not part of the discussion.	Fanny Brewer Statement	Quotes rumors of "unlawful intercourse."
Chauncy Webb Statement	Spoke anachronistically of a "sealing."	Elder's Journal	Printed three statements to defuse Oliver Cowdery's charges of adultery.	Emma Smith's Actions	Reportedly Emma sent Fanny out of the Smith home. Clearly she did not consider the relationship a legitimate plural marriage.
Eliza Jane Churchill Webb Statements	Quotes Fanny's mother saying a marriage occurred. Refers to relationship as a "sealing."	Martin Harris Statement	Spoke of "improper proposals" only.	Clark Braden Statement	Braden's late, second-hand, sensational claims must be evaluated carefully. Many are unsubstantiated.
Ann Eliza Webb Young Statement	Information is second-hand. Quotes Fanny's mother saying Fanny was "sealed" to Joseph Smith.	Fanny Alger's Actions	Her willingness to enter into a civil marriage in November 1836 can be interpreted as evidence that she considered her marriage to Joseph Smith dissolved or that she was never married.	Historicus [pseud.]	Late [1881] source that spoke of Joseph Smith's "free-loveism."
Webb Family Actions	The Webbs continued as active Church members at Nauvoo and later in Utah.	Fanny Alger's Statement	Later in life when asked about Joseph, she reportedly responded: "That is all a matter of my own, and I have nothing to communicate."		
Alger Family Actions	Remained active Church members in Nauvoo and later in Utah.				
John Hawley Statement	Second-hand and late. He calls the relationship a "sealing."				
Benjamin F. Johnson Statement	Late recollection. Considered it the first plural marriage.				

Summary

The issue of whether Joseph Smith was married to Fanny Alger or had an immoral sexual relationship with her has been debated for decades. Several documents combine to support what I consider to be persuasive evidence that a marriage ceremony occurred. Most notably are previously unpublished materials from Eliza R. Snow via Andrew Jenson describing Eliza as "well acquainted" with Fanny and listing Fanny as a wife. The behavior of men and women close to the proceedings, particularly the Webb and Alger families, appears to corroborate that a marriage occurred. It appears that there was an officiator—Levi Ward Hancock—and that he officiated by Melchizedek Priesthood authority, though not sealing priesthood, since those keys had yet to be given to Joseph Smith.

Despite the evidences of a marital ceremony, it is clear that Emma Smith, the Prophet's legal wife, and Oliver Cowdery did not accept the relationship as a legitimate marriage. Either they were unaware of the polygamous wedding ceremony or they did not think it valid. Their rejection created immediate turmoil in the Smith home, with close associates Oliver Cowdery and Martin Harris, and for Fanny, who was expelled from the house. Fanny soon left the area with her family and married a non-Mormon, apparently never again formally affiliating with the Saints.

Chapter 6

Oliver Cowdery and the Aftermath of the Alger-Smith Relationship

Joseph Smith's first plural marriage appears to have generated a huge amount of commotion for those closest to the proceedings, creating an immediate crisis for him, Emma, Fanny, Oliver Cowdery, and perhaps a few others. However, those individuals who knew firsthand regarding its details appear to have remained silent about the relationship. The one exception was Oliver Cowdery. He is documented as making statements that resulted in questions among his and Joseph's associates with which Joseph had to deal.

Oliver Cowdery: Early Polygamist?

Oliver Cowdery married Elizabeth Ann Whitmer on January 22, 1832, in Jackson County, Missouri; and together they had six children, only one of whom survived to adulthood.[1] Historians have long debated whether he entered a polygamous relationship during the early 1830s, but the question cannot be resolved on the basis of extant documentation. Credible evidence supports both a "yes" and "no" answer. Two reputable scholars who take the position that Oliver was a polygamist are Danel Bachman and Glen M. Leonard. Bachman wrote: "Before the close of the Kirtland period, Smith and Cowdery both began polygamous households."[2] Historian Glen M. Leonard, author of *Nauvoo: a Place of Peace, a People of Promise*, wrote: "In Kirtland, Oliver Cowdery knew of the revelation on marriage but was denied permission to take a plural wife. He proceeded anyway and engaged in an illicit relationship."[3]

They largely base this conclusion on several nineteenth-century Church leaders who accused Oliver Cowdery of either unauthorized polygamy or adul-

---

1. Four of the Cowdery children died in infancy: Elizabeth Ann (1836–37), Oliver Peter (1840) Adeline Fuller (1844), and Julia Olive (1846). Josephine Rebecca (1838–44) passed away at age six. The only child to live to adulthood was Maria Louise (1835–92). Ancestral File. http://www.familysearch.org/Eng/Search/frameset_search.asp. (accessed July 24, 2011).

2. Danel W. Bachman, "A Study of the Mormon Practice of Plural Marriage before the Death of Joseph Smith," 76; see the discussion 76–86.

3. Glen M. Leonard, *Nauvoo: A Place of Peace, a People of Promise*, 344.

tery. However, the earliest of the allegations was not voiced for more than twenty years after the reported event, and at least part of their motivation may have been to assure the Saints that Joseph Smith only reluctantly obeyed the divine commandment to accept both the principle and the practice of plurality. On August 26, 1857, Wilford Woodruff, then assistant Church historian recorded: "President Young stayed three-plus hours in compiling his history. He remarked that the revelation upon a plurality of wives was given to Joseph Smith. He revealed it to Oliver Cowdery alone upon the solemn pledge that he would not reveal it or act upon it. But he did act upon it in a secret manner and that was the cause of his overthrow."[4]

Oliver Cowdery. Photograph courtesy Library of Congress.

In 1872, Charles Lowell Walker wrote a full account in his journal of an address in which President Young, speaking at a Salt Lake 14th Ward meeting that was "crowded insomuch that many could not get in and had to stand by the door," also reportedly taught:

> While Joseph and Oliver were translating the Book of Mormon, they had a revelation that the order of Patriarchal Marriag and Sealing was right. Oliver said unto Joseph, "Br Joseph, why don't we go into the Order of Polygamy, and practice it as the ancients did? We know it is true, then why delay?" Joseph's reply was "I know that we know it is true, and from God, but the time has not yet come." This did not seem to suit Oliver, who expressed a determination to go into the order of Plural Marriage anyhow, altho he was ignorant of the order and pattern and the results. Joseph said, "Oliver if you go into this thing it is not with my faith or consent." Disregarding the counsel of Joseph, Oliver Cowdery took to wife Miss Annie Lyman, cousin to George A. Smith. From that time he went into darkness and lost the spirit.[5]

---

4. Scott G. Kenney, ed., *Wilford Woodruff's Journal, 1833–1898*, 5:84, August 26, 1857. See also Journal History of the Church of Jesus Christ of Latter-day Saints, August 26, 1857, in *Selected Collections*, Vol. 2, disk #3, for comments by Apostle Joseph F. Smith, July 7, 1878, *Journal of Discourses*, 20:29.

5. Andrew Karl Larson and Katharine Miles Larson, eds., *The Diary of Charles Lowell Walker*, July 26, 1872, 1:349.

Richard Van Wagoner, however, observes: "It would have been impossible for Cowdery to have been living polygamously during the period charged by Young (1827–30). Cowdery's marriage to his only wife, Elizabeth Ann Whitmer, occurred in 1832."[6] The alleged sequence of events is further problematized by terminology. If Oliver did, in fact, enter a relationship with Annie Lyman while he and Joseph were translating the Book of Mormon, it would have been fornication, not polygamy; but too much weight should not be placed on exact terminology, especially given the distance of these recollections from the alleged event.

The timetable implied is problematic in other ways. Brigham Young was not positioned in the early 1830s to know about Oliver's personal activities, although he might have learned about them second-hand at a later date. In an 1874 sermon, Brigham recalled that prior to his leaving for England in 1839: "Joseph had never mentioned this [plural marriage], there had never been a thought of it in the Church that I knew anything about at that time."[7] On January 23, 1865, speaking before the Utah Legislative Assembly, he explained: "Did we believe in polygamy when we were driven from Ohio, when we were driven from Jackson County, when we was driven from Missouri? No, we knew nothing about it, there was no such thing."[8] A quarter century after Brigham's death, Mary Elizabeth Rollins Lightner, one of Joseph's plural wives, corroborated Brigham's lack of knowledge about polygamy during the Kirtland period: "Brigham Young had not been in the church long enough to broach such a thing [as plural marriage] to Joseph, for I talked with him [probably Joseph, although the pronoun is ambiguous] about it."[9] If she is remembering accurately events that had occurred seventy years earlier, Brigham was unaware of the Fanny Alger plural marriage in Kirtland and probably any "polygamy"-related dealings of Oliver Cowdery as well.

Other Church leaders in the Utah territory were also critical of Oliver Cowdery's behavior. In 1878, Joseph F. Smith denounced Oliver for "taking liberties without license."[10] However, his information could have been only second-hand or even third-hand. Of all the General Authorities, George Q. Cannon's criticisms were the sharpest. But since he did not join the Church until 1840, he would have had no firsthand knowledge of the events. Regardless, in 1885 he wrote that Oliver "committed adultery," saying "the Spirit of God withdrew

---

6. Richard S. Van Wagoner, *Mormon Polygamy: A History*, 11–12.

7. Brigham Young, June 23, 1874, *Journal of Discourses*, 18:241.

8. Richard S. Van Wagoner, ed., *The Complete Discourses of Brigham Young*, 4:2259.

9. Mary E. Lightner, Letter to A. M. Chase, April 20, 1904, quoted in J. D. Stead, *Doctrines and Dogmas of Brighamism Exposed*, 218–19. See also Mary Rollins Lightner Carter, "Record Book of Mary R. L. Carter."

10. Joseph F. Smith, July 7, 1878, *Journal of Discourses*, 20:29; see also Joseph F. Smith, Statement on Oliver Cowdery and polygamy, March 3–4, 1883, Provo Utah Central Stake, Quarterly Stake Conference, p. 271.

from him, and he, the second elder in the Church, was excommunicated from the Church."[11] He also alleged: "Taking her [a plural wife] as he did [without permission] was a grievous sin and was doubtless the cause of his losing the Spirit of the Lord, and of being cut off from the Church."[12] Cannon's accusation places Oliver's indiscretion shortly before his 1838 excommunication.

Annie Lyman: Candidate Wife?

Although, as seen above, most of the comments denouncing Oliver Cowdery for engaging in unauthorized polygamy do not mention who the plural wife might have been, Charles Walker records Brigham Young as identifying Annie Lyman, a cousin of George A. Smith, as the woman in question. George A. was Brigham's close friend, a fellow apostle since 1839, and first counselor in Brigham's First Presidency from 1868 until his death in September 1875, three years after Walker recorded Young's comments. Thus, Brigham would have had ample opportunity to hear family stories from George A. Smith, who presumably would have been in a position to know their veracity first-hand, or at least second hand.

What is known about Annie Lyman? Scott H. Faulring, who did extensive research on this question for an unpublished "Documentary History of Oliver Cowdery," wrote:

> The identification of "Annie Lyman" is somewhat problematic. Our identification is tentative based on the brief details President Young provided, 1) her name and 2) her relationship to George A. Smith. We think that Mary A. [Ann?] Lyman is possibly who B [Brigham Young] was referring to. She was the daughter of Asa [Lyman] and Sarah Davis Lyman and was born in February 1817. Her father was a brother to George A. Smith's mother Clarissa Lyman Smith. Thus Mary Ann Lyman was a first cousin to George A. Smith. Exactly when Mary Ann arrived in Kirtland is difficult to date. From the MS [ambiguous but possibly referring to MS 27, the George A. Smith document] we know that her father, Asa Lyman, was in Kirtland in May 1833. There is the possibility that Mary Ann arrived sometime between May 1833 and mid-1834.[13]

---

11. George Q. Cannon, "Editorial Thoughts," *Juvenile Instructor* 20 (December 1, 1885): 360.

12. George Q. Cannon, "History of the Church," *Juvenile Instructor* 16 (September 15, 1881), 206. Heber J. Grant, Diary, June 11, 1881, states: "Bro Lysander Gee went with me. Retd to Tooele in the Evening Coming home Bro Gee told me that he had known Oliver Cowdery personally & that to his knowledge Cowdrey [sic] had committed adultry [sic] before he lost his faith—It strengthens my faith to learn that even the leading men of the Church cannot commit sin & remain in the Church, unless they repent."

13. Faulring cites as sources: George A. Smith, *Sketch of the Autobiography of George*

D. Michael Quinn lists Mary Ann Lyman as a plural wife for Oliver, dating the marriage in 1833, with the union dissolving the next year.[14] Quinn also asserts: "Smith had ignored Oliver Cowdery when he chose his counselors apparently because of Cowdery's sexual transgressions before and after his 1832 marriage. . . . His [Cowdery's] alienation during the Kirtland apostasy of 1837 . . . indicates his long-smoldering bitterness at Smith's double standard condemnations of Cowdery's 'evils' while the prophet at the same time was in a polygamous relationship with Alger."[15] Quinn does not substantiate this extreme interpretation of available evidence nor do his endnote references seem to support this view.

My personal conclusion about Annie Lyman as a candidate plural wife is that it begs the more important question of whether, in fact, Oliver Cowdery ever engaged in plural marriage. If Oliver was never a polygamist, then Annie's identity and relationship with Oliver, if any, is mostly moot. Without more information, including biographical details about Annie (or Mary Ann) herself, the questions regarding her remain open to further research.

Possible Chronologies

Reviewing the significant events in Oliver's life identifies only three time periods between his 1832 monogamous marriage and his 1838 excommunication when a polygamous union or adulterous relationship might have occurred. The three spans are separated by two events. First is Oliver's December 1834 ordination as associate president. The second occurred on April 3, 1836, when in a vision the Savior told both Joseph and Oliver: "Behold, your sins are forgiven you; you are clean before me; therefore, lift up your heads and rejoice" (D&C 11:5). Both of these experiences imply that at those times, Oliver was in the highest possible spiritual and ecclesiastical standing.[16] In addition, on January 25, 1836, Oliver recorded his intolerance for any behavior that might be interpreted as polygamy: "Settled with James M. Carrel, who left the office. I gave him a reproof for urging himself into the society of a young female

---

Albert Smith, MS 27 (15 July 1865): 438; and Lyman Coleman, *Lyman, from High Ongar in England, 1631* (Albany, N.Y.: J. Munsell, 1872): 122–23. Scott H. Faulring, "Documentary History of Oliver Cowdery," preliminary draft, Scott H. Faulring Collection, Marriott Library, Accn 2316, Box 23, fd. 3.

14. D. Michael Quinn, *The Mormon Hierarchy: Origins of Power*, 544.

15. Ibid., 43, 45.

16. A chart "Chronology on Oliver Cowdery and Polygamy," p. 4, by an unidentified author, presumably Faulring, posits a marriage between Oliver and Anne Lyman "between January and July 1833." The citations for this chronology are the quotations from Brigham Young and George Q. Cannon as quoted. The author, presumably Faulring, references no other documentation.

while he yet had a wife living, but he disliked my admonition: he however confessed his impropriety."[17]

The most likely period for an illicit plural marriage might have been between January 1832 and December 1834. Researcher David Keller wrote: "I suspect then, that if Oliver really did practice plural marriage, it would have been during the summer months [of 1834] when Joseph Smith was absent and hence not around to advise him about such a sensitive matter. Being away from his first wife for such a long time must have increased the temptation to act independently for the [S]econd Elder. In August of 1834, we can place Oliver in Asa (and Annie) Lyman's house."[18]

Robert G. Mouritsen, who wrote his dissertation on the little-known office of associate president, accepts the possibility of Oliver as a polygamist and proposes this time-frame: "The evidence does suggest, then, that the Second Elder entered upon his unauthorized course sometime between January 14, and late July, 1833, probably in the forepart of 1833."[19] Supporting this possibility, William McLellin wrote in 1848: "We attended a general conference, called at the instance of Joseph Smith in Clay County, Mo., on the 8th day of July 1834, at the residence of Elder Lyman Wight. And while the conference was in session, Joseph Smith presiding, he arose and said that the time had come when he must appoint his successor in office. Some have supposed that it would be Oliver Cowdery; but, said he, Oliver has lost that privilege in consequence of transgression."[20] The accuracy of McLellin's memory is unknown; his recollections sometimes reflected exaggeration and his personal biases.

No other evidence seems to support that Oliver Cowdery was involved in unauthorized polygamy or adultery during that time span. His later behavior also seems inconsistent with that conclusion; and as mentioned above, he was ordained as associate president in December of 1834. The other two time periods are even more problematic. (See Table 6.1.)

Don Bradley has proposed a plausible explanation, one that does not necessarily square precisely with the described timing. He suggests that Oliver may have engaged in a flirtation or possibly intimate relationship after he became engaged to Elizabeth Ann in 1830 but before their marriage in 1832, and that

---

17. Oliver Cowdery, "Sketchbook," January 25, 1836.

18. David Keller, "Annie Lyman."

19. Robert G. Mouritsen, "The Office of Associate President of the Church of Jesus Christ of Latter-day Saints," 84 note 121; see also 77–112. In support of this thesis, Mouritsen previously explained: "Oliver Cowdery was set apart as Associate President of the Church, December 5, 1834. . . . The probable reason that Oliver was not set apart on January 25 or April 26, 1832, was not because he 'was absent in Missouri,' but rather because he was at odds with the Prophet regarding the proper time for his entry into plural marriage" (83 note 118).

20. William E. McLellin, "The Successor of Joseph the Seer," 43.

TABLE 6.1
TIMELINE OF OLIVER COWDERY'S POSSIBLE PLURAL MARRIAGE/ADULTERY

Pre-1832	Impossible	The Book of Mormon translation was complete in June 1829. At that time, the unmarried Oliver could not have been involved with polygamy. However, he was implicated in minor misconduct when, after becoming engaged in 1830, he behaved as if he were not betrothed on his missionary trip to the Indians later that year.
1832	January 22	Oliver Cowdery married Elizabeth Ann Whitmer, at Kaw, Jackson County, Missouri.
Period #1	Possible.	William McLellin recalled that Cowdery had been censured for some offense in July 1834.
1834	December 5	Oliver was set apart as Associate Church President.
Period #2	Unlikely	Sometime prior to August 1835, Oliver wrote an "Article on Marriage," which specifies monogamy, as part of the Doctrine and Covenants. This may have been at Joseph Smith's request, as a censure to Joseph Smith, or to cover up Oliver's own polygamy.
1836	April 3	Joseph and Oliver receive a vision in the Kirtland Temple. Jesus Christ says, "Behold, your sins are forgiven you; you are clean before me; therefore, lift up your heads and rejoice" (D&C 11:5).
Period #3	Unlikely	During this two-year period, Oliver was vocal in his criticisms of Joseph Smith's involvement with Fanny Alger. His accusations were one of the reasons Oliver was ultimately excommunicated.
1838	April 12	Oliver was excommunicated but sexual misconduct was not identified as part of the misbehavior of which he was accused.

such an impropriety (whether mild or severe) may have been conflated with or inflated to include charges of polygamy.[21] According to this scenario, in October of 1830, Oliver, along with Peter Whitmer, Ziba Peterson, and Parley P. Pratt, set out on their mission to the Indians across the Missouri state line. Prior to leaving New York, Oliver became engaged to Elizabeth Ann Whitmer (Peter's sister).[22] However, during the journey, Oliver apparently ignored his betrothal and flirted with an unidentified woman. Ex-believer Ezra Booth wrote:

> While descending the Missouri river . . . two of my company, divulged a secret respecting Oliver, which placed his conduct on a parallel with Ziba.[23]

---

21. Don Bradley, email to Brian Hales, February 20, 2008.
22. See discussion in Stanley R. Gunn, *Oliver Cowdery: Second Elder and Scribe*, 211–12.
23. Ziba Peterson's specific impropriety is unknown, but the Far West High Council recorded on August 4, 1831, "Confession of br. Ziba Peterson of his transgressions which was satisfactory to the Church as approved by unanimous vote." Donald Q.

> . . . These two persons stated, that had they known previous to their journey to Missouri, what they then knew, they never should have accompanied Oliver thither. . . .
>
> If a pure and pleasant fountain can send forth corrupt and bitter streams, then may the heart of that man [Oliver Cowdery] be pure, who enters into a matrimonial contract with the young lady, and obtains the consent of her parents; but as soon as his back is turned upon her, he violates his engagements, and prostitutes his honor by becoming the gallant of another, and resolved in his *heart*, and expresses resolutions to marry her.[24]

Regardless, this indiscretion was still a concern among Church leaders as late as May 26, 1832, when the Far West High Council met

> to take into consideration a certain transgression of our br. Oliver committed in the fall of 1830 in the Township of Mayfield Cuyahoga County State of Ohio.
>
> Which after some discussion he having frankly confessed the same to the satisfaction of all present; it was resolved that these proceedings be recorded for the benefit & satisfaction of the Church of Christ.
>
> The reason why the above case was not taken into consideration by proper authority in the Church previous [to] this day, is that some of the Elders supposed that the affair had been adjusted last year when brother Oliver made his confession to the individuals injured & received their forgiveness.[25]

It is interesting that Oliver's questionable behavior in 1830 is referred to as an "affair" in the high council minutes, although it apparently had nothing to do with sexual misconduct, and it is true that it was not until our own day that the connotations have narrowed to refer almost exclusively to extramarital sex. Nevertheless, as Bradley suggests, this matter may lie at the root of later accusations directed at Oliver Cowdery of adultery or polygamy by individuals who were not personally involved with the proceedings. As noted above, the earliest of the allegations was made at least twenty years after its reported occurrence and several years after Oliver's own death. In addition, since Oliver "made his confession" on at least two occasions for a comparatively mild indiscretion, it seems that he would be less likely to commit a greater transgression at a later date.[26]

Cannon, and Lyndon W. Cook, eds., *Far West Record: Minutes of the Church of Jesus Christ of Latter-day Saints 1830–1841*, 9. Ziba left the Church in 1833 and later moved to California. Susan Easton Black, *Who's Who in the Doctrine & Covenants*, 222.

24. Ezra Booth, quoted in E. D. Howe, *Mormonism Unvailed*, 208, 218; emphasis in original.

25. Cannon and Cook, *Far West Record*, 49.

26. See discussion in Brian C. Hales, "'Guilty of Such Folly?': Accusations of Adultery or Polygamy against Oliver Cowdery," 279–93.

Also noteworthy is the fact that no accusations of sexual impropriety were included in the list of nine offenses against Oliver when the Far West High Council tried him for his membership in April 1838 and excommunicated him for six of the charges.[27] (See "Refuting the Rumors of Adultery" below.) Larry Foster concluded: "If Cowdery's character in this regard had been anything but spotless, there can be little doubt that he would have been thoroughly vilified for his indiscretions."[28] Given the tensions and extreme reactions of the time (not stopping short of death threats), I find Foster's conclusion credible.

One year before his reconnection with the Church, while living in Ohio on July 24, 1846, Oliver responded to his sister, Phebe Cowdery Jackson (wife of Daniel Jackson), who had earlier stated that Church members under the guidance of the Quorum of the Twelve were practicing plural marriage in Nauvoo and Iowa:

> I can hardly think it possible that you have written us the truth—that though there may be individuals who are guilty of the iniquities spoken of,—yet no such practice can be preached or adhered to as a public doctrine. Such may do for the followers of Mohamet; it may have done some thousands of years ago; but no people professing to be governed by the pure and holy principles of the Lord Jesus, can hold up their heads before the world at this distance of time, and be guilty of such folly—such wrong—such abomination.[29]

Oliver's surprise and disgust is consistent with his apparent continued disapproval of polygamy during his association with Joseph Smith and the Church.

A key factor contributing to the confusion surrounding Oliver's alleged plural marriage in the early 1830s might be an article on "Marriage" that he wrote sometime prior to August 17, 1835. The article will be discussed below, but it condemned polygamy, specifying monogamy as the only form of union accepted by the Church. It was included in the 1835 Doctrine and Covenants and remained there until 1876 as section CI (101). Critics of polygamy during the decades prior to 1876 would often refer to the article to demonstrate that Church members did not follow their own scriptures and laws. The RLDS Church was also aggressive referring to the "Marriage" article as "Joseph Smith's marital standard" and proclaiming that polygamy was Brigham Young's creation.[30]

---

27. Cannon and Cook, *Far West Record*, 163.

28. W. Lawrence Foster, *Religion and Sexuality: Three American Communal Experiments of the Nineteenth Century*, 300 note 35.

29. Oliver Cowdery, Letter to Daniel and Phebe Jackson, July 24, 1846, quoted in "An Old Document," *Salt Lake Tribune*, October 5, 1878, 2.

30. This theme is repeated over and over by RLDS attorneys E. L. Kelley and P. P. Kelley, Temple Lot Transcript, 1892.

Over time the article on "Marriage" caused some embarrassment to Church leaders who were practicing plural marriage between 1852 and 1890. It appears that they sought to place some distance between it and Joseph Smith.[31] Starting in 1869 with the visit of Joseph Smith's sons Alexander Hale Smith and David Hyrum Smith to Salt Lake City, Brigham Young reported to the Prophet's sons that the article was written by Oliver Cowdery without Joseph's approval. He also attributed it to Oliver's attempt to quell rumors that Oliver himself had started through his own polygamous activity.[32] Wilford Woodruff recalled in 1892: "I have heard representations that the doctrine [on "Marriage"] as put into the book of doctrine and covenants . . . by Oliver Cowdery . . . was represented as being contrary to the wishes of Joseph smith, but I couldn't swear that that was the fact."[33]

A review of contemporary documents describing Oliver's behavior and beliefs throughout the 1820s and up to his death is less than conclusive regarding any possible involvement or acceptance of plural marriage at any time.[34] After researching available evidence, I agree with Todd Compton who summarized: "Evidence of a plural marriage for Cowdery in Kirtland is not persuasive."[35]

Rumors of *Adultery*, Not *Polygamy*

It appears that rumors of the Joseph Smith—Fanny Alger relationship were circulating to some degree in the Kirtland area. The level of clamor is unclear. Benjamin F. Johnson wrote much later that references were "whispered . . . at the time there was little Said publickly upon the Subject."[36] In contrast, Eliza Jane Churchill Webb exclaimed, "What a talk the whole affair made," a comment that suggests more than whispers.[37] William McLellin stat-

---

31. See the discussion in Joseph Fielding Smith, *Doctrines of Salvation*, 3:195.

32. T. B. H. Stenhouse, *The Rocky Mountain Saints*, 193–94; Wilford Woodruff, Deposition, Temple Lot Transcript, Respondent's Testimony, Part 3, p. 70, question 769. See also the discussion in Richard and Pamela Price, "LDS Leaders Accused Oliver Cowdery of Polygamy," 25–27.

33. Wilford Woodruff, Deposition, Temple Lot Transcript, Respondent's Testimony, Part 3, p. 70, question 769.

34. See the discussion in Faulring, "Documentary History of Oliver Cowdery," unpaginated.

35. Todd Compton, *In Sacred Loneliness: The Plural Wives of Joseph Smith*, 645. See also Max H Parkin, "Conflict at Kirtland: A Study of the Nature and Causes of External and Internal Conflict of the Mormons in Ohio between 1830 and 1838," 169–72, esp. 172 note 100.

36. Dean R. Zimmerman, *I Knew the Prophets: An Analysis of the Letter of Benjamin F. Johnson to George F. Gibbs*, 38–39.

37. Eliza J. Webb [Eliza Jane Churchill Webb], Letter to Mary Bond, April 24, 1876.

ed that it caused "some scandal" at the time,[38] while Martin Harris reportedly recalled that it "created quite a talk amongst the people."[39]

Church member Fanny Brewer, who moved from Boston to Kirtland in the spring of 1837,[40] claimed in a September 13, 1842 letter: "There was *much excitement* against the prophet on another account, an unlawful intercourse between himself and a young orphan girl residing in this family, and under his protection!" (emphasis mine).[41] Published in John C. Bennett's exposé, *History of the Saints*, in 1842, Fanny Brewer's assertion has been reprinted so many times that it appears in virtually every description of the atmosphere in Kirtland, Ohio, during the admittedly troubled spring of 1837. It has also been misinterpreted as a reference to *polygamy*.

Even though some Ohio Saints were apparently aware of the eventual restoration of plural marriage, current research shows that the tales being "whispered" or causing "excitement" in Kirtland, Ohio, in 1837 were not about polygamy. That Joseph Smith was restoring plural marriage at that time does not seem to have been the general conclusion. Rather the rumored impropriety was *adultery*. In trying to reconstruct the events that describe the emergence of plural marriage in Joseph Smith's life, this is an important distinction.

As noted above, it appears that Oliver Cowdery may have been a primary source of the rumors of Joseph's alleged adultery. Apparently, he either did not know of the actual marriage ceremony or, if he was aware, he did not think it legitimate. How far Oliver's rumors had spread is not clear. In

---

38. J. H. Beadle, "Jackson County," 4.

39. Anthony Metcalf, *Ten Years before the Mast*, 72.

40. According to Samuel H. Smith, Journal, June 24, 1832: "In Boston. Held a meeting at Fanny Brewers." They also held other meetings at Fanny Brewer's on June 25, 27, July 1, 8, and on other dates. Samuel's entry for July 29, 1832, reads: "Held a meeting at Sister Brewer's. Preaching in the forenoon and then baptized two, Fanny Brewer and Mary Voce."

41. Fanny Brewer, quoted in John C. Bennett, *The History of the Saints: Or an Exposé of Joe Smith and Mormonism*, 85–86; emphasis mine. It is doubtful that Brewer had firsthand knowledge of the event, since Fanny Alger was not an orphan but a housemaid in the Smith home. In 1889, dissident Benjamin Winchester wrote a reminiscence about "Primitive Mormonism" that was published in the *Salt Lake Tribune*: "[In 1835] there was a good deal of scandal prevalent among a number of Saints concerning Joseph's licentious conduct, this more especially among the women. Joseph's name was then connected with scandalous relations with two or three families." Winchester, "Primitive Mormonism—Personal Narrative of It," 2. Winchester was present in Kirtland during the 1835–37 period, but he was born August 6, 1817; thus, his youth would have likely prevented him from becoming a confidante of Joseph Smith regarding his first plural marriage. Furthermore, Winchester's recollection of scandal "with two or three families" is unsubstantiated by any other witness. It appears Winchester was repeating rumors he had heard, rather than recording firsthand recollections.

September of 1837, Oliver's brother Warren Cowdery, who was the editor of the Church newspaper, *Messenger and Advocate*, wrote an open letter "To the Inhabitants of Milton and Palmyra, Portage County Ohio" defending the character of Joseph Smith against "rumors [that] were afloat . . . that were derogatory" to him.[42] He does not identify the rumors as being specific allegations of either adultery or polygamy, but it seems doubtful that Warren would have defended the Prophet if he believed him guilty of sexual misconduct.[43]

On November 2, 1837, a special council of Church members and leaders was convened in Far West. A number of business items were discussed and resolved, except for one. Joseph Smith recorded: "All difficulties were satisfactorily settled except a matter between Oliver Cowdery, Thomas B. Marsh, and myself, which was referred to us with the agreement that our settlement of the affair would be sufficient for the council."[44]

The issue was not resolved quickly or easily. Two and a half months later on January 21, 1838, Oliver wrote stiffly to Joseph Smith clarifying the depth of their estrangement: "I hear from Kirtland, by the last letters, that you have publicly said, that when you were here I confessed to you that I had willfully lied about you—this compels me to ask you to correct that statement, and give me an explanation—until then you and myself are two."[45] Apparently Joseph had previously combated the rumors that Oliver had started by saying Oliver had admitted to him (Joseph) that he (Oliver) had lied. Oliver wrote to his brother, Warren A. Cowdery, that same day:

> As God is to judge my soul at the last day, and as I hope for salvation in the world to come, I never confessed, intimated, \or admitted/ that I ever willfully lied about him. When he was here we had some conversation in which in every instance I did not fail to affirm that what I had said was strictly true. A dirty, nasty, filthy scrape ["affair" is written over scrape] of his and Fanny Alger's was talked over in which I strictly declared that I had never deviated from the truth on the matters, and as I supposed was admitted by himself.[46]

---

42. [Warren Cowdery], "To the Inhabitants of Milton and Palmyra, Portage County Ohio," 566.

43. Warren Cowdery mentioned polygamy only once in his editorials. In the February 1837 issue of the *Messenger and Advocate*, he referred to Old Testament marital practices: "Polygamy and concubinage were allowable, but adultery was discountenanced." "Ancient History," 455.

44. Cannon and Cook, *Far West Record*, 120; see also *History of the Church*, 2:521.

45. Oliver Cowdery, Letter to Joseph Smith, January 21, 1838; copied into a letter of Oliver Cowdery to Warren A. Cowdery for the same date, Oliver Cowdery Letterbook, 80, original at Huntington Library. In "Letters of Oliver Cowdery," 80–83. In *New Mormon Studies: A Comprehensive Resource Library*; emphasis mine. It is not known if Joseph ever received the original letter.

46. Ibid.

Excerpt from Oliver Cowdery's letterbook copied by his nephew, Warren F. Cowdery. Photo courtesy of the Huntington Library.

Evidently this letter was copied by Oliver's nephew, Warren F. Cowdery (son of Warren A. Cowdery), into Oliver's letterbook, before Oliver sent it to Joseph—and the original letter is not among Joseph Smith's surviving papers. Oliver's level of participation with the transcription process is unknown. He may have been absent and uninvolved, or he may have been closely monitoring the process when the copy was made.

Concerning this letter, Don Bradley has written:

> Though Cowdery's letter, with its talk of Smith's "dirty, nasty, filthy affair," would seem to explicitly identify the relationship as an extramarital affair, it does not. The letter stops short of an accusation of adultery. The key word is "affair." Although it has hitherto escaped comment, that word in Oliver's January 21, 1838 letter *overwrites* a pre-existing word. An examination of the overwriting on the manuscript letter, in the Oliver Cowdery Letterbook at the Huntington Library . . . confirms that the copyist first wrote another word after "dirty, nasty, filthy" and then replaced it with "affair." The original, underlying word appears to have been "scrape," a word also used in the trial testimony to narrate Cowdery's description of the trouble Smith and Alger had gotten themselves into.[47]

In the nineteenth century, both "scrape" and "affair" had similar meanings.[48] "Scrape" is no longer in current use and, as noted, "affair" has acquired

---

47. Don Bradley, "Mormon Polygamy before Nauvoo? The Relationship of Joseph Smith and Fanny Alger," 32.

48. The 1828 edition of Webster's *American Dictionary of the English Language* provides three definitions for "affair": "1. Business of any kind; that which is done, or is to be done; a word of very indefinite and undefinable signification. In the plural, it denotes transactions in general; as human affairs; political or ecclesiastical affairs: also the business or concerns of an individual; as, his affairs are embarrassed. 2. Matters; state; condition of business or concerns. 3. In the singular, it is used for a private dispute, or duel; as, an affair of honor; and sometimes a partial engagement of troops." Definitions for "scrape" from the same dictionary include: "difficulty; perplexity;

Cropped letters from the same page spliced together demonstrate the word underlying the overwritten "affair" is "scrape." Photo courtesy of the Huntington Library.

the almost exclusive meaning of extramarital sex. As noted above, Oliver's misconduct in 1830 was referred to as an "affair" by the Far West High Council in 1832, even though sexual impropriety was not part of his alleged misconduct. The 1830s definition of the word did not include or imply a sexual relationship.

Regrettably, several authors have abused the quotation (probably without having checked the original handwriting) by only citing the overwritten word "affair" (a word that cannot be directly traced to Oliver Cowdery) rather than "scrape," which was the first word transcribed. They also commonly apply twentieth-century interpretations of "affair" that include sexual immorality. Together these two processes have created a widespread interpretation of the Alger-Smith relationship as an extramarital sexual relationship. Based on this observation, some have concluded that Joseph was capable of arranging sexual trysts when the opportunity arose. However, as demonstrated, the manuscript documentation is at best ambiguous, if not contradictory.

Refuting the Rumors of Adultery

Evidence indicates that Joseph tried to quiet Oliver's allegations and make amends.[49] The January 21, 1838, letter quoted above explains Oliver's view of what transpired: "Just before leaving, he [Joseph] wanted to drop every past thing, in which had been a difficulty or difference—he called witnesses to the fact, gave me his hand in their presence, and I might have supposed of an honest man, calculated to say nothing of former matters."[50] Oliver bristled under the idea that Joseph had publicly declared he had lied and asked the Prophet to correct the misinformation and provide an explanation. In this

---

distress; that which harnesses." While either could be applied to a sexual relationship, neither conveyed the same meaning as having an "affair" does in today's vernacular.

49. Historian John J. Stewart, *Joseph Smith the Mormon Prophet*, 104, asserted: "Years later Cowdery told a Church audience that he, rather than Joseph, had been at fault." Stewart provides no documentation, nor have I located any evidence that supports this position.

50. Oliver Cowdery, Letter to Joseph Smith, January 21, 1838.

same letter, he declares to Joseph saying they are "two"—meaning decisively alienated from each other (see D&C 38:27 recorded January 2, 1831).

However, Joseph's disagreement with Oliver regarding Fanny Alger was not the only problem brewing. On April 12, 1838, the Far West High Council brought nine charges against Associate President Cowdery, although they did not include immorality or adultery. The most obvious explanation is that Oliver was not involved in such behaviors; or possibly, Joseph feared that accusations of immorality might prompt Cowdery to make similar public disclosures against him personally.[51]

The second of the nine charges against Cowdery read: "For seeking to destroying the character of President Joseph Smith jr. by falsly insinuating that he was guilty of adultery etc." During the trial, George W. Harris, identified as the tenth high councilor, testified: "He [Oliver] seemed to insinuate that Joseph Smith jr was guilty of adultery." Apostle David W. Patten similarly reported: "He [Patten] went to Oliver Cowdery to enquire of him if a certain story was true respecting J. Smith's committing adultery with a certain girl, when he turned on his heel and insinuated as though he was guilty; he [Cowdery] then went on and gave a history of some circumstances respecting the adultery scrape stating that no doubt it was true." Thomas B. Marsh, president of the Quorum of the Twelve and a witness in the proceedings, provided secondhand corroboration of Patten's account with additional details: "David W. Patten asked Oliver Cowdery if he Joseph Smith jr had confessed to his wife that he was guilty of adultery with a certain girl, when Oliver Cowdery cocked up his eye very knowingly and hesitated to answer the question, saying he did not know as he was bound to answer the question yet conveyed the idea it was true." Marsh continued: "He [Marsh] heard a conversation take place between Joseph Smith and Oliver Cowdery when J. Smith asked him if he had ever confessed to him that he was guilty of adultery, when after a considerable winking etc. he said no. Joseph then asked him if he ever told him that he confessed to any body, when he answered No."[52] Doubtless Oliver's winking undermined the validity of his denial and was construed as an affirmation of the allegation. At one point, Joseph addressed the assembled high councilors: Samuel H. Smith, Jared Carter, Thomas Grover, Isaac Higbee, Levi Jackman, Solomon Hancock, George Morey, Newel Knight, George M. Hinkle, George W. Harris, Elias Higbee, and John Murdock who was "President of the High Council." Joseph described Oliver Cowdery as "his bosom friend, therefore he intrusted him with many things," although no additional details were provided.[53]

---

51. See discussion in Bachman, "A Study of the Mormon Practice of Plural Marriage before the Death of Joseph Smith," 80–86.

52. Cannon and Cook, *Far West Record*, 167–68.

53. Ibid., 168.

Toward the end of the meeting, the delicate issue of Oliver's allegation regarding Joseph's adultery was directly raised. The minutes recount: "He [Joseph] then gave a history respecting the girl business."[54] Exactly what the Prophet said to the council members is not recorded, but it seems likely his "history" included a denial of any adulterous relations. If a marriage ceremony had been performed between him and Fanny, Joseph would have considered the union to be legitimate in the eyes of God and therefore not adultery.

According to all available records, no high council member called for a Church court to investigate allegations of Joseph Smith's improper moral conduct. It appears that they would not have tolerated fornication or adulterous behavior in any Church member including their prophet-leader. This is important because, in that setting, the Far West High Council had authority to initiate proceedings against even the Church president should he transgress (D&C 107:82, 74–76).

One explanation of the proceedings is that Joseph realized anew that the high council membership and the Church in general were not ready for a restoration of polygamy. As a result, he did not mention it, nor was plural marriage brought up for discussion before the Far West High Council. One wonders how the Prophet might have responded to a specific question about whether he had married Fanny polygamously. Regardless, Joseph's explanation apparently satisfied the Far West High Council members and Bishop Edward Partridge, who was also present.

Although Oliver was not in attendance, six of the nine charges, including the second, were sustained and he was excommunicated.[55] By judging Oliver guilty of "*falsly* insinuating that he [Joseph Smith] was guilty of adultery etc." (emphasis mine) the Far West High Council was essentially exonerating the Prophet of any charges of adultery.[56]

Subsequently, Joseph took action to suppress possible gossip among Church members that he had ever confessed to adultery. At his request, the next issue of the *Elder's Journal* published three statements by Church leaders

---

54. Ibid.

55. The nine charges were (1) "for stirring up the enemy to persecute the brethren," (2) by "falsly insinuating that he [Joseph Smith] was guilty of adultery," (3) for "not attending meetings," (4) for "declaring that he would not be governed by any ecclesiastical authority," (5) "for selling lands in Jackson Country," (6) "for writing and sending an insulting letter to President T. B. Marsh," (7) "for leaving the calling . . . for the sake of filthy lucre," (8) for "being connected in the 'Bogus' business," (9) "for dishonestly Retaining notes after they had been paid." Charges 1, 2, 3, 7, 8, 9, were sustained; 4, 5, 6 were not sustained.

56. A pamphlet entitled *Defense in a Rehearsal of My Grounds for Separating Myself from the Latter Day Saints* (Norton, Ohio: Pressley's Job Office, 1839), purportedly written by Oliver Cowdery, has been shown to be a forgery. Its true author is unknown.

and men present at the April 12 high council meeting, quashing any rumors that might have originated with Oliver Cowdery. The first was by Thomas B. Marsh, president of the Quorum of the Twelve Apostles:

> This may certify that I heard O. [Oliver] Cowdery say to Joseph Smith, Jr., while at George W. Harris' house in Far West, that he (Joseph) never confessed to him, (Oliver) that he was guilty of the crime alleged to him. And O. Cowdery gave me to understand that Joseph Smith, Jr. never acknowledged to him that he ever confessed to anyone, that he was guilty of the above crime. —Thomas B. Marsh.

George W. Harris, a member of the Far West High Council wrote a similar denial:

> This may certify that I heard Oliver Cowdery say in my house, that Joseph Smith, Jr. never confessed to him that he was guilty of the crime alleged against him and Joseph asked if he ever said to him (Oliver) that he confessed to anyone that he (Joseph) was guilty of the above crime, and Oliver, after some hesitation, answered no.

George M. Hinkle, also a member of the Far West High Council, corroborated:

> This may certify that having heard the report about the crime above referred to, I asked Oliver Cowdery last fall when Joseph Smith was in the Far West, if the report was true, for said I, if it is, as he is to be presented before the church, I wish to know of the truth of this matter beforehand. And he gave me to understand, either in plain words or implications, that it was false. I bear this testimony for the good of the honest hearted in the east and elsewhere, and for the good of Brother Joseph Smith, Jr. Brother Marsh will please copy this in the letter to the east and keep the original here.[57]

Richard Lyman Bushman, Joseph Smith's biographer, summarized:

> He [Joseph Smith] contended that he had never confessed to adultery. . . . In contemporaneous documents, only one person, Cowdery, believed that Joseph had had an affair with Fanny Alger. Others may have heard the rumors, but none joined Cowdery in making accusations. David Patten, who made inquiries in Kirtland, concluded the rumors were untrue. No one proposed to put Joseph on trial for adultery. Only Cowdery, who was leaving the Church, asserted Joseph's involvement. On his part, Joseph never denied a relationship with Alger, but insisted it was not adulterous. He wanted it on record that he had never confessed to such a sin. Presumably, he felt innocent because he had married Alger.[58]

---

57. "Minutes of the Proceedings of the Committee of the Whole Church in Zion," 45.
58. Richard Lyman Bushman, *Joseph Smith: Rough Stone Rolling*, 324–25.

Although Oliver's faith must have been shaken by his perception of Joseph's misbehavior and by what he would have considered betrayal and alienation, Fawn Brodie observed: "Cowdery had seen visions that were more real to him than meat and drink."[59] Despite his misgivings concerning polygamy, Oliver Cowdery's previous experiences prompted him to be rebaptized on November 12, 1848, by Orson Hyde, who was then a polygamist. Oliver had expressed a desire to eventually join the Saints in the West but died on March 3, 1850, before being able to make the trek. It appears, however, that he never was reconciled to the practice of plural marriage and undoubtedly would have confronted additional challenges with the new marriage practices had he lived long enough to join the polygamous Saints in the West.

No Rumors of Polygamy

As noted above, a review of available evidence suggests that some rumors of adultery involving Joseph Smith circulated in Kirtland after 1835–37, although listeners did not always take them seriously. But importantly, rumors of *polygamy* were apparently unknown among the Saints and nonmembers alike.[60] This pattern is consistent among loyal Church members who provided depositions, sometimes unwillingly, in the Temple Lot case between the Church of Christ (Temple Lot) and the RLDS Church in 1892. Emily Dow Partridge, daughter of Edward Partridge, the first presiding bishop of the Church, who died in 1840, reported that she "never heard anything at all

---

59. Fawn M. Brodie, *No Man Knows My History: The Life of Joseph Smith, the Mormon Prophet*, 208.

60. Juanita Brooks, *On the Ragged Edge: The Life and Times of Dudley Leavitt*, 53–54, includes an interesting account written by Rachel Judd Hamblin (born 1822 in Canada) titled "Polygamy in Missouri": "My sister Mary was married to Thomas B. Marsh, one of the first Quorum of the Twelve chosen in 1835. He was a good man, very loyal and active. When the law of plural marriage was started, I became his first and only plural wife. But many other things entered in, and he became estranged and dropped out, so that he did not come West." Some of the details in this account are problematic. For example, Thomas B. Marsh was excommunicated in 1839. If this recollection was accurate, plural marriage (beyond Joseph's marriage to Fanny Alger) would have been started in Ohio, not Illinois. However, it appears that Rachel's memory is faulty. Thomas B. Marsh was never a polygamist. He did in fact travel west in 1857, dying there in 1866. Rachel's sister, Mary Judd, was actually married to Apostle John E. Page, not Marsh. Page, indeed, was a polygamist in Nauvoo but did not remain with the Saints nor travel to the Rocky Mountains. Mary Page, who was violently opposed to plural marriage, remained in the Midwest, married William Eaton, and joined the Reorganized Church of Jesus Christ of Latter Day Saints in 1874. I am indebted to Don Bradley for his detective work in understanding this account. Todd Compton believes that either Dudley Leavitt or Juanita Brooks was the source of the confusion, not Rachel. Todd Compton, "Civilizing the Ragged Edge," 155–98.

about it [plural marriage] during the lifetime of my father.... I am certain that I never heard him [Joseph Smith] teach or preach polygamy in any way at all."[61] This chronological distinction is important, since Emily became one of Joseph Smith's plural wives in Nauvoo. Martin Harris left the Church in 1837. In an 1875 discussion, he assured his interviewer "that polygamy was not taught or practiced by Joseph Smith nor was it a doctrine of the Church in his day."[62] In an 1884 debate between Edward L. Kelley, future presiding bishop of the RLDS Church, and Church of Christ (Disciples) Clark Braden, who took the position that Joseph Smith was a womanizer in Kirtland and Nauvoo, Church member F. C. Rich testified on June 10, 1884:

> Q. Did you ever live in Kirtland?
> A. Yes, sir. I came here in 1831.
>
> Q. Did you know, or were you acquainted with Joseph Smith, Martin Harris and Sidney Rigdon, or either of them? Did you know their reputation for truth and veracity in the neighborhood [of Kirtland, Ohio] at the time they lived here? And were you acquainted with their moral character?
> A. I knew nothing against them. I was but a boy however, but the outsiders persecuted them on account of their religious views.
>
> Q. You had an opportunity to know?
> A. Yes, sir; my father was here in an early day and was connected with the church.
>
> Q. Were you in their meetings frequently?
> A. Yes, sir. Brought right up in the church. The first meeting I recollect very much about was after the temple was finished. I attended meetings right along after it was completed. I was too young during its building to take any particular notice outside.
>
> Q. Did you ever see anything of an immoral tendency in the meetings?
> A. Nothing that could be considered immoral. They shouted Hosannah, and seemed to enjoy their religion; and, of course, got excited as other people do....
>
> Q. You may state whether they believed in having more than one wife?
> A. I never heard they were in favor of anything of the kind here.
>
> Q. You heard them talk with your father, heard the elders preach, was in their meetings, and mixed with them in all the affairs of life; if there had been anything wrong or bad in their teachings and habits would you not have known it?
> A. I am perfectly satisfied that the church did not teach or practice polygamy, or any other immoral doctrine while they were in Kirtland.[63]

---

61. Emily D. P. Young, Deposition, Temple Lot Transcript, Respondent's Testimony, Part 3, p. 355, questions 103, 108.
62. Simon Smith, Letter to Joseph Smith III, December 29, 1880.
63. E. L. Kelley and Clark Braden, *Public Discussion of the Issues between the Reorganized Church*

As a youth, F. C. Rich may have missed discussions of plural marriage, but it seems likely that his involvement would have placed him in a position to hear any scandalous whispers.

Nonmember A. E. Sanborn came to Kirtland in 1836. When asked if Church members were ever practicing polygamy, he replied: "Not that I knew of." When further questioned whether he would have known about it if it were occurring, he responded: "I ought to, my father was a Mormon. . . . I attended meetings both in Nauvoo and here in Kirtland, both in the evenings and on the Sabbath, and I never heard anything of polygamy at all until after Smith's death."[64] In 1844, dissenter Benjamin Winchester wrote that nothing was taught regarding plural marriage, "from the time of the organization of the Church up to the year 1841." It was only after 1841 that, "this flagitious doctrine of polygamy was introduced into the church."[65]

Adultery Rumors Quickly Died

It appears that most individuals who believed the adultery gossip left the Church at Kirtland. Those who stayed with the body of the Saints included two groups: those who disbelieved the charges, and perhaps a dozen insiders who understood the Smith-Alger relationship to be a genuine plural marriage. Eliza R. Snow, who lived with the Smith family in the spring of 1836 and probably saw firsthand the conflict surrounding Fanny Alger, wrote three years later in 1839: "I now anticipate your question, Do you yet believe Joseph Smith is a prophet? I have not seen or heard anything which caus'd me to doubt it even for a moment: If possible, I have better testimony that J. Smith is a prophet, than that Jeremiah was one, altho' he has not been kept in prison quite so long."[66] Assuming that she was privy to the Fanny Alger relationship, it obviously did not affect her belief in Joseph Smith.

The shrewd and discerning William Law arrived in Nauvoo in November of 1839, apparently unaware of any Kirtland rumors of adultery or polyga-

---

of Jesus Christ of Latter Day Saints and the Church of Christ (Disciples) Held in Kirtland, Ohio, Beginning February 12, and Closing March 8, 1884 between E. L. Kelley, of the Reorganized Church of Jesus Christ of Latter Day Saints and Clark Braden, of the Church of Christ, 395. I have been unable to ascertain the full name of "F. C. Rich" or any biographical information about him.

64. Ibid., 394.

65. Benjamin Winchester, "Letter to the Editor." Many years later, Winchester, "Primitive Mormonism—Personal Narrative of It," 2, explained: "Up to the year 1843 'spiritual marriage' or polygamy had never been preached or inculcated as a doctrine of the church. Prior to that year my experience had been that the church was fully as strict and as pure with respect to virtue and morality as any other religious organization."

66. "Eliza R. Snow to Esqr. Streator," February 22, 1839, in F. Mark McKiernan, ed., "Eliza R. Snow Letter from Missouri," 549.

my. After observing the Prophet for one year, he wrote to his close friend and one-time idol, Isaac Russell, who was in the process of apostatizing: "It is needless for me to express my regret that you remain so long from the Body of the Church. . . . I have carefully watched his [Joseph Smith's] movements since I have been here, and I assure you I have found him honest and honourable in all our transactions which have been very considerable I believe he is an honest upright man, and as to his follies let who ever is guiltless throw the first stone at him, I shant do it."[67] In an 1871 letter, Law, who had become a counselor in the First Presidency in January 1841, further reflected: "In 1842 I had not heard of such teaching [of polygamy]. . . . I think it was in 1843 that I first knew of the 'plurality doctrine.' I believe, however, it existed possibly as early as 1840."[68]

When asked about the specific problems that Joseph Smith experienced in Kirtland, Williard Griffith, who was baptized in 1831, recounted no adultery or polygamy allegations. He identified other problems as the cause of the dissension that tore at the community:

> Some of the people were not satisfied with their position in the Church and others were not satisfied with the doctrine and so forth. There was dissatisfaction there at that time for five of the Quorum of the Twelve apostatised at one time and left the Church. . . . They persecuted him principally as I got the idea, because of his personal actions and the people or some of them were dissatisfied with his dignity, and they dissented from it, and were disfellowshipped.

He added: "I heard things said about him [Joseph Smith] from the very origin of his history, and I heard a great many things that had no grounds for being said whatever, and which were false hoods and proved to be so."[69] In other words, if he heard rumors about Fanny Alger, he rejected them as not credible.

Apparently the "whisperings" or "excitement" did not spread to the Saints in Missouri either. I have been unable to identify even one account from someone living in Missouri in the 1830s who remembered hearing about polygamy or Joseph Smith and Fanny Alger at that time. When asked in 1892: "Did you not hear some rumors or whisperings of the plural wife doctrine in 1838 in Far West, or in Caldwell County [Missouri], when you were there?" Bathsheba W. Smith responded: "No, sir . . . I am positive of that for I know I never heard of it."[70] Concerning teachings about the doctrine of polygamy

---

67. William Law, Letter to "Bro. Russell, Far West, Missouri," November 29, 1840, quoted in Lyndon W. Cook, "'Brother Joseph Is Truly A Wonderful Man, He Is All We Could Wish a Prophet to Be': Pre-1844 Letters of William Law," 217–18.

68. Stenhouse, *The Rocky Mountain Saints*, 198–99.

69. Williard Griffith, Deposition, Temple Lot Transcript, Part 4, pp. 68–69, questions 625–33, 639.

70. Bathsheba W. Smith, Deposition, ibid., Part 3, p. 295, questions 65–66.

during that period, Joseph Kingsbury agreed: "We never heard anything of the kind in those days at all."[71] Commenting on the Missouri problems in 1838, an Illinois paper wrote: "It has been stated by divers men, who stand fair in society, that the present difficulties with the Mormons amounts to a political quarrel."[72] Apparently they were unaware of any moral issues.

Mercy Rachel Fielding Thompson, who joined the Church in Canada in 1836 and moved to Far West, Missouri, recalled: "It [plural marriage] was not either taught or practiced until along about '41 or '42,—I would not say which,—but it was never taught or practiced until about that time. . . . I did not hear anything about it before 1841."[73] Lorenzo Snow, who joined the Church in 1836 at Kirtland, was asked: "When you were out in 1839 [serving as a missionary], were you instructed with reference to the law of marriage, to teach plurality of wives, or monogamy?" He answered: "No sir, I received no instructions to teach plural marriage . . . I never once heard of it."[74]

Cyrus Wheelock was baptized in September of 1839 while living in Pike County, Missouri. In 1892 he testified that he "never heard anything about it [plural marriage] at that time. . . . There was no practice of that kind then that I knew anything of."[75] When asked: "Did you think when you joined the church that you could be permitted to have more wives than one?" he answered: "I did not know anything about it at all. They preached the doctrine of the church to me, and I accepted it, and there was nothing said about it at that time."[76] John H. Carter also testified: "The polygamy doctrine was never taught in the early days up to 1843. I lived most [of] two years with Joseph Smith in the one place, and I have heard him preach, and the rest of the elders, Hyrum Smith[,] Oliver Cowdery, and the rest of them, and I never heard the doctrine of polygamy taught by any of them,—never in the world did I hear it taught." [77]

The Gentile Press and Other Writers Were Unaware

Among all the individuals and groups that failed to accuse Joseph Smith of either adultery or polygamy, the most significant was the media. Researcher Don Bradley and I made an exhaustive search of periodicals, books, and pamphlets published prior to July 1842 (when John C. Bennett made his first claims

---

71. Joseph C. Kingsbury, Deposition, ibid., Part 3, p. 208, question 665.

72. Article from *The Missourian*, reprinted under the title of "From the Missourian," *Peoria Register and North Western Gazetteer*, November 10, 1838.

73. Mercy Rachel Thompson, Deposition, Temple Lot Transcript, Part 3, pp. 238, 241, 245, questions 21, 46–52, 134–35.

74. Lorenzo Snow, Deposition, ibid., Part 3, p. 116, question 124–26.

75. Cyrus Wheelock, Deposition, ibid., Part 3, p. 544, questions 186–92.

76. Ibid., p. 544, question 197.

77. John H. Carter, Deposition, ibid., Complainant's Testimony, Part 2, pp. 375–76, question 25.

Oliver Cowdery and the Aftermath 149

in letters to the *Sangamo Journal*) to discover any published allegations of either polygamy or adultery directed toward Joseph Smith during that period. We also examined the voluminous data provided by Stanley S. Ivins in Notebooks 1–15.[78] Not a single allegation has been located. A review of that literature demonstrates that writers and newspaper reporters sometimes mentioned the "Mormons" and Joseph Smith in their periodicals.[79] Scattered articles referred to polygamy and "spiritual wifery."[80] Nevertheless, available evidence shows that journalists had not put the two subjects, Mormons and polygamy, together prior to 1842.

For example, the subscriber list in the *Cleveland Liberalist* for late 1836 and early 1837 included the names of several Kirtland men including Latter-day Saints.[81] An article in the February 4, 1837, issue, penned by a correspondent named "Enquirer," proposed to abolish the law against polygamy:

> It would be more desirable to be the second or even the third wife of a generous man than to remain an old maid, neglected and laughed at. It would relieve one wife from the burden of bearing many children and give the husband who had a barren wife the chance of having children by another. It would eminently lessen prostitution in one sex and ranging in the other. It would be no more expensive for a man to have two wives than to have one wife and hire a seamstress. It appears that a host of evils which now exist would at once cease.[82]

However, the context of "Enquirer's" proposal did not mention the Mormons, but the editor was undoubtedly aware of them since several had subscriptions to his paper. Eva Pancoast, in her 1929 master's thesis, accused Joseph Smith or some other Latter-day Saint of authoring the letter, but no evidence exists to support such a claim.[83] It seems obvious that if any tales of polygamy and Joseph Smith existed anywhere close to the ears of the *Cleveland*

---

78. Stanley S. Ivins Collection, Notebooks, 1–15.

79. For references to Joseph Smith, see *Adams Sentinel* (Gettysburg, Pa.), August 15, 1836; *Republican Compiler* (Gettysburg, Pa.), April 17, 1838; *Huron Reflector* (Norwalk, Ohio), September 3, 1839 and December 21, 1841; *Madison Express*, September 29, 1841; *Ohio Atlas and Elyria Advertiser*, December 1, 1841. For articles mentioning the Mormons, see *Huron Reflector*, November 28, 1831, May 20, 1834, December 8, 1840; *[Canton] Ohio Repository*, September 1, 1836; *Tioga Eagle* (Wellsboro, Pa.), August 18, 1841.

80. For references to polygamy, see *Sandusky [Ohio] Clarion*, September 28, 1831; *Star and Republican Banner* (Gettysburg, Pa.), July 23, 1833, August 29, 1836; *Alton [Illinois] Telegraph*, February 1, 1837; *Bangor [Maine] Daily Whig and Courier*, October 15, 1838; *Hagerstown [Maryland] Mail*, October 19, 1838; *Tioga Eagle* (Wellsboro, Pa.), October 2, 1839; *Adams Sentinel* (Gettysburg, Pa.), November 30, 1840.

81. "Subscriptions," *Cleveland Liberalist*, December 24, 1836, 11; February 10, 1838, 162.

82. Enquirer (pseud.), "Subscriptions," *Cleveland Liberalist* 1 (February 4, 1837): 164.

83. Eva L. Pancoast, "Mormons at Kirtland," 109.

Liberalist writer, he would have included—even exploited—them. Other newspapers would have been equally eager to republish those details.[84]

A New York City newspaper article written by an unnamed non-Mormon correspondent living in the western United States indicates that neither polygamy nor adultery rumors had reached Missouri in 1839:

> I have yet to learn that their [Mormon] faith taught them immorality. I have yet to learn that it encouraged disobedience to the laws or encroachments on the rights of any fellow-citizen.
>
> The Mormons were in truth a moral, orderly and sober population. They were industrious farmers, and ingenious mechanics. They were busy about their own affairs, and never intermeddled in the concerns of their neighbors. They were exceedingly peaceful and averse to strife, quarrels and violence. They had established schools, they encouraged education; and they all had the rudiments of learning taught under our school system at the East . . .
>
> They [the Missourians] were sagacious enough to know that their acts should have a "show of virtue," and they accordingly began to misrepresent the Mormons. The charges were at first general. The Mormons were a "mighty *mean* people." They were "great fools"—which in common acceptation is about as bad as being great villains. Then they were thievish (how ludicrous, when the Anti-Mormons had hardly anything worth stealing!) They "tampered with the negroes" . . . Finally, a fellow burnt his own corn crib and charged it on the Mormons.[85]

This unnamed writer seemed familiar with the Saints and was obviously willing to defend them, but he was apparently unaware of any polygamous activities among them including its president or most certainly he would have incorporated that information, if only to deny it.[86]

---

84. Four years later in 1841, antagonistic author E. G. Lee published *The Mormons, or, Knavery Exposed*. Despite an apparent desire to disparage the Latter-day Saints, he made no comments about alleged polygamy or sexual immorality among the Mormons. It seems likely he would have done so had any such rumors or reputed behaviors been whispered or otherwise circulated.

85. "From the *Boston Atlas*: Missouri and the Mormons. Letter from a Gentleman at the West to his friend in Boston," *Emancipator*, March 25, 1839; emphasis in original.

86. As late as 1881, newspapers bent on exposing Mormon polygamy were unaware of the Alger-Smith relationship. An article in the *Anti-Polygamy Standard* for January 1881 wrote that Louisa Beaman's 1841 sealing was Joseph Smith's first polygamous marriage. However, after recounting the event, the writer hedged: "These were the first plural marriages [in 1841] of which anything authentic is known, although the fact was well established that if he had been consistent, Joseph should long before that have been sealed to a large number of women." Historicus [pseud.], "Sketches from the History of Polygamy, The First Polygamous Marriages," 1.

Equally, a review of the Church's publications in Ohio at that time fails to demonstrate an emphasis on marital issues or a defensive stance to allegations of sexual misconduct.[87] The *Messenger and Advocate*, between October 1834 and September 1837, contained only three references to "adultery" and three to "polygamy."[88] Similarly, the *Elder's Journal* printed in 1837 and 1838 in Kirtland contained two references to "adultery," two to "more wives than one," and none to "polygamy."[89]

In summary, no matter what level of excitement actually existed in Kirtland regarding Joseph Smith and Fanny Alger or the topic of polygamy in the 1830s, the alleged excitement evidently never expanded to the newspapers of the day. Editors, then as now, were hungry for titillating gossip and information that would sell their papers. Yet not a single accusation has been located prior to July 1842. Tyler Parson, author of the 1842 publication, *Mormon Fanaticism Exposed*, wrote: "I am not aware that the Mormons claim the privilege of polygamy, as yet. I presume they will when they revise their creed."[90]

Summary

As the years passed, it appears that the knowledge of Joseph Smith's first polygamous marriage came full circle. I accept the evidence indicating that it was Joseph Smith's first plural marriage and that he and Fanny considered it as a valid relationship. Nevertheless, it initially created rumors of adultery. Then after the practice of plural marriage became known in Nauvoo and Utah, authors looked back to Kirtland and wrote, not of adultery but of polygamy. Despite the absence of credible evidence of Kirtland polygamy, many writers embraced unsubstantiated claims, shaping them into false traditions like the notion that Joseph Smith had a reputation during the 1830s that included polygamy.

---

87. The Church's first newspaper, *The Evening and the Morning Star*, published in Independence, Missouri, between June 1832 and July 1833 and then in Kirtland, Ohio, from January to September 1834, contains no references to "adultery" or "polygamy."

88. "Adultery" is mentioned in the *Messenger and Advocate* in "Let Every Man Learn His Duty," 2, no. 4 (January 1836): 250; "Persecution," 3, no. 4 (January 1837): 436, and Warren Cowdery, "Ancient History," 3, no. 4 (February 1837): 455. "Polygamy" is referred to in "General Assembly," 1, no. 2 (August 1835): 163; "Ancient History," 3, no. 4 (February 1837): 455, and "To Our Readers," 3, no. 7 (May 1837): 511.

89. "Adultery" is mentioned in twice in the *Elder's Journal*: "To Subscribers of the Journal," 1, no. 4 (August 1838): 59, and "More Wives than One" (editorial), 1, no. 2 (November 1837): 28, and "Editorial," 1, no. 3 (July 1838): 43.

90. Tyler Parson, *Mormon Fanaticism Exposed: A Compendium of the Book of Mormon or Joseph Smith's Golden Bible*, 5.

Chapter 7

Oliver Cowdery's Article on "Marriage"

Over the past decades, several writers have alleged a connection between Joseph Smith's relationship with Fanny Alger and Section CI (101) in the 1835 Doctrine and Covenants called the article on "Marriage."[1] Such assertions imply that the Prophet was battling reports of polygamy at that time; they also influence these scholarly attempts at constructing the chronology of the Alger-Smith union.

August 17, 1835, General Assembly

In 1818, Joseph Smith's maternal uncle, Stephen Mack, settled the township of Pontiac, Michigan. Shortly after the Church was organized in New York in 1830, one of Stephen's daughters, Almira Mack, traveled to visit her relatives in Manchester, New York, and was baptized into the new church, making her the first Michigan Mormon.[2] Robert Church, a writer for the Pontiac *Daily Press*, wrote in 1940: "When rich, handsome, adventurous Col. Stephen Mack founded Pontiac he also set the stage for the advent of the Mormons making Pontiac the earliest citadel in this part of the West. . . . Lucy Smith, mother of Joseph Smith, the Mormon prophet, and sister of Col. Mack, was desirous of founding a church in Pontiac, where fortune had favored her brother and where she had reason to believe there were Indians a plenty who were in sore need of religious teaching."[3] Lucy, accompanied by her son Hyrum and missionaries Lyman Wight, John Corrill, and John Murdock, visited Pontiac in the summer of 1831. Stephen Mack had died years earlier, but his widow Temperance and two daughters were soon baptized.

At his mother's urging, Joseph Smith visited Pontiac in October 1834.[4] The *History of the Church* records, as in Joseph's voice: "Hyrum Smith, and Elders

---

1. Todd Compton, *In Sacred Loneliness: The Plural Wives of Joseph Smith*, 36; George D. Smith, *Nauvoo Polygamy: ". . . but we called it celestial marriage,"* 43; Richard Abanes, *One Nation under Gods: A History of the Mormon Church*, 133.
2. John and Audrey Cumming, "The Saints Come to Michigan," 12–13.
3. Robert Church, "Historical News and Notes," 248–49.
4. Edward Stevenson, Autobiography, 7, and Hilda Faulkner Browne, "The

David Whitmer, Frederick G. Williams, Oliver Cowdery, and Roger Orton, left Kirtland for the purpose of visiting some Saints in the state of Michigan, where, after a tolerably pleasant journey, we arrived at Pontiac on the 20th."[5] Ten months later, Joseph, accompanied by Frederick G. Williams, a counselor in his First Presidency, made a second but very brief visit to Pontiac. Joseph was still in Kirtland on August 10, since he made a complaint before the high council on that date, and the two men returned to Kirtland on August 23.[6]

It appears that, shortly after the Prophet's departure from Kirtland, Oliver Cowdery and Sidney Rigdon hastily called a "General Assembly" of Church leaders and members specifically "for the purpose of examining a book of commandments and covenants, which [had] been compiled and written."[7] The General Assembly, which may have been announced on only twenty-four hours' notice, was held Monday, August 17. Its spur-of-the-moment nature is demonstrated by observing that a puzzling majority of Church leaders were absent. Missing from the meeting were all of the Twelve Apostles, eight of the twelve Kirtland High Council members, nine of the twelve Missouri High Council members, three of the seven Presidents of the Quorum of Seventy, Presiding Bishop Partridge, and, as noted, two of the three members of the First Presidency.[8]

Despite this startling absence of Church leaders, the assembly proceeded to accept the Doctrine and Covenants as a binding religious document for the Latter-day Saints. In addition, an article on "Marriage," written by Oliver Cowdery, was read aloud to the gathering. It specified: "Inasmuch as this Church of Christ has been reproached with the crime of fornication and polygamy, we declare that we believe that one man should have one wife, and one

---

Michigan Mormons," 1985, both refer to this 1834 visit to Pontiac. Unfortunately, neither mentions Joseph's August 1835 visit.

5. Journal History, October 16, 1834; see also *History of the Church*, 2:168.

6. Journal History, August 10 and 23, 1835; see also *History of the Church*, 2:242, 253. Regarding this trip, Richard Van Wagoner writes: "Oliver Cowdery would seem to be the likely person to go with Joseph Smith to Michigan, but his wife Elizabeth gave birth to a daughter, Maria, on 21 August 1835. Rigdon's health is still not good, and so the only other leader aware of the Fanny Alger situation is Frederick G. Williams, who accompanies Joseph to Michigan for this very quick 'missionary trip' (they are back in Kirtland only six days after the conference which has accepted the 'Article on Marriage'). Richard Van Wagoner, Letter to Linda King Newell, n.d., MS 447, Box 11, fd. 4, Linda King Newell Collection. It is unclear why Van Wagoner listed the journey as a "missionary trip"; although missionary work was undoubtedly performed, it may not have been the primary objective.

7. Fred C. Collier, ed., *Kirtland Council Minute Book*, September 19, 1835, 122.

8. H. Michael Marquardt, *The Joseph Smith Revelations: Text and Commentary*, 14; Robert J. Woodford, "The Historical Development of the Doctrine and Covenants," 44.

> ### SECTION CI.
> ### MARRIAGE.
>
> 1 According to the custom of all civilized nations, marriage is regulated by laws and ceremonies: therefore we believe, that all marriages in this church of Christ of Latter Day Saints, should be solemnized in a public meeting, or feast, prepared for that purpose: and that the solemnization should be performed by a presiding high priest, high priest, bishop, elder, or priest, not even prohibiting those persons who are desirous to get married, of being married by other authority. We believe that it is not right to prohibit members of this church from marrying out of the church, if it be their determination so to do, but such persons will be considered weak in the faith of our Lord and Savior Jesus Christ.
>
> 2 Marriage should be celebrated with prayer and thanksgiving; and at the solemnization, the persons to be married, standing together, the man on the right, and the woman on the left, shall be addressed, by the person officiating, as he shall be directed by the holy Spirit; and if there be no legal objections, he shall say, calling each by their names: "You both mutually agree to be each other's companion, husband and wife, observing the legal rights belonging to this condition; that is, keeping yourselves wholly for each other, and from all others, during your lives." And when they have answered "Yes," he shall pronounce them "husband and wife" in the name of the Lord Jesus Christ, and by virtue of the laws of the country and authority vested in him: "may God add his blessings and keep you to fulfill your covenants from henceforth and forever. Amen."
>
> 3 The clerk of every church should keep a record of all marriages, solemnized in his branch.
>
> 4 All legal contracts of marriage made before a person is baptized into this church, should be held sacred and fulfilled. Inasmuch as this church of Christ has been reproached with the crime of fornication, and polygamy: we declare that we believe, that one man should have one wife; and one woman, but one husband, except in case of death, when either is at liberty to marry again. It is not right to persuade a woman to be baptized contrary to the will of her husband, neither is it lawful to influence her to leave her husband. All children are bound by law to obey their parents; and to influence them to embrace any particular faith, or be baptized, or leave their parents without their consent, is unlawful and unjust. We believe that all persons who exercise control over their fellow

Article on "Marriage," Section CI [101] in the 1835 Doctrine and Covenants.

woman but one husband, except in case of death, when either is at liberty to marry again."[9] It was "accepted and adopted and ordered to be printed in said book, by a unanimous vote."[10] Accordingly, the marriage declaration was published in the very next issue of the *Messenger and Advocate* (dated August 1835 but printed sometime in September) and was included in the first edition of the 1835 Doctrine and Covenants as Section CI (101).[11] These circumstances resulting in the hasty approval of the article on "Marriage" raise some significant questions.

Historian Max Parkin wrote: "The 'Article on Marriage' was written because of rumors circulating concerning unorthodox marital relations among the Mormons. Although the Mormons continued to deny polygamy as a principle of faith, the complaint that it was being practiced among them was occasionally raised."[12] The compelling question revolves around the actual source of the alleged rumors and Cowdery's motivations. Was it Oliver Cowdery's actions, Joseph Smith's actions, a general misunderstanding regarding the law of consecration, or the misdeeds of other individual Church members (not involving Oliver Cowdery or Joseph Smith)? Or something else or a combination of these elements? And is Parkin accurate in deducing that rumors of polygamy (rather than other forms of sexual misconduct) prompted Cowdery to pen the article?

---

9. Doctrine and Covenants, 1835, Section CI:4 (p. 251); "General Assembly," *Messenger and Advocate* 1, no. 2 (August 1835): 163; *History of the Church*, 2:247.

10. "General Assembly," 162; *History of the Church*, 2:246.

11. "General Assembly," 162; *Doctrine and Covenants*, 1835, CI (pp. 251–52). Section CI, "The Article on Marriage," became Section 109 in the 1844 edition of the Doctrine and Covenants.

12. Max H Parkin, "Conflict at Kirtland: A Study of the Nature and Causes of External and Internal Conflict of the Mormons in Ohio between 1830 and 1838," 171.

A Reaction to Oliver Cowdery's Behavior?

One explanation for this article's creation (and presence in the LDS Doctrine and Covenants until 1876) dates back to the nineteenth century and accuses Oliver of attempting to cover his own polygamous misconduct; further, this explanation asserts, he deliberately seized an occasion to push its ratification through the hastily assembled General Assembly when Joseph was not present because Joseph was opposed to it.

There are four relevant sources. The earliest public statement seems to have been issued in Brigham Young's October 9, 1869 (Saturday morning) discourse. The *Deseret News* summarized: "President Young made some brief remarks in relation to the 109th section of the Book of Doctrine and Covenants, showing how it was introduced there by Oliver Cowdery, against the wish of the Prophet Joseph."[13] The *Deseret News* promised that "his [Young's] remarks would be published in full," which apparently never happened.[14] Nor was the discourse printed in the *Journal of Discourses*. Brigham Young's comments were no doubt calculated to combat the assertions of Alexander and David Hyrum Smith, missionaries from the RLDS Church and sons of Joseph and Emma, who had arrived in Salt Lake City just weeks before and who were publicly claiming that the article on "Marriage" was the only marital standard approved by their father, the Prophet Joseph Smith.[15] Apostle Joseph F. Smith's journal corroborated the *Deseret News* summary: "President Young spoke 12 minutes in relation to Sec. 109 Book of Doctrine and Covenants [article on "Marriage"] saying Oliver Cowdery wrote it, and insisted on its being inserted in the Book of D. & C. contrary to the thrice expressed wish and refusal of the Prophet Joseph Smith."[16] This account implies, but does not explicitly state, that Cowdery had powerful reasons for acting against Joseph's repeated and persistent opposition.

The missing piece—Oliver's motives—was added in what appears to be the earliest published version of this explanation, written by ex-Mormon T. B. H. Stenhouse in 1873:

> Brigham . . . made the damaging avowal that the Appendix [article on "Marriage"] was written by Oliver Cowdery against Joseph's wishes, and was permitted to be published only after Cowdery's incessant teasing and Joseph's warning to him of the trouble which his course would create. . . .

---

13. "Thirty-ninth Semi-Annual Conference," *Deseret News*, October 13, 1869, 6.
14. Ibid.
15. Our Own Correspondent, "The Mormon Church War," *Daily Evening Bulletin* (San Francisco), September 1, 1869.
16. Joseph F. Smith, Diary, October 9, 1869, in Richard E. Turley Jr., *Selected Collections from the Archives of the Church of Jesus Christ of Latter-day Saints*, Vol.1, DVD #26.

Cowdery would seem to have had either a glimpse of polygamy at that early day, or . . . he was, at the very moment of receiving revelations, a profligate in morals, for he insisted, Brigham says, upon adding to his marital relations a young woman familiar with his family, and did hold the relation of husband to her. To silence the clamour and surmising that arose over this "second wife," he wrote that Appendix.[17]

Similarly, in 1875 an unidentified Church correspondent (the first page of the letter is missing) wrote to John U. Stucki, president of the Swiss German Mission, stating that the article on Marriage "was written by Oliver Cowdery Just before his apostasy, to cover up some of his own conduct in disobedience to the command of God through Joseph Smith, and was doubtless that which lead [sic] to his apostasy; and it never had any business in the Book of Doctrine and Covenants."[18] Since this correspondent cannot be identified on the basis of the existing letter and since the extant portion of the letter does not say how the correspondent obtained his information, this assertion must be received with the caution due a third-hand source.

In 1878, Apostle Joseph F. Smith told a congregation in a Sunday morning service in the Tabernacle in Salt Lake City: "The publication, by O. Cowdery . . . of an article on marriage, which was carefully worded . . . afterwards found its way into the Doctrine and Covenants without authority."[19] It appears that the reference to "without authority" implied that Joseph Smith, being absent, did not authorize its inclusion. However, the article was approved by the same process and authority that canonized the rest of the 1835 edition of the Doctrine and Covenants.

In 1883, Joseph F. Smith gave an even more detailed account of his understanding at the Provo Utah Central Stake Conference. According to the conference clerk's record:

> Joseph received it [a revelation on plural marriage] in 1831 but he was told by the Lord that the time was not come to reveal it, and was forbidden to publish it save it be to a few. Joseph did entrust this to a few soon after 1831.
>
> Lyman E. Johnson one of the Apostles received this from Joseph, we also understand that Oliver Cowdery received it from Joseph also [sic]—did not know of any others that Joseph entrusted it to. L E Johnson testified of this to Orson Pratt as early as 1832 or a little later, and Brother Orson Pratt has left his written testimony of the facts relating to this matter: Oliver

---

17. T. B. H. Stenhouse, *Rocky Mountain Saints*, 193. Stenhouse may be recirculating a rumor that Oliver had established either a polygamous (not technically possible, since he was not married) or an extramarital relationship with Annie (or Mary Ann) Lyman. See discussion in Chapter 6.

18. [Unidentified correspondent], Letter to President John U. Stucki, April 2, 1875.

19. Joseph F. Smith, July 7, 1878, *Journal of Discourses*, 20:29.

Cowdery was not so discreet in regard to this matter but in consequence of his conduct brought reproach upon the Church bringing upon the Church the accusation of fornication & polygamy—he wrote an article to stave off the impression that had been made which was published in the Book of Doctrine and Covenants which has been left out of the New Edition because it was not one of the Revelations.[20]

Joseph F. was not, of course, an eyewitness, since he was not born until 1838; and it is not clear where he learned this information. As discussed in Chapter 4, Lyman E. Johnson told Orson Pratt that "Joseph had made known to him as early as 1831 that plural marriage was a correct principle."[21] As reviewed in Chapter 6, manuscript documentation of Oliver Cowdery's involvement with polygamy in Ohio is all late, third-hand, and has something of a scapegoating flavor. The dating that these four sources mention is also problematic. Importantly, there is no contemporaneous evidence that, in August of 1835, Oliver would have felt any need to publicly deny "fornication and polygamy" because of his personal behavior.

A Reaction to Joseph Smith's Behavior?

If the article on "Marriage" was not a response to Oliver Cowdery's actions, a more popular interpretation alleges that the morally indignant Cowdery wrote it as a public rebuke to what he viewed as Joseph Smith's scandalous behavior with Fanny Alger. A variation of this explanation is that Oliver and Joseph had strategized together about the best way to suppress gossip being circulated about Joseph and Fanny.

The first explanation hypothesizes that Oliver Cowdery was incensed by Joseph Smith's involvement with Fanny Alger and sought to curb his behavior by single-handedly persuading the hastily summoned General Assembly to adopt the article on "Marriage" along with the rest of the 1835 edition of the Doctrine and Covenants. According to this theory, if the Prophet had returned from Michigan, he would probably have asserted his influence to stop the article's acceptance. As cited above, Apostle Joseph F. Smith recorded an 1869 statement by Brigham Young that Joseph Smith "thrice" refused to include the article on "Marriage" in the 1835 edition of the Doctrine and Covenants but that "Cowdery wrote it, and insisted on its being inserted."[22] Although Oliver Cowdery was not a subservient man, especially when his differences with Joseph mounted to explosive proportions during 1838 in

---

20. Joseph F. Smith, Statement on Oliver Cowdery and Polygamy, Provo Utah Central Stake, Quarterly Stake Conference, Sunday afternoon session, 271–72.
21. Orson Pratt quoted in, "Report of Elders Orson Pratt and Joseph F. Smith," 788.
22. Joseph F. Smith, Diary, October 9, 1869.

Missouri, Joseph had no trouble rebuking Church members sharply when he felt they were in error. For example on December 26, 1833, the Prophet encountered Elder Ezekiel Rider and Brother Story [the article does not identify them further], due to their "murmuring and complaining," he "rebuked them sharply."[23] Knowing Joseph's likely reaction, it seems less probable that Oliver would have deliberately insisted on a course that he knew to be absolutely contrary to Joseph's wishes and done it in a way that involved the Mormon community in a public gesture. It is possible that at least part of these explanations that emerged during the late 1860s and 1870s when Church leaders were insisting on the significance of plural marriage and countering attempts to distance Joseph, the wellspring of sealing authority for plural unions, from a public document viewed as establishing monogamy as the law of the Church.

The second version—or "damage control" explanation—takes the position that Joseph Smith commissioned Oliver to present the "Marriage" article to help dispel the current rumors involving Fanny Alger and to do it during Joseph's absence to avoid embarrassing backlash or at least the need to answer questions privately. Details of Joseph's trip to Michigan are not available. It is 220 miles around Lake Erie to Pontiac, but they may have taken a boat across the lake, which would have reduced the travel time required. Furthermore, no corroborating evidence in the records of Joseph Smith, Frederick G. Williams, or Saints then living in Pontiac has been found of this visit—not even that Joseph and Frederick actually got to Pontiac.

Todd Compton argues for this "damage control" explanation and concludes that the article on "Marriage "represented an effort to counteract scandal and perhaps to defuse rumors of Fanny Alger's marriage, possible pregnancy, and expulsion."[24] This explanation, however, requires that the Fanny Alger scandal was in full bloom during the summer of 1835, probably no earlier than June and July. However, there is little or no evidence that Joseph was being charged with either "the crime of fornication or polygamy" in the summer of 1835. As discussed in Chapter 5, Eliza R. Snow went to live with the Smith family in the "spring of 1836"[25] and she "was well acquainted with her [Fanny Alger] as she [Eliza] lived with the Prophet at the time" that "Emma made such a fuss about" her.[26] The Levi Hancock autobiography as annotated by his son, Mosiah, records that Joseph asked for his help in dealing with the consequences in the summer of 1836.[27] A second-hand account

---

23. "History of Joseph Smith," *Times and Seasons*, (July 15, 1845) 6:961.
24. Compton, *In Sacred Loneliness*, 36.
25. Maureen Ursenbach Beecher, ed., *The Personal Writings of Eliza Roxcy Snow*, 10.
26. Document #10, Andrew Jenson Papers, Box 49, fd. 16.
27. Levi Hancock recalled that it was the summer of 1836 when Joseph Smith asked for his assistance in defusing the rumors concerning Fanny Alger. Levi Ward Hancock,

quotes Fanny Alger's mother as dating the marriage (not the aftermath) to 1835 or 1836.[28] In addition, the Kirtland Temple was dedicated in April of 1836. Accounts, both contemporary and late recollections, describing the events associated with the temple dedication contain no mention of rumors or "excitement" regarding the Prophet and a possible extramarital relationship that would have flourished during the summer of 1835.[29] As I discuss in Chapter 4, the most plausible timing for the Alger-Smith relationship to have become known with its explosive repercussions appears to be the summer of 1836, not 1835, and early in the summer—shortly after the Kirtland Temple dedication in late March 1836.

Second, the article on "Marriage" did not contain any new doctrines or directives. It simply restated commandments concerning marriage and the law of chastity that Joseph Smith had been teaching for several years. It specified that the marrying couple should keep themselves "wholly for each other, and from all others during your lives."[30] This language was similar to a revelation received in February 1831, also titled "The Laws for the Government of the Church"[31] "Thou shalt love thy wife with all thy heart, and shall cleave unto her and none else." That revelation was included in the Book of Commandments (44:22—approved for publication by a council on May 1, 1832)[32] and was also published in *The Evening and the Morning Star* in July 1832.[33] Importantly, it was part of the very set of revelations that Joseph and the committee had submitted to the general assembly for approval for publication in the 1835 Doctrine and Covenants (13:7; LDS D&C 42:22 today). In other words, the General Assembly that ratified the inclusion of the article on "Marriage" had, as part of the same meeting, ratified Joseph's February 1831 revelation that, in essence, made the article on "Marriage" redundant.

Another restrictive statement found in the article on "Marriage"—that a man "should have one wife"—was also not new. It had appeared in a March 1831 revelation: "And again, I say unto you, that whoso forbiddeth to marry, is

---

"Autobiography of Levi Ward Hancock," with additions in 1896 by his son Mosiah Hancock, 57.

28. Eliza J. Webb [Eliza Jane Churchill Webb], Lockport, New York, Letter to Mary Bond, April 24, 1876.

29. Steven C. Harper, "'A Pentecost and Endowment Indeed': Six Eyewitness Accounts of the Kirtland Temple Experience," in John W. Welch with Erick B. Carlson, eds., *Opening the Heavens: Accounts of Divine Manifestations, 1820–1844*, 327–71.

30. 1835 Doctrine and Covenants, Section CI, v. 2.

31. "Revelations: Extract from the Laws for the Government of the Church of Christ," *Evening and Morning Star* 1, no. 2 (July 1832): 9.

32. *History of the Church*, 1:149.

33. "Revelations: Extract from the Laws for the Government of the Church of Christ," 9.

not ordained of God, for marriage is ordained of God unto man: Wherefore it is lawful that *he should have one wife*, and they twain shall be one flesh" (Book of Commandments 52:16–17; emphasis mine). These verses were published in *The Evening and Morning Star* in Independence in the November 1832 issue[34] and were also included in the revelations approved by the assembly to be printed as the 1835 Doctrine and Covenants (65:3; LDS D&C 49:15–16 today). Furthermore, this affirmation of Christian monogamy would have been in every respect what conservative Mormon converts would have expected to hear, regardless of the scandalous variations of the Shaker and Oneida communities. Accordingly, it appears that the doctrine taught by the "Marriage" article was not new. Rather, it reiterated Joseph's earlier revelations and teachings, which were already published and circulated among the Latter-day Saints.

Third, available evidence shows that the model of Christian monogamy was so powerful that the concept of the restoration of Old Testament plural marriage with such complications as levirate marriage, concubinage, mandatory marriage in the case of rape, and differential inheritances for the children of wives of different status had little more than intellectual or metaphoric interest, even for the biblically schooled. However, it appears that Joseph's only justification for his plural marriage to Fanny was that Old Testament polygamy needed to be restored at that time and place.[35] Joseph apparently made an attempt to explain to Emma and Oliver Cowdery that it was a valid marriage, but both of them considered it an adulterous relationship. In the months that followed, Oliver spread rumors of adultery—not polygamy. In contrast, individuals who evidently learned of Fanny's involvement from Fanny herself, including Eliza R. Snow, the Webb family, and Fanny's parents and siblings, apparently believed her description that it was a marriage, a plural marriage; but for the next three decades, they kept quiet concerning it. When they did mention it, some referred to it anachronistically as a "sealing."[36] (See Appendix D in Volume 2 and Chapter 6 in Volume 3.)

Accordingly, if the article was designed to neutralize reports about Joseph Smith and his alleged "crimes," polygamy would not have been included because that allegation was not made then nor at any other time during

---

34. "Revelations: Revelation, Given May, 1831," *Evening and Morning Star* 1, no. 6 (November 1832): 47. This version mistakenly dates the revelation as being given in "May, 1831." The correct month is March.

35. See Benjamin F. Johnson's statement in Dean R. Zimmerman, ed., *I Knew the Prophets: An Analysis of the Letter of Benjamin F. Johnson to George F. Gibbs, Reporting Doctrinal Views of Joseph Smith and Brigham Young*, 38–39.

36. Michael Guy Bishop observed: "Very few Kirtland Saints actually had firsthand knowledge of this facet [polygamy] of their religion, and its practice was carefully circumscribed." Bishop, "The Celestial Family: Early Mormon Thought on Life and Death, 1830–1846," 11–12.

the Kirtland period according to any documentation currently available.[37] In other words, assuming that the denial of polygamy in the "Marriage" article was specifically tied to rumors of Joseph Smith's behavior is problematic, unless other corroborating evidence can be located.[38]

Fourth, it is unclear how being absent from Kirtland when the article on "Marriage" was presented for a sustaining vote would have benefited the Prophet. If Joseph was running away from the memory of his relationship with Fanny Alger or some problem associated with the article on "Marriage," why did he return only six days later and allow the unpublished pages to be printed and immediately shipped to the bindery?[39]

A review of the printing chronology of the 1835 Doctrine and Covenants shows that six of the galley sheets were completed by May 26.[40] A galley sheet contains eight pages on each side, which are afterwards cut and sewn to create one "signature." The various signatures are then bound together to form a book. Six galley sheets would comprise the first ninety-six pages. By August 15, publisher W. W. Phelps had undoubtedly finished ten more sheets for a total of fifteen signatures (or 240 pages of the book's eventual 288-page length).[41] He

---

37. While it is impossible to prove a negative, an in-depth review of available private journals and letters, published books, and periodicals fails to identify any allegations of polygamy against Joseph Smith during the 1830s. A May 29, 1835, journal entry written by John Murdock, then on a mission, recorded: "[At] Rufus Harwood's near Angelica, [southwest New York]. Conversed with Anderson a Methodist Priest. He lied and scandalized Brother Joseph the Prophet and said he sanctioned and upheld whoredom and he bore testimony against him." John Murdock, Journal, May 1835, 2:66. This is most likely a reference to the "common wives" or "community of wives" allegations made in conjunction with the united order attempts in Missouri and Ohio a few years earlier. It does not appear to be an accusation of polygamy or adultery against Joseph Smith based upon specific information. Angelica, New York, is more than two hundred miles from Kirtland, significantly removed from any rumors that might have been circulating there.

38. William Alexander Linn, *The Story of the Mormons from the Date of Their Origin to the Year 1901*, 156–57, tried to bolster the charge that Joseph Smith practiced polygamy in Kirtland by quoting Fanny Brewer's statement from Bennett's *History of the Saints* and quotations from the *Elder's Journal* and the *Messenger and Advocate*. Apparently he, too, was unable to locate a journal, letter, periodical, or other published work from the Kirtland period to substantiate his claims.

39. H. Dean Garrett, "The Coming Forth of the Doctrine and Covenants," 97.

40. W. W. Phelps, Letter to Sally Phelps, May 26, 1835. The "Lectures on Faith" comprise pp. 5–74 and were part of these first six sheets. Accordingly, Joseph Smith was undoubtedly aware and supportive of the Lectures' inclusion in the edition.

41. Printing on the presses of the time allowed for eight book-size pages on one side of a large sheet of printing paper or sixteen pages per two-sided sheet, constituting a signature. After the ink dried, the pages would be cut, folded, and sewn in as a section of the book. The number of the sheet is found at the bottom of the first page of the sixteen

was forced to stop because pages 255–57 (located on the sixteenth galley sheet) were reserved for an account of the proceedings of the General Assembly, which had not yet been convened.[42]

After completion of the August 17 General Assembly that ratified the book (including Oliver's article on "Marriage"), Phelps undoubtedly went right to work printing the last three galley sheets comprising the final forty-eight pages. Preparing these pages would have required making up a three-page table of contents and a twenty-five-page index that had yet to be compiled. Next, the eighteen stacks of 1,000 galley sheets had to be cut and sewn. Assembled but unbound books were delivered to the Cleveland bindery by early September. On September 16, Phelps wrote: "We got some of the Commandments from Cleveland last week."[43]

In looking at this timeline, it seems unlikely, if not impossible, that the described work could have been completed in the nine days between August 17 and August 26 when Joseph and Frederick returned. Doubtless the final pre-binding stages were accomplished after the Prophet's return to Kirtland. Accordingly, he could have intervened to eliminate or delay the publishing of the article on "Marriage," if he had felt it was necessary. He could even have hastily called his own "General Assembly" to address any concerns he felt, and probably, given the later date, more Church leaders would have been in attendance.

As a fifth objection, the specific wording of the document, "we believe that one man should have one wife, and one woman but one husband," might be read so that it does not technically prevent a man from having *more* than one wife—in other words, it may mean "we believe that one man should have [at least] one wife, and one woman but one husband." However, it does prohibit

---

pages being printed. Page 243 of the 1835 Doctrine and Covenants shows "16*" at its foot, meaning that fifteen sheets of sixteen pages each had already been printed. The next sheet, "17*" appears on the first page of the index, corresponding to page 259. Number 18 appears on the foot of p. 275 (roman numeral xvii of the index section). If the printing was done in numerical order, Section CI (109) was published before the last two sheets were printed, which would likely be at least a week or more later.

42. The minutes of the assembly, Collier, *Kirtland Council Minute Book*, August 17, 1835, mentioned a "book . . . [with] 284 pages" (with four blank pages totally 288). It seems probable that the scribe inserted the number of pages as he was transcribing the actual minutes weeks later. Since pp. 255–57 include an account of the meeting itself, the book circulated during the meeting could not have contained those pages. The minutes clearly state that a "book" was passed around. Most likely it consisted of 240 sewn but unbound pages from the first fifteen signature sheets then completed.

43. W. W. Phelps, Letter to Sally Phelps, September 16, 1835; quoted in Bruce Van Orden, "Writing to Zion: The William W. Phelps Kirtland Letters (1835–1836)," 566.

a woman from having more than one husband. RLDS Elder David H. Bays analyzed this passage in 1897:

> You may have observed the ingenious phraseology of that part of the document which is designed to convey the impression that the assembly, as well as the entire church, was opposed to polygamy, but which, as a matter of fact, leaves the way open for its introduction and practice. The language I refer to is this:
>
> "We believe that one man shall have *one* wife; and one woman *but one husband.*" Why use the restrictive adverb in the case of the woman, and ingeniously omit it with reference to the man? Why not employ the same form of words in the one case as in the other? Of the woman it is said she shall have *but one husband.* Why not say of the man, he shall have *"but one wife* except in case of death, when either is at liberty to marry again." We repeat the question with emphasis, Why not restrict the man to *one* wife in the same manner that the woman is restricted to *one* husband? The reason seems obvious.[44]

In 1902, LDS Church President Joseph F. Smith made the same observation: "The declaration . . . that 'one man should have one wife, and one woman *but* one husband,' bears the implication that a man might possibly be permitted at some time to have more than one wife, while a woman was to have *"but* one husband.'"[45] If the loophole terminology was intentional, it may have been due to Joseph Smith himself, since by 1835, the Prophet knew that the practice of plural marriage was one of the many things he was expected to restore.

Sixth, Brigham Young's 1869 statement about Joseph Smith's refusal to condone the article on "Marriage" loses a good deal of force when the historical record shows that Joseph himself referred to the article on "Marriage" as he performed several weddings after the Doctrine and Covenants was published. On December 3, 1835, for instance, he recorded in his journal:

> At Evening, was invited with my wife, to attend, at Thomas Caricoes [Carrico Jr.'s], to join W[arren] Parrish & Martha H. Raymond in matrimony, we found a verry pleasant and respectable company, waiting when, we arrived, we opened our interview with singing & prayer, after which, I delivered an address, upon the subject of matrimony, I then invited the \parties/ couple to arise, who were to be joined in wedlock, I and, solemnized the institution in a brief manner, and pronounced them husband and wife in the name of God according to the articles, and covenants of the \Church of the/ latter day Saints.[46]

---

44. Davis H. Bays, *Doctrines and Dogmas of Mormonism Examined and Refuted*, 328; emphasis his.

45. Joseph F. Smith, "The Real Origin of American Polygamy," 494; emphasis his.

46. Dean C. Jessee, Mark Ashhurst-McGee, and Richard L. Jensen, eds., *Journals. Vol. 1: 1832–1839*, 114–15; Scott H. Faulring, ed. *An American Prophet's Record: The Diaries and*

The only marriage ceremony found in any of the "articles and covenants of the Church" in December 1835 was that found in the article on "Marriage." Hence, it appears the Prophet used that specific language, or at least wording consistent with its guidelines.

On January 14 and again on January 20, he pronounced marriage ceremonies "according to the rules and regulations of the Church of the Latter Day Saints," which on that date, would have included the instructions contained in Section CI of the Doctrine and Covenants.[47] The Prophet's references to the article would be surprising if he did not believe it to be authoritative.

Seventh, some skeptical writers have suggested that since the article was not a revelation and was not written by Joseph Smith, but instead was penned by Oliver Cowdery, it could have been approved by the General Assembly only through some form of subterfuge. However, the 1835 Doctrine and Covenants contained another section that Cowdery had written, assisted by Orson Hyde. Section 5, "Minutes of the Organization of the High Council of the Church of Christ of Latter Day Saints" (pp. 95–98) was also approved for publication that day. Nine years later it was retained as Section 5 in the 1844 edition of the Doctrine and Covenants published in Nauvoo (p. 123; LDS D&C 102 today).

In summary, numerous observations support that the article on "Marriage" was not a response to Joseph Smith's relationship with Fanny Alger as a "crime of fornication" or as "polygamy." It appears he was not personally accused of "polygamy" in any venue until years later. When reports about fornication made a minor stir during the summer of 1836—a year after the article on "Marriage"—the Prophet straightforwardly and flatly denied them without resorting to elaborate public maneuvers, which were, according to available records, never needed.

A Reaction to Accusations of Communal Wives?

A third interpretation is that the article on "Marriage" was issued as a response to rumors that the Church practiced a form of communal wives. Elizabeth A. Clark and Herbert Richardson observed: "Nineteenth-century America abounded in utopian societies; as many as five hundred such communities may have flourished in this period."[48] Some experimented with novel

---

Journals of Joseph Smith, 70. The slash marks in the quotation indicate material added interlinearly.

47. Jessee, Ashhurst-McGee, and Jensen, *Journals: Vol. 1: 1832–1839*, 153, 165; Faulring, *An American Prophet's Record*, 104, 116. I am indebted to Michael Marquardt for bringing these sources to my attention.

48. Elizabeth A. Clark and Herbert Richardson, eds., *Women and Religion: The Original*

marital and sexual practices, which focused suspicion upon all of the groups. Mario S. De Pillis observed: "Polygamy should be mentioned as another communitarian institution, if only because it is interpreted in almost every other way. There is no need to cite the vast and sometimes obscene literature or to refute any of its bizarre claims. Suffice it to say that polygamy was first of all typically communitarian in that very many communitive sects experimented with sex and marriage."[49] Accordingly, early Latter-day Saint efforts to live the law of consecration, even though it sustained traditional monogamy, were instantly misunderstood.

The *Evangelical Magazine and Gospel Advocate*, published in Utica, New York, reported in its February 5, 1831, issue: "They [the Mormons] have all things in common, and dispense with the marriage covenant."[50] An issue four months later mentioned that the "Mormonites" lived in "common stock families" without defining precisely what that meant.[51] Henry Carroll, who was in the Kirtland area in 1832 recalled in 1885: "It was claimed all things were common, even to free love, among the Mormons at Kirtland."[52] John L. Brooke, fascinated by folk manifestations of the occult in antebellum America, wrote: "Among the non-Mormons in Ohio there were suspicions that the community of property dictated in the 'Law of Consecration' included wives."[53]

Historian Mark Staker observed: "As late as 1835, Joseph was still trying to counter outside rumors that had apparently arisen as a result of the Morley Family and early Mormonite confusion before his arrival in Kirtland."[54] The "family" was the appellation applied to a loose group of Christian seekers and restorationists, and the name honored Isaac Morley, a man of exemplary piety and generosity. Many members of this group had become Mormons on the whirlwind visit of the four Mormon missionaries to the Lamanites in October 1830, but the rapidity with which they had left Ohio for Missouri left their new converts attempting, with mixed success, to incorporate the new teachings, such as gathering and the redemption of Israel with the Christian forms with which the were already familiar. Staker points out that "several descriptions"

Sourcebook of Women in Christian Thought, 201.

49. Mario Stephen De Pillis, "The Development of Mormon Communitarianism, 1826–1846," 266 note 1.

50. J. M. H., "Editorial Correspondence," *Evangelical Magazine and Gospel Advocate* (Utica, N.Y), February 5, 1831, 47.

51. "Infatuation," *Evangelical Magazine and Gospel Advocate* (Utica, N.Y), June 18, 1831, 198.

52. Henry Carroll, "Statement," In Arthur H. Deming, ed., *Naked Truths about Mormonism*, April 1888, 2:3.

53. John L. Brooke, "'Of Whole Nations Being Born in One Day': Marriage, Money, and Magic in the Mormon Cosmos, 1830–1846," 115.

54. Mark Lyman Staker, *Hearken, O Ye People: The Historical Setting for Joseph Smith's Ohio Revelations*, 107.

of this group "use terms frequently applied to Owenite communities, such as calling them 'communistic.' One observer said they practiced 'free love.' No one in the Morley Family ever says what they believed or did as a group, ever."[55] The result is something of a descriptive vacuum, which could be readily filled by scandal. Thus, allegations of matrimonial improprieties followed the Church, inciting a variety of denials.[56] The April 1833 *Evening and Morning Star*, clarified: "It has been reported that the church had settled in this country [Independence, Missouri], and were living as one family. This is not so."[57] Eventually Joseph Smith addressed this concern in an 1840 article in the *Times and Seasons*:

> When we consecrate our property to the Lord, it is to administer to the wants of the poor and needy according to the laws of God, and when a man consecrates or dedicates his wife and children to the Lord, he does not give them to his brother or to his neighbor; which is contrary to the law of God, which says, "Thou shalt not commit adultery, Thou shalt not covet thy neighbors [sic] wife" "He that looketh upon a woman to lust after her has committed adultery already in his heart."—Now for a man to consecrate his property, his wife and children to the Lord is nothing more nor less than to feed the hungry, cloth [sic] the naked, visit the widows and fatherless, the sick and afflicted; and do all he can to administer to their relief in their afflictions, and for himself and his house to serve the Lord. In order to do this he and all his house must be virtuous and "shun every appearance of evil.["] Now if any person, has represented any thing otherwise than what we now write they have willfully misrepresented us.[58]

An interesting story printed in the May 24, 1837, issue of the *Missouri Republican* was obviously drawing on the image of the Mormons as exotics.

---

55. Mark Staker, email to Brian Hales, August 16, 2008.

56. Parley P. Pratt, *Late Persecutions of the Church of Jesus Christ of Latter-day Saints . . . with a Sketch of Their Rise, Progress, and Doctrine*, 10: "It is also a current report among the ignorant that we do away [with] matrimony, and that we allow unlawful intercourse between the sexes. Now this idea originated and has been kept alive by wicked and designing persons, and by the credulity of those who are more ready to believe falsehood than they are to believe truth. There has never been the shadow of anything to cause such a report." Erastus Snow and Benjamin Winchester printed a similar denial in 1841 in *An Address to the Citizens of Salem and Vicinity, by E. Snow and B. Winchester. . .*: "It has been stated in public journals that we hold all things in common, or that we have a community of goods, also of wives. These charges we positively deny: for we hold no such things nor never did. . . . The rules of the church forbid anything like unvirtuous conduct, and they are righteously enforced" (not paginated).

57. "Rise and Progress of the Church of Christ," *Evening and Morning Star* 1, no. 11 (April 1833): 84.

58. "Communications," *Times and Seasons* 1, no. 6 (April 1840): 85.

The author, whom Dale Morgan identified as Edmund Flagg, reported that, while traveling in Illinois in July 1836, he spent a day with a Mormon emigrant on his way to Jackson County, Missouri, with "a brace of wives and two or three braces of children, by way of stock in trade for community at Mount Zion."[59] This colorful narrative lacks even a shadow of probability. In the first place, the idea that a polygamist husband would have cheerfully disclosed his marital arrangements to a stranger encountered by chance is not credible. Furthermore, assuming that such a Mormon elder was so chatty, local newspapers would have rejoiced to spread the report clear to the eastern coastlines. Even at Nauvoo in the 1840s, plural marriage was kept very secret, almost as a matter of life and death. Prior to the migration west in 1846, no polygamist husband openly traveled with his wives as described. Additionally, the Saints left Jackson County in 1833 and, in 1836, were experiencing the end of their welcome in Clay County as well. It is more likely new converts would be traveling to Kirtland, Ohio, to see the Prophet and the newly dedicated temple there, rather than heading straight for Missouri.

It seems plausible, even likely, that beginning in 1831, some uninformed individuals assumed that the law of consecration included a community of wives as one of its tenets, even publishing such claims, although there is no indication that this is how the Mormons themselves interpreted the law of consecration. Understandably, Church leaders would actively seek to deny such untrue allegations in a document on marriage to be included in the 1835 Doctrine and Covenants.

A Reaction to Members' Personal Misconduct?

Besides general accusations against the Church, during the 1830s, several individual members were guilty of immoral practices that may have been labeled as "polygamy." Neither their nonmember neighbors nor their Church leaders shrugged off such activities. In 1892, Church member John Taylor (not the apostle) remembered that in Independence in 1832:

> I went about visiting and teaching the people, and visiting all the houses I saw. I went to a man by the name of Claudious Hendricks, and there was a woman living in his house, and I felt as though there was something wrong about it, although I had no evidence,—that is no proof. . . . There was a man,—this woman's husband was an elder and he was sent here on a mission, and she stayed there at Hendricks' place, and he went and got her with a child, the same as old David and Uriah's wife,—He got her with child

---

59. Edmund Flagg [published as E. F.], "Sketches of a Traveler," [*St. Louis*] *Missouri Republican*, May 24, 1837, 1. Earlier, Edmund Flagg published *The Far West* (1828). See Stanley S. Ivins Collection, Notebook #8, p. 186, Utah State Historical Society.

while her husband was gone. [A]nd he was brought up and cut off from the Church for it.[60]

On February 3, 1834, Joseph Wood was excommunicated reportedly for either fornication or some form of polygamy.[61] Oliver Cowdery wrote to a Brother Fosdick regarding this case of Church discipline:

> We were very sorry to learn that Bro. J. Wood had gone so far astray and offered such violence to the pure principles of the Gospel of Christ. But, alas! Such is the depravity of man when lost to a sense of the fear of God and of the ties which bind every virtuous man to the interest and happiness of his fellow man. Every principle incubated among you which is contrary to virtue, to industry, to wisdom, to good order, to propriety, and in fine, to the pure principles of godliness as contained in the Scriptures of the Old and New Testaments, the Book of Mormon and the revelations and commandments of Jesus Christ, which have been given to his church in these last days, is entirely foreign from the feelings of our breasts, and is that upon which we look down with feelings of the utmost disapprobation; and as conscientious men who expect to render an impartial account, before the searcher of hearts, of all our transactions here, we cannot look upon any principle contrary to the above with any degree of allowance.
>
> After some investigation of the case of Bro Wood, in council, it was decided that he should be cut off from the Church. Accordingly the Council lifted their hands against him and he was excluded from the church on this 3rd day of Feb. 1834 for indulging an idle, partial, overbearing and lustful spirit and not magnifying his holy calling whereunto he had been ordained. These things were plainly manifest to the satisfaction of all the council, and the spirit constrained us to separate him from the church.[62]

Benjamin F. Johnson reported a third case: "There was [in 1835] Some trouble with Jarid Carter. and through Bro Sherman, I learned that 'As he had built himself a new house, he now wanted another wife' which Joseph would not permit."[63] Carter had married Lydia Ames in 1823 and been converted to

---

60. John Taylor, Deposition, Temple Lot Transcript, Complainant's Testimony, Part 2, p. 398, questions 70–72.

61. Phillip R. Legg, *Oliver Cowdery: The Elusive Second Elder of the Restoration*, 80, considered Wood's behavior a form of polygamy. Available details suggest it may have been adultery.

62. Joseph Smith Jr., Letter to Bro. Fosdick, February 3, 1834.

63. Dean R. Zimmerman, ed., *I Knew the Prophets: An Analysis of the Letter of Benjamin F. Johnson to George F. Gibbs, Reporting Doctrinal Views of Joseph Smith and Brigham Young*, 38. Benjamin F. Johnson wrote in his autobiography, *My Life's Review*, 17–18: "Elder Jared Carter, a man then [summer of 1834] of great faith, came with other elders to our house, and seeing sister Nancy upon her crutches commanded her in the name of Jesus Christ of Nazareth to leave her crutches and walk, which she at once did, and never again did she use them."

the gospel in 1831. After serving several missions during the 1831–34 period, his convictions seemed to wax and wane. On September 19, 1835, Carter was brought before the Kirtland High Council for discipline, but the minutes contain no reference to polygamy. At the proceedings, Hyrum Smith stated: "Pride had engendered in his heart a desire to excel, and the spirit of meekness was withdrawn and he left to err."[64] Joseph Smith added: "His rebelling against the advise [sic] and counsel of the presidents was the cause of his falling to the hands of the Destroyer."[65] Precisely what Carter's aspirations were with respect to plural marriage, his new house, or simply an improper attitude are unknown, but he apparently quickly repented and was restored.

A fourth case developed just a week later. On September 28, 1835, the Kirtland High Council met and heard "charges preferred against Lorenzo L. Lewis for adultery according to general report amongst the brethren by P. R. Cahoon.

> The accused plead not guilty to the charge preferred above. The accusation is now preferred of an illicit intercourse with a female. The defendant confesses that he had disgraced the girl, himself, & the Church, but plead not guilty to the charge of illicit intercourse. . . . The accused was called upon & confessed that he had done wickedly & had made all the reparation he could in his confession in the early part of this litigation and requested his name to be taken off from the Church records, or dispose of him according to the mind of the Spirit.[66]

Accordingly, "The Presidency decided that Brother Loyd [sic] L. Lewis be cut off from the Church."[67]

Eight months later, the Kirtland High Council heard a similar case on May 14, 1836. Joseph brought the complaint, a second-hand one from Apostle William E. McLellin, who was excommunicated himself almost exactly two years later. According to Joseph, McLellin stated that he "had learned from the defendant [Jenkins Salisbury, who was married to Joseph's sister Katharine] that he had been intimate with every woman he could since he belonged to the Church."[68] Although Jenkins denied "the charge of unchastity to his wife," he was excommunicated briefly and rebaptized.

In the ninth case, "polygamy" was, in fact, the charge. William Perry accused an Elder Freeman on November 29, 1837, before the Kirtland Elder's Quorum

---

64. Collier, *Kirtland Council Minute Book*, September 19, 1835, 138.
65. Ibid., 139.
66. Ibid., September 28, 1835, 143–44. See also Legg, *Oliver Cowdery*, 95; *History of the Church*, 2:285.
67. Ibid.
68. Ibid., September 28, 1835, 172.

for the crime of polygamy. . . . Elder Freeman pled not guilty of the charge[.] [T] estimony for the Complainant came forward (Dexter Stilman) and Stated that Elder Freeman had a wife in Tollan township Co of Berksheir in Mass, and it was told him there that he (E. Freeman) Came a way without his wife Elder Harlow Redfield Stated that when he and Elder Stilman went to see Elder Freeman. Elder Freeman acknoledged before the quorum that he had left his first wife . . . and Soon Commenced living with another woman he further Stated he did not know but his first wife was yet living he further stated he would not go across the room to obtain a bill [of divorce] from her Elder Freeman Manifest a Carless indifferent spirit.[69]

It is unclear from the notes whether the high council excommunicated Freeman, but the last line suggests that the quorum did not sympathize with his position.

Doubtless, these cases were not kept secret. For example, Lorenzo L. Lewis regretted that he "had disgraced . . . the Church." Reports of these immoral behaviors probably spread beyond the confines of the Church membership. Cases such as these provided priesthood leaders with another reason to officially deny any endorsement of fornication or polygamy through a statement on marriage in the 1835 Doctrine and Covenants. By taking stern disciplinary action, they sent the message that such misbehavior was not tolerated within the Church.

Timing of Including "Marriage"

This discussion up to this point has found reasons to deny that the article on "Marriage" was a response to either Joseph's or Oliver's behavior, but instead was designed to establish that Christian monogamy was a law that they already accepted, and that infractions of this law were seriously disciplined. However, other questions persist: Who decided to include Section CI ("Marriage") as part of the 1835 Doctrine and Covenants? When was that determination made? Was the decision to hold the General Assembly made before or after Joseph Smith left for Michigan?

One interpretation is that Joseph Smith decided to include the article before leaving for Pontiac, but that Oliver Cowdery and Sidney Rigdon called the General Assembly hastily at W. W. Phelps's request. On November 14, 1835, three months after the General Assembly, Phelps proudly wrote to his wife: "My time and that of President John Whitmer is all taken up in the printing office. We have, when all are in the office, three apprentices and four journeymen, and we shall have to employ more men, as our work is so far

---

69. Lyndon W. Cook and Milton V. Backman Jr. eds., *Kirtland Elders' Quorum Record, 1836–1841*, 35. I have been unable to find any additional information about Freeman, suggesting that he drifted away from the Church soon after this episode.

behind."⁷⁰ It was important for Phelps to keep his crews busy and not to let external constraints slow down the printing firm's productivity.

The two-story printing office was located immediately behind the Kirtland Temple. Phelps was responsible for reprints of the *Evening and Morning Star* (edited by Oliver Cowdery) and the more recently established *Messenger and Advocate* (Oliver Cowdery, the first editor, was replaced by John Whitmer in May 1835). Undoubtedly both men were encouraging Phelps to keep up. I hypothesize that on Saturday, August 15, Phelps had either caught up with his printing obligations or felt that the enormous Doctrine and Covenants was an insurmountable roadblock to beginning any new project. As the former editor of one of the newspapers and the active editor of the other, Cowdery alone may have been personally motivated to also keep the printing presses working. If so, after Joseph Smith had departed for Michigan, Phelps, Cowdery, and Rigdon, may have decided to finish the Doctrine and Covenants, whose galley sheets and sewn signatures were demanding much storage space and other resources. If this scenario is accurate, then Cowdery and Rigdon would have announced the General Assembly during Sunday meetings on August 16 and convened the assembly the very next day on Monday.⁷¹

This reconstruction does not provide conclusive evidence about when the decision was made to include "Marriage" in the Doctrine and Covenants and whether Joseph Smith was part of that decision. However, helpful clues are found by examining the twenty-five-page "Contents" at the back of the book. (Despite its title, the "Contents" actually functions as an index.) It was clearly compiled after the decision was made by Joseph to include the article on "Marriage" (Section 101) because it refers to that section under four headings: "Husband and wife," "Marriage in this church," "One wife and one husband," and "Record all marriages."⁷²

If we could ascertain the date the "Contents" was compiled, it would be clear that the decision to include the article had occurred before the compilation. The "Contents" contains no page numbers—only sections and paragraphs—suggesting that page numbers were not yet available. They did not become available until the sixteenth galley was printed a few days after the August 17 General Assembly.

---

70. W. W. Phelps, Letter to Sally Phelps, November 14, 1835; quoted in Van Orden, "Writing to Zion," 568.

71. I am indebted to H. Michael Marquardt for his assistance in piecing together this interpretation of those events.

72. The "Contents" or functional index does not continue arabic numerals from the text, but is paginated separately using roman numerals. The headings are located on pages xii, xv, xvi, xix respectively.

If the "Contents" section was compiled before the page numbers became available, how much earlier might it have been? On August 4, 1835, before leaving for Michigan, Joseph Smith referred "to the book of covenants, 2nd section, 2nd part, and 12, paragraph" in a letter."[73] His reference did not include a page number—hence, he was using a reference system exactly like that of the "Contents." Whether the Prophet was working from unbound pages, a printer's copy, or some other collection is not known. However, his citation demonstrates that some form of an indexing system had been established at that point, perhaps even weeks before. If that indexing system included references to the article on "Marriage," then the decision to include it in the Doctrine and Covenants would have been made before Joseph Smith left for Michigan.

It is possible that at some point Joseph and Oliver differed about whether the article on "Marriage" should be included in the Doctrine and Covenants. Nevertheless, enough evidence is available to suggest that, if a disagreement existed, it was resolved before the Prophet left for Pontiac and that he accepted the article after its adoption. Importantly, this reconstruction of the events of that time period suggests that Joseph Smith's absence from the General Assembly on August 17, 1835, was not related to his first plural marriage to Fanny Alger.

If this reconstruction is accurate, then if Joseph Smith had attended the General Assembly, he would have been the first to sustain the proposal to include "Marriage" in the 1835 Doctrine and Covenants, since it simply echoed accepted revelations already published and clearly stated official Church teachings.[74]

Denials of Polygamy

In some ways, the 1835 article on "Marriage" can be counted as the first of a handful of denials issued by the Church and its leaders regarding sexual indecencies and polygamy. A second statement occurred on April 29, 1837, when the Seventies at Kirtland "Resolved: That we have no fellowship whatever with any elder belonging to the quorum of seventies who is guilty of polygamy in any shape and does not in all cases of like nature conform to the

---

73. The text of the letter was copied into Joseph Smith's Letterbook and appears to be an epistle from the High Council, although the recipient is unidentified. See August 4, 1835, Letterbook 1 (January 1834–August 1834 [sic]) for August 4, 1835," p. 91. In Turley, *Selected Collections*, Vol. 1, DVD #20.

74. The section is retained in the Community of Christ Doctrine and Covenants as Section 111. Kenneth L. McLaughlin, "Doctrine and Covenants Section 111: Another Look," 35–40.

Laws of the Church as made known in the book Doctrine and Covenants and in the Bible."[75] This resolution was published in the November 1837 issue of the *Messenger and Advocate*.[76]

Third, the *Elder's Journal* for that same month—November 1837—acknowledged twenty questions that were "daily and hourly asked by all classes of people whilst we are traveling" promising a response in the next issue.[77] The seventh question was: "Do the Mormons believe in having more wives than one?" The next number of the *Elder's Journal* was not printed until July 1838 and answered: "No, not at the same time. But they believe that if their companion dies, they have a right to marry again."[78] Significantly, the preceding question (No. 6) read: "Do the Mormons believe in having all things common? Answer. No." The Latter-day Saints had been accused of supporting a community of wives since 1831. Having these two questions addressed together may have been coincidental, but it seems likely to have reflected the continuing misrepresentation that Mormons believed in having common property and "common wives."

Fourth, a December 1838 letter from the Prophet to Church members also contained a denial of adultery:

> Was it for murder in Ray County, that we were thus treated? We answer no.... Was it for committing *adultery*? We are aware that false and slanderous reports have gone abroad, which have reached our ears, respecting this thing, which have been started by renegades, and spread by the dissenters, who are extremely active in spreading foul and libelous reports concerning us; thinking thereby to gain the fellowship of the world, knowing that we are not of the world; and that the world hates us. But by so doing they only show themselves to be vile traitors and sycophants. *Some have reported that we not only dedicated our property, but likewise our families to the Lord*, and Satan taking advantage of this has transfigured it into lasciviousness, a *community of wives*, which things are an abomination in the sight of God.[79]

In analyzing this last letter, historian Thomas F. O'Dea asserted: "It is curious also that in his [Joseph Smith's] letters from Liberty Jail in Missouri [December 1838 to April 1839], when he answered charges that the gentiles had made against his people, Joseph Smith denied *polygamy*—curious because it was one of the few things that had not been charged against them (empha-

---

75. "Minute Book of the Seventy," April 29, 1837, in Alan H. Gerber, comp., "Church Manuscripts," typescript, Vol. 2, p. 137.

76. "To Our Readers," *Messenger and Advocate* 3, no. 8 (May 1837): 511.

77. Joseph Smith, Editorial, *Elder's Journal* 1, no. 2 (November 1837): 28–29.

78. Joseph Smith, Editorial, *Elder's Journal* 1, no. 3 (July 1838): 43.

79. "Communications," (Joseph Smith, Letter to the Church (from Liberty Jail), December 16, 1838) *Times and Seasons* 1, no. 6 (April 1840): 84–85; emphasis mine.

sis mine).[80] It seems that the primary refutation was against "adultery" and "polygamy" was not mentioned. Perhaps O'Dea considered the disclaimer regarding a "community of wives," a behavior clearly never practiced by the Latter-day Saints, to constitute a actual denial of polygamy.

In interpreting the events of the Church and its members in Ohio, equating adultery with authorized polygamy creates confusion. For Joseph Smith, the two could not have been more different, with one leading to damnation (D&C 76:103), the other, when authorized, existing as a part of the new and everlasting covenant of marriage, which, according to his Nauvoo teachings, leads to exaltation.[81]

A fifth statement made by Joseph Smith on May 26, 1844, just a month before the martyrdom, is sometimes used as evidence that he was accused of polygamy at the time of his marriage to Emma Hale in 1827: "I had not been married scarcely five minutes, and made one proclamation of the Gospel, before it was reported that I had seven wives."[82] Concerning this statement, Dan Vogel wrote: "In 1844, while publicly denying apostate accusations of secret polygamy, he [Joseph Smith] admitted that similar charges on his character had been made as early as 1827."[83] Unfortunately, Vogel's interpretation ignores Joseph Smith's comment that the charge of polygamy came after two things had occurred: first, that he had married (which he did in January 1827) and second, had "made one proclamation of the Gospel." Although his meaning is less clear here, it suggests that he took up his public ministry at this point. Richard Bushman reported: "He [Joseph Smith] is not known to have preached a sermon before the Church is organized in 1830. He had no reputation as a preacher."[84] The Prophet did not specifically mention when he made that first "proclamation"; but later in this same discourse, he stated: "I am the same man, and as innocent as I was fourteen years ago."[85] Counting back fourteen years from 1844 brings us to 1830. As discussed above, published documents in 1831 accused the Church in general of practicing a "community of wives" or polygamy. It seems probable that, rather than establishing the chronology for the first "report" of polygamy charges against him personally, as Vogel asserts, Joseph Smith was

---

80. Thomas F. O'Dea, *The Mormons*, 61.

81. The revelation now canonized as LDS Doctrine and Covenants 132 was not dictated until July 12, 1843; however, it seems likely that the Prophet became aware of its doctrines years before. My research confirms that at no time did Joseph Smith tolerate adultery or fornication in himself or other Church members. See Chapters 2–3, 5.

82. Andrew F. Ehat and Lyndon W. Cook, eds., *The Words of Joseph Smith: The Contemporary Accounts of the Nauvoo Discourses of the Prophet Joseph Smith*, 375.

83. Joseph Smith, Statement, May 26, 1844, in Dan Vogel, ed., *Early Mormon Documents*, 4:206 note 9.

84. Richard L. Bushman, "A Historian's Perspective of Joseph Smith," CD-2, track 8.

85. Ehat and Cook, *The Words of Joseph Smith*, 377.

venting frustration of being a target of malicious gossip and was engaging in a little rhetorical hyperbole. Without additional evidence, it appears that the 1827 dating is unsupported. Months earlier the Prophet exclaimed: "No Crime can be done but what it is laid to Jo Smith."[86]

Significantly, authors throughout the decades have cited some of these denials as evidence that rumors of polygamy in 1827 or in the 1830s were perhaps "widespread."[87] Fawn Brodie assured her readers: "Rumors of polygamy among the Mormons were not loud, but they were persistent."[88] Ironically, these writers do not present verification from the rumor-mongers nor do they themselves provide evidence.[89] In essence, the primary evidence of Mormon polygamy at Kirtland (or before) is reduced to denials by Church authorities, rather than reprinted allegations from the accusers (assuming there were any).[90] Lawrence Foster concluded: "Although the Mormon movement during its initial decade of existence in the 1830s had become subject to hostility for a variety of religious, political, economic, and social reasons, sexual matters do not initially appear to have provoked much controversy."[91]

Importantly, adultery and polygamy were just two of many allegations that were leveled at the Church and its members. Oliver Cowdery wrote in the *Messenger and Advocate* in 1836: "It would be a Herculean task to point out the innumerable falsehoods and misrepresentations, sent out detrimental to

---

86. Ibid., 227.

87. Todd Compton, "Fanny Alger Smith Custer: Mormonism's First Plural Wife?" 181 note 24. See also Linda King Newell and Valeen Tippetts Avery, *Mormon Enigma: Emma Hale Smith*, 67; A. T[heodore]. Schroeder, *Some Facts Concerning Polygamy*, 9.

88. Fawn M. Brodie, *No Man Knows My History: The Life of Joseph Smith, the Mormon Prophet*, 186. Similarly, William D. Morain, *The Sword of Laban: Joseph Smith, Jr. and the Dissociated Mind*, 187, speculated in 1998: "[John C.] Bennett had perhaps been drawn to Nauvoo [in late 1840] by the rumors concerning polygamy." In fact, I have made strenuous but unavailing efforts to find any published or private document that accuses Joseph Smith of polygamy; the first such document dates from July 1842, a year and a half after Bennett's arrival in Nauvoo.

89. Danel W. Bachman, "A Study of the Mormon Practice of Plural Marriage before the Death of Joseph Smith," 88, assessed: "There appear to be no accusations of immoral conduct or polygamy in the public statements of anti-Mormon sentiment during these last days of difficulty. But an adverse undercurrent may have been beginning."

90. Of the nineteen historical documents listed in Table 5.1 that mention the Smith-Alger relationship, several authors, including William McLellin and Benjamin F. Johnson wrote late accounts referring to the affiliation as a plural marriage. However, as discussed in Chapter 5, no contemporary allegations have been located in private or published sources accusing Joseph Smith of polygamy in Ohio.

91. Lawrence Foster, "Sex and Conflict in New Religious Movements: A Comparison of the Oneida Community under John Humphrey Noyes and the Early Mormons under Joseph Smith and His Would-Be Successor," 34–58.

this society. The tales of those days in which Witches were burnt, and the ridiculous inconsistencies of those who directed the building of the funeral pyre, could be no more absurd than the every-day tales, relative to the conduct and professions of the 'Mormons.'"[92]

Apostasy at Kirtland

By early 1838, Joseph Smith and other leaders had escaped to Missouri. Researcher Karl Ricks Anderson observed: "At least two hundred to three hundred persons apostatized, representing a loss of 10 to 15 percent of the Kirtland membership. About one-third of the Church leaders were either excommunicated, disfellowshipped, or removed from their Church callings. Although almost half of the leaders later repented and returned, it took a heavy toll on the Church's administrative functioning."[93] In 1858, Apostle George A. Smith referred to the "spirit of adultery" as intensifying the apostasy at Kirtland:

> I believe, if you will take the whole circle of the history of apostates from this church, that in ninety-nine cases out of every hundred you will find that the spirit of adultery or covetousness was the original cause. . . . After the organization of the Twelve Apostles, and the so far finishing of the Kirtland Temple as to hold a solemn assembly and confer the Kirtland endowment therein, the spirit of apostacy became more general, and the shock that was given to the Church became more severe than on any previous occasion. The Church had increased in numbers, and the Elders had extended their labours accordingly; but the apostasy commenced in high places. One of the First Presidency, several of the Twelve Apostles, High Council, Presidents of Seventies, the witnesses of the Book of Mormon, Presidents of Far West, and a number of others standing high in the Church were all carried away in this apostasy . . . You may go to every one of these men—I care not which one; you cannot put your finger on any one of these thirty men but what you will find that the spirit of adultery or covetousness had got possession of their hearts; and when it did, the Spirit of the Lord left them. They had not sense enough to repent and put away their iniquity, but suffered themselves to be overthrown with the spirit of darkness; and they have gone to hell, and there they may lift up their eyes, asking for some relief or benefit from those they once tried to destroy; but if they get the privilege of waiting on a servant to those who have kept the laws of heaven, they will be exceedingly thankful and fortunate.[94]

---

92. Oliver Cowdery, Editorial, *Messenger and Advocate* 3, no. 1 (October 1836): 395.
93. Karl Ricks Anderson, *Joseph Smith's Kirtland: Eyewitness Accounts*, 216.
94. George A. Smith, January 10, 1858, *Journal of Discourses*, 7:115.

Several authors have concluded that the Joseph Smith-Fanny Alger relationship contributed to the Kirtland apostasy, which is probably true to some degree.[95] Max Parkin wrote: "It is impossible to ignore the evidence that the beginning of the practice of Mormon polygamy had a bearing upon the internal if not the external conflict of the Mormons in Ohio. It contributed to apostasy and disharmony among some of the Saints as well as suspicion by the non-Mormon community."[96] One year later, Kenneth Godfrey wrote: "Mormonism was never very popular with a majority of Ohio's citizens. Rumors of unusual marriage customs helped bring about this unpopularity."[97] However, the fact that the press remained unaware (see Chapter 6) provides circumstantial evidence that the gossip's spread was limited and its effects less influential on the apostates.[98] Furthermore, Ohioans outside of the Church were likely unaware of rumors of either adultery or polygamy arising from the Smith-Alger relationship. BYU history professor Kathryn M. Daynes assessed:

> Despite the persecution and continuing threats the saints suffered through the Kirtland period, attempts to introduce plural marriage then were relatively unsuccessful. A belief circulated among some saints that plural marriage was a correct principle and would be practiced in the church at some future time. Though the belief soured the minds of some, little evidence exists indicating that it alone had much impact on the community.[99]

---

95. Concerning "Mormons [taking] more wives than one" in the 1831–37 period, historian Carmon Hardy, *Solemn Covenant: The Mormon Polygamous Passage*, 6, wrote: "Men remembered this early period as one when leaders sometimes behaved in ways that later made them blush." Without further explanation, this description can be misleading. The reference is to Lorenzo Snow's 1882 statement: "I remember very well the cloudy and stormy days of Kirtland, and how foolishly some people acted. There were men who occupied high standing in the Church, who disgraced themselves, having behaved in a manner which afterwards brought the blush of shame to their cheeks." May 6, 1882, *Journal of Discourses*, 23:193. Snow's original statement does not appear to attribute the leaders' blushes to plural marriage or sexual impropriety but rather to the anger, uncertainty, and disaffection, primarily over financial matters, that resulted in episodes of disloyalty to Joseph as prophet. As discussed in Chapters 2–3, 5, my research supports only one plural marriage during the entire decade of the 1830s, that between Joseph Smith and Fanny Alger.

96. Max Parkin, "The Nature and Cause of Internal and External Conflict of the Mormons in Ohio between 1830 and 1838" (1966), 163.

97. Godfrey, "Causes of Mormon-Non-Mormon Conflict in Hancock County, Illinois, 1839–1846," 6.

98. As noted in the text, rumors of adultery and/or polygamy do not appear in the media of that era. Nor does it appear that the gossip followed Joseph Smith to Nauvoo. Robert Kent Fielding in his dissertation, "The Growth of the Mormon Church in Kirtland, Ohio," discusses the causes of the Kirtland conflict at length but does not include polygamy or alleged sexual indiscretions among those causes.

99. Kathryn M. Daynes, "Family Ties: Belief and Practice in Nauvoo," 66. Daynes,

An important question involves who was affected and to what degree. The specific reactions of informed individuals to the apparent polygamous relationship were quite varied. The actions of some of those who were closest to the proceedings, like Eliza R. Snow, Fanny Alger's parents, and the Webbs, indicate that they did not view the affiliation as adulterous. Other Church members, including Lyman Sherman and Benjamin F. Johnson seemed equally unaffected.

In contrast, Emma was understandably distraught and Oliver completely rejected the Smith-Alger union as a legitimate plural marriage. Todd Compton observed that "Cowdery and Smith became increasingly estranged in 1837 and early 1838. Smith's relationship with Alger seems to have been a major issue in their conflict, which strengthens the hypothesis that Cowdery never practiced polygamy. . . . The circumstantial evidence is strong that Cowdery's respect for Joseph diminished after that point."[100] Linda King Newell and Valeen Tippetts Avery likewise concluded: "The incident [with Fanny Alger] drove a serious wedge between Oliver Cowdery and Joseph."[101] Benjamin F. Johnson, writing long after the fact, likewise attributed the rift between Oliver and Joseph to the Fanny Alger relationship:

> There was Some trouble with Oliver Cowdery. and <u>whisper</u> Said it was Relating to a girl then living in his [Joseph Smith's] Family And I was afterwards told by Warren Parrish That He himself & Oliver Cowdery did know that Joseph had Fanny Alger as a wife for They were <u>Spied upon</u> & found together — And I Can now See that . . . the Suspician or Knowledge of the Prophets Plural Relation was one of the Causes of Apostasy & disruption <u>at Kirtland</u>, altho at the time there was little Said publickly upon the Subject.[102]

Although Warren Parrish himself left no account of which I am aware, he served during the 1835 to 1837 period as one of Joseph Smith's scribes and would therefore have been in a position to be aware of the relationship and perhaps any resulting pregnancy.[103] He wrote a February 5, 1838, letter to the

---

"Plural Wives and the Nineteenth-Century Mormon Marriage System: Manti, Utah 1849–1910," 48–49, also wrote: "The apostasy of so many leaders [at Kirtland, Ohio] and the subsequent expulsion of Mormons from Missouri were not caused by the introduction of polygamy, but the acceptance of plural marriage within Mormon community was facilitated by these events." Further research shows little evidence that the "Mormon community" in general was aware of the restoration of plural marriage in the Ohio period. See also Daynes, "Mormon Polygamy: Belief and Practice in Nauvoo," 132.

100. Compton, *In Sacred Loneliness*, 37–38. On May 24, 1868, "Pres H. C. Kimball Gave instructions about Prayer. The Revelation concerning polygamy was what sent O. Cowdery overboard." Heber C. Kimball, Statement on Oliver Cowdery and Polygamy, Provo Utah Central Stake General Minutes, p. 118.

101. Newell and Avery, *Mormon Enigma*, 66.

102. Zimmerman, *I Knew the Prophets*, 38–39.

103. Ibid., 38; Dean C. Jessee, "The Reliability of Joseph Smith's History," 32–33.

editor of the *Painesville Republican* reporting that he had "been Smith's private secretary" and criticized Joseph and other Church leaders saying: "They lie by revelation, swindle by revelation, cheat and defraud by revelation, run away by revelation."[104] Yet it doesn't appear that he ever accused the Prophet of sexual immorality.[105] Janet Ellingson observed: "Warren Parrish, who in 1837–38 did his best to publicly destroy Smith, failed to mention the alleged Alger pregnancy in all his verbal attacks; and the national press, which loved to extrapolate on Smith's foibles, ignored the polygamy angle during the 1830s."[106]

Similarly, the Far West High Council membership was evidently satisfied with an apparent brief synopsis of the "girl business" as the Prophet explained it to them in April 1838. It seems most likely to me that the question of plural marriage did not come up and that the Prophet, who would have made a sharp distinction between plural marriage and adultery, straightforwardly (and accurately) denied committing adultery. To my knowledge, no retrospective statements exist from high councilors who heard that first conversation but later learned about polygamy in Nauvoo and who might, therefore, have reappraised the information in the high council meeting. Likewise, when asked about the First Presidency's conduct at his excommunication trial on May 11, 1838, William E. McLellin told Joseph Smith that "he had seen nothing out of the way himself, but he judged from hearsay."[107]

Excommunicated in 1838, David Whitmer, one of the Three Witnesses of the Book of Mormon, likewise was unaware of any polygamy in Ohio. In 1887 he wrote: "I desire to speak here on the subject of polygamy. A few years ago I had doubts in regard to Brother Joseph's connection with the Spiritual Wife doctrine, but . . . I now have as much evidence to believe that Brother Joseph received the revelation on polygamy and gave it to the Church, as I have to believe that such a man as George Washington ever lived."[108] But if Joseph had confided the restoration of plural marriage to him in Ohio or Missouri (unlikely, given the growing alienation that began shortly after the April 1836 dedication of the Kirtland Temple), then Whitmer would have had no "doubts" about whether Joseph had received the revelation he mentions.

---

104. Warren F. Parrish, Letter to the *Painesville Republican*, February 5, 1838, *Painesville Republican* 2, nos. 14–15 (February 15, 1838).

105. Warren F. Parrish asserts that the leaders' "examples do violence to the system of morality, to say nothing about religion. . . . [And there are] many abominations that might be [stated] such as the prophet's fighting four pitched battles at fisticuff[s], within four years, one with his own natural brother. Ibid.

106. Janet Ellingson, "Alger Marriage Questioned," vi.

107. Jessee, Ashhurst-McGee, and Jensen, *Journals. Vol, 1: 1832–1839*, 268; Faulring, *An American Prophet's Record*, 182.

108. David Whitmer, *An Address to All Believers in Christ: By a Witness to the Divine Authenticity of the Book of Mormon*, 38.

The initial responses of other individuals, like Thomas B. Marsh and Frederick G. Williams, are not available, nor can the level of their personal knowledge of polygamy with Fanny Alger (or rumors of polygamy) be determined; but it appears that they were unfazed. An October 24, 1838, affidavit written by Marsh accused Joseph Smith of errors, like taking a warlike attitude towards the Missourians, but he includes no complaint of polygamy or sexual immorality.[109] First Presidency Counselor Frederick G. Williams also left an undated handwritten statement titled "Statement of Facts Relative to Joseph Smith and Myself," in which he airs grievances but says nothing about polygamy or sexual misconduct.[110] Elder Luman A. Shurtliff recalled discussing polygamy with Frederick G. Williams in March of 1838: "They [we] had talked it over and concluded it was ridiculous for an Elder to believe such an awful doctrine."[111]

Reviewing available literature gives a puzzling picture of the impact of Joseph Smith's first plural marriage on the 1837 apostasy at Kirtland. With the exception of Oliver Cowdery, no other contemporary voice declared it to be a problem. While rumors of adultery undoubtedly affected some in their estrangement from the Church, the degree of influence is difficult to determine and no accusations of *polygamy* (only adultery) against the Prophet have been identified. Several other issues, like the collapse of the Kirtland Safety Society, seemed to have had more influence than the Prophet's possible illicit relationship as primary contributors to the apostate flow of that era.

Summary

Some authors assert that Joseph Smith and the Latter-day Saints had a reputation for polygamy during the 1830s and cite the denials of Church leaders as evidence. They allege that the article on "Marriage," which was written by Oliver Cowdery and included in the 1835 Doctrine and Covenants, was somehow associated with Joseph Smith's behaviors because it explicitly condemned "fornication and polygamy." In fact, no evidence has been found to support that the Prophet was accused of either impropriety at that time. A year or two later, he would be charged with adultery, but not polygamy. Writers who assert that the Church or its leaders like Joseph Smith had a reputation for practicing polygamy during the 1830s need to produce some contemporary evidence to support the allegation.

It appears the decision to include the article on "Marriage" was made weeks or even months before the General Assembly held on August 17, 1835,

---

109. Thomas B. Marsh, Affidavit, 1838.
110. Frederick G. Williams, "Statement of Facts Relative to Joseph Smith and Myself."
111. Luman Andrus Shurtliff, "Autobiography," 116–18.

approved it for inclusion in the Doctrine and Covenants and that Joseph Smith's absence was unrelated to the article's approval.

By 1837, Church members who believed Joseph Smith's denials of adultery continued true to the faith, giving full support to their seer and president. In contrast, unbelievers generally withdrew from the body of the Saints, leaving their accusations to be muffled by time and frontier space.

Available evidence supports that Joseph was able to leave Ohio and Missouri to enter a new chapter of his life in Illinois effectively unfettered by credible accusations of previous immorality or even whispered allegations of restored plural marriage. By 1838, Joseph Smith had crossed the plural marriage threshold and endured its consequences, which undoubtedly transformed him and his feelings towards its practice. Bruised by the repercussions, he continued a monogamous path but not for long. Records indicate that soon the angelic visitor would return, bearing specific directives that the reluctant Prophet could not easily refuse.

Chapter 8

Pre-Nauvoo Preparations for Plural Marriage

As discussed in Chapters 2-3, several authors have speculated that, during the 1830s, Joseph Smith was involved in other pre-Nauvoo relationships or polygamous unions in addition to Fanny Alger. However, available documentation reveals important credibility and plausibility problems with each of the eleven reports that have been offered as evidence. In addition, a review of both published and unpublished documents indicates that the Prophet did not then possess a reputation as a womanizer.

During the late 1830s, the Prophet's life underwent several transformations. The apostasy at Kirtland necessitated a move to Missouri where war broke out between the Latter-day Saints and the inhabitants of the state in the fall of 1838. Church members were killed. Joseph was imprisoned. He eventually escaped, arriving safely in Quincy, Illinois, in April 1839. After acquiring tracts of land forty miles to the north, Joseph renamed a riverside hamlet "Nauvoo" and settled down. He must have been filled with hope that a templed city would soon arise there on the banks of the Mississippi River.

Church Members' Pre-Nauvoo Knowledge of Plural Marriage

As outlined in Chapter 4, Joseph Smith learned of the correctness of plural marriage in 1831 and informed a very few Church members, like Lyman E. Johnson and W. W. Phelps, about it.[1] About four years later, he entered his first plural marriage with Fanny Alger and, as a consequence, introduced the topic to a few more individuals including those who assisted with the ceremony. Precisely how many were then informed is difficult to assess. Those who appear to have learned of the relationship from the Prophet's mouth included Emma Smith, Oliver Cowdery, Martin Harris, Lyman R. Sherman, and Levi Hancock. Also informed at the time were Fanny Alger's parents,

---

1. For Lyman E. Johnson, see report of Orson Pratt, "Report of Elders Orson Pratt and Joseph F. Smith," 788. For W. W. Phelps, see W.W. Phelps, Letter to Brigham Young, August 12, 1861.

Chauncy and Eliza Churchill Webb, Clarissa Hancock, and Eliza R. Snow. It appears perhaps a dozen learned about the first plural marriage either directly from Joseph or from Fanny herself.

A letter from Franklin D. Richards to Joseph F. Smith, July 5, 1881, mentions an unidentified Church sister who seems to have been one of those the Prophet taught in Kirtland:

President Joseph F. Smith,

Dear Brother—In 1840 while on my first mission, my labors were mostly in the vicinity of Laporte, Plymouth, and Michigan City in the Northern Indiana where by the help of the Lord I raised up a Branch and added to Branches already formed.

In this region were quite a number of Saints who were on their way to Far West in Missouri at the time of the persecutions in 1838, who, When they learned of the expulsion to Illinois, located wherever they were at the time until another place of gathering should be designated—of this number was one a [sic] sister Akers[2] who represented herself to me as having lived in Kirtland and as being well acquainted with the Prophet Joseph and with many of the leading men and their families in that place.

She stated to me that the doctrine of "spiritual wives"[3] as she then termed it, was a true doctrine, that it had been revealed to the Prophet Joseph Smith and would sometime be put in practice in the Church—that it was not then permitted, but that I would live to see it taught accepted, lived in and practically adopted as a doctrine and ordinance of the Church.

Although in her statement she appeared honest and earnest, and for aught I knew was blameless in her life & conduct otherwise still I found that such whisperings were prejudicing unbelievers against the truth and souring the minds of some of the Saints, still I was obliged to put a stop to her unwise

---

2. I have been unable to further identify "sister Akers" in Church records and documents.

3. In the 1830s, observers commonly used "spiritual wife" to describe any non-monogamous matrimonial arrangements sanctioned by the different religious sects of the day. Samuel Harrison Smith, Diary, July 1, 1832, and Orson Hyde, "1832 Mission Journal," July 1, 1832. There is no contemporary evidence that Joseph Smith used the term to introduce the restoration of plural marriage, either at Kirtland, Ohio, or later at Nauvoo, Illinois. The first person to apply the term to the Prophet's teachings was John C. Bennett in 1842. Joseph Smith apparently used the phrase in derision on occasion after 1842. Andrew F. Ehat and Lyndon W. Cook, eds., *The Words of Joseph Smith: The Contemporary Accounts of the Nauvoo Discourses of the Prophet Joseph Smith*, 257. In later years, some Church members and even leaders adopted the term, which creates confusion for historians attempting to reconstruct the chronology associated with its use. See, for example, Heber C. Kimball, October 6, 1855, *Journal of Discourses*, 3:125; Emily D. Partridge Young, "Pioneer Day," 37.

conversation by threatening to disfellowship her if she did not desist. Sister Akers afterwards gathered to Nauvoo where some of her sayings come true.
Yours very truly,
[signed] F. D. Richards[4]

Chapter 3 analyzes the available reports that Joseph Smith was involved with plural marriage or other relationships between 1835 and 1841. Despite those few late narratives, it appears that, after Kirtland, Joseph Smith taught no one about plural marriage and did not even mention the subject for five or six years. If such discussions took place, they have yet to be documented. That span of silence could represent a postponement in the project of reestablishing polygamy. However, during that period, some Church members may have independently speculated on the subject. Luman A. Shurtliff described a conversation he had with another member, Leister Gaylor, about March 1838 in Ohio:

> While I and Br Leister was going from Kirtland to Sullivan to see about getting our Teems [i.e., about mid-March 1838] In our conversation on the advancement of the Kingdom of God on the Earth I told him I believed that the time would come when men \in this church/ would have more then \one/ Wife... I also read in the Prophets that in the latter days Seven women should take hold of one man saying we will Eat our own bread and wear our own cloths that we may be called by the name of one man then marry him Again I read in Acts that the Lord would restore all thing spoken \off/ or taught by all the holy Prophets since the World began Was the Polig\a/my of Abraham Jacob David Solomon and many others spoken of if so that must be restored. I also understand that the Gospel must be preached among all Nations and all those who believe and are baptised shall be saved and enjoy all the privileges of this Kingdom Also than one third of the Nations of the Earth are now in the belief and practice of polygamy. Now if you should be sent to preach the Gospel to or in a Nation practiceing poligamy and a man should believe and all his House or family And ask or demand Baptism at your hands What would you do[?][5]

As Joseph Smith's life calmed upon arriving in Illinois, his mind was free to reconsider previous doctrines that had been only partially revealed including plural marriage. Richard L. Bushman noted: "After this one unsuccessful attempt" of polygamous marriage with Fanny Alger, Joseph Smith "waited another five years. The delay showed an uncharacteristic reluctance, hard for one who

---

4. Franklin D. Richards, Letter to Joseph F. Smith, July 5, 1881, in *Selected Collections*, Vol. 1, DVD #27.

5. Luman Andros Shurtliff, Autobiography, typescript, 117. The slash marks indicate interlinear additions and corrections.

feared God. . . . Surely he realized that plural marriage would inflict terrible damage, that he ran the risk of wrecking his marriage and alienating his followers."[6]

Angel with a Drawn Sword

More than twenty documents support that Joseph Smith hesitated in Nauvoo to once again consider the principle of plural marriage. Helen Mar Kimball Whitney stated late in life: "Had it not been for the fear of His [the Lord's] displeasure, Joseph would have shrunk from the undertaking and would have continued silent, as he did for years."[7] "Joseph put off the dreaded day as long as he dared."[8] Lucy Walker reported that Joseph "had his doubts about it for he debated it in his own mind."[9]

The Prophet's nephew, Joseph F. Smith, summarized at a stake quarterly conference in 1883: "Joseph Smith was commanded to take wives, he hesitated and postponed it, seeing the consequences and the trouble that it would bring and he shrank from the responsibility, but he prayed to the Lord for it to pass as Jesus did, but Jesus had to drink it to the dregs so it was with Joseph Smith, the Lord had revealed it to him, and said now is the time for it to be practiced—but it was not until he had been told he must practice it or be destroyed that he made the attempt."[10]

Joseph Smith had other reasons to be hesitant. In 1832 he had been mobbed, tarred, and feathered in Hiram, Ohio, for attempting to establish the United Order. (See Chapter 2.) The memory of that experience may be why he lamented to Levi Hancock: "Brother Levi, if I should make known to my brethren what God has made known to me they would seek my life."[11] In 1843 Joseph observed: "Men will say I will never forsake you but will stand by you at all times but the moment you teach them some of the mysteries of God that are retained in the heavens and are to be revealed to the children of men when they are prepared, They will be the first to stone you & put you to death."[12] In addition, Richard Van Wagoner observed: "The difficulties [of] the Fanny

---

6. Richard L. Bushman, *Joseph Smith: Rough Stone Rolling*, 437–38.
7. Helen Mar Kimball Whitney, *Why We Practice Plural Marriage*, 53.
8. Jeni Broberg Holzapfel and Richard Neitzel Holzapfel, eds., *A Woman's View: Helen Mar Whitney's Reminiscences of Early Church History*, 142.
9. Lucy Walker, Deposition, Temple Lot Transcript, Respondent's Testimony, Part 3, p. 474, questions 600.
10. Joseph F. Smith, Statement on Oliver Cowdery and Polygamy, March 4, 1883, 271–72.
11. Joseph Smith, quoted in Mosiah Hancock, "Correspondence: The Prophet Joseph—Some of His Sayings," *Deseret News*, February 27, 1884, 15.
12. Ehat and Cook, *The Words of Joseph Smith*, 213.

Alger situation . . . seriously hampered Joseph Smith's apparent enthusiasm for plural marriage."[13]

So in the face of these anxieties, what might have prompted Joseph Smith to once again marry polygamously and teach others to do likewise? Twenty-one accounts by nine polygamy insiders left recollections that the Prophet told of one specific reason: an angel with a sword who threatened him if he did not proceed.[14]

All nine witnesses could have heard the statement from the Prophet himself; however, the narratives themselves suggest that Benjamin F. Johnson and Eliza R. Snow may have been repeating information gathered from other people. Joseph Lee Robinson's narrative is difficult to date and his actual source is not clear.[15] Lorenzo Snow, Erastus Snow, and Mary Elizabeth Rollins Lightner quote the Prophet directly and Mary Elizabeth provides details not available elsewhere. Unfortunately, with the possible exception of the Robinson account, all of the reminiscences date to at least twenty to thirty years after the event.

The identity of the angel is not revealed. It is possible that he was a prophet from a previous dispensation who had actively practiced plural marriage during mortality. Except for Abraham or Jacob, however, very few prophets mentioned in the scriptures were polygamists. Most prophets referenced in the Bible and Book of Mormon practiced monogamy.

The harshness of the described threats has caused some researchers to discount the "sword," considering it a later embellishment.[16] Expanding and enhancing the details of a narrative are not uncommon, even while the substance of the story is based in solid truth. For example, one twentieth-century

---

13. Richard S. Van Wagoner, *Mormon Polygamy: A History*, 12.

14. Three secondhand accounts can be identified. The first is from "Historicus" (1881): "Several persons have sworn to the fact that Joseph told them at different times, but always in strictest confidence, that the time had come for the practice of the doctrine and an angel with a drawn sword had appeared threatening him with eternal destruction, if he did not step forward and establish it." Historicus [pseud.], "Sketches from the History of Polygamy: Joseph Smith's Especial Revelations," 1. Second, Angus Cannon, "Ecclesiastes as an Interviewer," 6, related in 1885: "When he [Joseph Smith] felt to shrink from the responsibility, an angel from heaven stood before him with a drawn sword, saying if he did not move forward and set the example for his brethren by introducing plural marriage, his Priesthood would be taken from him, and he should be destroyed." Third, a non-Mormon, Emily Pfeiffer, wrote that same year: "He [Joseph Smith] accepted from an angel with a drawn sword, and under threat of destruction on refusal, the command to practice and to defuse [diffuse] the doctrine of polygamy." Pfeiffer, *Flying Leaves from East and West*, 147.

15. Lawrence Foster, *Religion and Sexuality*, 305 note 74, wrote: "The earliest manuscript evidence of this story known to me [in 1981] dates from 1846 in Joseph Lee Robinson's, Autobiography and Journal." The reference is dated in the early 1840s, but the journal does not begin daily entries until 1853, suggesting that it was a reminiscence penned at that time. Oliver Preston Robinson ed., *History of Joseph Lee Robinson*, 27, 103.

16. Foster, *Religion and Sexuality*, 305 note 74.

TABLE 8.1
REPORTS OF "ANGEL WITH A DRAWN SWORD"

Date	Source	Quotation	Reference
1853 or possibly earlier[a]	Joseph Lee Robinson	"The Lord instead of releasing [Joseph Smith] from that burden, he sent an holy angel with a drawn sword unto him, saying unto him, Joseph, unless you go to and immediately teach that principle (namely polygamy or plural marriage) and put the same in practice, that he, Joseph, should be slain for thus saith the Lord, that the time has now come that I will raise up seed unto me as I spoke by my servant, Jacob as is recorded in the Book of Mormon, therefore, I command my people."	Oliver Preston Robinson ed., *History of Joseph Lee Robinson*, 27.[b]
1869	Lorenzo Snow	"He [Joseph Smith] said that the Lord had revealed [the doctrine of the plurality of wives] unto him and commanded him to have women sealed to him as wives, that he foresaw the trouble that would follow and sought to turn away from the commandment, that an angel from heaven appeared before him with a drawn sword, threatening him with destruction unless he went forward and obeyed the commandment."	Affidavit signed August 18, 1869; Joseph F. Smith, Affidavit Books, 2:19.[c]
1892	Lorenzo Snow	"He [Joseph Smith] explained to me the principles of plural marriage distinctly and clearly, and told me that the Lord had revealed the principle and had commanded him to enter into that practice. And that he had received a revelation to that effect. He said that he had demurred to doing so as he foresaw the trouble that would ensue, but that an angel of the Lord had appeared before him with a drawn sword commanding him to do so and he could not go backward."	Testimony, Temple Lot Case, Respondent's testimony, Part 3, p. 124, question 258.
1896	Lorenzo Snow	"Pres[iden]t Lorenzo Snow stated that he was in England with Bro[ther] [Parley] Pratt when reports came from Nauvoo to the effect that the doctrine of plural marriage was bring taught. Upon his return to Nauvoo in the spring of 1843 he had a long talk with the Prophet Joseph Smith, who fully explained to him the doctrine of plural marriage, and stated that an angel with a drawn sword had visited him and commanded him to go into this principle, and President Smith told Bro[ther] Snow to enter into plural marriage."	Heber J. Grant, Diary, April 1, 1896.

a. Robinson places this quotation in 1841 of his autobiography. Lawrence Foster dates this account to 1846. It appears to be a recollection that may have been derived from a previously recorded 1841 or 1846 entry in his journal, a journal that is not currently available. If it is a recollection, then it could have been written in 1853 or even later. See Oliver Preston Robinson ed., *History of Joseph Lee Robinson*, 305 note 74. See also Joseph Lee Robinson Reminiscences and Journal, 25. *Three American Communal Experiments of the Nineteenth Century*, 305 note 74.

b. See also Joseph Lee Robinson Reminiscences and Journal, 25.

c. Quoted in Andrew Jenson, "Plural Marriage," 222; see also Joseph Fielding Smith, *Blood Atonement and the Origin of Plural Marriage*, 67 and comments made by President Snow on May 8, 1899, "Discourse," 348.

Benjamin F. Johnson			Eliza R. Snow		
1870	1896	1903	1880	1884	1887
"[Joseph Smith declared] that an angel appeared unto him with a drawn sword, threatening to slay him if he did not proceed to fulfill the law that had been given to him.	"Hyrum said to me, 'Now, Brother Benjamin, you know that Brother Joseph would not sanction this if it was not from the Lord. The Lord revealed this to Brother Joseph long ago, and he put it off until the Angel of the Lord came to him with a drawn sword and told him that he would be slain if he did not go forth and fulfill the law.'"	"Brother Hyram [sic] at once took me in hand, apparently in fear I was not fully Converted and this was the manner of his talk to me—"Now Benjamin, you must not be afraid of this new doctrine for it is all Right. You Know Brother Hyram dont get carried away by worldly things, and he taught this principle untill the Lord Showed him it was true. I know that Joseph was Commanded to take more wives and he waited untill an Angel with a drawn Sword Stood before him and declared that if he longer delayed fulfilling that Command he would Slay him.'"	"She [Eliza R. Snow] spoke of Plural marrage. Said it was a perfect law. Said she had her own prejuse about it. Said she did not know much about it when she was married to Joseph Smith. Said she did not know if ever she would be owned as a wife. Spoke of the Angel standing with a drawn sword in his hand and told Joseph if he did not comply with the requirement of heaven that his priesthood should be taken from him" (terminal punctuation and initial capitals added).	"Joseph told [my brother] Lorenzo Snow that he had 'hesitated and deferred from time to time, until an angel of God stood by him with a drawn sword and told him that, unless he moved forward and established plural marriage, his Priesthood would be taken from him and he should be destroyed!'"	"[Joseph Smith] received the revelation in 1837. but he was himself afraid to promulgate it until the angel came and stood beside him with flaming sword and bade him do the command of God. Not until then did Joseph enter into polygamy, or get any of his disciples to take plural wives."
Affidavit, March 7, 1870, Joseph F. Smith, Affidavit Books, 28.[d]	Benjamin F. Johnson, *My Life's Review*, 95–96.	Dean R. Zimmerman, ed., *I Knew the Prophets: An Analysis of the Letter of Benjamin F. Johnson to George F. Gibbs, Reporting Doctrinal Views of Joseph Smith and Brigham Young*, 43.	Glenwood Ward (Sevier Stake), Relief Society Minutes, 1873–1881, p. 224, September 28, 1880, LDS Church History Library.	*Biography and Family Record of Lorenzo Snow*, Salt Lake City: Deseret News Company, 1884, 69–70.	J.J.J., "Two Prophets' Widows A Visit to the Relicts of Joseph Smith and Brigham Young," *St. Louis Globe-Democrat*, August 18, 1887, 6.

d. Quoted in "Joseph the Seer's Plural Marriages," *Deseret News*, October 19 and 22, 1879. Also in Jenson, "Plural Marriage," 222.

TABLE 8.1 CONTINUED

Date	Source	Quotation	Reference
Pre-1881	Orson Pratt	"I had a pleasant conversation … of the trials of the Prophet Joseph in first introducing the doctrine of Celestial marriage in Nauvoo and quoted the statement of the late apostle and church Historian [Orson Pratt, d. 1881], that the angel of the Lord appeared unto the Prophet Joseph with a drawn sword and declared that if He, Joseph did not go to and teach and practice the Holy commandment He would slay him."	Quoted in A. Karl Larson and Katherine Miles Larson, *Diary of Charles Lowell Walker*, 2 vols. (Logan: Utah State University Press, 1980), 2:814–15, entry for March 5, 1896.[e]
1881	Zina Huntington	"Zina D. Young told of Bro. Joseph's remark in relation to the revelation on celestial marriage. How an angel came to him with a drawn sword, and said if he did not obey this law he would lose his priesthood; and in the keeping of it he, Joseph, did not know but it would cost him his life."	Quoted in "The Prophet's Birthday," *Deseret News*, January 12, 1881, 2.
1894		"[Joseph] sent word to me by my brother, saying, 'Tell Zina I put it off and put it off till an angel with a drawn sword stood by me and told me if I did not establish that principle upon the earth, I would lose my position and my life.'"	"Joseph, the Prophet, His Life and Mission as Viewed by Intimate Acquaintances," *Salt Lake Herald Church and Farm Supplement*, January 12, 1895, 212.[f]
1882	Helen Mar Kimball	"This angel, he [Joseph] states, stood over him with a drawn sword prepared to inflict the penalty of death if he should be disobedient."	Helen Mar Whitney, *Plural Marriage as Taught by the Prophet Joseph: A Reply to Joseph Smith [III], Editor of the Lamoni Iowa "Herald"* (Salt Lake City: Juvenile Instructor Office, 1882), 13.
1884		"This fact [plural marriage] the Lord revealed to His prophet, Joseph Smith, as early as the year 1831. And yet, had it not been for the fear of His displeasure, Joseph would have shrunk from the undertaking and would have continued silent, as he did for years, until an angel of the Lord threatened to slay him if he did not reveal and establish this celestial principle."	Helen Mar Kimball Whitney, *Why We Practice Plural Marriage* (Salt Lake City: Juvenile Instructor Office, 1884), 53.

e. Walker adds: "This statement was made by Joseph F. Smith many years ago and is in print in the Deseret News, where this Angel met the prophet Joseph in the woods and commanded him to go forth and obey and practice the Holy revelation." A. Karl Larson and Katherine Miles Larson, eds., *Diary of Charles Lowell Walker*, 2:815, March 5, 1896.
f. Comments made at a Memorial Services in honor of the Prophet Joseph Smith's Birthday; held in the Sixteenth Ward Meeting House, Sunday Evening, December 23, 1894. Quoted in Brian Stuy, *Collected Discourses*, 5:32.

Person	Quote	Citation	Year
Erastus Snow	"Spoke of the Angel of the Lord meeting Joseph with a drawn sword and of his going to slay him for his being neglectful in the discharges of his duties and of Joseph having to plead on his knees before the Angel for his Life."	A. Karl Larson and Katherine Miles Larson, *Diary of Charles Lowell Walker*, 2 vols. (Logan: Utah State University Press, 1980), 2:611, June 17, 1883.	1883
Erastus Snow	"The Prophet Joseph had said to him [Erastus Snow] also 'I have not been obedient enough to this holy law and the Lord was angry with me and an angel met me with a drawn sword but I pled with the Lord to forgive me and he did so and I made the sacrifice required of my hand and by the help of the Lord I will obey his Holy Law.'"	Erastus Snow, St. George Stake [Conference], General Minutes, Sunday, June 17, 1883, 2 p.m., LR 7836 11, Reel 1.	
Mary Elizabeth Rollins Lightner	"In 1834 he was commanded to take me for a wife. I was a thousand miles from him. He got afraid. The angel came to him [Joseph Smith] three times, the last time with a drawn sword and threatened his life."	"Statement" signed February 8, 1902, Vesta Crawford Papers, Marriott Library, University of Utah[g]	1902
Mary Elizabeth Rollins Lightner	"Joseph told me that he was afraid when the angel appeared to him and told him to take other wives. He hesitated, and the angel appeared to him the third time with a drawn sword in his hand and threatened his life if he did not fulfill the commandment."	Mary E. Lightner to A. M. Chase, April 20, 1904, quoted in J. D. Stead, *Doctrines and Dogmas of Brighamism Exposed* ([Lamoni, Iowa]: RLDS Church, 1911), 218–19.	1904
Mary Elizabeth Rollins Lightner	"An angel came to [Joseph Smith] and the last time he came with a drawn sword in his hand and told Joseph if he did not go into that principle, he would slay him. Joseph said he talked to him soberly about it, and told him it was an abomination and quoted scripture to him. He said in the Book of Mormon it was an abomination in the eyes of the Lord, and they were to adhere to these things except the Lord speak. ... The angel came to me three times between the years of 1834 and 1842 and said I was to obey that principle or he would slay me."	"Remarks" at Brigham Young University, April 14. 1905, vault MSS 363, fd 6, 2–3.	1905
Mary Elizabeth Rollins Lightner	"...he said I was the first woman God Commanded him to take as a plural wife, \in 1834/ he was very much frightened about [it] until the Angel appeared to him three times. It was in the early part of Feb, 1842 before \that/ he was compelled to reveal it to me personally, by the Angel threatening him'" [sword not mentioned].	Letter to Emmeline B. Wells, Summer 1905.	1905

g. Fawn Brodie erroneously attributes this quotation to "Extracts from Mrs. Lightner's autobiography, *Utah Genealogical and Historical Magazine*, 17 (1926), 193 ff." Fawn M. Brodie, *No Man Knows My History: The Life of Joseph Smith, the Mormon Prophet*, 467.

reference to the angel/sword accounts states: "The principle was then revealed by the Lord to Joseph. He was commanded to obey it. He did not immediately comply. Then, according to Apostle George A. Smith, an angel with a flaming sword appeared to the Prophet Joseph and warned him that unless he obeyed it, he would be destroyed."[17] In fact, the George A. Smith this author cites is quoting Lorenzo Snow and, while Snow mentions a sword, he does not describe it as "flaming." However, Lorenzo's sister, Eliza, does describe the sword as "flaming," although she is the only contemporary of Joseph Smith to do so.[18]

Reviewing God's previous dealings with Joseph Smith fails to identify any threats of this magnitude. When he and Martin Harris lost the 116 translated pages of the book of Lehi, the Lord admonished the Prophet, threatening the "vengeance of a just God upon him" (D&C 3:4) if he did not repent (D&C 3:4-6, 5:21, 10:1-2, 37). On this issue, four of the accounts describe him as "afraid"; six state that the angel "threatened" him; seven threaten him with possible death. Three of the statements declare that his priesthood would have been taken if he did not comply. Perhaps this was a threat to take away the keys he had been given by Elijah, releasing him as the "one" man controlling all eternal and plural marriages (see D&C 132:7, 18-19).

Mary Elizabeth Rollins Lightner recalled that the sword-threat was not symbolic: "Joseph told me that he was afraid when the angel appeared to him and told him to take other wives. He hesitated, and the angel appeared to him the third time with a drawn sword in his hand and threatened his life if he did not fulfill the commandment."[19] Erastus Snow claimed that Joseph had "to plead on his knees before the Angel for his Life."[20] On another occasion, Joseph reportedly affirmed: "God commanded me to obey it [plural marriage]. He said to me that unless I accept it and introduce it, and practice it, I, together with my people, should be damned and cut off from this time henceforth."[21] This statement refers to Joseph's salvation, rather than his mortal life, which seems more probable.

The Old Testament story of the prophet Balaam has some similarities to these accounts. When Balak enticed Balaam to curse Israel, an angel with a sword threatened the prophet: "And the ass saw the angel of the Lord standing in the way, and his sword drawn in his hand: and the ass turned aside out of

---

17. Don Cecil Corbett, *Mary Fielding Smith: Daughter of Britain*, 154.

18. Orson F. Whitney also mentioned a "flaming" sword. Orson F. Whitney, *Life of Heber C. Kimball, An Apostle; The Father and Founder of the British Mission*, 321.

19. Mary E. Lightner, Letter to A. M. Chase, April 20, 1904, quoted in J. D. Stead, *Doctrines and Dogmas of Brighamism Exposed*, 218-19.

20. Erastus Snow, quoted in Larson and Larson, *Diary of Charles Lowell Walker*, June 17, 1883, 2:611.

21. Dennison Lott Harris, Statement, May 15, 1881. See also Horace Cummings, "Conspiracy of Nauvoo," 251-60.

the way . . . Then the Lord opened the eyes of Balaam, and he saw the angel of the Lord standing in the way, and his sword drawn in his hand" (Num. 22:23, 31). Balaam later yields to the temptation for riches, curses Israel, and dies by the sword—not wielded by an angel, but in battle (Num. 31:8). For Balaam, the angel's sword became a shadow of his future demise if he continued to disobey.

Besides Balaam's experience, other threatening angels, sometimes with swords, are mentioned five times in scripture. As a consequence of his sins, King David "could not go before it to enquire of God: for he was afraid because of the sword of the angel of the Lord" (1 Chron. 21:30). If Joseph had dawdled in obeying the angel's initial instructions, he may have felt similar fear.

Isaiah related that, in the battle between Judah and the Assyrians, "the angel of the Lord went forth, and smote in the camp of the Assyrians a hundred and fourscore and five thousand: and when they arose early in the morning, behold, they were all dead corpses" (Isa. 37:36, see also 2 Kgs. 19:35). In addition King Herod was smitten by an angel:

> Herod, arrayed in royal apparel, sat upon his throne, and made an oration unto them.
>
> And the people gave a shout, saying, It is the voice of a god, and not of a man.
>
> And immediately the angel of the Lord smote him, because he gave not God the glory: and he was eaten of worms, and gave up the ghost. (Acts 12:21–23).

Future angels are prophesied who will be empowered to "hurt the earth and the sea," to cause "every living soul . . . in the sea" to die and "the rivers and fountains of waters [to become] blood," and "to scorch men with fire" (Rev. 7:2; 16:3–4, 8). In short, Joseph's description of a menacing angel with a sword is not unique.

It is possible that by February of 1842, Joseph Smith had provoked the heavens as never before in his life. The 1834 angelic command prompted Joseph's marriage to Fanny Alger, but that relationship turned into a huge debacle. During the next seven years the angel appeared again, but Joseph apparently demurred for good reasons. He had learned Emma was not ready to accept plural marriage and undoubtedly dreaded the consequences of proceeding without her knowledge or consent. Keeping the whole process secret would be a daunting task. Finding a woman to marry plurally without being exposed would not be easy. Yet the angel commanded compliance.

Evidence of foot-dragging in fulfilling the angelic directive may be identified in the historical record. Joseph Smith received the authority to seal eternal marriages, either monogamous and polygamous, in 1836, but waited five years to use it. Such a span is surprising for the Prophet. Within those years, Joseph may have experienced several opportunities to resist divine promptings and heavenly instructions if they occurred. As Mary Elizabeth Rollins Lightner described it, the angel brandished the sword only on the third visit. Perhaps this situation was unique in the Prophet's life, although, as an imperfect human being, he had faltered in smaller ways on other occasions. He reportedly confessed: "I have my failings and passions to contend with the same as has the greatest stranger to God. I am tempted the same as you are, my brethren. I am not infallible."[22] It seems that in most instances throughout his life, he immediately responded to the Lord's directives.[23] The command to practice polygamy appears to be the only occasion where such forceful admonishment was required to elicit obedience.

Reliability of the Angel-Sword Narratives

Some authors have questioned the overall reliability of any angel-sword narratives, and it is true that none are contemporary with the Prophet. The Joseph Lee Robinson account may be dated as early as 1843 or 1846, but the currently available typescript suggests it may have been written or transcribed in 1853 or even later. Another second-hand rendition, written in 1854 by non-Mormon Benjamin Ferris, who was appointed Secretary to Utah Territory in 1852, contains interesting details that are unsubstantiated and may be fictional. A follower of Swedenborgianism, Ferris clashed with the Mormons during his six months there and provided this account:

> He [Joseph Smith] told some of his most influential followers that if they knew what a hard and unpalatable revelation [regarding plural marriage] he had had, they would drive him from the city. The heavenly powers, however, were not to be trifled with, and a day was appointed when the important mandate was to be submitted to convocation of the authorities of the Church. The time arrived; but Joseph, in virtuous desperation, concluded rather to flee the city than be the medium of communicating a matter so repugnant to his mind. He mounted his horse and galloped from the town, but was met *by an angel with a drawn sword, and threatened with instant destruction* unless he immediately returned and fulfilled his mission. He returned, accordingly, in submissive despair, and made the important communication to the assembled notables. Such is substantially the account of the matter given by simple-minded believers at Salt Lake.[24]

---

22. John D. Lee, *Mormonism Unveiled; or The Life and Confessions of the Late Mormon Bishop, John D. Lee*, 111.

23. See D&C 5:24, 10:1–2. In 1891, Lorenzo Snow, then president of the Quorum of the Twelve, acknowledged: "I saw Joseph the Prophet do, and heard him say, things which I never expected to see and hear in a Prophet of God, yet I was always able to throw a mantle of charity over improper things." Quoted in Dennis B. Horne, ed., *An Apostle's Record: The Journals of Abraham H. Cannon*, January 29, 1891, 175.

24. Benjamin G. Ferris, *Utah and the Mormons: The History, Government, Doctrines, Customs,*

Ferris claimed that he was repeating the version recounted by "simple-minded believers in Salt Lake City" between 1852 and 1854. His narrative is unique in that it describes the angelic threat coming because Joseph delayed in sharing a revelation on plural marriage with Church authorities, rather than hesitating to personally enter polygamy. Regardless, Ferris's statement indicates that the Latter-day Saints were talking about an angel with a sword promoting plural marriage by 1854, a decade after the martyrdom.

Lawrence Foster comments: "Accounts of the 'angel with a drawn sword' story are widespread, although manuscript evidence for such a story apparently does not exist from the period when Joseph Smith was alive. Whether or not Joseph Smith ever made this particular statement, his actions in attempting to introduce polygamous belief and practice among his closest followers in Nauvoo suggest that he was, indeed, operating under a sense of intense inner compulsion."[25]

Researcher Don Bradley argues that contemporary evidence for at least some of the elements can be identified.[26] Associate Church President Hyrum Smith did not accept the principle of plural marriage until May 26, 1843.[27] Earlier that spring, he and others planned to trap the Nauvoo polygamists, possibly not realizing that Joseph was one of them.[28] Levi Richards recorded a portion of Hyrum's discourse on May 14, fervently denouncing polygamy:

> He said there were many that had a great deal to say about the ancient order of things as Solomon and David having many wives and concubines, but it is an abomination in the sight of God. *If an angel from heaven should come and preach such doctrine*, some would be sure to see his cloven foot and cloud of darkness over head, though his garments might shine as white as snow. A man might have one wife but concubines he should have none.[29]

Bradley theorizes that this 1843 quotation may have been referring to the same sword-wielding angel, without mentioning the sword. Hyrum may have been responding to rumors he had heard—rumors that were true and

---

and Prospects of the Latter-day Saints, 115; emphasis mine. This story is repeated in Pomeroy Tucker, *The Origin, Rise, and Progress of Mormonism*, 184; J. H. Beadle, *Polygamy; or Mysteries and Crimes of Mormonism*, 337–38, and James H. Kennedy, *Early Days of Mormonism: Palmyra, Kirtland and Nauvoo*, 272.

25. Lawrence Foster, "A Little-Known Defense of Polygamy from the Mormon Press in 1842," 32 note 4; see also 22. B. Carmon Hardy, *Solemn Covenant: The Mormon Polygamous Passage*, 9, echoed: "One need not be a psychoanalyst to recognize the symbolism in Joseph's claim that an angel appeared to him, sword drawn, commanding activity."

26. Don Bradley, email to Brian Hales, November 11, 2008.

27. George D. Smith, ed., *An Intimate Chronicle: The Journals of William Clayton*, 106.

28. Ibid., 105. See also Andrew F. Ehat, "Joseph Smith's Introduction of Temple Ordinances and the Mormon Succession Question," 46–47.

29. Levi Richards, Journal, May 14, 1843; emphasis mine.

which had originated with Joseph Smith, but which would not be recorded with their details until years later.[30]

A few recollections similarly relate an angelic visit to Joseph in the 1840s without mentioning a sword. In 1866, Brigham Young recalled an encounter between Joseph and William Law, his counselor in the First Presidency, who never accepted plural marriage: "In one council where Joseph undertook to teach the brethren and sisters, William Law was there and William and Hyrum and a few others were against Joseph. William Law made this expression: 'If an angel from heaven was to reveal to me that a man should have more than one wife, and if it were in my power I would kill him.'"[31] Emily D. Partridge recalled: "He [Joseph Smith] told me himself that he had had a revelation. . . . Joseph Smith told me that the angel had appeared to him and had given him that revelation" on plural marriage.[32] In 1848, dissenter Catherine Lewis wrote that plural marriage was restored by "an immediate revelation, and that by an Angel."[33]

Perhaps the most significant of these angel-without-a-sword accounts are those from Joseph B. Noble. He remembered in 1869: "In the fall of the year A.D. 1840 Joseph Smith, taught him the principle of Celestial marriage or a 'plurality of wives', and that the said Joseph Smith declared [sic] that he had received a Revelation from God on the subject, and that the Angel of the Lord had commanded him, (Joseph Smith) to move forward in the said order of marriage."[34] Eleven years later in 1880, Noble "spoke of Joseph unfolding to him the eternity of the marriage covenant to convince him of the truth of which was no small matter—Joseph bore testimony that he had received a revelation on this principle in Kirtland but the Lord then told him 'not yet.' The angel of the Lord came to him in Nauvoo and told him the time had come and Joseph's obedience should be followed by blessing."[35] In 1883 Noble

---

30. Joseph Smith received a vision on January 21, 1836, part of which included: "I saw Elder Brigham Young standing in a strange land, in the far south and west, in a desert place, upon a rock in the midst of about a dozen men of color, who appeared hostile. He was preaching to them in their own tongue, and *the angel of God standing above his head, with a drawn sword in his hand,* protecting him, but he did not see it." Scott H. Faulring, ed., *An American Prophet's Record: The Diaries and Journals of Joseph Smith*, 119; see also *History of the Church*, 2:381; emphasis mine.

31. Brigham Young, October 8, 1866, address in the Salt Lake Bowery, Ms d 1234, Box 49, fd. 13, quoted in Elden J. Watson, *Brigham Young Addresses, 1865–1869: A Chronological Compilation of Known Addresses of the Prophet Brigham Young*, 5:53.

32. Emily D. P. Young, Deposition, Temple Lot Transcript, Respondent's Testimony, Part 3, p. 352, questions 43–44.

33. Catherine Lewis, *Narrative of Some of the Proceedings of the Mormons, etc.; Giving an Account of their Iniquities*, 11.

34. Joseph B. Noble, Affidavit, in Joseph F. Smith, Affidavit Books, 1:38.

35. Noble quoted in St. George Stake Manuscript History, December 23, 1880.

again reminisced: "He [Joseph Smith] stated the angel of the Lord appeared to him and informed him that the time had fully come."[36]

Joseph Noble thus left three accounts that Joseph Smith received the commandment to practice plural marriage from an angel. However, he never describes the angel as bearing a sword. This may be because Noble was first taught plural marriage "in the fall of the year A.D. 1840."[37] Mary Elizabeth Rollins Lightner affirmed that the angel threatened Joseph with a sword only on the third visit, which occurred in February 1842.[38] Noble had undoubtedly heard the other stories about the angel with a sword, but he may have been recounting his own conversations with Joseph Smith that predated that final threatening visit.

Nearly a century later, Apostle Melvin J. Ballard was doubtless aware of some of the potential problems with the angel-sword accounts. He wrote to Mormon fundamentalist polygamist Eslie Jenson in 1934: "The statement . . . concerning the angel appearing with the drawn sword is not a matter that is in our own church history. While it may be all true, the church has not pronounced it authentic nor has it contradicted it."[39]

Future apostle Orson F. Whitney, grandson of Heber C. Kimball and son of Joseph Smith's plural wife Helen Mar Kimball Whitney, apparently believed the story genuine. His 1888 biography of Heber C. Kimball includes this statement:

> A grand and glorious principle had been revealed, and for years had slumbered in the breast of God's Prophet, awaiting the time when, with safety to himself and the Church, it might be confided to the sacred keeping of a chosen few. That time had now come. An angel with a flaming sword descended from the courts of glory and, confronting the Prophet, commanded him in the name of the Lord to establish the principle so long concealed from the knowledge of the Saints and of the world—that of plural marriage.[40]

It would not be surprising to learn that an angel, or even several angels, were involved with Joseph's 1841 decision to enter into his second plural marriage. Church scholar Alex Baugh has documented seventy-six "vision-

---

36. Notes from a quarterly stake conference held at Centerville, Davis County, Utah, June 11, 1883; spelling standardized, quoted in Jenson, "Plural Marriage," 232–33.

37. Noble, Affidavit, in Joseph F. Smith, Affidavit Books, 1:38. See also Joseph Bates Noble, Deposition, Temple Lot Transcript, Respondent's Testimony, Part 3, p. 412, question 384.

38. Mary Elizabeth Rollins Lightner, "Statement," February 8, 1902. See also Mary E. Lightner to A. M. Chase, April 20, 1904, quoted in Stead, *Doctrines and Dogmas of Brighamism Exposed*, 218–19; Rollins Lightner, "Remarks at Brigham Young University, April 14, 1905, 2–3.

39. Melvin J. Ballard, Letter to Eslie Jenson, August 14, 1934, quoted in Joseph W. Musser, *Marriage: Ballard/Jenson Correspondence*, 15.

40. Whitney, *Life of Heber C. Kimball*, 321.

ary experiences" of the Prophet between 1820 and 1844, thirty-one of which included angelic visits.[41] The importance of eternal marriage, including the principle of plural marriage, coupled with the obvious challenges both principles would present to Joseph, makes it a significant event in his life and a likely opportunity for an encounter with an other-worldly being.

To summarize, Mary Elizabeth Rollins Lightner reported that the Prophet informed her that the angel came three times, first in 1834: "In 1834 he [Joseph Smith] was commanded to take me for a wife.... The angel came to him three times."[42] She also quoted the Prophet: "The angel came to me three times between the years of 1834 and 1842 and said I was to obey that principle or he would slay me."[43] If these dates were accurate, the first angelic visit may have prompted the Alger plural marriage, probably in 1835.[44] It also possible that Joseph's poignant memories about the fiasco that resulted caused him to delay further efforts to engage in plurality. The timeline further supports that the angel may have returned for a second visit before April 1841 to admonish Joseph to contract his first plural sealing. The third visit in February 1842 corresponds chronologically to a shift in the Prophet's plural marrying patterns. (See Chapter 17.)

Priesthood Marriages for "Time"

It appears that Joseph Smith performed civil marriages in Ohio using priesthood authority. These ceremonies were for earth life only and did not invoke language that indicated an eternal affiliation was being formed, thus providing further evidence that he was not teaching plural marriage. The first such marriage occurred November 24, 1835, when the Prophet officiated at the wedding of Lydia Goldthwaite Bailey and Newel Knight.[45] Newel recorded:

---

41. Alexander L. Baugh, "Parting the Veil: Joseph Smith's Seventy-Six Documented Visionary Experiences," in John W. Welch and Erick B. Carlson, ed., *Opening the Heavens: Accounts of Divine Manifestations, 1820–1844*, 307–17; accounts #1, 2, 6, 7, 9, 10, 15, 16, 17, 18, 19, 21, 23, 24, 25, 26, 27, 28, 29, 30, 33, 36, 37, 39, 41, 43, 52, 53, 54, 59, and 67 report an angel interacting with Joseph Smith. The text specifies that these thirty-one accounts involved "angels" in general, not angels ordering plural marriage or bearing swords.

42. Rollins Lightner, Statement, February 8, 1902.

43. Rollins Lightner, "Remarks at Brigham Young University, April 14, 1905."

44. Rollins Lightner's "Remarks," 3, contains an inaccuracy: "I am the first being that the revelation was given to him for, and I was one thousand miles away in Missouri for we went up to Jackson County in 1841." The date should be 1831 as no Church members remained in Jackson County after 1833. Whether the discrepancy is due to her faulty memory or an error in the typed transcription is unknown.

45. William G. Hartley, "Newel and Lydia Bailey Knight's Kirtland Love Story and Historic Wedding," 6–22; M. Scott Bradshaw, "Joseph Smith's Performance of Marriages in Ohio," 23–68; Gregory A. Prince, *Power from On High: The Development of*

> Both myself & Lydia had desired that ~~it might be so that~~ the Prophet might seal the bond of matrimony for us, but had not made our desires known to any save the Lord. As Bro Hiram was going to invite the guests I requested him to ask Elder S. Brunson to come to marry us, not expecting Brother Joseph would attend to that ordinance, as he never had married anyone; he having no licence from the State, the state refused to give such licence to the Elders of this Church on the ground that they were not considered by the State [be pre]achers of the gospel, & if any attempted to marry [witho]ut such licence they reviled[?] & did cause them to pay a penalty, it being according to the law of the State of O But to return to the subject: when Brother Hiram invited the Prophet & his family he [Joseph] observed that [Hyrum] was going to invite Brunson to marry us, Joseph replied Stop I will marry them my self, this was good news to us; it seemed that the Lord had granted unto us the desires of our hearts; suffice to say the feast was prepared, the guests were ready, the Prophet & his Council were there, we received much Instruction from the Prophet concerning matrimony, & what the ancient order of God was, & what it must be again concerning marriage. In the name of the Lord, & by the authority of the preisthood which he held, he joined us in the bond of matrimony on Tuesday Nov 23rd [24th] 1835. The evening passed of[f] well, & all felt edefied & glad of the opportunity of enjoying instruction from the Lord through the beloved Prophet.[46]

As quoted earlier, Newel Knight also reported Joseph as saying: "I have done it by the authority of the holy Priesthood and the Gentile law has no power to call me to an account for it. It is my religious privilege, and the congress of the United States has no power to make a law that would abridge the rights of my religion."[47] The Prophet elaborated:

> I had an invitation, to attend a wedding at Br. Hiram [Hyrum] Smith's in the evening also to solemnize the matrimonial ceremony \between Newel Knights [Newel Knight] & Lydia Goldthwaite [Bailey]/ I and my wife, went,

---

Mormon Priesthood, 182.

46. Newel Knight, "Autobiography and Journal [ca. 1846]," 58–59; Joseph Smith's journal and the calendar affirm that Tuesday was the 24th. Dean C. Jessee, Mark Ashhurst-McGee, Richard L. Jensen, eds., *Journals, Vol. 1: 1832–1839*, 109.

47. Newel Knight, "Sketch of the Life of Newel Knight." Quinn identifies Knight's statement as a "first draft"; no notation to that effect is on the holograph, although it is the shortest of several in the collection. D. Michael Quinn, *The Mormon Hierarchy: Origins of Power*, 326 note 32. Lydia Knight quoted Joseph as saying: "Our Elders have been wronged and prosecuted for marrying without a license. The Lord God of Israel has given me authority to unite the people in the holy bonds of matrimony. And from this time forth I shall use that privilege and marry whomsoever I see fit. And the enemies of the Church shall never have power to use the law against me." Susa Young Gates [writing under the pseudonym "Homespun"], *Lydia Knight's History: The First Book of the Noble Women's Lives Series*, 31.

when we arrived a conciderable company, had collected, the bridegroom & bride came in, and took their seats, which gave me to understand that they were ready, I requesteded [sic] them to arise and join hands, I then remarked that marriage was an institution of h[e]aven institude [instituted] in the garden of Eden, that it was necessary that it should be Solemnized by the authority of the everlasting priesthood, before joining hands however, we attended prayers. I then made the remarks above stated; The ceremony was original \with me/ it was in substance as follows, You covenant to be each others companions through life, and discharge the duties of husband & wife in every respect to which they assented, I then pronounced them husband & Wife in the name of God and also pronounced the blessings that the Lord confered upon adam & Eve in the garden of Eden; that is to multiply and replenish the earth, with the addition of long life and prosperity; dismissed them and returned home.[48]

During the next two months, the Prophet solemnized an additional ten weddings.[49] Some writers have been critical of Joseph's actions, saying he was spurning the state laws regarding civil marriages.[50] However, attorney M. Scott Bradshaw reviewed the pertinent statutes in Ohio, then concluded: "Joseph was indeed within his statutory rights in assuming the authority to solemnize marriages. Moreover, he was correct when he stated that performing marriage was his 'religious privilege.' Ohio's marriage statute and the history and evolution of such laws in other states provided clear grounds for these conclusions."[51]

On January 20, 1836, Joseph performed the marriage of Apostle John F. Boynton to Susan Lowell. "I pronounced upon them the blessings of Abraham, Isaac, and Jacob, and such other blessings as the Lord put into my heart. . . . I

---

48. Jessee, Ashhurst-McGee, and Jensen, *Journals: Vol. 1: 1832–1839*, 109–10; Faulring, *An American Prophet's Record*, 67; see also *History of the Church*, 2:320.

49. Geauga County Marriage Records, Book C, microfilm of holograph, 141–42, 144, 165, 188–89, 233–34, LDS Family History Library, quoted in Bradshaw, "Joseph Smith's Performance of Marriage in Ohio," 50 note 5.

50. Among those who comment that Joseph's action was illegal are D. Michael Quinn, *The Mormon Hierarchy: Origins of Power*, 88; John L. Brooke, "'Of Whole Nations Being Born in One Day': Marriage, Money and Magic in the Mormon Cosmos, 1830–1846," 115; and Richard S. Van Wagoner, *Mormon Polygamy*, 7. Lydia remarried without obtaining a formal divorce from her abusive first husband, whom she had left. Danel Bachman commented: "It appears that in the few instances where the original marriages were performed prior to one's acceptance of the gospel but subsequently went bad, Joseph felt they could be abrogated for practical reasons if the candidates wanted to marry someone else." Danel Bachman, "Prologue to the Study of Joseph Smith's Marital Theology," xv + 788 pp., with notes and index, online version. This union could be characterized as "ceremonial polyandry," since two ceremonies were performed, one legal (without a subsequent divorce) and a second religious ceremony in Ohio. However, the first marriage persisted only as a legal formality that was ignored by all participants. See Chapters 12–16.

51. Bradshaw, "Joseph Smith's Performance of Marriage in Ohio," 31.

doubt whether the pages of history can boast of a more splendid and innocent wedding and feast than this, for it was conducted after the order of heaven."[52]

These priesthood marriages were different from those that would be performed later in Nauvoo. They were never called "sealings" and were believed to be equivalent to legal ceremonies that were for this life only—that is, "until death do they part."

A New Doctrine: Marriage beyond Death

It appears that, in the mid-1830s, Joseph Smith began privately teaching that marriage could continue beyond death—a novel doctrine for the times.[53] The practice of plural marriage could be found in the Bible, as with Abraham and Jacob. However, Jesus's statement "For in the resurrection they neither marry, nor are given in marriage, but are as the angels of God in heaven" (Matt. 22:30) was generally interpreted by Christian denominationalists to indicate that death ended earthly marriages. Accordingly, they still consider the teaching of eternal matrimony to be in error, if not blasphemous.[54]

Precisely when Joseph Smith first taught about the possibility of marriage beyond death is not known. Section 76 of the Doctrine and Covenants, given in 1832, describes the inhabitants of the celestial kingdom as "priests and kings" (v. 56); but the section uses only the masculine gender, leaving it unclear if there would also be "priestesses and queens" or if salvation was genderless, hence without the possibility of marriage. It does hint at loftier doctrines by stating that celestial beings will be "sealed by the Holy Spirit of Promise" (v. 53). The need for the active approval of the "Holy Spirit of Promise" for eternally sealed marriages is mentioned four times in the revelation discussing eternal marriage given in 1843 (D&C 132:7, 18, 19, 26).

Hints that marriage could last into the next life can be identified in Joseph Smith's teachings as early as 1835. In May, W.W. Phelps introduced a "new idea" to his wife in a letter: "A new idea, Sally, if you and I continue faithful to the end, we are certain of being one in the Lord throughout eternity; This is one of the most glorious consolations we can have in the flesh. Do not forfeit your birth right."[55]

---

52. Jessee, Ashhurst-McGee, and Jensen, *Journals: Vol. 1, 1832–1839*, 165; Faulring, *An American Prophet's Record*, 116–17; see also *History of the Church*, 2:377.

53. A few other religious movements have embraced a continuation of gender and even marriage after death. For example, Swedish scientist, theologian, and minister Emanuel Swedenborg (1688–1772) taught that marriage could continue in heaven. Swedenborg, *Heaven and Hell*, 382–83, and *The Delights of Wisdom Pertaining to Marriage Love*, 27–56.

54. Richard Abanes, *Becoming Gods: A Closer Look at 21st-Century Mormonism*, 220; George B. Arbaugh, *Gods, Sex, and Saints: The Mormon Story*, 33.

55. W. W. Phelps, Letter to Sally Phelps, May 26, 1835, in *Selected Collections*, Vol. 2, DVD #1. See also Bruce Van Orden, "Writing to Zion: The William W. Phelps

W. W. Phelps. Courtesy of the LDS Church History Library.

Phelps's contemporaneous writings show that he learned these "new ideas" from the Prophet. Phelps was at the time living in the Smith home and was thus well positioned to hear his new revelations.

The following month W. W. Phelps wrote in the Church's *Latter Day Saints Messenger and Advocate*:

> New light is occasionally bursting in to our minds, of the sacred scriptures, for which I am truly thankful. We shall by and by learn that we were with God in another world, before the foundation of the world, and had our agency: that we came into this world and have our agency, in order that we may prepare ourselves for a kingdom of glory; become archangels, even the sons of God *where the man is neither without the woman, nor the woman without the man* in the Lord: A consummation of glory, and happiness, and perfection so greatly to be wished, that I would not miss of it for the fame of ten worlds.[56]

Two months later in a letter from Kirtland, Church member John Corrill referred to his wife as "my companion forever."[57] On September 16, W. W. Phelps wrote again: "Brother Joseph has preached some of his greatest sermons on the duty of wives to their husbands and the rule of all women I ever heard. I would not have you ignorant, Sally, of the mystery of men and women, but I can not write all. . . . You will be mine in this world and in the world to come." But he also added "I have called you at the commencement of this letter, my only one, because I have no right to any other woman in this world nor in the world to come."[58] This last sentence indicates that Joseph's teachings of the continuation of matrimonial ties beyond death did not then include any discussion of plurality of wives.

Joseph and Emma used a variety of parting phrases in their correspondence. On May 5, 1837, Emma signed herself "Yours forever."[59] His parting words in a November 4, 1838, letter were "I am yours forever your husband

---

Kirtland Letters (1835–1836)," 550; M. Guy Bishop, "Eternal Marriage in Early Mormon Marital Beliefs," 78.

56. W. W. Phelps, "Letter No. 8"; emphasis mine.
57. John Corrill, quoted in D. Michael Quinn, *The Mormon Hierarchy: Extensions of Power*, 178.
58. Van Orden, "Writing to Zion," 564.
59. Emma Smith, Letter to Joseph Smith, May 5, 1837, in Joseph Smith Letterbook.

LATTER DAY SAINTS' MESSENGER AND ADVOCATE.

Vol. I. No. 9.]   KIRTLAND, OHIO, JUNE, 1835.   [Whole No. 9.]

Latter Day Saints' Messenger and Advocate, June 1835 issue.

and true friend," and on March 21, 1839, "Yours Forever."[60] Curiously, an 1840 note ended with "Yours in the bond of love your husband until death."[61] But an August 16, 1842, correspondence clarifies this to some degree: "Your affectionate husband until death, through all eternity; forevermore."[62] These early hints of the persistence of marriage beyond death constituted an introduction to doctrines that would be further elucidated in Nauvoo years later. Andrew Ehat explained the apparent limitations of their understanding at that time: "The only direct, contemporary evidences [of the knowledge of eternal marriage in 1835] are two statements by W. W. Phelps. Neither statement by Phelps suggests that since the civil marriage ceremonies were only 'until death do you part' that another marriage ceremony had to be performed before man and woman would be 'one' in the Lord throughout eternity. Phelps's statements seem to say that as long as a couple 'continue faithful' they will be together forever."[63]

In January 1840, Joseph Smith met in Philadelphia with several of the apostles who were on their way to England. Parley P. Pratt had private interviews in which the Prophet taught him about eternal marriage, apparently without mentioning polygamy:

> In Philadelphia I had the happiness of once more meeting with President Smith, and of spending several days with him and others, and with the Saints in that city and vicinity.
>
> During these interviews he taught me many great and glorious principles concerning God and the heavenly order of eternity. It was at this time that I received from him the first idea of eternal family organization, and the eternal union of the sexes in those inexpressibly endearing relationships which none but the highly intellectual, the refined and pure in heart, know how to prize, and which are at the very foundation of everything worthy to be called happiness.
>
> Till then I had learned to esteem kindred affections and sympathies as pertaining solely to this transitory state, as something from which the heart must be entirely weaned, in order to be fitted for its heavenly state.[64]

---

60. Joseph Smith, Letters to Emma Smith, November 4, 1838, and March 21, 1839. Joseph and Emma were not sealed until May of 1843.

61. Joseph Smith, Letter to Emma Smith, January 20, 1840.

62. Joseph Smith, Letter to Emma Smith, August 16, 1842.

63. Andrew F. Ehat, "An Overview of the Introduction of Eternal Marriage in the Church of Jesus Christ of Latter-day Saints, 1840–1843," 3.

64. Parley P. Pratt Jr., ed., *Autobiography of Parley Parker Pratt, One of the Twelve Apostles*

While this entry was recorded several years after the described meeting, other evidence supports the timeline. Also, it indicates that the Prophet was well acquainted with eternal marriage concepts years before publicly mentioning them. Pratt also added:

> It was Joseph Smith who taught me how to prize the endearing relationships of father and mother, husband and wife; of brother and sister, son and daughter. It was from him that I learned that the wife of my bosom might be secured to me for time and all eternity; and that the refined sympathies and affections which endeared us to each other emanated from the fountain of divine eternal love.
>
> It was from him that I learned that we might cultivate these affections, and grow and increase in the same to all eternity; while the result of our endless union would be an offspring as numerous as the stars of heaven, or the sands of the sea shore.
>
> It was from him that I learned the true dignity and destiny of a son of God, clothed with an eternal priesthood, as the patriarch and sovereign of his countless offspring. It was from him that I learned that the highest dignity of womanhood was, to stand as a queen and priestess to her husband, and to reign for ever and ever as the queen mother of her numerous and still increasing offspring.
>
> I had loved before, but I knew not why. But now I loved—with a pureness—an intensity of elevated, exalted feeling, which would lift my soul from the transitory things of this groveling sphere and expand it as the ocean. I felt that God was my Heavenly Father indeed; that Jesus was my brother, and that the wife of my bosom was an immortal, eternal companion; a kind ministering angel, given to me as a comfort, and a crown of glory for ever and ever. In short, I could now love with the spirit and with the understanding also.
>
> Yet, at that time, my dearly beloved brother, Joseph Smith, had barely touched a single key; had merely lifted a corner of the veil and given me a single glance into eternity.[65]

Whether these additional details were disclosed to Parley in 1840 or later in Nauvoo is unknown.

Elijah's Sealing Authority

Perhaps the most important event associated with the establishment of eternal and plural marriage occurred during the dedication of the Kirtland Temple on April 3, 1836. Joseph and Oliver Cowdery recounted an impressive vision, a visitation from Jesus Christ, Moses, and Elias (D&C 110:2–12).[66] Their account

---

of the Church of Jesus Christ of Latter-day Saints, 329–30; see also Benjamin E. Park, "Roundtable Discussion: Perspectives on Parley Pratt's *Autobiography*," 151–53.

65. Pratt, *Autobiography of Parley Parker Pratt*, 297–98.

66. Cynthia Doxey, "Elijah's Mission, Message, and Milestones of Development

Pre-Nauvoo Preparations for Plural Marriage

Kirtland Temple. Used by permission, Utah State Historical Society. All rights reserved.

then described the appearance of the Old Testament prophet Elijah who, Joseph Smith taught, was the last prophet to hold the keys of sealing authority:[67]

The veil was taken from our minds, and the eyes of our understanding were opened.

We saw the Lord standing upon the breastwork of the pulpit, before us; and under his feet was a paved work of pure gold, in color like amber . . .

After this vision had closed, another great and glorious vision burst upon us; for Elijah the prophet, who was taken to heaven without tasting death, stood before us, and said:

Behold, the time has fully come, which was spoken of by the mouth of Malachi—testifying that he [Elijah] should be sent, before the great and dreadful day of the Lord come—

To turn the hearts of the fathers to the children, and the children to the fathers, lest the whole earth be smitten with a curse. (D&C 110:1–2, 13–15.)

It appears that, shortly after this vision on April 3, Joseph Smith recorded a first-hand account or notes about the vision in his personal journal.[68] That original record has not been found and is probably lost. Nonetheless, these important visitations were documented in other contemporaneous records. Within a few days, the Prophet's secretary, Warren Cowdery, transcribed Joseph's first-hand account into a third-hand account to be used in the Church history then being composed.[69] Willard Richards made a separate private copy in 1843.[70]

---

in Family History and Temple Work," in W. Jeffrey Marsh, ed., *Joseph Smith and the Restoration: The 34th Annual Sperry Symposium*, 157–71.

67. Ehat and Cook, *The Words of Joseph Smith*, 43; original manuscript in Robert B. Thompson's hand, October 5, 1840. See also "Elijah," "Bible Dictionary," in the *Holy Bible*, LDS Edition of King James Version (1979), 664.

68. Prince, *Power from On High*, 35–45.

69. For photograph of holograph, see Jessee, Ashhurst-McGee, and Jensen, *Journals: Vol. 1, 1832–1839*, 219–22; *Selected Collections*, Vol. 1, DVD #20; Faulring, *An American Prophet's Record*, April 3, 1836, 157–58. Michael Marquardt observed: "This account was copied into Smith's journal by Warren A. Cowdery who arrived in Kirtland on 25 February 1836. . . . The entries of 2 and 3 April 1836 are written in third-person. It appears that Cowdery used a first-person account but recorded the entries in the third-person as he did for the 1835–36 History." Marquardt, *The Joseph Smith Revelations: Text and Commentary*, 279 note 26.

70. Robert J. Woodford, "The Historical Development of the Doctrine and Covenants," 1460, table 110.

Interior of the Kirtland Temple showing the podiums where Joseph Smith and Oliver Cowdery reported seeing Jesus Christ, Elijah, and other messengers. Used by permission, Utah State Historical Society. All rights reserved.

W. W. Phelps wrote a letter to his wife on April 3 mentioning the Lord's visit and Malachi's prophesy concerning Elijah: "On Sunday, April 3 [1836], the twelve held meeting and administered the sacrament. It was a glorious time. The curtains were dropt [from the ceiling] in the afternoon. And there was a manifestation of the Lord to Brother Joseph and Oliver [by] which they [were told] thus the great and terrible day of the Lord as mentioned by Malachi, was near, even at the doors."[71]

This letter indicates that the Prophet discussed these heavenly visitations with a few associates at that time. However, multiple evidences support that most Kirtland Latter-day Saints were either unaware of the visitation or at least uninformed regarding its significance.[72] It was not published at that time. This is curious because other revelations and accounts of important historical events, like the ordination from Peter, James, and John, had been published.[73] In fact, Church members would not learn about the vision in any printed venue until November 6, 1852 when the *Deseret News* published it.[74] Orson

---

71. William W. Phelps, Letter to Sally Phelps, April 1–3, 1836; quoted in Steven C. Harper, "A Pentecost and Endowment Indeed: Six Eyewitness Accounts of the Kirtland Temple Experience," in Welch and Carlson, *Opening the Heavens*, 349.

72. See discussion in David L. Paulsen, Kendel J. Christensen, and Martin Pulido, "Redeeming the Dead: Tender Mercies, Turning of Hearts, and Restoration of Authority," 49 note 66.

73. See 1835 D&C 50:3; David Patten, "To the Saints Scattered Abroad," 42.

74. "Life of Joseph Smith," *Deseret News*, November 6, 1852, 101.

Pratt converted the narrative to first-person and included it as section 110 of the 1876 Doctrine and Covenants.

Child-to-Parent Sealings

Despite the importance of Elijah and the Kirtland Temple visitations, Joseph Smith apparently did not refer to it throughout the remainder of the 1830s. In his discourses beginning in 1840s, the Prophet began emphasizing the importance of Elijah's mission and his priesthood authority. At that time, he might have also divulged the details of the heavenly visitations to his followers.[75] However, the historical record shows a public silence concerning that 1836 ordination throughout his life.[76] For example, on October 5, 1840, Joseph taught: "Elijah was the last prophet that held the keys of this priesthood, and who *will*, before the last dispensation, restore the authority and deliver the keys of this priesthood in order that all the ordinances may be attended to in righteousness."[77] He could have said that Elijah "has already restored the authority," but apparently he felt that level of disclosure was not yet appropriate.

---

75. Identifying Joseph Smith's first private and public discussions of Elijah's visit suggests that little was said prior to 1840. However, in Patten's, "To the Saints Scattered Abroad," 42, published in July 1838, he wrote: "Now my readers, you can see in some degree, the grace given to this man of God [Joseph Smith], to us-ward. That we, by the great mercy of God, should receive from under his hand, the gospel of Jesus Christ, and having the promise of partaking of the fruit of the vine, on the earth with him, and with the holy prophets and patriarchs our fathers. For those holy men are angels now. And these are they, who make the fulness of times complete with us. . . . And also Elijah, who holds the keys of committing the power, to turn the hearts of the fathers to the children, and the hearts of the children to the fathers, that the whole earth may not be smitten with a curse." This statement might be considered a direct reference to the visit of Elijah in the Kirtland Temple more than two years earlier, except that Patten is apparently simply quoting and paraphrasing D&C 27:5–13. Whether he was actually aware of the previous bestowal of sealing keys upon Joseph and Oliver is unclear.

76. In 1842, Joseph wrote about the sealing authority, implying that he held those keys: "It may seem to some to be a very bold doctrine that we talk of—a power which records or binds on earth and binds in heaven. Nevertheless, in all ages of the world, whenever the Lord has given a dispensation of the priesthood to any man by actual revelation, or any set of men, this power has always been given. Hence, whatsoever those men did in authority, in the name of the Lord . . . it became a law on earth and in heaven, and could not be annulled, according to the decrees of the great Jehovah." (D&C 128:9). This letter was published as "On Marriage," *Times and Seasons* 3 (October 1, 1842): 939–40.

77. Ehat and Cook, *The Words of Joseph Smith*, October 5, 1840, 43; holograph in Robert B. Thompson's hand; emphasis mine.

The exact reasons for Joseph Smith's public silence concerning Elijah's visit are unknown. However, a parallel event described in the New Testament may provide a clue:

> And after six days Jesus taketh Peter, James, and John his brother, and bringeth them up into an high mountain apart,
>
> And was transfigured before them: and his face did shine as the sun, and his raiment was white as the light.
>
> And, behold, there appeared unto them Moses and Elias talking with him.
>
> Then answered Peter, and said unto Jesus, Lord, it is good for us to be here: if thou wilt, let us make here three tabernacles; one for thee, and one for Moses, and one for Elias.
>
> While he yet spake, behold, a bright cloud overshadowed them: and behold a voice out of the cloud, which said, This is my beloved Son, in whom I am well pleased; hear ye him.
>
> And when the disciples heard [it], they fell on their face, and were sore afraid.
>
> And Jesus came and touched them, and said, Arise, and be not afraid. And when they had lifted up their eyes, they saw no man, save Jesus only.
>
> And as they came down from the mountain, Jesus charged them, saying, Tell the vision to no man, until the Son of man be risen again from the dead. (Matt. 17:1–9.)

Matthew outlines the visit of Elias and Moses to Christ and his three senior apostles in a visit that resembles Joseph and Oliver's experience in several ways. Importantly, after the theophany was finished, the Savior instructed them: "Tell the vision to no man, until the Son of man be risen again from the dead" (Matt. 17:9). Perhaps a similar injunction was included regarding the public disclosure of Elijah's visit, with the limiting factor being, perhaps, to wait until the Nauvoo Temple was completed. Joseph Smith reportedly encouraged the Latter-day Saints to "finish the temple" promising them that afterwards "God will fill it with power, and you will then receive more knowledge."[78] It is possible that the Prophet was waiting for some sentinel event before sharing the details of the visits of the Old Testament prophets on April 3, 1836, with Church members.

Without mentioning Elijah specifically, the function and significance of the priesthood keys he restored were eventually taught. In Joseph Smith's theology, it is the same power Christ gave to Peter as outlined in the New Testament. Jesus instructed his senior apostle saying: "And I will give unto thee the keys

---

78. Manuscript History of the Church, August 27, 1843, in *Selected Collections*, Vol. 1, DVD #1; *History of the Church*, 5:555. The specific knowledge promised was regarding the "patriarchal authority," but it seems likely that other important disclosures would be made in conjunction with the beginning of ordinance work in the temple.

of the kingdom of heaven: and whatsoever thou shalt bind on earth shall be bound in heaven: and whatsoever thou shalt loose on earth shall be loosed in heaven" (Matt. 16:19). Specifically, Elijah's authority could authorize eternal sealings in two directions: joining husbands and wives (horizontal) and joining children to parents (vertical). Notwithstanding, Joseph introduced Elijah's mission by almost exclusively emphasizing the sealings of parents and children (vertical). For example, on April 16, 1843, Joseph taught of the resurrection: "I actually saw men, before they had ascended from the tomb, as though they were getting up slowly, they took each other by the hand & it was my father & my son. my mother & my daughter, my brother & my sister when the voice calls, suppose I am laid by the side of my father.—what would be the first joy of my heart? where is my father—my mother—my sister. they are by my side I embrace them & they me."[79] Regarding this sermon, Andrew Ehat insightfully observed: "Joseph Smith poignantly described [in the discourse] how familial relationships can be expected to continue in the resurrection. But, Joseph during the sermon carefully avoided mentioning the possibility that eternal relationship could exist between husband and wife. From the five contemporary accounts of this discourse we find the prophet mentioned the titles 'Father' and 'Son,' 'Mother' and 'Daughter,' but not the titles 'husband' and 'wife.'"[80]

Just months before the martyrdom, on March 10, 1844, the Prophet gave a lengthy public discourse referring to Malachi's prediction emphasizing the need for inter-generational parents-to-children sealings: "Behold, I will send you Elijah the prophet before the coming of the great and dreadful day of the Lord. And he shall turn the heart of the fathers to the children, and the heart of the children to their fathers, lest I come and smite the earth with a curse" (Mal. 4:5–6).[81] However, even at that later date, he did not publicly teach eternal marriage so far as records indicate.

Private Teachings of Marriage Sealings

Multiple documents demonstrate that, in contrast to his public sermons, Joseph Smith privately taught that Elijah's authority could seal marriages, either monogamous or polygamous. In Ramus, Illinois, on May 16, 1843, William Clayton recorded:

> Prest. J. & I went to B.F. Johnsons to sleep. Before we retired the Prest. gave bro Johnson & wife some instructions on the priesthood . . .

---

79. Ehat and Cook, *The Words of Joseph Smith*, 195–96.
80. Andrew F. Ehat, "Joseph Smith's Introduction of Temple Ordinances and the Mormon Succession Question," 65.
81. Ehat and Cook, *The Words of Joseph Smith*, 327–31; citing Wilford Woodruff, Diary, March 10, 1844.

He said that except a man and his wife enter into an everlasting covenant and be married for eternity while in this probation by the power and authority of the Holy priesthood they will cease to increase when they die (ie. they will not have any children in the resurrection), but those who are married by the power & authority of the priesthood in this life & continue without committing the sin against the Holy Ghost will continue to increase & have children in the celestial glory.[82]

Clayton continued by recording part of this explanation. Decades later, Brigham Young directed Orson Pratt to extract it, and it first appeared as section 131 of the 1876 of the Doctrine and Covenants.[83]

It appears that Joseph Smith may have privately informed his inner circle that Elijah had bestowed the sealing authority upon him. His revelation on celestial marriage, recorded on July 12, 1843, states that "I have appointed unto my servant Joseph to hold this power [the authority to seal] in the last days" (D&C 132:7). On April 8, 1844, Hyrum Smith taught: "The Lord has given Joseph the power to seal on earth and in heaven [for] those who are found worthy; having the Spirit of Elijah and Elias, he has power to seal with a seal that shall never be broken, and it shall be in force in the morn of the resurrection."[84] Neither of these sources overtly acknowledged who bestowed the authority or when or where it was given, but clues are provided.

In 1852, Orson Pratt related items of instruction he likely received privately from the Prophet concerning the Kirtland events:

They are the sealing keys of power, or in other words, of Elijah, having been committed and restored to the earth by Elijah, the Prophet, who held many keys, among which were the keys of sealing, to bind the hearts of the fathers to the children, and the children to the fathers; together with all the other sealing keys and powers, pertaining to the last dispensation. They were committed by that Angel who administered in the Kirtland Temple, and spoke unto Joseph the Prophet, at the time of the endowments in that house.[85]

Evidently, Joseph Smith's only known *public* reference to eternal monogamous marriage occurred on July 16, 1843, just four days after he dictated the revelation on eternal and celestial marriage that is now Doctrine and Covenants 132.[86] (See Chapter 25.) Perhaps emboldened by the written

---

82. George D. Smith, *An Intimate Chronicle*, 102.

83. Woodford, "The Historical Development of the Doctrine and Covenants," 1724.

84. Hyrum Smith, Discourse of April 8, 1844, in *Selected Collections*, Vol. 1, DVD #1, internal pagination is Vol. 6, pp. 1984–91. The edited version of this discourse that was published in the *History of the Church*, 6:320–21, appears on page 11 of the addendum.

85. Orson Pratt, August 29, 1852, *Journal of Discourses*, 1:64. See also Parley P. Pratt, "Proclamation," 151; Pratt, "Celestial Family Organization," 193.

86. Two months earlier, he reportedly said: "We have no claim in our eternal comfort

revelation, the Prophet openly referred to eternal monogamous marriage, but the response of his audience convinced him that additional disclosures would not be well received. Teaching from the temple stand in Nauvoo, the Prophet instructed, according to Franklin D. Richards: "No man can obtain an eternal blessing unless the contract or covenant be made in view of eternity. All contracts in view of this life only terminate with this life."[87] According to William Clayton, he also "showed that a man must enter into an everlasting covenant with his wife in this world or he will have no claim on her in the next."[88] The official *History of the Church* version contains an amalgamation and commentary: "I . . . slightly touched upon the subject of the everlasting covenant, showing that a man and his wife must enter into that covenant in the world, or he will have no claim on her in the next world. But on account of the unbelief of the people, I cannot reveal the fullness of these things at present."[89] The actual source of the last sentence about the imposition of silence is unclear from the handwritten records, but it appears to accurately represent the receptiveness of the Saints at that time.[90]

By the end of 1843, the Prophet, either directly or through other leaders, taught of eternal marriage sealings. We have no record that the teachings were given publicly, but documents show that Church members were gradually informed during the last few months of 1843. On October 15, 1843, non-Mormon Charlotte Haven wrote to her sister: "I have heard that in some cases the marriage is not only for time but for eternity."[91] Similarly, in January 1844, Jacob Scott wrote to his daughter, Mary Warnock, explaining details of eternal marriage and proxy sealings that go beyond published discussions of the topic printed up to that date:

> Several Revelations of great utility, & uncommon interest have been lately communicated to Joseph & the Church; but where you are you cannot obey them; one Tis that all Marriage contracts or Covenants are to be "Everlasting["], that is: The parties (if the[y] belong to the Church) and will obey the will of God in this relationship to each other; are to be married for both Time and Eternity; and as respects those whose partners were dead,

---

in relation to eternal things unless our actions and contracts and all things tend to this end." Ehat and Cook, *The Words of Joseph Smith*, 205. While not specifically mentioning marriage, "eternal things" might be an allusion to eternal contracts, which could include matrimony.

87. Ibid., 232; citing Franklin D. Richards, "Scriptural Items," July 16, 1843.

88. Ibid., 233; citing William Clayton, Diary, July 16, 1843.

89. *History of the Church*, 5:510; see Manuscript History of the Church, July 16, 1843, in *Selected Collections*, Vol. 1, DVD #1.

90. This version was also published in "History of Joseph Smith," *Millennial Star* 21, no. 47 (November 19, 1859): 747.

91. Charlotte Haven, "A Girl's Letters from Nauvoo," 637.

before this Revelation was given to the Church; they have the privilege to be married to their deceased husbands, or wives (as the case may be) for eternity, and if it is a man who desires to be married to his deceased wife; a Sister in the Church stands as Proxy, or as a representative of the deceased in attending to the marriage ceremony; and so in the case of a widow who desires to be joined in a everlasting covenant to her dead husband—and if they are not thus married for Eternity, they must remain in a state of Celebacy [sic], & be as the angels, ministering spirits, r [are] servants to the married to all eternity, and can never rise to any greater degree of Glory.—

Many members of the Church have already availed themselves of this privilege, & have been married to their deceased partners; & in some cases where a Man has been married to 2 or three wives, and they are dead he has been married to them all; in the Order in which he was married to them while living & also widows have been married to their dead husbands . . . & I intend to be married to the wife of my youth before I go to Ireland, I would be unspeakably glad to have you all here to witness our Second Nuptials. The work of Generation is not to cease for ever with the Saints in this present life— There are many things connected with this subject which I am not at liberty to communicate to you, where you are living which would make the matter plainer to your minds & more satisfactory therefore, beware how you treat this subject for no doubt it is of God. Other revelations intimately connected with this momentous dispensation and which are almost ready to unfold themselves to us, I cannot communicate to you at present, altho' I know them in part for you could not bear them now. If you were living with the Church, your Spiritual advantages would be much greater than they now are.[92]

While some teachings of eternal marriage appear to have been discussed, perhaps even publicly (although not recorded), several witnesses declare that Joseph may have also openly mentioned *plural* marriage in Nauvoo on two occasions (once in 1841 and again in 1843). However, no record has been found documenting that he explained the principle in any detail. (See Chapter 24.) Plural wife Lucy Walker stated that plural marriage was not taught publicly in Nauvoo.[93] In 1892 another plural wife, Malissa Lot, similarly testified: "In the lifetime of Joseph Smith, it [plural marriage] wasn't presented to the Church to my knowledge."[94]

---

92. Jacob Scott (Nauvoo, Ill.), Letter to Mary Warnock (Trafalgar, Ontario), January 5, 1844. Many of these details are found in the first twenty-one verses of the revelation on celestial marriage dictated July 12, 1843, now Doctrine and Covenants 132. Whether Jacob Scott was aware of the remaining teachings found in the revelation is unknown.

93. Lucy Walker, Deposition, Temple Lot Transcript, Respondent's Testimony, Part 3, p. 480, questions 712–22. Virtually all of the witnesses in the Temple Lot Case denied that plural marriage was *publicly* taught in Nauvoo.

94. Malissa Lott, ibid., p. 102, question 181.

Reticence about "Eternal" Marriage?

The historical record indicates that Joseph Smith did not publicly teach eternal marriage for perhaps six years after he received the authority to perform those ordinances. On first glance, the doctrine of eternal marriage seems to be a very innocuous teaching that could provide comfort to couples who were deeply in love or who had lost a spouse to death. Accordingly, the question arises, "Why did Joseph Smith wait so long to teach this principle?"

The answer seems to be related to two factors: Joseph's new teachings regarding vicarious ordinances (like baptism for the dead) and the fact that his brother Hyrum was a widower. On April 8, 1844, Hyrum Smith explained eternal marriage to an eager audience in Nauvoo. In the process of explaining how marriage could last beyond death, Hyrum disclosed the undeniably close relationship that exists between eternal marriage on earth and eternal plural marriage after death:

> I married me a wife, and I am the only one who had any right to her. We had five children, the covenant was made for our lives. She fell into the grave before God showed us his order. God has shown me that the covenant is dead, and had no force, neither could I have her in the resurrection, but we should be as the angels—it troubled me. President Joseph said you can have her sealed to you upon the same principles as you can be baptized for the dead. I enquired what can I do for any second wife? You can also make a covenant with her for eternity and have her sealed to you by the authority of the priesthood.
>
> I named the subject to my present wife, and she said, "I will act as proxy for your wife that is dead, and I will be sealed to you for eternity myself for I never had any other husband. I love you and I do not want to be separate from you nor be forever alone in the world to come" . . . What honest man or woman can find fault with such a doctrine as this? None. It is a doctrine not to be preached to the world; but to the Saints who have obeyed the gospel and gathered to Zion. It is glad tidings of great joy.[95]

An edited account of this discourse was later published in the *History of the Church*, but the portion quoted above was not included.[96] Neither version was printed in the Church's newspaper *Times and Seasons*.

In his comments, Hyrum acknowledged that eternal marriages can be performed for the dead vicariously. This was important to him as a widower because he obviously wished to be married to his first (deceased) wife, Jerusha,

---

95. Hyrum Smith, Conference Minutes, April 8, 1844, in *Selected Collections*, Vol. 1, DVD #1, internal reference: Vol. 6, pp. 1985–88. The edited form of the discourse included in the *History of the Church*, 6:320–21, is found on page 11 of the addendum.

96. *History of the Church* 6:320–21.

in the next life. Hyrum also reported that his living wife, Mary Fielding, did not "want to be separate" from him and could also be sealed to him. Together, the two sealings established the principle of eternal polygamy or polygamy after death. Joseph Smith undoubtedly knew that, upon learning of these principles, his audience would ask the obvious question: "If a man can be sealed to a living wife and a deceased wife, can he be sealed to two living wives?" The truthful answer was quite simple, "Yes, plural marriage is a correct principle when authorized."

However, Joseph had already witnessed the no-holds-barred rejection of plural marriage by Emma, Oliver, and others in Kirtland, Ohio, who considered it straightforward adultery. He recognized that generally, the Saints would not easily understand or embrace plural marriage. In other words, it seems likely that after the Prophet received the authority to seal marriage in 1836, he realized that the minute he introduced *eternal* marriage, questions regarding *plural* marriage would quickly arise, questions he did not want to answer.[97] Accordingly, for several years he hesitated to discuss either teaching with the Latter-day Saints until compelled by an angel to do so.

A Commandment and a Privilege

Individuals who listened to Joseph teach during the Nauvoo period universally recall his reported reason for practicing plural marriage: *he had been commanded*. Brigham Young remembered: "He [Joseph Smith] often said to me when speaking upon polygamy . . . It is the work of God and he has revealed this principle and it is not my business to control or dictate it: to say it shall or shall not be."[98] Wilford Woodruff affirmed: "Joseph Smith claimed that he was commanded by the Lord."[99]

Several of the angel-sword accounts also emphasize that its practice was commanded. Lorenzo Snow testified in 1892:

> He [Joseph Smith] told me the principle of plural marriage for time and eternity was a revelation from God, and he was commanded to put it into practice. . . . He explained to me the principles of plural marriage distinctly and clearly, and told me that the Lord had revealed the principle, and had commanded him to enter into that practice, and that he had received a revelation to that effect. He said that he had demurred to doing so as he

---

97. M. Guy Bishop, "Eternal Marriage in Early Mormon Marital Beliefs," 79, wrote: "It was sealing for eternity that captivated early Mormons, not polygamy." It appears that Joseph Smith taught both topics with caution. See also Foster, *Religion and Sexuality*, 123–24.

98. Brigham Young, October 8, 1866, in Watson, *Brigham Young Addresses, 1865–1869*, 5:52.

99. Wilford Woodruff, Deposition, Temple Lot Transcript, Respondent's Testimony, Part 3, p. 63, question 656.

foresaw the trouble that would ensue, but that an angel of the Lord had appeared before him with a drawn sword commanding him to do so, and he could not go backward.[100]

Lorenzo's sister and plural wife of the Prophet, Eliza R. Snow gave this account:

> [In an 1843 interview with Lorenzo] the Prophet Joseph unbosomed his heart, and described the trying mental ordeal he experienced in overcoming the repugnance of his feelings, the natural result of the force of education and social custom, relative to the introduction of plural marriage. He knew the voice of God—he knew the commandment of the Almighty to him was to go forward—to set the example, and establish Celestial plural marriage. He knew that he had not only his own prejudices and prepossessions to combat and to overcome, but those of the whole Christian world stared him in the face; but God, who is above all, had given the commandment, and He must be obeyed. Yet the Prophet hesitated and deferred from time to time, until an angel of God stood by him with a drawn sword, and told him that, unless he moved forward and established plural marriage, his Priesthood would be taken from him and he should be destroyed![101]

In an 1866 discourse, Apostle John Taylor summarized: "Where did this commandment come from in relation to polygamy?" and then he answered: "It also came from God. It was a revelation given unto Joseph Smith from God, and was made binding upon His servants. When this system was first introduced among this people, it was one of the greatest crosses that ever was taken up by any set of men since the world stood."[102]

Besides a commandment, Joseph Smith also repeatedly referred to the opportunity to enter into eternal plural marriages as a *privilege*.[103] In 1842 he explained concerning polygamy: "Everything that God gives us is lawful and right; and it is proper that we should enjoy His gifts and blessings whenever

---

100. Lorenzo Snow, Deposition, Temple Lot Transcript, Respondent's Testimony, Part 3, pp. 114, 124, questions 87, 258.

101. Eliza R. Snow, *Biography and Family Record of Lorenzo Snow*, 69–70.

102. John Taylor, April 7, 1866, *Journal of Discourses*, 11:221.

103. George D. Smith asserts that Joseph Smith also used "favor" as a synonym for plural marriage. Smith, *Nauvoo Polygamy:* "... *but we called it celestial marriage,"* xiii, xv, 45, 47, 217, 241, 244, 245, 410, 453, 473, etc. John C. Bennett referred to plural marriage "favors" in *The History of the Saints: Or an Exposé of Joe Smith and Mormonism*, 224. I find no persuasive evidence that Joseph Smith taught Bennett plural marriage. Only one secondhand reference supports the possibility that Joseph Smith used "favor" to refer to plural marriage. On March 7, 1843, William Clayton recorded: "Elder Brigham Young called me on one side and said he wants to give me some instructions on the priesthood the first opportunity. He said the prophet had told him to do so and give me a favor which I have long desired." George D. Smith, *An Intimate Chronicle*, 94.

and wherever He is disposed to bestow; but if we should seize upon those same blessings and enjoyments without law, without revelation, without commandment, those blessings and enjoyments would prove cursings and vexations in the end, and we should have to lie down in sorrow and wailings of everlasting regret."[104] Although he does not use the term "privilege," his description certainly fits the definition of privilege.

Joseph Smith's intimate knowledge of the Book of Mormon assured him that polygamy was not always permitted, even among devout and worthy followers of God. Joseph Kingsbury recalled that the Prophet "said we had the privilege of having more than one wife. . . . He said it was the privilege of an able man to have more wives than one. . . . He said that a man had that privilege if he was considered worthy."[105] To William Clayton he advised: "It is your privilege to have all the wives you want."[106] George A. Smith recalled in 1869: "He [Joseph Smith] testified to me and to my father [John Smith, b. 1781] that the Lord had given him the keys of this sealing ordinance, and that he felt as liberal to others as he did to himself . . . and said to me 'you should not be behind in your privileges.'"[107] William Law recalled in 1885 that the Prophet "said it [plural marriage] was a great privilege granted to the *High Priesthood.*"[108] Apparently it was a commandment to marry at least one plural wife. If desired, the privilege to marry more was available.

Summary

The historical record demonstrates that, during the 1830s, the Latter-day Saints were generally aware of Old Testament polygamy and of a few sects that were practicing some form of extramarital unions often labeled "spiritual wifery." However, it appears that Church members generally had little expectation that plural marriage might be introduced as a religious practice among them.

Joseph Smith reported several times that an angel appeared, commanding him to enter into plural marriage. During one visit, the angel reportedly threatened the Prophet with a sword if he did not comply. Analyzing the vari-

---

104. "Sixth Letter from John C. Bennett," *Sangamo Journal*, Springfield Illinois, August 19, 1842; reprinted in John C. Bennett, *The History of the Saints*, 243–45. See also *History of the Church*, 5:134; and Joseph Fielding Smith, comp. and ed., *Teachings of the Prophet Joseph Smith*, 256.

105. Joseph Kingsbury, Deposition, Temple Lot Transcript, Respondent's Testimony, Part 3, p. 209–10, questions 681–89, 714.

106. William Clayton, Affidavit, February 16, 1874.

107. George A. Smith, Letter to Joseph Smith III, October 9, 1869.

108. William Law, Affidavit dated July 17, 1885. Quoted in Charles A. Shook, *The True Origin of Mormon Polygamy*, 126; emphasis in original.

ous accounts shows that angel-sword accounts can be reliably found as early as 1854.

In the mid-1830s, Joseph Smith apparently alluded to the possibility that marriage could last beyond death. He also used priesthood authority to perform marriage ceremonies, but the language used made it clear that the union would end when either of the companions died.

Joseph Smith reported receiving sealing authority from a resurrected Elijah in 1836 in the Kirtland Temple, but never specifically mentioned that visitation or ordination during his life. When introducing Nauvoo Church members to the importance of Elijah's mission and authority, the Prophet emphasized child-to-parent sealings, saying little about the possibility of eternal marriage, but privately he affirmed the reality of marriage in eternity. His reticence in discussing eternal marriage likely stemmed from the questions that he anticipated would follow. Those questions would probably necessitate the disclosure that eternal *plural* marriage was a correct doctrine, which was a declaration Church members were ill-prepared to hear.

When discussing plural marriage, Joseph consistently referred to it as a "commandment" and a "privilege" for him and other Latter-day Saints to practice.

Chapter 9

Eternal Plural Sealings Begin

The historical record indicates that perhaps a dozen trusted Church members learned of restored plural marriage in Kirtland. Throughout his life, Joseph Smith must have struggled as he chose the individuals to whom he would teach this lofty doctrine.[1]

Evidence indicates that the circle of insiders in Nauvoo expanded only slowly, reaching no more than 200–300. The precise number cannot be determined. I have identified by name 115 polygamists at the martyrdom: Joseph Smith, his thirty-five wives, and an additional twenty-nine men and their total of fifty plural wives. For every married polygamist, I presume that at least one or two others also knew but were not yet involved in the practice by the time of Joseph Smith's assassination in June 1844.

Facing the Challenges

Currently available evidence supports the argument that Joseph Smith, after one disastrous experience in Kirtland, resisted the divine command to enter plural marriage when it was renewed at Nauvoo. As discussed in Chapter 8, numerous narratives recount the commandment as transmitted by an angel who threatened him at various levels of seriousness for his reluctance. Benjamin F. Johnson remembered that Joseph "put it off" and "waited untill an Angel with a drawn Sword Stood before him and declared that if he longer delayed fulfilling that Command he would Slay him."[2] Lorenzo Snow recalled that the Prophet "hesitated and deferred from time to time" and that he "foresaw the trouble that would follow and sought to turn away from the commandment."[3] Erastus Snow reported that the angel accused the Prophet

---

1. See Andrew F. Ehat, "An Overview of the Introduction of Eternal Marriage in the Church of Jesus Christ of Latter-day Saints: 1840–1843," 6.

2. Benjamin F. Johnson, *My Life's Review*, 95–96; Dean R. Zimmerman, ed., *I Knew the Prophets: An Analysis of the Letter of Benjamin F. Johnson to George F. Gibbs, Reporting Doctrinal Views of Joseph Smith and Brigham Young*, 43. See also Zina Huntington quoted in "Joseph, the Prophet, His Life and Mission as Viewed by Intimate Acquaintances," *Salt Lake Herald Church and Farm Supplement*, January 12, 1895, 212.

3. Lorenzo Snow, quoted by Eliza R. Snow in *Biography and Family Record of Lorenzo Snow*, 69–70; Lorenzo Snow, Affidavit, August 18, 1869, in Joseph F. Smith, Affidavit Books, 2:19.

of "being neglectful in the discharges of his duties" and spoke "of Joseph having to plead on his knees before the Angel for his Life."[4]

Several of Joseph Smith's plural wives had similar recognitions. Eliza R. Snow described Joseph as "afraid to promulgate it."[5] Helen Mar Kimball remembered that, "had it not been for the fear of His displeasure, Joseph would have shrunk from the undertaking and would have continued silent, as he did for years, until an angel of the Lord threatened to slay him if he did not reveal and establish this celestial principle."[6] She also said that "Joseph put off the dreaded day as long as he dared."[7] Lucy Walker reported that Joseph "had his doubts about it for he debated it in his own mind."[8] Mary Elizabeth Rollins Lightner describes a conversation in which Joseph told her that "he [Joseph] talked to him [the angel commanding Joseph to practice plural marriage] soberly about it, and told him it was an abomination and quoted scripture to him. He said in the Book of Mormon it was an abomination in the eyes of the Lord."[9] She also related that the angel was required to visit Joseph three times between 1834 and 1842 before he fully complied:

> An angel came to him [Joseph Smith] and the last time he came with a drawn sword in his hand and told Joseph if he did not go into that principle, he would slay him. Joseph said he talked to him soberly about it, and told him it was an abomination and quoted scripture to him. He said in the Book of Mormon it was an abomination in the eyes of the Lord, and they were to adhere to these things except the Lord speak. . . . [The Prophet reported that] the angel came to me three times between the years of 1834 and 1842 and said I was to obey that principle or he would slay me.[10]

---

4. Erastus Snow quoted in A. Karl Larson and Katherine Miles Larson, *Diary of Charles Lowell Walker*, June 17, 1883, 2:611.

5. Eliza R. Snow quoted in J.J.J., "Two Prophets' Widows: A Visit to the Relicts of Joseph Smith and Brigham Young, the Present Occupants of the Lion House and Bee-Hive, A Peep into the Big Parlor Where Brigham Held Family Prayers—Aunt Zinah and Eliza R. Snow, the Poetess," *St. Louis [Mo.] Globe-Democrat*, August 18, 1887, p. 6, col. E.

6. Helen Mar Kimball Whitney, *Why We Practice Plural Marriage*, 53.

7. Jeni Broberg Holzapfel and Richard Neitzel Holzapfel, eds., *A Woman's View: Helen Mar Whitney's Reminiscences of Early Church History*, 142.

8. Lucy Walker, Deposition, Temple Lot Transcript, Respondent's Testimony, Part 3, p. 474.

9. Mary Elizabeth Rollins Lightner, "Remarks at Brigham Young University, April 14, 1905, 2–3.

10. Mary Elizabeth Rollins Lightner Smith, "Remarks at Brigham Young University, April 14. 1905," 2–3; Mary E. Lightner to A. M. Chase, April 20, 1904, quoted in J. D. Stead, *Doctrines and Dogmas of Brighamism Exposed*, 218–19; Mary Elizabeth Rollins Lightner, Letter to Emmeline B. Wells, Summer 1905, MS 282.

Despite angelic pressure, other constraints may have daunted the Prophet. Helen Mar Kimball recalled in 1883: "It was a strange doctrine, and very dangerous too, to be introduced at such a time, when in the midst of the greatest trouble Joseph had ever encountered. The Missourians and Illinoisans were ready and determined to destroy him. They could but take his life, and that he considered a small thing when compared with the eternal punishment which he was doomed to suffer if he did not teach and obey this principle." She also added: "The Prophet said that the practice of this principle would be the hardest trial the Saints would ever have to test their faith."[11]

In an 1869 letter to his first cousin once removed Joseph Smith III, Apostle George A. Smith reflected: "The obligation which rested upon your father to establish this order of Patriarchal marriage beyond the power of destruction seemed like a weight to crush him to the earth. . . . [But] notwithstanding the bigotry of his friends, the opposition of his own house, the universal tradition of the Christian world, and the law of Illinois against it, he felt to rejoice that he was enabled to fulfill his mission."[12]

T.B.H. Stenhouse acknowledged: "No one can fail to appreciate the difficulty of introducing a practice which the civilization of a thousand years had condemned as a relic of barbarism."[13] Lawrence Foster observed:

> Americans of Smith's day were not inclined to look kindly on polygamy, even in the Bible. . . . Even under ideal circumstances, polygamous practices could hardly have been introduced into nineteenth-century Illinois without provoking severe misunderstanding and conflicts.[14]
>
> Most people were already suspicious of individual immorality or deviance. To go further and claim that a deviant practice such as polygamy, which was illegal in Illinois, was authorized and indeed commanded by God seemed to undercut the very basis of moral authority itself . . . The opposition to polygamy was formidable.[15]

---

11. Holzapfel and Holzapfel, *A Woman's View*, 252–53, 140.

12. George A. Smith, Letter to Joseph Smith III, October 9, 1869, in Journal History, in *Selected Collections*, Vol. 2, DVD #5. The "A." stands for "Albert," but to prevent confusion with his grandson, LDS Church President George Albert Smith (1945–51), I refer to him consistently as "George A."

13. T. B. H. Stenhouse, *Rocky Mountain Saints*, 183. Stenhouse, a British convert, wrote this book several years after he had apostatized and been excommunicated for resistance to Brigham Young's theology and economic practices. His wife Fanny also wrote two exposés of Utah polygamy.

14. Lawrence Foster, *Religion and Sexuality: Three American Communal Experiments of the Nineteenth Century*, 132, 146.

15. Lawrence Foster, *Women, Family, and Utopia: Communal Experiments of the Shakers, the Oneida Community, and the Mormons*, 134.

Smith was well aware of the necessity for extreme caution in such a touchy area [as polygamy]. He had a canny sense of how fast he could move.... The Bible did not provide detailed guidelines as to how polygamy was to be practiced. Thus, it is not surprising that the development of Smith's thought in this and in many other areas of revelation appears to have been a gradual process, building "precept by precept, and line upon line."[16]

Francis M. Gibbons, secretary to the First Presidency (1970–86) and General Authority (1986–91), summarized in a biography of Joseph Smith: "After years of reluctance and trepidation, he [Joseph] had taken a step that he knew full well would further poison the public mind against him and the Church and would lead to scenes of violent persecution.... He knew also that regardless of how pure and circumspect a man might be in entering into this relationship [of plural marriage], he would be denounced by enemies who would ascribe to his actions the same base motives such a relationship might suggest to a carnal mind."[17]

1840 Nauvoo: Joseph Smith Cautiously Shares Plural Marriage Teachings

Joseph Smith left no record of his thoughts, feelings, and fears about polygamy in Nauvoo, Illinois. All of the information about his statements comes from reminiscences or from the diaries of associates like William Clayton. Only retrospective accounts exist, suggesting his concerns and worries as he introduced plural marriage to selected friends. Elizabeth Ann Whitney, first wife of Bishop Newel K. Whitney, remembered in the late 1870s: "He [Joseph] had been strictly charged by the angel who committed these precious things into his keeping, that he should only reveal them to such persons as were pure, and full of integrity to the truth, and worthy and capable of being entrusted with divine messages; that to spread them abroad would only be like casting pearls before swine; and that the most profound secresy [sic] must be maintained, until the Lord saw fit to make it known publicly through his servants."[18]

Despite the tendency of historians to focus almost exclusively upon the practice of plural marriage in Nauvoo, an examination of Joseph Smith's teach-

---

16. W. Lawrence Foster, "Between Two Worlds: The Origins of Shaker Celibacy, Onedia Community Complex Marriage, and Mormon Polygamy," 214. Foster is slightly misquoting KJV Isaiah 28:10 ("precept upon precept; line upon line"). D&C 98:12 and 2 Ne. 28:30 read "line upon line, precept upon precept." No scripture has "precept *by* precept."

17. Francis M. Gibbons, *Joseph Smith: Martyr, Prophet of God*, 285.

18. Elizabeth Ann Whitney, quoted in Edward W. Tullidge, *The Women of Mormondom*, 368; see also Carol Cornwall Madsen, ed., *In Their Own Words: Women and the Story of Nauvoo*, 201.

ings demonstrates that polygamy was introduced as a part of a new matrimonial system called the new and everlasting covenant of marriage. According to its teachings, couples wed in this new covenant remained married in the next life (see Volume 3, Chapter 8). While these two principles—eternal marriage and plural marriage—are clearly disconnected today, they were inextricably combined into one unfolding story in Nauvoo. Within Joseph Smith's expanding Nauvoo ideology regarding eternal families, plural marriage comprises one small, but necessary component (see Volume 3, Chapter 10). Both eternal and plural marriage were relatively novel in the 1840s, but only one defied the Christian monogamous mindset held by most religionists and consequently generated the greatest excitement and condemnation.

While eager to share *eternal* marriage with his followers, doubtless Joseph Smith did not relish the challenge before him to share the teachings about marital plurality. His closest confidants, members of his own family, would probably not be receptive. Emma had vehemently rejected polygamy in Kirtland. Among his brothers, Hyrum's piety seemed an immediate deterrent (he would not accept plural marriage until May 1843).[19] Don Carlos may have learned of it early, but the historical record contains two accounts concerning his reaction (see Chapter 10), one negative, the other positive. Samuel, the plodding, devoted, hard-working, sibling, seemed to be Joseph's confidant for meaty doctrines less frequently. William may have readily embraced the practice, but his mercurial devotions and inability to keep secrets would have generated immense reservations. It also seems unlikely that Joseph would have dared introduce it to his father or mother, despite their continued devotion.

Among the leading brethren of the Church, Joseph Smith's first counselor in the First Presidency, Sidney Rigdon, had participated minimally as new doctrinal teachings were introduced in Nauvoo. Although a partner in receiving a lengthy vision (now section 76) a decade earlier in 1832, the Prophet's confidence in Sidney had waned. Evidence suggests Joseph attempted to introduce Sidney to the principle in early 1842 through a plural marriage proposal to his daughter Nancy and a dictated letter on "happiness" that may have been directed to both of them. The results were catastrophic for everyone involved (see Chapter 17). On January 9, 1841, William Law was called as second counselor in the First Presidency (D&C 124:126), but he wrote that he learned of plural marriage in 1843.[20]

Beyond the First Presidency, a July 8, 1838, revelation specified that members of the Quorum of the Twelve Apostles were to leave from Far West, Missouri, for England on April 26, 1839. On that date, seven apos-

---

19. See George D. Smith, ed., *An Intimate Chronicle*, 106.

20. See William Law, Affidavit, July 17, 1885, in Charles A. Shook, *The True Origin of Mormon Polygamy*, 126.

tles—Brigham Young, Heber C. Kimball, Orson Pratt, John E. Page, John Taylor, Wilford Woodruff, and George A. Smith—gathered in a secret meeting, hiding from mob violence, to launch their missionary journey.[21] Missing were Parley P. Pratt (held in a Richmond jail) and Willard Richards (who was already in England). Also absent were Orson Hyde and William Smith whose faithfulness had been questioned. One vacancy remained to be filled. The Far West apostolic excursion returned to Nauvoo on May 2, 1839, and thereafter nine eventually united in England, taking different courses across the Atlantic. Neither John E. Page nor William Smith completed the mission.

In light of the complexities in the 1840–41 period surrounding Joseph Smith's family and Church leaders in Nauvoo, accompanied by the absence of his trusted apostles serving abroad, the Prophet was forced to look outside the structure of the general Church leadership in his first introductions to both eternal and plural marriage.

Finding Women to Marry as Plural Wives

Besides identifying men to embrace his new matrimonial teachings, Joseph Smith sought devout sisters who could understand and also participate. Apostle Joseph F. Smith taught that the Lord had prepared certain women to help the Prophet with this bold undertaking. In 1882 Joseph F. spoke at the funeral services of Elizabeth Ann Whitney. The correspondent who recorded his discourse misquoted him in a column printed in the *Deseret News*.[22] The next day, the paper published a clarifying letter from Elder Smith: "When the Prophet Joseph Smith received the revelation in relation to the eternity of the marriage covenant, which includes plural marriage, in 1831; the Lord showed him those women who were to engage with him in the establishment of that principle in the Church, and at that time some of these women were named and given to him, to become his wives when the time should come that this principle would be established."[23] Elder Smith, who was born in 1838

---

21. V. Ben Bloxham, "The Call of the Apostles to the British Isles," 70–71. See also James B. Allen and Malcolm R. Thorp, "The Mission of the Twelve to England, 1840–41: Mormon Apostles and the Working Classes," 501–6.

22. The original inaccurate account read: "The speaker said, perhaps, for the first time in public, that the women who entered into plural marriage with the Prophet Joseph Smith were shown to him and named to him as early as 1831, and some of them were given to him in marriage as early as that date, although it was not prudent, under the circumstances, to make these facts public." "Funeral Services of Sister Elizabeth A. Whitney," *Deseret Evening News*, February 17, 1882, 6.

23. Joseph F. Smith, Letter to the Editor, "Correction," *Deseret Evening News*, February 18, 1882, 2. An edited version of Elder Joseph F. Smith's remarks, containing the correction, appears in "Funeral Services of Sister Elizabeth A. Whitney," *Deseret News*

and would have been five at the deaths of Joseph and his own father, Hyrum Smith, provides no hint about the source of this information.

Joseph Smith, Emma, and their children moved to Nauvoo in May 1839. No documentation that mentions plural marriage during that year or any other time after his marriage to Fanny Alger in 1835–36 has been identified. In 1887, an interviewer quoted Eliza R. Snow who reportedly said: "In 1840 he [Joseph Smith] began to seal women to him and a few of his followers did the same."[24] In fact, the first known sealing occurred in 1841, not 1840, suggesting an error by the pseudonymous interviewer. However, it is possible that, in 1840, the Prophet began to teach selected individuals regarding God's command. Locating a woman who would agree to this novel marriage system without exposing him, and therefore had both explicit faith in him as God's prophet and in the restored gospel, might not have been easy. She would also have to be willing to seek her own divine confirmation of this system, all the more troubling because it was secretive and because it would likely be done without Emma's knowledge.

Zina Diantha Huntington may have been the first woman Joseph approached. Historians Martha Sonntag Bradley and Mary Brown Firmage Woodward, in their group biography, *Four Zinas: A Story of Mothers and Daughters on the Mormon Frontier*, record: "Joseph pressed Zina for an answer to his marriage proposal on at least three occasions in 1840, but she avoided answering him. Weighing against such a proposal was her affection for the prophet's first wife, Emma, her respect for traditional Christian monogamy, the strangeness of this new matrimonial system, and the secrecy it would require."[25]

This information—particularly the date of 1840—is based on a family tradition recalled by Mary Brown Firmage Woodward, a descendant of Zina Huntington. Reportedly, Zina Diantha Huntington gave this information to her daughter (by Brigham Young), Zina Presendia Young Williams Card, who told it to her own daughter, Zina Card Brown, who passed the information along to her own daughter Mary. Besides the family tradition, Martha Bradley reports viewing a single-page typescript of an "autobiography," then in Mary Brown Firmage Woodward's possession.[26] However, corroborating details are unknown: When it was written? By whom? Is the typescript the original or is it a transcription of the holograph? Typewriters became available for business offices in Utah in the 1890s [27]and for household use perhaps a decade later.

Weekly, February 22, 1882, 73.

24. J.J.J., "Two Prophets' Widows, p. 6, col. E.

25. Martha Sonntag Bradley and Mary Brown Firmage Woodward, *Four Zinas: A Story of Mothers and Daughters on the Mormon Frontier*, 108.

26. Martha Sonntag Bradley, March 27, 2008, email to Brian Hales.

27. See "Remington Standard Typewriter," advertisement, *Salt Lake Tribune*, January 25, 1891, 12.

Bradley reported that this typescript corroborated the oral tradition as cited in *Four Zinas* but of course was unable to determine whether it might also have been the source of the oral tradition. Apparently the document was misplaced before it and other papers were donated to the Harold B. Lee Library at Brigham Young University.[28] This page's current whereabouts are unknown.

This mysterious typescript is, however, only part of the problem involved in dating the commencement of plural marriage in Nauvoo to 1840.[29] For instance, interviewed by John W. Wright in 1898, Zina insisted that Joseph never directly discussed plural marriage with her prior to her October 27, 1841, sealing. Zina explained: "My brother Dimick told me what Joseph had told him" regarding plural marriage, and asserted: "Joseph did not come until afterwards. . . . The Lord had revealed to Joseph Smith that he was to marry me. I received it from Joseph through my brother Dimick."[30] The timeline is important because, as Todd Compton points out, Zina's plural marriage, if it occurred in 1840 or early 1841, may have been the first in Nauvoo.[31] Nonetheless, all available evidence seems to support a later sealing date including Zina's affidavit, signed on May 1, 1869.[32] In 1887, a journalist identifying himself only by initials, interviewed Zina Huntington and, based on that information, states: "Louisa Beman, married to the Prophet April 5, 1841 . . . the first woman

---

28. See Zina Diantha Huntington Young Papers, MSS SC 2184, Perry Special Collections.

29. Author George D. Smith writes that the death of Joseph Smith, Sr. on September 14, 1840 may have influenced the chronology associated with Joseph Smith, Jr.'s first plural marriage at Nauvoo, that perhaps due to embarrassment if his father discovered the practice, the Prophet waited for his father's passing.. Smith, *Nauvoo Polygamy:* "*... but we called it celestial marriage,"* 33. This theory is problematic because it is improbable that Joseph Smith Sr. would have learned about it at that time. Joseph Jr. successfully kept his brother Hyrum and many others unaware until mid-1843. While the Prophet acknowledged plural marriage to be a difficult principle, he never apologized for it, implied that it was sinful, or expressed embarrassment for its introduction.

30. John W. Wight, "Interview: Evidence from Zina D. Huntington-Young, October 1, 1898," *Saints' Herald* 52, no. 2 (January 11, 1905): 28–30. Also in J. D. Stead, *Doctrines and Dogmas of Brighamism Exposed*, 212–14.

31. Todd Compton, *In Sacred Loneliness: The Plural Wives of Joseph Smith*, 659, observed: "If Zina married Joseph soon after her marriage to [her legal husband Henry] Jacobs (in March 1841), this has important implications for the history of Nauvoo polygamy. She might have married Joseph before Louisa Beaman (on April 5), making her Joseph's first wife in the Nauvoo period." (See also ibid., 79–80, 658.) Also noting the same possibility that Zina was Joseph's first plural wife are George D. Smith, *Nauvoo Polygamy*, 74, and George D. Smith, "The Forgotten Story of Nauvoo Celestial Marriage," 145 and note 47.

32. Zina D. Huntington, Affidavit, May 1, 1869, Joseph F. Smith, Affidavit Books, 1:5, 4:5.

of modern times who ventured into polygamy."[33] If Zina's sealing preceded Louisa, it seems likely that she would have clarified it.[34]

In short, the chronological inconsistencies, the contradictions with other accounts by Zina, the current unavailability of any validating manuscript documentation, and our inability to further analyze the referenced document to address credibility issues, all support a conclusion that this family tradition with the date of 1840 should be used with caution.[35]

Louisa Beaman:
First Documented Eternal Plural Marriage

It appears the first Nauvoo plural sealing occurred between Joseph Smith and Louisa Beaman. Louisa Beaman died in 1850, leaving no accounts of the sealing ceremony or of her relationship with the Prophet. Everything known concerning the union is from secondary sources, primarily her brother-in-law Joseph B. Noble.

---

33. J.J.J., "Two Prophets' Widows," 6. This article quotes Zina Huntington who in turn recites Andrew Jenson's *Historical Record* where "Louisa Beman" is listed first and Fanny Alger second of Joseph Smith's plural wives.

34. Eliza R. Snow is interviewed later in the same article, but she does not comment on the chronology of Joseph Smith's plural sealings, including those to Louisa Beaman, Zina Huntington, and, more importantly, Fanny Alger's earlier in Kirtland.

35. D. Michael Quinn also accepts an 1840 sealing date for Joseph Smith and Zina Huntington, as well as for Joseph and Zina's sister Presendia (sealed according to her affidavit, December 11, 1841), writing that "the conventional dating of Zina's polygamous marriage as 1841, which was in her 1869 affidavit and its many repetitions thereafter" is in "error." Without providing documentation, he asserts that the ceremonies were performed twice, once in 1840 by a non-apostle and then again 1841 by Brigham Young: "Someone obviously decided that the easiest way to avoid confusion was to emphasize the month and day of the original ceremonies performed in 1840 by two rank-and-file Mormons, yet assign them to the year (1841) when the ceremonies were solemnized by apostolic authority." Quinn, "Evidence for the Sexual Side of Joseph Smith's Polygamy," 8–9. Quinn's interpretation is problematic for several reasons including the lack of documentation that Presendia's sealing was performed twice or ever by Brigham Young. He also dismisses firsthand notarized affidavits from Zina (Joseph F. Smith, Affidavit Books 1:5), Presendia (Joseph F. Smith, Affidavit Books 1:7), the officiator, Dimick Huntington, (Joseph F. Smith, Affidavit Books 1:19) and a witness, Fanny Huntington, (Joseph F. Smith, Affidavit Books 1:21) that affirm 1841 for both sealings. Instead, Quinn hypothesizes a cover-up and asserts that a more trustworthy source is the "Historian's Private Journal" (one volume, 1858–78, entries after July 1, 1866, LDS Church History Library), which lists an 1840 date but does not identify the source of that information. As a general rule, firsthand documents are preferred to second- and third-hand reports from unidentified sources.

Joseph Bates Noble, who turned thirty in 1840, grew up in Massachusetts, joined the Church in 1832, and attended Hebrew school in Kirtland. After leaving Missouri, he moved to Montrose, Iowa, across the Mississippi River from Nauvoo, in 1839, then settled in Nauvoo where he served as a bodyguard to Joseph Smith and as a bishop in 1841.[36] Noble himself left several relevant accounts, the first an affidavit phrased in third person for Joseph F. Smith in 1869, when he was fifty-nine: "In the fall of the year A.D. 1840 Joseph Smith, taught him the principle of Celestial marriage or a 'plurality of wives,' and that the said Joseph Smith declared that he had received a revelation from God on the subject, and that the angel of the Lord had commanded him, (Joseph Smith) to move forward in the said order of marriage, and further, that the said Joseph Smith, requested him, (Joseph Bates Noble) to step forward and assist him in carrying out the Said principle."[37] Those present in Joseph B. Noble's Montrose home that day included him, probably his wife, Mary Adeline Beman (sometimes Beaman), her sister, Louisa Beaman, and Church member Cyrus Wheelock.[38]

Born February 28, 1813, in Henderson, New York, Cyrus Wheelock converted to the Church in 1839 and shortly thereafter served a mission to Vermont. In 1892, he remembered some of the earliest teachings from the Prophet Joseph Smith regarding plural marriage. "The first time I recollect hearing him [Joseph Smith] teach was in Iowa, at a place called Montrose. It was at Montrose in Iowa at the house of one [Joseph] Bates Noble."[39] Since Noble moved to Nauvoo in late 1841, Wheelock's recollection dates to the 1840–41 period and identifies them both as perhaps the first to hear of plural marriage in Illinois period

The natural question is why Joseph Smith approached Noble and Wheelock at that time. In 1840, he faced two immediate challenges with respect to plural marriage. First was to identify faithful confidants to whom he could safely teach this dangerous doctrine that he knew would be disruptive and challenging. Second, Joseph Smith sought his first eternal plural wife. However, neither of those men had daughters of marriageable age.[40]

---

36. David L. Clark, *Joseph Bates Noble: Polygamy and the Temple Lot Case*, 60–66; Joseph B. Noble, Deposition, Temple Lot Transcript, Respondent's Testimony, Part 3, page 393, question 20.

37. Noble, Affidavit, Joseph F. Smith, Affidavit Book 1:38, 4:38; published in Andrew Jenson, "Plural Marriage," 221.

38. Joseph B. Noble, Deposition, Temple Lot Transcript, Respondent's Testimony, Part 3, page 395, questions 39–42.

39. Cyrus Wheelock, Deposition, Temple Lot Transcript, Respondent's Testimony, Part 3, page 533, question 42.

40. Noble wed in 1834 and Wheelock in 1835 (www.FamilySearch.com; accessed August 27, 2011).

The choice of Joseph Bates Noble may have been prompted by a couple of things. Noble had proven himself as a member of Zion's Camp in 1834, so he was not a stranger to the Prophet.[41] The following year in 1835 he was sustained as a member of the First Quorum of Seventy in Kirtland. After being encouraged by Joseph Smith, he attended the Hebrew class held there in the temple.[42] The Prophet had reasons to trust him after watching his devotion over the span of several years. Importantly, Joseph may have viewed Noble's sister-in-law, Louisa Beaman, as someone who might be receptive to plural marriage teachings and even a proposal to practice it.

Joseph Smith's reasons for allowing Cyrus Wheelock to witness his early instructions regarding plural marriage are less obvious. Wheelock, a man who could not and did not contribute to the Prophet's first plural marriage with Louisa so far as records indicate, was not positioned to help Joseph in any discernable way. If obtaining a plural wife was Joseph Smith's primary objective, then keeping outsiders outside of the proceedings seems to have been the most logical action. The inclusion of Wheelock in the discussions is puzzling because after hearing of the explosive doctrines, he was empowered to expose the Prophet if he chose to do so. Wheelock's privileged position as an early polygamy insider appears to be based upon two factors: first, Joseph Smith's belief that the teachings needed to be cautiously dispersed among the faithful membership and, second, upon the Prophet's confidence in Wheelock's devotion and ability to keep a secret.

Cyrus Wheelock's early introduction to polygamy apparently did not affect his convictions. Three years later, just before the martyrdom, he unsuccessfully defended Joseph Smith before Illinois Governor Thomas Ford.[43] In 1852 he served a mission to England presiding over the Manchester, Liverpool, and Preston Conferences.[44] Two years afterwards he was appointed as a captain of one of the pioneer companies that crossed the plains to Utah Territory.[45] Wheelock settled in Mount Pleasant, Utah Territory, and later composed the lyrics to several hymns, including "Ye Elders of Israel."[46] Called in 1878 as president of the Northern States Mission, he served faithfully in the Church.

Wheelock was one of the very first introduced to the polygamy inner circle of secret-keepers in Nauvoo. Although he did not become a polyga-

---

41. Clark, *Joseph Bates Noble*, 21–33.
42. See D. Kelly Ogden, "The Kirtland Hebrew School (1835–36)," 74.
43. "Cyrus Wheelock," in Andrew Jenson, *Latter-day Saint Biographical Encyclopedia*, 4:363.
44. Polly Aird. "Bound for Zion: The Ten- and Thirteen-Pound Emigrating Companies, 1853–54,"
45. William G. Hartley, "The Keokuk Encampment," 57.
46. "Cyrus Wheelock," in Jenson, *Latter-day Saint Biographical Encyclopedia*, 4:363.

mist during the Prophet's lifetime, he married several plural wives in Utah.[47] Wheelock represents a man who possessed a bird's-eye view of Joseph Smith's polygamy from its Illinois beginnings. Without personally committing himself to polygamy, he was positioned to watch the Prophet secretly establish the controversial practice among his fellow Latter-day Saints. Whatever his innermost doubts and thoughts, he remained true to his beliefs in Joseph Smith. This reaction is important because numerous antagonistic writers have depicted the Prophet as a libertine, and such behavior would likely have been apparent to men like Cyrus Wheelock. Wheelock's immediate non-participation left him free to decide, without having to weigh his own plurality and willingness to set aside his own polygamous wives. He could have exposed Joseph or quietly left his fellowship. He chose neither.

At some point Louisa Beaman became involved with Joseph Smith's quiet plural marriage conversations, eventually fielding a polygamous proposal from him. Whatever the dynamics, Louisa accepted.[48] Noble's 1869 affidavit, mentioned above, affirms: "On the fifth day of April A.D. 1841, At the City of Nauvoo, County of Hancock, State of Illinois, he married or sealed Louisa Beaman, to Joseph Smith."[49] If Joseph Smith's sole motive was to marry Louisa the timeline is a little curious, since several months passed between the introduction of the principle and the sealing ceremony. Noble testified that it was in the "fall of 1840" that he first heard of plural marriage, but the matrimony did not occur until April 5, 1841.

Joseph Noble left at least four personal statements, three of them after a second-hand account affirmed Noble's role in this first plural marriage with a documented date.

Noble evidently made this affidavit at Joseph F. Smith's invitation because he had, five months earlier, made what is his first known statement about his role in the Joseph-Louisa marriage. On Thursday, January 22, 1869, Franklin D. Richards recorded:

---

47. Wheelock married Olive Parrish on June 5, 1834. Later he wed five plural wives: Mary Ann Broomhead, July 1, 1847; Mary Ann Dallin, December 10, 1853; Desdemona Jemima Rose, December 11, 1853; Elizabeth Burgess Neslen, April 21, 1854; and Louisa Godsall, January 1, 1857. (www.FamilySearch.com; accessed August 23, 2011).

48. Clark, *Joseph Bates Noble*, 59–87.

49. Joseph B. Noble, Affidavit, Joseph F. Smith, Affidavit Books, 1:3. See also Scott G. Kenney, ed., *Wilford Woodruff's Journal, 1833–1898*, February 22, 1869, 6:452. Noble apparently did not always remember the same date. On Sunday, December 19, 1880, Charles L. Walker reported in his journal: "Br Nobles made a few remarks on the celestial order of marriage, He being the man who sealed Louisa Beaman to the Prophet Joseph Smith in 1840 under his instructions." A. Karl Larson and Katherine Miles Larson, *Diary of Charles Lowell Walker*, 2:515.

Eternal Plural Sealings Begin

Joseph Bates Noble. Courtesy of the International Society of Daughters of Utah Pioneers.

For many years sister Jane Blackhurst has invited the Presidency and the Twelve to her house during the Legislative session to Dine with her in pursuance of which I this day with my wife met. Br. Joseph B. Noble being the master of ceremonies was present and During the visit related he performed the first sealing ceremony in this Dispensation in which he united Sister Louisa Beman to the Prop[h]et Joseph in May—I think the 5th day in 1841 during the evening under an Elm tree in Nauvoo. The Bride disguised in a coat and hat.^{50}

The reference to a "coat and hat" is singular. No other accounts of this sealing include that detail nor do any other documents recalling plural marriages mention the use of a disguise or camouflage.

Another account is second hand, twelve years after the 1869 affidavit, but possibly the reason why Noble spoke more freely after that point. Ann Eliza Webb Young, by then launched on a career as an anti-Mormon speaker and writer as Brigham Young's ex-plural wife, constructed an interesting account that describes Joseph B. Noble as not only performing Joseph Smith's first sealing, but also marrying a plural wife at the same time:

> Among the earliest converts to the doctrine of plural wives was a Mr. Noble, who, more impressible, or, according to Joseph, "more faithful" than any others, opened his heart very readily to receive the teachings of the Prophet, and was willing to reduce the teachings to practice. Joseph had paid his addresses to Mr. Noble's sister-in-law, a very worthy woman, and had succeeded in overcoming her scruples so far that she had consented to be sealed to him.
>
> He then advised Noble to seek a second wife for himself, and to commence at once to "building up his kingdom." He was not slow in following his Prophet's advice, and together the two men, with their chosen celestial brides, repaired one night to the banks of the Mississippi River, where Joseph sealed Noble to his first plural wife, and in return Noble performed

---

50. Joseph Bates Noble, quoted in Franklin D. Richards, Journal, January 22, 1869. Both Brodie and Compton list Lucinda Pendleton Harris as Joseph's first plural wife after he received the sealing keys in 1838; I argue that they are mistaken and that Louisa was the first documented sealed plural marriage.

the same office for the Prophet and his sister. These were the first plural marriages that ever took place in the Mormon Church, and they were obliged to be very secretly performed, and kept hidden afterwards.[51]

Although Ann Eliza was not born until 1844, her parents were close to the Alger family and provided shelter to Fanny when she was expelled from the Smith home in Kirtland. Ann Eliza may be inaccurate in some of her secondhand reports, but her parents appear to be reputable witnesses where Fanny is concerned, even though they left the Church in Utah in the 1870s. (See Chapter 5.) However, their reliability comes into question as witnesses where Noble and Joseph's marriage to Louisa Beaman is concerned for two reasons: (1) There is no evidence that they were polygamy insiders in Nauvoo where Chauncy married his first plural wife January 21, 1846, in the Nauvoo Temple, just months before the Saints pulled out for the West. True, they lived in Nauvoo not far from the Smiths but they don't seem to have been prominent in any of his journals, and (2) the Webb account contradicts Joseph Noble's personal memories at several important points.

As one detail, Noble did not take his first plural wife, Sarah B. Alley, until April 5, 1843.[52] This date is the second anniversary of the sealing he performed for Joseph and Louisa. Whether it was purposeful or coincidental is not known, but the convergence of the dates may explain Noble's later fuzziness on consistently naming the same date. William Clayton provides some background on Noble's first plural marriage a month later on May 17, 1843: "Joseph said to Brother [Benjamin F.] Johnson and I that J[oseph] B. Noble, when he was first taught this doctrine set his heart on one and pressed J[oseph] Smith] to seal the contract but he never could get opportunity. It seemed that the Lord was unwilling. Finally another came along and he then engaged that one and is a happy man."[53]

---

51. Ann Eliza Webb Young, *Wife Number 19, or, The Story of a Life in Bondage, Being a Complete Exposé of Mormonism, and Revealing Sorrows, Sacrifices and Sufferings of Women in Polygamy*, 72. Five years later, the pseudonymous "Historicus" published the same charge in "Sketches from the History of Polygamy: The First Polygamous Marriages" in the January 1881 issue of the *Anti-Polygamy Standard*, 1. Ann Eliza's mother, Eliza Jane Churchill Webb, repeated this same claim in a letter to Mary Bond, April 24, 1876: "The sealing ordinance began like this, Joseph Smith took Louisa Beaman, and Joseph Bates Nobles took Sarah Alley one night about twelve o'clock and went down to the banks of the Mississippi and Joseph performed the ceremony for Bates and his girl, and then Bates sealed Joseph and Louisa." In fact, the plural sealing between Joseph B. Noble and Sarah B. Alley occurred two years later on April 5, 1843 (www.FamilySearch.com accessed August 23, 2011).

52. Gary James Bergera, "Identifying the Earliest Mormon Polygamists, 1841–1844," 61.

53. George D. Smith, ed., *An Intimate Chronicle: The Journals of William Clayton*, 103.

The third and fourth accounts date from June 1883. On Sunday, June 10, leaders of the Davis Stake quarterly conference held in Centerville, Utah invited the venerable Noble, who worked as a sheep rancher in the Bountiful area, to share a few recollections: In the audience was future apostle George F. Richards, who noted in his diary: "Brother Nobles [sic] also testified that he sealed to Joseph a relative of his own & that it was the first ceremony of the plural marriage performed in this dispensation and that it was done in a whisper."[54] Notes from the same conference, dated Monday the following day (June 11) were published by Andrew Jenson in his "Plural Marriage" article in the *Historical Record*. The date may have actually been June 10. A reporter for the conference wrote: "Elder Noble sealed his wife's sister to Joseph, that being the first plural marriage consummated [performed]. The Prophet gave the form of the ceremony, Elder Noble repeating the words after him. Elder Noble bore testimony to the purity of character of his sister-in-law, who was a woman of irreproachable morality, who entered into the plural marriage relation on a deep-seated conviction that the doctrine was from God."[55]

The fifth account dates from 1892 when Joseph Bates provided a deposition in the Temple Lot Case. E. L. Kelley, the attorney taking the deposition, asked what authority he used to seal Louisa Beaman to Joseph Smith. The eighty-two-year-old Noble stated with a hint of pride: "I know this, that the law giver [Joseph Smith] authorized it. . . . I got it all right—right from the Prophet himself. That is where I got it. . . . I sealed her to him and I did a good job too."[56]

In summary, Joseph B. Noble served as an intermediary, an arrangement that occurred in several of later plural marriages contracted by the Prophet and other Church members. Both Cyrus Wheelock and Noble were early polygamy insiders, but the historical record indicates they were afterwards not involved or instrumental in the expansion of plural marriage in Nauvoo. The detail that Louisa was "disguised in a coat and hat" is unique among all of Joseph Smith's plural marriages. Without question, this first plural marriage was an enormous step, taken in obedience to the angel. Unbeknown to him, his personal practice of polygamy would last only three and a half years and would ultimately contribute to his demise.

---

54. George F. Richards, Journal, June 10, 1883.

55. Joseph Bates Noble, quoted in Notes from a Stake Quarterly Conference, Centerville, Davis County, Utah, June 11, 1883; spelling standardized. Quoted in Jenson, "Plural Marriage," 232–33.

56. Joseph Bates Noble, Deposition, Temple Lot Transcript, Respondent's Testimony, Part 3, pages 432, 436, questions 793, 799, 861; sentence order reversed.

Instructing the Twelve Apostles

As discussed earlier in this chapter, nine apostles congregated in England on their mission: Brigham Young, Heber C. Kimball, Orson Pratt, John Taylor, Wilford Woodruff, George A. Smith, Parley P. Pratt, Orson Hyde, and Willard Richards.[57] Neither John E. Page nor William Smith accompanied their brethren (one position was vacant). The last general conference held by the nine apostles in England occurred April 16, 1841, in Manchester. Four days later, Brigham Young recorded:

> Elders H. [Heber] C. Kimball, O. [Orson] Pratt, W. [Wilford] Woodruff, J. [John] Taylor, Geo. [George] A. Smith, W. [Willard] Richards and family, myself and a company of 130 Saints, went on board the ship Rochester, Captain Woodhouse, at Liverpool, for New York. We gave the parting hand to Elders O. [Orson] Hyde [headed to dedicate Palestine] and P. [Parley] P. Pratt, [staying as mission president] and a multitude of Saints who stood upon the dock to see us start. We drew out into the river Mersey, and cast anchor in sight of Liverpool, where we spent the day and night.[58]

Upon reaching New York on May 20, several of the Nauvoo-bound apostles split up conducting business along the way as they felt inspired. The earliest apostles to make it to Nauvoo included Brigham Young, Heber C. Kimball, and John Taylor, arriving July 1, 1841.[59] George A. Smith joined them on July 13 with Orson Pratt following a couple of days later.[60] On August 1 the Prophet noted: "All the Quorum of the Twelve Apostles who were expected here this season, with the exception of Elders Willard Richards and Wilford Woodruff, have arrived."[61] Willard Richards reached Nauvoo on August 16, with Wilford Woodruff following on October 6.[62]

Months previous to the apostles' return, Lyman Wight was ordained on April 8, 1841, to fill the vacancy in the Quorum of the Twelve. However, his frequent absences from Nauvoo limited his interactions with Joseph Smith and fellow Quorum members. Superintending the procurement of lumber for the temple and Nauvoo House, he spent extended periods in the pine country at Black River, Wisconsin Territory. Several authors speculate that he married three plural wives prior to the martyrdom, supporting that Joseph Smith

---

57. Parley P. Pratt stayed in England until 1842, arriving in Nauvoo in spring of 1843. V. Ben Bloxham, "The Call of the Apostles to the British Isles," 114.
58. Elden Jay Watson, ed., *Manuscript History of Brigham Young, 1801–1844*, April 20, 1841.
59. *History of the Church* 4:381.
60. *History of the Church* 4:383, 389.
61. *History of the Church* 4:390.
62. *History of the Church* 4:402, 429.

confided his plural marriage teachings to him early.[63] However, other sources place the plural marriages several years later.[64] Available evidences indicate that if Joseph Smith ever personally instructed Lyman Wight, William Smith, and/or John E. Page regarding his lofty teachings about eternal and plural marriage, it did not occur in 1841 when several other apostles in Nauvoo likely became apprised.

As the apostles completed their trans-Atlantic mission and joined the Prophet in Illinois, polygamy's inner circle expanded. No contemporaneous documentation exists regarding how and when Joseph Smith introduced his trusted apostles to plural marriage. The historical record demonstrates that he met with at least some members of the Quorum of the Twelve at least thirty-two times between July 1841 and May 1842.[65] Lawrence Foster observed: "The impossibility of finding time and privacy to give detailed instructions even to the twelve apostles, Smith's closest associates, suggests how difficult translating such beliefs into practice for the general membership must have been."[66]

Of the seven apostles who returned in 1841, five left accounts of being taught about the restoration of this ancient practice: Brigham Young, Heber C. Kimball, John Taylor, Wilford Woodruff, and George A. Smith. Willard Richards apparently left no record of his initial introduction to plural marriage. Orson Pratt's case is much more complex for a couple of reasons. First, Orson's wife, Sarah Bates Pratt, later divorced him and burned his journals, so no contemporaneous diary entries are available.[67] In addition, evidence indicates that she and John C. Bennett experienced a sexual relationship while Orson was in England. Joseph Smith intervened and was afterwards accused by Sarah of making an improper proposal. Accusations subsequently flew in both directions. (See Chapter 21.) What is apparent is that even though the reported improprieties occurred prior to Orson's return in mid-July 1841, Pratt functioned as a devoted apostle until May of 1842. During that period he is numbered with his

---

63. See George D. Smith, *Nauvoo Polygamy: "... but we called it celestial marriage,"* 631; Bergera. "Identifying the Earliest Mormon Polygamists, 1841–1844," 71.

64. D. Michael Quinn, *The Mormon Hierarchy: Origins of Power,* 602, lists Mary Hawley 1845, Mary A. Otis about 1848, and Margaret Ballantyne about 1851; see also http://saintswithouthalos.com/b/wight_l.phtml (accessed August 26, 2010).

65. Dean C. Jessee, ed. *The Papers of Joseph Smith. Vol. 2: Journal, 1832–1842*; Watson, *Manuscript History of Brigham Young, 1801–1844*; and *History of the Church* for the following dates: July 15, 19, August 10, October, 30, 31, November 7, 28, 30, December 11, 13, 19, 26, 27, 1841; January 2, 17, 28, 29, 30, 31, February 13, 19, 28, March 1, 9, 11, 17, 26, 31, April 6, 12, 1842; May 4, 19. See also Tim Rathbone, "Brigham Young's Masonic Connection and Nauvoo Plural Marriages," 2 note 20.

66. Foster, "Between Two Worlds," 246.

67. Elden J. Watson compiled various references to Orson Pratt up to 1847, titling it *The Orson Pratt Journals* (Salt Lake City: Elden Jay Watson, 1975); however, it is not a true journal.

fellow Quorum of the Twelve members attending meetings and signing correspondence.[68] If Joseph Smith informed him regarding restored plural marriage during that time, which is very likely, his immediate response is unknown. However, by May of 1842, nearly a year after arriving in Illinois, a rift finally appeared between him and the Prophet. The actual event that provoked Orson's dissention in May 1842 is unknown. He may have become aware of the early 1841 accusations that had otherwise been kept secret. Possibly John C. Bennett was responsible or other concerns arose. Regardless, no evidence of discord between him and Joseph Smith prior to that time has been located.

Concerning the other four apostles who left reminiscences, Brigham Young returned to Nauvoo July 1, 1841, and immediately assumed a privileged position in Joseph Smith's confidence. Speaking at Third Ward Meeting House in Salt Lake City when he was seventy-three, he recalled his own spiritual preparation for Joseph Smith's disclosures:

> We came to Nauvoo, and the Twelve went to England. While we were in England, I think, the Lord manifested to me by visions and his spirit, things that I did not then understand. I never opened my mouth to any persons concerning them, until I returned to Nauvoo. Joseph had never mentioned this, there had never been a thought of it in the Church that I knew anything about at that time. But I had this for myself, and I kept it to myself, and when I returned home and Joseph revealed these things to me, I then understood the reflections that were upon my mind while in England. But this was not until after I had told him what I understood. I saw that he was after something by his conversation, leading my mind along, and others, to see how we could bear this. This was in 1841; the revelation was given in 1843, but the doctrine was revealed before this, and when I told Joseph what I understood which was right in front of my house in the street, as he was shaking hands and leaving me, he turned round and looked me in the eyes, and says he—"Brother Brigham, are you speaking what you understand,—are you in earnest?" Says I—"I speak just as the Spirit manifests to me." Says he—"God bless you, the Lord has opened your mind," and he turned and went off.[69]

Notwithstanding these intuitions, Brigham related in 1855 his initial anguish with the practice: "My brethren know what my feelings were at the time Joseph revealed the doctrine; I was not desirous of shrinking from any duty, nor of failing in the least to do as I was commanded, but it was the first time in my life that I had desired the grave, and I could hardly get over it for a long time.

---

68. See *History of the Church*, 4:389, 396, 400, 411, 414, 424, 428, 429, 438, 453, 463, 466, 475, 484, 490, 494, 509, 564, 589, 593, etc.

69. Brigham Young, June 23, 1874, *Journal of Discourses*, 18:241.

And when I saw a funeral, I felt to envy the corpse its situation, and to regret that I was not in the coffin."[70]

Forty years after its occurrence, Heber C. Kimball's daughter, Helen, vividly recalled his homecoming:

> On the 1st day of July my father with President Young and Brother John Taylor arrived home from their mission. . . . The Prophet and many more were there ready to greet and welcome them home again, Joseph would have them go home with him to dinner. . . . we thought this almost an unkindness for it seemed so long a time to us who were waiting and watching with impatience to see him. . . . My mother felt the presence of others at such a time almost an intrusion, but Brother Joseph seemed unwilling to part with my father; and from that time kept the Twelve in council early and late, and she sometimes felt nearly jealous of him but never dreamed that he was during those time revealing to them the *principles of celestial marriage* and... *they* little realized the meaning of his words when he said "he was rolling off the kingdom from his own shoulders onto the shoulders of the Twelve."[71]

In a discourse delivered on the tenth anniversary of the martyrdom, Apostle John Taylor recalled those early days when the Prophet introduced the principle to them:

> I remember being with President Young and Kimball and I think one or two others with Brother Joseph soon after we had returned from England. He talked with us on these principles and laid them before us. It tried our minds and feelings. We saw it was something going to be heavy upon us. it was not that very nice pleasing thing some people thought about it. It is something that harried up our feelings. Did we believe it? Yes we did. I did. The whole rest of the brethren did but still we should have been glad to push it off a little further. We [would have] been glad if it did not come in our day but that somebody else had something to do with it instead of us.[72]

Twenty-two years later, Apostle Taylor recalled: "[At] the time when men were commanded to take more wives. It made us all pull pretty long faces sometimes. It was not so easy as one might think. When it was revealed to us it looked like the last end of Mormonism. For a man to ask another woman to marry him required more self-confidence than we had."[73]

---

70. Brigham Young, July 14, 1855, *Journal of Discourses*, 3:266.
71. Helen Mar Kimball Whitney, "Scenes and Incidents in Nauvoo," *Woman's Exponent* 10 (August 15, 1881): 42; emphasis hers; see also Stanley B. Kimball, "Heber C. Kimball and Family: The Nauvoo Years," 454.
72. John Taylor, "Sermon in Honor of the Martyrdom," June 27, 1854, Disk 2, images 151–52. Terminal punctuation and initial capitals added.
73. John Taylor, "Report of the dedication of the Kaysville Relief Society House," November 12, 1876.

On October 13, 1882, President John Taylor received a revelation filling two vacancies in the Quorum of the Twelve (calling George Teasdale and Heber J. Grant) and discussing the need to continue the practice of plural marriage, which is part of Celestial and eternal marriage.[74] Wilford Woodruff reported that the following day the revelation was presented to the First "Presidency, Twelve Apostles, and Presidents of Stakes" and accepted by them.[75] Thereafter, the revelation received limited circulation.[76] The minutes for that October 14 meeting read:

> When this principle was first made known to us by Joseph Smith, it was in Nauvoo, and many of you will remember the place very well. We were assembled in the little office over the brick store, there being present Brs B. Young Heber C Kimball, Orson Hyde & myself. Br Willard Richards may have been present too, but I am not positive. Upon that ocassion [sic], Joseph Smith laid before us the whole principle pertaining to that doctrine, and we believed it. Having done this, Joseph felt, as he said, that he had got a big burden rolled off his shoulders. He felt the responsibility of that matter resting heavily upon him. Notwithstanding, however, that we received the principle & believed it, yet we were in no great hurry to enter into it.[77]

If President Taylor's memory was correct, the meeting referred to would have occurred after December 7, 1842, when Orson Hyde returned from Palestine. At that point, Brigham and Heber had each married one plural wife (Vinson Knight married polygamously but had died), but no one else.

Wilford Woodruff, who kept a voluminous journal, did not mention Nauvoo plural marriage in his daily entries, but did recall early polygamy in several recollections. In 1892 he recounted his feelings upon returning on October 5, 1841, from the apostolic mission:

> Joseph Smith of course taught that principle while in Nauvoo, and he not only taught it, but practiced it too . . . He taught it to the twelve apostles and to some other individuals. I mean to some other individuals who were not members of the quorum of twelve. . . . I heard him teach it,—he taught it to the quorum of twelve apostles, and he taught it to other individuals as they bear testimony. I know he taught it to us. . . . he taught me and others . . . In his addresses to the quorum of twelve apostles, when he visited us, he would teach that. . . . We were with him,—I don't know how many months,—but probably

---

74. For discussion that plural marriage is a principle that is part of the law of celestial marriage, see John Taylor, n.d., *Journal of Discourses*, 24:229; *On Marriage*, n.p., n.d., 5.

75. Scott G. Kenney, ed., *Wilford Woodruff's Journal*, 2:235; see also a synopsis of the revelation in John Taylor, Letter to Albert Carrington, October 18, 1882.

76. See James R. Clark, *Messages of the First Presidency*, 2:348–49.

77. John Taylor, quoted in *Minutes of the Apostles of The Church of Jesus Christ of Latter-day Saints, 1835–1893*, October 14, 1882, 342,

Apostle George A. Smith. Courtesy of the Utah State Historical Society.

as much as six months. . . . It was nearly six months, and he spoke of it frequently. . . . He taught it to us as a principle amongst other things.[78]

Apostle George A. Smith also remembered this period: "At one of the first interviews" he had with Joseph after returning from his mission to England on July 13, 1841, he "was greatly astonished at hearing from his lips that doctrine of Patriarchal marriage, which he continued to preach to me from time to time. My last conversation with him on this subject occurred just previous to my departure from Nauvoo (May 9, 1844) in company with Elder Wilford Woodruff, to attend Conference in Michigan. . . . He testified to me and to my father [John Smith] that the Lord had given him the keys of this sealing ordinance, and that he felt as liberal to others as he did to himself."[79]

Warren Foote, whose niece was one of George A.'s plural wives, recorded a conversation in which George A. related his struggle in accepting the revelation:

> [1846 January] 23rd. . . . After receiving our endowments, I and my wife went down to Bro. George A. Smith's who had married my sister Betsey's daughter Nancy for his third wife, Bro. Smith was at home. He related to us what a trial it was to him to receive the revelation on plural marriage. It was first made known to him by the Prophet Joseph. He did not feel at first at though he could receive it as from the Lord. But again he knew that Joseph was a prophet of God, and he durst not reject it. Thus he reasoned with himself, until he obtained a testimony from the Lord for himself.[80]

The "revelation" referred to is probably not the one recorded on July 12, 1843 (see Chapter 25), but rather an unwritten revelation (or more likely revelations) Joseph Smith had received from the angel and through inspiration that explained eternal and plural marriage and commanded its practice. George A. Smith returned from England on July 13, 1841, and undoubtedly was introduced to those teachings by the Prophet in the weeks thereafter.

---

78. Wilford Woodruff, Deposition, Temple Lot Transcript, Respondent's Testimony, Part 3, pp. 10, 58, questions 62–64, 573–80. Woodruff's recollection of a six-month teaching period fits quite well with the documented meetings from August 1841 to March 1842, with the most intense period being in the late fall and winter of 1841–42.
79. George A. Smith, Letter to Joseph Smith III, October 9, 1869, Journal History.
80. Warren Foote (1817–1903), Autobiography and Journal, 1:83.

By the end of 1841, the quorum had been completely filled by calling Lyman Wight to fill the vacancy; however, he left no account concerning his introduction to plural marriage. Among the remaining eleven, two were probably not immediately taught of the controversial doctrine, specifically William Smith and John E. Page (Page was absent from Nauvoo much of the year anyway). Orson Hyde returned to Illinois on December 7, 1842 (see Chapter 16) and Parley P. Pratt on April 12, 1843 (see Chapter 22), so their initial interactions with the doctrine were still in the future. While Willard Richards left no record, he was probably included with Brigham Young, Heber C. Kimball, John Taylor, Wilford Woodruff, and George A. Smith who received early instructions concerning eternal and plural marriage. Richards sealed Joseph's sealing to Patty Sessions on March 9, 1842.[81] As discussed above, Orson Pratt's level of understanding in the July 1841–May 1842 period is indiscernible.

These accounts describe how Joseph Smith directly, but cautiously taught some members of the Quorum of the Twelve regarding restored plural marriage soon after arriving in Illinois from their missionary journey to England. They also describe the apostles' consistent and poignant distaste for the practice, but also a willingness to accept it as the will of God. Perhaps not surprisingly, none entered into the practice until the spring of 1842 (at the earliest). Joseph Smith remained the lone authorized polygamist in Nauvoo until that time. It would take a third sword-bearing angel to get the apostles in gear with the command to move forward.

First Teachings, First Reactions

Throughout the Nauvoo period, no matter how trusted the confidant, Joseph Smith had to brace himself to deal with the same negative reaction manifested by his apostles as they learned of the principle and practice of plural marriage. Specific responses are discussed below; however, the documentation of revulsion to the teaching is nearly universal. Richard Ballantyne, then a missionary in India, commented in 1856: "This [Polygamy] is a large pill for many to swallow, and in fact the very first sight of it nauseates their stomachs, that at present they can scarcely receive anything else."[82] Lawrence Foster wrote: "In almost all recorded cases, initial presentation of the belief in plural marriage to either men or women produced shock, horror, disbelief, or general emotional confusion. Those who eventually accepted the principle almost invariably went through a period of inner turmoil lasting from several

---

81. Donna Toland Smart, ed., *Mormon Midwife: The 1846–1888 Diaries of Patty Bartlett Sessions*, 276–77.

82. Richard Ballantyne (Madras, India), Letter to his wife, September 6, 1856, quoted in David J. Whittaker, "Early Mormon Polygamy Defenses," 45.

days to several months."[83] Commenting on the Nauvoo period, LDS historian Kathryn M. Daynes observed, "In every recorded case, the initial attitude toward entering plural marriage was negative."[84] Psychologist Irwin Altman and anthropologist Joseph Ginat, in their ground-breaking *Polygamous Families in Contemporary Society*, wrote: "The resistance of even the most devoted followers was understandable, given the long-standing American and Christian heritage of monogamy. Moreover, plural marriages were illegal, they would require men to support multiple families, and in Smith's teaching they implied that civil marriages were not binding in the hereafter. Yet many eventually gave in, believing that if they did not do so they would be jeopardizing their salvation in the hereafter."[85]

Todd Compton concurred: "Many who have commented on their first introduction to polygamy wrote that they at first looked at it with revulsion and shock, and fought the idea for a time. Some Mormons, male and female, had suicidal feelings when they were first told that they were required to practice polygamy."[86] Attorney Sarah Barringer Gordon concluded: "Polygamy shocked and offended those outside the faith; and it was not readily accepted by many Mormons when they first learned of 'the Principle' of plural marriage."[87]

Despite this common reaction from the Latter-day Saints, many writers including most anti-Mormons, have assumed that Joseph Smith's personal reaction was exactly the opposite, despite ample second-hand testimony reporting that Joseph recoiled at the idea of polygamy.[88] As discussed earlier, he related to numerous listeners his resistance and frustrations. Joseph Smith had several very good reasons to be hesitant. First, he could easily recall the experience when he shared his First Vision with others. It resulted in his being persecuted and having "all manner of evil [spoken] against" him (JSH—1:25). The outcry against the Book of Mormon by those who rejected it as scripture gave him a second reason for suspecting that an unorthodox marriage system would be even less

---

83. Foster, *Religion and Sexuality: Three American Communal Experiments of the Nineteenth Century*, 153.

84. Kathryn M. Daynes, "Family Ties: Belief and Practice in Nauvoo," 68; Daynes, "Mormon Polygamy: Belief and Practice in Nauvoo," 135.

85. Irwin Altman and Joseph Ginat, *Polygamous Families in Contemporary Society*, 28.

86. Todd Compton, email to Brian Hales, August 27, 2008; compare Compton, *In Sacred Loneliness*, 238.

87. Sarah Barringer Gordon, *The Mormon Question: Polygamy and Constitutional Conflict in Nineteenth Century America*, 23.

88. See, for example, Mary Elizabeth Rollins Lightner, "Remarks at Brigham Young University, April 14, 1905, 2–3: "Joseph said he talked to him [the angel commanding Joseph to practice plural marriage] soberly about it, and told him it was an abomination and quoted scripture to him. He said in the Book of Mormon it was an abomination in the eyes of the Lord."

popular. Almost certainly some otherwise faithful Church members might also falter before such a demand. Mosiah Hancock wrote in 1884:

> Concerning the doctrine of celestial marriage the Prophet told my father [Levi] in the days of Kirtland, that it was the will of the Lord for His servants who were faithful to step forth in that order. But, said Brother Joseph, "Brother Levi, if I should make known to my brethren what God has made known to me they would seek my life." My Father [Levi] made some things known to me [Mosiah] concerning those days, and the part he took with the Prophet in trying to assist him to start the principle with a few chosen friends in those days.[89]

Second, the theological difficulties were substantial. The Book of Mormon confirmed in stern language that sexual relations out of lawful marriage constituted a sin next to murder (Alma 39:5), an increase in the seriousness from the general message of both the Old Testament and the New scripture forbidding adultery and fornication and reinforcing the ideal of monogamous marriage and devotion to parental responsibilities. The "law of the Church," received within weeks of Joseph's arrival in Ohio, likewise forbade sexual transgression in strict terms (D&C 42:24). Such declarations provided important obstacles to sexual experimentation, should Church members perceive plural marriage in that light.

Many converts considered the Book of Mormon to be primary evidence of Joseph's prophetic calling.[90] To defy its teachings would have undermined his claims as a seer and revelator. Doubtless, he understood the immense consequences to himself and the Church should he be seen as being guilty of immoral behavior. With so many eyes upon him, he could not easily hide any sexual duplicity. It appears that Joseph recognized that the only way to successfully introduce plural marriage to the Latter-day Saints was to present it to them as had been presented to him: as a commandment delivered by an angel to restore a biblical practice for the purpose of "raise up seed unto me" (Jacob 2:30), the one exemption allowed by the Book of Mormon.

A fourth—and formidable—source of apprehension would have been Joseph's concerns about his wife, Emma. She had been deeply hurt by his first plural marriage to Fanny Alger; and although she had ultimately forgiven him and proved her commitment with unwavering loyalty through the debacle of the Ohio apostasy and the chaos of the Mormon War in Missouri, Joseph had no reason to believe that she would be willing to share him with other

---

89. Mosiah Hancock, "Correspondence: The Prophet Joseph—Some of His Sayings, Spanish Fork, February 18, 1884," *Deseret News*, February 27, 1884, 15.

90. Mark R. Grandstaff, "The Impact of the Mormon Migration on the Community of Kirtland, Ohio, 1830–1839," 110, documents that nearly a third of converts near Kirtland in the 1830s joined the Church primarily due to the influence of the Book of Mormon.

women under any circumstances. Historian Lawrence Foster wrote: "The introduction of polygamy was complicated by the deep affection that Emma and Joseph had for each other, a bond which is unmistakably revealed in their personal letters. Emma was jealously devoted to Joseph. He, in turn, showed great love for her. The deep attachment between them must have made the introduction of plural marriage particularly painful."[91]

A Quincy Connection?

While it is impossible to identify the spread of the teachings on plural marriage in 1841, it is possible that Joseph Smith had divulged these doctrines to devout believers in Quincy, Illinois. Mary Isabella Hales Horne related to an unidentified interviewer that she first heard the doctrine of plural marriage while she lived in Quincy.[92] The Hornes did not move to Nauvoo until March of 1842.[93] Joseph Smith visited Quincy on June 4, 1841[94]:

> Bro. Joseph Smith and several of the brethren and sisters came to Quincy. They came to Mrs. Horne's house, partook of refreshments—and scattered. Bro. Joseph was in the best of spirits. He said laughingly, "Sister Horne if I had a wife as small as you, when trouble came I would put her in my pocket and run." Bros. Joseph, Bennet, Law and Mrs. Law remained with Mrs. Horne. The next day Bro. Joseph and some of the brethren called upon Gov. Carlin. He received them cordially and everything seemed satisfactory. Next morning the brethren started on their missions, the rest returning to Nauvoo. The prophet with Sister Snyder called in his buggy upon Sister Cleveland. Upon reaching Lima, between Quincy and Nauvoo, some 20 miles from Quincy, he was taken prisoner on a writ from Gove. Carlin and brought back to Quincy.[95]

This reminiscence could be significant because it names a "Sister Snyder," who could be Mary Heron Snider, the legal wife of John Snyder (usually Snider) who is a poorly documented plural wife of the Prophet. (See

---

91. Foster, *Religion and Sexuality: Three American Communal Experiments of the Nineteenth Century*, 149.
92. Mrs. Joseph Horne [Mary Isabella Hales Horne], "Migration and Settlement of the Latter Day Saints," 17; see also Lorraine Wight Hales, comp., *The Chronicles of the Hales Family in America: Book One, 1791 to 1867*, 80.
93. Hales, *The Chronicles of the Hales Family in America*, 85.
94. Journal History June 4, 1841; *History of the Church* 4:364.
95. This is an amalgamation of two accounts from Mary Isabella Hales Horne, "Migration and Settlement of the Latter Day Saints," 11–13 and "Testimony of Sister M. Isabella Horne," 1905, 2–3, MS 5302, LDS Church History Library, combined by Hales, *The Chronicles of the Hales Family in America*, 79.

Chapter 16.)⁹⁶ Unfortunately, no additional document places her in Quincy in 1841. Nauvoo tax records for 1842 identify nine male property owners with the surname of "Snyder" or "Snider," seven of whom were married: Henry Snider to Paulina Voorhees Snider, Isaac Snider to Louisa Comstock Snider, Jacob Snyder to Hannah Anderson Snider, Robert Snider to Almeda Melissa Livermore Snider, Samuel Snider to Henrietta Maria Stockwell Snider, Chester Snyder to Catharine Montgomery Snyder, and George G. Snyder to Sarah Wilder Hatch Snyder.⁹⁷ Any of these seven women could have been "Sister Snyder" if they had ventured to Quincy at that time. However, since the Prophet was apparently sealed to Mary Heron Snider at some point, she may have been the otherwise undefined "Sister Snyder."

Even more significant is the mention of "Sister Cleveland," who is undoubtedly Sarah Kingsley Cleveland, the spouse of a nonmember and a sealed wife of the Prophet who lived in Quincy at the time. The date of her sealing to Joseph is unknown; whether it was before or after this visit cannot be determined on the basis of currently available documentation. However, Joseph Smith preferentially sought sealings to legally married women up until the spring of 1842 and then began proposing to unmarried women. (See Chapters 13–16, 24.) Mary Isabella Hales Horne recounted:

> About noon the next day the Prophet came to our house and said, "Sister Horne, the Spirit always draws me to your home." "Brother Joseph," I said, "you are always welcome. But how is it you are here when I thought you were almost home?" "Haven't you heard that I have been in court all morning?" he asked. I replied that I had not. "Well I have," he said. "I told the officers that I would be forthcoming at any hour in the morning they might name, if they would let me go, so here I am. What am I to do? They won't let me have my trial in Nauvoo, but are going to take me to Walla Walla. I thought I should be at home by this time where my wife would look after my clothing, as it is in need of attention." "I will wash your clothing," I answered. "Indeed, Sister Horne, you do not look able to do it." I insisted saying I esteemed it an honor to wash and iron the clothes of the prophet of the last days, and he finally consented, as I told him my Saturday's work was all done. I prepared his clothing that afternoon (he was wearing white linen pants), so that he was ready for his journey in the morning. At five o'clock on Sunday morning he was ready to leave the house, having spent all the intervening time fasting and praying. Before leaving the house he blessed them all. Sister Cleveland, who had heard of the Prophet's arrest, came to

---

96. D. Michael Quinn affirms that the only possible identity of "Sister Snyder" is Mary Heron Snyder although, as discussed in the text, other candidates exist. Quinn, Evidence for the Sexual Side of Joseph Smith's Polygamy," 13.

97. These marriages are documented at www.ancestry.com and www.earlylds.com (accessed August 5, 2012).

see him, and met him at the door just as he was leaving. As she shook hands with him, she began speaking in tongues which the prophet interpreted. Brother Joseph listened until she had finished, then turned to us and said, "All shall be well; there are to be trials and tribulations but that he [sic] should be exalted in the presence of God" and much more to that effect. "You have no fears for me, as Sister Cleveland says, I shall have my trial and be acquitted." He was taken to a court some little distance above Nauvoo, tried and released.[98]

While it is unknown whether Joseph and Sarah Cleveland had been sealed at this time, it is interesting that she spoke in tongues, evidently prophesying that he would be "acquitted."

Little more is known about how Mary Isabella Hales Horne learned of plural marriage while living at Quincy. Did she hear it from Sarah Cleveland, from Joseph Smith himself, or from some other insider? Evidence suggests that, at that time, only a dozen or two individuals were informed about the restoration of this principle and the Prophet was the only male participant. Regardless, in a signed June 10, 1905, statement, Mary Isabella affirmed:

> I testify that Joseph Smith was the greatest Prophet that ever lived on this earth, the Savior, only, excepted. . . . I heard him relate his first vision when the Father and Son appeared to him; also his receiving the Gold Plates from the Angel Moroni. . . . While he was relating the circumstances, the Prophet's countenance lighted up, and so wonderful a power accompanied his words that everybody who heard them felt his influence and power, and none could doubt the truth of his narration. I know that he was true to his trust, and that the Principles that he advanced and taught are true.
>
> I solemnly testify that I know that the principle of Plural Marriage is true; that it came direct from God; I have had evidence of its truthfulness, and have lived in it for nearly fifty years. I counsel all my posterity to avoid condemning or making light of this sacred principle.
>
> I also testify that this Principle (Plural Marriage) was revealed by our Heavenly Father to the Prophet Joseph Smith and was taught and practiced by the Prophet.[99]

Mary Isabella and Joseph Horne lived monogamy for twenty-eight years until November 30, 1856, when he married twenty-year-old Mary Park

---

98. This is an amalgamation of two accounts from Mary Isabella Hales Horne, "Migration and Settlement of the Latter Day Saints," 11–13, and her "Testimony of Sister M. Isabella Horne," 2–3, combined by Lorraine Hales, *The Chronicles of the Hales Family in America*, 80.

99. Mary Isabella Hales Horne, "Testimony of Sister M. Isabella Horne," typescript, 3–4, last paragraph (about plural marriage) handwritten; see also M. Isabella Horne, "The Prophet Joseph Smith: Testimony of Sister M. Isabella Horne," 160.

Shepherd and forty-four-year-old Elizabeth Ashford on November 30, 1856, in the upper room of Brigham Young's office.[100] Like Cyrus Wheelock, Mary Isabella was one of the first to learn of plural marriage and did not immediately engage in it. As an early polygamy insider, she was positioned during the next three years to judge any impropriety connected with it and Joseph Smith's behavior. It is probable that she knew of his involvement with Sarah Cleveland; and if "Sister Snyder" was plural wife Mary Heron Snider, Mary Isabella may have been aware of that relationship, too. Either way, she apparently did not view "Sister Snyder's" buggy ride as inappropriate or as something that would reflect negatively on the Prophet's behavior. Mary Isabella Horne's testimony above indicates that she remained a strong believer in Joseph Smith and his prophetic calling throughout her life.

A "Testing the Waters" Sermon

While Joseph Smith mentioned polygamy publicly on a few occasions denying that he or the Church were involved (see Chapter 30),[101] evidence supports that on perhaps two occasions he openly attempted to discuss plural marriage in his Nauvoo discourses. Clark Braden, who never met the Prophet, asserted: "Smith declared in a sermon he preached in 1840, that polygamy was right."[102] No such declaration appears in any surviving sermons from 1840 although the record is incomplete.

Joseph Smith's earliest public reference to polygamy may have occurred in 1841. In his autobiography penned in 1853, Joseph Lee Robinson dates a discourse specifically to "fall 1841."[103] At the age of thirty-three, Robinson arrived in Nauvoo in August 1841, settling "three-fourths of a mile southeast of the temple on Warsaw Street, between Mulhollon and Parley Street."[104] Robinson reported:

> While speaking to the people in that place he supposed a [hypothetical] case, he said suppose we send one of our elders to Turkey or India or to a people where it was lawful to have several wives. Where they practiced

---

100. Hales, *The Chronicles of the Hales Family in America*, 368–69.

101. See for example, Editorial, *Elder's Journal*, 1, no. 3 (July 1838): 43, Kirtland, Ohio; Andrew F. Ehat and Lyndon W. Cook, eds. *The Words of Joseph Smith: Contemporary Accounts of the Nauvoo Discourse of the Prophet Joseph Smith*, 377.

102. E. L. Kelley and Clark Braden, *Public Discussion of the Issues between the Reorganized Church of Jesus Christ of Latter Day Saints and the Church of Christ (Disciples) Held in Kirtland, Ohio, Beginning February 12, and Closing March 8, 1884, between E. L. Kelley, of the Reorganized Church of Jesus Christ of Latter Day Saints and Clark Braden, of the Church of Christ*, 203.

103. Oliver Preston Robinson ed., *History of Joseph Lee Robinson*, History Comes Home, 2007, 27, 103.

104. Ibid., 27, 103.

polygamy and suppose he should say to them your laws are not good, you should put away your plural wives. What would they do to him? They would kick him out of their realm. Said he, what right has he to speak against their laws and usages. Said he, God doesn't care what laws they make if they will live up to them. What shall they preach? Said he, they shall preach the gospel and nothing but the pure gospel and some will believe and be baptized.

He shall say nothing about the gathering but confirm them members in the Church and give to them the Holy Ghost and he shall pass along, preaching and baptizing and a man shall receive the Holy Ghost, and that shall teach him of a land of Zion and of the gathering, and when the elders shall come around again, this brother shall accost him thus saying, elder, is there not a land of Zion, a place where the Saints should gather to?

The elder should not lie to him. He shall say, yes, brother, there is a land of Zion where Saints of God are required to gather to. Then, said he, to the elder, I have five wives and I love one equally as well as I do the other and now what are the laws in that land? Can I bring my five wives there and enjoy them there as well as I can here? Said the prophet, yes the laws in Zion are such that you can bring your wives and enjoy them here as well as there, the elder shall say to that brother.

The prophet went on preaching the gospel of the kingdom as if he had not said anything strange or awful, but this to me was the first intimation that I ever received that polygamy would ever be practiced or lawful with this people.

The prophet went to his dinner and as it might be expected, several of the first women of the Church collected at the prophet's house with his wife and said thus to the prophet Joseph. Oh Mr. Smith, you have done it now, it will never do for it is all but blasphemy. You must take back what you have said today. It is outrageous. It would ruin us as a people.

The prophet knew it would not avail anything to contend with the sisters. Said he, I will have to take that saying back and leave it as though there had been nothing said. For he was aware it was a very large pill for them or the people to swallow.[105]

Robinson's narrative wanders to other topics and then returns to the "fall 1841" discourse:

In the morning he declared the law of Zion should favor plural wives. It surprised me much. It was the first intimation that I ever had as we remarked in favor of polygamy. I retired to my dinner. Several of the brethren stopped into my house and we talked about the preaching. I remarked to them that it was not likely that we should have the privilege of getting more wives but that the law would be framed so that they that had several wives could retain them and they did not know any better.

---

105. Ibid., 25–27.

> We attended the meeting in the afternoon. The prophet Joseph came upon the stand. He arose to address the meeting. He said brethren and sisters, I take back what we said this morning and leave it as though there had nothing been said. It amused me somewhat, but did not take with me for I was satisfied that he meant what he had said in the morning.[106]

The accuracy of the dating of this recollection is uncertain. Robinson may have kept a journal or diary during that period from which he was quoting, a diary that is no longer available. In the nineteenth century, as individuals started a new "journal" or "history," a common practice was to summarize entries in an older journal up to the date that the new "history" was begun. If this was Robinson's approach, then his account of Joseph Smith's "fall 1841" sermon would be much more believable. If however in 1853, Robinson was using his natural memory to recall a verbatim report of the discourse, its reliability including the dating scheme would be suspect. Notwithstanding, three other recollections seem to describe this very same sermon, but none provides a date, nor year. Apostle George A. Smith recalled: "The Prophet goes up on the stand, and, after preaching about everything else he could think of in the world, at last hints at the idea of the law of redemption, makes a bare hint at the law of sealing, and it produced such a tremendous excitement that, as soon as he had got his dinner half eaten, he had to go back to the stand, and unpreach all that he had preached, and left the people to guess at the matter."[107]

Horace Cummings reported a similar reminiscence from his father, James Cummings (b. 1821):

> At a conference one time in Nauvoo, he [Joseph Smith] predicted that some day polygamy would be practiced in this church. This caused such consternation among the saints, that at a later meeting he soothed their feelings by explaining that the gospel had to be "preached to every nation, kingdom, tongue and people." If preached to them many would receive it, else what would be the use of preaching it? Since most of the earth's inhabitants now practice polygamy, what would a man with two or more wives do when he joined the Church? Would he have to discard all his family but his first wife and her children? NO; the gospel is not to break up families. They would all be received into the Church and continue to live as they always had lived in that respect as there was no crime in having more than one wife.[108]

Another possible reference to same sermon is in a remembrance of Helen Mar Kimball Whitney, who was sealed to the Prophet in May 1843, and who would have been only thirteen at the time of the discourse:

---

106. Ibid., 28–29.
107. George A. Smith, March 18, 1855, *Journal of Discourses*, 2:217.
108. Horace Cummings, "Excerpts from History of Horace Cummings as given to N. B. Lundwall," one typescript page. Cummings was quoting his father.

He [Joseph] astonished his hearers by preaching on the restoration of all things, and said that as it was anciently with Abraham, Isaac and Jacob, so it would be again, etc. He spoke so plainly that his wife Emma, as well as others, was quite excited over it. Seeing the effect his sermon had upon them, he consoled them in the afternoon by saying that the time of which he had spoken might be further off than he anticipated, at all events, the Lord would assist them to understand and perform His will in the matter if they were faithful.[109]

It is not clear how Helen Mar, as a young girl, would have known Emma's reaction; and her report of the details of the sermon differs, though not more markedly than can be accounted for by the vagaries of memory, from those reported by Joseph Lee Robinson, George A. Smith, and (third-hand) by Horace Cummings. In any case, it seems clear that Joseph preached a sermon ostensibly about missionary work and the gathering that introduced the element of plural marriage.

Reports of a second public reference to plural marriage by Joseph Smith that occurred in July 1843 have been found. (See Chapter 24.) Several individuals remembered the exact month and year he openly referred to the controversial subject, although the few discourses documented in that month do not include a plural marriage discussion. The question arises, are all of these references to one single sermon in 1843, or did the Prophet broach the topic publicly twice in Nauvoo? Without any contemporaneous records, later recollections support that two, one in the fall of 1841 and another in July 1843, occurred.

First, Joseph Lee Robinson recorded that "on Wednesday morning following [the discourse mentioning polygamy], as I was working with E[zra] T[aft] Benson, I received the first revelation upon that subject."[110] On that day Robinson received personal inspiration concerning plural marriage. Importantly, Ezra T. Benson's autobiography states that he arrived in Nauvoo in April 1841 and lived there, "the remainder of this year, and till June, 1842," adding that at that time he "labored on the temple."[111] At that same time Joseph Lee Robinson indicated that he also helped build the temple, giving a general time period for the discourse of April 1841 to mid-1842, which includes "fall 1841."[112] Benson served a mission to the eastern states from June 1842 to the fall of 1843, so he would not have been in Illinois in July 1843

---

109. Helen Mar [Kimball Smith] Whitney, *Plural Marriage as Taught by the Prophet Joseph: A Reply to Joseph Smith /III/, Editor of the Lamoni Iowa "Herald,"* 11; see also Holzapfel and Holzapfel, *A Woman's View*, 142–43.

110. Ibid., 29.

111. Ezra Taft Benson, "Autobiography," *The Instructor* 80 (1945): 53, 101–3, 162–64, 213–15; available at http://www.boap.org/LDS/Early-Saints/ETBenson.html (accessed August 27, 2011); digital version not paginated.

112. Ibid., 22–23, 35.

further supporting two separate references to polygamy in Joseph Smith's sermons in Nauvoo.[113]

Second, the fall of 1841 was a ramping-up period for polygamy. Joseph Smith was then secretly introducing a few members of the Quorum of the Twelve Apostles, and perhaps others, to the teaching. Third, although he had married one plural wife (Louisa Beaman on April 5), he was sealed to two additional plural wives, one in October and another in December, before the end of the year. It appears that the topic would have been on his mind even if his discussions were all otherwise private. Fourth, the simplicity of the example used, that of a missionary encountering polygamy in a foreign land, fits the theological developments of 1841 better than July 1843. On July 12, 1843, Joseph Smith dictated the revelation on celestial marriage (D&C 132) and then just four days later he publicly mentioned that "by the multiplication of Lives that the eternal worlds are created and occupied."[114] The revelation states that to "bear the souls of men" in the "eternal worlds" is one of several reasons for the practice of plural marriage (D&C 132:63). Two months earlier (May 16, 1843) he had privately discussed "children in the resurrection."[115] It seems that in July 1843, the Prophet would have been less inclined to use an example of a foreign polygamist to introduce plural marriage, when he might have instead mentioned it in the context of eternal marriage and/or eternal families.

Accordingly, it appears that Joseph Smith attempted to bring up the topic of plural marriage at least twice in Nauvoo, a simplistic and practical introduction in the fall of 1841 and a more doctrinally rich reference in July 1843. Neither was well-received and evidently due to a retraction or the brevity of the reference(s) or to some other factor, neither prompted even one record-keeper to make a contemporaneous report.

Reinforcing the negative reaction specific to this sermon, Latter-day Saints had no difficulty opposing polygamy as an aberrant and immoral practice, particularly since sexual experimentation and varieties of experimental families (i.e., the Shakers, the Cochranites, and the Oneida community) were part of the false practices they preached against. Missionaries sometimes encountered false doctrinal interpretations and spurious revelations authorizing sexual transgressions among investigators, which they were quick to suppress. Writing from England, Elder Joseph Fielding penned on September 2, 1841:

> There has been a certain Principle manifested here which I shall mention. There has been a select little Company who have looked upon them-

---

113. Benson, "Autobiography," 53, 101–03, 162–64, 213–15.

114. Andrew F. Ehat and Lyndon W. Cook, eds., *The Words of Joseph Smith: The Contemporary Accounts of the Nauvoo Discourses of the Prophet Joseph Smith*, July 16, 1843, 232; Franklin D. Richards reporting.

115. George D. Smith, ed. *An Intimate Chronicle: The Journals of William Clayton*, 102.

selves as better than the rest, they met together as a choice Band, where they obtained Manifestations which it was not lawful to tell to the common Saints, nor even to me, though [I was] at the time presiding, it was shewn to them who should be Companions in another World; that they would not be united as they are now, (these were mostly Females). They had many strange Visions, of these things I got to hear by degrees, and \one/ of their Company came to [me] a short time ago to ask my forgiveness, as she had pronounced a Curse or Woe upon me. . . . I did not get to know of the new Companion Revelation till a short time ago. I then said it was not of God, and if one of the Twelve should sanction it, I should still reject it, soon after I was with Elder P. P. Pratt, and asked him if it were of God, he said "no." . . .

Another thing I will mention here. There had been a too great Familiarity between the Brethren and Sisters in this Land, this I saw; but had not so much Firmness as I should have had, but rather partook in it, and when the 12 returned last year, to this Land they checked this Evil, yet some who came from America, went far beyond any thing we had ever done or sanctioned, so much so that E C [Elder "C," otherwise unidentified] went into Bed with different Women and endeavored to persuade them it was no harm. . . . It seems also that E[lder] T [Theodore Turley] has been cut off from the Church since he returned to America for the like Sin.[116]

Although the level of confusion Elder Fielding was encountering in the mission field seems extreme, his response accurately measures the cultural and religious resistance of the environment into which Joseph Smith was commanded to introduce plural marriage. (See Chapter 5 for the consistent Church teachings on sexual morality and action taken against violators.)

Summary

In Nauvoo, when Joseph Smith finally committed himself to introduce and practice plural marriage, multiple challenges confronted him. By April 1841, after significant pressure from the angelic messenger, he was sealed to Louisa Beaman. Joseph B. Noble, Louisa's brother-in-law, provided several accounts of the marriage ceremony, but little is known about the union itself. Louisa died in 1850 and, as far as is known, left no personal memoir or record. As seven of the apostles returned to Nauvoo in 1841 from their mission to England, Joseph cautiously and immediately began teaching selected members about the doctrine. Two and possibly more attempts to broach the topic publicly before his death were not well received by Church members.

---

116. Joseph Fielding, Journal, retained copy of letter, September 2, 1841 73–76; terminal punctuation and initial capitals added when necessary.

Chapter 10

October 1841 to June 1842: Ten Additional Sealings

The historical record indicates that, after Joseph Smith's April 1841 plural marriage to Louisa Beaman, he contracted perhaps ten more sealings by the end of June 1842, approximately a year later. Nine were to women who were legally married. The tenth woman was a widow.

Zina and Presendia Huntington, 1841 Sealings

Before the end of 1841, Joseph Smith was sealed to two additional plural wives, sisters Zina and Presendia Huntington.[1] Both women were civilly married to legal husbands at the time of their sealings to the Prophet.

Zina's legal marriage had occurred just months before her sealing to the Prophet. Oa Cannon, granddaughter of Zina and her legal husband Henry Jacob and also one of Zina's biographers, wrote:

> While Zina and her brothers were living with the Prophet and Emma she met and became engaged to Henry Bailey Jacobs. They asked the Prophet to perform their marriage ceremony [on March 7, 1841] which was to be held at the County [sic] Clerk's office. When the couple arrived the Prophet was not there. After a wait, they decided to ask the clerk, John C. Bennett, if he would perform the marriage, which he did. When the couple later met the Prophet, Zina asked him why he hadn't come as he had promised. He told her it had been made known to him that she was to be his Celestial Wife and he could not give to another one who had been given to him.[2]

Ms. Cannon was born in 1902, a year after her grandmother's death. Although she tells this family story with great confidence, she could only have learned it second-hand, most likely from her father, Henry Chariton Jacobs.

---

1. For a detailed description of Zina Huntington and her marriages, see Allen L. Wyatt, "Zina and Her Men: An Examination of the Changing Marital State of Zina Diantha Huntington Jacobs Smith Young."
2. Oa Jacobs Cannon, "History of Henry Bailey Jacobs," 1.

Zina Diantha Huntington Jacobs Smith Young. Courtesy of the LDS Church History Library.

Seven months later on October 27, Zina, who was about seven months pregnant with her and Henry's first child, was sealed to Joseph Smith.[3] Concerning it, she wrote later in an undated biographical sketch:

When I heard that God had revealed the law of celestial marriag that we would have the privilige of associating in family relationship in \the/ worlds to come I searched the scripture & buy [by] humble prayer to my Heavenly Father I obtained a testimony for himself [sic] that God had required that order to be established in his church. I mad[e] a greater sacrifise than to give my life for I never anticipated a gain to be look uppon as an honerable woman by those I dearly loved [How] could I compremise conscience [and] lay aside the sure testimony of the spiret of God for the Glory of this world[?][4]

In 1898, RLDS Elder John Wight questioned Zina concerning her relationship with the Prophet. At this time, she was seventy-one:

Q. You claim to have married Joseph Smith?
A. No, I do not claim any such thing; he married me. The Lord told him to take me and he did so.
Q. I believe you claim your brother officiated at the marriage?
A. He did. . . .
Q. Can you give us the date of that marriage with Joseph Smith?. . .
A. No I do not remember. It was something too sacred to be talked about; it was more to me than life or death. I never breathed it for years. I will tell you the facts. I had dreams. I am no dreamer—but I had dreams that I could not account for. I know this is the work of the Lord; it was revealed to me, even when young. Things were presented to my mind that I could not account for. When Joseph Smith revealed this order, I knew what it meant; the Lord was preparing my mind to receive it. . . .
Q. Can you tell me when you were married to Mr. Jacobs?
A. That is no matter . . .

---

3. Zina D. H. Young, Affidavit, May 18, 1869, in Joseph F. Smith, Affidavit Books, 1:5.
4. Zina D. H. Young, Biographical Sketch #1 (of three). N.d. In Zina Card Brown Family Collection, MS 4780, Reel 2, Box 2, fd. 17. The "\ /" marks indicate words inserted interlineally.

Q. Then it is a fact, Mrs. Young, is it not, that you married Mr. Smith at the same time you were married to Mr. Jacobs?

A. What right have you to ask such questions? I was sealed to Joseph Smith for eternity.

Q. Mrs. Young, you claim, I believe, that you were not married to him for time?

A. For eternity. I was married to Mr. Jacobs, but the marriage was unhappy and we parted. . . . [5]

Q. I presume you are aware of the fact that it is claimed by your church that the marriage with Mr. Jacobs was not an agreeable one?

A. That is true . . . [6]

Q. Did you hear the question of plural marriage discussed either privately or publicly, prior to your having been sealed to Joseph Smith?

A. No. We hardly dared speak of it. The very walls had ears. We spoke of it only in whispers.

Q. How, then, could you have been sealed to Joseph Smith without first having heard the doctrine of plural marriage?

A. Joseph Smith sent my brother Dimick to explain it to me.

Q. It is a fact, then, that you were never taught it by Joseph Smith himself?

A. My brother Dimick told me what Joseph had told him. I knew it was from the Lord, and I received it. Joseph did not come until afterward.

Q. You mean by that, then, that after your brother Dimick had returned to Joseph and given him the information that you had accepted such teaching, that Joseph then came to you, prior to having been sealed, and taught you the doctrine of plural marriage?

A. I told you that the Lord had revealed to Joseph Smith that he was to marry me. I received it from Joseph through my brother Dimick.

---

5. Biographer Oa Jacobs Cannon wrote: "Henry signed an agreement releasing Zina to the Prophet for eternity. This agreement is on file in the Salt Lake Temple. It was found by Rega Card, Zina's grandson." "A Brief History of Zina D. H. Young, by Oa Jacobs Cannon, a Granddaughter, Researched by David Henry Jacobs, a Great Grandson," n.d., 12. If such a document actually exists in the Salt Lake Temple, Henry would have signed it during the Nauvoo period, nearly forty years prior to the Salt Lake Temple dedication.

6. [Emmeline B. Wells], "A Distinguished Woman, Zina D. H. Young," 99, also reported: "It was a most unhappy and ill-assorted marriage, and she subsequently separated from the husband who was so little suited to be a companion for her through life. Joseph Smith taught her the principle of marriage for eternity, and she accepted it as a divine revelation, and was sealed to the Prophet." Wells is correct that Zina separated from Henry, but it did not occur until 1847. Zina was sealed to Joseph Smith in 1841 and then to Brigham Young in 1846. However, she bore Jacobs a son, Henry Chariton Jacobs, conceived approximately June 15, 1845, a year after Joseph Smith's death and months before her sealing to Brigham Young. The issue of whether she practiced sexual polyandry with her legal and sealed husbands is discussed in Chapters 14–16.

Q. Who was present at the time that Joseph taught you the doctrine of sealing, besides, yourself and Joseph?
A. My brother Dimick.[7]

Zina's experience has similarities to other plural courtships in that an intermediary was involved, in this case, Zina's brother Dimick, who was thirteen years her senior. However, it was unique in the fact that Dimick's role was so extensive that Joseph Smith did not need to personally teach her about plural marriage prior to her acceptance. Oliver Boardman Huntington, who was two years Zina's junior, recorded a family story, no doubt told to him by Dimick, that casts the plural marriage to Zina (and probably to Presendia as well) as a blessing bestowed by Dimick's request for closeness to the Prophet:

> Dimick was a shoemaker and was mending a pair of boots for the Prophet soon after Dimick had given our sisters Zina and Prescenda to Joseph as wives for eternity. Joseph was waiting for the boots to be mended and talking upon the gifts and powers of the priesthood, the future of this work and the great glory and high positions of the faithful hereafter. Joseph said to Dimick "ask of me what you will, and it shall be given you even to the half of my kingdom." Dimick studied a moment and with a heart full of liberality and unselfishness replied. "I ask not for riches nor worldly honors, but brother Joseph I ask that where you and your fathers family are, there I and my father's family may also be." Joseph replied "in the name of Jesus Christ it shall be even as you desire." This promise we all expect with the greatest confidence will be fulfilled in eternity.[8]

In another account, Zina affirmed:

> I received a testimony for myself from the Lord of this work, and that Joseph Smith was a Prophet of God before I ever saw him, while I resided in the state of New York, given in answer to prayer. I knew him in his lifetime, and know him to have been a great, true man, and a servant of God....
>
> I wish to bear my testimony to the principle of celestial marriage, that it is true . . .
>
> He [Joseph Smith] sent word to me by my brother, saying, "Tell Zina I put it off and put it off till an angel with a drawn sword stood by me and told me if I did not establish that principle upon the earth, I would lose my position and my life."[9]

---

7. John Wight, "Interview: Evidence from Zina D. Huntington Young," 29; see also Martha Sonntag Bradley and Mary Brown Firmage Woodward, *Four Zinas: A Story of Mothers and Daughters on the Mormon Frontier*, 114. For information on Dimick Huntington, see Andrew Jenson, *Latter-day Saint Biographical Encyclopedia*, 4:748.

8. Oliver Huntington, Diary and Autobiographical Sketch, 1835–1900, February 18, 1883.

9. Zina Huntington et al., "Joseph, the Prophet, His Life and Mission as Viewed by Intimate Acquaintances," 212.

Joseph's third plural sealing (fourth plural marriage counting Fanny Alger) was to Zina's sister, Presendia Huntington Buell, who was eleven years Zina's senior. A spiritually gifted woman, Presendia reported impressive experiences associated with the Kirtland Temple in March 1836:

Presendia Lathrop Huntington Buell Smith Kimball. Courtesy of the LDS Church History Library.

> On one occasion I saw angels clothed in white walking upon the temple. It was during one of our monthly fast meetings, when the saints were in the temple worshipping. A little girl came to my door and in wonder called me out, exclaiming, "The meeting is on the top of the meeting house!" I went to the door, and there I saw on the temple angels clothed in white covering the roof from end to end. They seemed to be walking to and fro; they appeared and disappeared. The third time they appeared and disappeared before I realized that they were not mortal men. Each time in a moment they vanished, and their reappearance was the same. This was in broad daylight, in the afternoon. A number of the children in Kirtland saw the same . . .
>
> At another fast meeting I was in the temple with my sister Zina. The whole congregation were on their knees, praying vocally. . . . While the congregation was thus praying, we both heard, from one corner of the room above our heads, a choir of angels singing most beautifully. They were invisible to us, but myriads of angelic voices seemed to be united in singing some song of Zion, and their sweet harmony filled the temple of God.[10]

Presendia was sealed to the Prophet on December 11, 1841.[11] Emmeline B. Wells wrote her biographical sketch in the *Woman's Exponent* in 1883:

> Sister Presendia . . . became more familiarly associated with the Prophet and his teachings. . . . Joseph himself taught the principle of plural marriage to Sister Presendia, and her heart was humble, and her mind open to receive the revelations of heaven. She knew Joseph to be a man of God, and she had received many manifestations in proof of this, and consequently when he explained to her clearly the knowledge which he had

---

10. Edward Tullidge, *The Women of Mormondom*, 207–8.
11. Presendia Lathrop Huntington Buell Smith Kimball, May 1, 1869, Joseph F. Smith, Affidavit Books, 1:7.

obtained from the Lord, she accepted the sealing ordinances with Joseph as a sacred and holy confirmation.[12]

At the time this sealing occurred, Presendia was thirty-one and had been married almost fourteen years. In 1881 at age seventy-one, Presendia recalled:

> I was maried to Norman Buell Jan 6th 1827. both joined the Church in in [sic] Kirtland Geauga Co Ohio he left the church in Mo in 1839 the Lord gave me strength to stand alone & keep the faith amid heavy persecution in 1841 I entered into the new & everlasting Covenant was sealed to Joseph Smith the Prophet & Seer & to the best of my ability I have honored Plural Marriage never speking one word against the principal.[13]

The marriage between Presendia and Norman appears to have been a troubled one, possibly because Presendia's devotion to Mormonism was stronger than her husband's. Although Presendia says that Joseph Smith personally taught her the principle of plural marriage, her brother Oliver Huntington reported in 1883 a parallel role for Dimick in Presendia's plural sealing: "Dimick [gave] our sisters Zina and Presendia to Joseph as wives for eternity."[14]

Eight More Sealings in 1842

Todd Compton identifies eight additional women who were sealed to Joseph Smith during the first six months of 1842.[15] (See Table 10.1.)

Regarding these additional eight sealings (identified by birth name), no information is available for Elizabeth Davis, Sarah Kingsley, and Lucinda Pendleton. Limited documentation has been located for Agnes Moulton Coolbrith Smith and Marinda Nancy Johnson Hyde. Both Mary Elizabeth Rollins Lightner and Patty Bartlett Sessions left personal accounts. Todd Compton's deduction that Sylvia Sessions Lyon was sealed to the Prophet in February 1842 may be in error; but she is a special case and will be discussed in Chapter 13.

Agnes Moulton Coolbrith: Levirate Marriage?

The first of three widows the Prophet married was Agnes Moulton Coolbrith Smith, the widow of his brother Don Carlos, who died on August 7,

---

12. [Presendia Lathrop Huntington Buell Smith Kimball.] "A Venerable Woman, Presendia Lathrop Kimball," *Woman's Exponent* 11, no. 21 (April 1, 1883): 163.

13. Presenda Lathrop Huntington [Buell Smith] Kimball, "Biographical Sketch," 1881, MS 742, first copy page 2 and variant copy page 2.

14. Oliver Huntington, Diary and autobiographical sketch, February 18, 1883.

15. Todd Compton, "A Trajectory of Plurality: An Overview of Joseph Smith's Thirty-Three Plural Wives," 33–35.

TABLE 10.1
JOSEPH SMITH'S PLURAL WIVES, 1841–42

Name	Marriage Year	Marriage Month
Louisa Beaman	1841	Apr
Zina Diantha Huntington		Oct
Presendia Huntington		Dec
Agnes M. Coolbrith	1842	Jan
Sylvia Sessions		Feb
Mary Elizabeth Rollins		Feb
Patty Bartlett		Mar
Marinda Nancy Johnson		Apr
Elizabeth Davis		<Jun
Sarah Kingsley		<Jun
Lucinda Pendleton	?	?

1841.[16] Married on July 30, 1835, they had three daughters, ages six months, two, and four at his death. Agnes was a dutiful and supportive wife to Don Carlos who worked in the printing business as their family lived above the *Times and Seasons* print shop. Brigham Young's journal for January 6, 1842, records: "I was taken in to the lodge J Smith was Agness."[17] According to Todd Compton, "was" is a probable abbreviation/code for "wed and sealed."[18]

This plural matrimony is consistent with the Old Testament Levirate marriage custom by which a man marries his brother's widow with the understanding that children born to them will be accounted as his dead brother's children. This law is expressed in Deuteronomy 25:5: "If brethren dwell together, and one of them die, and have no child, the wife of the dead shall not marry without unto a stranger: her husband's brother shall go in unto her, and take her to him to wife, and perform the duty of an husband's brother unto her." Notwithstanding, there is no evidence of sexual relations between Joseph and the thirty-year-old Agnes, although such would have been permitted by the sealing. It is probable neither of them would have felt any compulsion to follow the dead Levirate law to raise up children to Don Carlos or for any other reason.

---

16. Don Carlos was born March 25, 1816, the youngest brother of Joseph Smith.
17. Brigham Young, Journal, January 6, 1842.
18. Todd Compton, *In Sacred Loneliness: The Plural Wives of Joseph Smith*, 153.

Agnes Coolbrith Smith Smith Smith Pickett. (She successively married Don Carlos, Joseph, and George A. Smith.) Courtesy of the Community of Christ Archives.

Contradictory evidence exists concerning Don Carlos's feelings toward plural marriage. In 1890, Ebenezer Robinson, who was his partner in the printing operation in Nauvoo from November 1839 to February 1842 quoted him saying: "Any man who will teach and practice the doctrine of spiritual wifery will go to hell, I don't care if it is my brother Joseph." Robinson added: "He was a bitter opposer of the 'spiritual wife' doctrine."[19] By all accounts, including surviving love letters from Don Carlos to Agnes,[20] their marriage was an extremely tender and loving union. However, if Ebenezer is remembering Don Carlos's exact words and quoting him exactly (a somewhat dubious assertion after fifty years), then his description of plural marriage as "spiritual wifery" is problematic, since there is no contemporary evidence that Joseph Smith used the term at that time.

Contradicting this account is one that reports Don Carlos as supporting Agnes's sealing to the Prophet. It comes from Mary Ann Covington Smith Sheffield West, who boarded with Agnes in Nauvoo from early 1843 until after the Prophet's death. Like Robinson's recollection, West's is more than fifty years old. Mary Ann Covington married James Sheffield in England in 1836. She left him because "he drank too much" and then, without a divorce, sailed to America arriving in Nauvoo in the spring 1843.[21] In April, she first met William B. Smith, the Prophet's brother. She recounted that later that fall, Joseph Smith "told me that he had received a revelation from God that men could have more wives than one, and that men were now being married in plural marriage. He told me soon after that his brother William wished to marry me as a wife in plural marriage if I felt willing to consent to it."[22] Joseph Smith sealed her to William for "time

---

19. Ebenezer Robinson, "Items of Personal History," *The Return* 2, no. 7 (July 1890): 302; see also 2, no. 6 (June 1890): 287.

20. See, for examples, Letters of Don Carlos Smith to Agnes Coolbrith Smith, June 25, 1836, and July 25, 1839, in Lavina Fielding Anderson, ed., *Lucy's Book: A Critical Edition of Lucy Mack Smith's Family Memoir,* 762–65.

21. Mary Ann West, Deposition, Temple Lot Transcript, Respondent's Testimony, Part 3, p. 497, question 67.

22. Ibid. pp. 495–96, questions 13; see also p. 504, question 272.

and eternity" and she reported that thereafter she "roomed with him" and slept with him[23] and testified they did not stay together on their wedding night or were together often during their marriage.[24] However, none of William's plural wives physically lived with him, as he had no home in Nauvoo at that time.[25]

Fourteen months after William Smith's October 1845 excommunication, but without a formal or Church divorce, Mary Ann wed Joseph Albert Stratton. Mary Ann declared that William "had gone off and left the church," which justified her remarrying.[26] Stratton died just three years later leaving Mary Ann alone (she had no children by any husband). Months thereafter she was sealed by proxy to Stratton and was married for "time" as a plural wife of Bishop Chauncey Walker West with whom she lived in Ogden until her death in 1908.[27]

Mary Ann West's willingness to recount her early experiences with Nauvoo polygamy prompted the Church of Christ Temple Lot to call her as a witness in their 1892 litigation with the RLDS Church.[28] Mary Ann then recalled: "She [Agnes] told me herself she was [married to Joseph Smith].... She said it was the wish of her husband, Don Carlos that she should marry him [Joseph]."[29] Since both women lived together for over a year as secret plural wives (of Joseph and William Smith), it is not unreasonable that they would have shared their feelings concerning their marriages that were novel not only due to polygamy, but because they were sealed to two brothers who were leading Church authorities.

A columnist for the *Corrine Reporter*, LDS convert Charles Wesley Wandell, was baptized in 1837 and worked as an assistant to Church Historian Willard Richards in Nauvoo in 1844. Endowed in the Nauvoo Temple on January 3, 1846, and sealed to his legal wife three weeks later, he later became disenchanted with the Church's teachings regarding plural marriage. In 1873 he joined the RLDS Church where he proved to be a valiant missionary, dying in Sydney, Australia, on a mission. In 1871 he recounted this version of Agnes's marriage to Joseph Smith:

> Don Carlos Smith, brother to Joseph, died in Nauvoo, in 1842 [sic], leaving no male issue. After the usual period of mourning had passed away, Joseph went to Agnes, his brother's widow, and stated to her that it was not right that Don Carlos' name should be lost in Israel; and that it was the duty of his next of kin to fulfill a certain office for him, in the hope that a son might

---

23. Ibid., p. 501, questions 174, 187
24. Ibid., pp. 500–01, questions 169–93.
25. Ibid. p. 512, question 509.
26. Ibid., p. 501, question 200, see also 201–2; see also p. 499, questions 129–30.
27. Ibid., p. 499, questions 114–15.
28. Ibid., p. 517, questions 611–19.
29. Ibid., pages 521–22, questions 679, 687.

be born which would bear his name. During this conversation no pretense to any new "revelation" upon the subject; but simply quoted Deut. xxv: 5, 6, in support of his position. This conversation Agnes subsequently reported to my wife; and afterward to me. Like a true and proper woman, she told Joseph she preferred doing her own choosing in the matter which so nearly concerned herself; which she afterward did by marrying a Gentile, and leaving Nauvoo.[30]

Both Charles Wesley and his wife Mary Brown Wandell lived in Nauvoo, so it is possible Mary was acquainted with Agnes, but my research does not connect them in any formal way. Regardless, Wandell thus relates a version of the story in which Agnes refused Joseph. However, the evidence for the sealing is stronger than Wandell's description. Two and a half months after Agnes Coolbrith Smith's sealing to Joseph, Clarissa Marvel, who also lived with Agnes "was accused of scandalous falsehoods on the character of President Joseph Smith without the least provocation" on March 17, 1842.[31] She later recanted her comments, signing a statement on April 2 exonerating the Prophet; but it is possible she may have witnessed signs of the polygamous union between Joseph and Agnes without knowing that a plural marriage had occurred.

After the martyrdom, the twice-widowed Agnes received her endowments on December 10, 1845, in the Nauvoo Temple and then on January 28 was sealed to Apostle George A. Smith. Todd Compton wrote: "It was another quasi-Levirate marriage, a man marrying his cousin's widow.... Soon after this the main body of the Latter-day Saints, including George A., departed for the West, but Agnes stayed in Nauvoo for reasons that are not entirely clear."[32] In the spring of 1847 Agnes married William Pickett, who afflicted by gold fever, moved the family to California. They separated when his drinking became unmanageable. While always friendly to Mormon visitors, she never identified herself as a Latter-day Saint in California.

Mary Elizabeth Rollins

Mary Elizabeth Rollins, born April 9, 1818, was converted with her family in Kirtland. Regarding one of her first meetings with Joseph Smith in 1831, she recalled:

> The Smith family came to Kirtland early in the spring of 1831. After they were settled in their house, mother and I went to see them. We had

---

30. Argus [Charles Wesley Wandell], "History of Mormonism: The Revelation of Polygamy Invented by Joseph Smith as a Cover for Incest: Open Letter to Brigham Young," *Daily Corrine Reporter*, August 2, 1871, 2.

31. Relief Society, Minutes, March 17, 1842; see also Dean C. Jessee, ed., *The Papers of Joseph Smith: Vol. 2, Journal, 1832–1842*, 372.

32. Todd Compton, *In Sacred Loneliness: The Plural Wives of Joseph Smith*, 156–57.

heard so much about the Golden Bible, as it was then called, that we were very anxious to hear more. The whole Smith family, excepting Joseph, was there. As we stood talking to them, Brother Joseph and Martin Harris came in with two or three others. When the greetings were over, Brother Joseph looked around very solemnly (it was the first time some of them had ever seen him) and said, "There are enough here to hold a little meeting."

A board was put across two chairs to make seats. Martin Harris sat on a little box at Joseph's feet. They sang and prayed, then Joseph got up to speak. He began very solemnly and very earnestly; all at once his countenance changed and he stood mute. He turned so white, he seemed perfectly transparent. Those who looked at him that night said he looked like he had a searchlight within him. I never saw anything like it on earth. I could not take my eyes away from him. I remember I thought we could almost see the bones through the flesh of his face.

I shall remember him as he looked then as long as I live.

He stood some moments looking over the congregation, as if to pierce each heart, then said, "Do you know who has been in your midst this night?"

One of the Smiths said, "An angel of the Lord."

Martin Harris said, "It was our Lord and Savior, Jesus Christ."

Joseph put his hand down on Martin's head and said,

"The Spirit of God revealed that to thee. Yes, brothers and sisters, the Savior has been in your midst this night, and I want you all to remember it. There is a veil over your eyes, for you could not endure to look upon him. You must be fed with milk not with strong meat. I want you all to remember this as if it were the last thing that escapes my lips. He has given you all to me, and commanded me to seal you up to everlasting life, that where he is there you may be also. And if you are tempted of Satan say, 'Get behind me Satan, for my salvation is secure.'" Then he knelt down and prayed. And such a prayer, I never heard before or since. We all felt that he was talking to the Lord and that the Spirit of the Lord rested down on the congregation.[33]

The Rollins moved from Ohio to Missouri where Mary Elizabeth married Adam Lightner on August 11, 1835, with whom she had ten children, six of whom survived to adulthood. Although Adam never joined the Church, unlike Norman Buell, he was not bitter about Mormonism and accompanied Mary Elizabeth to Utah in 1863 where he died in 1885. She lived in Minersville in Beaver County, near her brother, James Henry Rollins.

She seemed reticent to talk about her experience until she was in her eighties. Then, through letters, affidavits, and public addresses, she left several interesting accounts discussing her decision to be sealed to the Prophet. Parts of these accounts have been quoted earlier. A question emerges regarding her

---

33. Mary Elizabeth Rollins Lightner, quoted in "Joseph Smith, the Prophet," *Young Woman's Journal* 16 (December 1905): 556–57.

motives for waiting so long to recount her experiences with Nauvoo plural marriage. One possibility is that as the years passed, she became less capable of discerning between fact and fantasy as she reminisced. Called "confabulation" by psychologists, such verbal meanderings often contain kernels of truth accompanied by elaborations. A second explanation is that by waiting for most of the early polygamists to die off, she could conflate or exaggerate her claims without the threat of exposure. I think these are less likely because even though she included details not found in other accounts, her narratives are internally consistent and similar to others currently available. Comparing her different recollections demonstrates one conflict regarding her sealing month to Joseph Smith among the various accounts; some say February of 1842 and others say March (see below).

Another more likely reason Mary Elizabeth Rollins Lightner waited to speak stems from the type of plural sealing she experienced with Joseph Smith and how it would be perceived by her listeners. In the 1890s, Church members were familiar with Joseph Smith's plural wives like Lucy Walker (d. 1910), Emily Partridge (d. 1899), and Malissa Lott (d. 1898), whose sealings were non-polyandrous. By waiting until Adam Lightner's death (1885), Mary Elizabeth was less likely to encounter inquiries concerning how her relationship as a plural wife of Joseph Smith differed from the non-polyandrous wives. (See Chapters 14–16.)

On January 21, 1892, Franklin D. Richards reported a pleasant conversation with Mary and included a detail of her reminiscences:

> Sister Mary E. Lightner Smith called with her sister Mrs Bingham (wife of Edwin Bingham) and visited us 2 or 3 hours–talking cheerfully over past experiences. She and her fathers [sic] family. She tells us that it was revealed to Joseph the Prophet in 1834 that she was to be his wife but that Joseph did not reveal it to her till 7 years after, in 1841.[34]

Ten years later in 1902, Mary Elizabeth wrote and signed the account below:

> I was sealed to Joseph Smith the Prophet by commandment, in the spring of 1831. The Savior appeared and commanded him to seal me up to everlasting life, gave me to Joseph to be with him in his kingdom even as he is in the Father's Kingdom. In 1834, he [Joseph] was commanded to take me for a wife. I was a thousand miles from him. He got afraid. The angel came to him three times, the last time with a drawn sword and threatened his life. I did not believe. If God told him so, why did he not come and tell me? The angel told him I should have a witness. An angel came to me—it went through

---

34. Franklin D. Richards, Diary, January 21, 1892. As discussed in Chapter 8, two other sources declare that the disclosure occurred in 1842. See Mary Elizabeth Rollins Lightner, "Remarks" at Brigham Young University, April 14, 1905; Letter to Emmeline B. Wells, Summer 1905.

Mary Elizabeth Rollins Lightner Smith. Courtesy of the LDS Church History Library.

me like lightning—I was afraid. Joseph Said he came with more revelation and knowledge than Joseph ever dare reveal. (Brigham Young sealed me to him, for time and all eternity—Feb. 1842.) Joseph said I was his before I came here and he said all the Devils in Hell should never get me from him.[35]

Mary Elizabeth made a similar statement to President John Taylor and his first counselor, George Q. Cannon, when they visited at her house in Minersville, Beaver County, Utah, on Friday, April 18, 1884, when she was sixty-six. She then quoted Joseph Smith: "He [Heavenly Father] has given me a commandment to give unto you, to seal you up unto everlasting life. he has given you to me to be with me in His Kingdom."[36] L. John Nuttall recorded for that evening: "He [John Taylor] had met with sister Leightner [sic] who was a wife of the Prophet Joseph Smith."[37] Three years later when Wilford Woodruff had succeeded John Taylor as Church president, Mary Elizabeth wrote him, affirming the sealing: "I was Sealed to Brother \Josephs/ family in the Spring of 1831."[38]

As early as October 25, 1831, Joseph Smith taught that high priests were given the authority to seal up individuals that were identified to them by revelation: "Br. Joseph Smith jr. said that the order of the High priesthood is that they have power given them to seal up the Saints unto eternal life. And said it was the privilege of every Elder present to be ordained to the

---

35. Mary Elizabeth Rollins Lightner, "Statement," February 8, 1902. Brigham Young apparently recorded nothing concerning his role in this sealing. See Elden Jay Watson, ed., *Manuscript History of Brigham Young, 1801–1844*, for February and March 1842.

36. Mary Elizabeth Rollins Lightner, Statement, April 18, 1884.

37. Jedediah S. Rogers, ed., *In the President's Office: The Diaries of L. John Nuttall, 1879–1892*, 123.

38. Mary Elizabeth Rollins Lightner, Letter to President Woodruff, Salt Lake City, October 7, 1887. It appears that D. Michael Quinn interprets this comment to mean that Joseph proposed marriage to Mary or was sealed to her in 1831. See *The Mormon Hierarchy: Origins of Power*, 89. His endnote for this assertion includes thirteen different books and articles. However, a review of their contents fails to identify any specific evidence supporting that conclusion.

High priesthood."[39] The next month he received a revelation stating: "And of as many as the Father shall bear record, to you shall be given power to seal them up unto eternal life" (D&C 68:12). As quoted above, Mary Elizabeth remembered that, in the 1831 meeting, Joseph Smith declared: "He [God] has given you all to me, and commanded me to seal you up to everlasting life, that where he is there you may be also."[40] The doctrine expanded in Joseph's public discourses in Nauvoo.[41]

Regardless, as discussed in Chapter 9, evidence for marriage "sealings" prior to the April 5, 1841, plural marriage between Joseph Smith and Louisa Beaman is problematic.[42] Mary's additional narratives provide multiple references that marriage proposals and/or sealings did not occur before that Smith-Beaman plural ceremony. She also outlined the chronology:

> I shall never forget her [Bishop Whitney's wife Elizabeth] as it was at her house [in Nauvoo] that the Prophet Joseph first told me about his great vision concerning me. He said I was the first woman God commanded him to take as a plural wife in 1834. He was very much frightened about until [it] until the angel appeared to him three times. It was in the early part of February, 1842 that he was compelled to reveal it to me personally, by the angel threatening him. I would not accept it until I had seen an immortal being myself.[43]
>
> After a long time of prayer and supplication to my heavenly Father for a witness of the truth I went forward and was sealed to him for time and all eternity. . . . I was sealed to him the fore part of February, 1842.[44]

Mary also left two long accounts detailing her experiences. In an undated autobiographical sketch, she penned:

> In January [1842] . . . Brother Joseph and Brother Brigham came to see me and invited me to go the next day to his office in the Brick Store. I was

---

39. Donald Q. Cannon and Lyndon W. Cook, eds., *Far West Record: Minutes of the Church of Jesus Christ of Latter-day Saints, 1830–1844*, 20–21. See also Gregory A. Prince, *Power from On High*, 157.

40. Mary Elizabeth Rollins Lightner, quoted in "Joseph Smith, the Prophet," *Young Woman's Journal* 16 (December 1905): 557.

41. Andrew F. Ehat, and Lyndon W. Cook, eds., *The Words of Joseph Smith: The Contemporary Accounts of the Nauvoo Discourses of the Prophet Joseph Smith*, 4–5, 14.

42. See Joseph Bates Noble, Deposition, Temple Lot Transcript, Respondent's Testimony, Part 3, pp. 432, 436, questions 793, 799, 861.

43. Mary Elizabeth Rollins Lightner, Letter to Emmeline B. Wells, Summer 1905; Mary Elizabeth Rollins Lightner, Statement, February 8, 1902.

44. Mary E. [Rollins] Lightner, Letter to A. M. Chase, April 20, 1904, quoted in J. D. Stead, *Doctrines and Dogmas of Brighamism Exposed*, 218–19. See also "Record Book of Mary R[ollins]. Lightner Carter, MS 748.

surprised at this. He asked me if I was afraid to go? I replied, "Why should I be afraid of a Prophet of God?" He said Brother Young would come for me.

That night I dreamed I was married to him and occupied an upper room in a new house. In the morning, we were called to breakfast. And I wondered what Emma would say to me for I was afraid of her, but Joseph took me by the hand and led me down stairs, at the foot of which, stood Emma smiling at us and conducted us to the breakfast room.

I awoke then and did not know what to think of my dream. But on going to the office [the] next day, I received the interpretation for what to my astonishment, when Joseph made known to me that God had commanded him in July, 1834, to take me for a wife. But he had not dared to make it known to me, for when he received the revelation, I was in Missouri and when he did see me, I was married. But he was again commanded to fulfill the first revelation or suffer condemnation, for I was created for him before the foundation of the earth was laid.

I said if the Lord told you such a thing, why doesn't He come and tell me? Furthermore, I never would consent to be sealed to him, unless I had a witness for myself. He told me a great many things concerning the order and the blessings pertaining to it etc. I felt that he and I were both wrong for I had dreamed for years that I belonged to him; and had besought the Lord to take away such thoughts from my heart. No human being can tell my feeling on this occasion. My faith in him, as a Prophet about failed me. I could not sleep, and scarcely eat.

Next day, Brother Young came to see me, and said after we left the office, Joseph told him that an angel appeared to him, and told him that the Lord was well pleased with him and that I should have a witness that what he told me was true. I marveled at this, but made it a subject of prayer, night and day. One night in February I felt impressed to pray as Moses did in the battle of Israel with the Amalekites, by holding up my hands towards heaven. I also covered my head with a white cloth and I prayed with all my soul, that if the doctrine was true, to give me a witness of the same.

One night I retired to bed, but not to sleep, for my mind was troubled so sleep fled from me. My Aunt Gilbert was sleeping with me at the time when a great light appeared in the room. Thinking the kindling wood was on fire, that was spread on the hearth, I rose up in bed to look. When lo, a personage stood in front of the bed looking at me. Its clothes were whiter than anything I had ever seen. I could look at its person, but when I saw its face so bright and more beautiful than any earthly being could be, and those eyes piercing me through and through, I could not endure it. It seemed as if I must die with fear. I fell back in bed and covered up my head so as not to see it. I pushed Aunt very hard to have her look up and see it too. But I could not wake her and I could not speak. I thought if she were awake, I would not feel so afraid. As it is, I can never forget that face. It seems to be ever before me.

A few days after this Joseph asked me if I had received a witness yet. I said no. He said you soon will have, for the angel expressly told me you should have. Then I told him what I had seen, for I fully realized what I had lost by my cowardice. The family all said they knew something had happened to me, for my countenance was almost transparent. And when I told them of it, there was great rejoicing and they felt that I had been highly favored of the Lord. As yet they knew nothing of what Joseph had said to me.

When Joseph had enquired about the appearance of the person, and I had told him, he seemed much affected and told me that it was an angel from God and that it came for aught with more knowledge and revelation, than he dare reveal at that time. And that if I had prayed in my heart to God, all fear would have left me. As it was, Satan snatched the cup from my lips. He told me of many things to take place soon in my life. As a sign of the truth of what he had revealed to me, his words were verified to the letter.

After receiving other testimonies, I felt I could no longer disbelieve and in the month of March, [1842], Brigham Young sealed us for time and all eternity. Willard Richards and Heber C. Kimball knew of it, but were not present on the 23rd of March.[45]

In 1905 when Mary Elizabeth was eighty-seven, she visited Brigham Young University and told a similar story to a group of elders preparing to leave on their missions, adding some details that do not appear in other narratives. At this point, the Woodruff Manifesto withdrawing Church support for new plural marriages was fifteen years old, and Joseph F. Smith had issued the sterner "Second Manifesto" in April 1904 warning that action would be taken on the membership of individuals who continued to make new plural marriages. However, thanks in part to the on-going hearings in the U.S. Senate about Apostle Reed Smoot's seat, "polygamy" was practically synonymous in the public mind with "Mormonism" and the missionaries had to balance the competing demands of truthfulness and obedience to the current policy. Having a witness from someone who had personally participated in the practice must have been reassuring to them. In Mary Elizabeth's account, she stressed the divine source of her testimony of plural marriage.

> When Joseph sent for me he told me all of these things. "Well," said I, "don't you think it was an angel of the devil that told you these things?" Said he, "No, it was an angel of God. God Almighty showed me the differ-

---

45. Mary Elizabeth Rollins Lightner, "Mary Elizabeth Rollins," photocopy of holograph, Susa Young Gates Papers. A major portion of this holograph has been published as *The Life and Testimony of Mary Lightner*, but the section quoted above, which would have appeared on p. 24, was omitted from the published version.

ence between an angel of light and Satan's angels. The angel came to me three times between the years of 1834 and 1842 and said I was to obey that principle or he would slay me. But," said he, "they called me a false and fallen prophet but I am more in favor with my God this day than I ever was in all my life before. I know that I shall be saved in the Kingdom of God. I have the oath of God upon it and God cannot lie; all that he gives me I shall take with me for I have that authority and that power conferred upon me."[46]

Well, I talked with him for a long time and finally I told him I would never be sealed to him until I had a witness. Said he, "You shall have a witness." Said I, "If God told you that, why does he not tell me?" He asked me if I was going to be a traitor. "I have never told a mortal and shall never tell a mortal I had such a talk from a married man," said I. "Well," said he, "pray earnestly for the angel said to me you should have a witness." Well, Brigham Young was with me. He said if I had a witness he wanted to know it. "Why should I tell you?" said I. "Well," said he, "I want to know for myself." Said he, "Do you know what Joseph said? Since we left the office the angel appeared to him and told him he was well pleased with him and that you should have a witness."

Brigham Young's apparent personal interest undoubtedly arose from the fact that, at this time, evidence indicates that Joseph Smith was also pressuring him and other members of the Quorum of the Twelve to enter into plural marriage. (See Chapter 17.) Mary Elizabeth's account continues:

I made it a subject of prayer and I worried about it because I did not dare to speak to a living being except Brigham Young. I went out and got between three haystacks where no one could see me. As I knelt down I thought, why not pray as Moses did? He prayed with his hands raised. When his hands were raised, Israel was victorious, but when they were not raised, the Philistines were victorious. I lifted my hands and I have heard Joseph say the angels covered their faces. I knelt down and if ever a poor mortal prayed, I did. A few nights after that an angel of the Lord came to me and if ever a thrill went through a mortal, it went through me. I gazed upon the clothes and figure but the eyes were like lightning. They pierced me from the crown of my head to the soles of my feet. I was frightened almost to death for a moment. I tried to waken my aunt, but I could not. The angel leaned over me and the light was very great, although it was night. When my aunt

---

46. In a 2011 article, senior research fellow at George Mason University, Carrie Miles expanded the last sentence of this paragraph. The words in italics are not in the original: "*It has been revealed to him . . . that he had the power to save anyone who was sealed to him*: All that he [God] gives me I shall take with me for I have the authority and that power conferred upon me." Carrie A. Miles, "'What's Love Got to Do with It?': Earthly Experience of Celestial Marriage, Past and Present," 190. The added sentence is not a quotation from Joseph Smith, nor does it accurately reflect his teachings.

woke up she said she had seen a figure in white robes pass from our bed to my mother's bed and pass out of the window.

Joseph came up the next Sabbath. He said, "Have you had a witness yet?" "No." "Well," said he, "the angel expressly told me you should have." Said I, "I have not had a witness, but I have seen something I have never seen before. I saw an angel and I was frightened almost to death. I did not speak." He studied a while and put his elbows on his knees and his face in his hands. He looked up and said, "How could you have been such a coward?" Said I, "I was weak." "Did you think to say, 'Father, help me?'" "No." "Well, if you had just said that, your mouth would have been opened for that was an angel of the living God. He came to you with more knowledge, intelligence, and light than I have ever dared to reveal." I said, "If that was an angel of light, why did he not speak to me?" "You covered your face and for this reason the angel was insulted." Said I, "Will it ever come again?" He thought a moment and then said, "No, not the same one, but if you are faithful you shall see greater things than that."[47]

Rollins's accounts are intriguing in their detail. Although Brigham Young was frequently present and supportive of Joseph's proposal, it was Joseph himself who taught Mary Elizabeth about plural marriage. He expressed concern that she "was going to be a traitor" and expose him and the new doctrines. Her willingness to argue with Joseph about gaining a testimony for herself and about the interpretation of the angel's message show discernment and spunk. She hardly fits the description of an easily duped woman so commonly presented in antagonistic literature.

Patty Bartlett

Born in Bethel, Maine, on February 4, 1795, Patty Bartlett was one of Joseph Smith's older plural wives, his senior by over ten years. At the age of seventeen on June 28, 1812, she married David Sessions with whom she had eight children born between 1814 and 1837 with only three living to adulthood. In 1834, she and David were baptized into the Church of Jesus Christ of Latter-day Saints and migrated to Far West, Missouri, in 1836. Driven out in 1838, they settled in Nauvoo.

On March 9, 1842, at age forty-seven, Patty was sealed to Joseph Smith. As will be discussed in Chapter 16, Patty Bartlett apparently kept a journal during her Nauvoo years, but it has been lost or destroyed. For reasons not entirely obvious, her June 1860 journal contains the following notation:

---

47. Mary Elizabeth Rollins Lightner, "Remarks at Brigham Young University, April 14. 1905," 2.

Ten Additional Sealings

Patty Bartlett Sessions Smith Parry. Courtesy of the LDS Church History Library.

I was sealed to Joseph Smith by Willard Richards March 9 1842 in Newel K Whitneys chamber Nauvoo for \time and all eternity/ Eternity ~~and I~~ and if I do not live to attend to it myself when there is a place prepared I want some one to attend to it for me according to order Sylvia \my daughter/ was present when I was sealed to Joseph Smith. I was after Mr. Sessions death sealed to John Parry senior for time on the 27 of March 1852 G.S.L. City[48]

Her statement "I want some one to attend to it for me" is apparently referring to a resealing by proxy in a temple that she believed needed to be done. Seven years later in 1867 in response to a "request" from an unidentified individual, perhaps Joseph F. Smith, Patty Bartlett, now age seventy-two, signed an affidavit providing much of the same information:[49]

I Patty Bartlett daughter of Enoch and Anna Bartlett was born February 4th 1795 town of Bethel State of Maine[.] I was Baptised into the church of Jesus Christ of Latter Saints July 2d 1834[. I] was sealed to Joseph Smith the Prophet by Willard Richards March the 9th 1842 in Nauvoo in Newel K Whitneys chamber Sylvia my Daughter was present[.] I received my Endowment in Nauvoo Dec 16 1845 I Never was sealed at the alter to any one.

Yours Truly Patty Sessions[50]

In 1845–46 after the completion of the Nauvoo Temple, many of Joseph Smith's plural wives were resealed to him by proxy. It was taught that all eternal sealings performed outside of a temple needed to be repeated, vicariously if necessary, within a dedicated temple walls.[51] Apparently Patty's concerns as

---

48. Donna Toland Smart, ed., *Mormon Midwife: The 1846–1888 Diaries of Patty Bartlett Sessions*, 276–77. In addition to the typeset text, Smart has reproduced the holograph on p. 277.

49. The first line of the affidavit begins "According to your request," but the intended recipient is not identified on either side of the single sheet. Salt Lake Temple Sealing Records, Book D, 243, April 4, 1899; Thomas Milton Tinney, *The Royal Family of the Prophet Joseph Smith, Jr*, 41. See Chapter 33.

50. Patty Sessions, Affidavit, n.d., received June 1867.

51. For example, in 1899, President Lorenzo Snow commissioned proxy marriage

expressed in the affidavit created some stir at Church headquarters. The next month, priesthood leaders invited Patty to be resealed to Joseph Smith, with Apostle Joseph F. Smith serving as proxy for his Uncle Joseph Smith. On July 3, 1867, Patty recorded:

> I was sealed to Joseph F. Smith for time and all eternity. . . . He Joseph F. Smith acting for and in behalf of his Uncle Joseph. Smith. The Prophet. Who was Martyred June 27th, 1844. in Carthage Jail with his Bro Hyram. Joseph Fs Father. [signed] Patty Sessions[52]

Patty's brief reference is unique among the affidavits and documents created by Joseph Smith's plural wives in that her original journal account stated that she was sealed to the Prophet "for eternity." A later insertion added: "for time and all eternity." However, a more common theme is the presence of her daughter Sylvia as an observer of this early plural sealing, which was consistent with other polygamous marriages where close family members were present as witnesses.[53]

Two Sealing Dates for Marinda Nancy Johnson Hyde

Born in 1815 to John and Alice Jacobs Johnson, Marinda Nancy Johnson married future apostle Orson Hyde on September 4, 1834. Marinda was discussed earlier in Chapter 2 in conjunction with allegations that an improper "intimacy" between her and Joseph Smith provoked the March 24, 1832, mobbing of him and Sidney Rigdon. She was also mentioned in Chapter 3 regarding a charge that, due to Orson Hyde's 1838 signed statement criticizing Joseph Smith and the Church, the Prophet demanded he deliver up his wife Nancy Marinda, to him. Neither allegation appears to be based on believable documentation.

Two separate sealing dates for Joseph Smith's marriage to Marinda Nancy Johnson are available. Joseph Smith's journal contains a list of plural marriages in the handwriting of Thomas Bullock, who served as his clerk from October of 1843 until the Prophet's death Bullock's writing occurs on a sepa-

---

sealings between Joseph Smith and any possible plural wife for which a temple sealing record could not be found. See Salt Lake Temple Sealing Records, Book D, 243, April 4, 1899; Tinney, *The Royal Family of the Prophet Joseph Smith, Jr.*, 41; Lisle Brown, *Nauvoo Sealings, Adoptions, and Anointings: A Comprehensive Register of Persons Receiving LDS Temple Ordinances, 1841–1846*, 282.

52. Smart, *Mormon Midwife* 276–77.

53. For example, monogamist parents Cornelius and Permelia Lott were present at the plural sealing of their daughter Malissa to the Prophet. Malissa's brother Joseph (b. 1834) and sister Amanda (b. 1836) also attended the ceremony. Malissa Lott, Deposition, Temple Lot Transcript, Respondent's Testimony, Part 3, p. 100, question 150.

Marinda Nancy Johnson Hyde Smith. Courtesy of the Utah State Historical Society.

rate page from the office diary portion. After the July 14, 1843, entry appears this notation: "Apri [could be "Spri"] 42 marinda Johnson to Joseph Smith."[54] Four months earlier on December 2, 1841, Joseph Smith had received a revelation for her:

> Verily thus saith the Lord unto you my servant Joseph, that inasmuch as you have called upon me to know my will concerning my handmaid Nancy Marinda Hyde [sic] —behold it is my will that she should have a better place prepared for her, than that in which she now lives, in order that her life may be spared unto her; therefore go and say unto my servant, Ebenezer Robinson, and to my handmaid his wife—Let them open their doors and take her and her children into their house and take care of them faithfully and kindly until my servant Orson Hyde returns from his mission, or until some other provision can be made for her welfare and safety. Let them do these things and spare not, and I the Lord will bless them and heal them if they do it not grudgingly, saith the Lord God; and she shall be a blessing unto them; and let my handmaid Nancy Marinda Hyde hearken to the counsel of my servant Joseph in all things whatsoever he shall teach unto her, and it shall be a blessing upon her and upon her children after her, unto her justification, saith the Lord.[55]

It is not known whether the instruction for Marinda to "hearken to the counsel of my servant Joseph in all things whatsoever he shall teach unto her" is a general admonition or a specific reference to plural marriage.

In May 1869 Marinda joined other plural wives of Joseph Smith in signing an affidavit at the invitation of Joseph F. Smith. She stated "that on the [blank] day of May A.D. 1843, at the City of Nauvoo, County of Hancock, State of Illinois, She was married or Sealed to Joseph Smith, President of the Church of Jesus Christ of Latter Day Saints, by Brigham Young, President of the Quorum of the Twelve Apostles, of Said Church, according to the laws of the same,

---

54. Photograph of holograph in *Selected Collections*, Vol. 1, DVD #20. See also Scott H. Faulring, ed., *An American Prophet's Record: The Diaries and Journals of Joseph Smith*, 396.

55. Jessee, *The Papers of Joseph Smith: Vol. 2, Journal, 1832–1842*, 361; the revelation is dated "Dcr 2d 1841." See also *History of the Church*, 4:467.

regulating Marriage; in the presence of Eliza Maria Partridge Lyman, and Emily Dow Partridge Young."[56] Whether one of these proposed sealing dates is in error or whether two ceremonies were performed is unknown.

Little additional information concerning her matrimony with the Prophet is available. Todd Compton assessed: "For such an important woman, Marinda is surprisingly under documented. I know of no holograph by her and have found only four letters to her."[57]

Sarah Granger Kimball's Refusal

While it appears that Joseph Smith was usually successful in his plural marriage proposals, acceptance was not guaranteed. Some of the women the Prophet approached rebuffed him quietly. Others, as we shall see, were offended, either because they or Joseph were already married.

During early 1842, when the Prophet was sealed to several legally married women, one civilly wed woman, Sarah Melissa Granger Kimball, calmly refused his proposal. Born December 29, 1818, in Ontario County, New York, to Lydia Dibble Granger and Oliver Granger, Sarah and the Granger family were converted to Mormonism in the early 1830s largely due to a dramatic vision of the Book of Mormon prophet Moroni (son of Mormon) experienced by her father. By 1833, they had moved to Kirtland. According to Sarah's biographer, Jill Mulvay Derr, "she attended the School of the Prophets, an irregular gathering where the priesthood-bearing elders studied the gospel and gospel-related topics."[58] At that point, Sarah would have been in her mid-teens. In Kirtland Sarah met and married, with her parents' blessing, non-member Hiram Kimball, on September 22, 1840. They became the parents of three sons. By 1840, the couple was living in Nauvoo where Hiram was a prosperous businessman. Derr continues:

> Later in life she confessed that she had not wanted to ask her nonmember husband for funds to contribute to the church for the building of the Nauvoo Temple, so when she bore their first son [Hiram, born November 22, 1841], she asked Hiram if she owned half of the boy. When Hiram said yes, she inquired as to the boy's worth, posing $1,000 as a reasonable estimate, and Hiram agreed. Sarah declared she was contributing her half

---

56. Marinda Nancy Johnson Hyde Smith, Affidavit, May 1, 1869, Joseph F. Smith, Affidavit Books, 1:15, 4:15.

57. Todd Compton, "'Remember Me in My Affliction': Louisa Beaman and Eliza R. Snow Letters, 1849," *Journal of Mormon History* 25, no. 2 (Fall 1999): 48.

58. Jill Mulvay Derr, "Sarah M. Kimball," 25; see also Augusta Joyce Crocheron, *Representative Women of Deseret: A Book of Biographical Sketches to Accompany the Picture Bearing the Same Title*, 25.

Sarah Melissa Granger Kimball. Courtesy of Alex Baugh.

to the church. When Hiram related this conversation to Joseph Smith, the Prophet told Hiram that he had the "privilege of paying [the Church] $500 and retaining possession, or receiving $500 and giving possession." Mr. Kimball paid the church in land, but Mrs. Kimball maintained that the contribution was hers.[59]

Sarah, Hiram, and their three children relocated in Utah in 1851. There, Sarah became a diligent ward president in the revived Relief Society and was also active in the suffrage movement as president of the Utah Woman Suffrage Association. Hiram joined the Church but died in a steamship explosion on May 1, 1863, while en route to a mission in Hawaii.

In 1869 as part of the larger attempt to collect affidavits from women who participated in plural marriage, Sarah submitted her own, an experience that could be considered an anomaly given her unwavering faith:

> Early in 1842, Joseph Smith taught me the principle of marriage for eternity, and the doctrine of plural marriage. He said that in teaching this he realized that he jeopardized his life; but God had revealed it to him many years before as a privilege with blessings, now God had revealed it again and instructed him to teach with commandment, as the Church could travel (progress) no further without the introduction of this principle. I asked him to teach it to some one else. He looked at me reprovingly and said, "Will you tell me who to teach it to? God required me to teach it to you, and leave you with the responsibility of believing or disbelieving." He said, "I will not cease to pray for you, and if you will seek unto God in prayer, you will not be led into temptation."[60]

Apparently this combination of blessing and warning failed to persuade Sarah, for she never married Joseph Smith during his lifetime. However, she was sealed to Joseph by proxy in the St. George Temple on March 2, 1877, twenty-one years before her own passing on December 1, 1898.[61]

---

59. Jill C. Mulvay, "The Liberal Shall Be Blessed: Sarah M. Kimball," 210.

60. Andrew Jenson, "Plural Marriage," 232.

61. Tinney, *The Royal Family of the Prophet Joseph Smith, Jr*, 29. See also Stanley S. Ivins Collection, Box 12, fd. 1, item 53. "Estate of Sarah Kimball," *Deseret News*, February 7, 1900, 2.

Summary

As the evidence presented in this chapter indicates, Joseph followed up his first plural sealing to Louisa Beaman, an unmarried woman, in April 1841. However, he went on to marry ten more women before mid-1842, nine of them legally married to other men and one of them his widowed sister-in-law. It is also plain that he was not always successful in his proposals. By mid-1842, he had been married to a total of perhaps eleven women, counting Fanny Alger.[62]

---

62. Tinney, *The Royal Family of the Prophet Joseph Smith Jr.*, 29. See also Ivins, "Wives of Joseph Smith," n.d., holograph.

Chapter 11

Sexuality in Joseph Smith's Plural Marriages

It is nearly impossible to mention polygamy without also addressing the issue of sexuality. The historical record provides few specific clues about the existence and degree of sexual relations in Joseph Smith's plural marriages. Several of his wives gave some hints; and on occasion, they provided direct indications of their physical relations with him.

Joseph Smith and Sexuality

Little or no evidence exists directly from Joseph himself explaining his personal feelings regarding sexuality. His teachings specify that sexual intercourse must occur only within the bounds of lawful heterosexual marriage; but beyond that, few other details have been found. The revelations that came through Joseph Smith also condemned lustful desires or licentious fantasies as well as illicit behavior: "He that looketh on a woman to lust after her, or if any shall commit adultery in their hearts, they shall not have the Spirit, but shall deny the faith and shall fear" (D&C 63:16).

Historical documents reporting both public and private conversations with Joseph Smith are free from either formal or slang references to sexual activities, vulgar terms, or lewd innuendos. My research has identified only four documents alleging that Joseph employed improper language when discussing sexual issues, and they are all from either anti-Mormon or non-LDS reporters.

The first is a statement attributed to Joseph: "Whenever I see a pretty woman, I have to pray for grace."[1] The statement itself is not necessarily improper, but it implies an almost instinctive reaction of lust in the presence of an attractive woman that would be inconsistent with the Prophet's teachings. The document in question is recorded in Wilhelm Ritter von Wymetal's pseudonymous account, published in 1886 under the name "W. Wyl." He says the statement was made by an unidentified "Mr. J. W. C." who was, in turn, quoting a "friend." At a minimum, the statement would be third-hand,

---

1. W. Wyl (pseud. for Wilhelm Ritter von Wymetal), *Mormon Portraits, or the Truth about Mormon Leaders from 1830 to 1886, Joseph Smith the Prophet, His Family and His Friends: A Study Based on Fact and Documents*, 55.

possibly fourth or more. Although nineteenth-century writers did not observe the same strict canons of attribution that we expect from contemporary histories, Wyl's vague identification makes it impossible to trace the statement to distinct individuals, thus diminishing the overall credibility of the statement. Of particular importance would be whether the person quoting Joseph had sufficient geographical and emotional closeness to have been the confidant for such a remarkable declaration, nor is there any evidence of how accurately the statement could have been preserved in the approximately forty years that passed between the alleged statement and its recording.[2] Readers familiar with Wyl's whole volume recognize this statement as fitting a frequent pattern of comments reflecting badly on Joseph Smith but without enough details to allow their validity to be investigated. Lawrence Foster adjudged this quotation as "probably apocryphal," and broadened the generalization beyond this statement: "Coming from Wyl . . . this statement is understandably suspect."[3] Despite its popularity with authors who seek to portray Joseph Smith as a libertine, multiple observations demonstrate this alleged quotation to be problematic.

Wyl is also the author of a second allegation, reportedly quoting Benjamin Winchester:

> A large, influential "branch of the Church" existed in Philadelphia, over which Ben Winchester successfully presided. Joe visited that church occasionally and enjoyed the associations much. On one occasion, it having been announced that the prophet was to preach, he sat on the platform by the side of his faithful presiding elder while awaiting the time to open services. Now and then as some handsome young woman came up the aisle and took a seat, Joe would turn to Elder Winchester and ask, "Who is that beautiful lady?" or, "Who is that fine, lovely creature?" On being told, "that is Miss So-and-so," or, "Mrs. So-and-so," or, "Sister So-and-so," he did not at all disguise his wishes; he made no "bones" of it; but would say in reply, "I'd just like [to] talk to her alone for a while," or "I would like her for a companion for a night," and other expressions too plain and vulgar for me to write.[4]

---

2. As partially quoted in Chapter 1, concerning the accuracy of Wyl's writings, non-Mormon author Thomas Gregg wrote: "The statements of the interview must be taken for what they are worth. While many of them are corroborated elsewhere and in many ways, there are others that need verification, and some that probably exist only in the mind of the narrator. One fact, however, will obtrude itself upon the mind of the reader—that while these seceders are making all these damaging statements against the Prophet and the leaders at Nauvoo, it is remembered that only a year or so earlier they were denying them when made by others. It is for them to reconcile these damaging facts." Thomas Gregg, *The Prophet of Palmyra*, 504.

3. W. Lawrence Foster, "Between Two Worlds: The Origins of Shaker Celibacy, Onedia Community Complex Marriage, and Mormon Polygamy, 235 and note 2.

4. Wyl, *Mormon Portraits*, 67.

As discussed in Chapter 3, Joseph Smith made only one journey to the Philadelphia area during his lifetime. He visited the city from December 21 to December 30, 1839, then returned the next month for a second visit spanning January 9–30. These thirty days are the only window of opportunity for this alleged sotto voce evaluation of women in the congregation. Joseph's visit encompassed five Sundays (December 22 and 29, and January 12, 19, 26), but he kept no journal for those dates and the *History of the Church* contains no references to Sunday activities of the Prophet in Philadelphia on those days. The dubious nature of this report is demonstrated in several observations. First, Joseph Smith had not yet begun practicing or teaching plural marriage (with the exception of the Kirtland union involving Fanny Alger). Thus, if he had made such comments to Winchester, Winchester could have interpreted this running commentary only as brazen lustfulness. Coming from a Church leader who preached against such behavior, Winchester would have struggled to make sense of this new side of the Prophet. If Benjamin were equally duplicitous, he might have enjoyed being his leader's confidant for such aggressively male sensuality. More likely he would have been repelled by such disgusting licentiousness and hypocrisy on the part of his prophet-leader. On February 10, 1840, Benjamin addressed a letter to a " Dear Brother in the Lord" declaring:

> We had a conference here the first of Jan. 1840, J. Smith, Jr. S. Rigdon, Orson , P. P. Pratt, and many other elders were present. . . . J. Smith, jr. bore testimony to [the] coming forth of the book of mormon [sic] which was means of doing much good * * [sic] The Lord has prospered me, and made me to see the fruits of my labors. And I feel myself authorized to say that the work of the Lord is taining [sic] ground, in this city: and I trust that it will still roll on.[5]

This letter is inconsistent with the allegation that Joseph Smith would have acted as Wyl asserted. That Winchester, a simple missionary attending along with several general and local authorities, would have been privy to the conversation described by Wyl is implausible. If such a discussion had happened, it seems likely that some of the other Church leaders might have also heard it and reacted. Winchester left the church, but again, sexual improprieties were not part of the reasons for his departure.

The second problem is the setting that Wyl reports. On December 23, two days after Joseph Smith arrived in Philadelphia, he presided over a conference at which he organized the Philadelphia Branch with Samuel Bennett as branch president. Winchester replaced Bennett as the presiding elder on April 5, 1840, more than two months after Joseph Smith left the city. Therefore, Winchester

---

5. Benjamin Winchester to "Dear Brother in the Lord," February 10, 1840, *Journal History*, in *Selected Collections*, Vol. 2, disk 1.

was not a "faithful presiding elder" seated next to Joseph Smith and listening to a succession of libinous comments before the meeting convened. Joseph was not in Philadelphia when Winchester presided.[6] Also, up to one hundred members had been baptized in the area by February 1840.[7] If all of them attended one of the meetings presided over by Joseph Smith (which seems less likely), then perhaps it could be classified as a "large" branch, but it would hardly be "influential" since it had just been organized on December 23.[8]

A third problem is that, with the exception of Wyl's statement quoted above and attributed to two anonymous/pseudonymous sources, no one else has left any reports of the Prophet's using this type of language or, indeed, of regarding women with such disrespect.

The fourth, and most damaging weakness with Wyl's allegation is that Winchester went on the record in a letter to the *New York Herald* on November 11, 1844, five months after Joseph's death, acknowledging that, prior to 1841, he knew nothing "contrary to the principles of morality and virtue" that Church leaders had "advocated":

> When I embraced what is called the Mormon faith, notwithstanding the distinguished peculiarities of the sect with regard to immediate revelation from heaven, literal fulfillment of prophecy, &c,. &c., which a great portion of the Christian community regard as absurdities, I had no idea that any thing contrary to the principles of morality and virtue, would be advocated by any of the leading men of the society; neither do I now believe that any thing of the kind transpired (with the exception of among a few refractory characters,) from the time of the organization of the church up to the year 1841, at which time this flagitious doctrine of polygamy was introduced into the church.[9]

These four problems with the statement that Wyl attributes to Benjamin Winchester undermine its credibility.

The third statement alleging sexual innuendos in Joseph's speech comes from the pseudonymous writer, "A Traveler," who wrote an undated letter to *The Warsaw Signal* that was published on March 20, 1844. (See Chapter 30.) The writer reported: "Being compelled to remain in that city [Nauvoo] on account of the closing of the river, I was happy to learn that there was to be a trial of one of their Priests. . . . On the day of the trial [November 25, 1843] I

---

6. "Minutes of the Church of Jesus Christ of Latter Day Saints in Philadelphia," December 23, 1839; see also Michael Marquardt, "Joseph Smith's Visit to Philadelphia, Pennsylvania," 6–7.

7. Lyman D. Platt, "Early Branches of the Church of Jesus Christ of Latter-day Saints 1830–1850," 36.

8. See David J. Whittaker, "East of Nauvoo: Benjamin Winchester and the Early Mormon Church," 39–41.

9. Benjamin Winchester, "Letter to the Editor," *New York Herald*, November 11, 1844, n.p.

repaired to the council chamber and by good luck, obtained a seat, the room being crowded to excess."[10] Before the high council court was a complaint issued by Joseph Smith against Harrison Sagers. Ultimately, the high council clerk, Hosea Stout, recorded: "The charge [of sexual misbehavior] was not sustained, but it appeared that he had taught false doctrine, which was corrected by President Joseph Smith, and the defendant was continued in the church."[11] During the proceedings, "A Traveler" summarized the Prophet's comments: "I must say that a more ungallant speech than that of the Prophet, was never spoken in the presence of females—in fact, so lewd and lascivious, that it was with difficulty that I could sit still and hear it."[12]

Wilford Woodruff attended the same meeting and recorded this synopsis:

> At the close President Joseph Smith made an address upon the subject which was highly interesting & its tendency was to do away with evry evil & practice virtue & Holiness before the Lord. That the Church had not received any license from him to commit adultery fornication or any such thing but to the contrary if any man Commit adultery He Could not receive the Ceslestial kingdom of God. Even if he was saved in any kingdom it could not be the Celestial kingdom.[13]

The contrast between the accounts of the two attendees is remarkable. It almost seems that "A Traveler" and Wilford Woodruff attended different meetings, but they did, in fact, witness the same proceedings. Undoubtedly both possessed personal biases concerning the Prophet which may account for the differing views.

Regardless, the "Traveler" in his accusation of nonspecific inappropriate language did not report overhearing a private comment or conversation of the Prophet. He claimed that Joseph Smith used "ungallant speech" in a room that was reportedly "crowded to excess" with men and women, both members and nonmembers. If Joseph Smith actually employed "ungallant speech" in such an open and routine setting, it seems likely that similar outbursts would have been a common occurrence and that many like reports in both private and public surroundings would be available in the historical record. However, no other comparable accounts or complaints have been found regarding that specific meeting or any others.

---

10. "A Traveler," "For the Warsaw [Illinois] *Signal*," 2. "A Traveler" states that he attended the trial "last December," but Sagers's case was addressed by the Nauvoo High Council on only one day, November 25. He was not mentioned in any of the December high council notes. See Fred C. Collier, *The Nauvoo High Council Minute Books of the Church of Jesus Christ of Latter Day Saints*, 127–30.

11. Collier, *The Nauvoo High Council Minute Books*, 127.

12. "A Traveler," "For the Warsaw [Illinois] Signal," 2.

13. Scott G. Kenny, ed., *Wilford Woodruff's Journal, 1833–1898*, November 25, 1843, 2:328.

It seems highly unlikely that Wilford Woodruff would have ignored "ungallant" and offensive speech by the Prophet or, indeed, how such terms could have formed part of the Prophet's address on "virtue and holiness." For these reasons, I also reject "Traveler's" allegations of Joseph Smith's lewd speech.

The fourth report of inappropriate speech comes from William Law who recorded in an 1885 affidavit that in 1843 Joseph Smith "Said it [plural marriage] was a great privilege granted to the *High Priesthood*. He spoke strongly in its favor. . . . He was very anxious that I would accept the doctrine and sustain him in it. He used many arguments at various times afterwards in its favor. . . . Joseph told me that he had several wives sealed to him, and that they afforded him a great deal of *pleasure*. He kept some of them in his own house."[14] Regarding Law's statement, Richard Lyman Bushman observes:

> We might expect that Joseph, the kind of dominant man who is thought to have strong libidinal urges, would betray his sexual drive in his talk and manner. Bred outside the rising genteel culture, he was not inhibited by Victorian prudery. But references to sexual pleasure are infrequent. William Law, Joseph's counselor in the First Presidency, said he was shocked once to hear Joseph say one of his wives "afforded him great *pleasure*." That report is one of the few, and the fact that it shocked Law suggests such comments were infrequent.[15]

Although Bushman does not rule out the possibility that Joseph might have used the term "pleasure" in the context of sexual pleasure, available documents from men and women who knew the Prophet contain no complaints of slang terms, sly innuendo, sexual jokes, or other forms of licentious speech. Danel Bachman wrote: "I think that you only find reverence and sensitivity regarding sex and marriage, nothing crude, obscene, offensive, off colored, or chauvinistic in his statements or conduct."[16]

Sexual Relations in Joseph Smith's Plural Marriages

Historical research shows that Joseph was sealed to perhaps thirty-five women during his lifetime and that some of these unions included sexual relations.[17] The Book of Mormon's strong prohibition against polygamy allows

---

14. William Law, Affidavit, July 17, 1885, in Charles A. Shook, *The True Origin of Mormon Polygamy*, 126; italics in original. See also Wilhelm Wyl, Interview, March 30, 1887, *Daily Tribune*, July 31, 1887; quoted in Lyndon W. Cook, *William Law: Biographical Essay, Nauvoo Diary, Correspondence, Interview*, 99.

15. Richard Lyman Bushman, *Joseph Smith: Rough Stone Rolling*, 441.

16. Danel Bachman, email to Brian Hales, April 12, 2007.

17. See Todd Compton, *In Sacred Loneliness*, 4–7, for the most accurate list. However, Compton does not differentiate the different types of sealing ceremonies that the

an exception only when God specifically commands plural marriage to "raise up righteous seed unto the Lord" (Jacob 2:30; see also D&C 132:63). Children could not be born if celibacy was maintained in plural relationships. Thus, one of the reasons for the establishment of plural unions, according to Joseph Smith, was to produce mortal children. (See Volume 3, Chapter 4).

However, it is a fact that Joseph did not openly acknowledge his paternity of any child born to a plural wife so far as the historical record documents. The evidence of the women themselves is also scanty, especially since many of the statements of cohabitation occurred in high-pressure settings such as questioning by Joseph III or being forced to provide depositions for the Temple Lot Case. As a result, Kathryn Daynes has cogently observed that any assertion that most of Joseph Smith's plural marriages included sexual relations is "a conclusion that goes beyond documentary evidence."[18] Occupying the other extreme is Fawn Brodie, who concluded that Joseph had sexual intercourse with most of his "wives," sometimes marrying them first and sometimes not.[19]

Throughout his book, *In Sacred Loneliness*, Todd Compton analyzes and interprets hundreds of historical documents that together supply a mixed assessment, including the implication that Joseph Smith was hypocritical in his sexual relationships with women. That is, without discussing the actual moral principles involved, Compton sometimes portrays Joseph Smith as teaching one ethical standard and personally obeying another.[20] Anti-Mormon writer Joel B. Groat admits: "While Compton never even suggests sexual impropriety on Joseph's part, perhaps it is enough that he provides sufficient documentation to enable the reader to draw his own conclusions."[21] Compton's book constitutes a huge contribution to Joseph Smith's polygamy historiography, but it also il-

---

women most likely experienced, a critical distinction in discussing the possibility of sexual relations as part of the relationship. No conclusive list exists of Joseph Smith's plural wives. (See Chapter 33.) Estimates range from Fawn Brodie's forty-six, to Danel Bachman's thirty-one, to George D. Smith's thirty-seven, to Gary Bergera's thirty-six, to Todd Compton's thirty-three. I find Compton's comparatively conservative list to be the most probable and best supported by the available evidence, to which I add two additional names.

18. Kathryn M. Daynes, *More Wives Than One: Transformation of the Mormon Marriage System, 1840–1910*, 29.

19. Brodie acknowledges marriage ceremonies in many instances, but depicts the unions with Fanny Alger and Lucinda Pendleton Harris as sexual liaisons. Fawn M. Brodie, *No Man Knows My History: The Life of Joseph Smith, the Mormon Prophet*, 181–82, 301.

20. Todd Compton, *In Sacred Loneliness: The Plural Wives of Joseph Smith*, 15–23, 36, 49–51, 79–82, 125, 179–84, 279, 391, 464, 500; pp. 91–92 depict Brigham Young's relationship with Zina Huntington as possibly manipulative and polyandrous.

21. Joel B. Groat, "Sacrificing Time for Eternity."

lustrates the difficulties dealing with the issue of sexuality in plural marriages and the need to not only cite historical accounts, but also to directly address contemporaneous doctrinal teachings in order to form a more accurate picture.

A review of available manuscripts supports that Joseph Smith practiced polygamy with some of his plural wives precisely as did his ancient prophetic counterparts. Sexual relations were included that could have resulted in offspring being born. Abraham's wife, Sariah, and at least two concubines bore him children (number not specified) (Gen. 25:6). Jacob had twelve sons and at least one daughter by four women (Gen. 35:23-26). Joseph Lee Robinson recalled the Prophet's teachings: "The Father had a large number of spirits, very intelligent, noble spirits, spirits that had been kept back, kept in reserve because they were needed to come forth to be born under or in the priesthood to perform a certain very important work. This is what the Lord meant, when [He instructed Jacob] I will [']raise up seed unto me. I will command my people.['] (Jacob 2:30)] The time now has fully arrived and it [plural marriage] became necessary to command His people"[22] According to Apostle Erastus Snow, "God has reserved to Himself this right to command His people when it seemeth to Him good and to accomplish the object He has in view—that is, to raise up a righteous seed, a seed that will pay respect to His law and will build up Zion in the earth."[23]

Joseph Smith also taught a second reason for plural sealings that had nothing to do with sexuality or "raising up seed." He explained that all men and women must be sealed to a spouse to be exalted (D&C 131:1-2; see Volume 3, Chapter 10). Such sealings could be monogamous or polygamous (D&C 132:19) and must be authorized by the "one" upon whom the sealing keys have been bestowed (D&C 132:7, 18). Individuals who are not sealed prior to the resurrection "remain separately and singly, without exaltation, in their saved condition, to all eternity" (D&C 132:16; see also 15). In other words, all women and men need to be sealed to an eternal spouse by the final judgment (see Chapter 15). For example, LDS women married to nonmembers would need to be sealed to a man for the next life only but would not necessarily be involved in earthly sexual relations with him.

Evidence of Sexual Relations

As I have appraised the documents, I have found credible evidence of sexual relations in twelve of Joseph Smith's plural marriages.[24] Ambiguous

---

22. Oliver Preston Robinson, ed., *History of Joseph Lee Robinson*, 30.
23. Erastus Snow, June 24, 1883, *Journal of Discourses*, 24:165.
24. Evidence for sexual relations with Mary Heron Snider will be discussed in Chapter 16.

documentation is available for another three, but reliable documentation is nonexistent for the remaining twenty. Importantly, convincing evidence is lacking regarding sexual relations between Joseph Smith and three subgroups of plural wives: (1) the two fourteen-year-olds, (2) non-wives—women to whom he was not married, and (3) all polyandrous wives who were experiencing conjugality with their legal husbands. (See below.)

Appendix E includes all of the manuscript documentation on this subject that I have been able to identify. Furthermore, I readily acknowledge the difficulties inherent in distinguishing between credible and unreliable evidence. Different conclusions can be reached from incomplete and ambiguous historical documents. However, to summarize, I accept documentary evidence as establishing conjugal relations between Joseph Smith and fewer than half of his plural wives. Claiming sexuality in more than twelve plural unions goes beyond the evidence. Nevertheless, twelve is still a significant number for monogamous minds to assimilate. Author Kimball Young acknowledged, "Surely the monogamous system was thoroughly entrenched in the Christian mores" of the Mormons.[25]

I include only a brief description of the primary evidence supporting sexuality in these twelve relationships and refer the reader to Chapter 33 and Appendix E for more details. (1) Several accounts record that Emma Smith, and possibly Warren Parrish and Oliver Cowdery, witnessed Joseph Smith and *Fanny Alger* together[26] and one source asserts that Fanny became pregnant.[27] (2) Providing a deposition in the Temple Lot Case, Joseph Bates Noble was asked: "Where did they [Joseph Smith and plural wife *Louisa Beaman*] sleep together?" His response: "Right straight across the river at my house they slept together."[28] (3) When under oath in a deposition in the Temple Lot Case, *Emily Partridge* was asked, "Do you make the declaration that you ever slept with him in the same bed?" to which she answered, "Yes sir."[29] (4) Concerning Emily's sister Eliza, Benjamin F. Johnson wrote in 1903: "The first plural wife brought to my house with whom the Prophet stayed, was *Eliza Partridge*."[30] (5) Lucy Walker's

---

25. Kimball Young, *Isn't One Wife Enough?* xii.

26. William E. McLellin, to President Joseph Smith [III], Independence, Mo., July 1872. Also printed in Stan Larson and Samuel J. Passey, eds., *The William E. McLellin Papers, 1854–1880*, 488; J. H. Beadle quoting William McClellan, "Jackson County," *Salt Lake Tribune*, October 6, 1875, 4; Benjamin F. Johnson in Dean R. Zimmerman, ed., *I Knew the Prophets: An Analysis of the Letter of Benjamin F. Johnson to George F. Gibbs*, 38.

27. Wilhelm Wyl quoting "Mr. W." [Chauncy Webb], *Mormon Portraits*, 57.

28. Joseph B. Noble, Deposition, Temple Lot Transcript, Respondent's Testimony, Part 3, p. 426, question 683.

29. Emily Partridge, Deposition, Temple Lot Transcript, Respondent's Testimony, Part 3, p. 384, question 752.

30. Benjamin F. Johnson, Letter to Anthon H. Lund, May 12, 1903; emphasis mine.

niece, Theodocia Frances Walker Davis, reported to Joseph Smith III in 1876, "*Lucy Walker* told her that she lived with Joseph Smith as a wife."[31] (6) Benjamin Johnson also affirmed that his sister *Almera Johnson* experienced sexual relations with the Prophet: "He [Joseph Smith] was at my house... where he occupied my sister Almera's room and bed."[32] (7) In a 1915 statement, Josephine Lyon declared that her mother, *Sylvia Sessions Lyon*, told her in 1882 that she (Josephine) was Joseph Smith daughter.[33] (8) On May 23, 1844, William Law who had apostatized months earlier over plural marriage, charged Joseph Smith in a Carthage court with living "in an open state of adultery" with *Maria Lawrence*.[34] (9) Several other statements document that her sister, *Sarah Lawrence* also lived with the Prophet as a plural wife. For example, Lucy Walker attested in 1902: "I know that [Emma] gave her consent to the marriage of at least four women [Emily and Eliza Partridge, and Mariah and Sarah Lawrence] to her husband as plural wives, and she was well aware that he associated and cohabited with them as wives."[35] (10) In an 1893 interview with RLDS Church President Joseph Smith III, *Malissa Lott*, asked if she was the Prophet's "wife in very deed?", answered, "Yes."[36] (11) Two sources state that *Olive Frost* gave birth to a baby by Joseph Smith.[37] Both Olive and her child died before the Saints left Nauvoo. (12) *Mary Heron*, who is discussed in Chapter 16.

Three other polygamous wives may have also been sexually involved with Joseph Smith. The best known is *Eliza R. Snow*, with Angus Cannon reporting her second-hand statement made to Heber C. Kimball, which Cannon afterward made to Joseph Smith III in 1905: "He [Joseph Smith III] said, 'I am informed that Eliza Snow was a virgin at the time of her death.' I in turn said, 'Brother Heber C. Kimball, I am informed, asked her the question if she

---

31. Joseph Smith III, Journal, November 12, 1876.

32. Benjamin F. Johnson, *My Life's Review*, 96.

33. Josephine F. Fisher, Certificate, February 24, 1915.

34. *People vs. Joseph Smith*, May 24, 1844, Circuit Court Record, Hancock County, Book D, pp. 128–29. See also William Clayton, *The Nauvoo Diaries of William Clayton, 1842–1846, Abridged*, May 23, 1844, 49; Thomas Gregg, *History of Hancock County, Illinois*, 301; Andrew F. Ehat and Lyndon W. Cook, eds. *The Words of Joseph Smith: The Contemporary Accounts of the Nauvoo Discourses of the Prophet Joseph Smith*, 375.

35. Lucy Walker [Smith] Kimball, "Oath of Lucy Walker Smith: Wife of Joseph Smith, Jr.," October 24, 1902, in Robert B. Neal, *Sword of Laban*, no. 10 (1905): 2. Its wording is identical to the December 17, 1902, Joseph F. Smith, Affidavit, October 24, 1902.

36. Malissa Lott Willes, Notarized Statement, August 4, 1893, to Joseph Smith III. Quoted in Raymond T. Bailey,. "Emma Hale: Wife of the Prophet Joseph Smith," 99–100; see also 100 note 9.

37. Joseph E. Robinson, Diary, October 26, 1902 (Ms 7866); James Whitehead, interviewed by Joseph Smith III, April 20, 1885. Original notes of interview in possession of John Hajicek.

was not a virgin although married to Joseph Smith and afterwards to Brigham Young, when she replied in a private gathering, "I thought you knew Joseph Smith better than that.""[38]

This third-hand account (Snow to Kimball to Cannon) seems to be contradicted by an 1877 letter from Eliza to RLDS missionary, Daniel Munns. Her correspondence indicates that either she was not sexually involved with the Prophet or she was carefully trying to avoid admitting to it, even though she freely implied that Joseph cohabited with other plural wives. :

> "You ask (referring to Pres. Smith), 'Did he authorize or practice spiritual wifery? Were you a spiritual wife?' I certainly shall not acknowledge myself of having been a carnal one'... I am personally and intimately acquainted with several ladies now living in Utah who accepted the pure and sacred doctrine of plural marriage, and were the bona fide wives of Pres. Joseph Smith." (Emphasis in original.)[39]

Another possible conjugal wife of Joseph Smith is Sarah Ann Whitney. In the only existing recorded sealing ceremony of any of the Prophet's plural marriages, a reference to the couple's "posterity forever" is made, ostensibly authorizing sexual relations.[40] No actual evidence has been located. *Hannah Ells* is the third possibility. In 1869, LDS Church member John Benbow signed an affidavit affirming: "President Smith frequently visited his wife Hannah at his (John Benbow's) house."[41] Whether those visits included conjugal relations is not clear, but possible.

In all, the historical record seems to support that sexual relations occurred with twelve of Joseph Smith plural marriages, with three more possibilities. This number, though fewer than half of Joseph's plural wives, is still substantial. That conjugal relations did not occur in some of Joseph Smith's plural marriages is not surprising or improbable. Jeffery O. Johnson credits Brigham Young with fifty-five wives, but he fathered children with only sixteen.[42] Similarly, Heber C. Kimball's biographer identifies sealings to forty-

---

38. Angus Cannon, Statement recalled from 1905 interview by Joseph Smith III.

39. Eliza R. Snow, Letter to Daniel Munns, May 30, 1877.

40. Joseph Smith, Revelation for Newel K. Whitney, July 27, 1842; reproduced in H. Michael Marquardt, *The Joseph Smith Revelations: Text and Commentary*, 315–16; see also Revelations in Addition to Those Found in the LDS Edition of the D&C in *New Mormon Studies: A Comprehensive Resource Library*.

41. Joseph F. Smith, Affidavit Books, 1:74. See also Andrew Jenson, "Plural Marriage," 223; Hannah Ells, Letter to Sister [Phoebe] Woodruff, May 4, 1845.

42. Jeffery Ogden Johnson, "Determining and Defining 'Wife': The Brigham Young Households," 58, 65–69; Leonard J. Arrington, *Brigham Young: American Moses*, 420–21, identifies sixteen plural wives by whom Brigham Young had children and nine other by whom he did not. However, Stanley P. Hirshson, *The Lion of the Lord*, 190–221,

three wives, but he had children with eighteen.[43] While these numbers are still startling from a monogamous context, and sexual relations do not always result in pregnancy, this research suggests that being sealed as a wife to a man does not necessarily confirm having a connubial relationship with him. Chapter 15 discusses why this may have happened.

Children from Joseph Smith's Plural Marriages?

During the nineteenth century, RLDS Church leaders, especially Joseph and Emma's sons, repeatedly attacked the LDS claim that Joseph Smith had restored polygamy by pointing to the absence of offspring from his polygamous wives. They made a double-pronged argument: that the absence of children meant either that Joseph Smith had not married plural wives or that, if he had, these marriages were purely ceremonial and had not included sexual relations. In 1903, Joseph Smith III asserted: "Joseph Smith could not have either taught or practiced contrary to this rule of marriage [monogamy]. To have done so he would have disregarded and disobeyed the commands of the Lord, as he and his associates understood them. The evidence that he did this is lacking or altogether inadequate. It is proof that no children were born to him except by his wife Emma."[44] Malissa Lott, giving her deposition in the Temple Lot Case, was asked if she knew of any children born to Joseph's polygamous wives. She answered: "I couldn't swear to any body else's children but my own"—by which she meant her own children by her husband, Ira Jones Willes, whom she married on May 13, 1849.[45] Emily Partridge, similarly questioned, responded: "No sir, I don't know of any."[46]

On June 7, 1892, George Reynolds, as Wilford Woodruff's secretary, answered a letter written to Church headquarters by "H. Neidig," a Latter-day Saint living in Wampum, Pennsylvania. Although Neidig's letter has not

---

identifies seventy wives.

43. Stanley B. Kimball, *Heber C. Kimball: Mormon Patriarch and Pioneer*, 307–16.

44. Emily P. Young, Deposition, Temple Lot Transcript, Respondent's Testimony, Part 3, p. 388, question 861. Joseph Smith III, "Plural Marriage in America," 465. Joseph Smith III was responding to LDS Church President Joseph F. Smith who had written months before: "He [Joseph Smith III] makes the bald assertion that there was no issue to any of these marriages. That is a mere assumption, which he is not able to prove, and which cuts no important figure in the dispute; for lack of offspring can scarcely be viewed as disproof of the marriage relation." Joseph F. Smith, "The Real Origin of American Polygamy," 493–94.

45. Malissa Lott Smith Willes, Deposition, Temple Lot Transcript, Respondent's Testimony, Part 3, p. 99, question 141.

46. Emily D. P. Young, Deposition, Temple Lot Transcript, Respondent's Testimony, Part 3, p. 388, question 861.

survived, apparently he asked why no documented children had been born to Joseph Smith's plural wives. Reynolds responded: "The facts you refer to are almost as great a mystery to us as they are to you; but the reason generally assigned by the wives themselves is, that owing to the peculiar circumstances by which they were surrounded, they were so nervous and in such constant fear that they did not conceive. It is known, however, that one at least did, become pregnant, but miscarried."[47] If Reynolds was aware of rumors of any other pregnancies or offspring, he did not share that information with Neidig.

When Lyman O. Littlefield published an 1888 collection of supportive reminiscences, he interviewed Lucy Walker, who had just turned sixty-two. She described being interviewed in the 1870s (probably 1876), by Joseph Smith's sons: "[They] seem[ed] surprised," Lucy recalled, "that there was no issue from asserted plural marriages with their father. Could they but realize the hazardous life he lived, after that revelation was given, they would comprehend the reason. He was harassed and hounded and lived in constant fear of being betrayed by those who ought to have been true to him."[48] These circumstances, while certainly true, might have been reasons to avoid the risks required by conducting conjugal encounters; but if those encounters occurred, "fear" and "hazards" would not have prevented conception. In an otherwise fertile woman (see below), only a lack of intercourse within twenty-four hours of ovulation or some form of contraception would have prevented her from conceiving.

After Brigham Young's death in 1877, his daughter Susa, an ardent defender of the faith, wrote: "Father and the Twelve Apostles felt the death of the Prophet far more keenly than did the people; and as we believe that children are a part of the glory we inherit hereafter, it seemed a cruel thing that the beloved leader and Prophet should be stricken down in the prime of life, and left without issue in this Church."[49]

---

47. George Reynolds, Letter to H. Neidig, June 7, 1892, Wilford Woodruff Letterbook 1352, vol. 10:350. Woodruff does not mention this query in his own diary.

48. Lucy Walker Smith Kimball, Statement, quoted in Lyman Omer Littlefield, *Reminiscences of Latter-day Saints: Giving an Account of Much Individual Suffering Endured for Religious Conscience*, 50.

49. Susa Young Gates, Undated and untitled handwritten statement, 78. Supporting that the apostles sought to raise up seed to the Prophet is the observation that, after his death, Brigham Young was sealed to eight of Joseph Smith's widows: Louisa Beaman, Emily Partridge, Zina Huntington, Eliza R. Snow, Maria Lawrence, Olive Frost, Mary Elizabeth Rollins, and Rhoda Richards. There are rumors that Brigham may have also approached Fanny Alger and possibly Emma Smith. Heber C. Kimball was sealed to seven of Joseph Smith's plural wives: Sylvia Sessions, Nancy Winchester, Sarah Lawrence, Martha McBride, Lucy Walker, Sarah Ann Whitney, and Presendia Huntington. Nancy Marinda Johnson was married to Orson Hyde. Eliza Partridge married Amasa Lyman.

The absence of documented offspring has posed a puzzle for both Joseph Smith's defenders and opponents. Fawn Brodie, among the most adamant in proposing an image of a libertine Joseph, wrote: "It is astonishing that evidence of other children . . . has never come to light."[50] She suggests that Joseph may have "learned some primitive method of birth control."[51] In the early 1840s, barrier forms of birth control were not generally available.[52] Other types— withdrawal, the rhythm method, and douching—were not reliable. It appears that Brodie was merely hypothesizing.

Dissident Sarah Pratt provided another unlikely explanation: "You hear often that Joseph had no polygamous offspring. The reason of this is very simple. *Abortion was practiced on a large scale in Nauvoo.* Dr. John C. Bennett, the evil genius of Joseph, brought this abomination into a scientific system. He showed to my husband and me the instruments with which he used to '*operate for Joseph.*'"[53] The instrument in Bennett's possession was likely a curette used to perform a uterine curettage, which would cause the demise of a fetus and hopefully remove it completely from the uterus. While it is likely that Bennett, as a licensed physician and experienced obstetrician,[54] knew how to perform abortions and may actually have done so in Nauvoo, the practice of abortion would clearly contradict the announced purpose of authorized plural marriage: to "raise up seed unto [God]" (Jacob 2:30).[55] Joseph Smith taught that a purpose of mar-

---

50. Brodie, *No Man Knows My History*, 346.

51. Ibid., 346.

52. Vulcanized rubber was developed in 1839, and rubber condoms were available by the mid-1840s. By that point, of course, Joseph Smith was dead.

53. John C. Bennett, quoted in Wyl, *Mormon Portraits*, 59; emphasis in Wyl. Sarah Pratt also allegedly stated: "[Joseph Smith] had mostly intercourse with married women, and as to single ones, Dr. Bennett was always on hand, when anything happened." Ibid., 61. As discussed in Chapter 19, little evidence supports John C. Bennett as a polygamy insider. Sarah Miller, who was interviewed by members of the Nauvoo High Council on May 24, 1842, stated that Chauncey Higbee "began his seducing insinuations by saying it was no harm to have sexual intercourse with women if they would keep it to themselves. . . . I told him it might be told in bringing forth [pregnancy]. Chauncey said there was no danger, and that Dr. Bennett understood it, and would come and take it away." "Take it away" is probably a reference to performing an abortion, although certain drugs could induce miscarriage. John S. Dinger, ed., *The Nauvoo City and High Council Minutes*, 415 note 40; photocopy of the holograph in Valeen Tippetts Avery Papers, Merrill-Cazier Library, Utah State University, Logan; photocopy in my possession.

54. In 1825 John C. Bennett passed the exam then required to practice medicine. Andrew C. Skinner, "John C. Bennett: For Prophet or Profit?" 249–50. In 1837 Bennett published *The Accoucheur's Vad Mecum*, an account of his obstetrical experiences. Andrew F. Smith, "John Cook Bennett's Nauvoo," 112.

55. Daniel H. Wells, appointed a counselor in Brigham Young's First Presidency in January 1857, taught two months later: "The principles of plurality have been

riage was to bring forth children (D&C 49:16–17). Plural marriage was also specifically designed "to multiply and replenish the earth . . . that they may bear the souls of men; for herein is the work of my Father continued" (D&C 132:63; see also Volume 3, Chapter 4). In short, Fawn Brodie and Sarah Bates Pratt are unreliable sources in associating Joseph with feticide, nor has more credible documentation been identified in the historical record.

An additional interpretation alleges that children were born to Joseph's plural wives, but they were kept hidden through two strategies. First, Lawrence Foster recalled a plausible but third-hand account that Joseph's children by plural wives were raised in other families:

> T. Edgar Lyon, a leading contemporary authority on the Nauvoo period, has related another account of how children by Smith's plural wives may have been handled. When Dr. Lyon was working in Nauvoo in 1968–69, a man introduced himself by saying: "How would you like to meet a descendant of Joseph Smith who has never been out of the Church!" Since none of Smith's children by Emma remained affiliated with the Utah Church, the man's statement showed that he considered himself descended from one of Smith's polygamous unions.
>
> The man told Dr. Lyon of three families—Farnsworth, Dibble, and Allred—in each of which lived one of Smith's plural wives. When each of the plural wives became pregnant, they as well as the recognized wife in the household both went into seclusion, as was the practice for visibly pregnant women at the time. After the plural wife's child was born, the recognized wife in the household reappeared and presented the child as belonging to her. At least one of the children was born from these polygamous unions before Smith's death. After his death, these plural wives went to Utah, were married to other men, and had children by them.[56]

If the narrative is correct, then a logical next question is which of the Prophet's wives may have lived in Nauvoo with an Allred, a Farnsworth, or a Dibble family? No evidence exists, to my knowledge, that any of Joseph Smith's known thirty-five plural wives boarded with any family with these surnames. Fourteen of the women had legal husbands so pregnancy in those marriages would be attributed to the civil spouse. Indeed several authors asserted that Joseph Smith preferentially sought to be sealed to married women

---

established, in order to raise up a righteous seed unto God." March 1, 1857, *Journal of Discourses*, 4:254.

56. T. Edgar Lyon, conversation with Lawrence Foster, June 27, 1974, quoted in W. Lawrence Foster, "Between Two Worlds," 252. See also Lawrence Foster, *Religion and Sexuality: Three American Communal Experiments of the Nineteenth Century*, 158. Despite attempts to do so, Foster was unable to further elucidate details concerning the three families mentioned. Lawrence Foster, email to Brian Hales, August 8, 2011.

in order to shield him from paternity suspicions. For example, Harry M. Beardsley, author of the 1931 *Joseph Smith and His Mormon Empire*, theorized: "Many of the members of Joseph's celestial harem were married women, and the offspring of such unions might easily be credited to the legal husbands in the official records."[57] Beardsley provided no documentation for his sensationalized claims. (The dynamics of Joseph's polyandrous unions are discussed in Chapters 12–16.)

Of the remaining twenty-one, none is an obvious candidate for pregnancy and inclusion in an Allred, Farnsworth, or Dibble family: Fanny Alger (Kirtland, Ohio plural marriage), Louisa Beaman (lived with widow Delcena Johnson but may have stayed with her sister Mary Adeline Beaman Noble if she became pregnant), Agnes M. Coolbrith (age thirty-three, a widow), Delcena Johnson (age thirty-seven, a widow), Eliza R. Snow (Nauvoo life too well documented for pregnancy to have gone unnoticed), Martha McBride (age thirty-seven, widow), Flora Ann Woodworth (lived with her parents), Emily Dow Partridge (lived in the Mansion House and then with Sylvia Lyon; available, though skimpy, documents provide no evidence of pregnancy), Eliza Maria Partridge (lived in the Mansion House and then with the Jonathan Holmes family), Almera Johnson (lived in Macedonia with her brother, Benjamin F. Johnson, and his wife), Lucy Walker (dictated several accounts of her Nauvoo polygamy experiences that indicate she was never pregnant by Joseph Smith), Sarah Lawrence (little information but lived in the Mansion House and later denied her plural marriage to the Prophet), Maria Lawrence (lived in the Mansion House; no additional information), Helen Mar Kimball (evidence supports she was not sexually involved with Joseph), Hannah Ells (lived outside of Nauvoo with the Benbow family), Rhoda Richards (fifty-eight at the time of sealing), Desdemona Fullmer (lived with Hyrum Smith and William Clayton families; no evidence of a pregnancy), Olive G. Frost (lived with her sister Mary Ann Frost and her husband Parley Pratt; Mary Ann might have feigned pregnancy instead of moving Olive to live with nonrelatives), Malissa Lott (lived with her parents outside of Nauvoo on Joseph Smith's farm), Nancy M. Winchester (almost no documentation of her marriage and relationship with the Prophet), Fanny Young (age fifty-six when sealed).

Among these women, sexual relations are not documented with the three widows (Agnes M. Coolbrith, Delcena Johnson, and Martha McBride) who were in their thirties when they were sealed to the Prophet. If conjugal relations had occurred and the woman became pregnant, it seems less likely that she would have joined another household at that point in which the mother would fake a pregnancy. The Nauvoo activities of Almera Johnson, Nancy M. Winchester, Sarah Lawrence, and Maria Lawrence, are so poorly documented

---

57. Harry M. Beardsley, *Joseph Smith and His Mormon Empire*, 390–91.

that any might have become pregnant and given birth. Others like Louisa Beaman, Flora Ann Woodworth, Eliza Partridge, and Hannah Ells may have chosen sequestration with the Allreds, Farnsworths, or Dibbles for the four or five months between the time of visible pregnancy until the baby's birth, and then moved back to her original locale.

Perhaps the most likely woman to have lived with an unrelated family due to pregnancy is Olive Frost although why she would have left the household of her sister, Mary Ann Frost Pratt, to do so is unclear. It appears she did become pregnant with Joseph's baby, but both she and the child died before the Saints left Nauvoo. The fact that almost nothing is known about Olive's child, including its birth date and gender (or if she had miscarried), demonstrates how little is known concerning the sexual and reproductive dynamics of Joseph Smith's plural marriages. This lack of documentation may create insurmountable difficulties when evaluating the truthfulness of rumors and traditions dealing with the Prophet's polygamous unions.

Several Nauvoo families had the surnames of Allred, Farnsworth, and Dibble.[58] Two Dibble families are listed. Very little is known of Ira T. and Luretia A. Dibble, but Philo Dibble and his wife, Hannah Ann Dubois Smith Dibble, are better known. (See Chapters 3 and 12.) Philo and Hannah married February 11, 1841, and had two children: Hannah Ann (b. January 7, 1842) and Loren (b. May 29, 1844). Four nineteenth-century writers identify her as a polygamous wife of Joseph Smith.[59] Even though both supportive and contradictory evidence exists, I do not count her as a plural spouse of the Prophet.

Several Allred families lived in Nauvoo. One is Levi Allred (b. 1800) and Abigail McMurtrey Allred (b. 1804). They had eleven children, but none was born after 1840, when Abigail would have turned thirty-six; she would not have been menopausal by 1844.

James Allred (b. 1784), a member of the Nauvoo High Council who heard the revelation on celestial marriage read on August 12, 1843, eventually accepted it and its teachings. However, his legal wife, Elizabeth Warren Allred (b. 1786) was beyond child-bearing years, thus preventing her from shielding a pregnancy. Four of James Allred's sons also lived in Nauvoo with wives who gave birth to children between 1841 and 1844. William Hackley Allred (b.

---

58. Data extracted from Family Group Sheets at www.FamilySearch.com; Susan Easton Black and Harvey Bischoff Black, *Annotated Records of Baptisms for the Dead, 1840–1845, Nauvoo, Hancock County, Illinois*; Lisle G Brown, *Nauvoo Sealings, Adoptions, and Anointings: A Comprehensive Register of Persons Receiving LDS Temple Ordinances, 1841–1846*; LDS Vital Records Library Infobase, 1997.

59. Johnson, *My Life's Review*, 96; John Hyde, *Mormonism: Its Leaders and Designs*, 84; Joseph Smith III, Letter to Bro. E. C. Brand, January 26, 1894; "Testimony of Benjamin Winchester," December 13, 1900. See Chapter 33.

1804) married Elizabeth Ivie (b. 1807), and she bore Amasa Lyman Allred (January 10, 1843). The second son, Wiley Payne Allred (b. 1818), married Sarah Zabriskie (b. 1814); among their five children was Elizabeth Hannah Allred (b. September 27, 1843). A third son, Reuben Warren Allred (b. 1815) married Lucy Ann Butler (b. 1814); they had ten children including Thomas Butler Allred (b. March 1, 1841) and Hannah Caroline Allred (b. July 27, 1843). No special ties between Joseph Smith and these members of the James Allred family have been identified.

James Allred's brother, Isaac Allred (b. 1788) also lived in Nauvoo. He married Mary Calvert Allred (b. 1793) and they had thirteen children, but Mary would have been past child-bearing age in the 1840s. Their son, Reddick Newton Allred (b. 1822) married Lucy H. Hoyt (b. 1824) and she bore at least nine children including a son, Isaac Newton Allred (b. October 1, 1844).

Apparently, the only Farnsworth family living in Nauvoo was that of Stephen Martindale Farnsworth (b. 1809) and Julia Ann Clark Farnsworth (b. 1819). Stephen was chosen as president of the priests' quorum there in Nauvoo.[60] He also reported a vision received in the spring of 1844 in which he saw the Saints moving toward the Rocky Mountains and God saving them from their enemies.[61] Among Stephen and Julia's nine children were Alonzo Lafayette Farnsworth (b. October 22, 1841) and Albert Stephen Farnsworth (b. May 22, 1844).

My research is not exhaustive, but nine children (two Dibbles, two Farnsworths, and five Allreds) could potentially fulfill T. Edgar Lyon's (1903–78) description, made in 1974. If the report is accurate, one or more of these children could have been fathered by the Prophet and one of his plural wives, and then adopted by one of these three families. However, such speculations are supported by little more than the observation that the children were conceived during the Prophet's lifetime. Also, the report raises concerns. Lyon stated that an unidentified man told this story in 1968–69—more than 120 years after the events reportedly occurred. What was the chain of transmissions before it reached him? Does the remaining narrative accurately represent the actual 1840s information? These questions cannot be answered. The originator would have had to be privy to three of the Prophet's plural marriages and have known details not available in any other account, although Mary Elizabeth Rollins Lightner stated in 1905: "I know he [Joseph Smith] had three children. They told me. I think two are living today but they are

---

60. "October Conference Minutes," *Times and Seasons* 5 (November 1, 1844); 693; *History of the LDS Church*, 6:175.

61. Ogden Kraut, *Visions of the Latter-days*, 85–87. See also Orson Hyde, n.d., *Journal of Discourses*, 5:143.

not known as his children as they go by other names."[62] DNA testing of these various individuals could yield certifiable results, but short of that level of research, it seems unlikely that any of the children mentioned are Joseph Smith's biological offspring.

Identities of Alleged Children

Available documents provide a basis for the possible existence of two, or possibly three children born to Joseph Smith's plural wives. A second-hand account from Lucy Meserve Smith,[63] who became a plural wife of Apostle George A. Smith in Nauvoo on November 29, 1844, stated that George A. "related to me the circumstance of calling on the Prophet one evening about 11, o clock, and he was out on the porch with a basin of water washing his hands, I said to him what is up, said Joseph one of my wives has just been confined and Emma was midwife and I have been assisting her. He said she had granted a no. of women for him."[64] Although this statement is undated, Lucy signed a very similar statement on May 18, 1892, when she was seventy-five. At that point, George A. had been dead for seventeen years.[65]

The best documentation for a child by Joseph Smith and his plural wife, Sylvia Sessions Lyon is that of daughter Josephine Lyon, born in 1844. (See Chapter 13.)[66] If her claim, based on her mother's deathbed statement, is correct, she is the only known child of Joseph and a plural wife to live to adulthood. The second is Olive Frost's child.[67] Joseph E. Robinson wrote: "During the afternoon I called on Aunt Lizzie [Joseph E. Robinson's aunt-in-law Mary Elizabeth

---

62. Mary Elizabeth Rollins Lightner, "Remarks at Brigham Young University, April 14, 1905," 5. Mary Ann Barzee Boice stated in her "History," that "some" of Joseph Smith's plural wives "had children." See also J. D. Stead, *Doctrines and Dogmas of Brighamism Exposed*, 218.

63. For a biographical sketch of Lucy Meserve Smith (1817–92), see Kenneth W. Godfrey, Audrey M. Godfrey, and Jill Mulvay Derr, eds., *Women's Voices: An Untold History of the Latter-day Saints, 1830–1900*, 261–71.

64. Lucy Meserve Smith, Statement, n.d., Wilford Wood Collection of Church Historical Materials, MS 8617, Reel 8, LDS Church History Library; internal reference within collection: 4-N-b-2.

65. Lucy Meserve Smith, Signed Statement, May 18, 1892; photocopy of holograph in Linda King Newell Collection, Marriott Library. See also Todd Compton, "A Trajectory of Plurality: An Overview of Joseph Smith's Thirty-Three Plural Wives," 16.

66. Josephine R. Fisher, Affidavit, February 24, 1915; see also Danel W. Bachman, "A Study of the Mormon Practice of Plural Marriage before the Death of Joseph Smith," 141; Richard S. Van Wagoner, "Mormon Polyandry in Nauvoo," 78 note 12; Ugo A. Perego, "Joseph Smith, the Question of Polygamous Offspring, and DNA Analysis," 250–55. This chapter summarizes the six cases.

67. Joseph E. Robinson, Diary, October 26, 1902. Olive Frost died October 6, 1845.

Green Harris, 1847–1911]. . . . She knew Joseph Smith had more than two wives. Said he Married . . . Olive Frost [and] had a child by him and that both died."[68]

Some evidence has been found supporting the birth of a third child, who may have been raised by the Dibble family. RLDS President Joseph Smith III noted in an 1894 letter to E. C. Brand, an RLDS missionary and leader in the Utah branch, that "Mrs. Philo Dibble . . . had a boy shown after father's [Joseph Jr.] death as his."[69] In addition, an 1876 memo from Joseph Smith III states: "A. B. Johnson says that he and Wm Lewis visited Mrs. Joseph Young, (brother of B Young) in 1853 and she showed him a son of Joseph Smith, a lad a few years old, by proxy."[70] This statement is confusing in several ways. Was "Mrs. Joseph Young" the mother of the proxy son of Joseph Smith or was she simply pointing him out? There is no evidence that Joseph Young married any of Joseph Smith's widows so "Mrs. Joseph Young" does not seem to be related to the child.[71] The reference, by proxy" is unhelpfully cryptic but most likely refers to a child of one of the Prophet's plural wives who remarried and gave birth to the "lad" mentioned. It does not confirm that the child was a biological son of Joseph Smith by one of his plural wives.

In addition to these two or three probable children, at least eighteen other children have been suggested as the Prophet's offspring. However, supportive evidence for the respective relationships is problematic and unconvincing. (See Table 11.1.)

Sexual Relations: An Apparent Rarity for Joseph Smith

Unfortunately, it is impossible to accurately determine how often Joseph Smith spent time with his plural wives, either in conjugal visits or otherwise. It does not appear that he ever appeared with any of them in a public setting or openly acknowledged them as a plural spouse. Accounts of him parading through Nauvoo with plural wives in tow or anything similar are fictional.[72] All public interactions

---

68. Joseph E. Robinson, Diary/Autobiography, October 26, 1902. See also James Whitehead, Interviewed by Joseph Smith III, April 20, 1885. This passage also states that Olive Frost bore a child to Joseph Smith. I saw this document and was present when Robin Scott Jensen read it aloud on September 25, 2009, at the home of John Hajicek in Independence, Missouri.

69. Joseph Smith III, Letter to E. C. Brand, January 26, 1894.

70. Joseph Smith III, Memo, 1876. Transcript in D. Michael Quinn Papers.

71. Joseph Young married his legal wife on February 18, 1834, and was later sealed to Lydia Caroline Hagar in July 1845; two other sealings in the Nauvoo Temple followed: to Lucinda Allen on January 16, 1846, and to Mary Ann Huntley on February 6, 1846. George D. Smith, *Nauvoo Polygamy: ". . . but we called it celestial marriage,"* 638 . None of these women has any apparent ties to Joseph Smith's plural marrying.

72. Reverend Samuel F. Whitney, Statement, p. 3, col. 7; Samuel M. Smucker and

were conducted without divulging the clandestine sealed marriages. While it is not possible to establish an accurate picture of his relations with his polygamous wives, several observations suggest that sexual relations occurred infrequently, at best.

Current evidence supports the births of two or three children to Joseph Smith's plural wives. Even if that number were doubled, it would still represent a surprisingly small number of children by thirty-five wives if sexual relations occurred often, considering that nineteenth-century monogamous families not infrequently produced from six to twelve children.[73] Out of the thirty-five women identified as wives, thirty were under age forty and therefore could be considered to be capable of conception if the timing was right. The Prophet was virile, having fathered eight children with Emma despite long periods of time apart and challenging schedules.[74] The required factors were apparently present to permit multiple pregnancies if sexual relations had been common.[75]

H. L. Williams, *Life Among the Mormons, or the Religious, Social, and Political History of the Mormons*, 148.

73. In his essay, "Evidence for the Sexual Side of Joseph Smith's Polygamy," D. Michael Quinn presents arguments to explain why few children were born to Joseph Smith's plural wives including the improbable: "Thus, his [Joseph Smith's] frequent intercourse with dozens of wives would (in his culture's view) make it very UNlikely that an otherwise-unmarried female would attract unwanted attention in Nauvoo by becoming pregnant" (page 19; emphasis Quinn's). Quinn's logic is problematic. Without any documentation of excessive sexuality in the Prophet's plural marriages, Quinn theorizes excessive conjugality lowered Joseph Smith's sperm counts to the point that his wives did not become pregnant. See Brian C. Hales, "A Response to D. Michael Quinn's, 'Evidence for the Sexual Side of Joseph Smith's Polygamy,'" unpublished manuscript, August 25, 2012.

74. These children were: Alvin Smith (b. and d. June 15, 1828); twins Thaddeus and Louisa (b. and d. April 30, 1831), Joseph Smith III (November 6, 1832–December 10, 1914); Frederick Granger Williams Smith (June 29, 1836–April 13, 1862); Alexander Hale Smith (June 2, 1838–August 12, 1909); Don Carlos Smith (b. 1840, died at fourteen months); and David Hyrum Smith (November 17, 1844–August 29, 1904). A misreading of Joseph Smith's journal for December 26, 1842, has resulted in the supposition that Emma suffered a miscarriage that day. The *History of the Church* 5:209, records: "I found my wife Emma sick. She was delivered of a son, which did not survive its birth." However, the original text reads: "Sister Emma sick, had another chill." Scott H. Faulring, ed., *An American Prophet's Record: The Diaries and Journals of Joseph Smith*, 258.

75. D. Michael Quinn affirms that sexual relations between Joseph Smith and his plural wives were a common occurrence. However, the evidence he presents is problematic. For example, he quotes a "phrenological chart" of the Prophet's head and concludes: "Joseph Smith was apparently virile enough to have sexual intercourse daily (or more than once daily) with one or two of his wives" ("Evidence for the Sexual Side of Joseph Smith's Polygamy," 17). Phrenology is a pseudoscience that measures the size of a person's skull and from those measurements derives the size of the brain and attributes certain physiological strengths and weaknesses to those measurements. See *History of the Church* 5:55.

TABLE 11.1
CHILDREN ATTRIBUTED TO JOSEPH SMITH

	Name	Mother	Birth Date	Evidence	Discussion
	\multicolumn{5}{c}{A. Probable Children of Joseph Smith}				
1.	Josephine Lyon	Sylvia Lyon	February 8, 1844	Mother's declaration	High probability
2.	"child"	Olive Gray Frost	Unknown; sealing occurred in summer of 1843	Joseph E. Robinson, "Diary/Autobiography," October 26, 1902.[a]	"During the afternoon I called on Aunt Lizzie[b] . . . She knew Joseph Smith had more than two wives. Said he Married . . . Olive Frost [and] had a child by him and that both died."
	\multicolumn{5}{c}{B. Eighteen Poorly Documented Allegations of Possible Paternity}				
1.	Orrison Smith	Fanny Alger (allegedly)	1834?	"tradition"[c]	Genetic testing demonstrates that Joseph Smith could not be the father.[d] The Smith-Alger plural marriage occurred (probably) in 1835; and if she was ever pregnant, it was after the marriage was over.
2.	Mosiah Lyman Hancock	Clarissa Reed Hancock	April 9, 1834	Observation	Genetic testing demonstrates that Joseph Smith could not be the father.[e]
3.	John Reed Hancock	Clarissa Reed Hancock	April 19, 1841	Family tradition	Genetic testing demonstrates that Joseph Smith could not be the father.[f]
4.	Sarah Elizabeth Holmes	Marietta Carter	January 24, 1838	Observation	Marietta Carter, Jonathan Holmes's first wife, died August 20, 1840. No evidence links her with Joseph Smith.

a. See also James Whitehead, interviewed by Joseph Smith III, April 20, 1885; see also D. Michael Quinn, *The Mormon Hierarchy: Origins of Power*, 588.
b. Probably Joseph E. Robinson's aunt-in-law, Mary Elizabeth Green Harris (1847–1911).
c. Although Orrison Smith is "regarded by some as a possible child of Joseph Smith and Fanny Alger," genetic testing establishes that Joseph could not have been the father. Ugo A. Perego, Natalie M. Myres, and Scott R. Woodward, "Reconstructing the Y-Chromosome of Joseph Smith: Genealogical Applications," 59.
d. Ibid.; see also Thomas Milton Tinney, "Fanny Alger, the First Plural Wife of the Prophet Joseph Smith Jr.: A Preliminary Genealogical Report," 13, 18.
e. Ugo A. Perego, Jayne E. Ekins, and Scott R. Woodward, "Resolving the Paternities of Oliver N. Buell and Mosiah L. Hancock through DNA," 128–36.
f. Ugo A. Perego quoted in Michael De Groote, "DNA Solves Joseph Smith Mystery," *Deseret News*, July 10, 2011, B1.

5.	Oliver Norman Buell	January 31, 1840	Mary Ettie V. Smith's statement	Genetic testing demonstrates that Joseph Smith could not be the father.[g]
6.	John Hiram Buell	July 13, 1843		Presendia was living thirty miles from Nauvoo when John Hiram was conceived. Stanley S. Ivins considered Mary Ettie V. Smith's book as "inaccurate and of no value."[h]
7.	Don Alonzo Smith	August 29, 1840	Family tradition	Genetic testing demonstrates Joseph Smith could not be the father.[i]
8.	Zebulon Jacobs	January 2, 1842	William Hall statement	Genetic testing demonstrates Joseph Smith could not be the father.[j]
9.	Hannah Ann Dibble	January 7, 1842	Benjamin Winchester	Winchester's described chronology contradicts the possibility that Joseph Smith was the father. Hannah Ann Dibble was born eleven months after her mother wed Philo Dibble.
10.	Loren Walker Dibble	May 29, 1844	John Hyde	Evidence of a plural marriage or sexual relationship between Joseph Smith and Hannah Dubois are problematic. John Hyde's additional claims concerning Loren Walker Dibble are contradicted by numerous evidences. However, Joseph Smith III recalled that a son of Hannah was "shown after father's death as his."[k]
11.	George Algernon Lightner	March 22, 1842	Observation	Joseph and Mary Elizabeth Rollins were sealed in February 1842, after George Algernon's conception. No evidence of sexual relations in their polyandrous relationship has been located.
12.	Florentine Mattheas Lightner[m]	March 23, 1844	Observation	Mary Elizabeth Rollins Lightner was living in Farmington, fifty miles east of Nauvoo, when Florentine was conceived.

g. Perego, Ekins, and Woodward, "Resolving the Paternities of Oliver N. Buell and Mosiah L. Hancock through DNA," 128–36.
h. Stanley S. Ivins Collection, Notebook 4, p. 63.
i. Ugo A. Perego, email to Brian Hales, December 6, 2011.
j. Perego, Myres, and Woodward. "Reconstructing the Y-Chromosome of Joseph Smith," 59–60.
k. See Chapter 12.
l. Joseph Smith III to Bro. E. C. Brand, January 26, 1894, 65.
m. Researcher Gregory L. Smith noted: "One bit of evidence often overlooked on potential children is Mary Elizabeth Rollins' remark that 'I knew he had three children. They told me.' (Mary Elizabeth Rollins Lightner, "Remarks,' given at BYU 14 April 1905, typescript BYU.) It would seem to me that this goes a long way to ruling out her children as Joseph's progeny—she obviously saw nothing wrong with Joseph having children, was before a sympathetic audience, and seemed keen to tell what she knew. If they had Joseph's children, you'd think she'd have been proud of it and told them. This seems to be the best she can do—she's heard about some (by rumor) but knows nothing more detailed." Gregory L. Smith, email to Brian C. Hales, October 19, 2009.

TABLE 11.1 CONTINUED

	Name	Mother	Birth Date	Evidence	Discussion
13.	Orson Washington Hyde	Marinda Johnson Hyde	November 9, 1843	Fawn Brodie[n]	No specific evidence available. Allegation is based on Brodie's speculation.
14.	Frank Henry Hyde		January 23, 1846	Observation	Birth date on his birth certificate and in his obituary would preclude Joseph Smith's being the father.[o]
15.	Josephine Henry or Hendry	Margaret Creighton	July 8, 1844	Rumor[p]	Chronology in available historical documents shows that Margaret became pregnant before the couple arrived in Nauvoo.
16.	Joseph Albert Smith	Esther Dutcher	September 21, 1844	Observation	Documentation supports an "eternity only" sealing to the Prophet. Other than observations, no supportive evidence has been found. Legal husband's name was Albert.[q]
17.	Moroni Llewellyn Pratt	Mary Ann Frost Pratt	December 7, 1844	Observation	Genetic testing demonstrates that Joseph Smith could not be the father and verifies Parley P. Pratt as the biological father.[r]
18.	Carolyn Delight	Lulu Vermillion	?	Unknown	Assertion made to Ugo Perego.[s] I have been unable to find additional information about Carolyn or her mother.

n. Fawn M. Brodie, *No Man Knows My History: The Life of Joseph Smith, the Mormon Prophet*, 345 note 464.

o. Frank Henry Hyde, Birth certificate, digital scan, http://wiki.hanksplace.net/index.php/Image:FrankHHyde.jpg (accessed August 27, 2009). My thanks to Gregory L. Smith for this reference. See also "Frank H. Hyde Dies Suddenly," *Ogden Standard*, June 29, 1908, 5.

p. See Chapter 12.

q. Esther Dutcher Smith did not conceive any children while her legal husband, Albert Smith, was on his mission between September 12, 1842, and August 22, 1843. Joseph Albert Smith was conceived about four months after his return (on approximately December 29, 1843). See David L. Bigler, transcriber, "Journal of Albert Smith, 1804–1889," pp. 2, 9, 17, holograph at LDS Church History Library; copy of transcription in my possession.

r. Perego, Myres, and Woodward. "Reconstructing the Y-Chromosome of Joseph Smith: Genealogical Applications," 55.

s. Perego, Ekins, and Woodward, "Resolving the Paternities of Oliver N. Buell and Mosiah L. Hancock through DNA," 129; see also Ugo A. Perego, "Joseph Smith, the Question of Polygamous Offspring, and DNA Analysis," 233–56.

A review of the child-bearing chronology of Joseph Smith's wives after his death and their remarriages demonstrates impressive fertility in several of the women. Most of them married within two years after the martyrdom and prior to the Saints leaving for the West. Three of the women became pregnant within weeks after remarrying. Sarah Ann Whitney who was sealed to Joseph Smith for twenty-three months (before his death), married Heber C. Kimball on March 17, 1845, and based on the birth date of their first child, became pregnant approximately June 15.[76] She bore Heber Kimball seven children between 1846 and 1858. Lucy Walker, who was sealed to the Prophet for fourteen months, also married Kimball. About three months after their February 8, 1845, marriage, she became pregnant.[77] She gave birth to nine of Kimball's children between 1846 and 1864. Malissa Lott who was sealed to Joseph Smith in September 1843 married Ira Jones Willes on May 13, 1849. Their first child was born April 22, 1850, with conception occurring approximately July 30, 1849 (or eleven weeks after the wedding ceremony). Seven Willes children were born between 1850 and 1863. Emily Partridge bore Brigham Young seven offspring between 1845 and 1862. Her sister Eliza married Amasa Lyman and together they had five children between 1844 and 1860. Several other plural wives, like Louisa Beaman, Martha McBride, and Nancy Winchester, also remarried and became pregnant. In light of the obvious fertility of many of Joseph Smith's plural wives, it seems that they either bore him children who are unknown today or that sexual relations in the marriages did not occur often.

As discussed above, it is possible that some of Joseph Smith's plural children were raised by other families and carried other surnames. However, after the Saints arrived in Utah, there would have been little motive to keep the paternity secret. Any child of the Prophet would have been regarded with special attention and perhaps have been looked upon as a legitimate future leader, similar to Joseph and Emma's sons who had remained in Nauvoo. In the 1860s and 1870s, when RLDS missionaries in Utah emphasized lineal succession in the Church presidency, LDS Church leaders would have been motivated to produce Joseph's offspring, not only to establish his role in Nauvoo polygamy, but also to dilute the succession claims of the three surviving sons of Joseph and Emma. However, LDS Church leaders never took such a step.

A review of Joseph Smith's hectic life in Nauvoo identifies several possible obstacles to achieving privacy where sexual intercourse was likely. He had heavy ecclesiastical and civic responsibilities as Church president and city mayor, entertained visitors and journalists, had parenting responsibilities in the Smith household, and intermittently went into hiding to avoid Missouri

---

76. Sarah's first child, David Kimball, was born March 8, 1846.

77. Rachel Sylvia Kimball was born January 28, 1846; assuming a full-term birth, conception occurred on approximately May 7, 1845.

lawmen. He also managed a complicated real estate business, preached at weekly services, and was even a candidate for U.S. president, which would further have limited his time.

In addition, secrecy was a major concern. Rumors of "spiritual wifery" were rampant after John C. Bennett wrote his mid-1842 letters accusing Joseph Smith of sexual improprieties. Joseph had nothing to do with Bennett's licentiousness (see Chapters 19 and 20), but the Prophet's teachings of restored Old Testament polygamy were still concealed, even from devout members, except in private settings. The scrutiny of the Latter-day Saints, supplemented by the stares of dissenters and unbelievers, heightened everyone's sensitivities to any extralegal intimacies and would have created challenges to his being able to slip away unnoticed with a plural wife.

Another huge restriction was likely Emma's vigilant and mostly intolerant eyes.[78] According to Joseph Lee Robinson, who turned thirty-two in 1843 and who supervised a school in Nauvoo, Emma even commissioned spies to prevent Joseph from having private moments with his plural wives.[79] As Joseph's first wife, Emma sought total control over his plural marriage activities after July 13, 1843. (See Chapters 25 and 26.)

An important consideration is the phenomenon of diminishing return. In other words, after a certain point, the addition of new plural wives did necessarily increase Joseph's opportunity for more numerous sexual relations, since the critical constraint would have been scheduling conflicts that prevented opportunities for private intimacies, rather than the absence of a plural marriage partner. Such a dynamic would, inevitably, have curtailed chances for conception on the part of his plural wives.

Summary

Beyond Joseph Smith's revelations and public utterances, little is known concerning his personal feelings about sexuality. Sexual relations occurred in some of the plural marriage relationships, but not all. The best evidence suggests that no more than two or three pregnancies resulted, leading to the conclusion that sexual relations were infrequent at best. At least eighteen additional allegations of specific children born to the Prophet have been made, but supportive evidence is currently unpersuasive.

---

78. See Emily Dow Partridge Young, "Incidents in the Early Life of Emily Dow Partridge," 5, written between December 1876 and January 7, 1877; see also Emily D. P. Young, Autobiographical Sketch: "Written Especially for My Children, January 7, 1877."

79. Oliver Preston Robinson, ed., *History of Joseph Lee Robinson*, 54. See Chapter 26.

Chapter 12

The Puzzle of "Polyandry"

According to Todd Compton and other authors, after Joseph's 1841 marriage to Louisa Beaman, nine of the next ten women sealed to the Prophet were already legally wed to husbands. In all, Compton identifies twelve civilly married women who were also sealed to Joseph Smith: Sylvia Sessions Lyon, Ruth Vose Sayers, Mary Elizabeth Rollins Lightner, Sarah Kingsley Cleveland, Presendia Lathrop Huntington Buell, Sarah Ann Whitney Kingsley, Zina Diantha Huntington Jacobs, Patty Bartlett Sessions, Marinda Nancy Johnson Hyde, Elvira Annie Cowles Holmes, Elizabeth Davis Durfee, and Lucinda Pendleton Morgan Harris.[1]

Many writers have labeled Joseph Smith's sealings to legally married women as "polyandrous" marriages.[2] The *American Heritage Dictionary* defines "polyandry" as "the condition or practice of having more than one husband at one time."[3] Pulitzer Prize-winning journalist and author Deborah Blum observed that, in human societies, polyandry is "extraordinarily rare."[4] According to Sarva Daman Singh, author of *Polyandry in Ancient India*, polyandry is "practically unknown to Hindu society" and the custom was unknown "at the time of the rise of Buddhism."[5]

Joseph Smith's sealings to legally married women constitute one of the most confounding details of his plural marriage practices. LDS scholar Andrew Ehat observed: "If polygamy is the most controversial story in the his-

---

1. Todd Compton, *In Sacred Loneliness: The Plural Wives of Joseph Smith*, 4–7.
2. Michael S. Riggs and John E. Thompson, "Joseph Smith, Jr., and 'The Notorious Case of Aaron Lyon': Evidence of Earlier Doctrinal Development of Salvation for the Dead and a Trigger for the Practice of Polyandry?" 118, theorize: "The incident between Aaron Lyon and Sarah Jackson was the likely trigger that stimulated Joseph Smith's receptiveness to consider 'taking another man's wife.'" Their discussion of Aaron Lyon's behavior, however, is not about a situation in which any of the participants believed themselves to be involved polyandrously, nor is there any evidence to suggest they would have accepted a polyandrous relationship. Riggs and Thompson's theory that the Aaron Lyon episode may have prompted Joseph Smith to think about polyandry is intriguing but purely conjectural, and seems incongruent with Nauvoo plural marriage practices and teachings.
3. *American Heritage Dictionary*, CD-ROM, 1992.
4. Deborah Blum, *Sex on the Brain: The Biological Differences between Men and Women*, 110.
5. Sarva Daman Singh, *Polyandry in Ancient India*, 24.

tory of Mormonism, 'polyandry' must surely be its darkest, least understood, and most troubling chapter."[6] Lawrence Foster wrote: "Perhaps the most puzzling and difficult-to-interpret behavior of Joseph Smith during this period is the evidence that he asked some of his closest associates to give their wives to him."[7] Returning to the topic in another essay, he commented: "How are such actions to be explained? Of course, one easily could make the assumption that most non-Mormons and anti-Mormons have that Smith simply was letting his sexual impulses get away with him in these or other cases. Or, as most Mormon writers have done, one could ignore the evidence entirely and hope that it would be forgotten."[8] Kathryn Daynes echoed: "Perhaps nothing is less understood than Joseph Smith's sealings to women already married, because the evidence supports conflicting interpretations."[9]

In 2006, Richard Lyman Bushman, author of *Joseph Smith: Rough Stone Rolling*, gave a lecture at Weber State: "A Historian's Perspective of Joseph Smith." In the accompanying question and answer period, he was asked regarding Joseph Smith's "polyandrous" marriages. He responded: "This is the single most puzzling part of Joseph Smith's life for Mormons. It's probably [puzzling] for non-Mormons too."[10] He also added: "There is just seemingly no answer. . . . How to explain it I think is very difficult. And probably you shouldn't even try. If you try to make up explanations, you get in more trouble."[11]

Historic Explanations

In 1854, Jedediah M. Grant, a counselor in Brigham Young's First Presidency preached: "Did the Prophet Joseph want every man's wife he asked for? He did not, but in that thing was the grand thread of the Priesthood developed. The grand object in view was to try the people of God, to see what was in them. . . . A man who has got the Spirit of God, and the light of eternity in him, has no trouble about such matters."[12] Fawn Brodie may have

---

6. Andrew Ehat, "Pseudo-Polyandry: Explaining Mormon Polygyny's Paradoxical Companion," 2.

7. Lawrence Foster, "Sex and Prophetic Power: A Comparison of John Humphrey Noyes, Founder of the Oneida Community, with Joseph Smith, Jr., the Mormon Prophet," 76–77.

8. W. Lawrence Foster, "Between Two Worlds: The Origins of Shaker Celibacy, Oneida Community Complex Marriage, and Mormon Polygamy," 256.

9. Kathryn M. Daynes, *More Wives Than One: Transformation of the Mormon Marriage System, 1840–1910*, 29.

10. Richard L. Bushman, "A Historian's Perspective of Joseph Smith," tracks 20–21.

11. Ibid.

12. Jedediah M. Grant, February 19, 1854, *Journal of Discourses*, 2:14. It is interesting that one year after this discourse, Grant stood as proxy as one of his wives, Rachel Ridgeway

been the very first to extract this declaration from the *Journal of Discourses*, using it as evidence that the Prophet practiced polyandry by demanding other men's wives.[13] In fact, no evidence has been found supporting that the Prophet made such demands and then was sealed to the already-married woman.[14] Regardless, others have followed Brodie's interpretation without attempting to contextualize the comment historically and theologically.[15] To date, no researcher has published a detailed analysis of Joseph Smith's practice of polyandrous marrying and his reasons for doing so. Todd Compton wrote: "There is a clearly discernible outline of ideology in the historical record that explains the development and rationale for the practice of Smith's polyandry."[16] However, Compton's explanation of the rationale and ideology is brief, comprising only a few pages and leaves many questions unanswered.[17]

Fawn M. Brodie's views are discussed more thoroughly in Chapter 14, but throughout *No Man Knows My History*, she consistently portrayed the Prophet as practicing sexual polyandry, a point useful in buttressing her characterization of Joseph Smith as a sexual libertine. At one point, in her interpretive way, she wonders about the polyandrous husbands' eternal welfare: "And what of the married women who gladly signed themselves and their children over to the Prophet's keeping and glory for eternity, leaving their unwitting husbands to be wifeless and childless in the celestial kingdom?"[18] Coming to the identical conclusion but from a defensive, rather than accusatory position, is Samuel Katich, who posted an article in 2003 on the website of the Foundation for Apologetic Information and Research (FAIR) concluding: "While it may seem

---

Ivins, was sealed to the Prophet for eternity. Evidence supports that Joseph proposed plural marriage to her in Nauvoo but she rejected his offer. (See Chapter 23.) See also handwritten entry in Thomas Milton Tinney, *The Royal Family of the Prophet Joseph Smith, Jr.*, 12; Ronald W. Walker, "Rachel R. Grant: The Continuing Legacy of the Feminine Ideal," 23–24.

13. Fawn M. Brodie, *No Man Knows My History: The Life of Joseph Smith, the Mormon Prophet*, 346.

14. None of the evidence available on the plural sealings of Joseph Smith's fourteen polyandrous wives confirms that the Prophet approached any of their husbands and requested that they relinquish their wives to him.

15. See Richard S. Van Wagoner, quoting "John R. Young," in "Mormon Polyandry in Nauvoo," 77; and Van Wagoner, "Sarah M. Pratt: The Shaping of an Apostate," 82; Todd Compton, "A Trajectory of Plurality: An Overview of Joseph Smith's Thirty-Three Plural Wives," 26; [anonymous], http://www.i4m.com/think/history/Joseph_Smith_mens_wives.htm (accessed September 14, 2011).

16. Compton, *In Sacred Loneliness*, 22.

17. See Danel Bachman, online review of Compton, "Prologue to the Study of Joseph Smith's Marital Theology," http://maxwellinstitute.byu.edu/publications/review/?vol=10&num=2&id=291 (accessed September 12, 2011).

18. Brodie, *No Man Knows My History*, 304.

more understandable, if not palatable, for some to comprehend these ['polyandrous'] marriages without this dimension [of sexual relations], the fact remains that such marriages did not prohibit its occurrence. . . . If there was an intimate dimension in every one of these particular marriages, it is ultimately a matter of no consequence as he [Joseph] could not commit adultery with wives who belonged to him."[19]

Anti-Mormon writer Richard Abanes, without documentation, takes Brodie's position to the extreme: "The wives continued to live with their husbands after marrying Smith, but would have conjugal visits from Joseph whenever it served his needs."[20] In another publication Abanes extended his fanciful assessment: "Although the wives continued to live with their husbands, they would receive conjugal visits from Smith whenever the need arose. . . .Wife-swapping was eventually looked upon as wholly acceptable if an influential church authority was involved."[21]

George D. Smith gave an explanation in 1994 that drew on feudal anthropology as an analogy: "Beginning in 1841, Joseph Smith took as plural wives several married women, as if exercising a variant of the feudal *droit du seigneur*: a king's right to [have sexual relations with] the brides [betrothed to other men] in his domain. This option was presented to the married woman as a favor to her."[22] In his full-length history, *Nauvoo Polygamy ". . . but we called it celestial marriage"*, George D. Smith notes the number of years that Joseph would have known several of his future "polyandrous" wives. For example, Sarah Ann Whitney was five when she first met the Prophet, Mary Elizabeth Rollins twelve, Marinda Nancy Johnson fifteen, Sylvia Sessions nineteen, Ruth Vose twenty-four, etc.[23] Although George Smith does not explicitly claim that Joseph Smith developed a sexual interest in these girls/women or groomed them for their future roles, he couples these observations with references to Joseph Smith's alleged "early struggles with chastity," stating that after 1828, "Joseph was haunted by the suspicion, which followed him from place to place, that he crossed moral boundaries in his friendship with other women" than Emma, although the supportive evidence he presents is slim.[24] George D.

---

19. Samuel Katich, "A Tale of Two Marriage Systems: Perspectives on Polyandry and Joseph Smith."

20. Richard Abanes, *One Nation under Gods: A History of the Mormon Church*, 193; see also John Cairncross, *After Polygamy Was Made a Sin: The Social History of Christian Polygamy*, 185.

21. Richard Abanes, *Becoming Gods: A Closer Look at 21st-Century Mormonism*, 237.

22. George D. Smith, "Nauvoo Roots of Mormon Polygamy, 1841–46: A Preliminary Demographic Report," 10.

23. George D. Smith, *Nauvoo Polygamy: ". . . but we called it celestial marriage,"* 36.

24. Ibid., 22, 28. As discussed in Chapters 2–3, while a few unpublished accusations surrounded Joseph Smith's first plural marriage in Kirtland, Ohio, no evidence has been found that his pre-Nauvoo reputation included licentiousness beyond a single problematic

Smith also asserts, "Joseph made other acquaintances in his early life that presaged the plural marriages he would consummate in the 1840s. His relationship in Ohio with various families and their daughters—some quite youthful at the time—allowed him to invite the young women into his further confidence when they were older."[25] George D. Smith does not specifically name the female "acquaintances" with whom Joseph would later "consummate" plural marriage, but his list includes all of Joseph Smith's future polyandrous wives.[26]

Todd Compton, although providing a list of twelve civilly married women who were also sealed to Joseph Smith,[27] takes the position that "it seems probable that Joseph Smith had sexual relations with his polyandrous wives."[28] This sentiment is reflected consistently throughout his text.[29] Two decades earlier in 1975, Danel W. Bachman tentatively concluded that Joseph Smith and Mary Elizabeth Rollins Lightner, who was legally married to Adam Lightner, "may well have had conjugal relations with Smith."[30] D. Michael Quinn takes a stronger position: "Mary Elizabeth Rollins Lightner also claimed that she 'was sealed to Joseph for Eternity.' However, this statement for the public was an effort to conceal the polyandrous circumstances of her marriage to Smith at a time when the twenty-five-year-old woman was also married to Adam Lightner and cohabiting with both men."[31] However, Quinn provides no evidence that Mary Elizabeth was sexually involved with Joseph Smith nor have I found any.

---

sentence from Levi Lewis published in 1834 in E. D. Howe, *Mormonism Unveiled*, 268.

25. George D. Smith, *Nauvoo Polygamy*, 30.

26. Ibid., 36, also adds three more names as polyandrous wives (Mary Ann Frost, Sarah Scott, and Phebe Watrous), although evidence that Joseph Smith was sealed to these women during his lifetime is unconvincing.

27. Compton, *In Sacred Loneliness*, 4–7.

28. Todd Compton, "Fawn Brodie on Joseph Smith's Plural Wives and Polygamy: A Critical View," 165.

29. Compton, *In Sacred Loneliness*, 50–51, 82, 124, 182–84, 671, 682.

30. Danel W. Bachman, "A Study of the Mormon Practice of Plural Marriage before the Death of Joseph Smith," 135. He also writes: "It is more likely that Smith sired Prescinda's seventh child. She does not give his birth date in her chronicle, but she does say that he lived two years, then died of the 'summer Complaint.' Her eighth child was conceived in about April of 1846, so one can guess that her seventh child was born before that year" (139). Her seventh child was John Hiram Buell, born July 13, 1843. (See Chapter 11.)

31. D. Michael Quinn, *The Mormon Hierarchy: Extensions of Power*, 184–85. See also Harold Bloom, *The American Religion: The Emergence of the Post-Christian Nation*, 105–6: "Historians both Mormon and Gentile have made clear that Smith went so far as to practice a kind of polyandry with the wives of several highly placed Mormons."

"Ceremonial Polyandry" Versus "Sexual Polyandry"

In order to comprehend the complex topic of polyandry, understanding definitions is important because of their different connotations. Todd Compton defines marriage "as any relationship solemnized by a marriage ceremony of some sort."[32] Therefore a woman married in a civil *ceremony*, who is subsequently married to another man in a religious *ceremony* would be considered as practicing *ceremonial* polyandry. A divorce of some kind either from the government or the Church would be necessary to terminate ceremonial polyandry in order to formally nullify the civil marriage or the religious matrimony.

Applying "polyandry" to women who have experienced two marriage ceremonies (one civil and one religious) seems to generate confusion, because it does not address the issue of sexuality. Theologically (and practically), there is a huge difference between ceremonial polyandry and sexual polyandry. If a civilly married woman who participated in a second, religious marriage, then ceased intimacies with her legal spouse because the religious marriage superseded the civil, even without a legal divorce, she would not be practicing sexual polyandry.

Proving the presence of *ceremonial* polyandry does not prove the presence of *sexual* polyandry. Scholars will generally require specific credible evidence of sexual polyandry before asserting its presence in any relationship—a task that is significantly more difficult than proving the existence of ceremonial polyandry. The best historical evidence would be the candid statement of the woman herself. Also useful could be an accusation or frank acknowledgement by either of the polyandrous husbands. Possibly a third party who was in a position to be privy to the private interactions of a woman and/or her "husbands" could also be trustworthy.

Without such reliable evidences, however, a child or children born in such a marriage can be considered tentative evidence as long as the requirements of geographical proximity are met; but in the days before DNA evidence was a possibility, establishing fatherhood, even in a monogamous marriage, is considerably less certain. As discussed in Chapter 11, DNA testing has recently been applied to seven candidates who have been identified on historical grounds or on the basis of family tradition as Joseph Smith's offspring; but in each case, the legal husband has been shown to be the biological father, not Joseph Smith.[33] Carrie Miles, writing in 2011, dismisses paternity as a non-issue: "It didn't matter with which of the husbands a woman slept or which fathered her children, as, once sealed to Joseph, any children were also accounted to Joseph's celes-

---

32. Compton, *In Sacred Loneliness*, 632.

33. Orrison Smith, Mosiah Lyman Hancock, John Reed Hancock, Oliver Norman Buell, Don Alonzo Smith, Zebulon Jacobs, and Moroni Llewellyn Pratt.

tial reckoning."³⁴ This position, however, is not helpful in determining whether marital intimacies were part of both relationships, nor does it take into account Joseph Smith's teachings concerning sexual polyandry.

The difficulty in proving sexual polyandry may be the reason many authors provide the evidence of ceremonial polyandry but fail to take the next step of establishing the proof (or plausibility) of sexual polyandry. In this chapter, I argue that sweeping assumptions of conjugal relations accompanying all instances of ceremonial polyandry are not warranted. Even specific allegations require definite supportive evidence. It might be argued that, from a practical standpoint, a "marriage" that excludes sexuality is not much of a marriage, irrespective of legal paperwork that exists concerning the union. If sexual relations were absent in "polyandrous" marriages as identified by Compton, perhaps other terms would generate less confusion. For example, Andrew Ehat explained: "I conclude that all such cases of apparent polyandry were not polyandry in reality. I have, therefore, chosen to call such cases instances of "pseudo-polyandry."³⁵

Perhaps a more useful definition of "marriage" is that proposed by the Royal Anthropological Institute: "A union between a man and a woman such that children born to the woman are the recognized legitimate offspring of both partners."³⁶ Using this classification, polyandry would require sexual relations with both husbands during the same time period. While Joseph Smith undoubtedly practiced "ceremonial polyandry," the question remains: Did he also practice "sexual polyandry"? Was he engaging in sexual activity with other men's wives during the same time period when those women were also experiencing connubial relations with their legal husbands?

Twelve Documents Supporting Joseph Smith's Sexual Polyandry

As demonstrated in the previous section, several authors like Fawn Brodie wrote confidently that Joseph Smith practiced sexual polyandry. However, the specific supportive evidence that they cited to support their views was minimal or nonexistent. I have found twelve documents that could be interpreted as supporting the observation that Joseph Smith practiced sexual polyandry. Nine are from published sources, and three are from private writings. I discuss

---

34. Carrie A. Miles, "'What's Love Got to Do with It?': Earthly Experience of Celestial Marriage, Past and Present," 196.
35. Ehat, "Pseudo-Polyandry," 19.
36. Royal Anthropological Institute, *Notes and Queries on Anthropology* (1951), 110, quoted in Stephanie Coontz, *Marriage, a History: From Obedience to Intimacy or How Love Conquered Marriage*, 27.

ten of these documents in this chapter. The eleventh, involving Sylvia Sessions Lyon, is investigated in Chapter 13 and the twelfth, concerning Mary Heron Snider, in Chapter 16. All twelve are examined to help determine the level of their reliability and believability. Eight of the accusers/reporters were openly anti-Mormon writers. (See Table 12.1.)

This chapter also examines newer assertions from researcher D. Michael Quinn and a possible case of sexual polyandry in Utah.

No. 1: John C. Bennett, 1842

The earliest allegation that Joseph Smith was involved in sexual polyandry was written July 2, 1842, by John C. Bennett, whose meteoric rise in Joseph Smith's favor in the fall and winter of 1841 was equaled only by his stunningly speedy fall from favor in the spring of 1842. His affidavit, the only allegation published during Joseph Smith's lifetime, appeared three weeks after its composition in *The Pittsburgh Morning Chronicle* on July 29. As was customary for nineteenth-century affidavits, the names of Joseph's alleged sexual partners were left blank.

Bennett asserted that Joseph Smith was sexually intimate with at least seven married women. The phrase "the blessing of Jacob" implies that plural marriages occurred between Joseph and each woman; however, it is also possible to interpret the statement as Joseph's quasi-biblical language used to persuade the women to become his sexual partners in relationships that were simply repeated adulteries.[37] More specifically, Bennett claims to have personally witnessed sexual relations between the Prophet and four of these women. On the face of it, the level of voyeuristic detail is quite improbable. Given the mores of sexual propriety that characterized the nineteenth century, it seems impossible that either Joseph or, perhaps even more improbably, a plural wife, would have allowed Bennett to observe these activities. Furthermore, my evaluation of the available evidence leads me to conclude that John C. Bennett never learned of eternal and plural marriage from Joseph Smith. Bennett's own sexual liaisons were not polygamous "marriages" because he did not require wedding ceremonies prior to sexual relations. (See Chapter 20.)

That Bennett did not identify the women by name may be due to ignorance of their identities (which seems unlikely if he was actually present, as he claims), to a desire not to embarrass the women, a nod in the direction of nineteenth-century conventions for treating scandalous material, fear of a suit for libel, or a combination of factors. Importantly, it appears that Bennett's accusation of numerous sexual polyandrous unions—perhaps the most explosive of all his charges—was published only in the *Pittsburgh Morning Chronicle*.

---

37. See Volume 2, Appendix E.

TABLE 12.1
TWELVE STATEMENTS ABOUT POSSIBLE POLYANDROUS WIVES

	Woman or Women Reportedly Involved	Year Allegation Was First Published	Author of Statement	Anti-Mormon Writer?	First-hand?	Second Witness?
1	Seven unnamed married women	1842	John C. Bennett	Yes	alleged	No
2	Marinda Nancy Johnson	1850	William Arrowsmith	Yes	No	No
3	Zina Huntington Jacobs	1851	William Hall	Yes	No	No
4	"Mrs. Dibble"	1857	John Hyde	Yes	No	No
5	Presendia Huntington Buell	1860	Mary Ettie Coray Smith	Yes	No	No
6	Zina Huntington Jacobs	1875	Ann Eliza Webb Young	Yes	No	No
7	"Merchant's wife"	1886	Wilhelm Wyl	Yes	No	No
8	Lucinda Pendleton Harris	1886	Sarah Pratt via Wilhelm Wyl	Yes	No	Possibly
9	Elvira Cowles Holmes	undated	Phebe Louisa Holmes Welling	No	No	No
10	Margaret Creighton	1929	Edwin Mace	No	No	No
11	Sylvia Sessions Lyon	1997	Todd Compton	No	No	No
12	Mary Heron Snider	1850	Joseph E. Johnson	No	Unknown	No

State of Illinois
Hancock County

Personally appeared before me, S. Marshall, a Justice of the Peace in and for said county, John C. Bennett, who being duly sworn, according to law, deposeth and saith—that the affidavit taken before Esq. Wells on the 17th of May, and the statement before the City Council of Nauvoo on the 19th, as published in the Wasp of the 25th of June, 1842, are false, and were taken under duresse, as stated in this letter—that he has seen Joseph Smith in bed with Mrs. _____, Mrs. _____, and that he has seen him in the act of cohabitation with Mrs. _____, and Mrs. _____, all four of whom he seduced by telling them that the Lord had granted the blessing of Jacob, and that there was no sin in it—that he told him that Bates Noble married him to ____ ____, and that Brigham Young married him to ____ ____, that he had free access to Mrs. _____, Mrs. _____, Mrs. _____, and various others, whose husbands he had sent off preaching, and not now necessary to mention—and further this deponent saith not.

JOHN C. BENNETT

Sworn to and subscribed this 2d day of July, 1842.

SAMUEL MARSHALL, J. P. [seal]

John C. Bennett's affidavit in the *Pittsburgh Morning Chronicle*, June 29, 1842.

The *Sangamo Journal*, which received much wider circulation in Illinois, published the same affidavit on July 15, 1842, two weeks before it appeared in the Pittsburgh paper—but only its first half. It stops after the phrase "He [John C. Bennett] has seen Joseph Smith in bed with Mrs _____" but there is no blank; instead he provides the name of "Fuller."[38] The repeated "Mrs. _____"s are absent.

"Mrs. Fuller" is undoubtedly Catherine Fuller Warren, who confessed to sexual relations with Bennett. Notes from her trial before the Nauvoo High Council relate:

> The defendant confessed to the charge and gave the names of several others [beside John C. Bennett] who had been guilty of having unlawful intercourse with her [Chauncey Higbee, Lyman O. Littlefield, Joel S. Miles,

---

38. John C. Bennett, "Further Mormon Developments!! 2d Letter from Gen. Bennett," *Sangamo Journal*, July 15, 1842; see also Bennett, *The History of the Saints*, 253.

State of Illinois
Hancock County

Personally appeared before me, Samuel Marshall, a Justice of the Peace in and for said County, John C. Bennett, who being duly sworn, according to law, deposeth and saith—that the affidavit taken before Esq. Wells on the 17th of May, and the statement before the City Council of Nauvoo on the 19th, as published in the Wasp Of the 25th of June, 1842, are false, and were taken under DURESSE as stated in this letter—that <u>He has seen Joseph Smith in bed with Mrs. Fuller.</u>

JOHN C. BENNETT
Sworn to and subscribed this 2d day of July, 1842.   SAMUEL MARSHALL, J. P. [seal]

Sangamo Journal, June 15, 1842. This version failed to include the expanded accusations found in the *Pittsburg Morning Chronicle*. Underlining added.

George W. Thatcher, and J. B. Backenstos] stating that they taught the doctrine that it was right to have free intercourse with women and that the heads of the Church also taught and practiced it which things caused her to be led away thinking it to be right but becoming convinced that it was not right and learning that the heads of the church did not believe nor practice such things she was willing to confess her sins and did repent before God for what she had done and desired earnestly that the Council would forgive her and covenanted that she would hence forth do so no more.[39]

If the *Pittsburgh Morning Chronicle* version was accurate (and the whereabouts of the original affidavit is not known), it is unclear what Bennett stood to gain by circulating two forms of the same July 2 affidavit, severely limiting the dissemination of the more damaging version. That Bennett chose to not include it in the *Sangamo Journal* or in his book suggests that they were overstatements, if not prevarications. Bennett obviously saw his scandalous disclosures as a money-maker, as witnessed by his rush to book publication followed by a lecture tour. If he had, in fact, witnessed such shocking activities as his affidavit implies, it seems more likely that he would have capitalized on them, even perhaps enhancing them with lurid details.

Another detail in Bennett's Pittsburgh affidavit is that the Prophet had sent men on missions so he could marry their wives in Nauvoo. This statement is contradicted by historical data. Of the twelve "polyandrous" husbands iden-

---

39. Nauvoo Stake High Council Minutes, 1839 October–1845 October, LR 3102 22, published in Fred Collier, *The Nauvoo High Council Minute Books of the Church of Jesus Christ of Latter Day Saints*, 57–58.

tified by Todd Compton,[40] ten were not on missions at the time Joseph was sealed to their legal wives. Of the two possible exceptions, only one, Orson Hyde, is documented as on a mission at the time of Marinda Johnson Hyde's sealing to Joseph Smith. The second possible case involves George Harris, who left on his fourteen-month mission in July 1840. His wife, Lucinda may have been was sealed to Joseph Smith at some point, but the date is unavailable.[41]

Undoubtedly the biggest problem with Bennett's accusations is Bennett himself. As shown in Chapter 20, the evidence is strong that Joseph Smith never privately instructed Bennett concerning plural marriage or authorized, by example or innuendo, Bennett's seduction of at least "six or seven" women in Nauvoo.[42] The record also provides evidence that Bennett lied; for example, he described the organization of three echelons of "spiritual wives" in Nauvoo.[43] No other author ever referred to them, leading to the conclusion that the three levels are fictional.[44]

A telling piece of corroboration to me is that Bennett portrays Joseph Smith as blatant, brazen, and aggressive in conducting sexual polyandry; yet the next allegation of sexual polyandry was not made until eight years later and, according to an unfriendly report, involved a different woman than any Bennett identified in his affidavit, letters to the *Sangamo Journal*, or his book, *History of the Saints*.

No. 2: John Bowes/William Arrowsmith

The second narrative, chronologically speaking, was published in 1850 and accused Joseph Smith of sexual polyandry with Marinda Nancy Johnson

---

40. Compton, *In Sacred Loneliness*, 49, 81, 123, 179, 185, 213, 239, 260, 278, 383, 548.
41. See "No. 8: Wilhelm Wyl quoting Sarah Pratt" later in this chapter and Chapter 16.
42. Hyrum Smith's comment at the trial of Francis Higbee, May 6, 1844, in "Municipal Court," *Times and Seasons*, 5 (May 15, 1844): 540.
43. Bennett, *The History of the Saints: Or an Exposé of Joe Smith and Mormonism*, 220–25. Lawrence Foster, *Religion and Sexuality: Three American Communal Experiments of the Nineteenth Century*, 173, suggested one possible parallel between Bennett's descriptions of polygamy in Nauvoo and Joseph Smith's teachings on plural marriage: "Thus, 'wives and concubines' could well correspond to Bennett's two upper levels of plural wives." There is no evidence of women being designated as concubines or of concubines being married in Nauvoo. Nor is there any form of official sanction of concubinage in the Church before or after Joseph Smith's death.
44. For example, at the time Bennett left Nauvoo, only three men and three women besides Joseph Smith had been sealed in authorized polygamous marriages. Brigham Young, Heber Kimball, and Vinson Knight each had married one plural wife. The numbers of participants implied in Bennett's descriptions have not been verified and appear to be fictional.

Hyde, wife of Apostle Orson Hyde. Methodist minister and anti-Mormon writer in England, John Bowes (1804–74), made many unsubstantiated claims in his 1850 exposé, including "hidden orgies of Mormonism practiced in the Nauvoo Temple."[45] In this exposé, he quotes William Arrowsmith, of Augusta, in Lee County, Iowa, which he locates as "about sixteen miles from Nauvoo" across the Mississippi River.

"He never was a Mormon," according to Bowes, "but he married the sister of the Mormon apostle John Taylor. The Mormons persuaded his wife to leave him and they robbed him of 100 dollars worth of property." According to Arrowsmith's March 27, 1849, statement given to Bowes, "He says. . . that he, William Arrowsmith, slept at his mother-in-law's, who was a Mormon, when Joseph Smith slept with Orson Hyde's wife, under the same roof."[46]

Some details are correct. On January 29, 1839, when both of them were twenty, Arrowsmith married in Hale, Westmoreland, England, Elizabeth Taylor, sister of future Church President John Taylor and daughter of Agnes Whittington Taylor and James Taylor. It is also true that Arrowsmith never joined the Church. Elizabeth left him and went west in 1847 with the company of her brother, Captain William Taylor, taking their son John Taylor Arrowsmith. Elizabeth married George Boyes on July 16, 1847, during the trek.

According to available documents, Marinda was sealed to Joseph Smith in April 1842, so the alleged cohabitation would have occurred during the next twenty-six months.[47] At that time, she lived in an apartment above the *Times and Season's* printing office while Orson was on a missionary trip to Palestine.[48] On December 7, he returned; and by summer they moved into a newly built home in Nauvoo. In mid-February 1843, Marinda became pregnant with Orson Washington Hyde (b. November 9, 1843). If Joseph had been experiencing conjugal relations with Marinda since the April 1842 sealing, it is curious that she did not become pregnant until a few weeks after Orson's return to Nauvoo. Orson served a two-month mission during September-October; and then in April 1844, he left for a mission to Washington, D.C., to meet with President John Tyler, returning after the martyrdom.[49] Since Agnes Taylor's home was located outside of Nauvoo, the described visit between Joseph Smith and Marinda would have likely occurred while Orson was gone. Plausibility issues arise regarding the Prophet's ability to slip out of Nauvoo to spend an entire night with Marinda, without other witnesses questioning the behavior.

---

45. John Bowes, *Mormonism Exposed*, 17.
46. William Arrowsmith, quoted in ibid., 63.
47. Scott Faulring, ed., *An American Prophet's Record: The Diaries and Journals of Joseph Smith*, 396.
48. Compton, *In Sacred Loneliness*, 235–40.
49. Howard H. Barron, *Orson Hyde, Missionary, Apostle, Colonizer*, 144–55.

Another problem involves how public Arrowsmith's allegations were. I have found no evidence of their specific reactions, but neither woman considered the tale a reason to lose faith in the Prophet Joseph or the Church. Agnes was endowed in the Nauvoo Temple on December 15, 1845, and was sealed to her husband on January 17, 1846. Elizabeth received her endowments on January 27, 1846. Both women lived the rest of their lives in Utah and died in Salt Lake City, Agnes on November 15, 1868, and Elizabeth on July 31, 1909.[50]

An additional concern surrounds John Bowes's willingness to exaggerate. He continued his exposé by accusing Joseph of "all kinds of evil, adultery, seduction, etc."[51] One section of his pamphlet warns his readers: "I trust that the fathers, and mothers, and husbands of England, will take care of their wives and daughters, and preserve them from ever being contaminated by the pestilential breath of adulterers and fornicators."[52] If Arrowsmith indeed made the charge as reported by Bowes, I have found no additional supportive evidence or corroborative witnesses to this particular allegation about Joseph and Marinda.

No. 3: William Hall

The next document dealing with Joseph Smith's alleged sexual polyandry was published in 1851, the year after Bowes's book appeared, and was, again, an exposé, suggesting that such denunciations in print were financially rewarding for their authors. This work, *The Abominations of Mormonism Exposed* by William Hall, contains three critical accounts concerning Joseph Smith and polygamy, one of which alleges polyandry. He dictated a questionable report regarding an 1839 incident with Orson Hyde and Marinda Nancy Johnson that was discussed in Chapter 3. A third story mentioning Jane Law will be addressed in Chapter 31. Larry Foster assessed: "William Hall's accounts are of extremely dubious accuracy and must be evaluated with the caution used in evaluating any malicious gossip."[53]

The specific allegation of sexual polyandry involves Zina Diantha Huntington Jacobs: "A Mr. Henry Jacobs had his wife seduced by Joe Smith, in his time, during a mission to England. She was a very beautiful woman, but when Jacobs returned, he found her pregnant by Smith. Jacobs put up with the insult, and still lived with her."[54]

---

50. www.FamilySearch.com (accessed September 14, 2011).

51. John Bowes, *Mormonism Exposed*, 12.

52. Ibid., 62.

53. Lawrence Foster, *Religion and Sexuality: Three American Communal Experiments of the Nineteenth Century*, 308 note 93.

54. William Hall, *The Abominations of Mormonism Exposed; Containing Many Facts and Doctrines concerning That Singular People during Seven Years' Membership with Them, from 1840 to 1847*, 43.

As already mentioned above, only one of the husbands of Joseph Smith's polyandrous wives was on a mission when the sealing was performed (and the date of sealing of a second cannot be determined). Henry Jacobs was a diligent elder who served several missions, but he was definitely in Nauvoo when Zina's sealing to Joseph occurred on October 27, 1841. Zina's only child conceived during Joseph Smith's lifetime was Zebulon William Jacobs whose conception date would have been about April 11, 1841, just a month after the couple's wedding on March 7.[55]

Recently geneticist Ugo A. Perego and his associates performed DNA testing comparing DNA from the Y chromosome of Joseph Smith's progeny to the Y chromosome of a descendant of Zebulon. They concluded: "We can confidently exclude Joseph Smith as Zebulon Jacobs's father and identify Henry Bailey Jacobs as his and his brother's likely father on the basis of combined genetic and genealogical evidence."[56] Fawn Brodie admitted: "There is no record other than this bald statement [from William Hall] that Zina ever bore Joseph a child."[57]

Regarding Joseph's sealing to Zina Diantha Huntington Jacobs, which occurred when she was pregnant by her legal husband, Compton accurately points out: "Nothing specific is known about sexuality in their marriage," but he then adds, "though judging from Smith's other marriages, sexuality was probably included."[58]

Martha Sonntag Bradley and Mary Brown Firmage Woodward, in their study of Zina Diantha, hypothesize: "Sexual relations with Joseph Smith [and Zina], if any, had been infrequent and irregular."[59] However, they include no documentary evidence either confirming or denying this hypothesis.

No. 4: John Hyde

The fourth document is an 1857 exposé written by excommunicated Mormon John Hyde, a British convert (no known relation to Orson Hyde): "There is a Mrs. Dibble living in Utah, who has a fine son. She was sealed, among others, to Joseph Smith, although living with her present husband before and since. On the head of her son, Smith predicted the most startling prophesies [sic] about wielding the sword of Laban, revealing the hidden Book of

---

55. Compton, *In Sacred Loneliness*, 80–81.
56. Ugo A. Perego, Natalie M. Myres, and Scott R. Woodward, "Reconstructing the Y-Chromosome of Joseph Smith: Genealogical Applications," 59–60.
57. Brodie, *No Man Knows My History*, 466.
58. Compton, *In Sacred Loneliness*, 82.
59. Martha Sonntag Bradley and Mary Brown Firmage Woodward, *Four Zinas: A Story of Mothers and Daughters on the Mormon Frontier*, 132–33.

Mormon, and translating the sealed part of the records. There is not a person at Salt Lake who doubts the fact of that boy being Smith's own child."[60]

Hyde thus posits a polyandrous marriage between Joseph Smith and Hannah Dubois Dibble and her legal husband Philo Dibble. Hannah married Philo on February 11, 1841, in Nauvoo with Joseph Smith performing the ceremony.[61] Compton lists her as one of the eight "possible" plural wives of the Prophet in part based on Hyde's assertion but also because of a comment by Benjamin F. Johnson, whose sister Almera was sealed to Joseph Smith and who had acted as Joseph's go-between in teaching his sister about plural marriage. Johnson stated: "At this time [May 16, 1843][62] I knew that the Prophet had as his wives, Louisa Beeman, Eliza R. Snow, Maria and Sarah Lawrence, Sisters Lyon and Dibble, one or two of Bishop Partridge's daughters, and some of C. P. Lott's daughters."[63] Out of the ten women whom Johnson links with Joseph, he is correct about eight: Beeman, Snow, the Lawrence sisters, Lyon, the Partridge sisters, and one of C. P. Lott's daughters. However, only one—Malissa—was married to the Prophet. No evidence has been found to support that either of her sisters, Mary Elizabeth (b. 1827) or Almira Henrietta (b. 1829), was sealed to Joseph Smith at any time. Therefore, despite Johnson's general reliability, he may also have been mistaken about a plural marriage between Hannah Dibble and the Prophet. No sealing date has been documented or even proposed for such a union. Also weakening the case for a sealing is that, unlike the Prophet's other plural wives, Hannah was not resealed to him when the Nauvoo Temple was completed. Instead, on January 15, 1846, she was married for eternity to Philo Dibble with Brigham Young officiating.[64]

The only Dibble son that fits Hyde's narrative is Loren Walker Dibble, born May 29, 1844 (conceived approximately September 6, 1843). As another anomaly, Hyde mentions "startling prophesies [sic] about wielding the sword of Laban, revealing the hidden Book of Mormon, and translating the sealed part of the records." Logically, such remarkable predictions would have been

---

60. John Hyde, *Mormonism: Its Leaders and Designs*, 84–85. I have found no evidence to corroborate this assertion. Hyde was capable of extreme claims, asserting that proxy marriages for the dead had "to be consummated in the same manner as that of the living. . . . And as a marriage ceremony is not valid till completed, there is practiced in consequence more abomination" (88–89). This claim is unfounded and is contradicted by more reliable evidence.

61. "Hannah Ann Dubois Dibble" (obituary), *Deseret News*, November 25, 1893, 32; see also "Philo Dibble's Narrative," 92–93.

62. George D. Smith, ed., *An Intimate Chronicle: The Journals of William Clayton*, May 16, 1843, 101.

63. Benjamin F. Johnson, *My Life's Review*, 96.

64. Lisle G Brown, *Nauvoo Sealings, Adoptions, and Anointings: A Comprehensive Register of Persons Receiving LDS Temple Ordinances, 1841–1846*, 83.

recorded, at least in family documents if not in more formal Church records. However, I have been unable to find corroborating evidence of these predictions or indications that Loren Dibble made remarkable contributions to the Church.[65] Hyde's assertion that Loren Dibble was widely known as Joseph Smith's child is completely unsupported by other reports, rumors, or even denials of Hyde's claim.

As discussed in Chapter 3, Benjamin Winchester launched the rumor that Joseph had fathered Hannah's son in 1839, which the Prophet flatly denied.[66] Chapter 11 examined the problems regarding a very late report that some of the children born to Joseph Smith's plural wives may have been raised in other families including one with the surname of "Dibble," but sexual polyandry was not alleged in either of these cases.

No. 5: Mary Ettie V. Smith

Mary Ettie V. Coray Smith (see Chapter 3), was born January 31, 1827, so she would have been seventeen when the Prophet died. Her brother, Howard Coray, served as a clerk and scribe of Joseph Smith. She can be identified with several different spellings of her first name besides "Mary Ettie," including "Mariette," "Marietta," Maryette," "Mary Eti," "Mary Etta," and "Mariet."[67] She married Samuel Goforth Henderson on January 30, 1844, and they were sealed in the Nauvoo Temple on January 20, 1846, by Brigham Young.[68] The couple apparently divorced, and Mary Ettie traveled to Salt Lake City where she received numerous plural marriage proposals and spent time in Heber C. Kimball's home.[69] She reported that Brigham Young arranged for her to be

---

65. The only biographical details I have found identify him as participating in an Indian altercation on June 26, 1866. Peter Gottfredson, *History of Indian Depredations in Utah*, 214. See also http://www.blackhawkproductions.com/diamondbattle.htm (access July 19, 2010). John W. Rockwell, *Stories from the Life of Porter Rockwell*, 145, calls him a "gunfighter."

66. Joseph Smith related on May 27, 1843: "I disagreed [with] him [Winchester] before the conference and to be revenged he told one of the most damnable lies about me. [I] visited Sister Smith, Sister Dibble [and]. . . told her to come to Nauvoo with me . . . and Benjamin Winchester set up a howl that I was guilty of improper conduct." Joseph Smith, in Quorum of the Twelve Apostles: Minutes of Meetings, May 27, 1843.

67. See, for example, listings in Brown, *Nauvoo Sealings, Adoptions, and Anointings*, 135; AncestralFile;http://www.findagrave.com/cgi-bin/fg.cgi?page=gr&GRid=33912889 (accessed September 14, 2011; and Lyndon W. Cook, comp., *Nauvoo Deaths and Marriages, 1839–1845*, 109.

68. Cook, *Nauvoo Deaths and Marriages*, 109; Brown, *Nauvoo Sealings, Adoptions, and Anointings*, 135.

69. Nelson Winch Green quoting Mary Ettie V. Smith in *Fifteen Years among the Mormons: Being the Narrative of Mrs. Mary Ettie V. Smith*, 172.

sealed to Nathaniel Vary Jones as a plural wife on May 12, 1851. Although the sealing was apparently for "time and eternity," she considered it as applying only after death.[70] Subsequently, Reuben P. Smith, an unbaptized Church attender arrived in town and began to court her. They were married on May 3, 1852, by Elder Jared Porter of the Fifteenth Ward in Salt Lake City, and the notice was published in the *Deseret News*.[71] Reuben's employment required him to travel to California the following year. Mary Ettie stayed behind until 1856 when she traveled to New York. There, in 1857, she dictated a narrative to her editor, Nelson Green, who may have also been her ghostwriter. Together they produced *Fifteen Years among the Mormons: Being the Narrative of Mrs. Mary Ettie V. Smith*. Reuben caught up with Mary Ettie in New York on August 13, 1858, and escorted her back to California where she died of "consumption" in San Francisco in January 1867.[72]

In her book, Mary Ettie V. Coray Smith asserts that she heard one of Joseph Smith's plural wives, Presendia Huntington Buell, "say afterwards in Utah, that she did not know whether Mr. Buel [her legal husband, Norman Buell] or the Prophet was the father of her son."[73] It is true that Presendia had been sealed to Joseph Smith on December 11, 1841. As discussed in Chapter 3, Fawn Brodie theorized that this child was Oliver Buell.[74] However, genetics researcher Ugo A. Perego has shown through DNA testing of parallel descendants that Oliver was not Joseph Smith's son.[75]

From internal evidence in Mary Ettie's narrative, the son in question could only have been John Hiram, who was conceived approximately October 20, 1842, when Presendia Huntington Buell lived at Lima, Illinois, thirty miles south of Nauvoo. According to Joseph Smith's journal, he was hiding from Illinois law officers who were cooperating with Missouri sheriffs in trying to extradite him to that state. Joseph was staying out of the public view in the home of James Taylor in Nauvoo; available records provide no support for a trip south to Lima or elsewhere. Also, there is no indication that Presendia made visits to Nauvoo at that time.[76]

---

70. Ibid., 182.

71. "Married," *Deseret News*, May 15, 1852, 2.

72. John W. McCoy, "True Grit and Tall Tales: How Mary Ettie Coray (1827–1867) Got Her Man," 9–11.

73. Green quoting Mary Ettie V. Smith, in *Fifteen Years among the Mormons*, 35.

74. Brodie, *No Man Knows My History*, 301–2.

75. Ugo A. Perego, Jayne E. Ekins, and Scott R. Woodward, "Resolving the Paternities of Oliver N. Buell and Mosiah L. Hancock through DNA," 128–36.

76. Dean C. Jessee, ed., *The Papers of Joseph Smith: Volume 2, Journal, 1832–1842*, 598. Presendia was a member of the Nauvoo Relief Society and traveled to Nauvoo to attend its meetings. However, its last meeting in 1842 occurred on September 28. See http://josephsmithpapers.org/paperSummary/nauvoo-relief-society-minute-

While several authors have treated Mary Ettie's statement as reliable,[77] it is problematic for four reasons. First, she wrote that she heard this report from Presendia personally. It appears that the two women may have crossed paths sometime after her arrival in Salt Lake City in early 1850: "I spent, during the winter, much of my time in the family of Heber C. Kimball who had over thirty wives; not all of whom were at home, however, as they lived in different houses."[78] If accurate, she might have met Presendia who became a plural wife (for "time") of Heber C. Kimball on February 4, 1846. Presendia joined Kimball's family during the western exodus and by the end of 1849 was settled in Utah. She did not live with Kimball's other wives during the early 1850s, so if Mary Ettie met her, it would probably have been as Presendia was visiting Kimball's primary residence; however, there is no evidence supporting this scenario.[79]

Second, it is questionable whether Mary Ettie was sufficiently close to Presendia in a social sense to have heard the admission. Mary Ettie mentions "Mrs. Buel" three times in her book, each time misspelling her name and never referring to her as "Presendia."[80] Presendia makes no mention of Mary Ettie in any known document. That Presendia would have confided in Mary Ettie, a divorced woman who had separated from her sealed husband and was also seventeen years her junior, seems less probable.

Third, it is equally unlikely that Presendia would have made the statement publicly. If she had, virtually all listeners would have been greatly surprised and scandalized. They could have interpreted the declaration in only one way, that Presendia experienced sexual relations during the same period with both Norman Buell and Joseph Smith so that when she became pregnant with her son, she could not accurately determine which man was the father. Such a bald announcement would have violated the reticence about sexual matters that was standard for nineteenth-century women.[81] As Todd Compton

---

book#86 (accessed September 14, 2011). It is unknown if she attended that particular meeting; but if conception had occurred on or around that date, Oliver, her sixth child, would have been three weeks overdue. Compton, *In Sacred Loneliness*, 122. Carrying a viable fetus during a sixth pregnancy two or three weeks past the due date would have been extremely rare.

77. See for example, George D. Smith, "Nauvoo Roots of Mormon Polygamy, 1841–46: A Preliminary Demographic Report," 11; Todd Compton, *In Sacred Loneliness*, 671, is skeptical but does not dismiss it completely. The statement is treated as credible on numerous anti-Mormon websites. For example, it is quoted in "Joseph Smith and Whorehouses," at http://www.mormoncurtain.com/topic_joesephsmith_section3.html (accessed September 17, 2011).

78. Green quoting Mary Ettie V. Smith in *Fifteen Years among the Mormons*, 172.

79. Compton, *In Sacred Loneliness*, 130–34.

80. Green quoting Mary Ettie V. Smith in *Fifteen Years among the Mormons*, 34, 35, 45.

81. Compton, "Fawn Brodie on Joseph Smith's Plural Wives and Polygamy: A

notes: "One wonders if Presendia would have said such a thing. Talk of sexuality was avoided by the Victorian, puritanical Mormons; in diaries, the word 'pregnant' or 'expecting' is never or rarely used."[82] In addition, polyandrous sexual relations violated accepted moral standards both in and outside of the Church in the 1850s. (See Chapter 14.) No Latter-day Saint would have then viewed sexual polyandry as an acceptable practice.

A fourth difficulty with Mary Ettie's statement is the implausibility of the declared activities themselves. Two factors would have greatly impeded such behavior, the thirty miles separating Presendia (in Lima) and Joseph (in Nauvoo) and the fact that her husband, Norman Buell, was antagonistic to the Mormons and would not have willingly shared his wife sexually with the Prophet under the guise of plural marriage. Mary Ettie's quotation requires Presendia to have rendezvoused with the Prophet for conjugal relations close to a time when she was sexually involved with her legal husband. Both the distance and Norman's presumably watchful eye would have made this difficult. Also important is whether Presendia herself, with her conservative Christian morals, could have accepted such conjugal arrangements.

In her 1875 exposé, Ann Eliza Webb Young repeated and embellished this allegation with patent falsehoods: "Some of these women [Nauvoo polygamous wives] have since said they did not know who was the father of their children; this is not to be wondered at, for after Joseph's declaration annulling all Gentile marriages, the greatest promiscuity was practiced; and, indeed, all sense of morality seemed to have been lost by a portion at least of the church."[83] Born in 1844, Ann Eliza could only have been restating secondhand information, most likely Mary Ettie's account, adding her own biased allegations.

In summary, no evidence exists supporting that Presendia and Mary Ettie were close friends in Utah. Nor are there reasons to believe Presendia would have confided such a scandalous detail to her. Mary Ettie also portrays Presendia making a startling confession in rather casual fashion. An admission of sexual polyandry would have created a stir among any who would have learned of it; and if it involved the Prophet, the publicity would likely have been much greater. Importantly, the thirty-mile distance between Joseph Smith and Presendia and Norman Buell's rejection of Mormonism represent significant obstacles to the behavior described. And finally, most historians do not consider Mary Ettie a credible witness. Stanley S. Ivins called her memories

---

Critical View," 166.

82. Ibid.

83. Ann Eliza Webb Young, *Wife No. 19, or, The Story of a Life in Bondage, Being a Complete Exposé of Mormonism, and Revealing Sorrows, Sacrifices, and Sufferings of Women in Polygamy*, 71,

"inaccurate and of no value."[84] In 1875, Fanny Stenhouse, who was writing an exposé of her own based on her disillusionment with polygamy, described Mary Ettie as "a lady who wrote very many years ago and in her writings, so mixed up fiction with what was true, that it was difficult to determine where the one ended and the other began."[85] A non-Mormon descendant of Mary Ettie, John W. McCoy, concluded:

> Mary Ettie does not seem to have kept a personal journal, and she is recounting events that occurred when she was very young. Moreover, the account was written down by Nelson Green, and then interpreted by the printer. . . . It will not take the reader very long to discover that Mary Ettie's account is skillfully written, if not deviously clever. Also, her literary license is stretched to the fullest possible extent for a variety of purposes. . . . The line between truth and fiction does not seem to have been regarded as an absolute in every instance. . . . Clearly, *Fifteen Years among the Mormons* is not a primary source. It is not even a reliable secondary source. The specific dates that it includes are most often wrong, and at least some of the names are reported incorrectly. . . . The level of credibility even for statements supported by external facts is reduced by the unavoidable presence of her editor, Nelson Green.[86]

In short, although Mary Ettie's report that Presendia Huntington "did not know whether Mr. Buell or the Prophet was the father of her son" is often quoted, its credibility is undermined by its numerous weaknesses.

No. 6: Ann Eliza Webb Young

Ann Eliza Webb Young, author of the sixth document reporting sexual polyandry, is, like all of the other authors reported thus far, writing an exposé, *Wife No. 19*, that had the alluring cachet of being written by one of Brigham Young's divorced plural wives. At one point, she comments: "One woman said to me not very long since, while giving me some of her experience in polygamy: 'The greatest trial I ever endured in my life was living with my husband and deceiving him, by receiving Joseph's attentions whenever he chose to come to me.'"[87]

Ann Eliza does not specifically name which of Joseph's wives she was allegedly quoting. However, her mother, Eliza Jane Churchill Webb, repeated the accusation in two private letters a year later specifying that Zina Diantha

---

84. Stanley S. Ivins, Notebook 4, Box 1, fd. 4, p. 63.
85. Fanny Stenhouse, *"Tell It All": The Story of a Life's Experiences in Mormonism*, 618.
86. McCoy, "True Grit and Tall Tales," 4–6, 13.
87. Ann Eliza Young, *Wife Number 19*, 71. See also Eliza Jane Webb, Letter to Mary Bond, August 27, 1876.

Huntington was the woman. I do not count Eliza Jane's letters as separate documentation because Ann Eliza specifies that her knowledge came from her personal conversation with "one woman," and Eliza Jane did not share the information until after her daughter had published the story. Eliza Jane's version of this account is: "There are women living in Utah now who were sealed to Joseph while living with their husbands, and they say it was the greatest trial of their lives to live with two men at the same time."[88] Four months afterwards, she clarified: "There is Zina,—whose maiden name was Huntington. She says the greatest trial of her life was, to live with her husband and Joseph too at the same time."[89]

Although Jerald and Sandra Tanner quote Ann Eliza's printed statement as primary evidence of sexual polyandry in Joseph Smith's plural marriages,[90] it raises several important questions. Perhaps foremost is the

Ann Eliza Webb Young. Courtesy LDS Church History Library.

issue of proximity. Ann Eliza was sealed to Brigham Young in 1868 when she was twenty-four but did not live in the Lion House with Zina and his other wives, but lived in her own house a few blocks away.[91] She apostatized and divorced Brigham in 1872, immediately suing him (unsuccessfully) for alimony.[92] Yet she claimed that, at some point during those four years, Zina Huntington, who was twenty-three years older, confided that her "greatest trial" nearly three decades earlier in Nauvoo was polyandrous sexuality involving both of her husbands: Joseph Smith and Henry Jacobs. Why she would have confided such a delicate and painful subject to this young and relatively inexperienced woman is not clear.

---

88. Eliza Jane Webb, Letter Mary Bond, April 24, 1876.

89. Eliza J. Webb, Letter to Mary Bond, August 27, 1876.

90. Jerald Tanner and Sandra Tanner, *Joseph Smith and Polygamy*, 51.

91. J.J.J. "Two Prophets' Widows: A Visit to the Relicts of Joseph Smith and Brigham Young, the Present Occupants of the Lion House and Bee-Hive, A Peep into the Big Parlor Where Brigham Held Family Prayers—Aunt Zinah and Eliza R. Snow, the Poetess," 6.

92. Edwin Brown Firmage and Richard Collin Mangrum, *Zion in the Courts: A Legal History of the Church of Jesus Christ of Latter-day Saints, 1830–1900*, 249.

In 1898 when Zina was interviewed by John Wight (1842–1921), an elder in the RLDS Church and son of excommunicated apostle Lyman Wight, she staunchly resisted disclosing details about her sealing to Joseph Smith: "It was something too sacred to be talked about; it was more to me than life or death. I never breathed it for years. . . . You are speaking of the most sacred experiences of my life."[93] It seems unlikely that, after the candid disclosure Ann Eliza reports, Zina would have done a complete about-face more than twenty years later.

Furthermore, about fifteen years after Ann Eliza's book appeared, Zina vigorously challenged both Ann Eliza's truthfulness and her general character in an 1887 interview:

> The trouble with Ann Eliza. . . was that she was not truthful. She was not grateful, and she was a very bad woman. She has convicted herself out of her own mouth. . . . She never lifted her finger to do a bit of work that she didn't want to do. She had servants and there was no necessity for her doing anything. She has asserted that President Young opened all his wives' letters, and that they couldn't visit anywhere or write to anybody, which is ridiculously untrue. President Young was occupied with too many important matters to give attention to such trivial things as his wives' letters or his wives' visits. We wrote to whom we pleased. . . . Ann Eliza knew she was misrepresenting the facts.[94]

Zina did not directly dispute Ann Eliza's claims regarding sexual polyandry probably because Ann Eliza's book did not identify her as the "one woman" who deceived her husband "by receiving Joseph's attentions whenever he chose to come to me"; and few individuals, including perhaps Zina herself, would have concluded that she was the woman in question.

Furthermore, given the attention that surrounded Joseph whenever he appeared on the streets of Nauvoo and the close-knit nature of the community, it seems unlikely that Zina might have been able to keep a sexually polyandrous marriage secret from her husband and to have been available "whenever [Joseph] chose."

Confusion regarding Zina's relationship with Joseph Smith has also arisen as the result of a misstatement in Martha Sonntag Bradley and Mary Brown Firmage Woodward's popular book, *Four Zinas: A Story of Mothers and Daughters on the Mormon Frontier.*[95] There Bradley and Woodward wrote, "Zina [Huntington] does not record if she and Joseph consummated their union, al-

---

93. Zina D. H. Young, Interviewed by John W. Wight, October 1, 1898, 29–30.
94. J.J.J., "Two Prophets' Widows," 6.
95. See, for example, "Extracts from Letters and Emails," *Salt Lake City Messenger*, no. 97 (October 2001).

though Zina later signed an affidavit that she was Smith's wife in 'very deed.'"[96] The affidavit appears in virtual duplicate in Joseph F. Smith, Affidavit Books 1:5, 4:5. However, neither affidavit mentions a consummation of the marriage in any terms, nor does it use the language of in "very deed."[97] The "very deed" language also does not appear in any of the eighty-eight affidavits contained in the four affidavit books. It is, however, the term used in an unrelated interview conducted by Joseph Smith III in 1893 who asked Malissa Lott, one of the Prophet's non-polyandrous plural wives, if she was Joseph Smith's wife "in very deed" and she answered in the affirmative.[98]

No. 7: Wilhelm Wyl

As discussed in Chapter 3, in 1886, Wilhelm Ritter von Wymetal, writing under the pseudonym, Wilhelm Wyl, produced yet another exposé about Joseph Smith, *Mormon Portraits* that was filled with sensationalized claims. Speaking on the subject of sexual polyandry, Wyl related: "There were in Nauvoo, when Joseph was in his glory as 'the greatest prophet that ever lived,' a young merchant and his wife whom he dearly loved. She bore to him several children, but became fascinated with Joe and with his claims to 'exalt' any woman who would yield to his wishes and become his 'wife.' The husband was sent on a mission, and during his absence Joseph 'gathered' the wife to his embraces, and she was 'sealed' as one of his harem."[99]

---

96. Bradley and Woodward, *Four Zinas*, 114–15.

97. Zina Diantha Huntington [Young], Affidavit, in Joseph F. Smith, Affidavit Book 1:5, affirms:

> Be it remembered that on this first day of May A.D. eighteen sixty nine before me Elias Smith Probate Judge for Said County personally appeared, Zina Diantha Huntington \Young/ who was by me Sworn in due form of law, and upon her oath Saith, that on the twenty-Seventh day of October A.D. 1841, at the City of Nauvoo, County of Hancock, State of Illinois, She was married or Sealed to Joseph Smith, President of the Church of Jesus Christ of Latter Day Saints, by Dimick B. Huntington, a High Priest in Said Church, according to the laws of the same; regulating marriage; In the presence of Fanny Maria Huntington.

The affidavit is signed by Zina and by Elias Smith. Affidavit 4:5 contains some minor word changes, but the content is not altered.

98. Malissa Lott Smith Willes, Notarized statement to Joseph Smith III, August 4, 1893.

99. Wilhelm Wyl, [pseud. for Wilhelm Ritter von Wymetal], *Mormon Portraits, or the Truth about Mormon Leaders from 1830 to 1886, Joseph Smith the Prophet, His Family and His Friends: A Study Based on Fact and Documents*, 69.

The Puzzle of "Polyandry" 327

Wilhelm Wyl's allegation regarding a nameless "merchant" and his nameless "wife" is difficult to investigate due to its vagueness. Researching Nauvoo merchants 1840–44 fails to identify one with a wife who might fit Wyl's description. The Prophet was sealed to Sylvia Sessions Lyon, the legal spouse of Windsor Lyon, who was, in fact a merchant; but he is the only merchant who was married to one of Joseph's plural wives. Furthermore, the date of their sealing is unknown; but when the Prophet wed Sylvia, Windsor had already been excommunicated so he could not have been serving a mission for the Church at that time. (See Chapter 13.)

Wyl's use of "harem" and describing Joseph as "the greatest prophet that ever lived" can be dismissed as rhetorical flourishes, meant to evoke socially negative images of Muslims. The 1830 Noah Webster's dictionary defines "harem" as "a place where Eastern princes confine their women, who are prohibited from the society of others."[100] While at least four of Joseph Smith's plural wives (Emily and Eliza Partridge and Sarah and Maria Lawrence) were living at the Nauvoo Mansion with Emma's permission when the Smiths moved in on August 31, 1843, Emily Partridge later testified that Emma forbade Joseph from cohabiting with them;[101] but they were not living in forced isolation and could hardly be considered to be a "harem." Without better documentation, Wyl's description of the merchant's wife can be dismissed.

No. 8: Wilhelm Wyl quoting Sarah Pratt

Wyl is also the source of the eighth document alleging sexual polyandry on Joseph's part, which was discussed (in Chapter 3), but is revisited here for completeness. In his 1886 exposé, Wyl quoted Sarah Bates Pratt who reported to him a dramatic account of how Joseph Smith had approached her in 1841 during the absence of her husband, Orson, then serving a mission, with a proposal that was described in different ways. In one account, Sarah was to become Joseph's "spiritual" or plural wife, although specifics of the type of eternal sealing may have been offered are still unclear.[102] In the Wyl account, Sarah called his offer a "dastardly attempt on me," asserting that the Prophet propositioned her for adulterous sexual relations.[103] The twenty-four-year-old Sarah apparently told Wyl that she subsequently confided her plight to an

---

100. Noah Webster, *An American Dictionary of the English Language; Exhibiting the Origin, Orthography, Pronunciation, and Definitions of Words*, 399.

101. Emily D. P. Young, Deposition, Temple Lot Transcript, Respondent's Testimony, Part 3, pp. 366, 384, questions 363, 747.

102. See John C. Bennett, The *History of the Saints: Or an Exposé of Joe Smith and Mormonism*, 228; *Minutes of the Apostles of The Church of Jesus Christ of Latter-day Saints, 1835–1893*, 15, January 20, 1843.

103. Wyl, *Mormon Portraits*, 60; see also Bennett, *The History of the Saints*, 175, 227.

older neighbor, Lucinda Pendleton Morgan Harris. According to the Wyl/Pratt version, Lucinda scoffed, "Why *I am his mistress since four years!*" (emphasis Wyl's).[104] Chapter 3 already outlined numerous credibility problems with this statement. Its ambiguous language does not specify a polyandrous arrangement; it could have been referring to non-polygamous adultery. (The interactions between Orson and Sarah Pratt, John C. Bennett, and Joseph Smith are analyzed in Chapter 21.)

No. 9: Phebe Louisa Holmes

In a refreshing change from the long series of exposés, the ninth document is a family record, though it contains some ambiguous elements. On December 1, 1842, Joseph Smith performed the civil marriage for thirty-six-year-old Jonathan Holmes to twenty-nine-year-old Elvira Ann Cowles in Nauvoo. Five months later, she was sealed to the Prophet on June 1, 1843. Jonathan joined the Mormon Battalion, and Elvira traveled west with the Jedediah M. Grant company, arriving in Salt Lake City October 2, 1847. They eventually settled in Farmington where they raised their family of five daughters, three of whom survived to adulthood. At his death in 1880, Jonathan Holmes was serving on the Davis Stake High Council.

The third of those children was Phebe Louisa, born in 1851 in Farmington. She married Job Welling on December 21, 1868, in Salt Lake City. In 1982, an unidentified descendant of Job Welling compiled historical documents titling the collection: "The Ancestors of Marietta Holmes, Phebe Louisa Holmes and Emma Lucinda Holmes, Daughters of Jonathan Harriman Holmes and Elvira Annie Cowles Smith."[105] It includes a section entitled: "Written by Phebe Louisa Holmes Welling 2/9/38," which would have been a year before her death on June 30, 1939, at eighty-eight. It reports: "I heard my mother testify that she was indeed the Prophet's (Joseph Smith) plural wife in life and lived with him as such during his lifetime."[106] Unfortunately, no other details regarding the declaration are available. The phrase "lived with him" as a "plural wife" in nineteenth-century parlance clearly suggested sexual activity.

It appears that all three individuals in the implied polyandrous triangle, Joseph, Elvira, and Jonathan, lived in Nauvoo during the year between Elvira's sealing to Joseph in June 1843 and his death in June 1844. However,

---

104. Wyl, *Mormon Portraits*, 60.
105. Phebe Louisa Holmes Welling, "The Ancestors of Marietta Holmes, Phebe Louisa Holmes, and Emma Lucinda Holmes, Daughters of Jonathan Harriman Holmes and Elvira Annie Cowles Smith," unpublished manuscript, 1982, LDS Family History Library.
106. Ibid., 25.

no specific evidence is available regarding the issue of sexual relations between them. Polygamy researcher Meg Stout wrote:

> Elvira's lack of children during this time [June 1, 1843 to June 27, 1844] indicates this sealing to Joseph was not physically consummated, despite Phoebe Holmes Welling's 1939 history (remembered hearsay recorded almost 100 years later). Family tradition and the lack of children also indicate that Jonathan didn't consummate his marriage to Elvira until after Joseph's death, as late as February 1845. Elvira's first child, Lucy, was born nine months later. Elvira's daughter, Marietta, would be born nine months after Jonathan returned from his Mormon Battalion service. Elvira continued to bear a child every two years thereafter until she was 43 years old.[107]

Stout's conclusions describe a strange relationship where Joseph Smith, her sealed husband, may have been sexually involved with Elvira, while Jonathan Holmes, her legal spouse, was not. This dynamic will be discussed in Chapter 15 but is supported by additional evidences.

Jonathan was a close friend of the Prophet and served as a pallbearer at the funeral. He apparently respected his wife's sealing to Joseph Smith, standing proxy in the Nauvoo Temple as she was resealed to Joseph vicariously for eternity.[108] Also, their decision to move west indicates a transfer of loyalty from Joseph as Church leader to Brigham Young and the Twelve. Elvira died March 10, 1871, so Phebe's recollection spanned at least sixty-six years, and the family records that preserve her recollection contain no indication that she made a written record earlier that would have preserved her mother's words closer to the time when they were spoken.

On June 2, 1931, seven years before Phebe made her report, William Wright, a member of the Church whom I have not been able to further identify, wrote a letter to the First Presidency containing a confusing reference to the relationship between Joseph, Jonathan, and Elvira in Nauvoo. This excerpt was transcribed by Michael Quinn in the 1980s and is found in his notes now housed at Yale University. The original letter apparently remains uncatalogued in the Church History Library. "I was well acquainted with two of Joseph's wives, LaVina [Elvira] and Eliza [Snow or Partridge?]. I came to Utah in '69, and rented LaVina Holmes farm. Before Joseph was shot, he asked Jonathan Holmes if he would marry and take care of LaVina, but that if LaVina wanted him to take care of her he would take her. He would fill that mission to please his Father in Heaven."[109]

---

107. "A Short History of Jonathan Holmes and Elvira Cowles," at http://www.megstout.com/blog/2010/02/19/a-short-history-of-jonathan-holmes-and-elvira-cowles/ (accessed September 19, 2011).

108. Brown, *Nauvoo Sealings, Adoptions, and Anointings*, 284 note 305.

109. William Wright, Letter to unidentified addressee but stamped as received in the

This letter is very late, secondhand, and somewhat garbled. It does not say whether Wright heard this claim of a protective marriage directly from Elvira, although it is implied and there is no other obvious source of the information. However, Wright does not remember Elvira's name correctly, creating concerns regarding its accuracy. Elvira was fifty-six in 1869 and died just two years later on March 10, 1871. The described "pretend" marriage to protect the Prophet was not completely outlandish, since Joseph Smith, after his sealing on July 27, 1842, to Sarah Ann Whitney, asked Joseph C. Kingsbury, then unmarried, to enter what Kingsbury called "a pretend marriage" on April 23, 1843, to conceal Joseph and Sarah Ann's relationship. (See Chapter 16.) In Elvira's case, an apparently legitimate civil marriage preceded the sealing by almost a year. There seems to be no reason why Jonathan and Elvira's marriage would not have included sexual relations, but the lack of children during Joseph Smith's lifetime coupled with Elvira's obvious fecundity afterwards is puzzling.

On August 28, 1869, Elvira Cowles signed an affidavit stating that she had been sealed to the Prophet on June 1, 1843, nearly a year after her legal marriage.[110] The year 1869—the same year William Wright says he learned about Joseph's assigning Jonathan Holmes to marry and take care of Elvira—may be significant in that the topic of establishing the validity of Joseph's plural marriages in Nauvoo was circulating in the community. Joseph's sons, Alexander Hale, and David Hyrum, came to Salt Lake City in 1869 with their anti-polygamy message fomenting new discussion of Nauvoo plural marriage. (See Chapter 13.) Nor can Wright's statement be explained as a copy-cat assertion of Kingsbury's "front" marriage. Kingsbury did not write his original account until May of 1870; it did not circulate at all. Kingsbury re-dictated his account May 22, 1886, and Andrew Jenson published it in his 1887 article, "Plural Marriage." (See Appendix C.)

One possibility is that Elvira misremembered the date of her sealing to Joseph Smith. If she had been sealed to him in 1842, then possibly Joseph Smith asked Jonathan Holmes to marry Elvira about a year later to serve, like Joseph Kingsbury, as a "front husband" to shield the Prophet from suspicion should a pregnancy result. In that case, the marriage to Jonathan would have been legal but without connubial relations. This scenario would be more consistent with William Wright's letter, but I stress that it is only conjecture and that the historical record fails to provide any further details about the sexual relations of Elvira with Joseph Smith.

First Presidency Office on June 2, 1931.

110. Elvira Ann Cowles Smith Holmes, Affidavit, August 28, 1869, in Joseph F. Smith, Affidavit Books 1:78. See Elvira Ann Cowles Holmes, Uncatalogued materials, in Andrew Jenson Collection, MS 17956, Box 49, fd. 16, docs. 6–7; see also Box 6, fd. 62.

Given the ambiguities in the historical record, I conclude that it is impossible to conclusively determine whether the elderly Phebe Louisa Holmes's recollection that her mother "lived with" Joseph Smith as his "plural wife" included polyandrous sexual relations (with both men), monogamous relations (with Holmes only), or polygynous relations (with Joseph Smith only). If Phebe's report accurately depicts conjugality between Joseph and Elvira during that period, proponents of the position that it also supports sexual polyandry must assume concomitant sexual relations with Jonathan because there is no evidence to support that they were also occurring at that time.[111] Importantly, the assumption that the legal marriage would have authorized connubial relations between Elvira and Jonathan after she had been sealed to Joseph for "time and eternity" may not be warranted in light of Joseph's teachings forbidding sexual polyandry. (See Chapters 13 and 14.)

In addition, for reasons that will be discussed in the next three chapters, if Joseph Smith had experienced sexual polyandry with Elvira, it seems that more evidence might be available than a single attestation related by one daughter nearly a hundred years after the events allegedly occurred.

No. 10: Edwin Mace

On February 15, 1858, Edwin Mace was born in Fillmore, Utah, to Hiram Mace and Elizabeth Armstrong Mace. Hiram and Elizabeth had been sealed in the Nauvoo Temple thirteen years earlier; and Edwin grew up in the Church, being baptized in 1877 and endowed in the Logan Temple in 1888. Sometime in the 1920s, for reasons that are unclear, Edwin was asked by Anthony W. Ivins, a counselor in the First Presidency, to write down his family's multi-generational tradition regarding the existence of a possible child of Joseph Smith.

In response, the seventy-year-old Mace produced a narrative describing his beliefs. Currently, a typed copy is available in the Stanley S. Ivins collection at the Utah State Historical Society. However, it is unknown whether Mace typed the copy, dictated it to a typist, or hand-wrote his account from which

---

111. D. Michael Quinn, "Evidence for the Sexual Side of Joseph Smith's Polygamy," Expanded version, 5–6, comments: "I find it difficult to believe that Elvira's 37-year-old widower-husband Jonathan stopped having sex with her only six months after their civil wedding, simply to accommodate the Prophet's sexual relations with her (which in June 1843 seemed likely to continue for many years)." As discussed in the text, there is no documentation to support sexual relations in the legal marriage between Elvira and Jonathan until approximately seven months after the martyrdom. The first child born to them was Lucy Elvira Holmes on October 11, 1845. According to available records, no children were conceived in the Holmes marriage during the Prophet's lifetime. Drawing additional conclusions is impossible due to a lack of documentation.

The following letter written by Edwin Mace, born in Fillmore 1858 at the age of 70.

Dear Prest Ivens
                According to request will say that my parents told me when rather a small boy that Josephine Henry as she was called, or Will King's mother was a daughter of Joseph Smith the prophet. That her mother Margrett(Creighton) had been married to The prophet and later married Andrew Henry who at that time was keeping the Postoffice in Fillmore and with whom I was well aquainted-both he and his wife. He also sold liquor or kept a kind of a saloon. I would think him to be partly Irish or a farmer. He was a large heavy set man, with deep red hair, a sandy rough beard, freckle face, and a coarce harsh voice; uncouth in his manners, and talk and unjentalmanly. His wife rather refined and lady like who looked more like an American. Her daughter Josephine was rather delicate in looks very refined and polite;-as is Will King and his sister Lilly; who married I.N.Hinckly who now lives on 1st.West and near 2nd North.There was a sister Josie who all like Will King resembled their mother Josephine also Sam King a brother to Will.

        Josephine in the yr 1844 the yr of the martyrdom. I also get this information from Lilly Hinckley. Josephine's birth may have been near enough a birth of a child of Andrew Henry's,(had he of had one) that he could partly lay claim to Josephine. You Prest Ivens can figure. Josephine grew up a playmate to one Arthur John Gab and adopted son to Andrew Henry. Now then is Andrew childless or not. I well remember one Brother William Felshaw a close neighbor to my father in Fillmore. They were so intimate that what one knew the other seemed to know also. I was also intimately aquainted with his daughter Julia all my life.When a widow she married Clarance Merrill. After having been married to Truscett and a man Rudd by name Culy made her home in Fillmore and later moved to Sugar house ward in S.L.C. I had lately moved to S.L.C. while she was living in Sugar house Ward. By this time I was getting to be near the age of 60 was married in S.L.C. to a Miss Clark who had lived here, and we used to visit July in Sugar hs Ward so I did not hesitate telling telling her privately what I had learned about Josephine Henry(as she was called). Julia ridiculed the thot of Josephine being a daughter of Andrew and so did I (as well as our parents)This being the first time I had ever told any body.

        I think she was surprised at me knowing what she had also learned;but talked to me freely;but was very careful not to be overheard;also made me a confident while talking about other things which I had not heard of.I talked with Julia several times and the last time not long before her death;not long before the death of Seymour B.Young I related to him what had been told me. I had been very intimate with Seymour and told him there was a person who would perhaps almost give her little finger(if such was the custom)to learn what I had told him;but she would not hear it from me;but sorry she did.I later or near that time heard a middle aged man.telling a croud of about a half dozen persons while grouped in the tabernacle yard and while Sam King was approaching, do you know who that man is; He is a grandson of Jos. Smith the prophet,but said he,I don't suppose there is a half dozen persons who knows it. My father worked on the Nauvoo temple until finished.He and Mother saw the Prophet and hid his bro Hyrum in their blood stained clothes after they had been fetched home and later heard Prest Young's sermon at which time the mantle of Jos.came upon him. He was sent to Fillmore by Brigham Young after reaching S.L.C.where he worked on the Statehouse until finished. I again repeat that I knew as well as Julia seemed to know that Josephine was not a daughter of Andrew Henry; and by all appearance and inquiry not even a relative.

Photo of Edwin Mace typescript, 1928. Used by permission, Utah State Historical Society. All rights reserved.

the typescript was made. The resulting document is comprised of one full single-spaced typed page with six typed words on a second sheet.

The Mace document discusses the possibility that a daughter of Margaret Creighton Henry named "Josephine" was fathered by Joseph Smith. The crucial sentence is: "My parents told me when rather a small boy that Josephine Henry as she was called or Will King's mother was a daughter of Joseph Smith the prophet."[112] Both families, the Maces and the Henrys, settled in Fillmore, Utah, in the early 1850s, so Edwin's parents would have been familiar with Josephine from the time she was about six through her teen years. Mace added his personal conviction that "Josephine was not a daughter of Andrew Henry; and by all appearances and inquiry not even a relative," although he did not claim to see a resemblance to the dead Prophet either.

A review of Mace's complete statement identifies three observations supporting that Joseph Smith fathered a daughter with Margaret Creighton. First is hearsay evidence from the author, Edwin Mace, that his "parents told" him. We have no way of knowing why they might have been privy to such a secretive relationship, especially in light of the absence of any other source to substantiate the claim. Second is the child's name: Josephine. Third, Edwin asserts that Josephine did not look like her father, Andrew Henry.

Records indicate that Andrew Henry, a twenty-seven-year-old carpenter from Drum, County Sligo, Ireland, who had joined the Church in 1837, was serving a mission to Great Britain in 1843, where he met and married Margaret Creighton, a twenty-six-year-old convert from Saintsfield, County Down, Ireland. On May 26, 1843, Andrew Henry recorded in his journal: "I went to Belfast and there got married to Sister Margaret Creighton of Hillsborough, and returned the same day."[113] Their first child, Josephine, was born July 8, 1844, with conception occurring approximately October 15, 1843, five months after their wedding. For Joseph Smith to be Josephine's biological father, Margaret must have been in Nauvoo near that date. However, according to the transcript of his diary, Andrew was still in the Liverpool area on August 23, 1843.[114] Parnell Hinckley, who wrote the history of Andrew and Margaret, recorded, "After Andrew's marriage as recorded in his diary, he spent six fruitless weeks as a missionary with his uncles and cousins and friends

---

112. Edwin Mace, Letter to [President Anthony] Ivens [sic], [no day or month] 1928.

113. Andrew Henry, quoted in Parnell Hinckley, *The Henrys and the Kings: Incidents Taken from the Lives of Andrew Henry, Margaret Creighton Henry, Josephine King Thornley, Samuel A. King, William Henry King, Lillian King Hinckley, William King, Thomas Rice King, Matilda Robison King*, 50. The author does not identify the location of the journal nor have I been able to locate it.

114. Ibid., 55.

in and around Sligo, Ireland. . . . The couple left England for America early in the year of 1844. . . . A baby girl was born to her in Nauvoo June 8, 1844."[115]

Accordingly, the timeline makes it impossible for Joseph Smith to have been Josephine's biological father. Even if Parnell Hinckley's additional history was inaccurate, Henry's journal places him in England on August 23, 1843, giving them insufficient time to have immigrated to Nauvoo and for Joseph Smith to be Josephine's father. The average length of a sea voyage from Liverpool to New Orleans, the most common port of entry for emigrating Saints in 1843, varied depending upon weather delays. However, at least two months was generally required. For example, Brigham Young, Heber C. Kimball, and John Taylor left Liverpool England on April 20, 1841, but did not arrive in Nauvoo until July 1.[116] In addition, there is no record of a sealing or any special relationship between Joseph and Margaret; in fact, available records fail to document that she was ever personally introduced to the Prophet.

Historian Larry R. King has researched the evidence in writing his family history and finds even more ambiguity:

> There is no information available on when Andrew and Margaret left England or when they arrived in Nauvoo. Based on Church records, three ships left England between August 23, 1843, and early 1844 with Mormon emigrants. The third carrying a group of Irish Saints.
>
> From these dates, it would appear to have been improbable for Josephine to have been conceived in Nauvoo and born there July 1844. For this to have occurred, Andrew and Margaret would have had to have reached Nauvoo by September or perhaps October 1843, but the earliest possible ship arriving in Nauvoo after Andrew's latest journal entry in Ireland, is November 11, 1843. The ship first landed in New Orleans on October 27, 1843 and the dating difference is the time the passengers spent traveling on board, but there are only 188 people accounted for. This leaves nearly a hundred people whose names have not been discovered by historians.
>
> A second thought that might be considered is the changing of the actual birthday of Josephine to create an illusion. This may sound farfetched, but stranger things happened in Nauvoo to maintain the confidentiality of Joseph's plural marriages. Along with this idea is the possibility [that] some diary entries may have been changed. The diary we have to work from is not the original, but a transcription. Furthermore, there are no known ship passenger records for the Henrys, there are no records confirming their marriage in Ireland in May 1843, and there are no known records in the LDS Church Archives identifying Andrew as a missionary in Ireland.[117]

---

115. Ibid., 55, 65.

116. Elden Jay Watson, ed., *Manuscript History of Brigham Young, 1801–1844*, April 20, 1841; *History of the Church* 4:381.

117. Larry R. King, *The Kings of the Kingdom: The Life of Thomas Rice King and His*

While all available evidence seems to contradict the possibility that Josephine could have been engendered in Nauvoo by Joseph Smith (or by Andrew Henry, for that matter), the documentation is not conclusive. What seems apparent, however, is that Edwin Mace's confidence in his 1928 statement may exceed its actual historical credibility.

Charles Edmund Richardson, Mary Ann Darrow, and Fredrick Walter Cox

One additional historical narrative suggests that Latter-day Saints in Utah practiced a form of sexual polyandry with "proxy husbands" being called to father children for missionaries who were serving in the field or for men who were sterile (see Volume 3, Chapter 14).[118] It involves the case of Charles Edmund Richardson and his legal wife, Mary Ann Darrow Richardson. Prior to their 1853 baptisms, they were members of a religious group that taught that only two children were permitted. After the births of their daughter Emma (b. 1841) and son George (b. 1846), Edmund submitted to a surgical procedure that rendered him sterile. Brigham Young sealed them in 1857 and counseled them to have more children who would be born "in the covenant." They explained their situation and sought his counsel. He explained to Edmund that any added children for him would have to come by proxy. Edmund's biographers quoted President Young: "You will need to give Mary Ann a civil divorce and allow her to have a civil marriage with another man. Any issue from such a marriage would belong to you because you and Mary Ann are sealed for eternity. This is possible only because the Lord has restored polygamy in time to help you."[119]

Their biographers outline how they overcame this huge trial of faith: "As governor of the State of Utah, Brigham Young granted Mary Ann Darrow Richardson a civil divorce from her husband Edmund Richardson. Then, on January 9, 1858, he performed a civil marriage between Mary Ann and Fredrick Walter Cox. . . . Edmund voluntarily moved away but sent regular checks or alimony to support his family."[120] Mary Ann bore two children during the next three years. According to family tradition, shortly after the second

---

Family, 317.

118. Lawrence Foster, *Religion and Sexuality: Three American Communal Experiments of the Nineteenth Century*, 163–64; Lawrence Foster, "Sex and Prophetic Power: A Comparison of John Humphrey Noyes, Founder of the Oneida Community, with Joseph Smith, Jr., the Mormon Prophet," 79; Quinn, "Evidence for the Sexual Side of Joseph Smith's Polygamy," MHA.

119. Annie R. Johnson and Elva R. Shumway, *Charles Edmund Richardson, Man of Destiny*, 28.

120. Ibid., 29.

child's birth on January 26, 1861, Edmund returned, and Brigham Young divorced her from Fredrick Walter Cox, remarrying her to Edmund.[121]

D. Michael Quinn has recently pointed out a few minor mistakes in the conventional family history presented above regarding the Richardson-Darrow-Cox relationship.[122] A primary concern for Quinn is whether a civil divorce and remarriage occurred. He points out that Brigham Young may not have been authorized to grant a legal divorce between Richardson and Darrow and to perform a legal marriage between Darrow and Fredrick Cox on January 9, 1858. Quinn correctly notes that a civil marriage between Darrow and Cox was an impossibility, because Cox was already legally married. Also, officially replaced as governor on April 12, 1858, by Alfred Cumming, Brigham Young would not have possessed authority as governor to perform a civil remarriage reuniting Richardson and Darrow in 1861.

While Quinn's observations require a rewording of the historical narrative, none of the participants would have doubted that Brigham Young's priesthood office allowed him to cancel and perform "time only" priesthood-sanctioned marriages, irrespective of the status of previous legal matrimonies. Joseph Smith performed the first such priesthood marriage on November 24, 1835, between Lydia Goldthwaite Bailey and Newell Knight. Lydia had not been legally divorced from her civil husband.[123] Priesthood marriages for time were considered even more valid to Church members than civil contracts and would not have affected the "eternity" portion of the sealing between Richardson and Darrow. In other words, in a strange series of priesthood marriages and cancellations, Richardson and Darrow were sealed for "time and eternity" on April 20, 1857.[124] Then in 1858, using the same priesthood authority, Brigham Young cancelled the "time" portion of that sealing and proceeded to marry Darrow to Cox "for time only" in order to permit her to conceive more children. In 1861, he canceled the Darrow/Cox union and performed a new priesthood marriage for time between Richardson and Darrow, thereby converting an "eternity only" sealing back into "time and eternity." Showing, as Quinn deftly does, that Brigham Young did not have legal author-

---

121. Ibid., 32–34; see also Jeff Richins, *After the Trial of Your Faith: The Story of Edmund and Mary Ann Richardson*, 267–326; Clare B. Christensen, *Before and after Mt. Pisgah*, 233–34.

122. Quinn, "Evidence for the Sexual Side of Joseph Smith's Polygamy," Expanded version, 68–70 note 196.

123. Lydia's legal husband had deserted her three years previously. Newel Knight, "Autobiography and journal [ca. 1846]"; William G. Hartley, "Newel and Lydia Bailey Knight's Kirtland Love Story and Historic Wedding," 6–22; M. Scott Bradshaw, "Joseph Smith's Performance of Marriages in Ohio," 23–68; Gregory Prince, *Power from on High*, 182.

124. Annie R. Johnson and Elva R. Shumway, *Charles Edmund Richardson, Man of Destiny*, 26.

ity to perform these marriages is of little consequence when priesthood power was deemed by all concerned to be superior and more than sufficient.

On October 17, 1859, Richardson and Darrow "met at the Endowment House in Salt Lake City, received their endowments and had their sealing repeated as the prophet had said any couple desiring to be sealed in the Endowment House could do."[125] Kathryn Daynes gives a slightly different version saying that Richardson "returned and took his wife to Salt Lake to be sealed again for eternity in the Endowment house."[126] Doubtless both were anxious to receive their endowments and be resealed for eternity in the Endowment House. Neither ordinance would have conflicted with the "for time" priesthood marriage she had experienced with Cox or the eternal sealing between her and Richardson.[127]

D. Michael Quinn concludes that the Richardson-Darrow-Cox interaction included polyandrous sexuality: "The known and knowable evidence indicates that the Richardson-Darrow-Cox marriages, cohabitations, and births constituted sexual polyandry in pioneer Utah."[128] He bases this conclusion on the observations discussed above and upon a "most crucial fact"—namely, the 1860 Manti, Utah, census, enumerated on June 1, lists Edmund Richardson as an occupant of the Richardson home where Mary Ann had continued to live even while married to Cox.[129] Mary Ann's second child was conceived approximately May 5, 1860, less than three weeks prior to the census visit of the marshal (or his assistant). It is unlikely that she would have been aware of her pregnancy on June 1. Accordingly, Quinn writes: "It seems very probable that Edmund resumed cohabiting with his wife months before she conceived Fredrick's second child and months before the census-taker's visit."[130]

Quinn's assumption that Edmund was then cohabiting with Mary Ann on June 1, 1860, is problematic for several reasons. First, the 1860 "Instructions to U.S. Marshals" regarding the census records states that the census is to include "the name of every free person in each family, of every age, including

---

125. Ibid., 32.

126. Daynes, *More Wives Than One*, 81.

127. Quinn asserts that through this Endowment House sealing "Edmund Richardson re-asserted his own spiritual rights to his 'former' wife." Quinn, "Evidence for the Sexual Side of Joseph Smith's Polygamy," Expanded version, 69 note 196. The eternal sealing between Mary Ann Darrow Richardson and Edmund Richardson was never cancelled, so Quinn's reference to her as his "former wife," would be referring to the temporary separation they experienced during her "time" marriage to Cox.

128. Ibid., 70 note 196; emphasis Quinn's.

129. 1860 U.S. Census, Manti, Sanpete County, Utah, Population Schedule, I, census information taken June 1, 1860; quoted in Daynes, *More Wives Than One*, 251–52 note 79.

130. Quinn, "Evidence for the Sexual Side of Joseph Smith's Polygamy," 70 note 196.

the names of those temporarily absent on a journey, visit, or for the purposes of education."[131] Accordingly, Edmund might have been living in the home as Quinn asserts, or his name may have been included even though he was "temporarily absent," living elsewhere as the family tradition supports. Doubtless, Mary Ann and Edmund considered their separation "temporary," and there was no change in ownership of the home. So to assume that Edmund was physically present in the house on June 1 is not justified.

Second, the Richardson family tradition describes a genuine separation, not cohabitation with two husbands. Annie R. Johnson and Elva R. Shumway wrote that, after her marriage to Cox, "As Mary Ann watched Edmund drive away into the loneliness of the next few years, she whispered these words after him: 'Greater love hath no man than this, that he giveth his life for another.'"[132] It is not clear whether this somewhat dramatic statement was part of the original family story or whether the biographers added it. In either case, such a reaction seems inconsistent with a sexually polyandrous relationship.

Third, it is probable that Edmund's sterility was due to an orchiectomy (surgical removal of the testicles), which would have also eliminated endogenous testosterone and his testosterone-based sex drive.[133] That he, or Mary Ann, who was cohabiting with Fredrick Cox, would have sought conjugal relations requires evidence, which is lacking.

Fourth, in a private council in December 1847 just a week before the reorganization of the First Presidency when Heber C. Kimball became first counselor, he anathematized such relations, "[T]here has been a doctrine taught that a man has can [sic] act as Proxy for another when absent—it has been practiced and it is known—& its damnable."[134] Another account of the same meeting quotes Elder Kimball, "[W]hat damnable doctrines are tau[gh]t that men may be proxy for others, [for] I wo[u]d, rather have my head brought to the block than do these things."[135] Five years later Brigham Young taught that a "woman having more husbands than one . . . [was] not known to the law."[136] In other words, there was no doctrinal justification for the scenario described by Quinn, a scenario that was "damnable" according to Heber C. Kimball and "not known to the law" according to Brigham Young. Therefore, the only

---

131. *Eighth Census, United States—1860; Act of Congress of Twenty-Third May, 1850. Instructions to U.S. Marshals. Instructions to Assistants,* Washington: Geo. W. Bowman, 1860, 14.

132. Johnson and Shumway, *Charles Edmund Richardson,* 29.

133. Vasectomies were performed in the mid-nineteenth century, but not for sterilization. See http://en.wikipedia.org/wiki/Vasectomy (accessed August 11, 2012).

134. *Minutes of the Apostles of the Church of Jesus Christ of Latter-day Saints, 1835–1893,* December 21, 1847, 160.

135. Ibid., 157.

136. Brigham Young, *Journal of Discourses,* 1:361, August 1, 1852.

context for the relationship would have been adultery, which would have been rejected by pious Latter-day Saints if ever proposed.[137]

Fifth, sexual polyandry is extraordinary in any society. Understandably, researchers would, like Quinn and Larry Foster, be motivated a hundred years later to investigate and report upon its novelty, if it actually occurred. Yet to assume that it happened, given that no one mentioned it in any context during the century afterwards, seems unjustifiable. In all, the preponderance of evidence does not support sexual polyandry between Mary Ann Darrow and her eternal husband, Edmund Richardson, and her "for time only" husband, Fredrick Cox.

Other problems can be identified with the idea that "proxy husbands" were ever called to take the place of missionaries in their families while the missionary served in the mission field. No manuscript has been found documenting the existence of even one such Church-sanctioned relationship. Husbands called on missions were undoubtedly daunted by the challenges confronting them as missionaries, traveling across the country and perhaps the world, enduring persecutions and deprivations, all to preach the gospel. How much greater would the sacrifices have been if, as the priesthood leader extended a missionary call, he also explained that a stay-at-home man would be providing maintenance for his wife and having children with her that would be part of the missionary's family? It seems highly unlikely that either the missionary or his wife would have accepted, let alone welcomed, such a process or that, even if they had initially accepted it, the missionary could have seamlessly resumed family life upon his return home, that ward members and older children would not have marked this odd arrangement, and that their reflections, commentary, and justifications or critiques would not have become part of the documentary record.

Additional Evidence from D. Michael Quinn

One of the firmest proponents of the position that Joseph Smith practiced sexual polyandry may be the accomplished scholar D. Michael Quinn.[138] He was the commentator at Mormon History Association annual meeting in Calgary, Canada, on June 29, 2012, in a session at which I presented a paper, "Joseph Smith's Sexual Polyandry and the Emperor's New Clothes: On Closer Inspection, What Do We Find?"[139] A few weeks later he expanded his response into a seventy-one page essay of over 10,000 words.[140]

---

137. For example, Apostle George A. Smith taught on October 8, 1869: "A plurality of husbands is wrong," *Journal of Discourses*, 13:40.

138. See, for example, D. Michael Quinn, *The Mormon Hierarchy: Origins of Power*, 89.

139. Quinn, "Evidence for the Sexual Side of Joseph Smith's Polygamy," MHA.

140. D. Michael Quinn, "Evidence for the Sexual Side of Joseph Smith's Polygamy,"

In his remarks, he affirmed polyandrous sexuality between Joseph Smith and at least six women. In the cases of Miranda Nancy Johnson and Elvira Cowles, he simply repeated the allegations already discussed in this chapter. Additionally, using circumstantial evidence and several assumptions, he postulated that Mary Ann Angell Young (wife of Apostle Brigham Young), Leonora Cannon Taylor (wife of Apostle John Taylor), and Flora Ann Woodworth (wife of nonmember Carlos Gove) experienced polyandrous sexuality with the Prophet. These relationships, along with Quinn's assertions, will be discussed in Chapters 26 and 28. He also described three more possible polyandrous situations, two involving Joseph Smith and one involving Brigham Young.

In his presentation, Quinn quoted the statement of Mary Elizabeth Rollins Lightner found in Chapter 11: "I know he [Joseph Smith] had six wives and I have known some of them from childhood up. I knew he had three children. They told me. I think two are living today but they are not known as his children as they go by other names."[141] Quinn commented: "Such a claim would occur only if the child's mother thought that Joseph Smith had impregnated her. DNA testing can disprove a woman's assumption about paternity, but cannot disprove the 1905 claim of Mary Elizabeth Rollins Lightner that three already married women besides herself, had borne a child that they each assumed was produced by their literal relationship with the Prophet Joseph Smith, not by their legally recognized husbands with whom they were cohabiting."[142]

Quinn misquotes Mary Elizabeth slightly but significantly; she did not speak, either in the statement quoted or elsewhere in her discourse, about "already married women" (i.e. polyandrous spouses) who were sealed to the Prophet. Her comments referred to Joseph Smith's plural wives generally, without differentiating their ages, sealing dates, or legal marital status. It is unclear why any interpreter would assume she spoke exclusively of "already married" wives of the Prophet nor did Quinn explicate his unique view of her remarks.

Quinn also asserted sexual polyandry in the case of Martha McBride Knight (who will be discussed in Chapter 17). Martha's husband, Church Bishop Vinson Knight, died July 31, 1842. Sometime prior to that date, he married a polygamous wife with Joseph Smith's permission. Also, his legal wife, Martha McBride Knight, signed an affidavit on July 8, 1869, affirming her sealing to Joseph Smith "in the summer of 1842."[143] Regarding these

---

July [no day] 2012; expanded version. Both versions have the same title but the expanded version contains elements not presented in Calgary due to time limitations.

141. Mary Elizabeth Rollins Lightner, "Remarks" at Brigham Young University, April 14, 1905, 5.

142. Quinn, "Evidence for the Sexual Side of Joseph Smith's Polygamy," 4.

143. Martha McBride, July 8, 1869, copied in Joseph F. Smith, Affidavit Books, 2:36;

plural marriages, Quinn declared: "Bishop Vinson Knight came to receive a plural wife in exchange for allowing his legal wife to become Joseph Smith's polygamous wife. Whether we call it polyandry or proxy husbands, Knight died shortly after the ceremony in 1842."[144]

Although it is true that Vinson Knight did not seem to be an obvious candidate to become a polygamist insider, Quinn's reconstruction includes a troubling number of assumptions. First, he speculates that Martha was sealed to Joseph Smith prior to Vinson's death. Martha stated that she was sealed in the "summer of 1842," technically between June 20 and September 21. Since Vinson died July 31, Quinn assumes that the sealing occurred between June 20 and July 31, not afterwards during the weeks of August and September. In contrast to Quinn, Todd Compton found an August date in her obituary: "I assume that the marriage was in August. This date is corroborated by her obituary: 'in August, 1842, she was sealed to the Prophet, Joseph Smith in the Nauvoo Temple [sic.].'" Quinn ... opts for an early summer date for the marriage, which would give us one more polyandrous relationship. However, I prefer not to posit a polyandrous marriage unless evidence is conclusive, and the obituary supports the August date."[145]

Another problem stems from idea the that Joseph Smith would have required Vinson to give him Martha as a plural wife (or sexual companion) as a condition for Vinson to marry plurally. Most Nauvoo polygamists did not want to participate in polygamy in the first place. So to believe that Vinson would have been enticed by the offer of a plural wife in order to give Martha, his wife of sixteen years and with whom he had had eight children between 1827 and 1841, seems less plausible. That Martha would have acquiesced without complaint or comment is also somewhat difficult to believe.

In addition, the issue of sexuality between Joseph and Martha is pure speculation. According to Compton: "We know virtually nothing about what Martha's and Joseph's married life was like, and little is known about Martha's life in Nauvoo from the time of Vinson's death to Joseph's."[146] She is not one of the fourteen plural wives discussed in the previous chapter as possibly involved with the Prophet sexually.

In his MHA presentation, Quinn also mentioned another possible example of sexual polyandry involving Augusta Cobb who was sealed to Brigham Young on November 2, 1843. (See Chapter 27.) Quinn prefaced his remarks by saying: ""Now I'm going to discuss evidence of sexual polyandry that Brian

---

3:36. See also Joseph Fielding Smith, *Blood Atonement and the Origin of Plural Marriage*, 86.

144. Quinn, "Evidence for the Sexual Side of Joseph Smith's Polygamy," MHA.

145. Compton, *In Sacred Loneliness*, 724. He is citing Quinn *The Mormon Hierarchy: Extensions of Power*, 189.

146. Ibid., 371.

Hales has not discussed. . . . I must also say it is the first time I have discussed this with anyone, even in private, in forty years." Then he proceeded:

> Senior Apostle Brigham Young began performing ceremonies that united Joseph Smith in some way with women who were already married to other men. Then, on 2 November 1843, Joseph united Brigham with already-married Augusta Adams Cobb, who had abandoned "her husband and five of her children in Boston" to travel with Brigham to Nauvoo. Thus, this apostle had direct knowledge of whether sexual intercourse was authorized by the secret ceremony uniting an already-married man with a woman who was already married to another husband.[147]

It is unclear why Quinn included these comments in his discussion of sexual polyandry. While Augusta (and Brigham) apparently ignored her legal marriage as they were sealed in plural marriage and thereafter may have engaged in connubial relations, Augusta was obviously not experiencing polyandrous conjugal relations with her legal husband who was still in Boston. The Augusta Cobb-Brigham Young relationship could be classified as "ceremonial polyandry," but not "sexual polyandry."

In his expanded printed version, Quinn also referred to the account from Lucy Meserve Smith, plural wife of Apostle George A. Smith, that I quoted in Chapter 11: "[George A.] related to me the circumstance of calling on the Prophet one evening about 11, o clock, and he was out on the porch with a basin of water washing his hands, I said to him what is up, said Joseph one of my wives has just been confined and Emma was midwife and I have been assisting her. He said she had granted a no. of women for him."[148] Quinn asserts that the pregnant woman was a polyandrous wife: "In view of Emma Smith's general hostility toward her husband's other wives, it's impossible to imagine her acting as 'the Midwife' for a woman whose relationship to him Emma knew about. Second, it's difficult to imagine that the Church President's wife would give implicit sanction to the pregnancy of an unmarried woman by serving as her midwife. . . . Therefore, Lucy Meserve Smith's account of what her husband learned directly from the Prophet must refer to a childbearing woman who was another man's legal wife. Unaware that this woman was also Joseph's polygamous wife, Emma would not object to acting as midwife, especially for one of her friends—as many of these already-married women were."[149]

Quinn's interpretation is problematic. Emma participated in four plural marriages including those of Joseph to Sarah and Maria Lawrence, whom

---

147. Quinn, "Evidence for the Sexual Side of Joseph Smith's Polygamy," 24.

148. Lucy Meserve Smith, Statement, n.d., Wilford Wood Collection of Church Historical Materials, MS 8617, Reel 8, LDS Church History Library; internal reference within collection: 4-N-b-2.

149. Quinn, "Evidence for the Sexual Side of Joseph Smith's Polygamy," 7; emphasis Quinn's.

she allowed to live in the Mansion indefinitely. Lucy Walker recalled that on at least one occasion, Emma "kept guard at the door to prevent disinterested persons from intruding when these ladies [Joseph's plural wives] were in the house."[150] Also, William Clayton remembered that, regarding several of Joseph's plural wives, Emma "generally treated them very kindly."[151] Quinn's allegation that the pregnancy was of "an unmarried woman" is puzzling, since George A. Smith refers explicitly to a plural wife. Perhaps the least likely element of Quinn's reconstruction is that Emma might have been completely unaware of facts that were plain to George A. Smith.

In all, Quinn's verbal and written responses to my presentation at the 2012 Mormon History Association meeting constitute the best accumulation of circumstantial evidence that will probably ever be collected on the topic. However, his interpretations of the historical data are consistently problematic. In virtually every case, there is a tendency to link assumption to assumption, producing some creative and internally consistent interpretations, but which are, nonetheless, lacking in solid documentation. Also, his essay ignores the contradictory evidence that will be presented in the next three chapters. The remainder of Quinn's specific assertions, those that merit response, will be addressed throughout the chapters of this book as the individual plural wives are discussed.[152]

Overview of the Evidence

The preceding documents, D. Michael Quinn's additional arguments, and the cases of Sylvia Sessions Lyon and Mary Heron Snider (discussed in Chapters 13 and 16), constitute the primary evidence I have currently identified that support the existence of sexual polyandry in some of Joseph Smith's plural marriages. A review of these specific accounts reveals important weaknesses in plausibility, clarity, accuracy, and motives of those producing them. The willingness of the reader to assume or not assume specific behaviors is often paramount to making the sexual polyandry case valid. Even the more credible declarations fail to document concomitant conjugality with the woman's legal husband, which would be helpful and is often deemed necessary. In my judgment, none of Quinn's allegations or the ten narratives rises to the level of "probable" alleged polyandrous behavior and most are more accurately classed as "possible," "ambiguous" or "unlikely." This pattern of shaki-

---

150. Lucy Walker, qtd. in Andrew Jenson, "Plural Marriage," 230.
151. William Clayton, Affidavit, February 16, 1874.
152. See also Brian C. Hales, " A Response to D. Michael Quinn's, 'Evidence for the Sexual Side of Joseph Smith's Polygamy,'" unpublished manuscript, August 25, 2012.

ness in report after report has the "halo" effect of undermining credibility in the body of documents as a whole.

Comparing the reliability of these statements to those corroborating sexual relations in the Prophet's *non*-polyandrous plural marriages reveals interesting contrasts. Non-polyandrous sexuality is documented by reliable first-hand or second-hand accounts in twelve of Joseph Smith's plural marriages. (See Chapter 11 and Appendix E.) In contrast, none of these ten accounts of polyandrous sexuality meets the same criteria; their authors did not practice plural marriage, nor were they confidants of the Prophet. Only John C. Bennett and Mary Ettie V. Smith lived in Nauvoo and personally knew Joseph Smith. For the reasons outlined in Chapter 20, I have concluded that Bennett did not learn about polygamy directly from Joseph Smith. Mary Ettie's declaration was dated later in Utah. The remaining informants were distant observers, both geographically and chronologically. (See Table 12.2.)

"Given to Multiply and Replenish"

Several authors have written that a primary reason Joseph Smith restored the practice of plural marriage was to obey the divine commandment to "multiply and replenish the earth" with a righteous generation (D&C 132:63). For example, Todd Compton wrote, "The command to multiply and replenish the earth was part of the polygamy theology, so non-sexual marriage was generally not in the polygamous program, as Smith taught it."[153] George D. Smith took an unnuanced stance: "Celestial marriage was all about sex and children."[154] Similarly, Gary Bergera affirmed: "Some researchers have asserted that Smith never planned to engage in sexual activity with any of his 'polyandrous wives,' at least while they remained legally bound to their husbands. Those holding such a view must convincingly explain, as historian George D. Smith has pointed out, how the Mormon prophet hoped to accomplish the reproductive purpose of plural marriage without engaging in sexual activity with his polyandrous wives."[155]

It is true that Joseph Smith taught reproduction as one of the reasons for the establishment of plural marriage.[156] However, it is less clear how sexual poly-

---

153. Compton, *In Sacred Loneliness*, 12.

154. George D. Smith, "Persuading Men and Women to Join in Celestial Marriage," 161.

155. Gary James Bergera, "*Vox Joseph, Vox Dei*: Regarding Some of the Moral and Ethical Aspects of Joseph Smith's Practice of Plural Marriage," 42; see also Gary James Bergera, Review of "Newell G. Bringhurst and Craig L. Foster, eds., *The Persistence of Polygamy: Joseph Smith and the Origins of Mormon Polygamy*," 111.

156. D&C 132:63. See also Charles Lambert, "Autobiography," quoted in Danel W. Bachman, "The Authorship of the Manuscript of Doctrine and Covenants Section 132," 43 note 44; Helen Mar Kimball Whitney, *Why We Practice Plural Marriage*, 7.

TABLE 12.2
WITNESS CREDIBILITY OF POLYGYNOUS (NON-POLYANDROUS) SEXUAL
RELATIONS COMPARED TO WITNESSES OF POLYANDROUS SEXUAL RELATIONS

Author of Statement	Plural Wife?	Nauvoo Polygamist?	Friend of Joseph Smith?	Distant Observer?	Anti-Mormon?	Ambiguous Statement?
Polygynous (Non-Polyandrous) Sexuality (see Chapter 11)						
Benjamin F. Johnson		YES	YES			
Joseph B. Noble		YES	YES			
Emily Partridge	YES	YES	YES			
Almera Johnson	YES	YES	YES			
Lucy Walker	YES	YES	YES			
Sylvia Sessions	YES	YES	YES			
Malissa Lott	YES	YES	YES			
Eliza R. Snow	YES	YES	YES			YES
John Benbow			YES			YES
Joseph Robinson			YES			YES
Polyandrous Sexuality						
John C. Bennett			Yes/No	Yes/No	YES	Yes/No
William Hall				YES	YES	
Ann Eliza Webb				YES	YES	
Wilhelm Wyl				YES	YES	
Sarah Pratt via Wilhelm Wyl				Yes/No	YES	YES
Mary Ettie V. Smith				YES		
William Arrowsmith				YES	YES	YES
Phebe Holmes Welling				YES		YES
John Hyde				YES	YES	
Edwin Mace				YES		
Todd Compton				YES		

andry would enhance "the reproductive purpose of plural marriage." Being married and sexually active with two husbands would generally not increase the fertility of a woman. Obstetrician-gynecologist Steven L. Johnson explains:

> In medical terms, a woman is capable of conception for approximately twenty-four hours after ovulation (release of the egg from the ovary) that occurs midway through her menstrual cycle or, on average, one day out of twenty-eight. Sperm are viable up to seventy-two hours, together creating a three day window wherein a sexual intercourse might result in pregnancy. Sexual relations at other times will not result in conception or enhanced reproduction. Fertilization occurs when one sperm enters the single ovum that has been ovulated during that menstrual cycle. The average male will release 80 to 600 million viable sperm through sexual intercourse that are available to combine with that single egg. Given the already overwhelming ratio of sperm to egg, additional conjugal relations during that conception window increase the chance of conception minimally if at all. The introduction of a second sperm donor at that time is unnecessary and generally would have little or no effect on pregnancy rate of the woman.[157]

One exception to this observation occurs if one of the husbands is sterile. If, for any reason, his sperm are incapable of fertilizing the ovum, then the addition of a second sperm sample would greatly enhance conception. Accurate statistical data regarding male infertility in the nineteenth century is inherently difficult to obtain, but Margaret Marsh and Wanda Ronner, authors of *The Empty Cradle: Infertility in America from Colonial Times to the Present*, observed that, "historians have estimated that about 8 percent of the marriages in colonial New England were childless," of which perhaps a third would be due to the husband.[158] Today infertility affects about 5 percent of the male population.[159] Accordingly, in a small subgroup of infertile couples, sexual polyandry would increase conception.

This physiology was obviously unknown to Joseph Smith, but evidence indicates that, in the first half of the nineteenth century, sexual polyandry would not have been considered by social traditions and medical science as enhancing fertility. Physician T. Bell discussed the common beliefs regarding infertility or a lack of "fecundity" in an 1820 publication: "Fecundity [fertility] may be prevented by many causes: such as a connexion physically or morally unsuitable, too early marriage, peculiar character or manner of things, strong passions, caprices, regrets, the notion of preserving beauty, intemperance, an

---

157. Steven Lowell Johnson, M.D., email to Brian Hales, September 26, 2011; used by permission.

158. Margaret Marsh and Wanda Ronner, *The Empty Cradle: Infertility in America from Colonial Times to the Present*, 12.

159. Ibid.

abuse of pleasure, the embarrassment of a family, &c. In general, the most fecund women are of sanguine temperament ... passions, and more especially the abuse of pleasure, and the physical insuitablenes [sic] of individuals, are the most frequent causes of sterility."[160]

Similarly, in his 1841 book, *Elements of Obstetric Medicine*, Dr. David D. Davis wrote: "It is a general opinion, and one it would seem well founded, that excess in the use of the means of impregnation is upon the whole unfavourable to the interests of fecundity. Hence the almost uniform sterility of the more public prostitutes."[161] In addition, we recall George Reynolds's reasons for why Joseph Smith's plural wives did not conceive as "the reason generally assigned by the wives themselves is, that owing to the peculiar circumstances by which they were surrounded, they were so nervous and in such constant fear that they did not conceive."[162] The women themselves viewed their own nervousness and fear as the reasons they did not conceive, two emotions that would likely have accompanied any polyandrous sexual relations at that time and place.

We do not know what scientific beliefs Joseph Smith and Nauvoo polygamists embraced regarding impregnation, but it seems likely they would have espoused the common perceptions that viewed unconventional sexual relations (like polyandrous conjugality) as antagonistic to fertility and therefore as hampering the mandate to "multiply and replenish" the earth. In addition, more than a century later, modern medicine has verified that sexual polyandry would generally contribute little to enhance a woman's fertility rate.

Summary

To date, authors chronicling Joseph Smith's plural marriages have documented the presence of ceremonial polyandry where a woman has experienced two marriage ceremonies, usually one legal and one religious. However, no one has provided credible evidence demonstrating the presence of sexual polyandry in any of those unions. The ten documents reviewed in this chapter along with the cases of Sylvia Sessions Lyon and Mary Heron Snider, constitute the most convincing documentation currently available. Nevertheless, whether grouped together or examined separately, they fail to provide even one convincing confirmation. These evidences might represent supplemen-

---

160. T. Bell, M.D., *Kalogynomia or the Laws of Female Beauty: Being the Elementary Principles of that Science*, 221.

161. David D. Davis, M.D., *Elements of Obstetric Medicine with the Description and Treatment of Some of the Principal Diseases of Children*, 369.

162. George Reynolds, Letter to H. Neidig, June 7, 1892, Wilford Woodruff Letterbooks, 1352, 10: 350.

tal corroboration that could be recruited to augment the credibility of other more reliable accounts. But the absence of even a single credible source that was close in proximity geographically and/or chronologically to the reported behavior, creates evidentiary challenges for all supporters.

While two accomplished polygamy researchers, Larry Foster and D. Michael Quinn, have presented the case of Mary Ann Darrow Richardson's marriages to Charles Edmund Richardson and Fredrick Cox as sexual polyandry, a close examination of documents supports, rather, a strange sequence of consecutive priesthood cancellations and marriages that did not include polyandrous conjugality.

In his well-researched essay, D. Michael Quinn has accumulated much circumstantial evidence, accompanied by his own interpretations, to assert the existence of sexual polyandry in several of Joseph Smith's plural marriages to legally wed women. However, this compilation once again lacks even one solid piece of documentation and manifests multiple analytic weaknesses.

Doubtless the reason commonly given (and developed in greater detail during the Utah period as polygamy became more widely practiced)—that plural marriage (polygyny) would fulfill the commandment "to multiply and replenish the earth" (D&C 132:63)—played a role in the development of polygamy theology, even as early as Nauvoo. However, Nauvoo pluralists would probably not have viewed such unconventional sexual relations as increasing fertility or assisting in replenishing the earth, a physiological reality verified a century later by medical science.

Chapter 13

Joseph Smith and Sylvia Sessions Lyon: Polyandry or Polygyny?

Todd Compton, in researching *In Sacred Loneliness*, reviewed the historical documentation supporting sexual polyandry and concluded: "In only one case do we have evidence."[1] That "one case" has been considered a firmly documented example of polyandrous sexual relations with the implication that conjugality was probably present in some or all of the rest. The case involved Joseph Smith, Sylvia Sessions Lyon, her legal husband Windsor Lyon, and her daughter Josephine Rosetta Lyon. Other authors have agreed with this interpretation.[2]

Evidence of Sexual Polyandry

Sylvia Sessions wed Windsor Lyon in a civil ceremony on April 21, 1838. Together they moved to Nauvoo and were comfortably established there by July 1840. At some point thereafter, Sylvia was sealed to the Prophet. Relevant questions about that relationship are: (1) When did that sealing occur? and (2) What was the status of her marriage to Windsor at that moment?

Despite the fact that Sylvia Sessions Lyon's sealing as a plural wife of Joseph Smith was known as early as 1869, it appears that Compton was the first author to consider whether she participated in polyandrous sexual relations with the Prophet.[3] Since his 1997 *In Sacred Loneliness*, most other writ-

---

1. Todd Compton, "Truth, Honesty and Moderation in Mormon History: A Response to Anderson, Faulring, and Bachman's Reviews of *In Sacred Loneliness*, Section titled: "Sexuality in the Polyandrous Marriages."

2. George D. Smith, *Nauvoo Polygamy: "... but we called it celestial marriage,"* 100; Compton, *In Sacred Loneliness*, 21, 183; D. Michael Quinn, The *Mormon Hierarchy: Origins of Power*, 642.

3. Three years prior to Compton's book, D. Michael Quinn made the same direct observation without providing any supportive evidence or argumentation. Quinn, *The Mormon Hierarchy: Origins of Power*, 642.

ers have followed this lead, holding that Josephine Rosetta Lyon, daughter of Sylvia Sessions, was conceived under polyandrous conditions.[4]

As support that Josephine was indeed the biological daughter of the Prophet, she signed the following statement in 1915:

> Fisher, Josephine Rosetta, a daughter of Sylvia Porter Sessions Lyon, was born in Nauvoo, Ill, Feb. 8, 1844, and when Mr. Lyon, her mother's husband died in Iowa, she was about five years old. Later her mother married Ezekiel Clark, a non-Mormon, who remained in the States when her mother migrated to Utah in 1854, taking her daughter Josephine R. and three children by Clark with her. Josephine was ten years old when she located in Bountiful, where she grew up and when 19 ½ years old she was married to John Fisher Aug. 15, 1863, John Straker performing the marriage ceremony. She is the mother of ten children, five whom were still living in 1915. Her husband died Oct. 23, 1905 at Bountiful. On the 24th of February, 1915, Elder Andrew Jenson, [Stake] Pres. Joseph H. Grant and Irvin Frederich Fisher (son of Sister Fisher) visited Sister Fisher at her home at Bountiful, on which occasion she gave the following testimony:
>
> Just prior to my mothers death in 1882 she called me to her bedside and told me that her days on earth were about numbered and before she passed away from mortality she desired to tell me something which she had kept as an entire secret from me and from others until no but which she now desired to communicate to me. She then told me that I was the daughter of the Prophet Joseph Smith, she having been sealed to the Prophet at the time that her husband Mr. Lyon had was out of fellowship with the Church. She also told me that she was sealed to the Prophet about the same time that Zina D. Huntington and Eliza R. Snow were thus sealed. In conclusion mother told me not to make her statement to me too public, as it might cause trouble and arouse unpleasant curiosity. I have followed her advice, and I am relating the facts to-day practically the first time, responding to the \ request/ desire or desire of one of the assistant Church Historians.
>
> Signed in the presence of Jos H Grant, I. F. Fisher, <u>Andrew Jenson</u>
>
> [signed] Josephine R. Fisher
> Bountiful, Utah, Feb. 24, 1915[5]

Not all researchers agree that this statement clearly declares Josephine to be the literal daughter of the Prophet. It is true that a few words are somewhat ambiguous and could possibly be interpreted to mean that Josephine was to be

---

4. Brian C. Hales, "The Joseph Smith—Sylvia Sessions Plural Sealing: Polyandry or Polygyny?" 41–57.

5. Josephine R. Fisher, Affidavit, February 24, 1915. See also Danel W. Bachman, "A Study of the Mormon Practice of Plural Marriage before the Death of Joseph Smith," 141; Richard S. Van Wagoner, "Mormon Polyandry in Nauvoo," 78 note 12.

Signed copy of Josephine Lyon Fisher's statement. Courtesy of the LDS Church History Library.

Joseph Smith's daughter only in eternity, without implying an actual paternal connection. Rex E. Cooper notes:

> I find the evidence to be less convincing on three different grounds. First, although the possibility that Josephine was a daughter of Joseph Smith was being discussed as early as 1905, the statement reports a conversation that took place twenty-three years before in 1882. Second, since the statement is transmitted through Andrew Jenson, it is a third-hand account of Sylvia P. Sessions's statement. And third, the statement is unclear about what it meant to be "a daughter of Joseph Smith." For example, because of his

Josephine Lyon Fisher. Photos courtesy of Clark Layton.

mother's matrimonial sealing to Joseph Smith, Heber J. Grant was regarded as a "son of Joseph Smith" even though he was born twelve years after the prophet's death.[6]

However, other details support that Josephine was the Prophet's biological offspring. If no biological connection existed between Josephine and Joseph Smith, it is strange that Sylvia would wait until her deathbed to dramatically reveal to Josephine that the Prophet was her father only in eternity.

Theologically, if Josephine were sealed as a daughter to Joseph Smith but was unrelated genetically, then Sylvia's other offspring born after the Prophet's death would share the same status. Yet none of those children reported a similar revelation from their dying mother.

Two of these children were sons of Sylvia and her legal husband, Windsor. Byron Windsor Lyon was born September 4, 1847, and David Carlos Lyon was born on August 8, 1848. However, these children would be sealed to Joseph Smith in eternity according to the Levirate law. After the martyrdom, dozens of women were also sealed to Joseph by proxy. All the children born to them—scores of offspring—would share the same relationship as Josephine with the Prophet, if she were not his biological daughter. And under the law of adoption as then practiced by Brigham Young, many Church members were subsequently adopted to Joseph Smith. To be sealed as one of his descendants was unexceptional. It conferred no unique or unusual status, required no special deathbed announcement, had no reason to be kept secret during most of the child's lifetime, and would not have been a matter of interest to Church historians.

---

6. Rex E. Cooper, *Promises Made to the Fathers: Mormon Covenant Organization*, 144 note 1.

Josephine's name also suggests the pattern of naming a child for its parent (with appropriate adaptation to communicate the child's sex). However, if the relationship producing the child had been an immoral connection—either because it was polyandrous or adulterous, then it seems reckless to give her a name that could raise suspicions concerning a possible relationship to the Prophet. In addition, if Sylvia sought to keep her relationship with Joseph Smith a secret from Windsor, as some writers have proposed,[7] then naming the child "Josephine" would actually invite Windsor's potential distrust and fears. Josephine's name, if it is indeed an indicator of her paternity, suggests that the relationship was considered legitimate by insiders and that Windsor was aware of that association. Nor was there anything inherently sinister in the name. Dozens of Nauvoo children, male and female, were named "Joseph," sometimes "Joseph Smith," although "Josephine" is rarer.

Sylvia Porter Sessions Lyon. Photo courtesy of Clark Layton.

It seems that some Church leaders became apprised of Sylvia's claims prior to Josephine's 1915 statement. In 1886, future BYU president George H. Brimhall recorded: "Went to Spanish Fork . . . Evening had a talk with Father Hales, who told me that it was said that Joseph Smith had a daughter named Josephine living in Bountiful, Utah . . . . Soon the contemporaries of the Prophet Joseph will be all gone."[8]

Similarly, in 1905, Angus Cannon, president of Salt Lake Stake, wrote this report concerning an interview he had with Joseph Smith III:

> Before we parted . . . I said, "Joseph, you have asked where is the issue in evidence of your father's having married plural wives." I will now refer you to one case where it was said by the girl's grandmother that your father has a daughter born of a plural wife. The girl's grandmother was Mother [Patty] Sessions, who lived in Nauvoo and died here in the valley. She was the grand-

---

7. Van Wagoner, "Mormon Polyandry in Nauvoo," 81; Todd Compton, *In Sacred Loneliness: The Plural Wives of Joseph Smith*, 179.

8. George H. Brimhall, "Diary of George H. Brimhall," Vol. 1, January 1, 1888. The most likely identity of "Father Hales" is Charles Henry Hales (1817–89)—incidentally, my great-great grandfather. Josephine Lyon married John Fisher on August 15, 1863. The Hales and Fisher families both emigrated from Kent, England, and may have known each other in Great Britain.

daughter of Mother Sessions. That girl, I believe, is living today in Bountiful, north of this city. I heard Prest. Young, a short time before his death, refer to the report and remark that he had never seen the girl, but he would like to see her for himself, that he might determine if she bore any likeness to your father. Joseph hereupon said, "Did you ever go and see her?" "No sir, I did not." "Then there is where you have not done what you ought to have done. You should have gone to see her for yourself, and so satisfied your own mind." I said, "The woman is now said to have a family of children, and I think she is still living.["] He replied, "I have heard of that case, but have understood that the girl was born more than a year after my father's death. I said, "I think you are mistaken or have been misinformed regarding this girl, for I have been told that her grandmother, Aunt Patty Sessions, asserts that the girl was born within the time after your father was said to have taken the mother."[9]

While all researchers do not agree, Josephine's affidavit provides the most credible known account of Joseph Smith's progeny from any of his plural wives.[10] As discussed in Chapter 11, I believe Josephine is one of the two documentable offspring from Joseph Smith's plural marriages and the only one to live to adulthood.

Dating Sylvia's Sealing

Many writers use Sylvia's 1882 disclosure to Josephine regarding her alleged paternity as evidence that Joseph Smith was having sexual relations with his "polyandrous" wives. Using the dating sequence of her marriages as described by Todd Compton might seem to support such a conclusion.[11] Compton gave a specific date for Sylvia's sealing to Joseph: "On February 8, when Sylvia was twenty-three, she was sealed to Joseph Smith."[12] Other authors have agreed.[13] The source of this information appears to be an unsigned document written in a notebook in 1869:

---

9. Angus Munn Cannon, "Statement of an Interview with Joseph Smith III, 1905, Regarding Conversation on October 12, 1905."

10. See also "Sylvia Porter Sessions Lyon Kimball," in Kate B. Carter, ed., *Our Pioneer Heritage*, 10:415.

11. Compton, *In Sacred Loneliness*, 179–83.

12. Ibid., 179; see also Todd Compton, "A Trajectory of Plurality: An Overview of Joseph Smith's Thirty-Three Plural Wives," 34.

13. Gary James Bergera, "Identifying the Earliest Mormon Polygamists, 1841–1844," 66; H. Michael Marquardt, *The Rise of Mormonism: 1816–1844*, 561; George D. Smith, "The Summer of 1842: Joseph Smith's Relationships with the 12 Wives He Married after His First Wife, Emma," 5; John S. Dinger, ed., *The Nauvoo City and High Council Minutes*, 431–32 note 77; Bachman, "A Study of the Mormon Practice of Plural Marriage before the Death of Joseph Smith, 350 #77; Quinn, *The Mormon Hierarchy:*

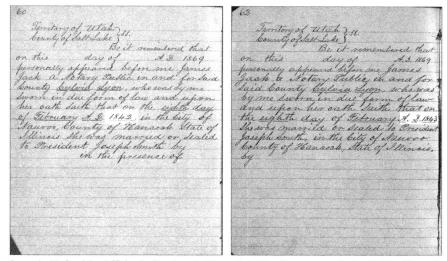

Joseph F. Smith Affidavit Books, 1:60 and 4:62. Courtesy of the LDS Church History Library.

> Territory of Utah   SS.
> County of Salt Lake
>   Be it remembered that on this [blank] day of [blank] A.D. 1869 personally appeared before me James Jack a Notary Public in and for Said County Cylvia Lyon [sic], who was by me sworn in due form of law and upon her oath Saith that on the eighth day of February A.D. 1842, in the City of Nauvoo, County of Hancock State of Illinois She was married or Sealed to President Joseph Smith by [blank] in the presence of [blank][14]

Several earlier historians, like Stanley S. Ivins or Fawn Brodie, did not specify a date for the sealing in their respective treatises on plural marriage.[15] It appears that the first person to list the February 8, 1842, date was Danel Bachman, but he also provided asterisks explaining that the document from which the date was taken was unsigned.[16] Compton also acknowledges that the document is "unfinished" (not specifically "unsigned") in a note, but in the text of *In Sacred Loneliness*, he uses the 1842 date without raising any questions about its reliability.[17]

Origins of Power, 587.
 14. Document mentioning Cylvia [sic] Lyons, Joseph F. Smith, Affidavit Books, 1:60.
 15. For Stanley S. Ivins's list, see Jerald Tanner and Sandra Tanner, *Joseph Smith and Polygamy*, 43; Fawn M. Brodie, *No Man Knows My History: The Life of Joseph Smith, the Mormon Prophet*, 486–87.
 16. Bachman, "A Study of the Mormon Practice of Plural Marriage," 108, 350, 354.
 17. Compton, *In Sacred Loneliness*, 179, 681–82.

On left: Joseph F. Smith. On right: Sitting: Lewis Bidamon (second husband of Emma Smith), Frederick G. Smith, Joseph Smith III. Standing left: David Hyrum Smith and Alexander Hale Smith. Both images courtesy Utah State Historical Society.

A second version of Sylvia's statement exists in a separate notebook and was apparently written at the same time. It contains similar wording and is also unsigned but has a different year (1843) for Sylvia's sealing to the Prophet.[18]

Whether Compton was aware of this important discrepancy is unclear from his writings.[19] Curiously, in a 1986 presentation, Andrew Ehat used the 1843 document but footnoted the 1842 affidavit.[20] An attempt to sort out these incongruities requires describing the affidavits compiled by Joseph F. Smith in 1869.

Joseph F. Smith's 1869 Affidavit Books

In the summer of 1869, Alexander Hale Smith and David Hyrum Smith, sons of Joseph and Emma Smith, traveled west as missionaries for the RLDS Church. On Sunday evening, August 8, they clashed with their Utah cousin, Apostle Joseph F. Smith, in the Fourteenth Ward meetinghouse in Salt Lake

---

18. Document mentioning Sylvia Lyon, unsigned and undated affidavit #1, in Joseph F. Smith, Affidavit Books, 1:60; unsigned and undated affidavit #2, in 4:62.

19. Compton, *In Sacred Loneliness*, 681–82; Todd Compton, "'Remember Me in My Affliction': Louisa Beaman and Eliza R. Snow Letters, 1849," 60; Bachman, "A Study of the Mormon Practice of Plural Marriage," 350 #77. Compton told me on July 22, 2008, that, in the early 1990s when he was researching at the LDS Church History Library, obtaining permission to view the four affidavit books took so long that he had only two hours to examine them on his final day.

20. Andrew F. Ehat, "Pseudo-Polyandry: Explaining Mormon Polygyny's Paradoxical Companion," 23.

Joseph Smith and Sylvia Sessions Lyon 357

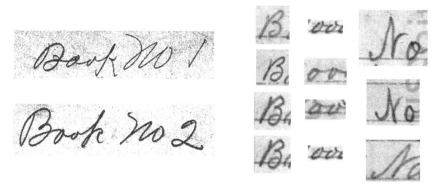

On left: Handwriting of an unknown scribe identifying two of the Affidavit Books as "Book No 1" and "Book No 2." On right: Letters cropped from the handwritten journal of Joseph F. Smith for October 31 and November 1, 1869, showing important differences. Courtesy LDS Church History Library.

City in a type of a debate.[21] Central to the discussion was whether the Prophet had practiced polygamy.

In the two months prior to Alexander and David's visit, Joseph F. Smith had accumulated thirty-five affidavits documenting the practice of polygamy in Nauvoo to dispute RLDS claims. Twenty-nine of them were recorded and notarized in each of two bound composition notebooks creating two nearly identical volumes. With the October 13, 1869, entries, both of these two books were full. The following March, Joseph F. Smith began two new record books of similar size and type where he recorded new testimonials and added transcriptions of the content of some affidavits on loose sheets that he had also collected. All of the affidavits were designed to prove that Joseph Smith taught and practiced plural marriage. (See Appendix C.)

At some point after 1869, an unidentified person, using a pencil, labeled one of the volumes "Book No 1" and another "Book No 2."[22] The other two books have been since labeled "Book No. 3" and "Book No. 4." Books 1 and 4 are nearly identical, as are Books 2 and 3.

Another distinguishing feature about Books 1 and 2 is an imprint stamped on the upper right corner of the first leaf that reads: "Joseph F. Smith, Salt Lake City, Utah," which is missing from Books 3 and 4. It seems likely that

---

21. Our Own Correspondent, "The Mormon Church War," *Daily Evening Bulletin* (San Francisco), September 1, 1869.

22. My comparison of the handwriting leads me to conclude that the words "Book 1" and "Book 2" were written by someone other than the books' compiler, Apostle Joseph F. Smith. See photograph.

Stamps "Joseph F. Smith, Salt Lake City, Utah" are found on the first page of Books 1 and 2 and are absent from Books 3 and 4. Courtesy of the LDS Church History Library.

Apostle Smith was making a private copy for himself (Books 1 and 2) and a second copy for the Church's archives (Books 3 and 4).

Books 1 and 4 have identical titles on the front cover, "40 Affidavits on Celestial Marriage," written in an ornate calligraphy that is apparently not Joseph F. Smith's handwriting. Books 2 and 3 have no title.

At some point, Book 3 was separated from Book 4 at the Church Historian's Office. Possibly because of the title displayed plainly on its cover, Book 4 was placed in the LDS Church Historical Department Archives vault. Sometime thereafter, Joseph F. Smith or his descendants donated Books 1 and 2 to the Church where they joined Book 3.

Danel W. Bachman, who examined the books in the early 1970s, explained:

> While examining two separate collections in the Church Archives the author [Bachman] found four small record books kept by Joseph F. Smith. Three were housed in his collection and the fourth was in a collection of affidavits and statements in the archives vault. Apparently Smith began the collection of these affidavits and statements in 1869 when Alexander Hale Smith and David Hyrum Smith, sons of Joseph Smith, came to Salt Lake City on a proselytizing mission for the RLDS church. They were denying that their father taught or practiced plural marriage. Joseph F. Smith collected these statements from personal witnesses to refute these missionaries. [sic. Joseph F. Smith gathered thirty-five attestations prior to the arrival of the Smith brothers.] Two of the three books in the [Joseph F.] Smith collection have identifying marks. The third one and the one in the vault have none. For convenience I have designated them as follows. The book titled "40 Affidavits on Celestial Marriage" is designated Book 1, the book designated as Book "2" will retain this number, and the unmarked one will be referred to as Book 3. The book in the vault will be designated Book 4. There are duplications in these volumes and it appears that two were intended as duplicates, but there are also unique items in each one.[23]

---

23. Danel W. Bachman, "New Light on an Old Hypothesis: The Ohio Origins of

Title stickers are found on books 1 and 4: "40 Affidavits on Celestial Marriage." Courtesy LDS Church History Library.

Although the books are pairs (1 and 4, 2 and 3), neither book is simply a handwritten copy of the other. The affidavits in both books contain genuine signatures and often a notary stamp.

The February 8, 1842, date for Sylvia Sessions's sealing comes from Book 1 and the February 8, 1843, date from Book 4. Book 4 is also unique because it contains two additional unfinished affidavits, one for Vienna Jacques, and a second affidavit, prepared by Judge Elias Smith that was started on June 26, 1869, but never completed. The Elias Smith affidavit reads: "Be it remembered that on this twenty-sixth day of June, A. D. 1869, personally appeared before me Elias Smith, Probate Judge for said county." It is canceled by a large "X" crossed through the entirety of the text.[24] There is no indication for whom the document was written or what information it was going to contain. Book 1 does not contain the aborted Vienna Jacques and Elias Smith affidavits.

Accordingly, it appears that, because Book 4 contains more documents than Book 1, it was in fact the primary of the two and was the first to receive entries, at least in those two instances. This observation suggests that Sylvia's sealing date of February 8, 1843, date could well be the most accurate, or at least the first recorded, even though it is found in a book currently referred to a "Book 4." Either way, it is a date with at least as much validity as the date of 1842 written in Book 1 and should not be dismissed on the inaccurate assumption that "1843" was simply a copyist's error that occurred as the contents of Book 1 were being duplicated in Book 4. In light of these observations, the best conclusion seems to be that the specific year of the sealing is unconfirmed in these documents.

A second observation also seems to undermine the day and month provided in the unfinished documents. February 8, the month and day that appears in both the 1842 and 1843 affidavits, is the birthday of Josephine Lyon (1844) and Windsor Lyon (1809). It is possible that Joseph and Sylvia were sealed on

---

the Revelation on Eternal Marriage," 21 note 6.

24. Joseph F. Smith, Affidavit Books, 4:3.

Windsor's birthday, exactly one or two years prior to Josephine's birth, but the likelihood is small. Accordingly, a rigid insistence upon a February 8 sealing date of either year seems unjustified.

A third observation is possibly the most important. By definition, an "affidavit" is a signed statement made before a notary public or a justice of the peace and subsequently validated by that official.[25] The two pages from the affidavit books discussed above do not qualify. Without signatures, they become documents that may or may not reflect the genuine beliefs of the scribe or intended signatory. One may argue that, in this case, the documents are found within a book containing many genuine affidavits but proximity does not confer affidavit status on these two unsigned documents. At best, Sylvia's unsigned statements are only "affidavit book documents."

Outside evidence can help determine the validity of the information they contain. However, these two documents provide contradictory data. Citing either of them preferentially as documenting a specific sealing date, either before (1842) or after (1843) Windsor's excommunication, is unjustified.

Sealing Dates: Late 1842 or Early 1843

Without the assistance of the affidavit books, other sources must be consulted to identify a sealing date for Joseph Smith and Sylvia Sessions Lyons. In a document undoubtedly used to write his 1887 *Historical Record* article on plural marriage, Andrew Jenson referred to Sylvia as "formerly the wife of Windsor Lyons [sic]."[26] He also drafted the following statement: "Sessions, Sylvia Porter, wife of Winsor [sic] Palmer Lyon, was born July 31, 1818, in Bethel, Oxford Co, Maine, the daughter of [blank] Sessions. sister of Perrigrine Sessions Became a convert to 'Mormonism' and was married to Mr. Lyons When he left the Church she was sealed to the Prophet Joseph Smith."[27] A second corroboration is found in the 1915 statement from Josephine who reported, as quoted above, that Sylvia "told me that I was the daughter of the Prophet Joseph Smith, she having been sealed to the Prophet at the time that her husband Mr. Lyon was out of fellowship with the Church."[28] Accordingly, these two documents place the sealing after Windsor's excommunication.

---

25. The *American Heritage Dictionary*, CD-ROM (Boston: Houghton-Mifflin, 1992), defines "affidavit" as: "a declaration made under oath before a notary public or other authorized officer."

26. Ruth Vose Sayers, Biographical information sheet, Andrew Jenson Papers, MS 17956, Box 49, fd. 16. Windsor's surname is actually "Lyon," but "Lyons" is sometimes substituted in error.

27. Biographical Information on Windsor and Sylvia Lyon, undated sheet in Andrew Jenson Collection, MS 17956, Box 10, fd. 81.

28. Josephine R. Fisher, Affidavit, February 24, 1915. See also Bachman, "A Study

Windsor Palmer Lyon. Photo courtesy of Edwin T. Alter.

Windsor Lyon experienced financial difficulties in the spring of 1842 and filed for bankruptcy in the District Court at Springfield, Illinois on May 2 and July 9. Notices were published in the June 4, July 30, and August 13, issues of *The Wasp* in Nauvoo.[29] While details are incomplete, part of his pecuniary problems stemmed from $3,000 he had earlier lent Nauvoo Stake President William Marks. Marks apparently could not repay the loan when it came due so Lyon sued him in civil court, filing his action on November 4.[30] Evidently Marks viewed this suit as a violation of Church standards that such matters were to be resolved without "going to law." Three days later, Marks wrote to the Nauvoo High Council: "I prefer a charge against Windsor P. Lyons for instituting a suit at law against me on the 4th of November, and for other acts derogatory to the character of a Christian."[31] The high council heard the case on November 19. The minutes read: "Defendant said that the suit was instituted by him, in another man's name, therefore, did not think he was in fault &c. Two were appointed to speak on the case, viz; (9) Knight and (10) Huntington. The charge was fully sustained. The president then decided that, unless he repent humble himself and repent, the hand of fellowship be with drawn from him, which decision was unanimously sanctioned by the Councillors."[32] Subsequently, according to a twentieth-century family account, he "left Nauvoo and went up to Iowa City, making his home there, but leaving his wife in Nauvoo, who apparently did not wish to leave the Church and go with him."[33]

Perhaps unaware of the dating discrepancies in the affidavits, several historians including Bachman and Compton cite only the 1842 document found in Book 1.[34] They conclude that Sylvia erroneously stated that she was "sealed

---

of the Mormon Practice of Plural Marriage," 141, 350 #77.

29. "District Court of the United States...," *The Wasp* 1, no. 8 (June 4, 1842): 4; 1, no. 16 (July 30, 1842): 1; 1, no. 17 (August 13, 1842): 4.

30. Fred C. Collier, *The Nauvoo High Council Minute Books of the Church of Jesus Christ of Latter Day Saints*, 74; Compton, *In Sacred Loneliness*, 181.

31. Collier, *The Nauvoo High Council Minute Books*, 74.

32. Ibid.

33. Irvin F. Fisher, Letter to A[nson]. B. Call, April 9, 1945.

34. Compton, *In Sacred Loneliness*, 179. See also Compton, "A Trajectory of Plurality," 34; Gary James Bergera, "Identifying the Earliest Mormon Polygamists, 1841–1844,"

to the Prophet at the time that her husband Mr. Lyon was out of fellowship with the Church." Compton wrote: "This scenario is not strictly consistent with the chronology provided by history, since Sylvia married Joseph Smith *before* Windsor was excommunicated. There are two possible explanations for this inconsistency. First, Sylvia may have been 'revising' history to explain to her daughter why she married Smith when she was already married to Windsor. Another possibility is that Sylvia meant that she had had sexual relations with Smith after Windsor was disfellowshipped, which is chronologically possible."[35]

Compton also wrote concerning the date on the unsigned affidavit: "Supporting evidence makes this marriage close to certain."[36] His confidence may have been derived in part from two observations. Reportedly, Sylvia stated to her daughter "that she was sealed to the Prophet about the same time that Zina D. Huntingon and Eliza R. Snow were thus sealed."[37] Zina was sealed to the Prophet on October 27, 1841, and Eliza on June 29, 1842, thus supporting an 1842 date. However, it is unlikely that Sylvia chose to compare her plural marriage to those of Eliza and Zina simply because their sealing dates were close to hers. It could be argued that, if Sylvia was sealed to Joseph Smith soon after Windsor Lyon's excommunication on November 19, 1842, they may have been married less than five months after Eliza's plural sealing date. Undoubtedly Josephine, like 99 percent of all Church members in 1882, was unaware of the chronology of the Prophet's plural marriage sealings in Nauvoo, since the first publication on the topic was Andrew Jenson's 1887 article, five years later.[38] Nor would she have recognized any dating discrepancy in her mother's story.

Instead, Sylvia knew that Josephine would be familiar with Eliza and Zina as plural wives of the Joseph Smith. In a letter to the *Deseret News* dated October 17, 1879, Eliza countered some claims of the RLDS Church leadership regarding Joseph Smith's polygamy, signing the letter: "Eliza R. Snow, A wife of Joseph Smith the Prophet."[39] Seven months afterwards—and a little more than a year after Emma Smith's death on April 30, 1879—she formally adopted his surname as her own married name, thereafter calling herself, Eliza R. Snow Smith (which ignored her "time only" marriage to Brigham

---

66; H. Michael Marquardt, *The Rise of Mormonism: 1816–1844*, 561; George D. Smith, "The Summer of 1842: Joseph Smith's Relationships with the 12 Wives He Married after His First Wife, Emma," 5; Dinger, *The Nauvoo City and High Council Minutes*, 431–32 note 77; Bachman, "A Study of the Mormon Practice of Plural Marriage before the Death of Joseph Smith, 350 #77; Quinn, *The Mormon Hierarchy: Origins of Power*, 587.

35. Compton, *In Sacred Loneliness*, 183; emphasis his.
36. Compton, "A Trajectory of Plurality," 34.
37. Josephine Lyons Fisher, Affidavit.
38. Jenson, "Plural Marriage," 233.
39. "Joseph the Seer's Plural Marriages," *Deseret News*, October 22, 1879, 604–5.

Young).[40] Two years later in 1882, when Sylvia was speaking to Josephine, Eliza was undoubtedly the most widely acknowledged wife of the Prophet, as well as the most prominent sister in the Church. Zina, too, was well known. Compton observed: "Zina [Huntington] was an extraordinary woman. She became the most important woman leader in the nineteenth-century Utah, after Eliza R. Snow."[41] Zina served as the second matron of the Endowment House and the Salt Lake Temple, succeeding Eliza.

An additional piece of evidence supporting an early 1842 sealing date for Sylvia involves her mother, Patty Bartlett Sessions. Sylvia was present for Patty's sealing to Joseph Smith on March 9, 1842.[42] Gary Bergera has asserted that Sylvia's attendance at that sealing probably could have occurred only if she was already a plural wife herself.[43] It is true that many of the individuals who witnessed these ultra-secret plural marriages were personally involved with polygamy. However, available evidence fails to support that it was ever a requirement. For example, James Adams, Joseph B. Noble, Dimick B. Huntington, Brigham Young, Willard Richards, and Newel K. Whitney all performed plural marriage ceremonies prior to becoming polygamists themselves.[44] In the latter half of 1841, Dimick Huntington's wife, Fanny, witnessed two separate polygamous ceremonies although she was not a plural wife and Dimick did not marry plurally during the Prophet's lifetime.[45] Two years later, Cornelius and Permelia Lott were present at the sealing of their daughter to the Prophet, but Cornelius would not become a polygamist until

---

40. According to Jill Mulvay Derr, "Mrs. Smith Goes to Washington: Eliza R. Snow Smith's Visit to Southern Utah, 1880–81," 5, 7: "'Aunt Eliza' or 'Sister Eliza' or 'Miss Eliza R. Snow' retained her maiden name until 1880, when in May, six months before she headed south [to Saint George, Utah] with Zina [Huntington], she took Joseph Smith's name and became known as Eliza R. Snow Smith. Eliza's new name and her declared relationship to Joseph Smith had significant repercussions throughout her southern tour. . . . At least two other wives of Joseph Smith—Zina D. H. Young and Emily Dow Partridge Young—experimented with taking the name Smith at this time. Ultimately, Eliza was the only one for whom the change of name endured."

41. Compton, *In Sacred Loneliness*, 72.

42. Patty Bartlett Sessions, Affidavit, n.d.

43. Gary James Bergera, Review of Newell G. Bringhurst and Craig L. Foster, eds., *The Persistence of Polygamy: Joseph Smith and the Origins of Mormon Polygamy*, 111.

44. All of the men listed performed plural marriages for Joseph Smith and perhaps others. See Compton, *In Sacred Loneliness*, 59, 81, 122, 179, 213, 298, 348, for marriage performance dates and sealer identities. For the dates on which the sealers themselves became polygamists, see George D. Smith, *Nauvoo Polygamy*, 574–656, and Bergera, "Identifying the Earliest Mormon Polygamists, 1841–1844," 1–74.

45. Fanny Maria Allen Huntington, Affidavits, both dated May 1, 1869, in Joseph F. Smith, Affidavit Books, 1:5, 7, 19.

1846.⁴⁶ Malissa's unmarried brother Joseph (b. 1834) and sister Amanda (b. 1836) also attended the ceremony.⁴⁷ At least five other non-polygamists witnessed plural sealings in Nauvoo: Benjamin F. Johnson, Elizabeth Ann Smith Whitney, Sarah Godshall Phillips, Julia Stone, and Hettie Stone.⁴⁸ In total, at least sixteen non-polygamists, besides Sylvia Sessions, can be identified in the very limited available documents as observing or participating. Hence, Sylvia's viewing of her own mother's sealing is inconclusive evidence of her personal involvement in plural marriage at that time.

To summarize: While circumstantial evidence and one unsigned document supports an early 1842 sealing date for Joseph and Sylvia, several other credible manuscripts indicate that Windsor and Sylvia separated after Windsor's excommunication (November 19, 1842) and that she was sealed to the Prophet after that date. Josephine was conceived approximately May 18, 1843; thus the plural marriage most likely occurred between the excommunication and that date.

A Legal Divorce between Windsor and Sylvia?

The question arises, did Windsor and Sylvia obtain a legal divorce or was she living in "ceremonial polyandry"? In the nineteenth century, civil divorces were generally difficult to obtain. Justices of the peace could marry a couple legally, but ironically, circuit courts and even state legislatures were then required to unmarry them or grant a divorce.⁴⁹

---

46. Cornelius and Permelia were sealed for time and eternity on the same day (September 20, 1843) that Joseph Smith was sealed to Malissa. Cornelius P. Lott, Family Bible, MS 3373. Cornelius was sealed to four plural wives in the Nauvoo Temple. Lisle G Brown, *Nauvoo Sealings, Adoptions, and Anointings: A Comprehensive Register of Persons Receiving LDS Temple Ordinances, 1841–1846*, 187–88.

47. Malissa Lott, Deposition, Temple Lot Transcript, Respondent's Testimony, Part 3, p. 100, question 150.

48. These assertions appear in the Joseph F. Smith Affidavit Books as follows: Benjamin F. Johnson, March 4, 1870, 2:3–9, 3:3–9; Elizabeth Ann Smith Whitney, August 30, 1869, 1:72, 4:74; and Sarah Godshall Phillips, Julia Stone, and Hettie Stone. See also Joseph Fielding Smith, *Blood Atonement and the Origin of Plural Marriage*, 58.

49. See, for example, *Acts of the General Assembly of the Commonwealth of Kentucky Passed at Called Session, August 1840 and at December Session, 1840*, 102, which states: "Chapter 41 . . . *Be it enacted by the General Assembly of the Commonwealth of Kentucky*, That the marriage contract now existing between Susan James and her husband, Thomas M. James, be, and the same is hereby, dissolved, so far as it relates to said Susan James; and she is hereby restored to all the rights and privileges of an unmarried woman. Approved, January 4, 1841." Other divorces were "enacted" during the two legislative sessions.

Currently, no documentation of a legal divorce between Windsor and Sylvia after his excommunication has been found. Several years earlier, on April 21, 1838, Joseph Smith had performed the civil marriage of Sylvia and Windsor.[50] It is possible, but unlikely, that the Prophet felt he had de facto authority to annul that same relationship as well.

The initial 1838 marriage ceremony between Windsor and Sylvia was performed by Joseph utilizing "priesthood authority," rather than civil authority formally granted to justices of the peace.[51] Regardless, the state of Missouri recognized religious marriages as legal.[52] While the extent to which Joseph, Windsor, and Sylvia complied with the law requiring the ceremony to be officially recorded, the wedding itself fulfilled Missouri state laws. However, county court records were destroyed in a courthouse fire, and recent attempts to identify a marriage document have been unsuccessful.

It is possible that Joseph saw himself as capable of single-handedly granting a divorce based on his position as mayor of Nauvoo. The Nauvoo Charter was a liberal document, which Nauvoo citizens interpreted very broadly. It granted the city the right to create the Nauvoo Municipal Court with "the Mayor as Chief Justice" and specified: "The Mayor shall have exclusive jurisdiction in all cases."[53] Three other Illinois city charters granted their respective cities the right to create a city municipal court, similar to Nauvoo's.[54] However, the Nauvoo Municipal Court was unusual in several ways, notably the powers attributed to it by Nauvoo citizens, especially Church leaders.

An 1827 Illinois law, still in effect in 1842–43, allowed divorce for biological impotence, adultery, desertion for two years, or "cruelty or habitual drunkenness for the space of two years."[55] Sylvia's case did not justify a divorce based on those criteria. Danel Bachman observed that, in the nineteenth

---

50. Emmeline B. Wells, "Patty Sessions," 86.

51. Newel Knight, "Sketch of the Life of Newel Knight." Quinn identifies this document as a first draft, although the manuscript does not make this identification. It is the shorter of two Knight autobiographies in the collection. Quinn, *The Mormon Hierarchy: Origins of Power*, 88, 326 note 32.

52. Unlike Ohio laws, Missouri statutes specified: "Every . . . ordained preacher of the gospel, may perform the ceremony of marriage in this state." *The Revised Statutes of the State of Missouri*, 401.

53. *City Charter: Laws, Ordinances, and Acts of the City Council of the City of Nauvoo and also, the Ordinances of the Nauvoo Legion from the Commencement of the City to this Date*, 6.

54. James L. Kimball Jr., "The Nauvoo Charter: A Reinterpretation." In Roger D. Launius and John E. Hallwas, eds., *Kingdom on the Mississippi Revisited: Nauvoo in Mormon History*, 40.

55. *Revised Laws of Illinois*, 233. Courts of Chancery were unique in that they did not have to call witnesses and were not always subject to other legal formalities. I am grateful to Raymond Collins, Reference Librarian at the Illinois State Library, for his assistance in locating pertinent historical documents defining legal procedures in Illinois in 1843.

century, "It appears that men or women were permitted to remarry without a divorce if it could be proven that their former spouses' conduct was adulterous or seriously marred by unfaithfulness. On the other hand, Saints who were considered guilty of gross marital misconduct were judged harshly."[56]

However, an 1832 Act, also in force in 1842–43, stated: "In addition to the causes already provided by law for divorces from the bands of matrimony, courts of chancery in this state shall have full power and authority to hear and determine all causes for a divorce, not provided for by any law of this state."[57] Typically, the Illinois Supreme Court would grant circuit courts the right to act as courts of chancery, but the Nauvoo Municipal Court never received this designation. John C. Bennett had been appointed as the Master in Chancery of Hancock County, but Joseph Smith was not so designated after Bennett's resignation as Nauvoo's mayor. It is possible but unlikely that Joseph Smith assumed authority as chief justice of the Nauvoo Municipal Court to deal with a divorce occurring within the city limits, reasoning that if other courts in the state were so empowered, then he and the citizens of Nauvoo should not be denied. Using such logic, he could have granted Sylvia a quasi-legal divorce.

Despite these observations, it is doubtful that Joseph Smith or Sylvia Sessions seriously considered the need for her to obtain a civil divorce from Windsor prior to her sealing to the Prophet. After the introduction of celestial marriage in Nauvoo, the covenants contracted through civil ceremonies were deemed inferior to the new and everlasting covenant of the eternal sealings.

A Religious Divorce between Windsor and Sylvia?

Given the inconclusive nature of a possible legal divorce between Windsor and Sylvia, the next logical question is whether a religious divorce or equivalent occurred. A number of factors suggest that some form of a religiously sanctioned separation or divorce accompanied Windsor's excommunication, even though clear nomenclature and explicit documentation are not available.

First, there is no question that, in special circumstances, Joseph Smith, as president of the Church, believed himself capable of granting permission to ignore legal unions, a decision that would constitute a religious divorce. As early as 1831, he recognized that a person might remarry without a legal divorce, if the circumstances warranted it. As quoted in Chapter 6, when the Prophet and several other men journeyed to Missouri as missionaries in the summer of 1831, he received a revelation that reportedly acknowledged: "It

---

56. Bachman, "A Study of the Mormon Practice of Plural Marriage," 133.

57. *Revised Laws of Illinois*, 234. See discussion in John G. Henderson, *Chancery Practice with Especial Reference to the Office and Duties of Masters in Chancery*, 48–49; emphasis mine.

has been made known to one, who has left his wife in the State of New York, that he is entirely free from his wife, and he is at pleasure to take him a wife from among the Lamanites." The man was Martin Harris who had not secured a legal divorce from his civil wife Lucy.[58]

Similarly, in October of 1835, the Prophet was consulted regarding the status of Lydia Goldthwaite Bailey's marriage to an abusive husband, Calvin Bailey, who had deserted her three years earlier. At that time, Lydia had received a marriage proposal from Newel Knight whom she wished to marry; the couple remained confused, however, since Lydia was not divorced from Bailey. Hyrum Smith took their concerns to his brother. Newel Knight recorded:

> Bro Hiram came to me said he had laid the affair before Bro Joseph, who at the time was with his council. Broth Joseph after p[ray]or & reflecting a little or in other words enquiring [of the] Lord Said it is all right, She is his & the sooner they [are] married the better. Tell them no law shall hurt [them]. They need not fear either the law of God or man for [it] shall not touch them; & the Lord bless them. This [is the] will of the Lord concerning that matter. . . . I told her all that had transpired, & we lifted our hearts with gratitude to our heavenly Father for his goodness towards us, & that we live in this mometuous [sic] age, & as did the ancients, so we have the privilege of enquireing through the prophet, & receiveing the word of the Lord concern\ing/ us.[59]

To summarize, after prayer and reflection, Joseph declared that Lydia was free to remarry. Interwoven in his directive was the acknowledgement that Lydia was, from a practical standpoint, divorced from Calvin Bailey. (See Chapter 14.) Given that the Prophet's jurisdiction concerned only religious laws, the separation or divorce granted could only be considered ecclesiastical. However, Joseph instructed that thereafter they need not "fear either the law of God or man." Joseph Smith evidently considered his judgment in that matter to satisfy all pertinent concerns including state and federal laws, so far as the participants were concerned.

The Nauvoo High Council also assumed authority to allow a new marriage to a man still legally married. On January 21, 1843:

> Henry H. Wilson appeared before the Council and desired to know, whether in his present condition, it would be wisdom, and also if it would be justifiable by the laws of God and man, for him to unite himself in matrimony, or not, as he had a living wife
>
> It appeared from evidence adduced that his wife was a very contentious, disobedient and ungovernable woman and that she would not submit to good order, or abide his counsel and altogether refused to live with [him]

---

58. Ezra Booth, "Letter IX," in Eber D. Howe, *Mormonism Unvailed*, 220. Harris did not avail himself of this permission. I am grateful to Don Bradley for this observation.
59. Newel Knight, Autobiography and journal ca. 1846, 57–58.

and that they had been apart for the last five years and many other things which was unbecoming &c.

After which it was decided by President Hyrum Smith and William Marks, that if he [Wilson] feels himself justified and can sustain himself against the laws of the land, that he is clear as far as they were concerned (i.e. the jurisdiction of the High Council) and was at liberty to marry again on the aforesaid conditions.[60]

In this instance, the Nauvoo Stake High Council was willing to ignore his civil marriage, telling him he was "at liberty to marry again," although they prudently added that he needed to be able to "sustain himself against the laws of the land"—meaning that he could have obtained a legal divorce if necessary. In fact, the five-year estrangement would have given the circuit court in Carthage very acceptable grounds for decreeing such a divorce. However, the high council did not require him to do so. Wilson was considered free from the civil union without a legal divorce as far as the Church leadership was concerned.

It is probable that participating parties understood that Sylvia's sealing to Joseph, accompanied by Windsor's excommunication and subsequent relocation away from his wife curtailed conjugal relations with Sylvia, a form of religious divorce. Historian Kenneth L. Cannon II recounts an example of a woman who automatically became divorced from her husband upon his excommunication. In 1857, John Hyde, a recent convert from London, accepted a mission to the Hawaiian Islands very soon after arriving in Salt Lake City, but his feelings soured toward polygamy; and by the time he reached Honolulu, he was in full apostasy. He published *Mormonism: Its Leaders and Designs*, which Cannon describes as "a vitriolic attack on the Church, which contains an early exposé of the 'mysteries' of the endowment and a bitter denunciation of the practice of plural marriage."[61]

Hyde's activities did not go unnoticed in Salt Lake City. On January 11, 1857, Heber C. Kimball publicly moved that the errant elder be "cut off root and branch" from the Church and "delivered over to Satan to be buffeted in the flesh" because "there is no sympathy to be shown unto such a man." After the motion carried unanimously, Kimball specified that Hyde's wife of three years, Lavinia Hawkins, was "not cut off from this Church, but she is free from him; she is just as free from him as though she never had belonged to him.—The limb she was connected to is cut off, and she must again be grafted into the tree, if she wishes to be saved."[62] Shortly afterward, Hawkins married Joseph Woodmansee in Salt Lake City on July 24, 1858.

---

60. Collier, *The Nauvoo High Council Minute Books*, 80.

61. Kenneth L. Cannon II, "A Strange Encounter: The English Courts and Mormon Polygamy," 76; see also John Hyde, *Mormonism: Its Leaders and Designs*; Edward L. Hart, "The Historian's Corner: "John Hyde, Junior—An Earlier View," 305–12.

62. Cannon, "A Strange Encounter: The English Courts and Mormon Polygamy,"

In 1861 Brigham Young reportedly taught that if a man becomes "unfaithful to his God and his priesthood," he also "forfeits his covenant with a wife" and that wife is "free from him without a bill of divorcement."[63]

Evidence Supporting a Post-Excommunication Sealing Date

Despite these observations, it is probable that Sylvia Sessions was not concerned about seeking a formal divorce from Windsor prior to her sealing to the Joseph Smith. The Prophet taught that his plural marriages were part of the "new and everlasting covenant" (D&C 132:4) and that the new and everlasting covenant causes "all old covenants" to be "done away" (D&C 22:1). Available evidence supports that this principle applied to polyandrous unions like Joseph's sealing to Sylvia, meaning that her sealing to Joseph would have caused her civil marriage (her "old marriage covenant") to have been "done away" as a consequence of the sealing ordinance. (See Chapter 14.) Stanley B. Kimball acknowledged: "Some church leaders at that time [of Nauvoo plural marriage] considered civil marriage by non-Mormon clergymen to be as unbinding as their baptisms. Some previous marriages . . . were annulled simply by ignoring them."[64] This interpretation places Windsor's excommunication as a chronological marker, but otherwise as a sideline issue, essentially unrelated to the actual status of the legal marriage after Sylvia's sealing to the Prophet.

Despite what has been written, no reliable evidence of sexual polyandry in Sylvia Sessions Lyon's life has been identified in the historical record. Everything presented by proponents is based upon assumptions. Understandably, writers usually assume sexuality in a monogamous marriages (and in biblical polygamy), even though history shows that such relations do not always exist. Yet, it could be argued that sexual polyandry deviates significantly from the biblical standard; therefore, drawing parallel assumptions may not be warranted. Instead, a new set of moral arguments or theological

---

76, quoting Heber C. Kimball, January 11, 1857, *Journal of Discourses*, 4:165.

63. Elden Jay Watson, ed., *Brigham Young Addresses 1836–1877: A Chronological Compilation of Known Addresses of the Prophet Brigham Young*, October 8, 1861, 4:139–40. Unfortunately the shorthand notes from George D. Watt for this discourse were never perfected by him or reviewed by Brigham Young. Watt's unfinished notes report Brigham saying: "If a woman can find a man holding the keys of the priesthood with higher power and authority than her husband, and he is disposed to take her, he can do so. . . . [T]here is no need for a bill of divorcement." Ibid., 4:138. See also B. Carmon Hardy, *Doing the Works of Abraham: Mormon Polygamy, Its Origin, Practice, and Demise*, 182; Catherine Lewis, *Narrative of Some of the Proceedings of the Mormons; Giving an Account of Their Iniquities*, 5.

64. Stanley B. Kimball, *Heber C. Kimball: Mormon Patriarch and Pioneer*, 95.

justifications would be needed for Christian women to embrace polyandrous sexuality. Such justifications are not found in the Prophet's teachings.

Supporters of sexual polyandry in Joseph Smith's plural marriage to Sylvia Sessions Lyon usually accept two assumptions regarding their behavior. They observe that Windsor Lyon fathered children with Sylvia prior to his excommunication (see chart of timeline) and then assume that Joseph also had sexual relations with her during that period. The second assumption is that, when she became pregnant with Joseph's daughter months later, she was also having conjugal relations with Windsor. As analyzed above, these two assumptions are not based upon historical documentation and therefore should be advanced with caution.

Three documents provide support for the argument that a formal separation or religious divorce occurred between Windsor and Sylvia after his excommunication. First, Andrew Jenson's notes refer to Sylvia as "formerly the wife of Windsor Lyons."[65] He also wrote that Sylvia "was married to Mr. Lyon. When he left the Church she was sealed to the Prophet Joseph Smith."[66] Third, Sylvia told Josephine, according to Josephine's 1915 statement, that she was "sealed to the Prophet at the time that her husband Mr. Lyon was out of fellowship with the Church."[67] Josephine's 1915 statement implies that either the excommunication or some other process at that time, like an eternal sealing, invalidated her legal marriage to Windsor allowing her to be lawfully (according to God's laws) sealed to Joseph Smith and to bear his child. Researchers who accept Josephine's 1915 statement as evidence that she was Joseph's offspring cannot easily reject the timetable presented or the implication that Josephine saw Windsor's estrangement as legitimizing Sylvia's eligibility to be sealed to the Prophet. None of these three documents suggests that she thought her mother was simultaneously married to two men polyandrously.

According to Josephine, Sylvia cautioned her to "not to make her statement to me too public" because "it might cause trouble and arouse unpleasant curiosity."[68] If Sylvia had been involved in sexual polyandry with Joseph Smith, it seems that knowledge would generate more than "unpleasant curiosity." People learning of the relationship in 1882 or anytime thereafter would have had no way to interpret it except as adultery. Accordingly, it seems more likely that, if Sylvia was trying to describe a polyandrous situation, she would have enjoined the utmost secrecy on Josephine, not just cautioned her about making

---

65. Sylvia Sessions, Biographical information sheet, n.d., Document 12, Andrew Jenson Papers, MS 17956, Box 49, fd. 16. Windsor Lyon died in Iowa in about 1849.

66. Windsor and Sylvia Lyon, Biographical information sheet, n.d., Andrew Jenson Papers, MS 17956, Box 10, fd. 81.

67. Josephine R. Lyons Fisher, Affidavit, February 24, 1915.

68. Ibid.

it "too public." In short, if Sylvia's relationship with Joseph Smith was in any way illicit, her concerns about divulging it to her daughter seem inadequate.

Childbearing Chronology Suggests Physical Separation

A review of Sylvia's child-bearing chronology suggests that she and Windsor were not cohabiting during the period when he was out of the Church. They were an otherwise fertile couple, conceiving three children during the four and a half years prior to his excommunication and two during the first two years after his rebaptism. The only child conceived during the three-plus years of his Church estrangement was Josephine. Historian Kathryn Daynes has reasoned, "If Sessions knew that Fisher was Joseph Smith's biological child . . . she could have been having sexual relations only with Smith, not with Windsor Lyon. . . . She could be certain of her child's paternity only if she restricted her sexual relationship to one husband at a time."[69] Daynes also found the timing of the births significant in lending some credence to her having denied Lyon cohabitation rights if Joseph Smith was the father of Josephine Fisher. Married to Lyon in March 1838, she gave birth to their first child sixteen months later, in July 1839. Their second child was born twenty-three months later, in June 1841, and another thirty months later their third child was born and died the same day, in December 1842, one month after Lyon had been excommunicated from the church. The next child, the purported daughter of Joseph Smith, was born in February 1844, fourteen months after Session's third child, a common interval between children when the previous child died as an infant (which would have eliminated any natural birth control secondary to breast-feeding). The child after Josephine Fisher, however, was not born until forty-two months later, in September 1847, over three years after Smith's death and nineteen months after Lyon was rebaptized a member of the Church. Sessions's sixth and last child was born only eleven months after the fifth, a surprisingly short interval. Only Josephine Fisher was conceived during the entire time Lyon was excommunicated from the Church.[70]

The question remains whether Windsor, after his excommunication, moved back in with Sylvia and resumed conjugal relations with her. He must have returned to Nauvoo within weeks after reuniting with the Church. Patty

---

69. Kathryn M. Daynes, *More Wives Than One: Transformation of the Mormon Marriage System, 1840–1910*, 29–30. In contrast, Todd Compton does not acknowledge the possibility of a non-physical pseudo-polyandrous arrangement stating: "How Sylvia was sure that Josephine was Joseph's, not Windsor's, is not clear." He further concludes that Sylvia's story "is convincing evidence that Smith had sexual relations with his wives, including his polyandrous spouses." Compton, *In Sacred Loneliness*, 183.

70. Daynes, *More Wives Than One*, 30.

Sessions's biographer dates Windsor's presence in Nauvoo three months after being cut off from the Church: "On the 12th of February [1843] . . . Bro. Joseph was at her house, and Mr. Lyons, Sylvia's husband, lent him five hundred dollars."[71] Significantly, the transaction did not take place at Windsor Lyon's residence, and Sylvia was evidently not involved. On June 5, 1843, Sylvia, apparently acting alone, bought a building lot from Joseph Smith for $500.[72]

A review of available historical documents from the 1842–44 period provides a few references to Sylvia or Windsor in Nauvoo, but they do not describe them as being together. Land records for Nauvoo show that Windsor owned a store with attached living quarters, as well as a house located less than a block away that was later converted to a store.[73] It is possible that the couple was separated but lived close to each other so Windsor could participate in parental responsibilities for their daughter Philofreen (b. June 1841).[74]

Several journal entries document that Sylvia lived in one of Windsor's dwellings, but none describe Windsor as being present there with her.[75] On Saturday April 15, 1843, for example, Eliza R. Snow recorded a visit to "Mr. Lyon's." Presumably Sylvia would have been hosting the gathering, but the diary entry does not specify whether Windsor was present: "Spent a very interesting and agreeable afternoon at Mr. Lyon's[,] present L[orenzo], Mrs. Scovill, Miss Geroot, &c."[76]

A couple of accounts refer to the residence of "Sister Lyons," without including any mention of Windsor. On September 18, William Clayton recorded: "Joseph and I rode out to borrow money, drank wine at Sister Lyons. P.M. I got $50 of Sister Lyons and paid it to D. D. Yearsley."[77] Another ex-

---

71. Wells, "Patty Session," 95.

72. "Nauvoo Project" cited in Compton, *In Sacred Loneliness*, 683.

73. Land records show a store on the corner of Main and Hotchkiss Street (no longer extant) and a home toward the east on Hotchkiss Street. The LDS Church has restored this home as a store typical of the 1840–46 period. Copy of city plats in my possession. See also Richard Neitzel Holzapfel and T. Jeffery Cottle, *Old Mormon Nauvoo and Southeastern Iowa: Historical Photographs and Guide*, 111–12.

74. The Lyons' children born prior to 1843 include Marian/Marion, born July 3, 1839, and died March 19, 1842. Their second daughter, Philofreen, was born June 11, 1841, and died January 2, 1844. Eliza R. Snow wrote "To Mrs. Sylvia P. Lyon: On the Death of Her Little Daughter," 479. See also Jill Mulvay Derr and Karen Lynn Davidson, eds., *Eliza R. Snow: The Complete Poetry*, 284–85. A second son, Asa Windsor Lyon, was born December 25, 1842, and died the same day. Only Philofreen was alive in 1843.

75. After Joseph Smith's death, Willard Richards wrote in his journal on December 20, 1844: "I went out with her [Jennetta] as far as Mr Lyons where we called and drank a glass of wine [and] were very kindly entertained by Mrs. Lyon."

76. Maureen Ursenbach Beecher, "Eliza R. Snow's Nauvoo Journal," 404.

77. George D. Smith, ed., *An Intimate Chronicle: The Journals of William Clayton*, 120.

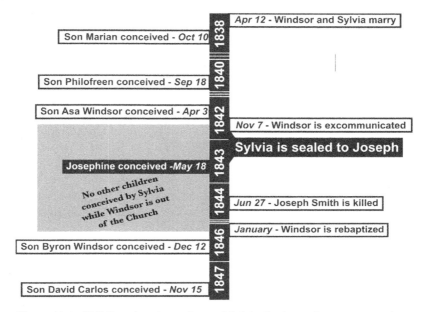

Figure 13.1. Childbearing chronology of Sylvia Session adjacent to prominent historical events.

ample is found when the Partridge sisters, Emily and Eliza, needed new lodgings in the latter half of 1843. Emily wrote: "My sister Eliza found a home with the family of Brother Joseph Coolidge, and I went to live with Sister Sylvia Lyons."[78] The differentiation between "the family of Brother Joseph Coolidge" and "Sister Sylvia Lyons" suggests again that the Windsor was not sharing the residence of his wife at that time.[79]

A few months after Joseph Smith's death in 1844, his plural wives were approached by several of the apostles and offered a sealing for time that would establish ties assuring material support. Reportedly the Prophet had previously "instructed the brethren in the Quorum of the Twelve to marry and care for the women who were sealed to him, that each should have her choice as to whom she would be married for time" should he be killed.[80] Sylvia was sealed for "time" to Heber C. Kimball in September.[81] Compton writes:

---

78. Emily Dow Partridge Smith Young, Autobiography, April 7, 1884, typescript, Perry Special Collections; unpaginated digitized copy.

79. Dr. James H. Lyon, no apparent relation to Windsor, was recruited as a witness of Joseph Smith's good character on June 26, 1844. *History of the Church*, 6:576.

80. Oa Jacobs Cannon, "History of Henry Bailey Jacobs."

81. Brigham Young, Journal, September 19, 1844, photocopy of holograph in my possession. The entry was coded: "Staed at home all day my wife is quite sick I saw

"Sylvia, however, continued to live with Windsor Lyon."[82] Unfortunately, no documentation is provided to support this assertion. That Sylvia and Windsor were living together in the same household or sharing the same bed after his excommunication remains undocumented and seems to contradict other available evidence.

Fifty years later, on January 6, 1894, RLDS President Joseph Smith III received a letter from RLDS Elder E. C. Brand, asking him to comment on a list of women who were reportedly plural wives of his father. Concerning Sylvia Sessions, Joseph III wrote: "There was a scandal about Mrs. Lyons, while yet in Nauvoo, but on inquiry was either fruitless of results; [or] it was hushed up, whitewashed. But she was then a married woman, her husband a storekeeper, his store known as the "Lion Store" because of a painted lion used as a sign."[83]

No additional details of a "scandal" involving Sylvia Sessions Lyon have been found. Joseph III's boyhood recollection could support a number of interpretations, including a dissolution of her legal marriage accompanying Windsor's excommunication, followed by a secret sealing to Joseph Smith and a child born from that union.

Available documents show that Sylvia rejoined Windsor shortly after his rebaptism on February 1, 1846.[84] The date is recorded by Enoch Tripp, a relative of Patty Sessions, who wrote: "On Sunday morning, February 1, 1846, Heber C. Kimball came to the house of Mr. Windsor P. Lyon in order to rebaptize him into the church and they sent up to the temple and got a large bath tub. The mob violence was so strong, Heber C. Kimball did not dare to do it in public."[85] Questions concerning the paternity of three-year-old

---

sister Louisa B. Smith H. C. Kimball & Silva L. Smith etc." Brigham Young, Journal, September 19, 1844, in Brigham Young, Office Files, 1832–1878. It appears that "saw" is short for "sealed and wed." According to "Sylvia Porter Session Lyon Kimball," in Kate Carter, ed., *Our Pioneer Heritage*, 10:415: "With full consent of Dr. Lyon, in Jan. 1846 Sylvia was sealed for eternity to the Prophet Joseph, and for time to Heber C. Kimball, '*that these were special sealings for spiritual reasons that did not constitute a husband and wife relationship in this life.*'" Emphasis in original; the significance, if any, is not explained. See also Lyndon W. Cook, *Nauvoo Marriages Proxy Sealings 1843–1846*, 42.

82. Compton, *In Sacred Loneliness* 184.

83. Joseph Smith III, Letter to Bro. E. C. Brand, January 26, 1894, 64.

84. No details are available to clarify what authority was used to reconfirm the marriage relationship between Sylvia and Windsor after their previous marital separation. Most likely the couple consulted with Brigham Young or Heber C. Kimball, who authorized their rejoining. Whether a private religious marriage ceremony for time was performed or whether the couple simply resumed their legal marriage is unknown. Importantly, even with the renewed conjugality between Windsor and Sylvia after Joseph Smith's death, no evidence has been found to support her involvement in sexual polyandry at any time.

85. Enoch Tripp, Journal, 9; quoted in Compton, *In Sacred Loneliness*, 185–86.

Josephine might have quickly faded after the couple reunited. Prior to Sylvia's 1882 confession, it appears that few individuals were privy to Josephine's paternity. For example, Nauvooan Eliza Jane Churchill Webb wrote in 1876: "Joseph never had any living children by his polygamous women."[86] When asked on November 1, 1879, "Why Joseph Smith the Prophet had no children?" Joseph F. Smith responded: "Because it would have been against him in the law of the state against bigamy. The children would have been proven to be his or the mothers would have been condemned for illicit intercourse, polygamous marriages not being considered legitimate marriages."[87]

Windsor and Sylvia became the parents of two more children prior to Windsor's 1849 death from tuberculosis.

DNA Testing to Establish Joseph Smith's Paternity?

Geneticist Ugo Perego examined DNA evidence attempting to scientifically prove a paternal connection between Joseph Smith and Josephine Lyon. He encountered two problems. First, existing scientific methods that allow verification of the paternity of a son or the maternity of a daughter do not permit the detection of a daughter's paternity. As he explained:

> The case of Josephine is interesting in that it is possibly the strongest case of an alleged biological child born to Joseph Smith through a polygamous union, but the well-developed sciences of Ycs [Y chromosome to verify paternity of a son] and mtDNA [mitochondrial DNA to verify the maternity of a daughter] testing cannot address their relationship at all. . . . Being a woman, she did not inherit the male-characteristic Ycs from her father and her mtDNA is not applicable in this situation as the mother's identity is not in question.[88]

To overcome these limitations, Perego utilized cutting-edge technology to analyze "hundreds of thousands of single nucleotide polymorphism (SNPs) from the autosomal genome." He explained that "the large amount of data produced through this method is phenomenal and was unthinkable just a few years ago. . . . Nearly one million SNPs were generated from a small number of carefully selected individuals belonging to both the Lyon and Smith families." Through testing, he theorized that "a measurable genetic contribution of Smith DNA among Lyon's descendants would be somewhat expected if

---

86. Eliza J. Webb [Eliza Jane Churchill Webb], Lockport, New York, Letter to Mary Bond, April 24, 1876.

87. Richard E. Turley, Jr., ed. *Selected Collections from the Archives of the Church of Jesus Christ of Latter-day Saints*, Vol. 1, DVD #26. Precisely when Sylvia Lyon made her disclosure to Church authorities is not known.

88. Ugo A. Perego, "Joseph Smith, the Question of Polygamous Offspring, and DNA Analysis," 249–50.

Joseph Smith was the actual father of Josephine." The testing was accomplished, but a second problem was encountered. "Considerable discrepancy was observed in the results," Perego wrote. To address this difficulty, "we evaluated the possibility of genetic contribution from other common ancestors in addition to the alleged ancestry linked to the union between Joseph Smith and Sylvia Sessions." To investigate this possibility, "family trees were provided by participants" and it was discovered that "a considerable number of additional ancestral relationships between the descendants [of] the Smith and Lyon families were catalogued."[89] In other words, cross marriages between ancestors of both Joseph and Josephine prevented the detection of a definitive genetic correlation between the two genetic lines. Perego summarizes:

> In light of the multiple familial relationships shared by both Josephine Lyons and Joseph Smith's descendants, it is clear that a lot of "genealogical noise" is also present. This complicates any attempt to identify a clear and straightforward genetic signal from Joseph Smith in Josephine's descendants. In other words, the challenge that researchers face is to be able to distinguish the genetic contribution by Joseph Smith in the purported paternity of Josephine, from all the other related Smiths who married ancestors of Josephine's descendants before and after Joseph Smith's time.[90]

Despite the immense resources spent investigating the possible genetic link between Joseph Smith and Josephine Lyon, Perego concludes: "It is possible that this paternity case may never be fully resolved by means of genetic testing."[91]

Summary

The historical data currently available do not conclusively describe the timeline or dynamics of Sylvia's marriages to either Windsor Lyon or Joseph Smith. However, significant evidence exists indicating that Windsor and Sylvia separated after his excommunication on November 19, 1842, and that she ceased cohabiting with him at that point, essentially comprising a practical but unofficial divorce. Available documents indicate that her sealing to Joseph Smith occurred after that date and would have caused the legal marriage to be "done away" during the remainder of the Prophet's life. Josephine was conceived during the time of her separation from Windsor. These observations combine to support the conclusion that Sylvia's case should be categorized as "ceremonial polyandry" due to the lack of a legal divorce but that it represents consecutive marriages with no evidence of "sexual polyandry" identified in Sylvia's marital relationships.

---

89. Ibid., 251–52.
90. Ibid., 255.
91. Ibid.

Chapter 14

Sexual Polyandry: Examining the Contradictory Evidence

As discussed in Chapter 12, Joseph Smith clearly practiced "ceremonial polyandry," which occurs when a woman experiences two marriage ceremonies, usually a legal matrimony and a priesthood sealing. Thereafter, two husbands can be identified for the woman from a ceremonial standpoint. However, the presence of ceremonial polyandry is not evidence of sexual polyandry; specific documentation of sexual relations with each husband during a specific time span is required. This chapter will review some of the data that contradict this possibility in Joseph Smith's polygamy. Since it is impossible to prove a negative, the observations and evidences can only support the absence of such behavior in the Prophet's life. The contradictory evidence is divided into two categories, theological and historical.

LDS Theology: Sexual Polyandry Is Nondoctrinal

Reviewing Joseph Smith's statements and revelations supports that, in his theology, sexual polyandry is *nondoctrinal*.[1] An evaluation of LDS scriptures and prophetic teachings fails to identify any statements that would authorize its practice. No ceremonies are described that would solemnize a true polyandrous relationship in which a woman was authorized to be sexually involved with two men during the same general time period.

The law of sexual morality, as emphasized in the Book of Mormon (Alma 39:4–6), describes the only acceptable sexual expression as *lawful* monogamous or polygynous[2] heterosexual marriage.[3] It is restated multiple times

---

1. See discussion in Helen Mar Kimball Whitney, *Why We Practice Plural Marriage*, 50–51.

2. Polygamy is the state of *multiple marriages* and includes *polygyny* (one man having more than one wife) and *polyandry* (one woman having more than one husband). I use "polygamy" interchangeably with "polygyny" except when I am specifically discussing polyandry.

3. Alma taught his son that breaking the law of chastity was "an abomination in the sight of the Lord; yea, most abominable above all sins save it be the shedding of innocent blood or denying the Holy Ghost" (Alma 39:5). This interpretation was specifically taught

in other LDS publications since 1830. The "law" referred to is divine law, not necessarily the laws of earthly governments. For example, legally permitting polyandrous marriages or same-sex marriages today would not create a "lawful" marriage according to Latter-day Saint beliefs.[4] Rex E. Cooper observed: "For a woman to be civilly married to one living man while matrimonially sealed to another does . . . present conceptual difficulties for Mormons. And for her to engage in sexual intercourse with both men would be regarded by most as a violation of divine law."[5]

Section 132 of the Doctrine and Covenants, recorded in July 1843, explains that the marriage of one man to more than one wife in polygamy (technically "polygyny") can be acceptable to God under certain circumstances. While plural marriage itself is not mentioned in the first thirty-three verses of the section, the remaining thirty-three verses discuss the doctrine and the underlying principles. Specifically, verses 41–44 and 61–66 explain how a man who is married in the new and everlasting covenant can marry another woman without committing adultery. In contrast, nothing has been taught that would authorize the practice of sexual polyandry.

Between 1851 and 1886, Church leaders in Utah provided for their conference discourses to be published in England to benefit the Latter-day Saints living there. The talks were compiled and printed in Liverpool in twenty-six volumes called the *Journal of Discourses*.[6] A computerized review of their contents reveals 220 references to "polygamy," 126 to "plural marriage," 42 to "many wives," 58 to "more wives," and 116 to "plurality of wives." These numerous references demonstrate the importance of plural marriage (multiple wives) during that period. Contrastingly, only three references to polyandry or a plurality of husbands can be identified, and they uniformly condemn the practice.[7]

---

by Apostles Orson Pratt (*The Seer* [Washington, D.C.] 1, no. 1 [January 1853]: 27) and Heber C. Kimball (January 11, 1857, *Journal of Discourses*, 4:175). For an alternative view that Alma 39:5 was not primarily referring to sexual immorality, see Michael R. Ash, "The Sin 'Next to Murder': An Alternative Interpretation," *Sunstone*, November 2006, 34–43; Bruce W. Jorgensen, "Scriptural Chastity Lessons: Joseph and Potiphar's Wife; Corianton and the Harlot Isabel," 7–34; and Brant A. Gardner, *Second Witness: Analytical & Contextual Commentary on the Book of Mormon, Volume Four: Alma*, 527–28.

4. Brian C. Hales, "Homosexuality and the Restored Gospel," chap. 3.

5. Rex E. Cooper, *Promises Made to the Fathers: Mormon Covenant Organization*, 143. Perhaps this obvious moral inconsistency is why antagonistic authors seem to accept uncritically the conclusion that Joseph Smith practiced sexual polyandry.

6. Ronald G. Watt, "The Beginnings of *The Journal of Discourses*: A Confrontation between George D. Watt and Willard Richards," 134–48.

7. See, in the *Journal of Discourses*: Brigham Young, August 1, 1852, 1:361; George A. Smith, October 8, 1869, 13:41; Orson Pratt, July 11, 1875, 18:55–56. For these quotations, see the next section.

LDS Theology: Sexual Polyandry Is Antidoctrinal

In addition to being nondoctrinal, a review of LDS theology shows that sexual polyandry is also *antidoctrinal*. In the revelation on celestial marriage, Joseph Smith referred to several situations where a married woman might "be with another man." If "another man" referred to was also her husband (through some ceremony), then polyandrous sexuality would been referenced:

> And as ye have asked concerning adultery, verily, verily, I say unto you, if a man receiveth a wife in the new and everlasting covenant, and if she *be with another man*, and I have not appointed unto her by the holy anointing, she hath committed adultery and shall be destroyed.
>
> If she be not in the new and everlasting covenant, and she *be with another man*, she has committed adultery. (D&C 132:41–42; emphasis mine.)

These verses will be analyzed in more detail in Chapter 15. However, what is clear is that the forms of sexual polyandry referred to are classified as "adultery" in both verses.[8] Verses 61–63 also mention another potentially polyandrous situation:

> And again, as pertaining to the law of the priesthood—if any man espouse a virgin, and desire to espouse another, and the first give her consent, and if he espouse the second, and they are virgins, and have vowed to no other man, then is he justified; he cannot commit adultery for they are given unto him; for he cannot commit adultery with that that belongeth unto him and to no one else.
>
> And if he have ten virgins given unto him by this law, he cannot commit adultery, for they belong to him, and they are given unto him; therefore is he justified.
>
> But if one or either of the ten virgins, after she is espoused, shall *be with another man*, she has committed adultery, and shall be destroyed; for they are given unto him to multiply and replenish the earth. (D&C 132:61–63; emphasis mine)

Verses 61–63 would universally condemn a virgin who is first sealed (in the new and everlasting covenant of marriage) and then thereafter legally married to another, if she is thereafter sexually involved with both husbands. Ironically, many observers assume that simply switching the chronology of the marriages would somehow allow polyandrous conjugality to not be adultery.

---

8. Verse 41 seems to imply a possible exception in that a woman who is sealed in the new and everlasting covenant could receive an "appointment" in the "holy anointing" (the marriage ceremony) and thereafter be authorized to experience conjugal relations with "another man," (possibly a legal husband). One interpretation is that this verse refers to "eternity only" sealings in the new and everlasting covenant that create a husband only for the next life with no conjugality on earth.

That is, if a woman is first legally married and then afterwards sealed to a second husband, proponents of sexual polyandry in Joseph Smith's plural marriages assume that she *could* experience conjugality with both husbands and it would not be sinful. In essence, the order of the marriages seems to make a difference, but nothing in the Prophet's teachings supports this scenario.

Also, the women mentioned in verses 61–63 are specifically described as "virgins." It is unknown whether the principles would also apply to unsealed, worthy, non-virgins. Likewise, it is unclear whether the requirement in verse 61, that the woman had previously "vowed to no other man," is referring to vows strictly within the "law of the priesthood" (sealings in the new and everlasting covenant) or to any marriage vow such as a legal marriage. Due to the brevity and ambiguity of some of the wording in these verses, it is impossible to fully identify all of the ramifications. However, what can be concluded is that all of the statements plainly label sexual polyandry as adultery in certain circumstances and none of the statements authorize it.[9] Whether they together describe a blanket condemnation of polyandrous conjugality in any and all circumstances is controversial.

Regardless, later statements from Church leaders are definite on this topic. As quoted in Chapter 13, Brigham Young asked in 1852, "What do you think of a woman having more husbands than one?" And then answered, "This is not known to the law."[10] Six years later Orson Pratt instructed: "God has strictly forbidden, in this Bible, plurality of husbands, and proclaimed against it in his law."[11] Pratt further explained: "Can a woman have more than one husband at the same time? No: Such a principle was never sanctioned by scripture. The object of marriage is to multiply the species, according to the command of God. A woman with one husband can fulfill this command, with greater facilities, than if she had a plurality; indeed, this would, in all probability, frustrate the great design of marriage, and prevent her from raising up a family. As a plurality of husbands, would not facilitate the increase of posterity, such a principle never was tolerated in scripture."[12]

In 1889, Joseph F. Smith, then a counselor in Wilford Woodruff's First Presidency, condemned polyandrous relationships: "Polyandry is wrong, physiologically, morally, and from a scriptural point of order. It is nowhere sanctioned in the Bible, nor by the law of God or nature and has no affinity with

---

9. The possible exception implied in D&C 132:41 is discussed in the next chapter dealing with "eternity only" sealings.

10. Brigham Young, August 1, 1852, *Journal of Discourses*, 1:361.

11. Orson Pratt, July 11, 1875, *Journal of Discourses*, 18:55–56.

12. Orson Pratt, "Celestial Marriage," *The Seer*, 1, no. 4 (April 1853): 60. As discussed in Chapter 12, Pratt was apparently reflecting the idea that unconventional sexual relations, which would have included polyandry, decreased fecundity (fertility).

'Mormon' plural marriage."[13] His son Joseph Fielding Smith, then an apostle, agreed in 1905: "Polygamy, in the sense of plurality of husbands and of wives never was practiced in the Church of Jesus Christ of Latter-day Saints in Utah or elsewhere."[14]

The Apostle Paul also denounced polyandry, calling it "adultery":

> For the woman which hath an husband is bound by the law to her husband so long as he liveth; but if the husband be dead, she is loosed from the law of her husband.
>
> So then if, while her husband liveth, she be married to another man, she shall be called an adulteress: but if her husband be dead, she is free from that law; so that she is no adulteress, though she be married to another man. (Rom. 7:2-3)

In addition, Mormon theology assigns specific responsibilities to parents regarding their own children: "And again, inasmuch as parents have children in Zion, or in any of her stakes which are organized, that teach them not to understand the doctrine of repentance, faith in Christ the Son of the living God, and of baptism and the gift of the Holy Ghost by the laying on of the hands, when eight years old, the sin be upon the heads of the parents" (D&C 68:25). Correspondingly, a father is not held accountable for teaching and disciplining his neighbor's children. Instead, "great things" are expected from fathers concerning their own offspring (D&C 29:48). Polyandry would unavoidably introduce confusion into this strict injunction. How could either husband be held stringently responsible for the mandated fatherly duties in a polyandrous family?

LDS scripture states that God will give us "a pattern in all things, that [we] may not be deceived" (D&C 52:14). The family pattern in Mormon theology is patriarchal where the father presides as patriarch, prophet, priest, and king, and the mother presides as matriarch, prophetess, priestess, and queen over their offspring.[15] Importantly, in patriarchal marriages or matrimonies within the new and everlasting covenant, the father ultimately presides.[16] Brigham Young taught in 1847:

---

13. Joseph F. Smith, Letter to Zenos H. Gurley, June 19, 1889, in Richard E. Turley Jr., *Selected Collections from the Archives of the Church of Jesus Christ of Latter-day Saints*, Vol. 1, DVD #29.

14. Joseph Fielding Smith, *Blood Atonement and the Origin of Plural Marriage*, 48.

15. See Andrew F. Ehat and Lyndon W. Cook, eds. *The Words of Joseph Smith: Contemporary Accounts of the Nauvoo Discourse of the Prophet Joseph Smith*, 233-34, 245; John Taylor, "Lines, Written in the Album of Miss Abby Jane Hart, of New York City," 178. John Taylor taught: " Adam was the (natural) father of his posterity, who were his family and over whom he presided as patriarch, prophet, priest, and king." John Taylor, "Patriarchal," *Times and Seasons* 6, no. 10 (June 1, 1845): 921.

16. Pratt, "Celestial Marriage," 153-54.

The man is the head and God of the woman, but let him act like a God in virtuous principles and God like conversation, walk and deportment and such men will continue to gain influence and power and advance in glory to all eternity. But should they use their power in wickedness as a tyrant they soon will be called to render an account of their stewardship. If not found worthy they will be hurled down to perdition and their family and kingdom be given to another that is more worthy. Some say that a woman cannot be saved without a man. Neither can a man without a woman.[17]

A polyandrous marriage would, confusingly, present two husbands who would be understood to preside over the wife and also over the children. Confusion would unavoidably result, creating disorder, and contradicting the LDS doctrine which specifies: "All things must be done in order" (D&C 28:13, 132:8, 18). In short, the practice of polyandry appears to contradict theological principles that are vital to Latter-day Saints.[18]

Feminist evaluators may criticize doctrines that allow a man to be sealed polygynously to more than one wife but prevent woman from being sealed polyandrously to more than one husband.[19] These gender-specific differences constitute LDS doctrines that are incompletely understood at present. Nevertheless, the expected sexual behavior is not misunderstood; it does not permit sexual polyandry.[20] It appears that even those who argue that Joseph Smith practiced sexual polyandry have yet to present any accompanying authoritative teachings to support it.

---

17. Scott G. Kenney, ed., *Wilford Woodruff's Journal, 1833–1898*, 3:131.

18. John D. Lee asserted: "After the death of Joseph, Brigham Young told me that Joseph's time on earth was short, and that the Lord allowed him privileges that we could not have." John D. Lee, *Mormonism Unveiled or the Life and Confessions of the Late Mormon Bishop*, 147. While we cannot corroborate the accuracy of Lee's recollection, this quotation might be used to support the belief that Joseph could have participated in a variety of transgressions including sexual polyandry, which emphasizes the need for evidence, not assumption, in evaluating his behaviors.

19. Currently, women can be eternally sealed to only one husband while they are living. Personal communication with a temple sealer July 20, 2006. Permitting a living woman to be sealed to two or more individuals would be a new doctrine. Church leaders today allow a deceased woman to be sealed to all the men to whom she was legally married on earth, so long as they are also deceased. However, it is not considered eternal polyandry; it is believed that at some point in the future prior to the resurrection, the woman will choose one husband as her eternal husband. President Joseph F. Smith stated in 1915: "We may bind on earth and it will be bound in Heaven, and loose on earth and it will be loosed in Heaven." In James R. Clark, ed., *Messages of the First Presidency*, 4:330–31.

20. For an antiquated (1868) look at a "plurality of husbands," see "Marrying and Giving in Marriage," 126–27.

The "New and Everlasting Covenant"

Joseph Smith's revelations provide a specific explanation regarding the reason why authorized sexual polyandry could not occur. He taught that during mortality, sexual relations can be experienced only within "lawful" marriage (D&C 49:16; see also 42:22). A "lawful" marriage requires both a *covenant* between a husband and a wife and official *authority* ratifying that covenant. Otherwise there is no marriage and sexual relations are adultery.

Making covenants alone is insufficient. Official Church doctrines do not permit a man and a woman to make a covenant with each other and thereafter consider themselves married or authorized to share sexual activity. Heber C. Kimball instructed in 1848: "No woman can covenant with a man & on that covenant live with them as man & wife[.] this [is] always true, & I heard it from Joseph himself & my senses teach me so."[21] Similarly, official authority alone cannot create a marriage. In other words, an officiator (e.g., a justice of the peace, a bishop, other religious clergy) could not pair up random men and women, pronounce them married by his authority, and expect them to begin to live as couples. Both a mutual covenant and proper authority are always required.

Joseph Smith taught that both elements of this dual dynamic—both covenant and authority—were new in the restored gospel. The *new* authority was the restored priesthood with the power to "seal on earth" in the assurance that such a sealing "shall be eternally bound in the heavens" (D&C 132:46; see also Matt. 16:19). This authority is strictly controlled and "there is never but one on the earth at a time on whom this power and the keys of this priesthood are

---

21. *Minutes of the Apostles of the Church of Jesus Christ of Latter-day Saints, 1835–1893*, 168. Heber C. Kimball also taught on December 21, 1847: "There has been a doctrine tau[gh]t—if a man & woman makes a Cov[enan]t. they have a right to connect themselves—[but] this is wrong…" *Minutes of the Apostles of the Church of Jesus Christ of Latter-day Saints, 1835–1893*, 157. This sentiment may contrast with private counsel given decades later on April 5, 1894, in a meeting of the First Presidency and Twelve when George Q. Cannon, a counselor in the First Presidency, stated: "I believe in concubinage, or some plan whereby men and women can live together under sacred ordinances and vows until they can be married. Thus our surplus girls can be cared for, and the law of God to multiply and replenish the earth be fulfilled. There is the danger of wicked men taking license from such a condition." In the same meeting Lorenzo Snow commented: "I have no doubt but concubinage will yet be practiced in this Church, but I had not thought of it in this connection. When the nations are troubled good women will come here for safety and blessing, and men will accept them as concubines." Church President Wilford Woodruff seemingly agreed: "If men enter into some practice of this character to raise a righteous posterity, they will be justified in it" Abraham H. Cannon, Diary, April 5, 1894, in Dennis B. Horne, *An Apostle's Record: The Journals of Abraham H. Cannon*, 314–15.

conferred" (D&C 132:7). During Joseph Smith's lifetime, this sealing power was conferred exclusively on him.

The *new* covenant introduced by Joseph Smith is called "the new and everlasting covenant." It is comprised of many spiritual covenants, but central to this constellation is the new and everlasting covenant of marriage (D&C 131:2). The new and everlasting covenant of marriage between a man and a woman requires the priesthood seal "for time and all eternity" through the power of the "one" man who holds the sealing keys (D&C 132:7, 18).

Importantly, if a covenant ratified by earthly authority (e.g., a legal marriage) conflicts with a covenant solemnized by the sealing authority of the "one" man (e.g., an eternal marriage), questions arise: Which covenant is valid? Can both be? For example, if a woman is legally married and is subsequently sealed to another man for "time and eternity," which husband does she retain afterwards or is she married to both at the same time? An important clue was mentioned in Chapter 13 and is found in one of Joseph Smith's April 1830 revelations: "Behold, I say unto you that *all old covenants* have I caused to be *done away* in this thing; and this is *a new and an everlasting covenant*" (D&C 22:1; emphasis mine). The specific covenant in question in 1830 was baptism. This revelation clarified that all old baptismal covenants, covenants performed by authority other than true priesthood, were "done away" through a baptism in the new and everlasting covenant.

The new and everlasting covenant includes many covenants, besides baptism. Thirteen years later, Joseph Smith dictated another revelation regarding eternal and plural marriage that he also referred to as a "new and an everlasting covenant" (D&C 132:4). The question arises whether a marriage in the new and everlasting covenant would cause a legal marriage covenant to be "done away"? We have no record of Joseph Smith addressing this question, but the revelation (D&C 22:1) declares that the new and everlasting covenant does away with "*all* old covenants," which seemingly would apply to matrimonial covenants as well. If so, then after a plural sealing in the new and everlasting covenant, a legal marriage covenant would not be binding upon the woman *and* her bystander civil husband so far as the Lord was concerned. Legal documents could remain filed at the courthouse, and the neighborhood might be unaware of the priesthood sealing ordinance, but due to the woman's new marriage covenant, the "old covenant" would no longer authorize sexual relations in that union. Martha Sonntag Bradley and Mary Brown Firmage Woodward observed: "In Nauvoo one way the Mormons dissolved civil marriages was by superseding them with a covenant of eternal marriage, a 'higher law' that overrode previous marriages without the necessity of a divorce."[22]

---

22. Martha Sonntag Bradley and Mary Brown Firmage Woodward, *Four Zinas: A Story of Mothers and Daughters on the Mormon Frontier*, 130.

These observations are consistent with the instructions regarding polyandrous sexuality outlined in verses 41–42, and 61–63.

Of all of Joseph Smith's ceremonial polyandrous marriages, evidence is available supporting that three sealings exhibited this dynamic—the plural unions to Sylvia Sessions Lyon (discussed in Chapter 13), Sarah Ann Whitney and Mary Heron Snider (both discussed in Chapter 16). Currently, there is no documentation showing that any of Joseph Smith's polyandrous marriages were sealed for "time and eternity" without the knowledge of the civil husband who was thereafter disfranchised from the marriage. Admittedly, if such eternal marriage sealings were ever contracted without the legal husband's knowledge, problems would have arisen as the woman thereafter felt unilaterally divorced from him. If any such sealings did occur, the prevailing "culture of honor" might have empowered the civil husband to retaliate against the sealed husband. However, no available documents describe such an occurrence, and it seems safe to conclude that such an occurrence never happened.

In summary, both authorities—civil and priesthood—can create lawful marriages between a man and a woman on earth; but according to Joseph Smith's teachings, either together or separately, they are unable to authorize full polyandry (with sexuality). If a woman is wedded to a husband by each authority—that is, if she is legally married to a husband but is also sealed in the new and everlasting covenant of marriage to a second husband—the new covenant ratified by priesthood authority overrides the earthly contract. By accepting the new covenant, the participants acknowledge a practical dissolution of the union in what might be considered a "religious divorce." For them, the legal marriage becomes dead and is ignored, as an effect of an eternal nuptial.

Writing about the sealing authority of the new and everlasting covenant of marriage, Todd Compton asserted, "Thus all couples in Nauvoo who accepted Mormonism were suddenly unmarried, granted Joseph's absolutist, exclusivist claims to divine authority."[23] Compton overstates the case. Nauvoo couples were never viewed as being "unmarried" if their weddings had been legally performed according to the laws of the land but were not yet sealed by priesthood authority. During the 1839–45 period, Church leaders performed civil marriages at members' request. Based on existing records, leaders officiated at the civil weddings of at least two couples in 1839, thirty in 1840, forty-five in 1841, sixteen in 1842, sixteen in 1843, twenty-seven in 1844, and twenty-eight in 1845.[24] Joseph personally performed at least twelve and Hyrum Smith twenty-six.[25] Accordingly, the view that accepting Mormonism

---

23. Todd Compton, "A Trajectory of Plurality: An Overview of Joseph Smith's Thirty-Three Plural Wives," 23.

24. Lyndon W. Cook, comp., *Nauvoo Deaths and Marriages, 1839–1845*, 89–114.

25. Ibid.

instantly dissolved civil marriages making new members "unmarried" is inaccurate. However, Compton is not completely in error because one aspect of "Mormonism" could apparently override and dissolve a civil marriage: an eternal sealing—a marriage performed by priesthood authority in the new and everlasting covenant.

This confusion highlights the perceived differences between earthly marriages and the newly described eternal marriages sanctioned by priesthood keys. John D. Lee provided this recollection describing the feelings of some Church members upon learning of eternal and celestial marriage:

> About the same time the doctrine of "sealing" for an eternal state was introduced [1842–43], and the Saints were given to understand that their marriage relations with each other were not valid. That those who had solemnized the rites of matrimony had no authority of God to do so. That the true priesthood was taken from the earth with the death of the Apostles and inspired men of God. That they were married to each other only by their own covenants, and that if their marriage relations had not been productive of blessings and peace, and they felt it oppressive to remain together, they were at liberty to make their own choice, as much as if they had not been married.[26]

While Lee's declarations cannot always be taken at face value,[27] in this case his description seems to have been accurate, especially regarding the possibility that a woman could have been sealed for eternity to someone other than her legal husband.

Some Researchers Ignore Joseph's Smith's Theological Positions

One aspect common to most researchers who depict Joseph Smith as practicing sexual polyandry is a lack of attention to his theology. According to the Prophet's instructions, the practice is both nondoctrinal and antidoctrinal. However, some researchers take the position that Joseph Smith was a deceiver and that his revelations and sermons therefore represent only his public position, not his private opinions or behavior.

For example, Dan Vogel in his *Joseph Smith: The Making of a Prophet*, concludes: "One cannot ignore Smith's capacity to deceive. One of the clearest

---

26. Lee, *Mormonism Unveiled*, 146.
27. John D. Lee's purported autobiography, *Mormonism Unveiled; or the Life and Confessions of the Late Mormon Bishop, John D. Lee* was edited by his attorney, William W. Bishop and published posthumously. Bishop claimed that the volume contains "simply true copies of material furnished me by John D. Lee," (viii) but Bishop's editing may have affected Lee's original text to an extent that cannot be determined, since no earlier drafts have survived.

evidence of this is his repeated public denials during the early 1840s of his own and other's plural marriages."[28] Vogel is correct in observing that the Prophet used carefully constructed statements to publicly deny the practice of polygamy several times during his lifetime, even while he was indisputably involved in the practice privately. When addressing twenty separate "questions which are daily and hourly asked by all classes of people whilst we are traveling"[29] in the July 1838 issue of the *Elder's Journal*, one inquirer asked: "Do the Mormons believe in having more wives than one?" Joseph Smith replied: "No, not at the same time."[30] This statement is accurate although incomplete. It was true because "the Mormons," as a religious group in July 1838, did not believe in polygamy. "Having more wives than one" was not then a "Mormon" doctrine or practice. Nevertheless, it is apparent that at least a few then believed it to be a correct principle and that Joseph Smith had already engaged in one such marriage.

Similarly, in 1844, one month before the martyrdom, the Prophet stated: "What a thing it is for a man to be accused of committing adultery, and having seven wives, when I can only find one."[31] The accuracy of this statement hinged upon how much effort Joseph Smith might have invested at that moment in order to "find" his other wives. Since he had then been sealed to over two dozen women, one can only conclude that, at that moment, he was

---

28. Dan Vogel, *Joseph Smith: The Making of a Prophet*, ix. In addition to the sources cited in this section, other researchers who similarly imply that Joseph Smith commonly preached one position while privately practicing another include B. Carmon Hardy, *Solemn Covenant: The Mormon Polygamous Passage*, 365–67; George D. Smith, *Nauvoo Polygamy: ". . . but we called it celestial marriage,"* 411–19; D. Michael Quinn, *The Mormon Hierarchy: Origins of Power*, 89; and Susan Staker, "'The Lord Said, Thy Wife Is a Very Fair Woman to Look Upon': The Book of Abraham, Secrets, and Lying for the Lord."

29. Joseph Smith, Untitled editorial beginning "We would say to the patrons . . .," *Elder's Journal*, 1, no. 2 (November 1837) 28. This journal was then being published in Kirtland, Ohio.

30. Joseph Smith, Untitled editorial beginning "In obedience to our promise...," *Elder's Journal* 1, no. 3 (July 1838): 43.

31. Ehat and Cook, *The Words of Joseph Smith*, May 26, 1844, 377; *History of the Church*, 6:411. For other general denials of the practice of polygamy, see "Apostacy," *Millennial Star* 3, no. 4 (August 1, 1842): 74; Parley P. Pratt, "Fragment of an Address, by P. P. Pratt," *Millennial Star* 6, no. 2 (July 1, 1845) 22–23; "Who Is the Liar," *Millennial Star* 12 (January 15, 1850) 29–30; Untitled notice beginning "Inasmuch as the public mind...," *Times and Seasons* 3 (September 1, 1842): 909; "On Marriage," *Times and Seasons* 3 (October 1, 1842): 939–40; H. R. Letter from Boston, Massachusetts, *Times and Seasons* 4 (March 15, 1843) 143; "Notice," *Times and Seasons* 5 (February 1, 1844): 423; Hyrum Smith, Letter to the Editor, *Times and Seasons* 5 (March 15, 1844): 474; Letter from "An Old Man of Israel," *Times and Seasons* 5 (November 15, 1844): 715; E. M. Webb, "Mormonism Unveiled," *Times and Seasons* 6 (May 1, 1845): 893–94.

not looking very hard. These types of denials naturally bring criticisms from observers today and seem somewhat clumsy attempts to avoid detection while obeying God's directive: "thou shalt not lie" (D&C 42:21). Despite these weaknesses, RLDS leaders during the nineteenth century apparently took these statements at face value.[32]

Writers who observe the disharmony between Joseph Smith's public denunciations of polygamy and his private practices may take the position that none of his theological positions need be taken seriously because, in their view, he himself did not observe them. I take the contrary position: that historical reconstructions of Joseph Smith's actions and behaviors must, in a creditable way, account for the doctrines he taught. This position is particularly important given the numerous questions raised by the Prophet's sealings to already-married women.

As I study the documentary evidence, it appears that Joseph Smith used careful language to secretly defy public laws that contradicted directives that he accepted as divine commandments. However, to conclude that he employed similar tactics in other aspects of his life or to generalize this strategy beyond the issue of acknowledging the practice of plural marriage requires specific evidence. Stated another way, in order to obey God, Joseph Smith may have publicly feigned obedience to the laws of the land while privately disobeying them. However, assuming that he also publicly feigned obedience to *God's* laws while privately disobeying them is not warranted without specific documentation. The two processes are very dissimilar.

A second problem with assuming that Joseph was not obeying the theological beliefs that he himself taught is that his faithful followers, even those closest to him, apparently saw no such inconsistency.[33] For some writers at-

---

32. RLDS Church President Joseph Smith III, Letter to John Smith (Church patriarch and son of Hyrum Smith), wrote on December 28, 1876: "To admit that Joseph and Hyrum publicly denied, but secretly practiced polygamy, or plurality of wives, was to admit they were deceivers, double dealing, two-faced men" (pp. 11–17).

33. Certainly many of Joseph's followers became disillusioned over various issues and at various stages of their association with him. Examples are David Whitmer's resistance to the increasingly refined structure of Church administration, Oliver Cowdery's frustrations with Joseph Smith's authoritative leadership and his first polygamous marriage to Fanny Alger, and William Law's ultimately wholesale rejection of plural marriage. All three of these men were part of Joseph Smith's inner circle who shared administrative power with him. However, their disillusion rapidly led to disaffection; they did not pretend to continue to support Joseph after they concluded that he was wrong, had disobeyed God's instructions, or had become a "fallen prophet." Where polygamy is concerned, I find it difficult to believe that even Joseph Smith's acknowledged charisma could have convincingly arrayed immorality in divine garb without more than a few people becoming rattled and breaking ranks.

Sexual Polyandry: Examining the Contradictory Evidence   389

tempting to explain this anomaly, the answer was not faith but gullibility. George T. M. Davis wrote in 1844: "From personal observation, I am convinced that there are many poor, unfortunate, deluded beings there, who are naturally honest, and who, under the influence of good example and upright leaders, would 'act well their part' in society. That class, however, are, generally speaking, of weak intellect, to a great extent uneducated, and easily made the dupes of the vicious."[34] Similarly, Mrs. Benjamin G. Ferris, based on her observations of Latter-day Saints in Utah during one winter twelve years later, asserted: "Anyone with half an eye can see the object of the prophet Smith, in promulgating such a doctrine [of plural marriage]; and the wonder is, that its transparency is not obvious to all. . . . The effect of the Mormon creed is, evidently, to gather together a low class of villains, and a still lower class of dupes."[35] Statements of this type are self-serving. The authors, though sometimes being in contact with Mormons only indirectly or for a few months, present themselves as more discerning than the Latter-day Saints who personally lived through the events in question and still found reasons to believe.

Steven C. Harper, in his study of the lives of Nauvoo polygamists, further challenges the accuracy of such "explanations."[36] It is significant that early polygamists typically reacted to their first exposure to plural marriage with shock and revulsion, struggled to come to terms with the doctrine and practice, and did so by utilizing, rather than denying, their strong spirituality, piety, and scriptural knowledge. Non-Mormon Bernard DeVoto observed in 1930: "He [Joseph Smith] attracted to his support not only the ordinary fanatics who gave the American Pentecost its hundreds of sects and supported them all, but also such superior and more significant men as [Sidney] Rigdon, Orson and Parley Pratt, Orson Hyde, W. W. Phelps, and Brigham Young."[37] Fawn Brodie agreed: "The best evidence of the magnetism of the Mormon religion was that it could attract men with the quality of Brigham Young, whose tremendous energy and shrewd intelligence were not easily directed by any influence outside himself."[38]

---

34. George T. M. Davis, *An Authentic Account of the Massacre of Joseph Smith*, 38. Davis lived in Alton, Illinois, over 170 miles south of Nauvoo. Shortly after the martyrdom, he traveled to Hancock County to interview apostates and nonmembers in preparation for his book.

35. Mrs. Benjamin G. Ferris, *The Mormons at Home, with Some Incidents of Travel from Missouri to California*, 130–31. For other examples, William Harris, *Mormonism Portrayed: Its Errors and Absurdities Exposed, and the Spirit and Designs of Its Authors Made Manifest*, 35, called Mormons "dupes and fanatics." See also Rev. F. B. Ashley, *Mormonism: An Exposure of the Impositions Adopted by the Sect Called "The Latter-day Saints*, 8.

36. Steven C. Harper, "'By No Means Men of Weak Minds': The Gullible Bumpkin Thesis and the First Mormons," 39–48.

37. Bernard DeVoto, "The Centennial of Mormonism," 5.

38. Fawn M. Brodie, No *Man Knows My History: The Life of Joseph Smith, the Mormon*

Accordingly, to assume that Joseph Smith could have callously transgressed his own teachings without disillusioning followers like Brigham Young, John Taylor, Eliza R. Snow, Zina Huntington, and many others is problematic. Most of Joseph's closest followers were too perceptive to be bamboozled and too religious to become accomplices in a deliberate deception. When asked in 1859: "Is the system of your church [a plurality of wives] acceptable to the majority of its women?" Brigham Young replied: "They could not be more averse to it than I was when it was first revealed to us as the Divine will. I think they generally accept it, as I do, as the will of God."[39] On August 18, 1887, the aged Eliza R. Snow declared: "It [plural marriage] is so great and grand an institution that only the good and god-like can understand and appreciate it."[40] Dismissing these comments as the babblings of dupes or the cover-ups of confederates seems insufficient. The documented behavior of men and women like Brigham Young and Eliza R. Snow suggests that, from their viewpoint, Joseph Smith lived his religion with integrity.

The sections above have discussed *theological* teachings that present doctrinal reasons why devout followers of Joseph Smith would not have readily engaged in polyandrous sexuality. Importantly, the historical record supports that the Prophet's teachings were not ignored by Nauvoo polygamists but were used to guide their beliefs and behaviors. While it is impossible to prove that something did not happen, the following sections of this chapter will investigate historical observations that raise important questions regarding the possibility that Joseph Smith practiced sexual polyandry.

No Complaints from Joseph Smith's Polyandrous Wives

An important potential source of historical evidence for sexual polyandry in Joseph Smith's life would be his polyandrous wives. Logically, even in the highly patriarchal nineteenth century and even given Joseph Smith's recognized charisma, it seems unlikely that he could have created and taught

---

Prophet, 126–27. In 1885, Joseph Johnson, *The Great Mormon Fraud*, 17, disagreed: "He [Brigham Young] must have been an idiot, or thought he was addressing idiots."

39. Horace Greeley, "Overland Journey #21: Two Hours with Brigham Young," 718; also quoted in Horace Greeley, *An Overland Journey from New York to San Francisco in the Summer of 1859*, 138, and reprinted as "Two Hours with Brigham Young," *Millennial Star* 21 (September 17, 1859): 608–11, with the following qualification: "Although the wording of the conversation might not be exactly as spoken, on the whole, we have no hesitation in endorsing it by republication" (605). The endorsement is part of the editorial discussion of the article printed later in that issue of the *Millennial Star*.

40. J.J.J., "Two Prophets' Widows: A Visit to the Relicts of Joseph Smith and Brigham Young," 6.

a nondoctrinal and antidoctrinal sexual standard to LDS women without serious repercussions. No religious precedent could be cited as an example. The Bible describes no prophetess or priestess who engaged in polyandry. No scriptures were available justifying it. Joseph Smith would have been starting from scratch to defend such a principle to women who possessed a familiarity with the Old Testament and a professed devotion to biblical moral standards.

Among the polyandrous wives of Joseph Smith were strong women who went on to become political and social activists during the Utah period and open proponents of polygamy after its announcement in 1852. In addition, many nonpolyandrous wives were aware of Joseph Smith's sealings to legally married women. None of these women seem to have been the gullible and easily duped creatures that are stock characters in lurid nineteenth-century anti-Mormon novels or, more tellingly, in works that present themselves as historical. Zina Huntington reported visionary experiences, exercised the gift of tongues, and was pregnant with the child of her legal husband, Henry Jacobs, when she was sealed to Joseph Smith in October 17, 1841. Concerning Lucy Walker, Mary Elizabeth Rollins Lightner, Emily Dow Partridge, and Eliza Partridge, historians Martha Sonntag Bradley and Mary Brown Firmage Woodward observe: "All were intelligent, sensitive young women of deep spirituality, perplexed by the doctrine [of polygamy] and struggling with its ramifications."[41]

Available evidence indicates that these women were committed to their matrimonial covenants and the moral standard of the day. They understood their obligations of wifehood to include strict marital fidelity. They would have had only one interpretation for having another "husband" in any kind of a sexual relationship: marital infidelity and a violation of their marriage vows. Thus, the category of "celestial marriage" and the instruction of a man they accepted as God's prophet would have presented them with a heart-wrenching conundrum. Even without the violation of their religious convictions, they would have feared the social consequences of what would have been universally seen as adultery. Fear for themselves would have been intensified by fear for Joseph Smith's safety and even for the impact of such revelations on the Church.

It is most unfortunate that none of these women left a specific record of how Joseph Smith explained the principle of plural marriage to them, the specific path they followed to come to an acceptance of the principle, or what exactly it meant to them in terms of their daily lives and activities. I also find it significant that no known documentation exists establishing that these women saw themselves as practicing polyandry or that they had any interest in such social experiments as sexual polyandry.[42] Lawrence Foster wrote, "I

---

41. Bradley and Woodward, *Four Zinas*, 115.

42. For example, as discussed in Chapter 4, Jacob Cochran promoted novel marriage practices among his religious adherents that the courts judged to be adultery, resulting

see no evidence that the behavior in which Joseph Smith apparently engaged was viewed, either by the Mormon prophet himself or by his close followers who knew about it, as a form of 'polyandry.'"[43] The historical record is replete with complaints about nonpolyandrous polygamy from participants in both Nauvoo and afterwards.[44] However, no similar complaints about polyandrous polygamy are found, despite the fact that it would have been considered a much more shocking practice.

No Complaints from Witnesses and Officiators

Joseph's eternal sealings involved witnesses and officiators, often family members of the plural brides. At the time of Joseph Smith's death, a total of 115 men and women had been sealed in plural marriages. (See Chapters 1 and 29.) Dozens more were aware of the teachings. Although polyandrous relationships were a fraction of this total, they would have been known; and participants and observers would have needed to be convinced of the propriety of sexual polyandry. Dimick Huntington was the officiator in separately sealing two of his sisters, Zina and Presendia, to Joseph; Dimick's wife, Fanny, willingly served as a witness for both sealings.[45] How readily would these individuals have accepted and participated in a practice that they must have defined as adultery? Difficult though polygamy must have been to accept, the evidence tilts toward their viewing the relationships as consistent with Joseph's strict moral teachings.

---

in his incarceration in 1819. In 1837, John Humphrey Noyes began gathering followers to his Oneida, New York, community; that group practiced complex marriage, where any member could experience sexual relations with any other member. Lawrence Foster, *Religion and Sexuality: Three American Communal Experiments of the Nineteenth Century*, 72–122. Other nineteenth-century experiments with marital and family arrangements flourished, but they were not models that Mormonism's Bible-based New England women would have respected, sought out, or followed, even assuming they knew about them.

43. Lawrence Foster, "Plural Marriage, Singular Lives," 185; see also Lawrence Foster, "Sex and Prophetic Power: A Comparison of John Humphrey Noyes, Founder of the Oneida Community, with Joseph Smith, Jr., the Mormon Prophet," 77.

44. See for example, Mary Isabella Hales Horne [catalogued as Mrs. Joseph Horne]; "Migration and Settlement of the Latter Day Saints, Salt Lake City, 1884," 17; see also Bathsheba W. Smith, Deposition, Temple Lot Transcript, Respondent's Testimony, Part 3, p. 292, question 21.

45. Zina D. H. Young, Affidavit, May 18, 1869; and Presendia Huntington Buell Kimball, May 1, 1869, in Joseph F. Smith, Affidavit Books, 1:5, 1:7 respectively. The discrepancy between the dates and the page numbers result from Smith's leaving some blank pages at the beginning of the affidavit book before beginning to write on May 1. He used one of these blank pages for Zina's affidavit on May 18.

Belinda Marden Pratt, a plural wife of Parley P. Pratt, wrote in 1854: "'Why not a plurality of husbands as well as a plurality of wives?' To which I reply: 1st God has never commanded or sanctioned a plurality of husbands."[46] On October 8, 1869, Apostle George A. Smith taught that "a plurality of husbands is wrong."[47] His wife, Bathsheba Smith, was asked in 1892 if it would "be a violation of the laws of the church for one woman to have two husbands living at the same time." She replied: "I think it would."[48] All of these individuals were involved with Nauvoo polygamy, and several were undoubtedly aware of Joseph Smith's sealings to legally married women, yet they made no effort to condone sexual polyandry, nor is there any evidence that any man but Joseph Smith engaged in polyandry in Nauvoo.

No Complaints from Legal Husbands

Another potential source of information regarding the presence of sexual polyandry are the legal husbands. Todd Compton acknowledges that sexual polyandrous relationships would be difficult for the men involved: "One wonders why these 'first husbands' apparently acquiesced to their wives' marriages to Smith,"[49] adding, "If polygyny offended against the American cult of true womanhood, polyandry offended even more."[50] Richard L. Bushman admits: "The practice [of polyandry] seems inexplicable today." Then he asks: "Why would a husband consent?"[51]

Another relevant question is whether the first husband was kept in the dark about his wife's polyandrous sealing. Richard Van Wagoner concluded: "The legal husband did not usually know about the extralegal husband."[52] Richard L. Bushman, however, asserted: "In most cases, the husband knew of the plural marriage and approved."[53] Todd Compton attempted to answer this question husband by husband (see Table 14.1) but concluded that we lack reliable evidence describing the husband's knowledge of or immediate response the polyandrous sealing in eleven of twelve cases—at least at the time they were performed.

---

46. Belinda Marden Pratt, "Defense of Polygamy: By a Lady of Utah, in a Letter to Her Sister in New Hampshire," 471.
47. George A. Smith, October 8, 1869, *Journal of Discourses*, 13:41.
48. Bathsheba Smith, Deposition, Temple Lot Transcript, Respondent's Testimony, Part 3, p. 347, question 1142.
49. Todd Compton, *In Sacred Loneliness: The Plural Wives of Joseph Smith*, 21.
50. Ibid., 80.
51. Richard Lyman Bushman, *Joseph Smith: Rough Stone Rolling*, 439.
52. Richard S. Van Wagoner, "Mormon Polyandry in Nauvoo," 81.
53. Bushman, *Joseph Smith: Rough Stone Rolling*, 439.

Table 14.1
Polyandrous Husbands Identified by Compton: Known Attitudes

Husband	Church Member?	Civil Marriage Date	Wife	Sealing to Joseph Smith	Husband's History	Husband's Death
Henry B. Jacobs	Yes, baptized 1832	March 7, 1841	Zina Diantha Huntington	Oct. 1841	Henry witnessed Zina's sealing to Joseph Smith for eternity and Brigham Young for "time," on Feb. 2, 1846.	1886 Utah
Norman Buell	Yes, baptized 1836, disaffected 1838	Jan. 6, 1827	Presendia Lathrop Huntington	Dec. 11, 1841	Norman "felt the difficulties were too much, and would have persuaded her, if possible, to leave the Church, but she remained firm and steadfast."[a]	1872
Adam Lightner	No	Aug. 11, 1835	Mary Elizabeth Rollins	Feb. 1842	Adam apparently remained a nonmember his entire life.	1885 Utah
Windsor Lyon	Yes, Excommunicated. Nov. 1842 Rebaptized Jan. 1846	April 21, 1838	Sylvia Sessions	After Nov. 19, 1842	Windsor fathered three children with Sylvia prior to his excommunication and two after his 1846 rebaptism. The only child conceived while he was out of the Church was Josephine, allegedly Joseph Smith's daughter.	1849 Iowa
David Sessions	Yes, baptized 1834	June 28, 1812	Patty Bartlett	March 9, 1842	David married two wives polygamously and largely abandoned Patty.	1850 Utah
Orson Hyde	Yes, reinstated in 1839	Sept. 4, 1834	Marinda Nancy Johnson	April 1842	Served as apostle and member of the Quorum of the Twelve. Marinda divorced Orson in 1870.[b]	1878 Utah

a. "Death of Presendia Kimball," *Deseret News Weekly*, February 6, 1892, 14.

b. Exposé author Ann Eliza Webb Young claimed that Orson Hyde, on learning of Marinda's sealing to the Prophet, was "in a furious passion." Ann Eliza Webb Young, *Wife Number 19*, 325–26. Ann Eliza's account is questionable in many ways; but even assuming Hyde's misgivings were real at one point, they were not permanent. Within months, Orson appealed to Joseph to perform his own plural marriage.

Sexual Polyandry: Examining the Contradictory Evidence 395

Jabez Durfee	Yes	March 3, 1834	Elizabeth Davis	Prior to June 1842?	Jabez and Elizabeth divorced prior to January 1846.	1867 Kansas
John Cleveland	No, friendly at first then hostile.	June 10, 1826	Sarah Kingsley	Prior to June 1842?	On August 2, 1850, Sarah wrote: "Your Father would by no means go to live with the Mormons, therefore I beg of you not to ask us any more, it offends him."c	1860 Illinois
George Harris	Yes, baptized 1834	Dec. 3, 1830.	Lucinda Pendleton	?	Served on Nauvoo High Council. George stood proxy as his wife was sealed to Joseph Smith for eternity on Jan. 22, 1846. Divorced by 1853. Did not move to Utah.	1857 Iowa
Edward Sayers	Nod	Jan. 23, 1841	Ruth Vose	Feb. 1843	Edward lived among the Saints until his death.	1861 Utah
Jonathan Holmes	Yes, baptized 1832	Dec. 1, 1842	Elvira Annie Cowles	June 1, 1843	Jonathan was always a faithful Mormon, Joseph's bodyguard and pallbearer. He was proxy when Elvira was sealed to Joseph Smith in the Nauvoo Temple.	1880 Utah
Joseph C. Kingsbury	Yes	April 29, 1843	Sarah Ann Whitney	July 7, 1842	This marriage was a front, apparently to dispel suspicions then focused on the Prophet. Sarah Ann and Joseph C. Kingsbury never consummated the union.	1898 Utah

c. John L. Smith, Letter to First Presidency, March 8, 1895, communicates that Sarah was sealed to Joseph only for "eternity": "In the days of Joseph. Mother [Sarah M. Kingsley (Howe)] Cleveland by advice, was sealed to the prophet in Nauvoo but lived with her husband John Cleveland." John Lyman Smith (1823–98) was the son of John Smith (Joseph Sr.'s brother) and Clarissa Lyman Smith, and a brother to George A. Smith—hence was Joseph Jr.'s first cousin. He married Sarah Kingsley Cleveland's daughter, Augusta Bowen Cleveland.

d. Andrew Jenson's personal notes state that Edward was not a member. Andrew Jenson Papers, Box 49, fd. 16, item 5.

These twelve husbands manifest great diversity in their relationships to the Church and its leaders. There are friendly nonmembers (Cleveland, Lightner, and Sayers), and members ranging from antagonistic (Buell) and unpredictable (Jacobs)[54] to active (Durfee, Harris, and Sessions), and stalwart (Kingsbury, Holmes, and Hyde).

On the basis of the scanty evidence available no husband is known to have reacted either positively or negatively toward Joseph Smith in a situation where the most predictable reaction would have been negative.[55] In fact, given the marital dynamic that was being disrupted by these polyandrous sealings, the lack of a negative reaction can be evaluated as positive unless one of three possible explanations prevailed: (1) the husband was completely ignorant of the polyandrous ceremony, a condition that would have imposed an enormous psychological burden on the wife; (2) the husband accepted the sealing as completely righteous in God's eyes, or (3) the husband accepted the polyandrous sealing and, however he interpreted it, understood that it did not require sexual relations between his wife and the Prophet.

No Complaints from Detractors

A fourth group of polygamy insiders who may have left a record is comprised of the detractors. William Law, though a member of Joseph Smith's First Presidency, denounced plural marriage and accused Joseph Smith of adultery. His affidavit to that effect launched the proceedings that ended with the martyrdom. (See Chapter 31.) Joseph personally instructed Law about

---

54. Jacobs experienced at least two failed marriages, besides his union to Zina. Caroline Barnes Crosby noted in her diary on January 11, 1852: "There were two couples married in our chamber. Mr. John M Horner officiated. Henry B. Jacobs to Mary Clawson." Two months later on March 20, 1852, "Mary Clawson called. She looked very sad, said she had been weeping, gave us an account of her late husband Henry B. Jacobs leaving her in consequence of his old wife [Asenath Babcock married in 1848] coming and claiming her previous right."

55. Chapter 15 discusses the case of Esther Dutcher, a polyandrous wife not included by Todd Compton. Dutcher's legal husband expressed disappointment when he learned that his wife had chosen the Prophet as an eternal mate. D. Michael Quinn affirmed that the legal husband's reaction is evidence that "contradicts his [Brian Hales's] claim that there were 'No Complaints from Legal Husbands' (his emphasis) of the Prophet's already-married wives." "Evidence for the Sexual Side of Joseph Smith's Polygamy," expanded version, July 2012, 3. Quinn asserts that disappointment voiced by a legal husband that his wife chose Joseph Smith as an eternal husband constitutes a complaint against the Prophet, with which I disagree. Understandably, the husbands may have been disheartened, but according to available evidence, none of the legal spouses accused or criticized Joseph Smith for his willingness to allow the sealings.

celestial and plural marriage,[56] and Law undoubtedly knew of some of his sealings to legally married women. In his split with Joseph Smith in the spring of 1844, the fact that Law did not accuse the Prophet of sexual polyandry and never mentioned it so far as available documents indicate, is surprising. Polyandrous sexuality would have been more shocking than adultery at that time and place. So the absence of any reference to it suggests that Law was unaware of conjugality in those unions or purposefully chose to ignore them altogether. In the end, Law settled for a less explosive charge of adultery. (For Law's role as a polygamy insider, see Chapter 31.)

Even more impressive is the fact the John C. Bennett, who claimed knowledge of seven (see Chapter 12) of Joseph Smith's plural marriages to civilly married women and even identified three by name (Presendia Huntington, Elizabeth Davis Durfee, and Patty Sessions), did not accuse the Prophet of sexual polyandry.[57] He reported polyandrous marriages without distinguishing them from nonpolyandrous polygamous unions and without recruiting the presumably offended husbands to join his crusade against Joseph. In his letters published in the July 15, 1842, edition of the *Sangamo Journal*, Bennett invited several individuals by name to join his crusade: Francis M. Higbee, George W. Robinson, Chauncey L. Higbee, Henry Marks, Martha Brotherton, and "Messrs. Kilbourne."[58] The editor of the *Sangamo Journal*, Simeon Francis, expanded Bennett's request in his next edition by identifying other possible supporters for Bennett's allegations: Sidney Rigdon, Orson Pratt, Mrs. Sarah M. Pratt, Nancy Rigdon, William Marks, Henry Maiker, "Miss Mitchell," "Rev. Samuel James," and "Capt. John F. Olney." Francis solicited their cooperation as part of their "sense of duty to the community . . . to come out with published statements."[59] In other words, Bennett and Francis together named more than a dozen persons who they thought were likely candidates to join in denunciations of Joseph Smith's improprieties; but none of these individuals were polyandrous husbands (who, logically speaking, would have been prime candidates to protect their family's honor) nor did they mention sexual polyandry as one of Joseph's alleged numerous misdeeds.

If any of Joseph Smith's opponents had suspected the presence of sexual polyandry, their silence on the subject is puzzling. The standard of frontier justice regarding a sexually molested woman generally allowed a father, husband,

---

56. William Law, Affidavit, July 17, 1885; quoted in Charles A. Shook, *The True Origin of Mormon Polygamy*, 126.
57. John C. Bennett, *The History of the Saints: Or an Exposé of Joe Smith and Mormonism*, 256.
58. John C. Bennett, Letter, June 27, 1842, published as "Bennett's Second and Third Letters," *Sangamo Journal*, July 15, 1842.
59. Ibid.

brother, or son to exact revenge by beating, horsewhipping, or even killing the perpetrator. Richard Bushman explained:

> The culture of honor bred deep loyalties to friends and family, while instilling a fierce urge to avenge insults. Andrew Jackson killed a man in a duel over a perceived slight to his wife's honor. The greatest fear in life, a fear stronger than death or damnation, was public humiliation. A man must fight for honor, whether in a duel like Jackson's or Hamilton's at the upper levels of society, or in a brawl among ordinary people. . . . In the culture of honor, one would battle to the death in defense of reputation. An honorable man who suffered an insult would spare nothing to get even.[60]

No American law would recognize a polygamous marriage, so polyandrous sexuality would be considered adultery. The non-LDS and anti-Mormon husbands would never have acknowledged polyandry as a legitimate religious practice. Even Church member Benjamin F. Johnson, who greatly admired the Prophet, threatened fatal retaliation should any improper sexual interaction occur between his sister and Joseph. In 1869 he recalled:

> I sincerely believed him [Joseph Smith] to [be] a prophet of God, and I loved him as such, and also for the many evidences of his kindness to me, yet such was the force of my education, and the scorn that I felt towards anything un-virtuous that under the first impulse of my feelings, I looked him calmly, but firmly in the face and told him that, "I had always believed him to be a good man, and wished to believe it still, and would try to;"— and that, "I would take for him a message to my sister, and if the doctrine was true, all would be well, but if I should afterwards learn that it was offered to insult or prostitute my sister I would take his life." With a smile he replied "Benjamin, you will never see that day, but you shall live to <u>know</u> that it is true, and rejoice in it."[61]

Historian Craig L. Foster provided an example dating from 1851 when the Saints were in Utah, which captures what seems to be a widely shared community expectation among the Mormons:

> Howard Egan . . . in 1851, killed James Monroe. Monroe had an affair with Egan's first wife, Tamson. Monroe wisely chose to get out of town before Egan's return from a prolonged journey to California. However, Egan followed Monroe and finally caught up with him close to the Utah border,

---

60. Bushman, *Joseph Smith: Rough Stone Rolling*, 294–95.
61. Benjamin F. Johnson, Affidavit, March 4, 1869, Joseph F. Smith, Affidavit Books, 2:3–4. On another occasion Johnson said that he told Joseph Smith: "If I ever Should know that you do this [plural marriage] to Dishonor & debauch my Sister I will kill you as Shure as the Lord Lives." Dean R. Zimmerman, ed., *I Knew the Prophets: An Analysis of the Letter of Benjamin F. Johnson to George F. Gibbs, Reporting Doctrinal Views of Joseph Smith and Brigham Young*, 41.

where he shot and killed him. Egan was later brought to a trial. . . . During the closing arguments, [George A.] Smith [his defense attorney] stated, "In this territory it is a principle of mountain common law, that no man can seduce the wife of another without endangering his own life. . . . The man who seduces his neighbor's wife must die, and her nearest relative must kill him!" Egan was acquitted.[62]

In 1855, Eleanor McComb McLean was sealed to Parley P. Pratt as his eleventh plural wife. However, at that time, she was the legal wife of Hector McLean. The couple had met and married in New Orleans in 1838 and had five children together. However, soon after the marriage, they experienced problems largely due to Hector's heavy drinking. They separated first in 1844 but subsequently reconciled and moved to San Francisco. On several occasions thereafter, Eleanor sought a permanent separation, but Hector would not allow it. In 1851, they came in contact with Parley P. Pratt and Mormonism. Eleanor wished to join, but Hector refused and even purchased a sword-cane and threatened to kill her and any minister who would baptize her. However, three years later Hector gave written permission, and she was baptized on May 24, 1854. Eleanor clung to the Church, having their children baptized unbeknownst to Hector who responded by having Eleanor committed to an insane asylum. She escaped with her children and made her way to New Orleans where they lived for a few months with her father. Dissatisfied, she traveled to Salt Lake City and married Parley P. Pratt on August 18, 1855.[63]

In the meantime, Hector McLean learned of the plural marriage and sought revenge upon Parley who managed to evade him for several months as he served a mission to the southern states. However, Hector eventually tracked down the unarmed Parley in Arkansas, fatally stabbing and shooting him to death. T. B. H. Stenhouse wrote that, shortly after the cold-blooded murder, Hector "walked through the town with his friends, and in the evening took the passing steamer for the South. No one seemed to think that he should be arrested. . . . There is always a feeling of sympathy for the injured when domestic intrusions are before the public."[64]

Polyandry would have certainly been considered such a "domestic intrusion" in Joseph's day, and public sympathy would have been on the side of the betrayed legal husband.[65] Joseph Smith's explanations would have been inad-

---

62. Craig L. Foster, "The Butler Murder of April 1869: A Look at Extralegal Punishment in Utah," 109. See also Kenneth L. Cannon II, "'Mountain Common Law': The Extralegal Punishment of Seducers in Early Utah," 308–27.
63. Steven Pratt, "Eleanor McLean and the Murder of Parley P. Pratt," 225–34.
64. T. B. H. Stenhouse, *The Rocky Mountain Saints*, 430.
65. In another example, the record of the Morgan County, Utah, Probate Court, Book "A", March 1869 term, pp. 17–22 reports that Charles A. Walker was convicted

equate, leaving him exposed to the Bible-based cultural standard of the day that required men to defend the virtue of their womenfolk by force. Proverbs expressed a common standard of retribution:

> He that goeth in to his neighbour's wife; whosoever toucheth her shall not be innocent.
> Men do not despise a thief, if he steal to satisfy his soul when he is hungry;
> But if he be found, he shall restore sevenfold; he shall give all the substance of his house.
> But whoso committeth adultery with a woman lacketh understanding: he that doeth it destroyeth his own soul.
> A wound and dishonour shall he get; and his reproach shall not be wiped away.
> For jealousy is the rage of a man: therefore he will not spare in the day of vengeance.
> He will not regard any ransom; neither will he rest content, though thou givest many gifts. (Prov. 6:28-35)

In other words, a thief can be pardoned by restoring sevenfold, but the adulterer cannot "wipe away" his sin; on the contrary, the woman's husband is justified in exacting a severe revenge—"not spar[ing] in the day of vengeance."

In light of these traditions and the reprisals that might be demanded by at least some of the husbands of Joseph Smith's polyandrous wives, it is perplexing that John C. Bennett did not exploit Joseph's alleged violation of the cultural and biblical norm. Equally surprisingly, he did not appeal to their code of manhood and justice (frontier or otherwise) when he sought collaborators to help expose Joseph Smith and his alleged immoralities.

The Calendar of Sexual Polyandry

A careful tracing of the chronology of what can be determined about the period of polyandry in Nauvoo reveals a curious pattern. After twenty months of sealings to legally married women, Joseph Smith dictated a revelation explaining the doctrines behind the practice of polygamy (now D&C 132). Creating a record of the revelation provided Joseph Smith with a perfect opportunity to justify sexual polyandry if it had been practiced.

---

of raping a married woman, Palia Swensen. The jury recommended a prison term of fifteen years, and Probate Judge Jesse Haven pronounced the sentence on March 16. The prisoner was ordered committed to the penitentiary. But when court convened on March 20, Sheriff Josiah Eardly reported that Neils Swensen, Palia's husband, had killed Walker. On March 22, the grand jury indicted Swensen for murder. He was tried the same day and the jury returned "a verdict of 'not guilty' it being justifiable homicide." Quoted in Stanley S. Ivins Collection, Notebook #8, 166.

According to available documents, Joseph was sealed to his first polyandrous wife, Zina Huntington Jacobs, on October 27, 1842, followed by sealings to possibly thirteen more women who had legal husbands. (Compton identified twelve to which I add two more, Esther Dutcher and Mary Heron, for a total of fourteen—see Chapters 15–16.) Five of the polyandrous sealings are undated but the last known occurred on June 1, 1843, to Elvira Cowles Holmes, nineteen months after the first such sealing. The existence of these unions is not in doubt, but considerably less certain is whether such sealings included sexual relations with the polyandrous wife.

The Prophet dictated the revelation on celestial and plural marriage on July 12, 1843. Although there is some evidence that he had received portions of this revelation earlier,[66] producing a written manuscript of the revelation was an important landmark in articulating the boundaries governing the practice of plural marriage. By any logic, given his practice of being sealed to civilly married women (i.e., ceremonial polyandry) for the previous twenty months, this revelation should have contained explicit authorization of sexual polyandry if such relations had been included. Such a doctrinal declaration would have retroactively authorized polyandrous conjugality and theologically assuaged criticisms, should any have arisen.

Surprisingly however, the revelation on celestial marriage contains no such directives. As noted above, the verses that refer to potential sexual polyandrous situations all condemn it as "adultery" (D&C 132:41–42, 61–63). In short, if Joseph Smith was engaged in sexual polyandry with his polyandrous wives up until at least June 1, reproving that very behavior on July 12 in the revelation made little sense. How could those aware of these relationships, including the wives themselves, have interpreted such condemnation except as hypocrisy once they became aware of the revelation? (See Chapter 25.) Joseph dictated it to his scribe in the presence of others, allowed a copy to be made, authorized Hyrum to use it to persuade Emma to comply, and also allowed him to read it to the Nauvoo High Council. Thus, it was on a very different order of information than gossip and rumors about "spiritual wifery" and clandestine licentiousness.

Sexual Polyandry:
A Non-Issue for Nauvoo and Utah Polygamists

As observed above, evidence of complaints of sexual polyandry from the men and women who were aware of Joseph Smith's sealings to legally married women have not surfaced. The "polyandrous" wives apparently did not

---

66. Danel W. Bachman, "A Study of the Mormon Practice of Plural Marriage before the Death of Joseph Smith," 50.

murmur. Their husbands left no known grievances. Officiators and witnesses evidently mounted no protest. Even anti-Mormon William Law was silent on the subject in his journal, publications, and recollections. John C. Bennett reported that his own voyeurism included witnessing sexual polyandry on several occasions, yet he did not exploit that potentially devastating charge.[67] The earliest accusation of which I'm aware was first published six years after the martyrdom in an anti-Mormon pamphlet published in England—a confusing statement by William Arrowsmith quoted by avid anti-Mormon John Bowes discussed in Chapter 12.[68]

It is easy to reason that devout women might have withheld their complaints. However, a greater surprise is that among contemporaneous manuscripts and later reminiscences, no defenses of sexual polyandry are found. If this practice had occurred, even on a limited basis, by Joseph Smith and his polyandrous wives, it seems probable that the women involved and their families might have generated discussions and justifications that would have survived in the historical record today. Even the most basic of all justifications—that Joseph Smith announced that God had approved or ordered this practice—is absent. Additional rationalizations might have appealed to scripture or other religious principles, but none are extant.

For example, in 1869 when seeking affidavits documenting Nauvoo polygamy, Joseph F. Smith made no apparent distinction between polyandrous and nonpolyandrous wives. (See Appendix C.) He entered his first affidavits on three dates in May (1, 18, and 20)—a total of ten attestations.[69] Of those, four were from polyandrous wives (Ruth Vose Sayers, Marinda Johnson Hyde, Presendia Huntington Buell, and Zina Huntington Jacobs) and two were witnesses from two of these sealings (Dimick and Fanny Huntington). The other four affidavits were from nonpolyandrous plural wives (Rhoda Richards, Malissa Lott, and Emily and Eliza Partridge). The order of the entries demonstrates no attempt to segregate polyandrous from nonpolyandrous wives. Instead, the testimonials of the various wives occur in no particular order. Possibly of greater importance is that, throughout the sixty-two affidavits and other documents written in the four affidavit books (forty-one in Books 1 and 4 with twenty-one in Books 2 and 3), not a single complaint, report, or defense of sexual polyandry is found.

The same phenomenon appears to have occurred eighteen years later in 1887 as Andrew Jenson, who became an assistant Church historian in 1891, published his "Plural Marriage" article in his periodical, *Historical Record*. (This

---

67. John C. Bennett, Affidavit, *Pittsburgh Morning Chronicle*, July 29, 1842.

68. William Arrowsmith, quoted in John Bowes, *Mormonism Exposed*, 63.

69. Joseph F. Smith, Affidavit Books, 1 and 4. See my Volume 2, Appendix C for page numbers and dates.

issue is, confusingly, dated as May 1887 but was not actually printed until July.)[70] He includes the names of twenty-seven of Joseph Smith's plural wives; nine were involved in polyandrous marriages but he does not differentiate them from the nonpolyandrous wives in any way. Five are identified by their maiden names with no mention of their legal husbands in Nauvoo: Sarah Ann Whitney, Mary Elizabeth Rollins, Sylvia Sessions, Zina Huntington, and Presendia Huntington. Two of the women are listed by their married surnames: Lucinda [Pendleton] Harris, and Sarah [Kingsley] Cleveland—also without reference to their legal husbands. Elvira A. Cowles is inaccurately identified as "afterwards the wife of Jonathan H. Holmes." According to available documents, she married Jonathan prior to her sealing to the Prophet. Surprisingly, the entry for Ruth Vose Sayers could support a polyandrous interpretation that apparently was not then viewed as problematic: "Ruth D. Vose, known as the wife of Edward Sayers." Throughout Jenson's listing of twenty-seven plural wives, there is little evidence that polyandry was an issue to be avoided or clarified. Importantly, the remainder of the twenty-one-page article quotes affidavits, letters, testimonials, and other statements from twenty-four men and women who lived in Nauvoo during Joseph Smith's lifetime and were privy to his plural marriage teachings. Yet no complaints, reports, or defenses of sexual polyandry are identified in the documents recorded.

The evident disregard for whether a sealing was polyandrous or polygynous could be interpreted in several different ways, and it must be remembered that the absence of evidence does not prove that something did not happen. However, these observations are consistent with an interpretation that sexual polyandry was not practiced by Nauvoo polygamists and therefore, they felt no need to defend or hide it in their later recollections. The apparent indifference of early polygamists to such a potentially problematic topic in the decades after the martyrdom is puzzling if it was practiced in any degree. The historical record indicates that sexual polyandry was, for them personally, a nonissue.

Polyandry and the Temple Lot Depositions

The existence of polyandrous sexuality (or the lack thereof) seems to have impacted the process of choosing witnesses to testify in the Temple Lot trial in 1892. During the proceedings, Church of Christ (Temple Lot) attorney, Colonel John N. Southern, was generously assisted by LDS Church leaders who were anxious to dispute RLDS claims that plural marriage was not sanctioned by Joseph Smith in Nauvoo. The Church of Christ (Temple Lot) goals ran parallel; by showing that the Prophet taught and practiced full conjugal polygamy, they would demonstrate that the Reorganized Church of

---

70. Andrew Jenson, "Plural Marriage," 233–34.

Jesus Christ of Latter Day Saints, which did not permit plural marriage, was not the natural successor to Joseph Smith's original organization and did not own the Independence, Missouri, temple site outright.[71] Any evidence of polygamous sexuality (polygynous or polyandrous) would support the Church of Christ (Temple Lot) position.

Nine of Joseph Smith's plural wives were still living when depositions started at Salt Lake City on March 14, 1892.[72] Three were polyandrous wives (Zina Huntington Jacobs Young, Mary Elizabeth Rollins Lightner, and Patty Bartlett Sessions) and six were nonpolyandrous (Helen Mar Kimball, Martha McBride, Almera Johnson, Emily Partridge, Malissa Lott, and Lucy Walker). Factors evidently affecting the choice of witnesses involved the health and travel distances for the women, and importantly, whether their polygamous marriages to the Prophet included conjugality. Non-sexual sealings would have been treated as spiritual marriages of little importance and would have played right into the hands of RLDS attorneys Parley Pratt Kelley (b. 1848) and Edmond Levi Kelley (b. 1844). The transcripts of the questioning show that the first plural wife called by the Church of Christ (Temple Lot) attorneys was Malissa Lott Willes, who resided in Lehi, thirty miles south of Salt Lake City.[73] When questioned, "Did you ever room with Joseph Smith as his wife?" she declared, "Yes sir."[74] The second wife to be deposed was Emily Partridge, a resident of Salt Lake City. During her testimony, she was asked, "Did you ever have carnal intercourse with Joseph Smith?" Emily answered directly, "Yes sir."[75]

At this point, a peculiar thing occurred. All three of Joseph Smith's polyandrous wives lived in or relatively near Salt Lake City and were apparently willing to testify but were bypassed. General Relief Society President Zina D. Huntington was in good health, living only a few blocks from the deposition room. Yet she was not summoned. Likewise, polyandrous wife Mary Elizabeth Rollins was well known to Church leaders and resided in Ogden, thirty-eight miles north of Salt Lake City. She was not requested to appear, nor was Patty

---

71. R. Jean Addams, "The Church of Christ (Temple Lot) and the Reorganized Church of Latter Day Saints: 130 Years of Crossroads and Controversies," 29–53.

72. Presendia Huntington died February 1, 1892, before the deposition process began in Utah the following month. See Emily Partridge, Temple Lot Transcript, Complainant's Testimony, Part 2, p. 369, introduction.

73. Malissa Lott testified on March 17. Emily Partridge had been called by the RLDS attorneys three days earlier but was deposed by the respondents on March 19. Lucy Walker testified on March 22. See Temple Lot Transcript.

74. Malissa Lott, Temple Lot Transcript, Respondent's Testimony, Part 3, p. 105, question 227.

75. Emily Partridge, Temple Lot Transcript, Respondent's Testimony, Part 3, p. 384, question 756.

Bartlett Sessions, who lived in Bountiful ten miles north of Salt Lake City. Patty was ninety-seven, probably a sufficient reason to pass her by.

The third polygamous wife called, Lucy Walker, lived in Logan, eighty-two miles to the north in Cache Valley.[76] At President Wilford Woodruff's personal request, she made the journey to Salt Lake City, probably traveling on the Utah Northern Narrow Gauge Railroad line (completed in 1873).[77] When asked during her deposition, "Did you live with Joseph Smith as his wife?" she responded "He was my husband sir."[78] Elsewhere she more plainly confirmed connubial relations with the Prophet.[79]

Among nonpolyandrous wives who were not summoned was Martha McBride who lived in Hooper, Utah (thirty-seven miles to the north). McBride's relationship with Joseph Smith is poorly documented, with no evidence of sexual relations.[80] Almera Johnson was in poor health and lived at Parowan, Utah, 232 miles to the south. She was not called.[81] Also passed by was Salt Lake resident Helen Mar Kimball who had written two books defending the practice of plural marriage. Her sealing to the Prophet occurred when she was only fourteen and the presence or absence of sexual relations in her plural marriage is debated by historians. (See Chapters 23 and 33.)

Throughout the lengthy question-and-answer sessions with Malissa Lott, Emily Partridge, and Lucy Walker, the details of their polygamous marriages with Joseph Smith were paramount; the physical aspect of sexuality was a core issue. If Zina and/or Mary Elizabeth could not testify to such relations, their testimonies as the Prophet's polygamous wives could hurt the Church of Christ (Temple Lot) cause. On the other hand, it might be reasoned that they avoided testifying because their answers might have revealed polyandrous sexuality, which would have been embarrassing and doctrinally problematic.

This second option seems less likely because, six years later, Zina willingly engaged in a formal interview (later published) with an RLDS elder, John Wight, who at one point asked: "Then it is a fact, Mrs. Young, is it not, that you married Mr. Smith at the same time you were married to Mr. Jacobs?"

---

76. Lucy Walker, Deposition, Temple Lot Transcript, Respondent's Testimony, Part 3, p. 449, question 2; see also Compton, *In Sacred Loneliness*, 471.

77. During the deposition, Walker was asked, "Who called you here?" to which she answered, "President Woodruff told me that I was wanted here." Lucy Walker, Temple Lot Transcript, Respondent's Testimony Part 3, p. 478, question 584.

78. Walker, Deposition, pp. 450–51, 468, 473, questions 29–30, 463–74, 586.

79. Lucy Walker, "Lucy Walker Statement," n.d., quoted in Rodney W. Walker and Noel W. Stevenson, *Ancestry and Descendents of John Walker [1794–1869] of Vermont and Utah, Descendants of Robert Walker, an Emigrant of 1632 from England to Boston, Mass.*, 35; D. H. Morris, "Statement," June 12, 1930; Joseph Smith III, Journal, November 18, 1876.

80. Compton, *In Sacred Loneliness*, 371.

81. Ibid., 304, 380.

to which Zina immediately responded: "What right do you have to ask such questions? I was sealed to Joseph Smith for eternity."[82] Zina's willingness to be interviewed by an RLDS inquisitor in 1898 suggests she would have been equally willing to face RLDS attorneys in 1892. However, her 1898 responses would not have been helpful to the Church of Christ (Temple Lot) at that time, had she been asked to testify.

Similarly, in 1905, Mary Elizabeth spoke freely to missionaries at BYU and even answered a direct question "concerning her husband [Adam Lightner]." She explained: "My husband did not belong to the Church. I begged and pled with him to join but he would not. He said he did not believe in it though he thought a great deal of Joseph. He sacrificed his property rather than testify against Joseph, Hyrum, and Geo. A. Smith. After he said this I went forward and was sealed to Joseph for Eternity."[83] In other words, she, like Zina, explained that she was "sealed to Joseph for Eternity." This testimony, which stopped short of sexual relations, would not have strengthened the Temple Lot Church's case.

In their responses, both women spoke of their polyandrous relationships with Joseph Smith without any hint of *sexual* polyandry or the need to justify and defend it. Also, documents indicate that if Church leaders in 1892 were worried about hiding Joseph Smith's polyandrous marriages (because of sexuality or other concerns), it would have been the first time such anxieties are identifiable in the historical record. As discussed above, when Joseph F. Smith in 1869 gathered his affidavits and in 1887 when Andrew Jenson accumulated his notes and statements, neither seemed to treat polyandrous plural marriages as problematic.

Contemporary Confidence That Joseph Smith Practiced Sexual Polyandry

The preceding three chapters have attempted to present the bulk of the pertinent available evidence, both supportive and contradictory, surrounding the question of whether Joseph Smith practiced sexual polyandry. It is certain that scholars and historians will weight differently the specific strength of the

---

82. John Wight, "Evidence from Zina D. Huntington Young," 29; see also Bradley and Woodward, *Four Zinas*, 114.

83. Mary Elizabeth Rollins Lightner, "Remarks" at B.Y.U. April 14, 1905. On other occasions, Mary Elizabeth stated she had been sealed to the Prophet for "time and eternity." Mary Elizabeth Rollins Lightner, Affidavit, March 23, 1877; Rollins Lightner, Letter to A. M. Chase, April 20, 1904, in Stead, *Doctrines and Dogmas of Brighamism Exposed*, 218–19; Mary Elizabeth Rollins Lightner, "Mary Elizabeth Rollins," copy of holograph in Susa Young Gates Papers; Rollins Lightner, "Statement," February 8, 1902.

Sexual Polyandry: Examining the Contradictory Evidence 407

TABLE 14.2
PLURAL WIVES AS CANDIDATES FOR TEMPLE LOT DEPOSITIONS IN 1892

Plural Wife	Residence	Distance (miles)	Called to testify?	Polyandrous marriage?	Notes
Emily Partridge	Salt Lake City		Yes	No	Testified of sexual relations with Joseph Smith
Zina Huntington	Salt Lake City		No	Yes	Available to testify
Helen Mar Kimball			No	No	Sealed at age 14
Patty Bartlett	Bountiful	10	No	Yes	Elderly, born in 1895
Malissa Lott	Lehi	30	Yes	No	Testified of sexual relations with Joseph Smith
Martha McBride	Hooper	37	No	No	Poorly documented
Mary E. Rollins	Ogden	38	No	Yes	Available to testify
Lucy Walker	Logan	82	Yes	No	Testified of sexual relations with Joseph Smith
Almera Johnson	Parowan	232	No	No	Poor health

documentation on either side. It is also possible that new evidence may come to light in the future. In the end, readers must draw their own conclusions.

Regardless, it appears that no document currently available represents a plain first-person attestation from the wives, legal husbands, or other insiders, that Joseph Smith engaged in polyandrous sexual relations with any of the women sealed to him who were already legally married to other men. D. Michael Quinn criticized my evidentiary expectation in his comments presented at the 2012 Mormon History Association meeting in Calgary, Canada: "NOTHING—can satisfy Brian Hales' calculatedly stringent requirements that are impossible to achieve, unless he finds a Victorian American woman who said, wrote, or testified that she (as a devout Mormon) alternated sexual intercourse with two husbands during a period of time."[84] In fact, Quinn's emotional assessment overstates the necessary threshold for convincing evidence, but his admission that such documentation is unavailable is helpful. If at least one—but preferably two or three—reliable, first-person narratives existed describing polyandrous sexuality—then some of the remaining accounts would be much more believable as secondary evidence supplementing

---

84. Quinn, "Evidence for the Sexual Side of Joseph Smith's Polygamy," expanded version, 66 note 183; emphasis Quinn's.

the core of credible documents, but no such reliable manuscript evidence has been found. In addition, none of the writers who argue in favor of sexual polyandry have attempted to account for the contradictory evidence presented in these chapters. An important question for such proponents is whether they believe Joseph Smith practiced sexual polyandry in *accordance* with his teachings or in *contradiction* to them.

Also, authors who write of Joseph Smith's polygamy usually document the presence of ceremonial polyandry without discussing the historical and theological evidences surrounding the possibility of polyandrous conjugality. Instead, they leave the readers to draw their own conclusions that sexual polyandry also existed. Consequently, audiences respond with intrigue, disgust, and/or condemnation as they imagine Joseph Smith having sexual relations with a married woman in full polyandry. If imagined sexual activity can elicit such responses 150 years after it reportedly occurred, how improbable, then, is the conclusion that earliest polygamists failed to have similar reactions on learning of such associations firsthand? And how likely is it that none of them would have confided such troubling feelings to a diary, a letter, a reminiscence, or a confidant who left such a record? This sweeping absence of documentation despite the scores of opportunities for someone to have made such a record must be accounted for at least on the basis of probability.

Ironically, the dearth of credible supportive evidence for sexual polyandry accompanied by tenuousness of proponents' arguments has not created a traditional view that such relations did not occur. Just the opposite exists today. Almost everyone who has written about Joseph Smith's plural marriages has expressed at least limited confidence that he engaged in polyandrous sexuality. As discussed, such depictions and declarations do not seem to be evidence-based; the confidence seems to outdistance the historical record. One may wonder how this came to be. This seemingly secure position appears to have developed as a result of four phenomena.

First is the important observation that the lack of evidence is not evidence of a lack—the famous logical inability to prove a negative. However, while it is impossible to demonstrate that something did not happen, this truism should not be mobilized as evidence that that something *did* happen. The absence of supportive evidence cannot disprove a theory, but it can supplement other contradictory evidence and implausibility evaluations.

Second, during the hundred years after William Arrowsmith's 1850 allegation of sexual polyandry against Joseph Smith, anti-Mormon literature sometimes included the charge on their laundry lists of the Prophet's alleged improprieties.[85] Those accusations were mostly ignored by Church leaders

---

85. See for example, F. B. Ashby, *Mormonism: An Exposure of the Impositions*, 8; Sparrow Simpson, *Mormonism: Its History, Doctrines and Practices*, 51; Benjamin G. Ferris, *Utah and*

along with other over-the-top allegations. Although few in number, all direct references by LDS authorities to polyandry or "multiple husbands" during this period condemned the practice. They reflected the feeling that sexual polyandry needed no defending (for whatever reason), that the Prophet's relationships with his polyandrous wives did not constitute adultery, and that he was not a hypocrite who was disobeying his own counsel.

Third, 1945 ushered in a new chapter in the Joseph Smith and sexual polyandry saga. Arguably the most influential book written dealing with the subject, one that seems to have single-handedly changed both LDS and non-LDS views on the topic, was Fawn Brodie's *No Man Knows My History: The Life of Joseph Smith, the Mormon Prophet*, published by the eminent Alfred A. Knopf of New York City in 1945. Throughout its pages, she consistently described Joseph Smith as a sexual polyandrist, a charismatic leader who was undeniably sharing his wives conjugally with their legal husbands all under the guise of polygamy. She confidently wrote: "Joseph could with a certain honesty inveigh against adultery in the same week that he slept with another man's wife, or indeed several men's wives, because he had interposed a very special marriage ceremony."[86] Her self-assured view is somewhat ironic because she was working from much skimpier documentation than that presented in Chapters 12 and 13. Still, lacking solid evidence did not hamper her in depicting Joseph Smith's sexual polyandry with total certainty.

Unfortunately for historical scholarship, Fawn Brodie's portrayal was not immediately questioned by historians in or out of the LDS Church. Nor did Mormon apologists rally to demand documentation of her claims. Hugh Nibley rebutted some of Brodie's general treatment of polygamy but did not touch on her interpretation of polyandry.[87] In the ensuing decades, LDS scholars have generally avoided the topic even though they realized that sexual polyandry was nondoctrinal and even antidoctrinal. In some ways, it might be argued that, in 1945, Brodie placed an elephant in the living room of LDS Church history. The elephant was comprised of her reports that Joseph Smith experienced polyandrous sexuality with some of his plural wives, reports that unbelievers readily accepted, but which believers evidently did not want to acknowledge or actively address. Perhaps LDS apologists did not ask to see

---

the Mormons: The History, Government, Doctrines, Customs, and Prospects of the Latter-day Saints, 134; Sir Richard Burton, *The City of the Saints, and across the Rocky Mountains to California, 1860*, 426; Correspondent, "The Mormon Church War," *Daily Evening Bulletin* (San Francisco), September 1, 1869: Jennie Anderson Froiseth, *The Women of Mormonism: The Story of Polygamy*, 37–38; Winifred Graham, *The Mormons*, 8.

86. Fawn M. Brodie, *No Man Knows My History: The Life of Joseph Smith, the Mormon Prophet*, 308.

87. Hugh Nibley, *No Ma'am, That's Not History: A Brief Review of Mrs. Brodie's Reluctant Vindication of a Prophet She Seeks to Expose*, 103–6.

her evidence because they were afraid she might actually have found some. Undoubtedly it was Brodie's cool assurance, more than her documentation, that shook her LDS audiences and reassured Mormon critics. Decades passed before any author openly questioned her assertions to determine whether the elephant was real or just an inflatable decoy.

Fawn Brodie's confidence continues to be echoed today. It is also enhanced by a fourth phenomenon, the willingness to make assumptions regarding Joseph Smith's motives and then to treat those assumptions almost as documented evidence. Deciphering religious claims is a complex matter and the willingness of observers to assume sexuality in all or most of Joseph Smith's plural marriages (polyandrous or otherwise) is not surprising. Individuals who do not accept his claims of being a prophet may naturally conclude he was a fraud, whether hypocritical or self-deceived. Once an observer has factored out God as a possible motivator, libido emerges as a high probability, producing the belief that, consciously or unconsciously, Joseph Smith saw in plural marriage a way to fulfill a desire for expanded sexual opportunities. With such a perspective, it is only natural to express skepticism in a scenario showing that Joseph was sealed to a legally married woman but did not have sexual relations with her. Such skepticism is not based on strong evidence supporting sexual polyandry but on the improbability that any other reason than sex would be a motive for such a marriage in the first place. Hence, for unbelievers, libido exists as essentially the only plausible incentive, and nonsexual plural marriages make no sense. These natural feelings may infuse unjustified confidence into assumptions used to interpret Joseph Smith's plurality.

At the other end of the spectrum are those who believe that God commanded Joseph Smith to practice polygamy and who accept him as a prophet. Such belief is ultimately a matter of faith in his teachings, not logic or even evidence. Brigham Young described these feelings: "The doctrine he [Joseph Smith] teaches is all I know about the matter, bring anything against that if you can. As to anything else I do not care. If he acts like a devil, he has brought forth a doctrine that will save us, if we will abide it. He may get drunk every day of his life, sleep with his neighbor's wife every night, run horses and gamble, I do not care anything about that, for I never embrace any man in my faith. But the doctrine he has produced will save you and me, and the whole world."[88] Thus, it is critical for believing and unbelieving investigators, apologists and antagonists, to be rigorously aware of their own *a priori* biases and assumptions and to work closely with the evidence, ever seeking to avoid substituting intuition for documentation.

---

88. Brigham Young, November 9, 1856, *Journal of Discourses*, 4:78.

Summary

This chapter outlined the primary contradictory evidences against the practice of sexual polyandry in Joseph Smith's plural marriages. That the teaching is both nondoctrinal and antidoctrinal is supplemented by analyses of contemporary LDS scripture pronounced by Joseph Smith and his own public teachings. Another strong counter-indication that these polyandrous marriages involved sexual relations is that no polyandrous wife, legal husband, officiator, or witness mentioned its existence or expressed confusion or dismay about it. Even fervent anti-Mormons like William Law and John C. Bennett failed to exploit any such examples of resistance in their opposition to Joseph Smith. The revelation on celestial marriage given July 12, 1843, condemns sexual polyandry, labeling it as adultery. Such condemnation is counterintuitive, given that Joseph had been marrying polyandrously for the preceding twenty months and married his final polyandrous wife in the month just prior to dictating the revelation.

The treatment of Nauvoo polygamy in 1869 by Joseph F. Smith as he gathered affidavits and in Andrew Jenson's 1887 "Plural Marriage" article supports the view that sexual polyandry was a non-issue for them. Assisted by LDS Church leaders, Church of Christ (Temple Lot) attorney, Colonel John N. Southern's choices of witnesses in the Temple Lot litigation is also consistent with a lack of sexual relations in Joseph Smith polyandrous marriages to Zina Huntington Jacobs Young and Mary Elizabeth Rollins Lightner. Fawn Brodie's *No Man Know My History* is arguably the most influential book dealing with Joseph Smith's polyandry, despite the fact that its depiction of the practice was based upon little supportive evidence.

Joseph Smith's revelations supply a plausible reason why he would not have allowed sexual polyandry in the first place. (See Chapter 15.) The new and everlasting covenant of marriage supplanted all old marriage covenants, causing them to be "done away" (D&C 22:1). Neither covenant system allows sexual polyandry, so practicing would have been doubly condemned, not permissible, under the new covenant of eternal and celestial marriage.

The assumption of sexual polyandry in Joseph Smith's life thus lacks even one solid piece of documentary evidence of its existence in Nauvoo, and is further hampered by contradictory evidence. However, many observers understandably cannot imagine a marriage of any kind (monogamous or polygamous) being contracted without sexual relations as an integral component. Hence, skepticism is high and the willingness of many to assume the existence of poorly documented behaviors is impressive.

Chapter 15

Sealings for "Time and Eternity" and for "Eternity Only"

LDS theology acknowledges the existence of several types of matrimonial relations, each enduring for different chronological spans. From the beginning of history, the most common has been marriage relationships that end with death. In contrast, Joseph Smith introduced a novel form of marriage through his teaching of the doctrine of "the new and everlasting covenant of marriage." This teaching allows marital unions to be bound or "sealed" and hence to persist after mortality (D&C 128:8, 132:7, 19; Matt. 16:19, 19:5–6). His theology also includes two forms of *eternal* sealings, one for "time and eternity" and the second exclusively for "eternity."

Duration of Three Forms of Marriage

In 1951, Apostle John A. Widtsoe acknowledged: "Several approaches to eternal marriage may be made: Two living persons may be sealed to each other for time and eternity. . . . It is also possible, though the Church does not now permit it, to seal two living people for eternity only, with no association on earth."[1] Concerning these "eternity only" sealings, he explained:

> [One] kind of celestial marriage seems to have been practiced in the early days of plural marriage. It has not been practiced since Nauvoo days, for it is under Church prohibition. Zealous women, married or unmarried, loving the cause of the restored gospel, considered their condition in the hereafter. Some of them asked that they might be sealed to the Prophet for eternity. They were not to be his wives on earth, in mortality, but only after death in the eternities. This came often to be spoken of as celestial marriage. Such marriages led to misunderstandings by those not of the Church, and unfamiliar with its doctrines. To them marriage meant only association on earth. Therefore any ceremony uniting a married woman, for example, to Joseph Smith for eternity seemed adulterous to such people.[2]

---

1. John A. Widtsoe, *Evidences and Reconciliations*, 340.
2. John A. Widtsoe, *Joseph Smith: Seeker after Truth, Prophet of God*, 240; see also Widtsoe, *Evidences and Reconciliations*, 343.

All three types of marriages were contracted in Nauvoo: "time only," "time and eternity," both of which may have included earthly conjugality, and marriages for "eternity only" that did not. However, sealings for eternity only were rare, even in Joseph Smith's day.

Previous to the performance of eternal marriage ceremonies, individuals probably chose their spouses without thinking of eternity. Christian dogma generally taught that marriage did not persist after the resurrection. Hence, as eternal marriage was introduced, husbands and wives confronted the possibility that they could be joined to their spouses forever. Some may have longed to keep their companions beyond the grave and rejoiced in the new doctrines. However, two classes of husbands and wives may have felt differently. Individuals whose spouses were nonmembers, inactive, or antagonistic could not be sealed because of worthiness and willingness issues to contract the sacred ordinances. A second group comprised men and women who found themselves in unhappy marriages; they may have quietly or openly balked at the offer to be sealed eternally to their problematic companions, even though they may have felt obligated to remain in the marriage during life, either through duty, for the sake of their children, or because of financial and social considerations.[3]

Once the teaching of eternal marriage was known among the unmarried members, they were expected to weigh potential marital companions as mates, not only for mortality, but also for eternity. Thereafter "eternity only" sealings were discontinued. Andrew F. Ehat assessed: "Joseph Smith only expected pseudo-polyandry to be a temporary catalyst essential to his first attempt to simultaneously introduce to the corporate consciousness of the Church the concepts of priesthood legitimacy [of marriages], eternal marriage, and polygyny."[4]

---

3. Primary examples are the women who were already legally married but who chose to be sealed to Joseph Smith for eternity. There is no evidence that the Prophet coerced these women to be sealed to him. For example, Joseph married two widows, Delcena Johnson Sherman and Martha McBride Knight. When the women appeared at the Nauvoo Temple to be resealed for eternity by proxy, Delcena was sealed vicariously to her deceased legal husband, Royal Lyman Sherman, while Martha McBride was sealed to Joseph Smith, not to her civil spouse, Vinson Knight. Lisle G Brown, *Nauvoo Sealings, Adoptions, and Anointings: A Comprehensive Register of Persons Receiving LDS Temple Ordinances, 1841–1846*, 272, 283. Marinda Nancy Johnson Hyde apparently changed her mind after the Prophet's death and was sealed to her legal husband, Orson Hyde, in the Nauvoo Temple. Brown's entry (285 note 323) showing Marinda Nancy Johnson sealed to Joseph Smith in the Nauvoo Temple on January 11, 1846, is in error. In a November 23, 2008, email to me, Brown clarified: "The information in the NSAA [*Nauvoo Sealings, Adoptions, and Anointings*] is not correct.... Marinda Nancy Johnson was sealed to Orson Hyde on Jan 11, 1846 for time and eternity. The sealing records do not show it as a proxy sealing to Hyde. Compton is correct." Used by permission. See also Todd Compton, *In Sacred Loneliness: The Plural Wives of Joseph Smith*, 243.

4. Andrew F. Ehat, "Pseudo-Polyandry: Explaining Mormon Polygyny's Paradoxical

Joseph Smith and Sealings for Eternity Only

A few authors have taken the position that none of the Prophet's sealings were exclusively for eternity.[5] Concluding that all of Joseph Smith's marriages fell into two categories—either for "time only" or "time and eternity"—implies that all of his unions might also have included conjugal relations. Todd Compton observes: "Though it is possible that Joseph had some marriages in which there were no sexual relations, there is no explicit or convincing evidence for this (except perhaps, in the cases of the older wives, judging from later Mormon polygamy)."[6] But even for Joseph Smith's "older wives," Compton is hesitant to suggest that their sealings might have been for "eternity" (without sexual relations) writing: "There are no known instances of marriages for 'eternity only' in the nineteenth century."[7]

Consistent with this assumption, throughout his impressive and comprehensive volume, *In Sacred Loneliness* Compton carefully avoids describing Joseph Smith's marriages as only for "eternity," even if he concludes that they did not include sexual relations. Instead, he substitutes other words that have the same practical meaning. For example, he wrote: "Patty [Sessions] married Joseph when she was forty-seven, well into middle age, so the marriage may have been *ceremonial only*, without a sexual dimension. . . . The ceremony was probably *purely religious in nature* and no cohabitation took place."[8] The terms "ceremonial only" and "purely religious" seem to reflect the characteristics of a sealing for eternity only. Concerning another union, Compton writes similarly: "Rhoda [Richards] was one of Joseph Smith's older wives and their marriage is a pure example of dynastic matrimony. . . . [T]here was no romantic involvement in the union. . . . [S]he expected to be married to [Joseph Smith] in eternity."[9]

D. Michael Quinn's thesis and dissertation provided this perspective in the 1970s:

> It has been suggested that the ordinance of sealing a living man and woman did not always involve the physical union of marriage, but instead

---

Companion," 27.

5. Compton, *In Sacred Loneliness: The Plural Wives of Joseph Smith*, 298, also 295, for Delcena's "time only" marriage to Joseph Smith, although no evidence exists to verify it. Contrast his pp. 14 and 500 for his argument that the lack of evidence may be evidence that "eternity only" sealings may never have occurred. See also Gary James Bergera, "The Earliest Eternal Sealings of Civilly Married Couples Living and Dead," 51, 59.

6. Compton, *In Sacred Loneliness*, 15. He also writes: "It is possible that Smith did not have sexual relations with his older wives" (281; see also 558; contrast 682).

7. Ibid., 14; see also 500.

8. Ibid., 171–72, 179; emphasis mine.

9. Ibid., 558.

was regarded as solemnizing a spiritual union that had reference only to life after death. Such an interpretation can be supported by several evidences.[10]

Even when the sealing involved a living man and woman, literal marriage was not always regarded as incumbent upon the participants in the ceremony. . . . At least one of the plural wives of Joseph Smith specified that she had been sealed to him "for eternity," thus precluding the actuality of a marriage relation during his life.[11] Thus, the sealing of living couples in the Mormon Church may not always have been synonymous with marriage in its conventional form.[12]

By contrast, twenty years later, Quinn emphasized the lack of explicit evidence for such sealings:

There are clear problems of evidence in claiming that a relationship remained celibate for a man and woman who received an LDS sealing ordinance as living persons. First, the original records of sealings in the nineteenth century used variations of only two phrases to define each marriage: "for time and eternity," and "for time only," both of which gave the sanction of the church for sexual intercourse between the living persons thus sealed. If the phrase "eternity only" ever appeared in an *original* record of LDS sealing in the nineteenth century, I have not discovered it while examining thousands of such manuscript entries.[13]

Quinn's observations are undoubtedly accurate regarding "original records" of "sealings of the nineteenth century" in general. However, they may have little application to sealings in Joseph Smith's time. Prior to Joseph's death, more than four dozen plural sealing ceremonies were performed for thirty men and their polygamous wives.[14] Unfortunately, only one contemporary document is available providing the terminology that was used. Joseph dictated a ceremonial prayer uniting him to previously unmarried Sarah Ann Whitney that was pronounced by Sarah Ann's father, Newel K. Whitney: "You both mutually agree calling them by name to be each others companion so long as you both shall live . . . and also through out all eternity."[15] Otherwise,

---

10. D. Michael Quinn, "Organizational Development and Social Origins of the Mormon Hierarchy, 1832–1932: A Prosopographical Study," 154–55.

11. Quinn is probably referring to Patty Session. See D. Michael Quinn, *The Mormon Hierarchy: Extensions of Power*, 184.

12. D. Michael Quinn, "The Mormon Hierarchy, 1832–1932: An American Elite," 64.

13. Quinn, *The Mormon Hierarchy: Extensions of Power*, 183–84; emphasis his.

14. It appears that thirty-four of the sealing ceremonies were for Joseph Smith (Fanny Alger is not included); in addition, twenty-nine men married fifty plural wives prior to the Prophet's death. See Chaps. 1, 29, and 33.)

15. Quoted in H. Michael Marquardt, *The Joseph Smith Revelations: Text and Commentary*, 315–16; see also "Revelations in Addition to Those Found in the LDS Edition of the D&C," *New Mormon Studies: A Comprehensive Resource Library*.

the wording employed in the dozens of plural sealing ceremonies performed during Joseph Smith's lifetime was apparently never recorded, either at the time of the ceremony or shortly thereafter. Regardless, it has not been preserved and is not currently unavailable to researchers. Accordingly, there is a lack of documented sealings using "for eternity" language during Joseph Smith's day, just as there is a similar lack of documentation of the phrase "for time and eternity" during that same period.

It is true that some later reminiscences state that their sealings in Nauvoo were for "time and eternity." However, the women may have been applying current language to sealing ceremonies performed up to fifty years earlier. When asked in 1892 if she could remember the words used to seal her to Joseph Smith, Malissa Lott replied: "I don't know that I can go and tell it right over as it was. . . . I don't remember the words that were used."[16] Similarly, Emily Partridge testified: "I can't remember the exact words, that he said."[17]

Most late recollections were recorded at a time when ceremonial sealing language had been standardized to include "time and eternity." For example, Brigham Young's sister Fanny was sealed to Joseph to assure she would have a husband in the next life with no expectation of an earthly relationship.[18] Yet Harriet Cook Young, who witnessed the ceremony, recalled in 1870 that the marriage was "for time and eternity."[19] Whether individuals would have been aware of early variations in the wording of the earlier ceremonies is unclear. Furthermore, to presuppose that sexual relations were present based solely on a late memoir that declared a Nauvoo marriage was for "time and eternity" would be to draw conclusions that go well beyond the evidence.

Michael Quinn has also asserted that no "eternity only" sealings could have occurred prior to May 28, 1843, because on that date Joseph Smith was sealed to Emma Smith, which Quinn affirms was the first eternal marriage in the new and everlasting covenant.[20] This view is problematic because it assumes that, having received the sealing keys in 1836, Joseph Smith would not have used them to seal his plural marriages prior to his sealing to Emma, an interpretation that is without corroborative evidence. As quoted above,

---

16. Malissa Lott, Deposition, Temple Lot Transcript, Respondent's Testimony, Part 3, pp. 95–96, questions 54, 70.

17. Emily Partridge, Deposition, Temple Lot Transcript, Respondent's Testimony, Part 3, p. 359, question 198.

18. Brigham Young, August 31, 1873, *Journal of Discourses*, 16:166–67.

19. Harriet Cook Young, Affidavit March 4, 1870, Joseph F. Smith, Affidavit Books, 1:14, 4:14.

20. Quinn explains: "The evidence shows . . . that Emma Smith was the FIRST woman ever 'sealed in the new and everlasting covenant,' and that this 'eternity' ceremony of marriage was never performed until May 1843." Quinn, email to Brian Hales, May 17, 2011; emphasis Quinn's. Used by permission.

the revelation specifying the wording that Newel K. Whitney used to seal his daughter, Sarah Ann, to the Prophet on July 27, 1842, declared their union to be unquestionably "through [o]ut all eternity"—an eternal marriage.[21] In addition, Joseph Bates Noble reported that the sealing he performed uniting Joseph Smith and Louisa Beaman on April 5, 1841 (which was the very first plural sealing performed under Joseph's direction, according to available historical data), was "according to the order of Celestial Marriage" and "celestial marriage" is by definition, eternal marriage.[22] (The same caveats about the accuracy of Noble's memory of this distant event should be kept in mind.) Similarly, on February 22, 1869, Wilford Woodruff recorded Noble's declaration: "Joseph B. Nobles said that he performed the first Marriage Ceremony according to the Patriarchal order of Marriage ever performed in this dispensation By sealing Eliza [sic] Beman to Joseph Smith."[23]

It is apparent that Joseph Smith did not teach of the "new and everlasting covenant" of marriage in a quorum setting until May 26, 1843, two days prior to his sealing to Emma.[24] Andrew Ehat acknowledges that Joseph Smith's sealing on May 28 was the first "in a Quorum context," but not that it was the first such sealing ever performed.[25] Furthermore, it does not appear that the words "new and everlasting covenant" are needed to perform a binding eternal matrimony. The revelation on celestial marriage speaks of the requirements to create an eternal marriage. It must include a "covenant" that is "for time and for all eternity," which is according to God's "word" and "law," and is "sealed by the Holy Spirit of promise through him whom I have anointed and appointed unto this power" (D&C 132:18). Assertions that these conditions were not met prior to May 28, 1843, are without documentary foundation.

Evidence of Nauvoo Sealings for "Eternity"

It appears that the primary argument supporting the claim that all of Joseph Smith's sealings were for either for "time" or for "time and eternity" is based on the negative evidence that the wording for "eternity," or for "eternity only," has not been located in the historical record. Notwithstanding, several observations and general documents assert that "eternity only" sealings oc-

---

21. Joseph Smith, Revelation for Newel K. Whitney, July 27, 1842.

22. Joseph B. Noble, Affidavit, Joseph F. Smith, Affidavit Books, 1:3.

23. Joseph B. Noble, quoted in Scott G. Kenney, ed., *Wilford Woodruff's Journal*, 6:452, February 22, 1869.

24. Andrew F. Ehat, "Joseph Smith's Introduction of Temple Ordinances and the Mormon Succession Question." 63.

25. Ibid.

curred during Joseph Smith's lifetime. Nauvooan Justus Morse recounted in an affidavit dated March 23, 1887:

> In the year 1842, at Nauvoo, Illinois, Elder Amasa Lyman, taught me the doctrine of *sealing*, or marrying for eternity, called *spiritual wifery*,[26] and that within one year from that date my own wife and another woman were sealed to me for eternity in Macedonia, by father John Smith, uncle to the Prophet. This woman was the wife of another man, but was to be mine in eternity and the said father John Smith, also taught me that if an unmarried woman was sealed to me that she was mine for *time* as well as eternity and that I was not limited as to number.[27]

Another late account is the second-hand recollection of Eliza M. A. Munson in 1931: "Eliza B. Manwaring was my mother's name. . . . The Prophet Joseph came to her and wanted her to help introduce plural marriages, so she was sealed to Orson Spencer . . . but [she] never lived with [Spencer] as husband and wife."[28]

---

26. Lawrence Foster, "Between Two Worlds: The Origins of Shaker Celibacy, Oneida Community Complex Marriage, and Mormon Polygamy," 277 note 3, observed: "This author [meaning himself] has never encountered the term 'plural marriage,' and almost never encountered the term 'celestial marriage,' in Mormon or non-Mormon accounts from the Nauvoo period."

27. Justus Morse, Affidavit, March 23, 1887, in Charles A. Shook, *The True Origin of Mormon Polygamy*, 169–70; emphasis in original. Justus Morse served as an elder, a seventy, and a high priest under Joseph Smith and joined the RLDS Church in 1870. His son, Joseph Riley Morse, wrote of his father in an 1895 letter to an aunt: "He was a good man. His word was as good as his note any place we ever lived." Quoted in Michael S. Riggs "'His Word Was as Good as His Note,' The Impact of Justus Morse's Mormonism(s) on His Families," 80. Nevertheless, Gary Bergera discounts the accuracy of Justus's memory by observing: "John Smith did not take his first plural wife until August 1843, and Lyman not until September 1844." Gary James Bergera, "'Illicit Intercourse,' Plural Marriage, and the Nauvoo Stake High Council, 1840–1844," 74 note 73. While Bergera's observations appear to be correct, the historical record demonstrates that Joseph Smith did not require men to be polygamists for them to teach the principle to others or to perform plural sealings and that he had authorized John Smith to perform eternal sealings. Robert Crookston Sr., "Autobiography," wrote in 1864: "Uncle John Smith, who was President of the Branch and was also a Patriarch, came to our house and always gave us blessings. He also sealed my Father's [James Crookston b. 1785] two wives to him for time and eternity [on December 28, 1846]. Joseph had authorized him to seal the old people that might not live to see a temple constructed. We were happy about this." See also Benjamin F. Johnson, Testimony, Joseph F. Smith, Affidavit Books, March 4, 1870, 2:9; and "Benjamin F. Johnson's Testimony," in Andrew Jenson, "Plural Marriage," 221, recalled that John Smith sealed his plural wife, Mary Ann Hale, to him on the "14th of November, 1844."

28. Eliza M. A. Munson, "Statement Dictated to N. B. Lundwall, June 1931, at

President Joseph F. Smith testified at the Reed Smoot hearing before the U.S. Senate's subcommittee in 1904 that "eternity only" sealings were indeed accepted in Church doctrine. (Tayler was the committee's attorney, and VanCott was the Church's attorney):

> Mr. TAYLER. Living persons have been united for eternity, have they not?
> Mr. SMITH. I think there have been some few cases of that kind.
> Mr. VANCOTT. To what time, Mr. Tayler, do you limit your question?
> Mr. TAYLER. I was going to ask him. How recently have you known that kind of a marriage?
> Mr. SMITH. Not very recently.
> Mr. TAYLER. Do you mean five years or twenty-five years?
> Mr. SMITH. Oh, twenty years or more.
> Mr. TAYLER. Is there any rule of the church prohibiting that kind of marriage?
> Mr. SMITH. Not that I know of.
> Mr. TAYLER. It has merely fallen into disuse; is that all?
> Mr. SMITH. It has merely fallen into disuse; that is all. I do not know that it could be said to have fallen absolutely into disuse.
> Mr. TAYLER. Or rather, that the principle which still adhere[s] has not been invoked or exercised so often.
> Mr. SMITH. No, sir; it has not been invoked. . . .
> The CHAIRMAN. You have heard of instances where two living persons have been sealed for eternity?
> Mr. SMITH. Yes, sir.
> The CHAIRMAN. According to the doctrines of your church, did that carry with it the right of earthly cohabitation?
> Mr. SMITH. It was not so understood.
> The CHAIRMAN. Then, what is your—
> Mr. SMITH. It does not carry that right.[29]

"Eternity only" marriages also occurred shortly after Joseph Smith's death. LDS historian Jeffery O. Johnson explained: "After Joseph Smith's death but before the temple in Nauvoo was completed, Brigham Young was sealed to fifteen women in secret ceremonies. Brigham Young recorded them in code in his diary as 'M E' (marriage for eternity) or 'M T' (marriage for time) capitalized and underlined at the top of the diary pages when his marriages were performed. For example, on 10 September 1844 he wrote, 'This day I visited Br. Isac Chace. Br. H.C. Kimball was with me. Br & Sister Chase Bountiful Utah."

---

29. *U.S. Senate, Committee on Privileges and Elections, Proceedings . . . in the Matter of the Protests against the Right of Hon. Reed Smoot, a Senator from the State of Utah, to Hold His Seat,* 1:185, 479–80.

with their daughter Claricy was at home. We had a good visit . . . .' 'M. E.' is written on that page."[30]

It appears that "eternity only" sealings were also performed in the Nauvoo Temple. Irene M. Bates and E. Gary Smith explain:

> On January 24 John [Smith, the uncle of Joseph Smith] was sealed to Aseneth Hubert, Rebecca Smith, and Julia Hills for eternity. All of these women were between fifty and sixty years of age, and it seems John might have married them to care for them during the removal from Illinois and on the journey to Salt Lake. It is also possible that the women requested marriage to Uncle John.[31]

Another example reportedly occurred in the 1850s. Mary Ettie V. Coray Smith was a member for several years who afterwards disaffiliated and wrote a memoir with the help of an editor; as a result, the memoir cannot always be relied on for accuracy. She reported meeting Brigham Young whom she had known earlier in Nauvoo:

> Upon going to his office, I found the Prophet alone. He said to me kindly: "Nett, you are determined, I see, to uphold Mormonism, notwithstanding it goes against your natural feelings. Being in something of a hurry, I must be brief with you. I suppose you understand that I have selected the Bishop of your ward for your 'spiritual' husband for eternity . . . He is a good man, such as would suit me if I were a woman. You need not live with him on earth unless you wish. But it is necessary to have a husband to 'resurrect' you. And more than that, it has become your duty to have children; but I do not now feel at liberty to insist upon such a thing."[32]

If Mary Ettie's recollections are accurate, Brigham Young instructed her to marry her local bishop in order to have a husband to effect her resurrection and to be her spouse in eternity.

Joseph Smith's "Eternity Only" Sealings

Several researchers have concluded that some of Joseph Smith's sealings were exclusively for "eternity." Lawrence Foster estimated that "approximately one-third" of Joseph Smith's plural marriages were in this category,[33] adding

---

30. Jeffery Ogden Johnson, "Determining and Defining 'Wife': The Brigham Young Households," 60.

31. Irene M. Bates and E. Gary Smith, *Lost Legacy: The Mormon Office of Presiding Patriarch*, 114.

32. Nelson Winch Green, ed., *Fifteen Years among the Mormons: Being the Narrative of Mrs. Mary Ettie V. Smith*, 181. Although Mary Ettie Smith's report appears reasonable and accurate, her testimony should not be relied on heavily, as she had a reputation for exaggeration.

33. Foster, "Between Two Worlds," 241 note 1, see also 248; Lawrence Foster, *Religion*

in another source: "Joseph Smith took as plural wives a number of women who had living husbands. . . . Some of these marriages may have been only for 'eternity.'"[34] Michael Marquardt observed with restraint: "Exactly what arrangement was made between those women who had a living husband and were sealed to Joseph Smith is not known."[35] Andrew Ehat was more expansive: "All polyandry-like marriage sealings performed under Joseph Smith's direction were specified as marriages for 'eternity only,' unless the first husband either gave explicit consent to a new marriage relationship or had abandoned his wife."[36]

In 1944, Dale Morgan wrote to Fawn Brodie, who was completing her biography of Joseph Smith: "I presume in your text itself that you have made allowance for the fact that some of the marriages were merely 'sealings for eternity' and that they may have had no force, and entitled Joseph to no privileges in 'time.' This might have some importance in cutting across some of the marriages already existing; at least, the viewpoint should be taken into consideration."[37] Brodie argued from the perspective that Joseph Smith's polygamy resulted primarily from his largely unchecked libido, but she also conceded: "Many Mormons have believed that Joseph Smith's marriages were entirely spiritual, with consummation left to the eternal state. And with some of his wives this was no doubt the case." She adds that some wives were married "chiefly for reasons of security [and] were probably married only 'for eternity.'"[38]

Available documents indicate that many of Joseph Smith's plural marriages were "eternity only" sealings and therefore without sexual relations.[39] Andrew Jenson's research notes contain this statement:

> \Sister Ruth/ Mrs. Sayers was married in her youth to Mr. Edward Sayers, a thoroughly practical horticulturist and florist,[40] and though he was not a member of the Church, yet he willingly joined his fortune with her and they reached Nauvoo together some time in the year 1841;

---

and Sexuality: Three American Communal Experiments of the Nineteenth Century, 159.

34. Foster, *Religion and Sexuality*, 159.

35. H. Michael Marquardt, *The Rise of Mormonism: 1816–1844*, 561.

36. Ehat, "Pseudo-Polyandry," 16.

37. Dale Morgan, Letter to Fawn M. Brodie, June 24, 1944.

38. Fawn M. Brodie, *No Man Knows My History: The Life of Joseph Smith, the Mormon Prophet*, 338.

39. Recognizing that Joseph Smith's marriages could have been for either "time and eternity" or "eternity only," P. P. Kelley questioned Malissa Lott in 1892 regarding the type of sealing ceremony that she experienced with the him: "Did you live with Joseph Smith as his wife, or were you just simply sealed to him for eternity?" Malissa Lott, Deposition, Temple Lot Transcript, Respondent's Testimony, Part 3, p. 97, question 94. Malissa, who was single at the time of her sealing to the Prophet, had earlier stated: "I was married to him for time and all eternity." Ibid., p. 95, question 56.

40. "Horticulture," *Times and Seasons* 3 (February 1, 1842): 678.

Andrew Jenson's handwritten notes tell of the "eternity only" sealing of Ruth Vose Sayers to Joseph Smith. Photo courtesy LDS Church History Library.

While there the strongest affection sprang up between the Prophet Joseph and Mr. Sayers.[41] The latter not attaching much importance to \the/ theory of a future life insisted that his wife \Ruth/ should be sealed to the Prophet for eternity, as he himself should only claim her in this life. She \ was/ accordingly the sealed to the Prophet in Emma Smith's presence and thus were became numbered among the Prophets plural wives. She however \though she/ \continued to live with Mr. Sayers / remained with her husband \until his death.[42]

Another somewhat garbled document apparently dating to 1843 appears to be in the hand of excommunicated Mormon Oliver Olney, whose wife, Phebe Wheeler, worked as a domestic in Hyrum Smith's home: "What motive has [S]ayers in it—it is the desire of his heart. . . . Joseph did not pick that

---

41. Joseph Smith stayed with the Sayerses during August 11–17, 1842, while hiding from Missouri lawmen. Dean C. Jessee, ed. *The Papers of Joseph Smith: Volume 2, Journal, 1832–1842*, 403–18.

42. Ruth Vose Sayers, "Draft biographical sketch," Document 5, Andrew Jenson Papers (ca. 1871–1942), Box 49, fd. 16, pp. 1–2. Jenson apparently used the documents in these folders to compile his 1887 *Historical Record* article, "Plural Marriage." This sealing is dated "February A.D. 1843" in Ruth Vose Sayers's Joseph F. Smith, Affidavit Books, May 1, 1869, 1:9. However, the affidavit states that Hyrum Smith performed the sealing, which is unlikely because Hyrum did not accept plural marriage until May 1843.

woman [Ruth Vose Sayers]. She went to see whether she should marry her husband for eternity."[43] Evidently, Olney was gathering information through his wife and learned of the episode involving the Sayers and Joseph Smith.

The second example of an eternity only sealing among Joseph Smith's plural marriages appears in a letter from Daniel H. Wells to Joseph F. Smith, June 25, 1888. Apostle Wells speaks of Albert Smith (no relation to Joseph Smith or George A. Smith), whose wife, Esther Dutcher (b. 1811), had died in 1856: "He [Albert Smith was] also much afflicted with the loss of his first wife. It seems that she was sealed to Joseph the Prophet in the days of Nauvoo, though she still remained his wife, and afterwards nearly broke his heart by telling him of it, and expressing her intention of adhering to that relationship. He however got to feeling better over it, and acting for Joseph, had her sealed to him, and to himself for time."[44]

None of the details surrounding this sealing have been discovered, nor does Wells explain how he learned about it. Did Esther, like Ruth Vose Sayers, actively petition Joseph to be sealed to him? What role did the Prophet play in the proceedings? Wells's description of Esther as "sealed to Joseph the Prophet in the days of Nauvoo, though she still remained his [Albert's] wife" is consistent with an "eternity only" sealing between Joseph Smith and Esther Dutcher. However, drawing reliable conclusions is impossible without additional historical information.

Albert and Esther Smith had five children: Azariah (b. 1828), Emily (b. 1832), Candace (b. 1833), Joseph Albert (b. 1844), and Esther (b. 1849).[45] Esther did not conceive any children while her legal husband, Albert Smith, was on his mission between September 12, 1842, and August 22, 1843. Joseph Albert Smith was conceived about four months after his return (on approximately December 29, 1843).[46] Michael Quinn has suggested that Joseph Albert may have been the biological son of Joseph Smith, a hypothesis that supports the possibility that the

---

43. [Oliver Olney], typescript excerpt in Quinn Papers, WA MS 244 (Accession:19990209-c) Box 1. I have been unable to identify the primary document to verify this quotation.

44. As discussed in Chapter 14, page 396 note 55. Daniel H. Wells, Letter to Joseph F. Smith, June 25, 1888. I am indebted to Michael Marquardt for bringing this source to my attention. D. Michael Quinn affirmed that Albert Dutcher's reaction is evidence that "contradicts his [Brian Hales's] claim that there were 'No Complaints from Legal Husbands' (his emphasis) of the Prophet's already-married wives." "Evidence for the Sexual Side of Joseph Smith's Polygamy," expanded version, July 2012, 3. Albert was understandably disheartened, but according to available evidence, he did not accuse or criticize Joseph Smith for his willingness to allow the sealing.

45. Albert Smith, "Journal of Albert Smith, 1804–1889," 2.

46. David L. Bigler, transcriber, "Journal of Albert Smith, 1804–1889," 2, 9, 17.

Prophet practiced sexual polyandry.[47] The child's first name is perhaps supportive, but his middle name of "Albert" seems less consistent with that interpretation. Besides this observation, there is no evidence identifying Joseph Smith as the father of Joseph Albert Smith (b. 1844). The given name may have been a tribute to the Prophet who had been martyred less than three months prior to his birth.

The only author to list Esther Dutcher Smith as a plural wife of Joseph Smith was polygamy researcher Stanley Ivins, and he identifies the sealing as having occurred by proxy after Joseph's death. He lists her as wife number 56: "Esther Dutcher Smith, wife of Albert Smith. Born in Cherry Valley, New York, February 15, 1811. She married Albert Smith in 1826. . . . On October 10, 1851 she was sealed to Joseph Smith, her husband standing as proxy for the Prophet. She died in Manti, Utah, September 17, 1856."[48] Ivins was apparently unaware of any Nauvoo sealing. According David L. Bigler, biographer of Esther's son, Azariah, she was a literate and "gentle woman," beloved of her family.[49] After several years of ill health, she died on September 17, 1856, at Manti, Utah.

Other more nuanced evidence of eternity only sealings can be located like Oliver Huntington's reference to how his brother "Dimick had given our sisters Zina and Prescenda to Joseph as wives *for eternity.*"[50] While it is true that historical documents dealing with Joseph Smith's plural marriages are few and often problematic, strong evidence of "eternity only" sealings does exist and a dogmatic view that they did not occur seems unjustified both historically and theologically.

Joseph Smith's Nauvoo Plural Marriage Chronology

After Joseph Smith began his plural marriages by being sealed to Louisa Beaman in April 1841, eight of the next nine marriage proposals were to already-married women. Compton's research would add two more, for a total of ten of the next eleven.[51] According to Mary Elizabeth Rollins, a sword-wielding angel appeared for the third time in "early February" of 1842 commanding

---

47. Michael Quinn, email to Brian C. Hales, May 17, 2011.

48. Stanley S. Ivins, "Wives of Joseph Smith," Ivins Papers, Box 12, fd. 1, no. 56. Ivins's entry is faithfully transcribed in Jerald Tanner and Sandra Tanner, *Joseph Smith and Polygamy*, 45.

49. David L. Bigler, ed., *The Gold Discovery Journal of Azariah Smith*, viii.

50. Oliver Huntington, Diary [and autobiographical sketch], 1835–1900, February 18, 1883; emphasis mine.

51. Compton, *In Sacred Loneliness*, 4, lists the sealing dates for Elizabeth Davis (Jabez Durfee's legal wife) as "<June 1842" and that of Sarah Kingsley (John Cleveland's legal wife) as "<29 June 1842." While these estimates are likely accurate, there is no accompanying manuscript documentation so I have chosen a more conservative approach. Compton also dates the sealing of Sylvia Sessions (Windsor Lyon's legal wife) as "8 Feb. 1842" but that dating is problematic. (See Chap. 13.)

the reluctant Joseph Smith to practice plural marriage.[52] Since he had married several plural wives by that time and may have been rejected twice, the angel's appearance and threats at that point are puzzling.

The various recollections state that the sword-bearing angel commanded the Prophet to "establish that principle upon the earth,"[53] to be "obedient,"[54] to "proceed to fulfill the law that had been given to him,"[55] to no "longer delay fulfilling that Command,"[56] to "move forward and establish plural marriage,"[57] "to have women sealed to him as wives . . . and obey the commandment."[58] Apparently his sealings to Louisa and to several already married women showed insufficient compliance.

The historical record shows that within weeks of the last angelic visit, the Prophet dramatically changed his pattern of proposing plural marriages. In April he proposed to Nancy Rigdon—the first time in Nauvoo after Louisa that he had approached a single woman in perhaps a dozen proposals. (See Chapter 17.) From that point onward, the great majority of polygamous marriages were to unmarried women, with sexual relations documented in at least ten cases. (See Chapter 11 and Appendix E.)

One interpretation is that Joseph Smith attempted to assuage the angel's pre-1841 demands by marrying Louisa Beaman and then engaged in multiple "eternity" sealings to legally married women, thus expanding his count of *eternal* plural wives but without augmenting the number of *earthly* polygamous spouses beyond Emma (who was unaware of polygamy at that point) and Louisa. This behavior, however, was unacceptable to the angel who evidently expected him to practice polygamy as ancient patriarchs did, with the possibility of children being born. Accordingly, the angel delivered a stern commandment to the Prophet in February of 1842, requiring him to marry for "time and eternity" and thus fulfill the entire commandment.

Joseph Smith's motivations for seeking "eternity" sealings may have also been due to their quasi-legal status; he would not be prosecuted for bigamy since

---

52. Mary Elizabeth Rollins Lightner, Letter to Emmeline B. Wells, Summer 1905.

53. Zina D. H. Smith, Statement, December 23, 1894, quoted in "Joseph, the Prophet, His Life and Mission as Viewed by Intimate Acquaintances," *Salt Lake Herald Church and Farm Supplement*, January 12, 1895, 212. Zina's comments are republished in Brian H. Stuy, ed., *Collected Discourses*, 5:31–32.

54. Helen Mar Whitney, *Plural Marriage as Taught by the Prophet Joseph: A Reply to Joseph Smith [III], Editor of the Lamoni, Iowa "Herald,"* 13.

55. Benjamin F. Johnson, March 4, 1870, in Joseph F. Smith, Affidavit Books, 2:8. See also Jenson, "Plural Marriage," 222.

56. Dean R. Zimmerman, ed., *I Knew the Prophets: An Analysis of the Letter of Benjamin F. Johnson to George F. Gibbs, Reporting Doctrinal Views of Joseph Smith and Brigham Young*, 43.

57. Eliza R. Snow Smith, *Biography and Family Record of Lorenzo Snow*, 69–70.

58. Lorenzo Snow, Affidavit, August 18, 1869, in Joseph F. Smith, Affidavit Books, 2:19; see also Jenson, "Plural Marriage," 222.

the state would not recognize the sealing as a bona fide marriage and sexual relations were absent. Possibly even more important was that Emma would have been less concerned because conjugal relations were not included. See Table 15.1

Other Evidence of "Eternity" Sealings

Besides these observations, other evidence exists supporting Joseph Smith's personal involvement with "eternity only" sealings. On March 8, 1895, John Lyman Smith, the son of John Smith (Joseph Smith's uncle), wrote to the First Presidency, describing what seems to be a sealing for eternity between Joseph Smith and Sarah M. Kingsley Howe Cleveland: "In the days of Joseph. Mother Cleveland by advice, was sealed to the prophet in Nauvoo but lived with her [non-LDS] husband John Cleveland."[59] In the Nauvoo Temple, Sarah was sealed "for time" to John Smith (John L.'s father) before being sealed for eternity to Joseph Smith by proxy.[60]

Another example already mentioned involves Patty Sessions who recorded in an 1860 diary entry that she had been married to Joseph Smith in Nauvoo "for eternity."[61] Seven years later, the ordinance was repeated by proxy using the standard language of that time: "time and all eternity."[62] Shortly thereafter, Patty apparently returned to her original entry and inserted "time and eternity" above her initial recording,[63] but it appears that her first reference specified an "eternity only" sealing.

---

59. John L. Smith, holograph letter to David H. Cannon, February 27, 1895, attached to a letter of the First Presidency, March 8, 1895.

60. Brown, *Nauvoo Sealings, Adoptions, and Anointings*, 280, 282 note 253.

61. Donna Toland Smart, ed., *Mormon Midwife: The 1846–1888 Diaries of Patty Bartlett Sessions*, 276–77.

62. Patty's diary contains a separate sheet dated July 3, 1867, affirming a "time and all eternity" sealing to Joseph Smith with Joseph F. Smith acting as proxy and also receiving her higher temple ordinances. This document undoubtedly refers to temple work performed shortly before in Salt Lake City. Smart, *Mormon Midwife*, 276–77.

63. Ibid. Smart is confident that Patty made the addition at a later date. Todd Compton agrees with Smart. Personal conversation with Brian Hales, August 17, 2008; notes in my possession. Don Bradley and I also believe that the writing added above the original text is in Patty's hand. However, Michael Quinn disagrees: "Patty Bartlett Sessions . . . specified that she had been sealed to Joseph Smith 'for eternity' in an ordinance for which there is no original record. This would preclude the sexual cohabitation of a marriage 'for time and eternity.' Her sealing to the thirty-six-year-old living prophet occurred when she was forty-seven and cohabiting with her legal husband." Quinn, *The Mormon Hierarchy: Extensions of Power*, 184. Quinn's endnote for this paragraph is insightful: "Patty Bartlett Sessions holographic 1856–66 diary, LDS Archives, entry between 16 June and 17 June 1860, which has a later addition in another person's handwriting of the words 'time and all' before the word 'Eternity.'" Brodie, *No Man Knows My History*, 445, and Claire Noall, *Intimate Disciple: A Portrait of Willard Richards*,

Table 15.1
Plural Sealings and Proposals in Nauvoo

Nauvoo Plural Sealings and Proposals	Sealing Date	Year	Legal Husband?	Sexuality?
1. Louisa Beaman	April 5	1841		Yes
Sarah Bates Pratt Proposal	< July		Orson Pratt	
2. Lucinda Pendleton	< July		George Harris	
3. Zina Huntington	Oct.		Henry B. Jacobs	
4. Presendia Huntington	Dec. 11		Norman Buell	
5. Agnes Moulton Coolbrith	Jan. 6	1842	[widow]	
Sarah Granger Kimball proposal	early		Hiram Kimball	
Angel Visit Early February 1842				
6. Mary Elizabeth Rollins	Late Feb.	1842	Adam Lightner	
7. Patty Bartlett	March 9		David Sessions	
8. Marinda Nancy Johnson	April		Orson Hyde	
April 1842 - Shift in Joseph's Plural Proposals				
Nancy Rigdon Proposal		1842		
9. Delcena Johnson	< July			
10. Eliza R. Snow	June 29			possible
11. Sarah Ann Whitney	July 27		[Joseph Kingsbury]	possible
12. Martha McBride	Aug.			
13 Sylvia Sessions	Early	1843	[Windsor Lyon]	Yes
14. Ruth Vose	Feb.		Edward Sayers	
15. Flora Ann Woodworth	Spring			
16. Emily Dow Partridge	March 4			Yes
17. Eliza Maria Partridge	March 8			Yes
18. Almera Woodard Johnson	April			Yes
19. Lucy Walker	May 1			Yes
20. Sarah Lawrence	May			Yes
21. Maria Lawrence	May			Yes
22. Helen Mar Kimball	May			
23. Hannah Ells	mid year			possible
24. Elivira Annie Cowles	June 1		Jonathan Holmes	
25. Rhoda Richards	June 12			
26. Desdemona Fullmer	July			
27. Olive G. Frost	Summer			Yes
28. Malissa Lott	Sept. 20			Yes
29. Fanny Young	Nov. 2			
30. Nancy M. Winchester	Unknown			
31. Elizabeth Davis			Jabez Durfee	
32. Sarah Kingsley			John Cleveland	
33. Esther Dutcher			Albert Smith	
34. Mary Heron			[John Snider]	Yes

Sealings for "Time and Eternity" and for "Eternity Only"

Patty Bartlett Sessions's original journal entry read: "I was sealed toe Joseph Smith . . . for Eternity." Courtesy LDS Church History Library

When seventy-seven-year-old Zina D. Huntington Jacobs Smith Young was interviewed in 1898 by RLDS elder John W. Wight, her answers also provide the impression that her sealing to Joseph Smith was only for "eternity."

Q. "Then it is a fact, Mrs. [Zina] Young, is it not, that you married Mr. Smith at the same time you were married to Mr. [Henry] Jacobs?"

A. "What right have you to ask such questions? I was sealed to Joseph Smith for eternity."[61]

Q. "Mrs. Young, you claim, I believe, that you were not married to him for time?"

A. "For eternity. I was married to Mr. Jacobs, but the marriage was unhappy and we parted." . . .

Q. "I presume you are aware of the fact that it is claimed by your church that the marriage with Mr. Jacobs was not an agreeable one."

Apostle to Joseph Smith — Cousin of Brigham Young, 611, quoted the edited phrase as if those were original words in the Sessions diary. This change was probably made by a member of the Sessions family before the diary's donation to the Church Historian's Office or by a staff member after the diary's donation. The apparent purpose of the addition was to defeat the argument of the Reorganized Church of Jesus Christ of Latter Day Saints that any woman "sealed" to Joseph Smith during his lifetime was for "eternity only" and was not an actual wife. Whoever added the phrase "time and all eternity" did not apparently realize that this revision did more than disprove RLDS claims: The revised diary asserts that Patty, an already married woman, was sealed to Joseph Smith in a ceremony that allowed sexual intercourse. Quinn, *The Mormon Hierarchy: Extensions of Power*, 497–98.

64. In her biography of Zina Huntington, Oa Cannon corroborated this view: "Seven months after their marriage, Zina was sealed to the Prophet Joseph Smith for eternity. This sealing took place on October 27, 1841 with Zina's brother, Dimick, officiating and Fanny A. Huntington present as a witness. Three months later Zina gave birth to her first son, Zebulon." Oa Jacobs Cannon, "Zina D. H. Young."

A. "That is true." . . .

Q. "It is a fact then, Mrs. Young, that Joseph was not married to you only in the sense of being sealed for eternity?"

A. "As his wife for time and eternity."

Q. "Mrs. Young, you have answered that question in two ways; for time, and for time and eternity."

A. "I meant for eternity."[65]

Thus, when Wight pointed out the contradiction in her answers, Zina clarified that her sealing was "for eternity."[66] But other comments in this interview are less clear, and Compton concludes that it "cannot be used as solid evidence" that the marriage was "spiritual" only.[67] Nevertheless, it appears to be useful evidence that sealings for "eternity," as well as "time and eternity," were then a possibility and, hence, should not be discounted.[68] It seems from the conversation that Zina wanted Wight to conclude that the sealing was for eternity, not time.[69] This would be a strange assertion if "eternity only" marriages were not possible.

Antagonistic writers might assert that Zina was attempting to cover up polyandrous sexual relations. However, Zina was undoubtedly aware that the RLDS interviewer was trying to establish that Joseph Smith did not have conjugal relations with anyone but Emma, his legal wife. An admission by Zina that her marriage was for "eternity" and without sexual relations would have played right into Wight's hands by providing him with the exact evidence he was seeking. Nonetheless, Zina knew that *some* of Joseph's plural marriages were for "time and eternity" and included connubial relations. As a conse-

---

65. John W. Wight, "Evidence from Zina D. Huntington Young, October 1, 1898," 29.

66. Family tradition supports this interpretation. Oa Jacobs Cannon, granddaughter of Zina Huntington, wrote: "Henry obeyed the voice of the Prophet and signed a slip which is still in the Salt Lake Temple agreeing that his marriage (civil) should remain for time only and allowing her to be sealed for eternity to the Prophet Joseph Smith." Oa Jacobs Cannon, "Zina D. H. Young."

67. Compton, *In Sacred Loneliness*, 15.

68. Quinn, "Organizational Development and Social Origins of the Mormon Hierarchy," 167, wrote in 1972: "Joseph Smith also proposed spiritual marriage, for eternity only, to the wives of several of his close associates in the hierarchy."

69. Martha Sonntag Bradley and Mary Brown Firmage mistakenly assert that Zina Diantha Huntington Jacobs stated that she was Joseph Smith's wife "in very deed" in an affidavit signed May 1, 1869, in Joseph F. Smith, Affidavit Books, 1:5, 4:5. Martha Sonntag Bradley and Mary Brown Firmage Woodward, *Four Zinas: A Story of Mothers and Daughters on the Mormon Frontier*, 114–15, 137. Those affidavits document a marriage ceremony between Joseph and Zina but do not refer to a physical dimension. The only plural wife of Joseph Smith to affirm she was his wife "in very deed" was Malissa Lott, notarized statement to Joseph Smith III, August 4, 1893.

quence, she may have been reticent to answer Wight's question by providing evidence that might have used to perpetuate a deception.

It is interesting that three of the polyandrous wives (Zina Huntington Young, Patty Bartlett Sessions, and Mary Elizabeth Rollins Lightner) on at least one occasion indicated that their sealing was for "eternity only," and yet apparently none of the nonpolyandrous wives ever made such a claim.[70]

Potentially important is a rumor recorded by John D. Lee: "[A] report said that [Orson] Hyde's wife, with his consent, was sealed to Joseph for an eternal state, but I do not assert the fact."[71] Ann Eliza Webb Young agreed: "It was hinted to him [Orson Hyde] that Smith had had his first wife sealed to himself in his absence, as a wife for eternity."[72]

Bathsheba Smith believed the Prophet and Jane Law, wife of second counselor in the First Presidency William Law, were sealed for "eternity." In testimony during the Temple Lot Court Case in 1892 she testified:

> Q. Did you ever see him [Joseph Smith] out to church with any one except Emma as his wife?
> A. Yes, sir.
> Q. Take them home with him, and to and from church?
> A. Yes Sir, I have seen them hanging on his arm.
> Q. Who have you seen hanging on his arm?
> A. Well, I have seen Mrs. Law, if you want to know.
> Q. William Law's wife?
> A. Yes sir.
> Q. Well, that is one?
> A. Yes sir.
> Q. Well, who else have you seen? Was he married to her?
> A. To whom?
> Q. To William Law's wife?
> A. You can't prove it by me for I was not present, but I believe it.
> Q. Did she not have a husband at that time?
> A. Yes sir.
> Q. Well how could she be married to Joseph Smith if she had a husband living at that time?
> A. Well I believe she was sealed to him for eternity.
> Q. Sealed to who for eternity?
> A. To Joseph Smith.

---

70. Wight, "Evidence from Zina D. Huntington Young," 29; Patty Sessions, Journal, page after June 16, 1860, entry, in Smart, *Mormon Midwife*, 276–77; Mary Elizabeth Rollins Lightner, "Remarks at B.Y.U. April 14, 1905," 7.

71. John D. Lee, *Mormonism Unveiled*, 147.

72. Ann Eliza Webb Young, *Wife Number 19, or, The Story of a Life in Bondage, Being a Complete Exposé of Mormonism, and Revealing Sorrows, Sacrifices and Sufferings of Women in Polygamy*, 325–26.

Q. Is that what you mean by "marrying" or "married,"—sealed to one for eternity?

A. Yes sir.

Q. That is what you mean by being his "wife"?

A. Yes sir, but sometimes they are married for time and eternity, and sometimes only for time. Sometimes for time and sometimes for eternity.

Q. And she was sealed to him for eternity?

A. I believe she was.

Q. But you don't mean to say that Joseph Smith had that man's wife living with him as his wife?

A. No sir, I mean that she was sealed to him for eternity, and I think that it was a good thing for her, for she will be much better off in eternity,— much better off in the next world than if she had stuck to Law.[73]

The evidence regarding Joseph Smith's relationship with Jane Law is puzzling and inconclusive. (See Chapter 31.)[74] But Bathsheba's testimony suggests that sealings for "eternity" did occur prior to the Prophet's death.

In early 1887 when Andrew Jenson was compiling his notes on the Prophet's polygamous wives, ten of Joseph's widows were still living.[75] Jenson spoke with at least three (Eliza R. Snow, Malissa Lott Willes, and Helen Mar Kimball Whitney) and tried to contact Mary Elizabeth Rollins Lightner. He used the information they provided to help compile a list of all of Joseph's known plural wives.[76] For example, Helen Mar Kimball Whitney recorded on June 27, 1887: "Bro. Gensen [sic] called to see me—wants me to write up incidents of my life as soon as I can. I gave him a few incidents of Flora [Woodworth] Gove's life who was a wife of Joseph Smith."[77] In characterizing the relationships of Joseph with his plural wives, Jenson consistently used "sealed" to describe the relationship between Joseph Smith and three of the women who were civilly married to other men but consistently (thirteen times) used "married" to describe the union between Joseph and previously unmarried women. (Jenson's only inconsistency was in describing Fanny Alger as

---

73. Bathsheba Smith, Deposition, Temple Lot Transcript, Respondent's Testimony, Part, p. 318, questions 564–77.

74. Laura Owen, "History of Laura Owen," 8.

75. Included were Zina Diantha Huntington (d. 1901), Presendia Huntington (d. 1892), Mary Elizabeth Rollins (d. 1913), Patty Bartlett (d. 1892), Martha McBride (1901), Emily Dow Partridge (d. 1899), Almera Johnson (d. 1896), Lucy Walker (d. 1910), Helen Mar Kimball (d. 1896), and Malissa Lot (d. 1898).

76. Zina D. H. Young, Letter to Mary Elizabeth Rollins Lightner, June 8 and June 22, 1887; Emmeline B. Wells, Letters to Mary Elizabeth Rollins Lightner, February 10 and March 12, 1887.

77. Charles M. Hatch and Todd M. Compton, eds., *A Widow's Tale: The 1884–1896 Diary of Helen Mar Kimball Whitney*, 246.

"sealed.") Ten women (including four who were already married) are listed without either "married" or "sealed" being specified. It is unlikely that this constant distinction was coincidental.[78]

Resistance to mentioning eternity-only sealings was also manifest by Apostle George A. Smith in a letter to Joseph Smith III on October 9, 1869.[79] To create an accurate register of Joseph Smith plural wives, George A. Smith used the 1869 affidavits collected by fellow apostle and mutual cousin of both men, Joseph F. Smith. Joseph F. Smith had obtained official declarations from Zina D. H. Young and Presendia Huntington Kimball, Ruth Vose Sayers, and Marinda Johnson Hyde—women who were already legally married when they were sealed to the Prophet. However, George A. Smith omitted them and limited his list to previously unmarried women: Louisa Beaman, Eliza R. Snow, Malissa Lott, Lucy Walker, Rhoda Richards, Desdemona Fullmer, and Emily and Eliza Partridge.[80] Perhaps he simply did not wish to introduce the complexities of polyandry into his discussion with Joseph III. Or more likely, George A. knew that "eternity" sealings would not prove his point—that Joseph Smith practiced full marriage including conjugal relations with some of his plural wives.

While it is possible that other priesthood leaders contracted sealings strictly for "eternity," undoubtedly Joseph Smith experienced more than any other man. Brigham Young appears to have contracted a few of the same kinds of relationships. In 1863, staunch Methodist Alexander C. Badger, who was serving as a member of the California Volunteers, visited Salt Lake City and wrote to his sister living in St. Louis: "Brigham says he don't know how many wives he has got—that is, spiritual wives. He says that he has never refused yet to marry any respectable woman that wanted to marry him. Some that he marries he never sees again after the marriage ceremony is performed. These spiritual wives may become *temporal* wives of other men."[81]

The Silence of "Eternity Only" Wives

Concerning the confusion surrounding some of Joseph Smith's "polyandrous" wives, Todd Compton insightfully observes: "It would help [the] case [that sealings were performed only for 'eternity'] if they found polyandrous

---

78. See correspondence and other notes in Andrew Jenson Collection, MS 17956, LDS Church History Library; and Mary Elizabeth Rollins Lightner Collection, MSS 363, fd. 2, items 10–13, Perry Special Collections.
79. George A. Smith, Letter to Joseph Smith III, October 9, 1869, in Journal History.
80. Ibid.
81. Alex Badger, Salt Lake City, Letter to Alice E. Badger Cayton, St. Louis, January 19, 1863, p. 75.

wives who explicitly, unambiguously stated that their marriages were for eternity only, not for time."[82] Such clear statements, however, do not exist, thus raising the question of why "eternity only" wives maintained silence on their marriage type.

Unfortunately, two processes seem to limit the amount of information recorded from the thirteen polyandrous wives. While ten polyandrous wives were living in 1869 when Joseph F. Smith recorded his affidavits, he obtained attestations from only six of them (Zina Huntington, Presendia Huntington, Marinda Nancy Johnson, Sarah Ann Whitney, Ruth Vose, and Elvira Cowles).[83] However, his purpose was to simply verify Nauvoo polygamy, not to document particulars of the relationships. Consequently, the affidavits reveal essentially nothing concerning the possibility of sexual relations in those polyandrous unions.

Eighteen years later when Andrew Jenson sought to archive more detailed information, only five of the thirteen were still living, Zina Huntington (d. 1901), Presendia Huntington (d. 1892), Mary Elizabeth Rollins (d. 1913), Patty Bartlett (d. 1892), and Marinda Nancy Johnson (d. 1886). Of these five, only two, Zina Huntington and Mary Elizabeth Rollins, left detailed references to their sealings to Joseph Smith. Presendia Huntington and Patty Bartlett left brief narratives; no record has survived from Marinda Johnson.

Zina Huntington separated from her legal husband, Henry Jacobs, after Joseph's death and was sealed to Brigham Young for time, bearing him two children. Throughout her life in Utah she was known as a plural wife of Joseph Smith who married Brigham Young, just like Eliza R. Snow. Few Church members would have known the details of her life sufficiently to ask about her polyandrous marriages.

In contrast, Mary Elizabeth Rollins Lightner lived with her legal husband, Adam Lightner, until his death in 1885. When approached in 1887 to help Andrew Jenson in his quest to publish the names of the Prophet's plural wives, she was reticent to respond.[84] Mary Elizabeth's delay sharing her recollections of her marriage to Joseph could be explained several ways. Cynics may assert she was simply avoiding questions about sexual polyandry that

---

82. Todd Compton, "Truth, Honesty, and Moderation in Mormon History: A Response to Anderson, Faulring and Bachman's Reviews of *In Sacred Loneliness*, section titled "Sexuality in the Polyandrous Marriages."

83. Three (Lucinda Pendleton, Sarah Kingsley, and Esther Dutcher) were deceased. Elizabeth Davis was in Kansas; an aborted affidavit in the books named Sylvia Sessions (see Chapter 13), Mary Elizabeth Rollins was uncooperative at that time, and Patty Bartlett had already signed a statement in 1867.

84. Emmeline B. Wells, Letter to Mary E. Lightner, March 12, 1887.

may have brought up charges of adultery.[85] However, the evidence for such relations in any of the Prophet's polyandrous marriages is extremely weak.

Three other possibilities appear to be more likely. One motivation was apparently Joseph Smith's instructions not to talk about it. In a letter to Emmeline B. Wells that no longer exists, Mary Elizabeth explained: "I could tell you why I stayed with Mr. Lightner. Things the leaders of the Church does not know anything about. I did just as Joseph told me to do, as he knew what troubles I would have to contend with."[86] Another compelling reason for Mary Elizabeth's silence undoubtedly arose from her desires to not appear as a second-class or inferior wife to women who had been Joseph's "time and eternity" spouses and had experienced full husband-wife relations with him. Throughout the nineteenth century, all of the Prophet's plural wives were revered by Church members for their sacrifices and proximity to the Church's founding leader. However, an "eternity only" wife, who had perhaps experienced little more than the sealing ceremony, might have been considered less than those who had participated in a full plural marriage. Mary Elizabeth outlived all of Joseph Smith's other plural wives, dying in 1913. In 1905 when

---

85. Michael Quinn, email to Brian Hales, May 17, 2011, wrote that in a 1906 letter from Joseph F. Smith to Emmeline B. Wells, the apostle declared that he "didn't want 'Aunt Mary E. Rollins' talking about it" with "it" being the alleged sexual dimension of polyandry. Apparently Quinn did not have a copy of the entire letter. While it does refer to Joseph F. Smith's desire that Mary E. not discuss a particular topic, that topic was that she had received her temple endowments twice and had nothing to do with polyandry, which is not mentioned or inferred in the letter. His letter reads: "There are somethings in her [Mary Elizabeth Rollins Lightner] letters, which I think would be very interesting to publish, and there are others which would be unwise to make public. I think her memory is remarkable for one of her age, but sometimes the memory grows a little with age. Receiving her endowments while the Prophet was living in P. P. Pratts house in Nauvoo, is of course, new to me. but do you think She was correct in Saying She "received them the Second time in the Nauvoo Temple"? If so it is the first case of the kind I have heard of. And was no doubt done without knowledge of having had them. However not knowing the facts, I will not presume to Judge. She may be mistaken about Endowments, one time or the other. I would not like the idea to go out that She received them twice—at least for herself. I have no doubt She could tell me many things I have never known. There are many people who could do likewise. But we ourselves know of some things which would be hard for even Aunt Mary to explain. And those things—although in them selves right and proper under the circumstances and conditions existing, would hardly be proper to expound to the world." Joseph F. Smith, Letter to Emeline B. Wells, January 20, 1906, in Richard E. Turley Jr. *Selected Collections from the Archives of The Church of Jesus Christ of Latter-day Saints*, Vol. 1, DVD #30; emphasis Smith's.

86. Mary Elizabeth Rollins Lightner, Letter to Emmeline B. Wells, November 21, either 1870 or 1880, typed excerpts; location of original letter unknown.

she gave her most detailed recollection to a group of missionaries at BYU,[87] only one other plural wife was still living, Lucy Walker (d. 1910).

In addition, Mary Elizabeth waited until her husband, Adam, had been dead for more than fifteen years before talking openly about her experiences with Nauvoo polygamy.[88] By that time, most other Nauvoo polygamists had also passed away. Thus, she could more easily discuss her marriage without pointed questions about polyandry. Her 1905 audience was probably unaware that "eternity" wives even existed and with the memory of her legal husband minimized, her status as a plural wife of Joseph Smith would seem equal to that of other plural wives. Even when Mary Elizabeth began to discuss her Nauvoo plural marriage, however, she spoke only of events leading up to her sealing. She said nothing concerning her relationship with Joseph Smith as his wife. Unlike many of the "time and eternity" wives who related their interactions with the Prophet after being married to him, Mary Elizabeth Rollins Lightner had nothing to say about post-sealing marital contacts with Joseph. On January 17, 1846, in the Nauvoo Temple she was resealed to Joseph Smith by proxy.[89]

An 1892 letter that Mary Elizabeth Rollins Lightner wrote to John Henry Smith, the apostle son of George A. Smith, shows her hesitancy to write a detailed account; but her wording suggests the sealing performed while Joseph was alive was for "eternity":

> I hope you will not think me intrusive, I am sure I do not wish to be— If I could have an oportunity of conversing with you, and Brother Joseph [F. Smith] I could explain some things in regard to my living with Mr L, after becoming the *Wife* of *another*, which would throw light, on what *now* seems mysterious—and you would be perfectly satisfied with me. I write this; because I have heard that it had been commented on to my injury. I have done the best I could, and Joseph will sanction my action—I cannot explain things in this Letter—some day you will know *all*. That is, if I ever have an oportunity of conversing with either of you.[90]

---

87. Rollins Lightner, "Remarks at B.Y.U., April 14, 1905."

88. Mary Elizabeth Rollins Lightner, "Statement," February 8, 1902; Rollins Lightner, Letter to A. M. Chase, April 20, 1904, quoted in J. D. Stead, *Doctrines and Dogmas of Brighamism Exposed*, 218–19; Rollins Lightner, "Remarks at Brigham Young University, April 14, 1905," 2–3.

89. Brown, *Nauvoo Sealings, Adoptions, and Anointings*, 282.

90. Mary Elizabeth Rollins Lightner, Letter to John Henry Smith, January 25, 1892; emphasis in original. Danel W. Bachman also quotes this letter. "A Study of the Mormon Practice of Plural Marriage before the Death of Joseph Smith," 135. Bachman lists the recipient as John A. Young in the text and John A. Smith in the footnote. Richard S. Van Wagoner, "Mormon Polyandry in Nauvoo," 77, 82, cites it as a letter to "John R. Young," dated January 25, 1892; also in his *Mormon Polygamy: A History*, 43, 232. Apparently Van Wagoner did not locate the original, but repeated

Mary Elizabeth does not explain what information would make John Henry Smith "perfectly satisfied" regarding the apparent "polyandrous" arrangements. Yet if she had reported having sexual relations with Joseph Smith and her legal husband during the same period, John Henry Smith would probably not have been "perfectly satisfied." In 1892, Church members would have considered sexual polyandry to be adultery.

D&C 132:41: ". . . Not Appointed unto Her"

Doctrine and Covenants 132:41 contains teachings that have supported a variety of interpretations over the years, yet a computerized search of LDS databases fails to identify even one General Authority who has commented on its meaning.[91] It reads: "And as ye have asked concerning adultery, verily, verily, I say unto you, if a man receiveth a wife in the new and everlasting covenant, and if she be with another man, *and I have not appointed unto her by the holy anointing*, she hath committed adultery and shall be destroyed" (emphasis mine).

Although the language is somewhat ambiguous, it describes a woman who is sealed to one man in the new and everlasting covenant but is sexually involved with another; this situation constitutes adultery unless she has received a special appointment in a "holy anointing." What could this appointment and "holy anointing" represent?

Antagonistic authors have suggested that Joseph Smith was describing a ceremony by which he quickly "appointed" a married woman to immediately become his wife. For example, Wilhelm Wyl wrote: "An old Mormon, who had been very intimate with Joseph in Nauvoo, assured me that the prophet always carried a small bottle with holy oil about his person, so that he might 'anoint' at a moment's notice any woman to be a queen in Heaven."[92] This interpretation is problematic, since Doctrine and Covenants 132:41 specifies that the woman anointed has been previously sealed to a man "in the new and everlasting covenant." Therefore, it could not be applied to the unsealed women that Wyl describes.[93]

Bachman's information and assumed that the recipient was John R. Young. Bachman was unable to recall the precise primary reference. Bachman, mail to Brian Hales, June 14, 2008. I am indebted to Don Bradley for solving this mystery.

91. In an 1855 editorial, "Family Relations," 726, Franklin D. Richards quotes vv. 41–44 of D&C 132 in conjunction with the "law of forfeiture," but without specifically addressing the meaning of verse 41.

92. W. Wyl [pseud. for Wilhelm Ritter von Wymetal], *Mormon Portraits*, 55; emphasis his. See also Foster, "Between Two Worlds," 260–65, and Jason W. Briggs, *The Basis of Brighamite Polygamy: A Criticism upon the (So-Called) Revelation of July 12th, 1843*, 4.

93. By Joseph Smith's death, several dozen women had been sealed to husbands in the new and everlasting covenant. The Prophet had personally authorized each one. I

A key to understanding this verse may lie in identifying the type of sealing "in the new and everlasting covenant" the woman received. As discussed above, two forms exist. The sealing could be for either "time and eternity" or for "eternity only." A "time and eternity" sealing creates a wife on earth and in heaven, therefore authorizing conjugal relations in mortality. An "eternity only" sealing creates a wife only after death and would not authorize sexual relations on earth.

If the statement, "appointed unto her by the holy anointing," refers to an "eternity only" sealing in the new and everlasting covenant, that is, the woman is "appointed unto" the husband only for "eternity," then afterwards she would be free to marry civilly (for "time" only) and to have conjugal relations with her legal husband without committing adultery. To alter a "time and all eternity" sealing ceremony to make it for "eternity only," the sealer shortens the phrase "for time and all eternity" to "for all eternity" while performing the "holy anointing" (the sealing ceremony).[94] This interpretation would read: "And as ye have asked concerning adultery, verily, verily, I say unto you, if a man receiveth a wife in the new and everlasting covenant, and if she be with another man, and I have not appointed unto her [as a wife for eternity only] by the holy anointing,[95] she hath committed adultery and shall be destroyed."

Two additional verses in Section 132 briefly discussed in the previous chapter support this interpretation. Verse 42 states: "If she be not in the new and everlasting covenant, and she be with another man, she has committed adultery." This verse condemns sexual polyandry because, if a man receives a wife but not in the new and everlasting covenant, then it must be a marriage for "time" only (or she would not be a "wife"); such a marriage would naturally include sexual relations. Sexual involvement with "another man" thereafter would unavoidably be an adulterous relationship as defined in scripture (D&C 42:24–25, 74–83; 63:14–21, Alma 39:3–5). Verse 63 also specifically addresses the circumstances of virgins who are sealed in the new and everlasting covenant, stating that if a woman, "after she is espoused, shall be with another man, she has committed adultery, and shall be destroyed."[96]

---

have found no evidence that Joseph ever invited any of them to be resealed to him or to be involved in any illicit relations.

94. Eternity-only sealings are not permitted today. In 1853, Orson Pratt published the ceremony "for time and all eternity" sealings in "Celestial Marriage," *The Seer* 1, no. 2 (February 1853): 31–32, a disclosure that displeased Brigham Young. Scott G. Kenney, ed., *Wilford Woodruff's Journal, 1833–1898*, September 17, 1854, 4:288.

95. The "holy anointing" appears to be the sealing ceremony although there is no actual "anointing" with oil. The "holy anointing" could refer to the priesthood power that is invoked to seal the marriage in the ceremony. Joseph Smith received this authority and was designated the one "anointed and appointed unto this power" (D&C 132:18; see also v. 7).

96. D. Michael Quinn disagrees with this interpretation: "THE REVELATION

These observations support the interpretation of Doctrine and Covenants 132:41 as describing an "eternity only" sealing that would allow the woman the option of a second marriage for "time" to a different husband. The woman is thus married to two husbands in succession, one for "time" (with conjugal relations during mortality) and the other a sealing for "eternity" (without sexual relations on earth). Additionally, these verses condemn sexual polyandry in all of the situations specified, if not universally.

Sexual Relations in "Time Only" or "Time and Eternity" Sealings

Several documents show that some women who were sealed to men for "time" only or for "time and eternity," did not experience conjugal relations with their respective husbands. LDS scholar Alma G. Allred observed:

> When church leaders implemented ordinance work in the Nauvoo temple, they [also] repeated the sealing ceremonies that had been performed before the temple was available. In every instance, a woman was first sealed for time before being sealed to Joseph Smith for eternity. Where the woman had a living husband who was not LDS, she was sealed for *time* to another individual [who was a member of the Church], but that did not constitute a marriage allowing cohabitation. For example, Mary Elizabeth Rollins Lightner had a non-Mormon husband with whom she lived throughout her life. In the temple, she was sealed to Brigham Young for "time" before being sealed to Joseph Smith.[97] She never lived with Brigham Young and the intent of her sealing with him seems merely to have been to qualify for the eternal sealing.[98]

Another example, mentioned above, is Sarah M. Kingsley Cleveland, who was sealed to Joseph Smith by proxy in the Nauvoo Temple but was

---

DID NOT DISCUSS THE CIRCUMSTANCE THIS VERSE ONLY IMPLIED—WHEN GOD APPOINTS ANOTHER MAN UNTO A WOMAN WHO IS ALREADY MARRIED. CONSISTENT WITH THE ABOVE VERSE, THERE WOULD BE NO ADULTERY ON THE PART OF THE WOMAN OR ON THE PART OF THIS OTHER MAN WHOM GOD HAS "APPOINTED" TO BE WITH HER SEXUALLY." "Evidence for the Sexual Side of Joseph Smith's Polygamy," expanded version, July 2012, 34; emphasis Quinn's. Quinn contends that this verse allows sexual polyandry so long as the woman is properly "appointed"; however, his interpretation is without any clear historical or theological support and it directly contradicts verses 61–63. As discussed in the text, an eternity only "appointment" would allow a legal marriage and family, while a time and eternity "appointment" would not (and would be adultery), which is consistent with verses 61–63.

97. Brown, *Nauvoo Sealings, Adoptions, and Anointings*, 351. See also Quinn, *The Mormon Hierarchy: Extensions of Power*, 185.

98. Alma G. Allred, "Variations on a Theme," 8.

civilly married to nonmember John Kingsley. Sarah was sealed "for time" to John Smith (Joseph Smith's uncle) before being sealed for eternity to Joseph Smith by proxy.[99] There is no indication that Sarah and John ever cohabited.[100] Sylvia Sessions Lyon was sealed to Heber C. Kimball in September 1844, but no historical documentation exists suggesting that Sylvia and Heber's relationship included conjugal relations.

Other similar sealings were performed in the Nauvoo Temple just months—sometimes only weeks—before the Saints abandoned the city to move West. The participants knew that a new temple and the benefits it afforded would not be available for several years after their establishment in the Rocky Mountains. Women were sealed to men with whom they never lived as actual wives. Fanny Stenhouse, a British convert of 1849, recalled meeting Heber C. Kimball sometime after she arrived in Salt Lake City in 1857. By then he had married at least forty-three plural wives:[101]

> He said that he would introduce me to *his wife*. Every one liked Heber for his outspoken, honest bluntness. He took me up the hall and introduced me to five wives in succession! "Now," said he, "I think I'll quit; for I fancy you are not over strong in the faith."
>
> I asked, "Are these all you have got?"
>
> "O dear! no," he said; " I have *a few more at home*, and *about fifty more* scattered over the earth somewhere. I have never seen them since they were sealed to me in Nauvoo, and I hope I never shall again."[102]

If Fanny's recollection is accurate, Heber C. Kimball probably dreaded the possibility that women with whom he had experienced nothing more than a sealing ceremony, might reappear with expectations of economic support.

Brigham Young was asked in 1859: "What is the largest number of wives belonging to any one man?" He answered: "I have fifteen.[103] I know no one who has more. But some of those sealed to me are old ladies, whom I regard rather

---

99. Brown, *Nauvoo Sealings, Adoptions, and Anointings*, 280, 282 note 253.

100. Compton, *In Sacred Loneliness*, 281–83.

101. Stanley B. Kimball, *Heber C. Kimball: Mormon Patriarch and Pioneer*, 307.

102. Mrs. T. B. H. [Fanny] Stenhouse, *Exposé of Polygamy in Utah: A Lady's Life among the Mormons: A Record of Personal Experience as One of the Wives of a Mormon Elder during a Period of More than Twenty Years*, 91–92; rpt., Linda Wilcox DeSimone, ed., *Fanny Stenhouse: Exposé of Polygamy, A Lady's Life among the Mormons*, 84–85; emphasis by Stenhouse.

103. By 1859, Brigham Young had been sealed to at least forty-nine women (George D. Smith, *Nauvoo Polygamy*, 635–37), so his definition of a "wife" was obviously not strictly dependent upon a sealing ceremony. He eventually married a total of fifty-five wives. Jeffery Ogden Johnson, "Determining and Defining 'Wife': The Brigham Young Households," 58. However, he had children by only sixteen of his wives but may have experienced conjugal relations with other wives who did not bear him children.

as mothers than wives; but whom I have taken home to cherish and support."[104] President Young's description of his relationship to some of his older plural wives indicates that they constituted nonsexual "time and eternity" sealings.

Summary

LDS theology teaches that marriages can exist beyond death if proper authority is used to perform the marriage ceremony and if the couple lives worthily. Called "sealings in the new and everlasting covenant of marriage," such unions would endure for "time and eternity" or, in other words, for mortality and beyond. They were first introduced by Joseph Smith in Nauvoo in the early 1840s.

The Prophet also taught the possibility that a woman might be married to one man on earth and to another man in the next life. Such marriages are referred to as "eternity" sealings and are not permitted today. The historical record shows that such sealings were performed in Nauvoo, including some of Joseph Smith's own plural marriages. Doctrine and Covenants 132:41, an admittedly puzzling verse, may be a reference to "eternity" sealings, and how such sealings allow the woman to marry for time (legally) and have a family with "another man" without committing adultery.

Existing documentation shows that "time" sealings did not always include physical intimacy, regardless of the actual wording used in performing the sealing ordinances. To assume that a woman's recollection of a "time and eternity" sealing was also a declaration that sexual relations existed in the union is a conclusion that goes beyond available evidence.

---

104. Horace Greeley, "Overland Journey, #21: Two Hours with Brigham Young," 718.

Chapter 16

The Fourteen "Polyandrous" Wives

After reviewing the general evidences, both historical and theological, concerning polyandry, it appears that more than one marital dynamic was occurring. Currently fourteen possible "polyandrous" wives have been identified, twelve listed by Todd Compton and two more: Esther Dutcher Smith, plus a fourteenth, Mary Heron Snider. Based on the evidence presented in Chapter 13, I conclude that Sylvia Sessions Lyon's relationship with Joseph Smith constituted consecutive marriages, rather than a polyandrous marriage, with the possibility that Windsor may have served as a "front husband" to some degree after his excommunication. Joseph Smith's sealings to Ruth Vose Sayers and Esther Dutcher Smith were "eternity only" marriages. That leaves the eleven remaining marriages to investigate.

The "Pretended" Marriage of Joseph C. Kingsbury and Sarah Ann Whitney

The relationship between Sarah Ann Whitney, Joseph Smith, and Joseph C. Kingsbury is unique and will be discussed in more detail in Chapter 18. However, from a ceremonial standpoint, it is apparently the only polyandrous marriage where the eternal sealing preceded the legal marriage.[1] Joseph Kingsbury referred to the marriage ceremony as "pretended" indicating that it was never consummated. Todd Compton wrote:

> One wonders what the dynamics of a pretend marriage would have been—there would have been no sexual dimension, but Joseph Kingsbury and Sarah must have lived as close friends. . . . We do know that Sarah Ann continued to live with her parents after the marriage to Smith; and Kingsbury, the day after the "pretend" marriage, apparently moved in the Whitney house also. Sarah became generally known as Mrs. Kingsbury, and she and Joseph

---

1. H. Michael Marquardt, *The Strange Marriages of Sarah Ann Whitney to Joseph Smith the Mormon Prophet, Joseph C. Kingsbury, and Heber C. Kimball*, 18.

C. attended public functions together. Outsiders would have suspected nothing unusual in the relationship.[2]

Years later in 1880, Kingsbury, then sixty-eight years old, submitted a bill to the Church for his financial support of Sarah Ann, which he refined on November 23, 1880, by asking Church President John Taylor that an $8,000 payment due him from the Church "be remitted in consideration of services he had rendered in Nauvoo, and after leaving there, to the Prophet Joseph, in keeping one of his wives, Sarah Whitney, daughter of Bishop N. K. Whitney."[3] I have found no evidence that Taylor honored the claim.

The Kingsbury/Whitney pretended marriage demonstrates that Joseph Smith facilitated the creation of at least one "front husband." Apparently, the Prophet was comfortable having a legal husband serve as a caregiver for one of his "time and eternity" wives. The legal husband would not experience connubial relations with the wife but could have plural wives of his own besides the one he was sheltering. This process, though strange and unconventional, could have been repeated, creating other "front husbands." It is possible that, after Windsor Lyon's excommunication and religious separation from Sylvia Sessions Lyon, Joseph Smith asked him to serve as a front husband to Sylvia, although the documentation for this is scant. Windsor was not rebaptized until 1846, but evidence indicates that he remained friendly toward Joseph during the entire span of their relationship.

Kingsbury's relationship with Sarah Ann shows that Joseph Smith's plural wives could enter a legal marriage with another man to shield the Prophet from suspicion by the public and by law enforcement officers. Importantly, it also demonstrates that a woman living under the same roof as a man to whom she was legally married does not automatically verify a sexual connection between her and her legal husband.[4] In other words, assuming conjugality from outward appearances may not be warranted. These observations complicate the already complex process of trying to document the presence or absence of sexual polyandry in Nauvoo polygamy. They also demonstrate the potential missteps in drawing specific conclusions without evidence.

---

2. Todd Compton, *In Sacred Loneliness: The Plural Wives of Joseph Smith*, 352.

3. L. John Nuttall, Notes for John Taylor's Office Journal.

4. Sarah Ann Whitney's marital circumstances were discussed in the revelation on celestial marriage dictated July 12, 1843, which states: "As pertaining to the law of the priesthood—if any man espouse a virgin, and . . . if one . . . after she is espoused, shall be with another man, she has committed adultery, and shall be destroyed" (D&C 132:61–63). Joseph Smith espoused Sarah Ann who thereafter became the legal wife of Joseph C. Kingsbury, but was never "with" him in a conjugal sense. Such relations would have been, according to these verses, "adultery."

In other words, documenting sexual polyandry generally requires specific evidence of conjugality between the woman and both husbands during the same time period. Such evidence is not easy to obtain; but without it, the accuracy of reconstructions portraying polyandrous sexuality is undermined to some degree. Importantly, such evidence has not been identified in any of the fourteen alleged polyandrous marriages. Therefore, authors who affirm the practice of sexual polyandry in some of Joseph Smith's plural unions should inform their readers that such conclusions are based at least partially upon assumption, not solid evidence. For example, Todd Compton wrote: "Zina [Huntington] and Henry [Jacobs] stayed married, cohabiting, throughout Smith's life."[5] Compton provides no corroborating evidence, nor am I aware of any.[6] (See Chapter 11.) Hence, any declaration that Zina was a sexual polyandrist is based, at least in part, upon a degree of speculation, and readers should be advised of that fact. Otherwise, authors' opinions may be misinterpreted as documented history by their readers.

Women Married to Nonmembers or Anti-Mormons

As already discussed, several "polyandrous" wives appear to have experienced "eternity only" marriage to the Joseph Smith. Esther Dutcher Smith's brief account indicates that she was the "wife" only of her legal husband during mortality (See Chapter 15). The Prophet also contracted at least four other probable "eternity only" sealings.

Historical documents show that Joseph Smith began teaching about eternal marriage (independent of plural marriage) as early as January 1840.[7] Among his eventual listeners were four women who could not be eternally sealed to their earthly spouses. As discussed, Ruth Vose Sayers, at the encouragement of her nonmember husband, privately requested a sealing to Joseph Smith. In addition, both Mary Elizabeth Rollins Lightner and Sarah Kingsley Cleveland were married to non-Mormons; and Presendia Huntington's husband, Norman Buell, though a Mormon at one point, became an anti-Mormon, who would not have participated in a Church-sponsored marriage of any kind. These four women had ample reason to seek an "eternity" sealing to Joseph Smith.

---

5. Compton, *In Sacred Loneliness*, 81.

6. Martha Sonntag Bradley and Mary Brown Firmage Woodward, *Four Zinas: A Story of Mothers and Daughters on the Mormon Frontier*, 114–15, wrote that Zina reported she was Joseph Smith's wife "in very deed," but this is an error. The term is actually Malissa Lott's.

7. Parley P. Pratt Jr., ed., *Autobiography of Parley Parker Pratt, One of the Twelve Apostles of the Church of Jesus Christ of Latter-day Saints*, 329–30.

Without specific documentation, a few writers have alleged that sexual relations might have existed in some of these relationships. (See Chapter 12.) If so, such intimacies probably could not have occurred with the consent of the respective legal husbands; most men simply would not have allowed it. Some writers have suggested that Joseph Smith might have engaged in clandestine sexual encounters. I find such conclusions dubious. For one reason, there is no persuasive evidence to support such a scenario. Second, as discussed previously, such relationships are nowhere authorized in Joseph Smith's teachings on the subject and are otherwise condemned (see D&C 132:42, 63). Third, Joseph Smith's experience in Hiram, Ohio, with a mob who tarred and feathered him likely created a lasting memory. Numerous witnesses recalled that he expressed fears that restoring Old Testament polygamy could get him killed and went to great lengths to ensure he did so in a way that would not compromise his safety.[8] The Prophet was unquestionably aware of the prevailing code of honor and frontier justice that exonerated a man's killing, wounding, beating, or otherwise threatening another man who took sexual advantage of his wife or sister. Although it is impossible to prove a negative, it seems that the fear of such retribution would be a natural deterrent were Joseph Smith to contemplate a sexual polyandrous arrangement in these four instances. Certainly such recklessness does not characterize most of the Prophet's decisions.

Fourth, Todd Compton identified another reason for "eternity only" sealings: "Sometimes these sacred marriages were felt to fulfill pre-mortal linkings and so justified a sacred marriage superimposed over a secular one."[9] He adds: "Heavenly marriages in the pre-existence require earthly polyandry here. Certain spirits were 'kindred,' matched in heaven, were born into this life, and, because of unauthorized marriages performed without priesthood sealing power, became linked 'illegally' to the wrong partners."[10] Possibly one of the Prophet's marriages was motivated by a premortal connection. Mary Elizabeth Rollins Lightner remembered Joseph telling her that "I was created for him before the foundation of the Earth was laid."[11] On another occasion,

---

8. See Sarah M. Kimball's statement in Andrew Jenson, "Plural Marriage," *Historical Record* 6 (July 1887): 232; Mary Elizabeth Rollins Lightner, "Remarks at Brigham Young University, April 14, 1905"; "Testimony of Mary Elizabeth Lightner," 2; Desdemona Fullmer, Autobiography, typed excerpt in D. Michael Quinn Papers; Joseph A. Kelting, "Statement," *Juvenile Instructor*, 29 (May 1, 1894), 289–90; Mosiah Hancock, "Correspondence: The Prophet Joseph—Some of His Sayings," *Deseret News*, February 27, 1884, 15.

9. Compton, *In Sacred Loneliness*, 22. Anti-Mormon J. H. Beadle wrote in 1870: "In the pre-existent state souls are mated, male and female, as it is divinely intended they shall fill the marriage relation in this life; or, in more poetic phrase, 'marriages are made in heaven.'" John Hanson Beadle, *Life in Utah: Or, the Mysteries and Crimes of Mormonism*, 340.

10. Compton, *In Sacred Loneliness*, 19.

11. Mary Elizabeth Lightner, Letter to Emmeline Wells, Summer 1905.

she recalled: "Joseph said I was his, before I came here and he said all the Devils in Hell should never get me from him."¹² And she noted her own feelings: "I had been dreaming for a number of years I was his wife."¹³

To recap the apparent status of the fourteen polyandrous marriages, I categorize five as "eternity only" sealings: Ruth Vose Sayers, Esther Dutcher Smith, Mary Elizabeth Rollins Lightner, Presendia Huntington Buell, and Sarah Kingsley Cleveland. In addition, two involved "time and eternity" sealings with one well-documented "front husband" (Sarah Ann Whitney Kingsbury) and a second with consecutive marriages (Sylvia Sessions Lyon). This chapter now investigates the six polyandrous unions involving: Patty Bartlett Sessions, Elizabeth Davis Durfee, Lucinda Pendleton Harris, Elvira Cowles Holmes, Marinda Nancy Johnson Hyde, and Zina Huntington Jacobs. The last section discusses the poorly documented plural relationship with Mary Heron Snider.

The Next Six "Polyandrous" Husbands

Before examining the women involved in these next six polyandrous marriages, a look at their legal husbands (David Sessions, Jabez Durfee, George Harris, Jonathan Holmes, Orson Hyde, and Henry B. Jacobs) demonstrates that they all share a powerful common trait: They were all committed Latter-day Saints. This trait increases the possibility that, if the woman had preferred Joseph Smith as her eternal husband, the husband might very well have willingly allowed her to marry the Prophet in an "eternity only" sealing. The devotion of these men to Joseph Smith and the Church might also have prompted them to relinquish their wives, with whatever degree of willingness, if any of the women chose a sealing to the Prophet for "time and eternity," with the husband thereafter serving as a "front husband."

If it occurred in any of these six relationships, it would have been a monumental sacrifice, but first-generation Mormons made sacrifices that are equally staggering in their scope to modern Mormons. Todd Compton observes: "One might conjecture that a 'first husband' very devoted to Smith would, at his command, refrain from sexual relations with his wife."¹⁴ But he also finds the idea improbable and instead offers another hypothesis:

> The "pretended" marriage opens up the possibility of other "front husbands" in Smith's polyandrous marriages. But the evidence generally does

---

12. Mary Elizabeth Rollins Lightner, "Statement," February 8, 1902; see also Compton, *In Sacred Loneliness*, 19, 212.

13. Mary Rollins Lightner, Remarks at Brigham Young University, April 14, 1905, 2.

14. Todd Compton, "Fawn Brodie on Joseph Smith's Plural Wives and Polygamy: A Critical View," 165.

not support front husband marriages in the other unions of the Mormon leader. In a pretend marriage we would expect a sealing to Smith, then a subsequent civil ceremony with the front husband, but most of Joseph's polyandrous wives married "first husbands" before him; and there is no evidence that any of them agreed to become front husbands *after* Smith married their wives. In fact, such a marriage—living with a wife and not having sexual relations with her after a period of full marriage—would probably have been impracticable.[15]

Compton's logic is valid primarily if Joseph Smith initiated the polyandrous sealings. However, if a woman found herself in a difficult marriage, she may not have desired to be sealed to her legal spouse forever. She may have also viewed the Prophet as a superior husband in eternity and even during this lifetime, prompting her to negotiate the marital change. It is important to point out that no specific supportive or contradictory evidence has been found that the women sought a different eternal husband; historical documentation of the dynamics of these marriages is almost nonexistent. In addition, Joseph and the legal husband would have had to agree. Again, we are moving into the logically difficult area of proposing a negative which is, by its nature, impossible to prove; and there is no evidence that any legal husband either accepted or declined to become "front husbands." Admittedly, such a marital adjustment would be difficult to accept unless he, too, was dissatisfied with the marriage relationship. Some observers may speculate that such sacrifices are beyond mortal capability. The absence of clarifying manuscript data prevents absolute confidence in any specific interpretation.

Regardless, several of the men married plural wives within a few months or years of the polyandrous sealings, but such unions cannot be taken as dissatisfaction with the first and legal marriage, as mixed feelings (repugnance for plurality clashed with a commitment to obey what they saw as God's law) are too well documented for other pluralists of unquestioned loyalty such as Brigham Young and Heber C. Kimball. Three polyandrous husbands who became polygamists are Orson Hyde in February or March of 1843, David Sessions in 1845, and Jabez Durfee in 1846.[16] Like Windsor Lyon, both Jonathan Holmes and Henry Jacobs had children with their plural wives after the martyrdom. These observations seem to generate more questions than answers.

The Next Six "Polyandrous" Wives

A closer look at the next six polyandrous wives provides additional insights, but falls short of definitive conclusions:

---

15. Compton, *In Sacred Loneliness*, 351–52; emphasis in original.
16. George D. Smith, *Nauvoo Polygamy: ". . . but we called it celestial marriage"*, Appendix B.

Patty Bartlett Sessions

Patty Bartlett Sessions kept a journal in Nauvoo in which, without special emphasis, she mentions her interactions with Joseph Smith along with other reports of her doings, meetings attended, women assisted in childbirth, etc. She was sealed to Joseph Smith on March 9, 1842, but the exact nature of that sealing (eternity only? time and eternity?) is not known. Emmeline B. Wells, editor of the *Woman's Exponent* in Salt Lake City, paraphrased multiple entries from this diary in an article published on November 15, 1884: "On the 13th [of December, 1842] she was very sick, the Prophet came and laid hands on her and she was healed. From that time she speaks of Joseph having visited at her house almost daily. . . . On the 30th [June 1843] she says Bro. Joseph is at home again; she went to see him, and then heard him address the people. . . . Oct. 3rd [1843] she took dinner at the Prophet Joseph's."[17] The whereabouts of Session's holograph Nauvoo journal is unknown, nor have Emmeline's prepublication notes for this article been located. Many documents housed in the *Woman's Exponent* office were destroyed due to a fire and a flood, but whether the Sessions diaries or other important manuscripts were among them is not clear.[18]

David Sessions and Patty Bartlett Sessions received their endowments together in the Nauvoo Temple on December 15, 1845, but they were not sealed in marriage, nor was Patty resealed to Joseph Smith at that time, as was customary for many of Joseph's plural wives. Patty's later diaries recount several difficult periods in her marriage to David after Nauvoo, particularly after he married a plural wife who seems to have been immature and selfish and who eventually abandoned the Saints.[19] Did Patty's status as Joseph Smith's eternal wife contribute to these difficulties? Was she actually sealed to Joseph for "time and eternity," thus positioning David as an unenthusiastic "front husband"? Was her sealing to the Prophet unrelated to apparent marital discord? The evidence is insufficient to draw any confident conclusions.

Elizabeth Davis Durfee

The date of Joseph Smith's sealing to Elizabeth Davis Durfee has not been verified, and whether such a sealing was actually performed has been questioned. If it occurred, the most likely time was spring of 1842. There is no doubt, however, that she was a member of the polygamy inner circle in Nauvoo.[20] Among Emily Partridge's reminiscences is a conversation that

---

17. [Emmeline Wells], "Patty Sessions," 95.
18. Carol Cornwall Madsen, telephone conversation, October 5, 2008.
19. Donna Toland Smart, ed., *Mormon Midwife: The 1846–1888 Diaries of Patty Bartlett Sessions*, 22, 58, 60, 140, etc.
20. Richard Lloyd Anderson and Scott H. Faulring, "Review of *In Sacred Loneliness:*

occurred in late 1842 or early 1843 (possibly May) after Emily married the Prophet. "Mrs. Durfee invited my sister Eliza and I to her house to spend the afternoon. She introduced the subject of spiritual wives as they called them in that day. She wondered if there was any truth in this report she heard. I thought I could tell her something that would make her open her eyes if I chose, but I did not choose to. I kept my own counsel and said nothing."[21] If Elizabeth Davis was, in fact, a plural marriage insider, it is strange she would have voiced her ignorance in this visit with the Partridge sisters. Perhaps she was just testing their knowledge, or using the comment to open a discussion on the topic.

Even though Elizabeth's legal husband, Jabez Durfee, was an active Latter-day Saint, he was endowed on a different day than Elizabeth when the Nauvoo Temple opened in the winter of 1845.[22] The two formally divorced the following year, but they had apparently separated previous to that time. Elizabeth, who was fifty-four, was resealed by proxy to Joseph Smith in the Nauvoo Temple on January 22, 1846, but Jabez did not participate either as a proxy husband or witness. Cornelius Lott represented the Prophet in the vicarious ordinance.[23] Was Elizabeth sealed to Joseph Smith for "eternity only" or "time and eternity"? Did she seek to be sealed to him, like Ruth Vose Sayers, due to problems in her marriage with Jabez, or did an eternal sealing generate conflict between them? Again, the lack of evidence prevents a clear understanding of what transpired.

Lucinda Pendleton Morgan Harris

Lucinda Pendleton Morgan Harris, the widow of a presumably murdered Mason in New York, occupies a somewhat ambiguous role. A date of sealing is not known, and she reportedly told Sarah Pratt in 1841 when Sarah expressed outrage that Joseph Smith had proposed to make her a plural wife: "Why *I am his mistress since four years!*"[24] As discussed in Chapter 3, multiple problems can be identified with her account, including plausibility, Pratt's credibility, and what seems a most unlikely window when a sealing between Joseph and Lucinda could have occurred. In my view, documentation sup-

---

The Plural Wives of Joseph Smith," by Todd M. Compton," 74–76.

21. Emily D. P. Young, Autobiographical Sketch, "Written Especially for My Children, January 7, 1877."

22. Lisle G Brown, *Nauvoo Sealings, Adoptions, and Anointings: A Comprehensive Register of Persons Receiving LDS Temple Ordinances, 1841–1846*, 88.

23. Ibid., 282 note 264.

24. Wilhelm Wyl [pseud. Wilhelm Ritter von Wymetal], *Mormon Portraits, or the Truth about Mormon Leaders from 1830 to 1886, Joseph Smith the Prophet, His Family and His Friends: A Study Based on Fact and Documents*, 60.

porting her inclusion as a plural wife of the Prophet is the weakest of all thirty-five women.

Whatever the relationship between Lucinda and Joseph Smith, records show that her legal husband, George Harris, eventually became aware of it. He stood proxy for the Prophet in the Nauvoo Temple on January 22, 1846, as Lucinda was sealed to the Prophet for eternity.[25] It is the indisputable fact of this sealing ordinance that provides the strongest evidence that Joseph and Lucinda were sealed or at least discussed the possibility of a plural marriage prior to his death. Otherwise, little is known concerning the polyandrous arrangement. George and Lucinda divorced by 1853 and neither party traveled west with the Saints. Lucinda apparently lived afterwards with a daughter in Tennessee and George died in 1857 in Iowa.[26] Unanswerable questions exist regarding the timing of the sealing (if one occurred), whether it was "eternity only" or "time and eternity," and George Harris's initial level of involvement.

Elvira Annie Cowles Holmes

The Nauvoo Marriage Record lists Elvira Annie Cowles and Jonathan Holmes marrying on December 1, 1842.[27] Jonathan, a close friend of the Prophet's, served as a pall-bearer at his funeral. Elvira signed an 1869 affidavit saying she was sealed to Joseph Smith June 1, 1843.[28] As discussed in Chapter 12, Church member William Wright wrote on June 2, 1931: "Before Joseph was shot, he asked Jonathan Holmes if he would marry and take care of LaVina [Elvira]."[29] This very late second-hand report suffers from numerous weaknesses, including the fact that almost a century had elapsed between the episode and the letter, but it could be evidence of a "front husband" role for Jonathan.

Other supporting evidence consists of a note penned by historian Andrew Jenson in 1887 which identifies Elvira as "one of Joseph's first plural wives" who "afterwards married Jonathan H. Holmes."[30] Both Jenson's note (he does not identify the source) and the Wright letter support a sealing to the Prophet as preceding Elvira's legal marriage to Holmes. Elvira conceived her first child with Jonathan three years and two months after their legal marriage ceremony (nineteen months after the martyrdom), which is consistent with the possibility

---

25. Brown, *Nauvoo Sealings, Adoptions, and Anointings*, 282 note 268.
26. William Leon Cummings, *Bibliography of Anti-Masonry*, 28.
27. Lyndon W. Cook, comp., *Nauvoo Deaths and Marriages, 1839–1845*, 103.
28. Joseph F. Smith, Affidavit Books, 1:78, 4:80.
29. William Wright, Letter to unidentified recipient but stamped as received in the First Presidency Office on June 2, 1931.
30. Andrew Jenson Papers, MS 17956, Box 49, fd. 16, document 7: "Elvira Cowles biographical information sheet."

that she was not experiencing sexual relations with Jonathan during Joseph's lifetime because he was only a "front husband" at that point. The Holmeses eventually had five children together. Jonathan obviously respected his wife's sealing to the Prophet, standing proxy for Joseph Smith in the Nauvoo Temple when she was resealed to the Prophet vicariously for eternity.[31] Without additional documentation, it is impossible to discern the precise marital dynamics of this polyandrous marriage.

Jonathan and Elvira Cowles Holmes. Courtesy International Society of the Daughters of Utah Pioneers.

Marinda Nancy Johnson Hyde

Joseph Smith first met Marinda Nancy Johnson at the home of her parents, John and Elsa Johnson, in Hiram, Ohio; and two of her brothers became apostles. Her own commitment seems to have been strong throughout her life, but few specifics are known about her relationship to Joseph. In Nauvoo, twenty-seven-year-old Marinda, who was married to Apostle Orson Hyde, served as an intermediary in helping the Prophet to propose to Nancy Rigdon, a prospective plural wife in April 1842. (See Chapter 17.) Although Nancy indignantly repudiated the offer, the episode is evidence that Marinda was then a member of Nauvoo polygamy's inner circle. A late second-hand report from exposé author Ann Eliza Webb Young tells a similar story:

> When Joseph Smith first taught polygamy, and gave the wives as well as the husbands opportunity to make new choice of life-partners, Mrs. Hyde, at that time a young and quite prepossessing woman, became one of the Prophet's numerous fancies. . . . Hyde was away on a mission at the time, and when he returned, he, in turn, imbibed the teachings of polygamy also, and prepared to extend his kingdom indefinitely. In the mean time it was hinted to him that Smith had had his first wife sealed to himself in his absence, as a wife for eternity. Inconsistent as it may seem, Hyde was in a furious passion."[32]

---

31. Brown, *Nauvoo Sealings, Adoptions, and Anointings*, 284 note 305.

32. Ann Eliza Webb Young, *Wife Number 19, or, The Story of a Life in Bondage, Being a Complete Exposé of Mormonism, and Revealing Sorrows, Sacrifices and Sufferings of Women in*

The Fourteen "Polyandrous" Wives 453

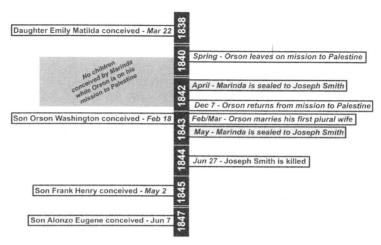

Figure 16.1. Marinda Johnson's childbearing chronology and other historical events.

Ann Eliza's ambiguous wording does not confirm whether this sealing was for "eternity only" or "time and eternity" and her reliability is questionable. Since she was born in 1844, the actual source of her information is unknown.

As discussed in Chapter 12, a slightly more credible tale was published secondhand by anti-Mormon John Bowes claiming that William Arrowsmith, the non-Mormon husband of John Taylor's sister, Elizabeth, witnessed Joseph Smith and Marinda sleeping together "under the same roof."[33]

Adding to the ambiguity is the fact that two different sealing dates are associated with Marinda and the Prophet.[34] The first, "Apr 42," is written by Thomas Bullock on a blank page at the back of the second of four small books Willard Richards used to record Joseph Smith's journal between December 1842 and June 1844.[35] The second sealing date, "May A. D. 1843," is recorded

---

Polygamy, 325–26.

33. William Arrowsmith, quoted in John Bowes, *Mormonism Exposed*, 63.

34. Gregory L. Smith, email to Brian Hales, November 2, 2009, observed: "The repeated sealings may simply have been a way for the husband to give consent or ratify a sealing that had taken place in his absence (e.g., Orson Hyde was away when his wife was first sealed to Joseph). This would be particularly important if those involved saw polyandrous sealings as establishing an eternal connection between Joseph and *both* spouses. It is also possible that in some cases husbands were unaware of the first sealing, but Joseph simply chose to (re)seal them when he had permission (one sees this with Joseph's second sealing to the Partridge sisters after Emma had chosen them as plural wives)."

35. Joseph Smith, Journal, Willard Richards scribe, notation by Thomas Bullock on undated page following final dated entry, July 14, 1843. Reproduced in Richard E.

on a affidavit that Marinda signed on May 1, 1869, and, except for the inevitable problems associated with memory and the passage of time, would generally be considered the most reliable because it comes from Marinda herself, unless more than one ceremony was performed.[36]

As the timeline establishes, Apostle Orson Hyde served a mission to dedicate Palestine for the return of the Jews. Prior to his departure from Nauvoo in the spring of 1840, Marinda conceived a daughter, Emily Matilda Hyde, on approximately March 22, 1838. Orson returned December 7, 1842; and weeks later, approximately February 16, 1843, Marinda became pregnant with their second child, Orson Washington Hyde, who was born on November 9, 1843. No evidence has been found to connect Joseph Smith with this child. (See Chapter 11.) If Joseph Smith was cohabiting with Marinda as a plural wife while Orson was away, pregnancies might have been expected, but none are evident. Regarding this possible sexual polyandrous situation, Todd Compton observes: "It is striking that Marinda had no children while Orson was on his mission to Jerusalem, then became pregnant soon after Orson returned home."[37]

Fawn Brodie has proposed that Marinda's third child, Frank Henry Hyde, was fathered by Joseph Smith, but she assigns him a birth year too early—January 23, 1845, meaning that he was conceived approximately May 2, 1844, the month before Joseph was killed.[38] In fact, both Frank Hyde's birth certificate and his obituary corroborate a birth date of January 23, 1846 (conception approximately May 2, *1845*), thus excluding the Prophet as a possible father.[39]

If Joseph and Marinda were sealed in April 1842, then Joseph may have been sealed to Marinda without Orson Hyde's knowledge. However, John D. Lee remembered that Orson gave his permission: "Hyde's wife, with his consent, was sealed to Joseph for an eternal state."[40] If Lee's reminiscence is correct (and his book is not without questions about its reliability), then the most probable sealing date would be the one Marinda herself gave of May 1843.

Turley, ed., *Selected Collections from the Archives of the Church of Jesus Christ of Latter-day Saints*, Vol. 1, DVD #20, MS155_1_6_320.jpg. For transcript, see Scott H. Faulring, ed., *An American Prophet's Record: The Diaries and Journals of Joseph Smith*, 396.

36. Joseph F. Smith, Affidavit Books, 1:15.

37. Compton, "Fawn Brodie on Joseph Smith's Plural Wives and Polygamy," 165.

38. Fawn M. Brodie, *No Man Knows My History: The Life of Joseph Smith, the Mormon Prophet*, 345; Ugo A. Perego, Natalie M. Myres, and Scott R. Woodward, "Reconstructing the Y-Chromosome of Joseph Smith: Genealogical Applications," 43.

39. Frank H. Hyde, Birth certificate, January 23, 1846. My thanks to Gregory L. Smith for identifying this document. See also "Frank H. Hyde Dies Suddenly," *Ogden Standard*, June 29, 1908, 5.

40. John D. Lee, *Mormonism Unveiled, or, The Life and Confessions of the Late Mormon Bishop*, 147. Lee added, "But I do not assert the fact."

These scanty data support at least three scenarios. First, Marinda many have been sealed to Joseph for "eternity only" in "Apr 1842." If so, she apparently changed her mind because she chose to be sealed to her legal husband, Orson Hyde, in the Nauvoo Temple on January 11, 1846.[41] Another possibility is that the first (April 1842) sealing was for "eternity only" and the second (May 1843) was for "time and eternity." However, at that point, she would have been about three months pregnant with Orson's child, making such a sealing seem less likely—though not impossible. Zina Diantha Huntington was pregnant with Henry Jacobs's child when she was sealed to Joseph Smith. It is intriguing, however, that Marinda had no additional pregnancies after the second sealing date until well after Joseph Smith's death.

Whatever the sequence, Orson appealed to Joseph to perform the sealing to his own first plural wife just months after returning from his Palestine mission. He wrote a statement in 1869: "In the month of February or March, 1843, I was married to Miss Martha R. Browitt, by Joseph Smith, the martyred prophet, and by him she was sealed to me for time and all eternity in Nauvoo, Illinois."[42] Interestingly, a Hyde family tradition states that before Orson Hyde married Marinda, Joseph Smith cautioned him against marrying her. Myrtle Stevens Hyde wrote: "With Orson, the Prophet talked gently about Orson's courtship of Marinda nine years before. Joseph Smith had then, in earnest, pronounced the warning words: 'God has given that woman to me. Do not marry her.' He had refrained from belaboring the statement, letting Orson think the words jestful."[43]

Zina Diantha Huntington Jacobs

Chapter 12 discusses two documents dealing with Zina as a polyandrous wife of Joseph Smith and Henry B. Jacobs. That written by William Hall suffers from gross historical inaccuracies, and I do not accept it as reliable. The

---

41. Brown, *Nauvoo Sealings, Adoptions, and Anointings*, 285 note 323, showing Marinda Nancy Johnson sealed to Joseph Smith in the Nauvoo Temple on January 11, 1846, is in error. Brown, email to Brian Hales, November 23, 2008, clarified: "The information in the NSAA [*Nauvoo Sealings, Adoptions, and Anointings*] is not correct.... Marinda Nancy Johnson was sealed to Orson Hyde on Jan 11, 1846, for time and eternity. The sealing records do not show it as a proxy sealing to Hyde." (Used by permission.) Thomas Milton Tinney, *The Royal Family of the Prophet Joseph Smith, Jr.*, 8, dates Marinda's first proxy sealing to the Prophet at January 12.

42. Orson Hyde, Affidavit, September 15, 1869; copied into Joseph F. Smith, Affidavit Books, 2:45; published in Joseph Fielding Smith, *Blood Atonement and the Origin of Plural Marriage*, 74.

43. Myrtle Stevens Hyde, *Orson Hyde: The Olive Branch of Israel*, 160.

other from Eliza Jane Churchill Webb and her daughter Ann Eliza Webb, later a divorced and hostile wife of Brigham Young, is only slightly more reliable.

Twenty-year-old Zina married twenty-three-year-old Henry Jacobs March 7, 1841, and became pregnant only a few weeks later.[44] Five months after her legal nuptials, Dimick Huntington, Zina's brother, performed her plural sealing to Joseph Smith on October 27, 1841, with his own wife, Fanny, acting as witness.[45] Curiously, Zina testified that her sealing to Joseph was performed a second time: "When Brigham Young returned from England, he repeated the ceremony for *time and eternity*."[46] She does not specify why the first sealing was inadequate. Brigham had arrived from England in July of 1841 and could therefore have performed the first sealing as well. After the birth of Zebulon William Jacobs, the firstborn son of Henry and Zina, she did not conceive again until June 1845 when she became pregnant with Henry Chariton (named for his birthplace, the river near which they were camped on their way west). Henry Jacobs was also the father of this second son. In other words, she did not conceive any children between either of her sealings to Joseph and his death.

What was the relationship between Joseph, Henry, and Zina?[47] One possibility is an "eternity only" sealing, since there is no evidence of sexual relations between Joseph Smith and Zina. A second possibility is that the first sealing on October 24, 1841, was for eternity and that a second ceremony performed by Brigham Young was for "time and eternity." The fact that Zina immediately became pregnant after her legal marriage to Henry B. Jacobs (prior to her sealing to Joseph), but then had no other children with him until well after Joseph Smith's death could support the tentative hypothesis that Henry served as a "front husband" during that period. According to Zina herself, Henry believed that "whatever the Prophet did was right, without making the wisdom of God's authorities bend to the reasoning of any man."[48] He also stood as a witness as Zina was resealed to Joseph Smith by Heber C. Kimball

---

44. Allen L. Wyatt, "Zina and Her Men: An Examination of the Changing Marital State of Zina Diantha Huntington Jacobs Smith Young."

45. Zina Huntington Jacobs Young, Affidavit, May 18, 1869, Joseph F. Smith, Affidavit Books, 1:5, 4:5; Fanny M. Huntington, Affidavit, May 1, 1869, Joseph F. Smith, Affidavit Books, 1:21, 4:21.

46. Zina D. Huntington Jacobs Young, quoted in John Wight, "Interview: Evidence from Zina D. Huntington Young, October 1, 1898," 29; emphasis mine.

47. Compton, *In Sacred Loneliness*, 84, theorizes that Zina may have been involved with sexual polyandry with Brigham Young. However, no documentation showing cohabitation between Zina and both men during the same period is available (see also 83–86).

48. Zina Diantha Huntington Young, Autobiography, Oa Jacobs Cannon, "History of Henry Bailey Jacobs," 5.

with Brigham Young acting as proxy in the Nauvoo Temple on February 2, 1846.[49] Thereafter, Kimball married Zina to Brigham Young for time only.[50]

Zina's Nauvoo journal, which she began June 5, 1844, contains ambiguous references to her two husbands.[51] Zina's biographers, Martha Sonntag Bradley and Mary Brown Firmage Woodward comment:

> [Zina] observed the necessary "double speak" in her journal, frequently using code names for Joseph and writing around "dangerous" subjects. For example, her first diary entry dated "June 5, 6, 7, 8, 9" [,] 1844, makes veiled reference to a meeting where some type of secret ceremonies were performed. "Went with Henres uncles family upon the hill," she writes. "From this day I understand the Kinsman degree of freemasonry. My husband, being a Master Mason, attended meeting…" "The hill" was the bluff above the Mississippi River where the temple was being built. There is no Kinsman degree in Freemasonry, suggesting that the meeting contained a ceremony of equal secrecy. Because Henry had been in Tennessee on a mission since 15 April, Zina's reference to "my husband" must have meant Joseph Smith, an admitted Master Mason.[52]

During the three weeks prior to the martyrdom, she mentions Henry only four times in her journal and Joseph Smith ten, but at that time of intensifying turmoil surrounding the Prophet, many Nauvooans may have been prompted to closely follow their leader's day-to-day circumstances. Zina's entries in those days immediately prior to the martyrdom include specific details, but I have been unable to determine whether she was recording generally known news or privileged information indicating her greater access, based on their sealing. Her references to Henry during those three weeks prior to the martyrdom are inconclusive regarding the possibility that the legal union was a "pretended" marriage (though, not surprisingly, she does not mention sexual relations), and she was definitely pregnant with Henry's child by June 1845 (a year after the Prophet's death). The fact that she conceived no children after her October 27, 1841, sealing to the Prophet and his death is curious, since she seemed to have quickly conceived after her legal marriage to Henry (and years later after consummating her union with Brigham Young; see below).

Zina's polygamous life after the martyrdom created a second polyandrous relationship. During the next twelve months, she remained with Henry as his monogamous wife and conceived a son approximately June 30, 1845. As mentioned, when Henry and Zina attended the Nauvoo Temple on February

---

49. Brown, *Nauvoo Sealings, Adoptions, and Anointings*, 284.
50. Ibid., 353.
51. Maureen Ursenbach Beecher, ed., "'All Things Move in Order in the City': The Nauvoo Diary of Zina Diantha Huntington Jacobs," 290–91.
52. Bradley and Woodward, *Four Zinas*, 124.

2, seven months later, Henry stood as a witness as Zina was resealed to Joseph Smith for eternity. At this point, a strange thing occurred. Zina, who was seven months pregnant with Henry's child, was sealed to Brigham Young for "time." The motivations for this sealing are unclear. Reportedly, Joseph Smith asked the Twelve to marry his widows to take care of them, but Zina needed no such support as Henry was a dutiful husband.[53] Zina's dissatisfaction with her marriage to Henry may have played a role. She later told an interviewer: "I was married to Mr. Jacobs, but the marriage was unhappy and we parted."[54] She also characterized the union as "a most unhappy and ill-assorted marriage."[55] Whether she had privately met with Brigham Young and requested a separation from Henry is unknown.

Despite her February 2, 1846, temple marriage for "time" to Brigham, Zina was traveling with Henry as they left Nauvoo for the West just five days later. Henry cared for pregnant Zina who delivered their second child, Henry Chariton Jacobs, on March 22 at the crossing of the Chariton River in Iowa. A little over two months later while camped at Mt. Pisgah, Iowa, Brigham Young called Henry on a mission to England, apparently informing him that Zina was no longer his wife and advising him to marry another wife. Regarding this event, anti-Mormon writer William Hall reported:

> At a place called, by the Mormons, Pisgah, in Iowa, as they were passing through to Council Bluffs, Brigham Young spoke in this wise, in the hearing of hundreds: He said it was time for men who were walking in other men's shoes to step out of them. "Brother Jacobs," he says, "the woman you claim for a wife does not belong to you. She is the spiritual wife of brother Joseph, sealed up to him. I am his proxy, and she, in this behalf, with her children are my property. You can go where you please and get another, but be sure to get one of your own kindred spirit."[56]

Hall's biases are evident and the source of his information is unidentified, but the general description may be accurate. Despite these heart-wrenching proceedings, Henry Jacobs remained true to his faith and to Brigham Young, writing to Zina on June 25, less than a month after leaving on his mission: "I

---

53. Susa Young Gates, Undated and untitled statement, Susa Young Gates Papers, Box 12, fd. 2, p. 78 (quoted in Chapter 11).

54. Zina D. Huntington Jacobs Young, quoted in Wight, "Interview: Evidence from Zina D. Huntington Young, October 1, 1898," 29; see also Bradley and Woodward, *Four Zinas*, 114.

55. [Emmeline B. Wells] "A Distinguished Woman: Zina D. H. Young," 99. It is possible that this is Wells's assessment, rather than a quotation from Zina. However, Zina lived until 1901, and the women were neighbors and associates in the Relief Society and other organizations.

56. William Hall, *The Abominations of Mormonism Exposed*, 43–44.

do not blame any person . . . may the Lord our Father Bless Brother Brigham and . . . tell him for me I have no feelings against him nor never had."[57] Within weeks as a missionary, Henry had proposed to two different women.[58] He went on to wed three more times with each union ending in divorce.[59]

In the wake of her religious divorce from Henry, Zina moved closer to the inner circle of Brigham Young's plural wives where she was accepted and cared for until arriving at Salt Lake City on September 20, 1848. With Brigham's help and assistance from her brothers Dimick, Oliver, and William, she was established in a small cabin in the central fort. Zina's biographers recount the next events:

> In early February 1849, Brigham stopped by—apparently unannounced—one Sunday evening, and the two "had a very agreeable veset.". . . The next week, on 13 February, Zina for the first time invited Brigham to her home for supper. Zina does not mention seeing her husband again for a month. Then on 15 March Brigham reappeared, and this time, she records briefly, he "stayed the night." The next day Zina "prepared to move"—evidently as a result of Brigham's instructions the previous night.[60]

The following day Zina reflected in her journal: "Many are the reflections of my minde. My Father & mother is not[;] Joseph is not[;] BY is very kinde indeed."[61] Regarding this entry, Bradley and Woodward ask: "Why, on the eve of this public change in her marital status, twenty-four hours after what was probably the consummation of her marriage with Brigham Young, does she linger over the fact that her father, mother, and idolized prophet-husband Joseph Smith are dead before reminding herself that Brigham 'is very kinde indeed'? . . . Conspicuous by his absence from this list of loved ones is the still-living Henry Jacobs who, by every indication, loved her passionately. Where were her memories of him?"[62]

One month later when she learned her room in Brigham Young's home was ready for her to occupy, she was overcome with emotion: "O did I not seek a lone retreat beside a murmering [stream] the water rolled over a fall about 3 feet whare the sound of my voice would not be herd there. I wept yes wept bitterness of Soul."[63] This rush of sentiment could be interpreted several ways. Bradley and Woodward observed: "Despite her tears, there is no evidence Zina found Young personally distasteful. She never spoke of him except with

---

57. Henry Bailey Jacobs, Letter to Zina D. H. Young, June 25, 1846, Zina D. H. Young Collection, quoted in Bradley and Woodward, *Four Zinas*, 153.
58. Bradley and Woodward, *Four Zinas*, 153; Compton, *In Sacred Loneliness*, 88.
59. Compton, *In Sacred Loneliness*, 660.
60. Bradley and Woodward, *Four Zinas*, 183.
61. Ibid.
62. Ibid., 184.
63. Quoted in ibid., 186.

deep respect amounting to reverence."⁶⁴ Nevertheless, she does not reflect a romantic attraction to him either. Plural marriage for her may have been more than just sharing a husband, but being bound to one to whom she was otherwise minimally attracted. Bradley and Woodward wrote: "Zina made no comment that illuminates her own preference in the matter [of plural marriage], but her behavior was consistent with her past obedience to priesthood authority. . . . [S]he seemed not to doubt that this arrangement was 'fair' or 'right.'"⁶⁵

Like the experiences of Sylvia Sessions Lyon (see Chapter 13) and Mary Ann Darrow Richardson (see Chapter 14), Zina's plural marriages are odd by even polygamy standards. They are polyandrous in a ceremonial sense, but sexually, they seem to represent consecutive matrimonies, where she shared the marriage bed with only one husband at a time. Her specific relationship with Joseph Smith and whether Henry was a front husband during the Prophet's life are currently unanswerable.

Zina Diantha Huntington Jacobs Smith Young. Courtesy LDS Church History Library.

Mary Heron Snider—Fourteenth Polyandrous Wife

Besides the thirteen women discussed above, Michael Quinn proposes a fourteenth woman as a polyandrous wife, Mary Heron Snider, the legal wife of John Snider (sometimes Snyder).⁶⁶ According to one isolated source, she was sexually involved with Joseph Smith. As reviewed in Chapters 2–3, a number of claims of illicit sexuality were leveled at the Prophet in the 1830s, none of which seems to represent credible evidence of impropriety. Bennett issued a few additional allegations in 1842, which lack reliability (Chapters 19–21).

---

64. Ibid., 187–88.
65. Ibid., 133.
66. After graciously agreeing to review an early draft of my chapters dealing with polyandry, Michael Quinn wrote: "My main objection to your approach is that you intentionally withhold the most explicit statement by a DEVOUT MORMON that Joseph Smith had sexual intercourse with an already married Mormon woman." Quinn, email to Brian Hales, May 17, 2011; used by permission; emphasis his. He was referring to the statement of Joseph E. Johnson discussed in this section.

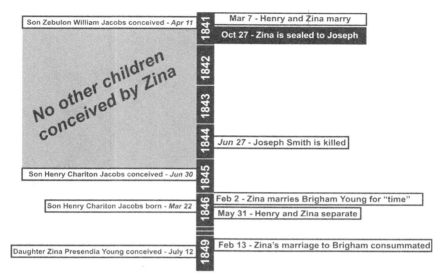

Figure 16.2. Zina Huntington's childbearing chronology and other historical events.

The reference by Michael Quinn, however, cannot be easily dismissed because it was made by a devout Mormon, Joseph Ellis Johnson and recorded in 1850.

Joseph E. Johnson and Hannah Goddard

Before addressing the account of Mary Heron Snider, a somewhat complex back story must be introduced involving the witness, Joseph Ellis Johnson, to provide context for his report concerning the Prophet and Mary. Johnson was born April 28, 1817, to Ezekiel Johnson and Julia Hills Johnson, a family destined to be prominent in early Mormonism. His younger brother by one year, Benjamin F. Johnson, would become a very close friend of the Prophet; and two of his sisters, Delcena and Almera, became Joseph's plural wives. On October 6, 1840, Joseph Ellis Johnson married Harriet Ellen Snider, oldest daughter of John Snider and Mary Heron Snider, in a ceremony performed by the Prophet.

On January 19, 1845 Brigham Young sealed Lorenzo Snow to Hannah M. Goddard (b. 1828), sister of his legal wife.[67] After the sealing, but apparently

---

67. Snow, Diary, 51, LDS Church History Library; quoted in D. Michael Quinn, "Evidence for the Sexual Side of Joseph Smith's Polygamy," 47–48 fn68. Quinn recorded as one of Lorenzo Snow's wives: "Hannah M. Goddard 1845 (no children), separated 1845, remarried 1849 but not divorced until 1882." D. Michael Quinn, *The*

prior to consummating the union, Lorenzo left on a mission. Around April 21, 1849, Joseph E. Johnson became intimately involved with Hannah who became pregnant with his child, Joseph Eugene Johnson, born January 3, 1850 (died March 7, 1852). Upon learning of the incident, Lorenzo Snow relinquished his claim to Hannah Maria, allowing her to eventually be sealed to Johnson. Endowment House records indicate that Joseph Ellis Johnson and Hannah Goddard Johnson were sealed on November 17, 1861. Together, they had eight children, six before the sealing and two afterwards.[68] Nearly twenty years later, Joseph E. Johnson wrote to Church President John Taylor seeking permission to have their six children sealed to them. The presiding apostle responded straightforwardly:

Joseph E. Johnson. Courtesy of LDS Church History Library.

> There is one thing that must be remembered that she [Hannah Goddard] was Elder Lorenzo Snow's wife, that she had been sealed to him for time and for eternity [in the 1840s], and until a dissolution of the former contract was had, by and with his consent, unless he himself had transgressed the former arrangement still held good. This, Bro. Snow stated, he never gave, and it must be remembered that it was yourself and Bro. Snow's wife that violated your contracts, and not him; and while he might be willing to pass by your transgression and not prosecute you for your liaison with his wife, yet it does not follow that she was legitimately yours. We cannot suppose for a moment that an act of transgression gives any rightful claim or privilege to a transgressor. It would be a most singular doctrine to assert that a man who seduces the wife of an honorable brother, and then when he has accomplished the foul deed, is to be rewarded for his crime with the gift of the man's wife, who he has sinned against. Bro. Lorenzo Snow protested against such action, with I think perfect consistency.... When it comes to asking the privilege of further sealings, the adoption of children, and the confirmation of these dishonorable things ... he cannot with propriety permit other acts of adoption, sealing etc. and thus violate his sacred covenant [and] desecrate the Temple Ordinances.[69]

Mormon Hierarchy: Extensions of Power, 701.

68. Joseph Ellis Johnson and Hannah Goddard Johnson, family group record, www.FamilySearch.com (accessed March 16, 2012).

69. John Taylor, Letter to President John D. T. McAllister, St. George Temple President, June 9, 1880.

Despite President Taylor's declaration, St. George Temple records show that a second marital sealing occurred on June 6, 1882; several of the couple's children were sealed to them a week and a half later. Possibly Lorenzo Snow had experienced a change of heart, allowing those ordinances to be performed.

Joseph Ellis Johnson's Statement

Returning now to their original transgression in April 1849, even at that time with polygamy secretly gaining momentum among Church members, LDS leaders were intolerant of adultery regardless of the setting. Hence, upon learning of Hannah Maria's pregnancy and the circumstances, Joseph Ellis Johnson's Church membership was in jeopardy. He attended a council of priesthood leaders in the Salt Lake Valley on September 2, 1850, that discussed the case.[70] Brigham Young presided at the meeting, which was also attended by Heber C. Kimball, Willard Richards, Orson Hyde, Parley P. Pratt, Ezra Taft Benson, George A. Smith, Orson Spencer, Daniel Carn, Alexander Neibaur, Joel H. Johnson, Benjamin F. Johnson, and Joseph Kelly (secretary).[71] Notes from that council explain:

> O. Hyde [speaking] there is a matter of bro: Johnson to be laid before the Council—this matter was brot. before Council in Kanesville his Priesthood was required to be laid down until he came here—a Miss Goddard wife of Lorenzo Snow became in a family way by Bro Johnson—she was living in his house—we deemed it improper for her to be there he sent her away to a retired place—she was delivered of a child—she is again living at his house in Kanesville—he wishes to retain his fellowship in the Church. He says he has bro: Snow & he was satisfied.
>
> "Joseph E. Johnson [speaking]—I am come purposely if possible to get the matter settled & atone for the wrong I av done—I av neglected to lay it before you before this—bro Hydes statements r all correct—true—all I can do is beg for mercy—I became acquainted with the girl, & the consequences r as the[y] r—I saw bro. Snow at Kanesville & he was satisfied—I am come here to atone for the wrong I av done.[72]

---

70. See Rufus David Johnson, *J. E. J. Trail to Sundown: Cassadaga to Casa Grande 1817–1882*, 125–30.

71. The precise decision of Church leaders regarding the Johnson-Goddard sexual transgression is unknown, but it appears he was soon restored to full fellowship. Concerning the event, Michael Quinn wrote: "BY [Brigham Young] reproves him and has him rebaptized." D. Michael Quinn Papers.

72. Miscellaneous Minutes, September 2, 1850, Brigham Young Collection, d 1234, restricted; excerpts transcribed by D. Michael Quinn, Box 3, fd. 2, Quinn Papers, Yale Library. This document is available on Richard E. Turley Jr., ed., *Selected Collections from the Archives of the Church of Jesus Christ of Latter-day Saints*, Vol. 1, DVD #18 , but that

During the proceedings, secretary Kelly recorded Joseph Ellis Johnson's explanatory comments that make it clear he was not attempting to justify his conduct:

> I never heard any conversation to say it was right to go to bed to a woman if not found out—I was aware the thing was wrong.—had been with—he sd. He was familiar with the first frigging [slang for sexual relations]—that was done in his house with his mother in law—by Joseph.[73]

The "mother in law" was Mary Heron Snider.

John Snider and Mary Heron Snider

Interpreting Joseph E. Johnson's statement is difficult due to a lack of historical documentation regarding the relationship between Joseph Smith, Mary Heron Snider, and her legal husband, John Snider. However, an examination of available evidence provides important clues.

Born February 11, 1800, at New Brunswick, Nova Scotia, the son of Marlin Snider and Sarah Armstrong Snider, John Snider moved with the family to Toronto, Upper Canada (now Ontario), where he worked as a mason. On February 28, 1822, he married Mary Heron, four years his junior. The daughter of Richard Heron and Harriet Hill Heron, she was born November 10, 1804. Together the Sniders had four children, Harriet Ellen (b. September 4, 1823), Edgerton (b. January 9, 1826), John Jr. (born May 3, 1828), and Julia (born in 1833) who apparently did not live long. John and Mary associated with fellow Canadian John Taylor in studying scriptures in 1833. Three years later they were converted and baptized through the instrumentality of Parley P. Pratt.

The Sniders left Upper Canada to join the body of the Latter-day Saints in Kirtland, Ohio, in the spring of 1837. A June 4, 1837, revelation to Joseph Smith, instructed Heber C. Kimball to lead a group of missionaries to England.[74] John Snider was among that vanguard of Mormon emissaries, the first to ever preach in Great Britain.[75] He arrived in Liverpool July 18, 1837, and stayed until October when he boarded a ship back to America. He joined Mary and his children in Far West, Missouri; they were forced to leave within a year, traveling east to Springfield, Illinois. There they were befriended by the Ezekiel Johnson family, including Ezekiel's son, Joseph Ellis Johnson, who eventually married John and Mary's oldest daughter, Harriet. Ordained

---

entry is blacked out, restricted because it deals with Church disciplinary proceedings.

73. Ibid.

74. Stanley B. Kimball, ed., *On the Potter's Wheel: The Diaries of Heber C. Kimball*, 4–5.

75. Scott G. Kenney, ed. *Wilford Woodruff's Journal*, 2:235; see also *History of the Church*, 1:153, June 12, 1837.

a Seventy on January 19, 1839, John was appointed four months later to serve a second mission to England with the apostles but apparently did not go.[76]

Joseph Smith stayed in the Snider home in Springfield while en route to Washington, D.C., to plead with federal officials for redress regarding Missouri persecutions.[77] On November 9, 1839, the Prophet wrote to Emma: "We have done all that we could for the safty of Elder Rigdon on account of his week state of hea[l]th and this morning we are under the ~~neces~~ nesesity of leaveing him at Brother Snyders and pesueing our Journy without him."[78] The Sniders stayed in Springville a year, after which they united with the Saints in Nauvoo. The 1842 census placed the John Snider family, consisting of John and Mary, and children Egerton, John Jr., and Sarah, in the third ward.[79] Their home was situated below the temple then being constructed, just under a mile from Joseph Smith's Homestead and Nauvoo Mansion.[80]

On January 19, 1841, John was appointed as a member of the committee to build the Nauvoo House (D&C 124:22, 62, 70). Before the revelation authorizing that building's construction, a bill had already been presented to the Illinois state legislature for the incorporation of an association to sell stock for the purpose of constructing a hotel in Nauvoo. That act, approved on February 23, 1841, named four trustees: George Miller, Lyman Wight, John Snyder, and Peter Haws. They were authorized to sell $150,000 worth of stock, from the proceeds of which the hotel would be built. In early February, Snider was also appointed to the Board of Trustees of the University of the City of Nauvoo.[81] John also served on the personal staff of the Prophet as an assistant aide-de-camp in the Nauvoo Legion.

John is mentioned several times in Joseph Smith's Nauvoo journals, which were begun on December 19, 1841:

> December 22, 1841: The word of the Lord came unto Joseph the Seer, verily thus saith the Lord, Let my servant John Snider take a mission to the Eastern continent, unto all the conferences now sitting in that region, and let them carry a package of Epistles that shall be written by my servants the

---

76. Lyndon W. Cook, *The Revelations of the Prophet Joseph Smith*, 277.
77. "History of Joseph Smith," *Deseret News*, June 8, 1854, 1.
78. Dean C. Jessee, ed., Joseph Smith to Emma Smith, November 9, 1839, in *The Personal Writings of Joseph Smith*, 448.
79. Nauvoo Ward Census, 1842, p. 47, LR 3102 27.
80. Nauvoo land records show the Sniders on Block 82, lot 2, two blocks below the temple then under construction. Also listed as John Snider's property is block 156, the location of the Nauvoo House. Both Peter Haws, another Nauvoo House Committee member, as well as Joseph Smith, are listed as owners of block 156. John Snider also owned land near Ramus, Illinois, the home of his daughter Harriet. Nauvoo Land and Records Research Center, P.O. Box 215, Nauvoo, IL 62354.
81. John S. Dinger, ed., *The Nauvoo City and High Council Minutes*, 7.

Twelve, making known unto them their duties concerning the building of my houses [Nauvoo House and Nauvoo Temple].[82]

December 27, 1841.—Joseph. Was with. Brigham [Young], Heber C [Kimball], Willard [Richards]. & John [Taylor] of the twelve, at his office. Instructing them in the principles of the kingdom. & what the twelve should do in relation to the mission of John Snider. & the European conferences.[83]

January 28, 1842—At the office . . . present H[eber] C. Kimball. W[ilford] woodruff. B[righam] Young. & received instruction concerning John Snider.[84]

Joseph decided that Elder John Snider should go out on a mission, and if necessary some one go with him. And raise up a Church. And get means to go to England. & carry the Epistles required in the Revelation page 36.— and instructed the Twelve, B[righam] Young H[eber] C. Kimball. W[ilford] woodruff. &— W[illard] Richards—being present. To call Elder Snider into their council & instruct him in these things & if he will not do these things he shall be cut off from the Church. & be damned.[85]

January 31, 1842—. . . in the <evening> was in council with Brigham [Young], Heber. C. [Kimball]—Orson [Pratt]. WIllford [Wilford Woodruff]. & Willard [Richards]. concring [concerning] Bro [John] Snider.[86]

March 26, 1842—Elder John Snider Recivied his final inst[r]uctions from the President, & received his blessing from Prest B[righam] Young. With the Laying on of the hands of Prest. Joseph. J[ohn] E. Page. & W[illard] Richards. & Started for England same day.[87]

Elder Snider hesitated to fulfill the December 22, 1841, revelation, apparently because he felt that the Quorum of the Twelve should furnish him means.[88] Church historians made this assessment in 1855: "Elder Snider had appeared very backward about fulfilling the revelation concerning him, and felt that he could not do it unless the Twelve would furnish him means, when he was more able to furnish his own means as all the elders were obliged to do when they went out on missions"[89] (see D&C 24:18, 84:78, 86; Luke 10:4). Under more intense pressure, as these entries show, he accepted his mission and departed on March 26. He journeyed in England until September 29,

---

82. Andrew H. Hedges, Alex D. Smith, and Richard Lloyd Anderson, eds., *Journals, Volume 2: December 1841–April 1843*, 16–17.
83. Ibid., 18.
84. Ibid., 31.
85. Ibid., 38.
86. Ibid., 32.
87. Ibid., 47.
88. Ibid., 31 note 99.
89. "History of Joseph Smith," *Deseret News*, August 1, 1855, 1.

1842, when he and 157 converts under his direction boarded the ship *Henry* and sailed from Liverpool for New Orleans.[90] The group arrived in Nauvoo on January 23, 1843. Weeks after arriving home, on February 18 and 19, John Snider was asked to serve as a "pro tem" member of the Nauvoo High Council.[91] Two months later, James Allred, John Snider, and Aaron Johnson were appointed to administer baptisms for the dead in the river while the font could not be used.[92] On January 3, 1844, Joseph Smith, acting as mayor, directed the marshal to bring Snider before the Nauvoo City Council to testify on his behalf against William Law, who was accusing the Prophet of sexual improprieties.[93] On June 28, the day after Joseph Smith's death, John Snider was invited to serve as a member of "Joseph's bodyguard" escorting the bodies of Joseph and Hyrum back into the city.[94] On July 18, 1844, John served as proxy in being baptized for ten of his deceased ancestors.[95]

Unfortunately, Mary Snider's activities before and after the death of Joseph Smith are poorly documented. Her reactions to the multiple separations from her husband as he served the Church are unknown, but her trials would not have been significantly different from those of many other wives whose husbands had similar leadership responsibilities. While it appears that Mary was not present at the organization of the Relief Society on March 17, 1842, Emma presented her name along with those of six others for admittance.[96] On May 26, 1842, Mary contributed fifty cents to the Relief Society. There is no record that Mary participated in baptisms for the dead.

According to a 1909 "Life Sketch" penned by Edwin George Snider, after the Prophet's death, "The family returned to Toronto, the object being to give the sons Edgerton and John Junior, a chance to learn the masons' trade."[97] Their exit from Nauvoo at that time is strange, because John was also a mason and there was probably ample work in Nauvoo, especially since the temple was being constructed at that time. Their absence from Illinois explains why

---

90. Andrew Jenson, *Church Chronology: A Record of Important Events Pertaining to the History of the Church of Jesus Christ of Latter-day Saints*. 2d ed., 21–22.

91. Dinger, *The Nauvoo City and High Council Minutes*, 447–48.

92. "Elders Conference," *Times and Seasons* 4, no. 10 (April 1, 1843): 158.

93. Dinger, *The Nauvoo City and High Council Minutes*, 199.

94. *History of the Church*, 7:135.

95. Susan Easton Black and Harvey Bischoff Black, eds., *Annotated Records of Baptisms for the Dead, 1840–1845, Nauvoo, Hancock County, Illinois* 6:3428–31.

96. Maurine Carr Ward, "'This Institution Is a Good One': The Female Relief Society of Nauvoo, 17 March 1842 to 16 March 1844," 184. The other six women were Sarah Higbee, Thirza Cahoon, Kezia A. Morrison, Miranda N. Hyde, Abigail Allred, and Sarah Granger.

97. Edwin George Snider, "Another John Snider [1800–1875] Life Sketch," unpublished, 1909, 2.

neither John nor Mary was endowed in the Nauvoo Temple or received other ordinances there. In the fall of 1847, the family moved to Iowa and then six months later, back to Nauvoo, where John assisted in disposing of Mormon properties after the Saints began the exodus west.[98]

In 1850, John journeyed alone to California in search of gold, leaving Mary and the children in the Midwest.[99] Mary crossed the plains in the Almon W. Babbitt Company in the spring of 1851 with their two sons, arriving July 17, 1851.[100] Fellow traveler Mary Augusta Hawkins Snow recorded on May 23, 1851: "We are all rejoicing to day in a glorious sunshine inward as well as outward I trust for all seem happy—particularly the children after being confined in the wagons so long . . . Mrs Snider is quite sick and has been made as comfortable as possible, her canaries, the only ones with us, are gaily singing quite unconscious that the hand which has tended them so faithfully thus far is able to do it no longer."[101]

John joined Mary months later in Salt Lake City. Whether she suffered a lingering illness, or experienced bouts of different sicknesses, she died January 31, 1852. A search of all available obituaries for Utah and the region for that period fail to identify any details concerning her death. John was never sealed to Mary during their lifetimes, even though a proxy sealing after her death would have been possible. Curiously, John waited until two weeks after Mary's passing away to obtain his own temple endowments.[102] Perhaps the timing of John Snider's first temple visit was coincidental, or possibly a sealing between Mary and Joseph Smith had created an awkward situation while they were both living.

John Snider remained in Salt Lake City, an active member of the Church, and married Sylvia Ameretta Meacham (Mecham) on November 3, 1855. The couple had three children, Marlin (b. 1856), Martin Henry (b. 1859), and John Hyrum (b. 1860) and were sealed in the Endowment House on February 16, 1867.[103] John lived the remainder of his life in the Seventeenth Ward, dying December 17, 1875. The notice of his death read: "Deceased was a veteran in the Church of Jesus Christ of Latter-day Saints, having been connected with it in the days of the Prophet Joseph Smith and ever since. He was a man much respected, being true to his convictions of right."[104] Two weeks later, Apostle John Taylor, who had joined the Church in Toronto, Canada,

---

98. Kenney, *Wilford Woodruff's Journal*, 2:235; see also *History of the Church*, 3: 311, 314, January 21, 25, 1848.

99. Susan Easton Black, *Who's Who in the Doctrine & Covenants*, 305.

100. Joseph E. Johnson's sister was Almon W. Babbitt's wife.

101. Mary Augusta Hawkins Snow, Journal, May 23, 1851.

102. John Snider and Mary Heron Snider, family group record, www.FamilySearch.com (accessed May 22, 2011).

103. John Snider and Sylvia Ameretta Meacham (Mecham), family group record, www.FamilySearch.com (accessed April 8, 2012).

104. "A Veteran Gone" [John Snider], *Deseret News*, December 22, 1875, 9.

in 1836 with John, penned a second obituary that was also published, which stated: "He [John Snider] gathered to Utah in 1851, where he has since continued a steadfast, faithful and honorable member in the Church. . . . Having been well acquainted with him for upwards of forty years, I thought it proper to give the above short statement."[105] There is no mention of his marriage to Mary Heron in either obituary notice.

Joseph Ellis Johnson's "House" in Ramus, Illinois

With that background, we now return to the event described in 1850 by Joseph Ellis Johnson. Johnson settled in Ramus, Illinois, located about twenty-five miles east of Nauvoo in 1840. He traveled to Nauvoo in October to marry Harriet Snider, and the couple returned to Ramus to set up housekeeping. The town was growing rapidly; it was renamed Macedonia in 1843; today it is called Webster. After three years in Ramus, Joseph Johnson finally built a "comfortable home in town and with good society lived happily with little means."[106] If his comment concerning sexual relations "done in his house" referred to this structure, then it would have occurred in Ramus/Macedonia in 1843.[107] Since both Joseph Smith and the Sniders lived in Nauvoo, they would have needed to travel to Ramus for any personal interaction.[108]

---

105. "Obituary" [John Snider], *Deseret News*, January 5, 1876, 14.

106. Joseph E. Johnson quoted in Rufus David Johnson, *J. E. J. Trail to Sundown: Cassadaga to Casa Grande 1817–1882*, 75.

107. Michael Quinn, email to Brian Hales, May 17, 2011, used by permission, proposed that sexual relations between Joseph Smith and Mary Heron Snider occurred while John Snider was on his mission in 1842. However, if these alleged relations occurred in their new home, then the time would have been in 1843—after John had returned from England.

108. As discussed, the Sniders owned lot 2 on block 82 in Nauvoo, and Joseph Ellis Johnson owned lot 3, block 7, in Ramus, also called Macedonia. Nauvoo Land and Records Research Center, P.O. Box 215, Nauvoo, IL 62354. Michael Quinn asserts that Joseph Ellis built a home in Nauvoo and that the sexual relations occurred there, but he provides no evidence beyond the observation that Joseph Ellis apparently bought property there on December 21, 1841 and he was not designated a "non-resident" in that paperwork. Based upon this single observation, Quinn concludes that Joseph E. Johnson and Harriet were "living in Nauvoo in 1841." "Evidence for the Sexual Side of Joseph Smith's Polygamy," 13–14. Quinn's reconstruction is contradicted by several evidences. In his biography of Joseph E. Johnson, *J. E. J. Trail to Sundown: Cassadaga to Casa Grande 1817–1882*, Rufus David Johnson describes how Joseph Ellis migrated from Springfield, Illinois, in the "summer of 1840" and stopped "20 miles from Nauvoo" purchasing land that would become Ramus-Macedonia (73). Joseph E. Johnson visited Nauvoo in the fall to marry Harriet Snider on October 6, 1840, but "the next day Joseph and his bride [returned] to Ramus." (Ibid.) Their first child, Mary Julia Johnson

Having returned from his English mission in January of 1843, John Snider was probably not in the mission field during the Prophet's alleged sexual relations with his legal wife. However, there is no documentation on when a relationship might have begun or when a plural marriage between Joseph and Mary was performed. According to available records, the Prophet visited Ramus, Illinois, on five different occasions during the 1840s. The first occurred on March 11, 1843, with subsequent visits on April 1, May 17, October 20, and the following March 27, 1844.[109] Hence for Joseph to have experienced conjugal relations with Mary, she would have also needed to have been in Ramus on one of those occasions, with or without her legal husband accompanying her to the town.

Observations

The research presented above supports several observations. First, John Snider remained devoted to Joseph Smith and the Church throughout his life. This behavior could be explained in at least two ways. One is that John was completely unaware of Joseph Smith's relationship with Mary. In this case, all those aware of the association would have needed to keep it secret. It seems probable that, if Joseph Ellis Johnson knew of the connection, at least one or two others would have also known. Hence, to keep John Snider completely in the dark might have required a conspiracy among those informed. Maintaining the deception would have included certain risks and moral concerns, in addition to their possible discomfort with the behavior itself. Hypothesizing such a dynamic raises the question of what arguments the Prophet could have employed to justify such activities and to successfully win promises of silence from those apprised.

The other possibility is that John Snider knew of the relationship and accepted it. This, too, is difficult to fathom unless his marriage to Mary had experienced significant problems prior to their settlement in Nauvoo; and even then, it would not have been an easy emotional transition. How readily men and women were permitted to choose a different spouse to marry in the new and everlasting covenant when it was first introduced is not revealed in the historical record; but if it was ever allowed, it apparently did not happen often.

---

was born December 24, 1841, not in Nauvoo, but in Macedonia. Similarly, their second child, Eliza Antoinette Johnson, was also born at Macedonia on November 17, 1843. The only house built by Joseph Ellis Johnson, according to any record, was in Ramus-Macedonia.

109. Faulring, *An American Prophet's Record*, 332, 338, 423, 435, 461, 472; George D. Smith, ed., *An Intimate Chronicle: The Journals of William Clayton*, 101–4.

Second, little can be concluded regarding the relationship between John and Mary in Nauvoo. While conjugality is documented up through 1833 (the birth of their last child), the lack of pregnancy after that point could have been either the result of limited sexual relations or sterility in Mary, who was in her thirties and theoretically, still very capable of conception. That John was able to father three children with his second wife demonstrates that he was not sterile. The fact that John and Mary were not sealed during Mary's lifetime may have been due to their absence from Nauvoo and consequent lack of access to the Nauvoo Temple and the lack of opportunity afterwards. However, the fact that the sealing was not performed vicariously thereafter, especially in 1867 when John was sealed to his second wife, supports the possibility that Mary may have been sealed to Joseph Smith.

Third, Mary appears to have been an active Latter-day Saint as corroborated by her 1842 admittance into the Relief Society. Worthiness was an important criterion for all members. That Emma recommended her admission suggests that either there was no known relationship between Joseph and Mary at that point or that the relationship existed but was unknown to Emma who did not accept plural marriage until the spring of 1843. (See Chapter 24.) Whether Mary would have willingly engaged in an illicit relationship with Joseph Smith is unknown, but it would seem inconsistent with her apparent moral character.

Fourth, little can be said regarding general interactions between Joseph Smith and Mary. He undoubtedly met her for the first time when he, along with Sidney Rigdon, and others, boarded at the Sniders' residence in Springfield, Illinois, in 1839 and she may have been the "Sister Snyder" mentioned by the Mary Isabella Hales Horne in Quincy, Illinois in June of 1841: "The prophet with Sister Snyder called in his buggy upon Sister Cleveland."[110] That their paths would have crossed in Nauvoo seems certain, but nothing beyond Joseph E. Johnson's statement places them reliably together.

Fifth, the faith of Joseph E. Johnson does not seem to have been negatively affected by what he learned about the Prophet and his mother-in-law in 1843. It is probable that, if he viewed the relationship as immoral, his testimony may have been compromised. Similarly, when he discussed his case with the council in 1850, the minutes do not record any reaction from the leaders to his comment about Joseph and his mother-in-law.[111] That they convened in part to

---

110. Hales, *The Chronicles of the Hales Family in America*, 79.

111. Other pertinent comments in the council meeting, as transcribed by Michael Quinn, are difficult to understand, although it does appear that the secretary, "J. Kelly," was surprised. Quinn's transcription reads: "O.H. sd. Kelly told him Johnson knew what he was about—it was done in his house by bro Joseph that the Ch had tried to break down bro. Babbitt & the Ch Therefor—I knew at the time I was doing

consider Joseph E. Johnson's membership status due to his adultery (he was disfellowshipped), demonstrates a lack of tolerance of sexual transgressions. That they would have disciplined Johnson but dismissed similar conduct by Joseph Smith without comment seems less likely. If the Prophet was guilty of adultery, Johnson could have claimed hypocrisy, which he was careful to not do.

Possible Interpretations

It appears that the one-sentence record of Joseph E. Johnson's statement during the council meeting constitutes the primary evidence of a relationship between Joseph Smith and Mary Heron Snider that can currently be identified. Several interpretations are possible. One view assumes that Joseph Johnson overstated his impression or claimed knowledge he did not actually possess in an attempt to exonerate himself. Excommunication in 1850 would have been a difficult challenge for a man who came from a very prominent family in the Church. Joseph E. Johnson's brother, Benjamin F. Johnson, recalled that in the early 1840s, "In Macedonia the Johnsons were quite numerous and influential and the envious dubbed us the 'Royal Family.' When Joseph [Smith] heard of the *honor* conferred upon us by our neighbors, he said the name was and should be a reality; that we were a royal family."[112] Despite these concerns, Joseph E. Johnson appears to be a trustworthy witness whose comments were probably quoted correctly by the secretary Joseph Kelly.

A second interpretation acknowledges that sexual relations did indeed occur between Joseph Smith and Mary Heron but assumes that no plural marriage ceremony had been performed, thus documenting Joseph and Mary as adulterers. However, the behavior of Joseph E. Johnson and Mary's husband, John Snider, both of whom remained true to the faith, seems to contradict this view. If they were privy to such hypocrisy, it seems less likely that they would have continued to hold to their beliefs in Joseph Smith and the Church he restored. We also note that thirteen men were in attendance at the 1850 council where Johnson made his defense, yet his comments did not seem to have affected anyone's convictions.

A third explanation also acknowledges the existence of sexual relations between Joseph Smith and Mary Snider and assumes that the two were sealed in a plural marriage making Mary Heron Joseph Smith's thirty-fifth plural

---

wrong—I never av taken any body as a excuse—I never plighted my faith on Joseph's transactions. . . . J. Kelly—It as taken me by surprise—in our conversation—Johnson introduced the subject—as to himself—& many scenes that r familiar in the Ch—he sd. It was a matter of his own concern & interested nobody else but those he wod. av to bow to him." Miscellaneous Minutes, September 2, 1850.

112. Benjamin F. Johnson, *My Life's Review*, 93.

spouse. It also assumes that, at the time, Mary's legal marriage was still "lawful" in God's eyes, thereby permitting sexual relations between her and John Snider—relations that did not result in pregnancy—and producing a sexually polyandrous situation. D. Michael Quinn concurred with this view, writing in his notes (now housed at Yale University): "If the statements about Joseph Smith in this trial are accurate, and they do not seem to be disputed with respect to the impropriety of circulating them, then JOSEPH SMITH HAD SEXUAL INTERCOURSE (AND PRESUMABLY PLURAL MARRIAGE) WITH MARY HERON SNIDER" (emphasis in original).[113] This option seems to contradict Joseph Smith's teachings regarding sexual polyandry.

A fourth interpretation also acknowledges conjugality between Joseph Smith and Mary Heron, and assumes that a plural sealing in the new and everlasting covenant occurred that would have caused the legal marriage to be "done away" (D&C 22:1) with John continuing as a "front husband" to shield Joseph Smith from suspicion. This explanation absolves Joseph of charges of both adultery and hypocrisy but raises plausibility issues about John Snider's willingness to give up his wife and to thereafter serve as a "front husband." In support of this possibility are the observations that John Snider and Mary Heron seem to have endured significant periods of estrangement after 1833, with no pregnancies after Mary turned twenty-nine. Also, the couple's marriage was apparently never sealed, although the option was available.

Without any additional evidence, it is impossible to conclusively identify the nature of Joseph Smith's relationship with Mary Heron, if any special relationship ever existed. Readers' conclusions will be based on their willingness to accept and reject certain assumptions. Included are (1) assuming that, without additional supportive evidence, Joseph E. Johnson's story was correct and accurately reported; otherwise there was *no relationship*, (2) assuming that sexual relations occurred without a plural sealing resulting in *adultery*, (3) assuming that sexual relations occurred with a plural sealing between Joseph Smith and Mary Heron and that Mary continued conjugal relations with her civil husband, thus practicing *sexual polyandry*, (4) assuming that sexual relations occurred with a plural sealing that caused her legal marriage to be "done away" and that her legal husband, John Snider, agreed to serve as a "front husband" for the Prophet, thus creating *consecutive marriages*. It is probable that one of these four possibilities describes the actual dynamic in the Joseph Smith-Mary Heron relationship. However, without additional documentation, reliable conclusions are unattainable.

---

113. D. Michael Quinn, Box 3, fd. 2, Quinn Papers, Yale Library; emphasis in original. Compton, *In Sacred Loneliness*, 632, lists Mary Heron as a "possible wife." Compton cites "Quinn, MHOP [*Mormon Hierarchy: Origins of Power*], 587." Quinn includes her in a long list of Joseph Smith's wives writing: "Mary Heron (Snider) 1842/43."

Table 16.1
Possible Dynamics of Polyandrous Unions

Joseph Smith's "Polyandrous" Wives	Legal Husband	Eternity Only Sealing	Sealing with "Front" Husband
1. Ruth Vose	Edward Sayers	Yes	No
2. Esther Dutcher	Albert Smith		
3. Mary Elizabeth Rollins	Adam Lightner		
4. Presendia L. Huntington	Norman Buell		
5. Sarah Kingsley	John Cleveland		
6. Patty Bartlett	David Sessions	Probable	Unlikely
7. Elizabeth Davis	Jabez Durfee		
8. Lucinda Pendleton	George Harris		
9. Elvira Annie Cowles	Jonathan Holmes	Probable	Possible
10. Marinda Nancy Johnson	Orson Hyde		
11. Zina Diantha Huntington	Henry B. Jacobs		
12. Sylvia Sessions	Windsor Lyon	No	Yes
13. Sarah Ann Whitney	Joseph C. Kingsbury		
14. Mary Heron	John Snider		Probable

Summary

A review of Joseph Smith's polyandrous marriage demonstrates the importance of clarifying the meaning of "polyandry." The Prophet unquestionably participated in "ceremonial polyandry," whereby a woman was married to him in a second marriage ceremony. However, to assume Joseph also was involved with "sexual polyandry" requires specific evidence of sexual relations between the wife and both husbands during the same time period. To this point researchers have failed to identify such evidence in the historical record.

Table 16.1 outlines the probable dynamics of Joseph Smith's fourteen polyandrous marriages.[114]

---

114. Ironically, only six of these fourteen women were implicated in the eleven situations discussed in Chapters 12 and 13. Proposed relationships of sexual polyandry also include three women who are not otherwise identified as Joseph's polyandrous wives. "Mrs, Dibble," a "merchant's wife," and Margaret Creighton. See discussion in Chapter 12. Also Bennett listed seven married women without providing names. Also discussed in Chapter 12.

Chapter 17

Nauvoo Plural Marriage Slowly Expands

As discussed in Chapter 10, available evidence indicates that the first plural sealing performed in Nauvoo occurred between Joseph Smith and Louisa Beaman on April 5, 1841. The Prophet was also sealed to two additional wives before the year's end, but I have found no evidence that any other LDS men entered the practice until 1842.

Besides Joseph Smith, two other men are sometimes described as 1841 polygamists. George D. Smith lists Zebedee Coltrin as entering a plural marriage to Mary Mott on February 5, 1841—two months before Joseph Smith's sealing to Louisa Beaman.[1] In early 1841, Zebedee was a resident of Kirtland, Ohio, having been called as a member of its stake presidency on May 22, 1841.[2] His wife, Julia Ann Jennings Coltrin, whom he had married in 1828, died there on October 24, 1841.[3] Zebedee soon left Kirtland, returned to Nauvoo briefly, then filled a mission to Wisconsin. Biographer Calvin Robert Stephens describes Zebedee's next marriage: "While he was serving as a missionary in Wisconsin, Zebedee met Mary Mott. She was lighting a lamp in the Church when he saw her and he said to himself, 'There is my future wife.' Zebedee records that after a brief courtship they were married February 5, 1843."[4] Obviously Coltrin could not have married Mary Mott in Kirtland in 1841 or practiced plural marriage at that time because he did not meet Mott until well after his first wife's death.[5]

The second case cited by George D. Smith quotes a Reynolds Cahoon "family tradition" that Reynolds married Lucina Roberts Johnson, a widow, in

---

1. George D. Smith, *Nauvoo Polygamy: "... but we called it celestial marriage"*, 585. Smith's data are invaluable, but are derived from family group sheets and may therefore contain some inaccuracies.

2. "Minutes of a Conference, Held in Kirtland, Ohio, May 22nd 1841," *Times and Seasons* 2 (July 1, 1841): 458.

3. Familysearch.com reports that the International Genealogical Index also gives a death date of October 24, 1840 (accessed June 10, 2012).

4. Calvin Robert Stephens, "The Life and Contribution of Zebedee Coltrin," 10. See also Mary Mott, *LDS Vital Records Library* CD-ROM (Salt Lake City: Infobase, 1996).

5. While www.FamilySearch.com and other sources give the marriage date as 1841, the record for Mary Mott, *LDS Vital Records Library*, lists the later date.

late 1841 or 1842.⁶ Without more reliable information, 1841 seems less plausible.⁷ While Reynolds Cahoon served on the building committees for the Nauvoo House and the temple, there is no indication that in 1841 he was one of the very first to learn of restored plural marriage and imprecise family traditions should be believed with caution. He may have married Lucina in 1842, but the primary expansion of polygamy beyond Church leaders occurred in 1843, when at least sixteen additional men, including ten who were not General Authorities, married plural wives. (See Chapter 29.) Hopefully additional documentation will be identified clarifying Cahoon's plural marriage.

As discussed in Chapter 14, it was apparently in early February 1842 when an angel with a sword sternly threatened Joseph Smith that he must comply more fully with the instructions to enter plural marriage. On April 9, 1842, he proposed plural marriage to nineteen-year-old Nancy Rigdon, Sidney and Phoebe Rigdon's daughter. She was single, making her, after Louisa Beaman, the second unwed woman whom the Prophet had approached in Nauvoo. In addition, he thereafter largely abandoned sealings to women who were legally married, contracting only three more such unions prior to his death.⁸ Instead, he appears to have sought "time and eternity" marriages to single women,

---

6. Gary James Bergera, "Identifying the Earliest Mormon Polygamists, 1841–1844," 6.

7. www.FamilySearch.com lists "about 1842" for the marriage date. Other sources like *LDS Vital Records Library* provide no date. www.EarlyLDS.com lists only 1842, without a specific day and month.

8. On October 12, 1905, Joseph Smith III interviewed the Salt Lake Stake president, Angus M. Cannon. Cannon reported telling Joseph: "The late President John Taylor, who was one of his father's closest friends and one of his most devoted associates, remarked to me during his presidency of the Church, 'You must not sustain men as President of the Stake who are preaching that men can obtain the blessings pertaining to the patriarchal order of marriage, upon getting dead women sealed to them for eternity, for such was not the instructions received from Joseph Smith as a Prophet of the Lord, during his life.'" Angus Munn Cannon, "Statement of an Interview with Joseph Smith, III, 1905." While we do not know the date of the Smith-Taylor conversation that Cannon reported, Taylor did not marry his first plural wife until December 12, 1843. Bergera, "Identifying the Earliest Mormon Polygamists, 1841–1844," 69. Possibly Joseph Smith may have instructed Taylor at the end of June 1842 as part of his own commission from the angel to begin practicing full plural marriage. Concerning this event, historian Don Bradley observed: "President Taylor describes his own resistance to polygamy, and commandment to enter it by Joseph Smith, in the context of instructing Cannon that a man having dead women sealed to him for eternity was not sufficient to comply with the law. In context, the implication of Taylor's narrative is that he had been instructed by Joseph Smith that he must truly *marry* living women, that eternal sealing was not enough— and that *this issue had already been considered and settled before that time.* It therefore dovetails with the interpretation that Joseph Smith himself had attempted to evade the full living of plural marriage, by merely having legally married women sealed to him, rather than marrying them in the full, temporal sense." Bradley, email to Brian Hales, October 2, 2007.

with sexual relations being documented in several cases. A third identifiable change came as three Church leaders—Bishop Vinson Knight and Apostles Brigham Young and Heber C. Kimball—were each subsequently married to one plural wife by summer 1842.[9]

Failed Proposal to Nancy Rigdon

Joseph Smith facilitated his proposal to Nancy Rigdon in April 1842 by enlisting the help of Marinda Nancy Johnson Hyde. As discussed in Chapter 10, Marinda may have been sealed to the Prophet that same month.[10] In any case, Marinda willingly cooperated with the Prophet's request and invited Nancy Rigdon to her home on April 9, 1842.[11] One account from Marinda's brother-in-law, Oliver Olney, who was excommunicated on March 17, 1842, states:

> Nancy Rigdon had repeated calls to visit [Marinda] Nancy [Johnson] Hyde. When she did make a visit, Smith was there and "told her that he had the word of God for her, that God had given her to him for a wife." Miss Rigdon said to him, "you have a wife." "Well," said he, "you know the ancient order was, one man had many wives, that is again to be." Miss Rigdon was obstinate. He then got Mrs. Hyde to come in, and made use of her persuasive arguments, that she was first unbelieving in the order, but had been better informed; although she had long been acquainted with Miss Rigdon, but her many arguments were of no account. Mr. Smith again used his influence by more rash means, that Miss Rigdon threatened to call for help, that he let her go, but soon a letter was conveyed to her, written by some one of the clan, that argued the doctrine of polygamy.[12]

Olney may have been piecing together his own observations with rumors and the claims of John C. Bennett. If he had a specific insider source of information, he did not reveal his or her identity.

---

9. The exact date of Heber C. Kimball's sealing to Sarah Peak Noon is unknown. That Sarah was "seven months pregnant" in October corresponds with conception in March-April, meaning that the sealing could have taken place no later than that time. Stanley B. Kimball, *Heber C. Kimball: Mormon Patriarch and Pioneer*, 100.

10. Photograph of holograph, Joseph Smith's journal, list of plural marriages in the handwriting of Thomas Bullock, on a separate page after July 14, 1843, entry: "Apri 42 marinda Johnson to Joseph Smith," in Richard E. Turley Jr., ed., *Selected Collections from the Archives of the Church of Jesus Christ of Latter-day Saints*, Vol. 1, DVD #20. See also Scott H. Faulring, ed., *An American Prophet's Record: The Diaries and Journals of Joseph Smith*, 396.

11. The date is derived from Bennett's claim that Nancy was first approached on the day of Ephraim Marks's funeral. John C. Bennett, *The History of the Saints: Or an Exposé of Joe Smith and Mormonism*, 241. The funeral is recorded in Dean C. Jessee, ed., *The Papers of Joseph Smith: Vol. 1, Autobiographical and Historical Writings*, 375.

12. Oliver H. Olney, *The Absurdities of Mormonism Portrayed: A Brief Sketch*, 16.

Researcher Richard Van Wagoner gave this view of Nancy's resistance: "Despite her tender age [nineteen years old], she did not hesitate to express herself. . . . [S]he rebuffed him in a flurry of anger."[13] Her younger brother, John Wickliffe Rigdon, recalled the incident in 1905:

> Joseph the Prophet, at the City of Nauvoo, Illinois, some time in the latter part of the year 1843, or the first part of the year 1844 [sic; should be April 1842], made a proposition to my sister, Nancy Rigdon, to become his wife. It happened in this way: Nancy had gone to Church, meeting being held in a grove near the temple lot on which the "Mormons" were then erecting a temple, an old lady friend who lived alone invited her, which Nancy did. When they got to the house and had taken their bonnets off, the old lady began to talk to her about the new doctrine of polygamy which was then being taught, telling Nancy, during the conversation, that it was a surprise to her when she first heard it, but that she had since come to believe it to be true.
>
> While they were talking Joseph Smith the Prophet came into the house and joined them, and the old lady immediately left the room. It was then that Joseph made the proposal of marriage to my sister. Nancy flatly refused him, saying if she ever got married she would marry a single man or none at all, and thereupon took her bonnet and went home, leaving Joseph at the old lady's home.[14]

Wickliffe Rigdon's description of the go-between as an "old lady" is somewhat puzzling, since Marinda Hyde would, at that point, have been only twenty-six. Despite being repelled, the Prophet dictated a letter to Nancy containing doctrinal teachings that he evidently hoped she would find persuasive:

> Happiness is the object and design of our existence; and will be the end thereof, if we pursue the path that leads to it; and this path is virtue, uprightness, faithfulness, holiness, and keeping *all* the commandments of God. But we cannot keep *all* the commandments without first *knowing* them, and we cannot expect to know *all*, or more than we *now* know unless we *comply* with or keep those we have *already received*. That which is *wrong* under one circumstance, may be, and often is, *right* under another.
>
> God said, *thou shalt not kill.*—at another time He said, *thou shalt utterly destroy*. This is the principle on which the government of heaven is conducted—*by revelation* adapted to the circumstances in which the children of the kingdom are placed. *Whatever God* requires is *right*, NO MATTER WHAT IT IS, although we may not see the reason thereof till long after the events transpire. If we seek first the kingdom of God, *all good things* will be added. So with Solomon: first he asked wisdom, and God gave it him, and with it every desire of his heart, even things which might be considered *abominable* to all

---

13. Richard S. Van Wagoner, *Sidney Rigdon: A Portrait of Religious Excess*. 295.

14. John Wickliffe Rigdon, Affidavit, July 28, 1905, quoted in Joseph Fielding Smith, *Blood Atonement and the Origin of Plural Marriage*, 83–84.

who understand the order of heaven only in part, but which in reality were right because God gave and sanctioned by special revelation.

A parent may whip a child, and justly, too, because he stole an apple; whereas if the child had asked for the apple, and the parent had given it, the child would have eaten it with a better appetite; there would have been no stripes; all the pleasure of the apple would have been secured, all the misery of stealing lost.

This principle will justly apply to all of God's dealings with His children. Everything that God gives us is lawful and right; and it is proper that we should enjoy His gifts and blessings whenever and wherever He is disposed to bestow; but if we should seize upon those same blessings and enjoyments without law, without revelation, without commandment, those blessings and enjoyments would prove cursings and vexations in the end, and we should have to lie down in sorrow and wailings of everlasting regret. But in obedience there is joy and peace unspotted, unalloyed; and as God has designed our happiness—and the happiness of all His creatures, he never has—He never will institute an ordinance or give a commandment to His people that is not calculated in its nature to promote that happiness which He has designed, and which will not end in the greatest amount of good and glory to those who become the recipients of his law and ordinances. Blessings offered, but rejected, are no longer blessings, but become like the talent hid in the earth by the wicked and slothful servant; the proffered good returns to the giver; the blessing is bestowed on those who will *receive* and *occupy*; for unto him that hath shall be given, and he shall have abundantly, but unto him that hath not or will not receive, shall be taken away that which he hath, or might have had.

> *Be wise* TO-DAY; *'tis* MADNESS *to defer*;
> Next day the fatal precedent may plead.
> Thus on till wisdom is pushed out of time
> Into eternity.

Our heavenly Father is more liberal in His views, and boundless in His mercies and blessings, than we are ready to believe or receive; and, at the same time, is more terrible to the workers of iniquity, more awful in the executions of His punishments, and more ready to detect every false way, than we are apt to suppose Him to be. He will be inquired of by his children—he says, ["]ask and ye SHALL RECEIVE, *seek* and ye shall find;" but, if you will take that which is not your own, or which I *have not given* you, you shall be rewarded according to your deeds; but no good thing will I withhold from them who walk uprightly before me, and do my will in *all things*—who will listen to *my* voice and TO THE VOICE OF MY SERVANT WHOM I HAVE SENT; for I delight in those who seek diligently to know my precepts, and abide by the law of my kingdom; for all things shall be made known unto them in mine own due time, and in the end they shall have joy.[15]

---

15. John C. Bennett, "Sixth Letter, *Sangamo Journal*, August 19, 1842, emphasis in Bennett's

The location of the original letter, if still extant, is unknown, leaving the question open whether the emphasis was Joseph Smith's, Bennett's, or the editor of *Sangamo Journal*'s.[16]

Even though this correspondence was intended to be private, it apparently fell into the hands of Francis M. Higbee, a suitor of Nancy's. Francis's brother Chauncey obtained it for Bennett who published it on August 19 in the *Sangamo Journal*.[17]

Even though the original letter was apparently lost, Church leaders after Joseph Smith's death recognized it as containing valid teachings by the Prophet and have attributed it to him to this day. In 1855 Thomas Bullock, a clerk in the Church Historian's Office, copied the letter into the Manuscript History of the Church. Two years later, the *Millennial Star* reprinted the version found in Bennett's *History of the Saints*, eliminating his emphasis.[18] The official *History of the Church* includes it in its entirety with a footnote written by B. H. Roberts: "It is not positively known what occasioned the writing of this essay; but when it is borne in mind that at this time the new law of marriage for the church—marriage for eternity, including plurality of wives under some circumstances—was being introduced by the Prophet, it is very likely that the article was written with a view of applying the principles here expounded to the conditions created by introducing said marriage system."[19]

This letter continues to be quoted in other Church-endorsed publications and by General Authorities today.[20] Had Nancy Rigdon kept the letter and the proceedings secret, subsequent generations might never have learned of the event.[21] However, as John Wickliffe Rigdon continued in his 1905 affidavit:

---

version; rpt. in Bennett, *The History of the Saints*, 243–45; see also *History of the Church*, 5:134; in Joseph Fielding Smith, comp. and ed., *Teachings of the Prophet Joseph Smith*, 256.

16. Van Hale, "The Purported Letter of Joseph Smith to Nancy Rigdon," *Mormon Historical Studies*, forthcoming.

17. George W. Robinson, Letter to John C. Bennett, July 3, 1842, printed in Bennett, *The History of the Saints*, 44.

18. Turley, *Selected Collections*, Vol. 1 DVD #1, v5\MH5_283.jpg; and "History of Joseph Smith," *Millennial Star* 19, no. 49 (December 5, 1857): 774–75.

19. *History of the Church*, 5:134 note. See also Dean C. Jessee, ed., *The Personal Writings of Joseph Smith*, 506–9.

20. Joseph Fielding Smith, *Teachings of the Prophet Joseph Smith*, 255–57; K. Codell Carter, "Godhood," 2:553; Bruce R. McConkie, "Joy," *Mormon Doctrine*, 397; and the following *Ensign* articles: Marion G. Romney, "Joy and Happiness," September 1973, 2; Thomas S. Monson, "An Invitation to Exaltation," July 1984, 69; James E. Faust, "Our Search for Happiness," October 2000, 2; Russell M. Nelson, "Divine Love," February 2003, 20; Thomas S. Monson, "Hallmarks of a Happy Home," October 2001, 3.

21. Lawrence Foster comments: "Joseph Smith's marriage proposal to Nancy Rigdon highlights both the positive valuation he placed on human sexuality and the

Nancy told father and mother of it. The story got out and it became the talk of the town that Joseph had made a proposition to Nancy Rigdon to become his wife, and that she refused him. A few days after the occurrence Joseph Smith came to my father's house and talked the matter over with the family [and] my sister. . . . The feelings manifested by our family on this occasion were anything but brotherly or sisterly, more especially on the part of Nancy, as she felt that she had been insulted. A day or two later Joseph Smith returned to my father's house, when matters were satisfactorily adjusted between them and there the matter ended.[22]

The year previous Wickliffe Rigdon had shared additional details in a letter to a correspondent:

Joseph Smith made a proposition to my Sister Nancy Rigdon to marry him but she refused. She told her Mother & Father what Joseph had done— the story had got out [and] was the talk of the People of Nauvoo. Joseph came to my Fathers house when he was sick abed & attempted to deny it & sister Mrs Athalia Robinson was present. Nancy was in an other room. She heard what Smith said She came rushing into the room & said to Smith You are a cursed liar You did ask me to become your wife. My Father was horror stricken to think he had a daughter who would call Joseph Smith \a/ liar[.] Smith went a way some few days; he came back again he was crying[.] [H]e asked Fathers & Mothers forgivness & shook hands with all the family that were present & Nancys [hand] & went away & there the matter rested. My Fathers cousin[23] who lived at Laharp 25 miles from Nauvoo quite a prominent Mormon was at the ducation [dedication] at Kirtland Ohio came to Nauvoo to learn if it

---

necessity he felt for placing it under proper controls. Marriage and sexual expression were described as a 'gift and a blessing' that could be compared to a desired apple, but they should only be experienced under proper authority." Lawrence Foster, "Sex and Prophetic Power: A Comparison of John Humphrey Noyes, Founder of the Oneida Community, with Joseph Smith, Jr., the Mormon Prophet," 76.

22. John Wickliffe Rigdon, Affidavit, quoted in Joseph Fielding Smith, *Blood Atonement and the Origin of Plural Marriage*, 83–84.

23. This is probably Peter Boyer who married Sidney's sister Lacy in about 1816 and moved to La Harpe, Illinois, in the early 1840s. Peter and Lacy Rigdon Boyer, along with Lacy's brother Carvel Rigdon (who married Peter's sister Sarah Boyer) were converted to Mormonism in 1831 due to the preaching of Sidney, their mutual brother or brother-in-law. Peter Boyer was living in Allegheny, Pennsylvania, when the 1840 census was taken, but moved to La Harpe, Illinois, shortly thereafter. By mid-1843, perhaps as a reaction to plural marriage at Nauvoo, the Boyers returned to their hometown. Peter Boyer was an elder and member of the high council in Sidney Rigdon's Mormon splinter group in and around Pittsburgh after the summer of 1844. He later returned to the Baptist faith, died after 1879, and was buried in the Peters Creek Baptist Church cemetery at Library, Pennsylvania. Peter Boyer, http://sidneyrigdon.com/RigHist/RigGenl1.htm#24b (accessed March 11, 2012).

was true that Polygamy was being taught then he called on Joseph Smith with whom he had been Well acquainted Ever since the building of the temple at Kirtland Ohio & told Smith what he had come for & pretended if it was taught he was in favor of \it/ Smith said it was & said to him at that ~~interview that~~ he had made a proposition to Nancy Rigdon to become his wife & she like a fool had to go & blab it.[24]

In an 1845 discourse given after Sidney Rigdon's excommunication, Marinda Hyde's husband, Apostle Orson Hyde, offered another explanation regarding the Prophet's proposal to Nancy that portrays her as a woman of loose morals:

> During my absence to Palestine, the conduct of his [Sidney Rigdon's] daughter, Nancy, became so notorious in this city, according to common rumor, she was regarded generally, little if any better than a public prostitute. Joseph Smith knowing the conduct she was guilty of, felt anxious to reprove and reclaim her if possible. He, accordingly, requested my wife to invite her down to her house. He wished to speak with her and show her the impropriety of being gallanted about by so many different men, many of whom were comparatively strangers to her. Her own parents could look upon it, and think that all was right; being blind to the faults of their daughter. Miss Nancy, I presume, considered her dignity highly insulted at the plain and sharp reproofs she received from this servant of God. She ran home and told her father that Mr. Smith wanted her for a spiritual wife, and that he employed my wife to assist him in obtaining her. . . . Miss Nancy is made, therefore, to attribute to Joseph Smith and to my wife, language which neither of them ever used.[25]

By Orson's own account, he was not in Nauvoo at the time of this incident; but he presumably obtained his information from Marinda. Possibly given the dimensions of the scandal, Marinda was anxious to minimize her own role in the episode. Further complicating the narrative, Orson was highly critical of Sidney at the time he related this version (almost a year after Joseph's death), since Rigdon and the Twelve were locked in a power struggle over prophetic succession. Accordingly, Hyde's observations were not without bias.

Precisely how far the rumors of Joseph Smith and Nancy Rigdon spread during the days immediately after the event is difficult to determine. However, within a few months, it would be broadcast through the efforts of John C.

---

24. John W. Rigdon, Brooklyn, New York, Letter to "Arthur Willing, Elder," February 20 1904, 7–8.

25. Orson Hyde, *Speech of Elder Orson Hyde, Delivered before the High Priests Quorum, in Nauvoo April 27th 1845, upon the Course and Conduct of Mr. Sydney Rigdon, and upon the Merits of His Claims to the Presidency of the Church of Jesus Christ of Latter-day Saints*, 27–28.

Bennett, an enraged apostate, creating a second wave of gossip for the participants to combat.

Why Nancy Rigdon?

Joseph Smith's choice of Nancy Rigdon to receive this plural proposal, the first he had apparently offered to a previously unmarried woman since he wed Louisa Beaman, is puzzling. With many potential possibilities in Nauvoo, why did the Prophet choose the daughter of his first counselor in the First Presidency? Also, assuming his authorship of the "Happiness" letter, why did he write such a detailed doctrinal exposition to teach her about polygamous marriage?

Drawing of Sidney Rigdon. Courtesy Utah State Historical Society.

One possible answer is that Joseph was attempting either to introduce the topic of plural marriage to Sidney through his daughter or to test Sidney's devotion to him. The letter, ostensibly written only to Nancy, contains a curious amount of expansive doctrinal discussion if she was indeed the only intended audience. Its primary focus is the theme: "Whatever God requires is right, no matter what it is, although we may not see the reason thereof till long after the events transpire."[26] The text includes a simple story about a child who steals an apple that would have been freely offered if the child had simply asked for it, a story Nancy could have easily understood.

However, also within the letter are quotations using specific language found in Old Testament scriptures (Exod. 20:13; Deut. 7:2, 12:2, 20:17). Joseph also referred to King Solomon's interactions with the Lord (2 Chron. 1:8–12; 1 Kgs. 4:29) and alludes to the issue that prompted the July 12, 1843, revelation on celestial marriage, specifically Solomon's "many wives and concubines" (D&C 132:1). Also included is a brief reference to Christ's parable of the talents (Matt. 25:14–30).

It is possible that Nancy Rigdon, the nineteen-year-old daughter of a prominent Campbellite preacher turned Mormon leader would have been familiar with these scriptural passages. She might have also understood the letter's references to ethical, and theological issues. Regardless, Joseph's doctrinal exposition in this situation is surprising. Its tone and approach do not seem to convey a message that would successfully persuade a teenager to join him in a

---

26. John C. Bennett, "Sixth Letter."

secret plural marriage. (And, in point of fact, it was not successful.) Absent are appeals to loving feelings he may have possessed for her or an offer to marry him in order to enjoy conjugal bliss. Neither does he remind her of the special status that she would receive being a plural wife of the prophet and Church president. Importantly, no coercive time-sensitive threats were declared that God had commanded her to comply or damnation would follow.[27]

These characteristics make the other possibility likely—that Joseph's real target audience was Sidney and that the Prophet was trying to instruct him and gain his support. In early 1842, neither William Law, the second counselor in the First Presidency, nor Hyrum Smith, associate president of the Church, was aware of Joseph's teachings on the subject.[28] It seems probable, therefore, that Sidney was equally uninformed. Possibly Joseph hoped that Nancy would respond favorably and, through her participation, her father would become converted to the principle. There is no evidence that Sidney Rigdon ever accepted plural marriage as a correct doctrine.[29]

Heber C. Kimball, Second Plural Husband

While the evidence is not conclusive, it appears that Heber C. Kimball was the second authorized polygamist in this dispensation. Lorenzo Snow shared a cell at the Territory of Utah's penitentiary with Helon H. Tracy in 1886 when both were incarcerated for practicing polygamy. Snow, who

---

27. The only known plural proposal that contained a time limit was issued to Lucy Walker who was introduced to the principle by Joseph Smith in 1842. She subsequently agonized for many months as the Prophet patiently waited. Lucy related: "I was tempted and tortured beyond endurance until life was not desirable. Oh that the grave would kindly receive me, that I might find rest. . . . Oh, let this bitter cup pass. And thus I prayed in the agony of my soul. The Prophet discerned my sorrow. He saw how unhappy I was." Lyman Omer Littlefield, *Reminiscences of Latter-day Saints: Giving an Account of Much Individual Suffering Endured for Religious Conscience*, 46. Only after witnessing her turmoil and having waited a minimum of several months, in May of 1843 Joseph instructed Lucy: "I have no flattering words to offer. It is a command of God to you." Then he gave a singular directive, "I will give you until tomorrow to decide this matter." This twenty-four-hour time limit is sometimes quoted to assert that Joseph gave ultimatums to his potential plural spouses to quickly press them into compliance. See, for example, George D. Smith, "The Forgotten Story of Nauvoo Celestial Marriage," 157. In reality many months passed between the two events.

28. William Law, Affidavit, July 17, 1885, quoted in Charles A. Shook, *The True Origin of Mormon Polygamy*, 126. On May 26, 1843, William Clayton recorded: "Hyrum received the doctrine of priesthood." George D. Smith, ed., *An Intimate Chronicle: The Journals of William Clayton*, 106.

29. Thomas J. Gregory, "Sidney Rigdon: Post Nauvoo," 61.

had served as an apostle while Heber C. Kimball was a member of the First Presidency, reportedly told Tracy:

> Speaking as. to the love that ought to exist between husband and wife Bro. S[now] said , No man should not or ought not to take a wife unless it was One he could truly love he related an anecdote about Bro H. C. K. [Heber C. Kimball] an affair that occured at Nauvoo when plural marriage was first introduced The principle was quite a trial to Sister V. K. [Vilate Kimball] but she essayed to submit to it and went and chose two very old maids of quite plain and homely Appearance for her husband Bro K spoke to the Prophet Joseph about it and he said, Bro K that arrangement is of the devil you go and get you a young wife one you can take to your bosom and love and raise children by. A man should choose his own wife and one he can love and get children by in love.[30]

Orson F. Whitney, grandson of Heber C. Kimball, also acknowledged the severity of "Vilate's trial" regarding "the doctrine of plurality of wives."[31] Their daughter (and Orson's mother), Helen Mar, provided this account of the ongoing test of faith:

> In Nauvoo the Prophet's life was in constant jeopardy, not only from outside influences and enemies, who were seeking some plea to take him back to Missouri, but from false brethren, who had crept into his bosom and then betrayed him. Therefore, when he told my father to take a second wife, he requested him to keep it a secret and not divulge it even to my mother, for fear that she would not receive the principle. Father realized the situation fully, and the love and reverence he felt for the Prophet was so great that he would rather have laid down his own life than have betrayed him. This was the greatest test of his faith he had ever experienced.
>
> When first hearing the principle taught, believing that he would be called upon to enter into it, he thought of two Sisters Pitkin, who, as they were both elderly ladies and great friends of my mother's, he believed would cause her little if any unhappiness. The woman he was commanded [by the Prophet] to take, however, was an English lady nearer my mother's age. . . . The thought of deceiving the kind and faithful wife of his youth, whom he loved with all his heart, and who with him had borne so patiently their separation and all the trials and sacrifices they had been called to endure, was more than he felt able to bear. He realized not only the addition of trouble and perplexities that such a step must bring upon him, but his sorrow and misery were increased by the thought of my mother hearing of it from some other source which would no doubt separate them forever, and he shrank

---

30. Helon Tracy, Diary, undated, 72, quoted in Stan Larson, ed., *Prisoner for Polygamy: The Memoirs and Letters of Rudger Clawson at the Utah Territorial Penitentiary, 1884–87*, 12.

31. Ibid., 324.

from the thought of such a thing, or of causing her any unhappiness. Finally he was so tried that he went to Joseph and told him how he felt—that he was fearful if he took such a step he could not stand, but would be overcome. The Prophet went and inquired of the Lord; His answer was: "Tell him to go and do as he has been commanded, and if I see that there is any danger of his apostatizing, I will take him to myself."

Father was heard many a time to say that he had shed bushels of tears over this order, the order of "celestial or plural marriage."

The Prophet told him the third time before he obeyed the command. This shows that the trial must have been extraordinary, for he was a man who from the first had yielded implicit obedience to every requirement of the Prophet.

My mother had noticed a change in his looks and appearance, and when she enquired the cause he tried to evade her question, saying it was only her imagination, or that he was not feeling well, etc. But it so worked upon his mind that his anxious and haggard looks betrayed him daily and hourly, and finally his misery became so unbearable that it was impossible to control his feelings. He became sick in body, but his mental wretchedness was too great to allow of his retiring at night, and instead of going to bed he would walk the floor; and the agony of his mind was so terrible that he would wring his hands and weep, beseeching the Lord with his whole soul to be merciful and reveal to his wife the cause of his great sorrow, for he himself could not break his vow of secrecy. His anguish, and my mother's, were indescribable, and when unable to endure it longer, she retired to her room, where, with a broken and contrite heart she poured out her grief to Him who has said: "If any lack wisdom let him ask of God, who giveth to all men liberally and upbraideth not." "Seek and ye shall find, knock and it shall be opened unto you."

My father's heart was raised at the same time in supplication, and while pleading as one would plead for life, the vision of her mind was opened, and as darkness fleeth before the morning sun, so did her sorrow and the groveling things of earth vanish away, and before her she saw the principle of celestial marriage illustrated in all its beauty and glory, together with the great exaltation and honor it would confer upon her in that immortal and celestial sphere if she would but accept it and stand in her place by her husband's side. She was also shown the woman he had taken to wife, and contemplated with joy the vast and boundless love and union which this order would bring about, as well as the increase of kingdoms, power and glory extending throughout the eternities, worlds without end.

Her soul was satisfied and filled with the Spirit of God. With a countenance beaming with joy she returned to my father, saying, "Heber, what you kept from me the Lord has shown to me."

She related the scene to me and to many others, and told me she never saw so happy a man as father was, when she described the vision and told him she was satisfied and knew that it was from God.[32]

The date of Heber's plural marriage to Sarah Noon is not known but probably occurred early in 1842.[33] Several months later on October 16, 1842, Vilate wrote to Heber, who was then on a mission in England, alluding to her sister-wife:

> Our good friend [Sarah Noon, Heber's plural wife] is as ever, and we are one. You said I must tell you all my feelings; but if I were to tell you that I sometimes felt tempted and tried and feel as though my burden was greater than I could bear, it would only be a source of sorrow to you, and the Lord knows that I do not wish to add one sorrow to your heart, for be assured, my dear Heber, that I do not love you any the less for what has transpired, neither do I believe that you do me; therefore I will keep my bad feelings to myself, as much as possible, and tell you the good.[34]

Nine days later, Heber wrote a tender letter reflecting his own love for Vilate and compassion for her sorrows:

> My dear companion: I have just returned from the office where I found a letter from you, and I need not tell you that it was a sweet morsel to me. I could weep like a child if I could get away by myself, to think that I for one moment have been the means of causing you any sorrow. I know that you must have many bad feelings and I feel to pray for you all the time, I assure you that you have not been out of my mind many minutes at a time since I left you. My feelings are of that kind that it makes me sick at heart, so that I have no appetite to eat. My temptations are so [indecipherable] it seems [indecipherable] I should [indecipherable] if I must sink beneath it. I go into the woods every chance I have, and pour out my soul before God that he would deliver me and bless you my dear wife, and the first I would know I would be in tears, weeping like a child about you and the situation that I am in, but what can I do but go ahead?
>
> My dear Vilate, do not let it cast you down for the Lord is on our side; this I know from what I see and realize and I marvel at it many times. You are tried and tempted and I am sorry for you, for I know how to pity you. I can

---

32. Helen Mar Kimball Whitney, "Scenes and Incidents in Nauvoo," *Woman's Exponent* 10, no. 10 (October 15, 1881): 74; rpt. in Jeni Broberg Holzapfel and Richard Neitzel Holzapfel, eds., *A Woman's View: Helen Mar Whitney's Reminiscences of Early Church History*, 136–39. See also Helen Mar Kimball Whitney, *Why We Practice Plural Marriage*, 56–59; Orson F. Whitney, *Life of Heber C. Kimball* (1945 edition), 326–27.

33. Stanley B. Kimball, *Heber C. Kimball: Mormon Patriarch and Pioneer*, 93–98.

34. Vilate Kimball, Letter to Heber C. Kimball, October 16, 1842; quoted in Helen Mar Kimball Whitney, "Scenes and Incidents in Nauvoo," *Woman's Exponent* 11 (June 1, 1882): 1–2.

say that I never suffered more in all my life than since these things come to pass; and as I have said, so say I again, I have felt as if I should sink and die.[35]

Then Heber's letter shifted to a solemn petition to the Lord:

Vilate Murray Kimball. Courtesy Utah State Historical Society.

Oh my God! I ask thee in the name of Jesus to bless my dear Vilate and comfort her heart and deliver her from temptation, and from sorrow. Be pleased to look upon thy poor servant and handmaid and grant us the privilege of living the same length of time that one may not go before the other, for thou knowest that we desire this with all our hearts . . . and then Father, when we have done with our career in this probation, in the one to come may we be still joined in one, to remain so to all eternities.[36]

A year later Vilate referred to a secret Sarah Peak learned from Joseph B. Noble's plural wife, Sarah Alley:

I have a secret to tell you, but I am almost afraid, it was committed to Sarah and she was requested not to tell me, but she said she considered me a part of herself and she would tell me, and I might tell you for it was just what you had prophesied would come to pass. Now if you know what you have said about Sarah Ally then you have got the secret, for it is even so, and she is tickled about it.[37] And they all appear in better spirits than they did before. How they will carry it out, is more than I know, I hope they have got more faith than I have.[38]

---

35. Heber C. Kimball, Letter to Vilate Kimball, October 25, 1842; quoted in Helen Mar Kimball Whitney, "Scenes and Incidents in Nauvoo," *Woman's Exponent* 11 (July 15, 1882): 26.

36. Heber C. Kimball, Letter to Vilate Kimball, October 25, 1842; quoted in ibid.

37. The first baby born from a sealed polygamous marriage was Adelbert Kimball, son of Heber C. Kimball and Sarah Peak, who was born in late 1842 or early 1843 and died in infancy. Stanley B. Kimball, *Heber C. Kimball*, 311. Sarah Alley, plural wife of Joseph B. Noble, delivered the second, George Omer Noble, on February 2, 1844. Andrew Jenson mistakenly wrote: "He [George Omer Noble] is supposed to have been the first polygamous child born in this dispensation." "Plural Marriage," 239.

38. Vilate Kimball, Letter dated June 27, 1843, to Heber C. Kimball; qtd. in part in Helen Mar Kimball Whitney, "Scenes and Incidents at Nauvoo," *Woman's Exponent* 11 (September 15, 1882): 58.

Brigham Young. Courtesy LDS Church History Library.

Heber and Vilate weathered the immediate storm, but another trial awaited them months later when their only daughter, Helen Mar, was sealed, through Heber's efforts, as one of Joseph's plural wives.

Brigham Young First Polygamous Proposal

During the spring of 1842, the time when Heber C. Kimball was seeking a second wife, Brigham Young and other Quorum of the Twelve members were reluctantly engaged in the same enterprise. Apostle John Taylor recalled that this commandment "made us all pull pretty long faces sometimes. It was not so easy as one might think. When it was revealed to us it looked like the last end of Mormonism. For a man to ask another woman to marry him required more self-confidence than we had."[39] Brigham related: "My brethren know what my feelings were at the time Joseph revealed the doctrine; I was not desirous of shrinking from any duty, nor of failing in the least to do as I was commanded, but it was the first time in my life that I had desired the grave, and I could hardly get over it for a long time. And when I saw a funeral, I felt to envy the corpse its situation, and to regret that I was not in the coffin."[40]

Despite his reluctance, Brigham Young obediently overcame his anxieties early in 1842, only to meet with a rebuff. The young lady selected was Martha Brotherton, a British convert whom Brigham had known on his mission in England. Brigham's fears of rejection or exposure would logically have prompted him to choose a woman who was extremely devout in her testimony of Joseph Smith as a prophet, but Martha's background did not match that profile. Martha came from Manchester, England, with her father, Thomas Brotherton, her mother, two sisters (Elizabeth and Mary), and Mary's husband, John McIlwrick. In November 1841, they and over two hundred other Saints disembarked from a steamboat at Warsaw, Illinois, twenty miles south of Nauvoo. They settled at Warren, a community of Saints one mile south of Warsaw. Martha's parents had struggled in their beliefs prior to arriving in Nauvoo. While crossing the ocean, Joseph Fielding, a leader in the company, reported:

---

39. John Taylor, "Report of the Dedication of the Kaysville Relief Society House, November 12, 1876," 148.

40. Brigham Young, July 14, 1855, *Journal of Discourses*, 3:266.

> We had in our company some who had not the spirit and would have quarreled often. . . . I preached many times by the light of the moon while sailing in the trade winds, and we enjoyed ourselves very much. My object was to speak on the subject of the gathering, chiefly, for I saw that this was not well understood by some of the Saints; one or two were rather hurt at my plain way of telling them what tribulations they might expect (I could almost give the names of some, knowing they will send home an evil report); such as a brother B. [Brotherton] from Macclesfield.[41]

Information is lacking on whether Martha had had experiences with Brigham Young in England that had impressed him with her devoutness; but in their absence, why he selected her for his first plural offer is perplexing. Antagonistic writer John Bowes suggested a reason in 1850: "William Arrowsmith talked to Joseph Smith about Martha Brotherton's case. Smith did not deny what Martha relates, but stated that Brigham Young . . . did it to try her, as they had heard an evil report of her."[42]

Of all the polygamous marriage proposals made in Nauvoo during Joseph Smith's lifetime, Brigham's involvement with Martha Brotherton may be the most detailed.[43] Although the account is from an antagonistic source and appears to be somewhat tainted, it is contemporary and contains many interesting particulars. Rejecting Brigham, polygamy, and the Church simultaneously, Martha and her parents fled to St. Louis. With the help of John C. Bennett who traveled there to request her help, she drafted an affidavit of her experience on July 13, 1842, and willingly allowed Bennett, by then a vindictive enemy to Joseph Smith, to publish it in a series of exposé letters. In this affidavit, Martha described her experience with Brigham Young:

> I had been at Nauvoo near three weeks, during which time my father's family received frequent visits from Elders Brigham Young and Heber C. Kimball, two of the Mormon Apostles; when, early one morning, they both came to my brother-in-law's (John McIlwrick's) house, at which place I then was on a visit, and particularly requested me to go and spend a few days with

---

41. Joseph Fielding, "Joseph Fielding's Letter," *Millennial Star* 3 (August 1842): 76–77. Earlier in the article, Fielding wrote: "Old Mr. B [Brotherton]—and daughter, like many others, were assailed by the apostate crews, who lay scattered on the banks of the river; and all manner of evil reports were sounded in their ears, until they became discouraged; and, finally almost denied the faith before they came near Nauvoo. People coming here with their minds thus prejudiced, will naturally construe everything they see and hear into evil and will imagine evil where there is none. In this state the B—ton [Brotherton] family came, and were something like spies afraid to be spoken to by any one, lest they should be ensnared, and especially afraid to meet Joseph Smith, lest he should want their money." Ibid., 75.

42. John Bowes, *Mormonism Exposed*, 64.

43. See Lawrence Foster, *Women, Family, and Utopia: Communal Experiments of the Shakers, the Oneida Community, and the Mormons*, 143–47.

them. I told them I could not at that time, as my brother-in-law was not at home; however, they urged me to go the next day, and spend one day with them. The day being fine, I accordingly went.[44]

Martha dutifully called on the apostles the next day. Her affidavit suggests that she had no inkling regarding the doctrine that would be introduced. This is understandable; while a few hushed rumors of polygamy might have existed in early 1842, most Nauvoo residents were probably unaware of its restoration.

> When I arrived at the foot of the hill, Young and Kimball were standing conversing together. They both came to me, and, after several flattering compliments, Kimball wished me to go to his house first. I said it was immaterial to me, and accordingly went. We had not, however, gone many steps when Young suddenly stopped, and said he would go to that brother's, (pointing to a little log hut a few yards distant,) and tell him that you (speaking to Kimball) and brother Glover, or Grover, (I do not remember which,) will value his land.[45]

Brigham's sudden departure might have been due to the immediate need to transact business nearby, but it is also possible that he was apprehensive or desired Heber to introduce the topic to Martha first, without his being present. As Heber and Martha walked to Joseph Smith's store, Heber sought to discern Martha's feelings toward the Prophet and the Restoration, as well as emphasizing the need for confidentiality:

> As we were going along, he said, "Sister Martha, are you willing to do all that the Prophet requires you to do?" I said I believed I was, thinking of course he would require nothing wrong. "Then," said he, "are you ready to take counsel?" I answered in the affirmative, thinking of the great and glorious blessings that had been pronounced upon my head, if I adhered to the counsel of those placed over me in the Lord. "Well," said he, "there are many things revealed in these last days that the world would laugh and scoff at; but unto us is given to know the mysteries of the kingdom." He further observed, "Martha, you must learn to hold your tongue, and it will be well with you. You will see Joseph, and very likely have some conversation with him, and he will tell you what you shall do."

---

44. Martha H. Brotherton, Affidavit, July 13, 1842, *Native American Bulletin* (St. Louis), 1 (July 16, 1842); rpt., *Sangamo Journal* (Springfield, Ill.), 10 (July 22, 1842); *Warsaw Signal*, July 23, 1842; *New York Herald* 8 (July 25, 27, 1842); extracted in *Louisville Daily Journal* 12 (July 25, 1842): 183; *Alton [Ill.] Telegraph and Democratic Review* 7 (July 30, 1842); *Quincy [Ill.] Whig* 5 (August 6, 1842): [2]; and Bennett, *The History of the Saints*, 236–40. Additional details of Martha's experience are all drawn from this July affidavit.

45. This individual was possibly Thomas Grover (1807–86), baptized in 1834 and a member of the Nauvoo High Council.

When they reached the Red Brick Store, Heber ushered Martha into the upper office where Joseph Smith and Brigham Young awaited them. Her narrative continues:

> ... Kimball came in. "Now, Martha," said he, "the Prophet has come; come up stairs." I went, and we found Young and the Prophet alone. I was introduced to the Prophet by Young. Joseph offered me his seat, and, to my astonishment, the moment I was seated, Joseph and Kimball walked out of the room, and left me with Young, who arose, locked the door, closed the window, and drew the curtain. He then came and sat before me, and said, "This is our private room, Martha." "Indeed, sir," said I, "I must be highly honored to be permitted to enter it." He smiled, and then proceeded—"Sister Martha, I want to ask you a few questions; will you answer them?" "Yes sir," said I. "And will you promise not to mention them to any one?" "If it is your desire, sir," said I, "I will not." "And you will not think any the worse of me for it, will you, Martha?" said he. "No, sir," I replied.

It appears that Joseph and Heber had arranged to leave Martha and Brigham alone so that he could discuss the sensitive topic of plural marriage with his candidate, without fear of interruption. Martha was understandably surprised and confused. Knowing that polygamy constituted meaty doctrine that could be easily misunderstood, Brigham again emphasized the need for confidentiality. Martha naturally agreed but without knowing what she was going to need to keep secret. Then Brigham broached the subject headlong:

> "Well," said he, "what are your feelings towards me?" I replied, "My feelings are just the same towards you that they ever were, sir." "But, to come to the point more closely," said he, "have not you an affection for me, that, were it lawful and right, you could accept of me for your husband and companion?"

Brigham's reported statement is problematic. For him to perceive that Martha possessed "an affection" for him presupposes that either Martha knew about the possibility of polygamy, that she would be attracted to a married man in contradiction to Church standards, or that Brigham had been flattered in England by her natural admiration for a competent and charismatic leader and surmised that these feelings could be made to take a more intimate form. Although doubtless nervous and somewhat awkward, Brigham Young proposed plural marriage in unmistakable terms. Martha reacted with shock:

> My feelings at that moment were indescribable. God only knows them. What, thought I, are these men, that I thought almost perfection itself, deceivers!" and is all my fancied happiness but a dream? 'Twas even so; but my next thought was, which is the best way for me to act at this time? If I say no, they may do as they think proper; and to say yes, I never would. So I considered it best to ask for time to think and pray about it. I therefore said, "If it was lawful and right, perhaps I might; but you know, sir, it is not."

Joseph Smith's Red Brick Store in Nauvoo. Courtesy LDS Church History Library.

Like almost all other women, Martha's initial reaction was revulsion. But unlike most, she stated that her faith in the Restoration was instantly shaken, leaving her feeling deceived and disheartened. Sensing her concern, Brigham offered additional encouragement and instruction:

> "Brother Joseph has had a revelation from God that it is lawful and right for a man to have two wives; for as it was in the days of Abraham, so it shall be in these last days, and whoever is the first that is willing to take up the cross will receive the greatest blessings; and if you will accept of me, I will take you straight to the celestial kingdom; and if you will have me in this world, I will have you in that which is to come. . . . Brother Joseph will marry us here today. . . ."

The offer that Martha Brotherton reports here is not a free-wheeling "spiritual wifery" sexual connection, but an actual plural marriage, performed by Joseph Smith's priesthood authority. However, Martha probably misunderstood Brigham's claim that such a marriage would guarantee her admittance "straight to the celestial kingdom." Her plural marriage to Brigham Young could not obviate the need for continued obedience to the other commandments throughout the remainder of her life. (See Vol. 3, Chapter 12.)

Despite the shock Martha had received, she kept her wits and refused to give either a yes or a no answer. Her world had been severely traumatized, either by a profoundly new religious teaching or by an unsavory offering from one of her Church leaders. Martha was unsure which was correct. Sensing her reaction, Brigham went out and brought in Joseph, to whom he reported:

"Well," said Young, "sister Martha would be willing if she knew it was lawful and right before God." "Well, Martha," said Joseph, "it is lawful and right before God—I know it is. . . . I have the keys of the kingdom, and whatever I bind on earth is bound in heaven, and whatever I loose on earth is loosed in heaven, and if you will accept of Brigham, you shall be blessed—God shall bless you, and my blessing shall rest upon you; and if you will be led by him, you will do well; for I know Brigham will take care of you."

Martha remained unpersuaded by these assurances; and when she requested time to think it over, they agreed:

Said I, "do let me have a little time to think about it, and I will promise not to mention it to any one." "Well, but look here," said he [Joseph]; "you know a fellow will never be damned for doing the best he knows how." "Well, then," said I, "the best way I know of, is to go home and think and pray about it." "Well," said Young, "I shall leave it with brother Joseph, whether it would be best for you to have time or not."

"Well," said Joseph, "I see no harm in her having time to think, if she will not fall into temptation." "O, sir," said I, "there is no fear of my falling into temptation." "Well, but," said Brigham, "you must promise me you will never mention it to anyone." "I do promise it," said I. "Well," said Joseph, "you must promise me the same." I promised him the same. "Upon your honor," said he, "you will not tell?" "No, sir, I will lose my life first," said I. "Well, that will do," said he; "that is the principle we go upon. I think I can trust you, Martha," said he. "Yes," said I.

Once out of the store, Brotherton no doubt thought about this strange arrangement as promised but found nothing appealing in it. Although she had promised to keep the proceedings a secret, the promise had come before understanding the subject that was to be discussed. She returned to her home and shared the experience with her parents. They instantly lost faith and together with their daughter fled downriver to St. Louis.

It is apparent that rumors of the conversation spread about Nauvoo sometime thereafter. On April 6, 1842, in general conference, the Prophet "spoke in contradiction of a report in circulation about Elder Kimball, B. Young, himself, and others of the Twelve, alleging that a sister had been shut in a room for several days, and that they had endeavored to induce her to believe in having two wives."[46] The rumors may have contained elements of truth, but Joseph's denial also contained elements of exaggeration, no doubt with the purpose of discounting the whole story. Four days later, Joseph's history records: "I preached in the grove, and pronounced a curse upon all adul-

---

46. "Conference Minutes," *Times and Seasons* 3 (April 15, 1842): 763. The proposed time frame is my reconstruction; but no firmer dates are available.

terers and fornicators, and unvirtuous persons and those who have made use of my name to carry on their iniquitous designs."[47]

Martha's younger sister, Elizabeth Brotherton, must also have been shaken by her sister's experience; but instead of leaving Nauvoo with the family, she remained in the city and affirmed her belief in the truthfulness of the gospel. She wrote to friends in England on April 20:

> These are trying times for us all, but I know this is the work of the living God, and though earth and hell should combine to stop its progress, they cannot prevail. I beg of you not to listen to reports, but know for yourself. . . . My parents have turned their backs upon me, because I would not leave the Saints, and have told my elder sister [Mary Brotherton McIlwrick] not to own them until she abandoned "Mormonism;" but with all this she is unmoved, and is still contending for the faith once delivered to the Saints, for she and many other of the English Saints have proved that the statements made by my sister [Martha] are falsehoods of the basest kind.[48]

Despite this early failure, Brigham Young conducted a more successful approach later that year and was sealed to Lucy Ann Decker on June 14, 1842.[49] No details of that courtship and sealing have been located in the historical record.

Vinson Knight's Polygamous Marriage

A family history provides a report that Vinson Knight, before his death on July 31, 1842, was sealed to a plural wife, Philinda Clark Eldredge Merrick.[50] Vinson served as a bishop in Nauvoo and also assisted the Prophet's own family: "If Bro. Joseph were away," according to this family sketch, "it was he who looked after the wants of his [Joseph's] family. He was always ready to look after the widows and orphans."[51] Another late, secondhand family account relates:

> Martha [McBride Knight] was told by Joseph Smith that she was the first woman to give her consent for her husband to enter into plural marriage. The story is told that Martha knew something was worrying her husband and he couldn't seem to tell her about it. One evening as Martha was sitting in the grape arbor behind the house, Vinson returned home carrying a basket. He explained to Martha that he had taken some fruit and veg-

---

47. Andrew F. Ehat and Lyndon W. Cook, eds., *The Words of Joseph Smith: The Contemporary Accounts of the Nauvoo Discourses of the Prophet Joseph Smith*, 114.

48. Elizabeth Brotherton, Letter to correspondent identified only by an underline, April 20, 1842, *Millennial Star* 3 (August 1842): 74.

49. Bergera, "Identifying the Earliest Mormon Polygamists," 42–44, 72–73.

50. See Della Belnap, "Martha McBride Knight," qtd. in Todd Compton, *In Sacred Loneliness*, 722, 724.

51. Lola Belnap Coolbear, "Vinson Knight—Biographical Sketch," 54–55.

etables to the widow of Levi N. Merrick,[52] whose husband had been killed at Haun's Mill. Vinson explained to Martha that he had been told to enter plural marriage and that, if he had to, this Sister Merrick would be the one he could help best. Martha's reply is said to have been, "Is that all."[53]

Concerning Vinson's plural marriage, Hyrum Belnap, a member of the Church in Ogden, wrote a reminiscence to Andrew Jenson in 1899: "At the \time/ plural marriage was reviled. There was difficulty to find [sic] Persons that would consent to go into it on the female side. Martha Knight says the Prophet Joseph told her that she was the first one who concented [sic] to her Husband to have an other [sic] wife. and her Husband Vinson Knight did take another woman and was sealed to her. A Mrs Merrick."[54] Additional details are unavailable, but presumably Martha would have been sealed to Joseph Smith for time after Vinson's death.[55]

Summary

In 1842 Joseph Smith's polygamy expanded in two ways. The Prophet began seeking time-and-eternity sealings with unmarried women, and three other men also entered the principle. He apparently proposed plural marriage to Nancy Rigdon, daughter of his first counselor, Sidney Rigdon, but she rejected the offer and the event became public, creating embarrassment for Joseph and hampering additional dissemination of the teachings.

The first men in Nauvoo to contract plural marriages after Joseph Smith led the way were apparently Heber C. Kimball, Brigham Young, and Vinson Knight. Their accounts indicate that, like their prophet-leader, they believed themselves commanded by God to proceed. Their actions entering into polygamy otherwise seem unremarkable, manifesting the concerns and clumsiness of real people facing real challenges.

---

52. Levi N. Merrick married Philinda Clark Eldredge on November 18, 1827. He was killed at Haun's Mill, Missouri, on October 31, 1838, and Philinda was sealed to Vinson Knight in early 1842. Widowed a second time, she married Daniel Keeler on February 6, 1843. They were endowed in the Nauvoo Temple on January 17, 1846, where Brigham Young sealed them "for time" on February 6. Currently available documents do not clearly identify to whom she was sealed for eternity.

53. Brent J. Belnap, "Life Story of Martha McBride Knight Smith Kimball." See also Bergera. "Identifying the Earliest Mormon Polygamists," 14.

54. Hyrum Belnap, Ogden, Utah, Letter to Andrew Jenson, December 30, 1899, 2.

55. Martha was sealed to Joseph Smith for eternity as well in a proxy ceremony performed in the Nauvoo Temple on January 26, 1846. Brown, *Nauvoo Sealings, Adoptions, and Anointings*, 283.

Chapter 18

Joseph Smith Marries Additional Plural Wives

Between the end of June and September in 1842, Joseph Smith was sealed to four additional plural wives: Delcena Johnson, Martha McBride, Eliza R. Snow, and Sarah Ann Whitney. Limited evidence of the Prophet's relationships with Delcena and Martha is available, while multiple documents concern Eliza and Sarah Ann's interactions with him.

Delcena Johnson and Martha McBride

Both Delcena Johnson and Martha McBride were widows at the time of their sealing to Joseph Smith. Delcena's husband, Lyman Royal Sherman, was a close friend of the Prophet and died in early 1839. She left no record of her relationship with Joseph. Her brother, Benjamin Franklin Johnson, provided the sole evidence corroborating her sealing, dating it to "before my Return to Nauvoo," which occurred on July 1, 1842.[1] Delcena was married to Joseph Smith for "time" and was later sealed for eternity to Lyman Sherman by proxy in the Nauvoo Temple.[2]

Martha McBride was married to Vinson Knight, a bishop of one of the Nauvoo wards. He died in August of 1842, and Martha signed an 1869 affidavit declaring that "in the summer of the year 1842 at the city of Nauvoo, County of Hancock, State of Illinois, She was married or sealed to Joseph Smith President of the Church of Jesus Christ of Latter-day Saints, by Heber C. Kimble [sic] one of the Twelve Apostles in said Church according to the law of the same regulating marriage."[3] Martha's affidavit does not specify

---

1. Dean R. Zimmerman, ed., *I Knew the Prophets: An Analysis of the Letter of Benjamin F. Johnson to George F. Gibbs, Reporting Doctrinal Views of Joseph Smith and Brigham Young*, 45, see also 40, 43. For the date of Benjamin's return to Nauvoo, see Benjamin F. Johnson, *My Life's Review*, 90, see also 95. For discussion of minor discrepancies in the dating, see Todd Compton, *In Sacred Loneliness: The Plural Wives of Joseph Smith*, 710.

2. Lisle G Brown, *Nauvoo Sealings, Adoptions, and Anointings: A Comprehensive Register of Persons Receiving LDS Temple Ordinances, 1841–1846*, 272.

3. Martha McBride Kimball, Affidavit, July 8, 1869; digital photo MS 3423. Affidavit copied in Joseph F. Smith, Affidavit Books, 2:36; 3:36. See also Joseph Fielding Smith,

whether the marriage performed in 1842 was for "time" or for "time and eternity." I hypothesize that it was for "time," designed to "raise up seed" to Vinson, similar to Delcena Johnson Lyman's sealing to the Prophet. When the ceremony was repeated vicariously in the Nauvoo Temple on January 26, 1846, Martha was sealed to the Prophet, not Vinson, for eternity.[4] In this arrangement, she was unlike Delcena, who was vicariously sealed to her legal husband. The differences in eternal sealings of these two women presumably reflected their own preferences. It also suggests that Delcena saw no eternal advantage to being sealed to the Prophet rather than to Lyman, her civil spouse.

Delcena Diadamia Johnson (Sherman Smith Babbitt). Courtesy of Todd Compton.

Sealing to Eliza R. Snow

Eliza R. Snow is the most widely known of Joseph Smith's plural wives. The sealing ceremony occurred on June 29, 1842, the day she began keeping her journal; but she alludes to the marriage ceremony only obliquely. That first entry reads:

> This is a day of much interest to my feelings. Reflecting on past occurrences, a variety of thoughts have presented themselves to my mind with regard to events which have chased each other in rapid succession in the scenery of human life.
>
> As an individual, I have not passed altogether unnoticed by change, in reference to present circumstances and future prospects . . . though I rejoice in the blessing of the society of the saints, and the approbation of God; a lonely feeling will steal over me before I am aware, while I am contemplating the present state of society—the powers of darkness, and the prejudices of the human mind which stand arrayed like an impregnable barrier against the work of God. While these thoughts were revolving in my mind, the heavens became shadowed with clouds and a heavy shower of rain and hail ensued, and I exclaimed "O God, is it not enough that we have the prepossessions of mankind—their prejudices and their hatred to contend with; but must we also stand amid the rage of elements?" I concluded within myself that the period might not be far distant, that will require faith to do so; but the grace of God is

---

Blood Atonement and the Origin of Plural Marriage, 72.
4. Brown, *Nauvoo Sealings, Adoptions, and Anointings*, 283.

Martha McBride (Knight Smith Kimball). Courtesy International Society of the Daughters of Utah Pioneers.

sufficient, therefore I will not fear. I will put my trust in Him who is mighty to save; rejoicing in his goodness and determined to live by every word that proceedeth out of his mouth.[5]

Eliza gave the exact date in a signed 1869 affidavit.[6] In a 1887 interview with a newspaper reporter, Eliza stressed the secrecy surrounding her sealing: "She lived in the same cottage with another lady for two years after she had been sealed, but said not a word to her friend and neighbor. At last Joseph told her one day that she might talk with her neighbor on the subject, and then for the first time she revealed her connection with plural-marriage. 'We women kept secrets in those days,' she added."[7] The reported timeline is problematic. Eliza arrived in Nauvoo in July 1839.[8] By August 19, 1842, she was living with Sarah Cleveland; however, it is unknown whether Eliza had boarded exclusively with Sarah those previous two years.[9] On August 19, Eliza was forced to leave the Cleveland residence and subsequently received an invitation to live with the Smiths, an arrangement that lasted until February 11, 1843.[10] Sarah Cleveland may have been the "lady" referred to because she had been sealed to Joseph Smith as a polyandrous plural wife on an unknown date, but likely by the spring of 1842.[11] Since Eliza wed the Prophet on June 29, the two women would have lived together as Joseph's plural wives, but unknown to each other, for only seven weeks, not two years. On February 11, Eliza moved from the Smiths to board at the home of Jonathan Holmes and Elvira Cowles Holmes. Elvira, sealed as a polyandrous wife to Joseph Smith, could

---

5. Maureen Ursenbach Beecher, ed., "Eliza R. Snow's Nauvoo Journal," 394.

6. Joseph F. Smith, Affidavit Book, 1:25. Compton, *In Sacred Loneliness*, 714, reports "an alternate date for the marriage" between Joseph and Eliza, March 1842, citing several sources that refer to her being sealed to the Prophet prior to the March 1842 organization of the Relief Society.

7. J.J.J., "Two Prophets' Widows: A Visit to the Relicts of Joseph Smith and Brigham Young," 6.

8. Jill Mulvay Derr and Karen Lynn Davidson, eds., *Eliza R. Snow: The Complete Poetry*, x.

9. Maureen Ursenbach Beecher, ed., *The Personal Writings of Eliza Roxcy Snow*, 54.

10. Ibid., 80.

11. Compton, *In Sacred Loneliness*, 4, 280.

have been the "lady," except that Eliza's stay there lasted only five months, until July 21, when she moved to the Morley settlement. (Her sister Leonora would become Isaac Morley's plural wife.) That Joseph would have arranged for Eliza to stay with another of his plural families or with a trusted friend is consistent with his general pattern of meeting the material needs of all of his wives.

Despite the apparent discrepancies, the exact chronology is less important than the point that Eliza was trying to make, that the secrecy of her marriage (and probably all discussions of plural marriage in Nauvoo in early 1842) was so profound, that two of Joseph Smith's polygamous wives could have lived in the same dwelling for weeks or months without either knowing about the other's plural union. It seems that if Eliza could keep her marriage to Joseph Smith concealed from her cottage-mate, then Joseph's visits to both wives were infrequent, brief, and without conjugal involvement. Otherwise either would have immediately suspected the other's marital ties.

Eliza Roxcy Snow Smith Young. Courtesy LDS Church History Library.

To the same reporter in 1887, Eliza declared:

> When first plural marriage was suggested to me . . . I would not listen to the matter. The idea was repugnant, abhorrent. I was like any other young woman who had beaux and suitors for her hand. I wanted to share a husband with no woman. But I was told it was God's command, and I went to God and asked God to enlighten me, and he did. I saw and felt that plural marriage was not only right, but that it was the only true manner of living up to the gospels and I quenched my womanly emotions and entered the order.[12]

A third document, a personal history penned in 1885, reflects again on her feelings when she was first introduced to plural marriage:

> In Nauvoo I first understood that the practice of plurality of wives was to be introduced into the church. The subject was very repugnant to my feelings—so directly was it in opposition to my educated prepossessions, that it seemed as though all the prejudices of my ancestors for generations

---

12. J.J.J., "Two Prophets' Widows," 6.

past congregated around me: But when I reflected that I was living in the Dispensation of the fulness of times, embracing all other Dispensations, surely Plural Marriage must necessarily be included, and I consoled myself with the idea that it was far in the distance, and beyond the period of my mortal existence. It was not long however, after I received the first intimation, before the announcement reached me that the "set time" had come—that God had commanded his servants to establish the order, by taking additional wives—I knew that God . . . was speaking. . . . As I increased in knowledge concerning the principle and design of Plural Marriage, I grew in love with it. . . .

I was sealed to the Prophet, Joseph Smith, for time and eternity, in accordance with the *Celestial Law of Marriage* which God has revealed—the ceremony being performed by a servant of the Most High—authorized to officiate in sacred ordinances. This, one of the most important circumstances of my life, I have never had cause to regret.[13]

As discussed above, Eliza boarded at the Smiths' first Nauvoo home, the Homestead, with Joseph and Emma for almost six months (August 14, 1842, to February 11, 1843) after her sealing to Joseph.[14] However, she never lived with the Smiths while they resided in the two-level Mansion, completed on August 31, 1843.[15] Eliza R. Snow expressed concern regarding plural marriage: "Polygamy did not hurt Me but to be looked upon as A Woman of light Character that did hurt me The very idea of my not being a virtuous Woman."[16]

Conflicting stories exist regarding the relationship between Emma and Eliza. A third-hand account suggests that Emma had consented to Eliza's plural sealing. Two years before Eliza's death in 1887, John Hawley wrote in his 1885 autobiography: "What Erastus Snow and toald me in the year 1870/?/ they Said him and his first wife was present at the time Elisa R Snow was given to Joseph and Emma Josephs wife was presant, and they both testify that Emma took E Snows hand and plased it in the hand of Joseph as giveng hur consent."[17] This recollection is undoubtedly in error. Eliza later testified that

---

13. Eliza R. Snow, "Sketch of My Life," 13; emphasis hers. See also Beecher, *The Personal Writings of Eliza Roxcy Snow*, 16–17.

14. Adiah Winchell Clements claimed: "That once when she was at her work that Emma went up stairs and pulled Eliza R. Snow down stairs by the hair of her head as she was staying there although she had contesended [consented] to give him one or more women in the beginning." Quoted in John Boice and Mary Ann (Barzee), Boice "Boice Record," 178–79. This account is problematic because Emma first gave her consent for Joseph to marry plural wives in May of 1843 but Eliza R. Snow had moved out of the Smith residence three months earlier.

15. Snow, "Sketch of My Life," 15.

16. Payson Ward, Utah Stake, Relief Society Minutes, September 26, 1872, 162–63. I am grateful to Jill Mulvay Derr for these minutes.

17. John Hawley, Autobiography, January 1885, 97.

Emma had consented to four other plural sealings, but she never mentioned Emma's involvement with her own. In addition, the timing is too early. Emma did not accept plural marriage until about a year after Eliza's sealing to Joseph.

Other accounts suggest that Emma and Eliza had a violent conflict, marked by hair pulling, Emma's attacking Eliza with a broom stick, and even pushing her down a staircase, possibly resulting in a miscarriage that left Eliza unable to bear children. (See Chapter 25.) In 1872, Eliza shared her convictions concerning plural marriage in the Payson Ward Relief Society. According to the secretary's minutes, she said: "Plurality of Wives is a great trial if you want to sit in the courts of Heaven honor Polygamy dont suffer your lips to say ought even if you do not believe in it When I entered it I had no anticipation of ever being acknowledged As a lawful Wife I beleived [sic] in it because I felt the work was true and I longed to see a Prophet. I feel proud that I ever embraced it."[18]

Sarah Ann Whitney's Two Husbands

As mentioned in Chapter 16, Sarah Ann Whitney, the daughter of Newel K. Whitney and Elizabeth Ann Whitney, was sealed to the Prophet on July 27, 1842.[19] This marriage was distinctive in four ways. First, her father and mother were the earliest parents to give their explicit permission for their daughter to enter plurality. Second, they unitedly received a confirming witness, prompting their approval. Third, Newel Whitney himself performed the ceremony, and fourth, he used language that Joseph Smith had received by revelation.

Helen Mar Kimball Smith Whitney, who was sealed to Joseph Smith and married Sarah's brother, Horace, after the martyrdom, remembered:

> Bishop Whitney was not a man that readily accepted of every doctrine, and would question the Prophet very closely upon principles if not made clear to his understanding. When Joseph saw that he was doubtful concerning the righteousness of this celestial order he told him to go and enquire of the Lord concerning it, and he should receive a testimony for himself.
>
> The Bishop, with his wife, who had for years been called Mother Whitney, retired together and unitedly besought the Lord for a testimony whether or not this principle was from Him; and they ever after bore testimony that they received a manifestation and that it was so powerful they could not mistake it. The Bishop never afterwards doubted, and they willingly gave to him their daughter, which was the strongest proof that they could possibly give their faith and confidence in him as a true Prophet of God.[20]

---

18. Payson Ward, Utah Stake, Relief Society Minutes, September 26, 1872, 162–63.
19. Joseph F. Smith, Affidavit Books, 1:36, 1:72.
20. Helen Mar Kimball Whitney, "Scenes in Nauvoo after the Martyrdom of the

Elizabeth recalled:

> Joseph had the most implicit confidence in my husband's uprightness and integrity of character, and so he confided to him the principles set forth in that revelation, and also gave him the privilege of reading and making a copy of it, believing it would be perfectly safe with him. . . . My husband revealed these things to me. We had always been united, and had the utmost faith and confidence in each other. We pondered upon the matter continually, and our prayers were unceasing that the Lord would grant us some special manifestation concerning this new and strange doctrine. The Lord was very merciful to us; He revealed unto us His power and glory. We were seemingly wrapt in a heavenly vision, a halo of light encircled us, and we were convinced in our own bosoms that God heard and approved our prayers and intercedings before him. Our hearts were comforted and our faith made so perfect that we were willing to give our eldest daughter, then seventeen years of age, to Joseph, in the order of plural marriage. Laying aside all our traditions and former notions in regard to marriage, we gave her with our mutual consent.[21]

Sarah Ann Whitney (Smith Kingsbury Kimball). Courtesy LDS Church History Library.

Orson F. Whitney, son of Helen Mar Kimball and Horace Whitney, wrote this account. which was doubtless based on his mother's report:

> This bond of affection [between the Whitneys and Joseph Smith] was strengthened and intensified by the giving in marriage to the former of the Bishop's eldest daughter, Sarah, in obedience to a revelation from God. This girl was but seventeen years of age, but she had implicit faith in the doctrine of plural marriage, as revealed to and practiced by the Prophet, was of celestial origin. She was the first woman, in this dispensation, who was given in plural marriage by and with the consent of both parents. Her father himself officiated in the ceremony. The revelation commanding and consecrating this union, is in existence, though it has never been published. It bears the date of July 27, 1842, and was given through the Prophet to the writer's

---

Prophet and Patriarch," *Woman's Exponent* 11, no. 19 (March 1, 1883): 146.

21. Edward Tullidge, *The Women of Mormondom*, 368–69; Elizabeth Ann Whitney, "A Leaf from an Autobiography," *Woman's Exponent*, 7, no. 14 (December 15, 1878): 105; see also Carol Cornwall Madsen, ed., *In Their Own Words: Women and the Story of Nauvoo*, 202.

grandfather, Newel K. Whitney, whose daughter Sarah, on that day, became the wedded wife of Joseph Smith for time and all eternity.[22]

Despite the spiritual confirmations, the process was nevertheless difficult for Sarah's mother, Elizabeth. John Wycliffe Rigdon, Sidney's son, was apparently aware of the proceedings. He wrote in 1904 to a correspondent:

> Was Polygamy taught & practiced [by] Joseph Smith at Nauvoo[?] I say yess, but it was not taugh [sic] openly it was done secretly It was commenced some time the latter part of the year of 1842 that is it was talked about & in 1843 & 1844 it was the common talk of the members of the church Joseph Smith married at Nauvoo Sarah Ann Whitney . . . I talked with her Mother Old Mrs Whitney at Salt Lake City in 1863—the old Lady told me how bad she felt when Joseph Smith first broched the subject to her, how she cryed about it \but/ the Prophet at last obtained her consent.[23]

At Mother Whitney's 1882 funeral, Apostle Joseph F. Smith eulogized her: "She was one who received in her heart the doctrine of plural marriage from the lips of the Prophet Joseph; and she was one of the first mothers in Israel who gave her daughter in the bond of marriage to the Prophet; and she stood by her daughter, and was true to Joseph in the trying circumstances of his life in Nauvoo, which grew out of his endeavors to establish this doctrine in the Church."[24]

The fourth singular element of Sarah Ann Whitney's sealing to Joseph Smith was that Joseph received a revelation on July 27, 1842, dictating the language that Bishop Whitney would speak in performing the ceremony:

> Verily thus saith the Lord unto my se[r]vant N. K. Whitney the thing that my se[r]vant Joseph Smith has made known unto you and your Famely and which you have agreed upon is right in mine eyes and shall be crowned upon your heads with honor and immortality and eternal life to all your house both old & young because of the lineage of my Preast Hood saith the Lord it shall be upon you and upon your children after you from generation to generation By virtue of the Holy promise which I now make unto you saith the Lord.
>
> [T]hese are the words which you shall pronounce upon my se[r]vant Joseph and your Daughter S. A. Whitney. They shall take each other by the hand and you shall say[:]

---

22. Orson F. Whitney, "Life of Heber C. Kimball," *The Contributor* 6, no. 4 (January 1885): 131.

23. John Wickliffe Rigdon (Brooklyn, N.Y.), Letter to "Arthur Willing, Elder," February 20, 1904.

24. "Death of Mother Whitney," *Deseret News Weekly*, February 22, 1882, 9. See also Journal History, February 17, 1882.

Joseph Smith Marries Additional Plural Wives

> [Y]ou both mutu[al]ly agree calling them by name to be each others companion so long as you both shall live presser[v]ing yourselv[es] for each other and from all others and also through [o]ut all eternity reserving only those rights which have been given to my servant Joseph by revelation and commandment and by legal Authority in times passed.
>
> If you both agree to covenant and do this, then I give you S. A. Whitney my Daughter to Joseph Smith to be his wife to observe all the rights betwe[e]n you both that belong to that condition. I do it in my own name and in the name of my wife your mother and in the name of my Holy Progenitors by the right of birth which is of Priest Hood vested in me by revelation and commandment and promise of the living God obtained by the Holy Melchizedek Gethrow [Jethro] and other of the Holy Fathers commanding in the name of the Lord all those powers to concentrate in you and through [you] to your po[s]terity for ever
>
> [A]ll these things I do in the name of the Lord Jesus Christ that through this order he may be gloryfied and through the power of anointing Davied may reign King over Iseral which shall hereafter be revealed let immortality and eternal life henc[e]forth be sealed upon your heads forever and ever.[25]

This revelation, interestingly, begins by referring to a "thing" Joseph had taught the Whitneys. From the context, this "thing" was undoubtedly the principle of eternal marriage including plurality of wives. (See Vol. 3, chap. 12.) The revelation assures Newel that this "thing" that had been "agreed upon," was "right," presumably authorizing the plural marriage between the Prophet and Sarah Ann. The wording specifies that the marriage is "as long as you both shall live" and "also throughout all eternity." In other words, it was a marriage for time and eternity. It contains references to "all the rights between you both that belong to that condition . . . [and] all those powers to concentrate in you and through to your posterity forever" suggesting that both mortal and post-mortal children might be born to the union. The authority of the priesthood is also acknowledged, invoking the unusual authority of the prophet " Gethrow " or Jethro, who gave the Melchizedek Priesthood and perhaps the sealing keys, to Moses.

Apparently Joseph Smith was concerned that Sarah Ann's brother, Horace Whitney, would try to prevent her marriage to the Prophet. Helen Mar, who married Horace after the Prophet's death, recalled:

> It was not till the summer [of 1842] . . . that I [Helen] learned of the existence of the plural order of marriage. . . . My father [Heber C. Kimball]

---

25. Joseph Smith, Revelation for Newel K. Whitney, July 27, 1842, published in H. Michael Marquardt, *The Joseph Smith Revelations: Text and Commentary*, 315–16; bracketed clarifications both Marquardt's and mine; paragraph indentations mine. See also "Revelations in Addition to Those Found in the LDS Edition of the D&C."

was the first to introduce it to me. . . . [H]e took the first opportunity to introduce Sarah Ann to me as Joseph's wife [married July 27, 1842]. This astonished me beyond measure; but I could then understand a few things which had previously been to me a puzzle, and among the rest, the meaning of his words at her party. I saw, or could imagine in some degree, the great trial that she must have passed through and that it had required a mighty struggle to take a step of that kind and had called for a sacrifice such as few can realize but those who first rendered obedience to this law. . . .

Sarah Ann took this step of her own free will, but had to do it unbeknown to her brother [Horace], which grieved her most, and also her mother, that they could not open their hearts to him. But Joseph feared to disclose it, believing that the Higbee boys [Francis and Chauncey] would embitter Horace against him, as they had already caused serious trouble, and for this reason he favored his going East, which Horace was not slow to accept. He had had some slight suspicions that the stories about Joseph were not all without foundation, but had never told them, nor did he know the facts till after his return to Nauvoo, when Sarah hastened to tell him all. It was no small stumbling-block to him when learning of the course which had been taken towards him, which was hard for him to overlook. But Joseph had always treated him with the greatest kindness from the time he came to live in his father's house in Kirtland. . . .

Sarah felt when she took this step that it would be the means of severing her from the happy circle in which she had moved as one of their guiding stars. She was called proud and somewhat eccentric, but the influence that she seemed to hold over one was almost magnetic.[26]

One month after her marriage, the Prophet was in hiding from Missouri law officials and alone. He wrote a touching letter to Newel K. Whitney, Elizabeth Ann Whitney, and Sarah Ann Whitney, on August 18, 1842:

I take this oppertunity to communi[c]ate, some of my feelings, privetely at this time, which I want you three Eternaly to keep in your own bosams; for my feelings are so strong for you since what has pased lately between us, that the time of my abscence from you seems so long, and dreary, that it seems, as if I could not live long in this way: and if you three would come and see me in this my lonely retreat, it would afford me great relief, of mind, if those with whom I am alied, do love me, now is the time to afford me succour, in the days of exile, for you know I foretold you of these things. I am now at Carlos Graingers, Just back of Brother Hyrams farm, it is only one mile from town, the nights are very pleasant indeed, all three of you can come and See me in the fore part of the night, let Brother Whitney come a little a head, and nock at the south East corner of the house at the window;

---

26. Helen Mar Kimball Whitney, "Scenes in Nauvoo after the Martyrdom of the Prophet and Patriarch," 146.

it is next to the cornfield, I have a room intirely by myself, the whole matter can be attended to with most perfect safty, I know it is the will of God that you should comfort me now in this time of afiliction, or not at [al]l[;] now is the time or never, but I hav[e] no kneed of saying any such thing, to you, for I know the goodness of your hearts, and that you will do the will of the Lord, when it is made known to you; the only thing to be careful of; is to find out when Emma [Smith] comes then you cannot be safe, but when she is not here, there is the most perfect safty: only be careful to escape observation, as much as possible, I know it is a heroick undertakeing; but so much the greater frendship, and the more Joy, when I see you I will tell you all my plans, I cannot write them on paper, burn this letter as soon as you read it; keep all locked up in your breasts, my life depends upon it. one thing I want to see you for it is to git the fulness of my blessings sealed upon our heads, &c. you will pardon me for my earnestness on this subject when you consider how lonesome I must be, your good feelings know how to make every allowance for me, I close my letter, I think Emma wont come tonight[,] if she dont dont fail to come to night. I subscribe myself your most obedient, and affectionate, companion, and friend.[27]

George D. Smith and Larry Foster have suggested that Joseph's plea for the Whitneys to come and "comfort him" implied a sexual rendezvous.[28] In his book, *Nauvoo Polygamy*, George D. Smith refers to this incident multiple times, each time implying that a tryst was being proposed.[29] I find this interpretation problematic. Besides requesting "comfort," he asks them to afford him "relief of mind" and "succor." Neither of the latter terms naturally carries an erotic connotation. An examination of twelve other separate uses of "comfort" or "comforted" by Joseph Smith in his speeches and writings likewise fails to identify even one that carried a sexual overtone.[30] In addition, intermixed with Joseph's pleas for a consoling visit were triple references to all three of the Whitneys. His message was directed to the parents, as well as to Sarah Ann,

---

27. Joseph Smith Jr., Letter to Newel K. Whitney, Elizabeth Ann Whitney, etc.," August 18, 1842. The text and the signature are in Joseph Smith's handwriting. Reproduced in Dean C. Jessee, ed., *The Personal Writings of Joseph Smith*, 539–40.

28. See for example, George D. Smith, "The Summer of 1842: Joseph Smith's Relationships with the 12 Wives He Married after His First Wife, Emma," 515. William Lawrence Foster, "Between Two Worlds: The Origins of Shaker Celibacy, Oneida Community Complex Marriage, and Mormon Polygamy," 248.

29. George D. Smith, *Nauvoo Polygamy: "... but we called it celestial marriage,"* ix, 142, 147, 185, 236 twice, 453, 459. On one occasion, he uses ellipses to omit Sarah Ann's parents (53).

30. Scott H. Faulring, ed., *An American Prophet's Record: The Diaries and Journals of Joseph Smith*, 17, 28, 90, 140, 141, 160, 192, 367, 369, 380; and Andrew F. Ehat and Lyndon W. Cook, eds., *The Words of Joseph Smith: The Contemporary Accounts of the Nauvoo Discourses of the Prophet Joseph Smith*, 119.

Drawing of Newel K. Whitney and photo of Eliza Ann Whitney. Courtesy LDS Church History Library.

who was not singled out at any time. It also seems unlikely Joseph would have been so audacious as to allude to a sexual encounter in front of his plural wife's parents, nor does the unedited text seem to authorize that interpretation.

Linda King Newell and Valeen Tippetts Avery wrote: "This letter clearly indicates that Emma was unaware of Joseph's marriage to Sarah Ann."[31] Hence, there was a need to avoid a confrontation between Emma and the three Whitneys in the proposed "fore part of the night." In the letter Joseph also mentioned his desire to "get the fullness of my blessings sealed upon our heads," an allusion to eternally sealing Newel and Elizabeth's own marriage.

Apparently, the Whitneys did not make the proposed visit that night. Todd Compton explains his reading of the letter: "There are evidently further ordinances that Smith wants to perform for the Whitneys. This is not just a meeting of husband and plural wife; it is a meeting with Sarah's family, with a religious aspect. . . . Three days later, on August 21, Newel and Elizabeth Whitney were sealed to each other for time and eternity."[32]

Several months later on March 23, 1843, Joseph Smith gave Sarah Ann Whitney a special blessing:

> Oh let <it> be sealed this day on high that she shall come forth in the first resurrection to recieve the same and verily it shall be so saith the Lord if she remain in the Everlasting covenant to the end as also all her Father[']s house shall be saved in the same Eternal glory and if any of them shall wan-

---

31. Linda King Newell and Valeen Tippetts Avery, *Mormon Enigma: Emma Hale Smith*, 125.
32. Compton, *In Sacred Loneliness*, 350.

der from the fo<a>ld [fold] of the Lord they shall not perish but shall return saith the Lord[33] and be saived and by repentance be crowned with all the fullness of the glory of the Everlasting Gospel."[34]

As discussed in Chapter 16, Sarah Ann's relationship with Joseph Smith was distinct in another way. Apparently sometime in the first half of 1843, suspicions arose concerning the possibility of their plural marriage. To deflect such suspicions, the Prophet requested that thirty-year-old Joseph C. Kingsbury, a clerk in the Red Brick Store, marry Sarah Ann civilly. I have found no evidence of a plot to expose the Prophet and Sarah Ann and no record of rumors (although this absence of a record does not prove the absence of either plot or rumors), so possibly some other motivation may have prompted the performance of this pretended marriage.

For Kingsbury, the promises of an eternal family through Joseph Smith's sealing keys motivated him to assist the Prophet:

> [I] was imployed in Joseph Smith's Store under the direction of Bishop Newel K Whitney untill the fall of 1842 and on the 16th day Oct Caroline my Wife Died [. . .] how thankfull I feal thinking I shall see & meat her again to enjoy each other society for ever to part no more & also my little sons [. . .] and on the 29th of April 1843 I according to President Joseph Smith council & others agreed to stand by Sarah \Ann/ Whitney as supposed to be her husband & had a pretended marriage for the purpose of bringing about the purposes of God in the last days as spoken by the mouth

---

33. This statement may have inspired a popular declaration originally voiced in April 1929 general conference by Sarah Ann Whitney's nephew, Apostle Orson F. Whitney, who said: " The Prophet Joseph Smith declared—and he never taught more comforting doctrine—that the eternal sealings of faithful parents and the divine promises made to them for valiant service in the Cause of Truth, would save not only themselves, but likewise their posterity. Though some of the sheep may wander, the eye of the Shepherd is upon them, and sooner or later they will feel the tentacles of Divine Providence reaching out after them and drawing them back to the fold. Either in this life or the life to come, they will return. They will have to pay their debt to justice; they will suffer for their sins; and may tread a thorny path; but if it leads them at last, like the penitent Prodigal, to a loving and forgiving father's heart and home, the painful experience will not have been in vain. Pray for your careless and disobedient children; hold on to them with your faith. Hope on, trust on, till you see the salvation of God." Orson F. Whitney, *Conference Report*, 110.

34. Quoted in H. Michael Marquardt, *The Rise of Mormonism: 1816–1844*, 586. In the early 1970s, a typescript of the revelation was part of the Joseph Smith Collection (MS 155), but since it was not an original document, it was removed for further research. Randall W. Dixon, email to Brian Hales, September 15, 2012. Currently it is filed as, "Blessing given to Sarah Ann Whitney. March 23, 1843." MS 23156. Whitney Family Documents. 1843-1844, 1912. CHL.

of the prophet Isiah Jeremiah Ezekiel and also Joseph Smith, & Sarah Ann should rec-d a great glory Honner & Eternal Lives and I Also Should Rec-d a Great Glory Honner & Eternal Lives to the full desire of my heart in having my companion Caroline in the first resurrection to hail her & no one to have power to take her from me & we Both shall be crowned & enthroned togeather in the Celestial Kingdom of God Enjoying Each others Society in all of the fullness of the Gospel of Jesus Christ & our little ones with us as is Recorded in this blessing that President Joseph Smith Sealed upon my head on the Twenty third day of March 1843 as follows.[35]

Joseph C. Kingsbury served as a "front husband," living in the same house with Sarah Ann Whitney, but without experiencing conjugal relations, apparently to shield the Prophet from suspicion.

Oliver Olney: An Outsider's View in Nauvoo

One of the very few contemporary historical documents from the Nauvoo area during 1842 comes from Oliver Olney, the husband of Alice Johnson. Alice was Marinda Nancy Johnson Hyde's sister, making her a sister-in-law to Apostle Orson Hyde. As discussed, Marinda herself was sealed to the Prophet and had served as an intermediary in at least one of his plural marriage proposals—that to Nancy Rigdon. Oliver undoubtedly enjoyed and exploited this tie as much as possible. However, it was diminished or terminated when his wife died in July of 1841, leaving Olney with two young daughters, ages six and eight. (It would have been unusual for a single father to care for his children, except to provide family finances, in these circumstances; the normal pattern would have been for a female relative or a hired woman to step into the mother's role.) Whether Alice's death greatly affected Oliver's mental stability is unknown, but it appears that something happened in 1841 to alter the trajectory of his life.

In early 1842, Oliver claimed to be in visionary contact with the "Ancient of Days," presumably Adam.[36] He reported teachings that were contradictory to Church doctrines and was excommunicated on March 17, 1842. In conjunction with his Church discipline, the *Times and Seasons* printed: "Mr. Olney has also been tried by the high council and disfellowshipped because he would not have his writings tested by the word of God; evidently proving that he loves darkness rather than light because his deeds are evil."[37]

---

35. Joseph C. Kingsbury, "History of Joseph C. Kingsbury," 13. Bracketed ellipses and virgules by Don Bradley.

36. Charlotte Haven, "A Girl's Letters from Nauvoo," 630.

37. "Try the Spirits," *Times and Seasons* 3 (April 1, 1842): 748.

His excommunication apparently provoked Olney to begin keeping a personal record of his experiences. While it is one of the most detailed contemporary records of life in Nauvoo during 1842, its usefulness is limited by his critical point of view and his tortured writing style. Olney fancied himself as rhetorically gifted and elected to write his historical notes in an abstract prose style. Consequently, many of his compositions are difficult to read and repetitious. Oliver penned on May 13, 1842:

> Respecting the plurality of wives,
> They will be a trouble to you
> As they will harass you
> Both by knight and day
> They will depend on you for a living[38]

Oliver's humorous reference to polygamy at that time is somewhat surprising, since only Joseph and perhaps two or three other men had married plurally. Possibly he was reacting to rumors of John C. Bennett's "spiritual wifism." Or perhaps rumors had significantly outdistanced the practice at that point. It is also possible that Oliver had received privileged communications directly from Marinda or he may have simply been repeating gossip he had heard in his movements about Nauvoo.

The following month, on June 15, Oliver recorded his suspicions: "They [Church leaders] have abused their own companions by being free with females of ill fame and others they have taken the advantage of by saying thus and thus saith the Lord."[39] On July 7, he wrote:

> To move in power and wisdom
> In this and foreign lands
> Also go ahead in polygamy
> And raise up a righteous branch
> Some where near the Rocky Mountains
> In the far west,
> Where no law can trap you
> Or hinder you on the way[40]

This passage interestingly demonstrates that Joseph Smith was talking about migrating to the West in 1842. Concerning this possibility, Dale Morgan referenced Olney's writings and concluded that the Prophet contemplated a westward movement within three years of settling Nauvoo: "Joseph Smith was ready to abandon Nauvoo and take his church west to the Rockies at this early date [1842]."[41]

---

38. Oliver Olney, Untitled journal, etc., May 13, 1842, Olney Papers, item 8.
39. Ibid., June 15, 1842.
40. Ibid., July 7, 1842.
41. Dale Morgan, "The Olney Papers: Foreword and Calendar of the Documents."

On February 10, 1843, Oliver was brought before the Nauvoo Municipal Court, presided over by Mayor Joseph Smith. Olney reported that the "Ancient of Days" had instructed him to steal goods from a local merchant, Moses Smith. In his defense, he stated: "David Patten [an apostle killed in 1838 at the Battle of Crooked River] appeared to me & conversed with me. . . . I took those things I did not care any thing about them."[42] The court decided that Olney must post bail of $5,000 or be committed to Carthage Jail. Joseph said: "This is the most painful thing I ever had to do . . . [but I] cannot swerve from the path of duty." An article in *The Wasp* reported on February 15:

> A bill of Grand Larceny and Burglary was found against him, and as he did not procure bail, he was committed to the county jail, to await the decision of the Circuit Court. Since the above was sent to the compositors we have been informed that Oliver Olney has broke loose from his keepers. . . . We do not wish to attach any particular blame to the officer having him in charge, as Olney was a large, powerful, athletic man. . . . We are informed that the constable had a pair of hand cuffs made to take the prisoner to Carthage with; but they were too small, and while they were getting them altered the prisoner decamped.[43]

Two weeks later Olney gave himself up to the marshal, Henry G. Sherwood,[44] although the record of Olney's legal imbroglio apparently ends there.

Less than a month later, Olney published one of the few books printed during the Nauvoo era that mentioned polygamy: *The Absurdities of Mormonism Portrayed. A Brief Sketch by Oliver H. Olney, Hancock Co., Illinois, March 3, 1843* (n.p.).[45] This thirty-two-page pamphlet contained a number of interesting assertions: "Polygamy was first introduced in Kirtland, Ohio about eight years ago. Hint after hint has been going, until we have to say, they have begun to do, as well as say. This subject has been kept in the dark, as long as it could be, as it was first said to be too strong meat for the Latter Day Saints to bear. . . . Many are actually attached to the second living companion; and a door is fast opening on this subject that many is arguing it to be the will of God."[46] The mention of Kirtland eight years earlier (1835) suggests that he had heard about Joseph's first plural marriage to Fanny Alger; but Olney's suggestion that "many" were involved

---

42. *Joseph Smith v. Oliver Olney*, February 10, 1843, in "Nauvoo Records."

43. "Outrageous Theft," 4.

44. Andrew H. Hedges, Alex D. Smith, and Richard Lloyd Anderson, eds., *The Joseph Smith Papers: Journals, Volume 2: December 1841–April 1843*, 260 note 385.

45. Oliver Olney had been working on the book for several months; he referred to its upcoming publication in a letter written September 18, 1842 (published October 7) to the *Sangamo Journal*.

46. Oliver H. Olney, *The Absurdities of Mormonism Portrayed: A Brief Sketch*, 10.

in ongoing plural marriage is an exaggeration. Only a half a dozen men were polygamists at the time of Olney's publications. (See Chapter 27.)

Rank-and-file Church members may have taken note of Olney's claims but largely dismissed them as remnants of the John C. Bennett scandal, which peaked in the summer of 1842. Olney again tried to capitalize on his association with the Mormons by publishing *Spiritual Wifery at Nauvoo Exposed* (1845). Despite the title, it contains even fewer references to Nauvoo polygamy than his earlier publication.

Summary

During the summer of 1842, the Prophet married additional plural wives. Little is known regarding Martha McBride Knight and Delcena Johnson. In contrast, more details are available concerning his plural marriages to Eliza R. Snow and Sarah Ann Whitney. Sarah Ann's sealing had several distinctive elements. Her parents gave their approval, and her father performed the ceremony, using words that Joseph received by revelation. Apparently to deflect suspicions arising from those nuptials, the Prophet asked the widowed Joseph Kingsbury to marry Sarah legally and to serve as a "pretended" husband.

Oliver Olney, whose wife was a sister to Marinda Johnson Hyde and Benjamin F. Johnson, kept a journal beginning on the day he was excommunicated for receiving spurious revelations. His diary entries do not represent the views of a Church insider, but they are instructive and sometimes entertaining.

Chapter 19

John C. Bennett Impacts Plural Marriage in 1842

Concerning a newcomer to Nauvoo, the controversial John C. Bennett, Todd Compton wrote: "In 1841 Smith cautiously added three wives. But in 1842 he married eleven wives in the first eight months of the year. New marriages then stopped for five months—a significant gap—perhaps caused by the John Bennett exposé."[1] Bennett published his first charges of impropriety against Joseph Smith in letters to the *Sangamo Journal* beginning in July of that year. The historical record shows that Bennett impacted Nauvoo plural marriage perhaps more than any other person besides Joseph Smith and that his influence continues to shape public opinion even today.[2]

John C. Bennett's Arrival in Nauvoo

John C. Bennett's first encounter with Mormonism came in 1832 as he was introduced to Joseph Smith and Sidney Rigdon in Kirtland, Ohio.[3] As the Latter-day Saints were building up Nauvoo in 1840, Bennett wrote several letters to the Prophet offering to help the Saints. Bennett, a licensed physician and a self-trained lawyer, had already established himself in Illinois with an appointment as Brigadier General of the "Invincible Light Dragoons." In response to the doctor's offer of assistance, Joseph Smith wrote, "Let all that will, come, and partake of the poverty of Nauvoo freely."[4]

Bennett arrived in Nauvoo in September of 1840 and boarded with the Smith family for the next thirty-nine weeks (or until the following May), for which he paid three dollars a week.[5] At that time, a power vacuum existed

---

1. Todd Compton, *In Sacred Loneliness: The Plural Wives of Joseph Smith*, 2.
2. It could be argued that William Law's rejection of polygamy was more important because his actions were the primary catalyst leading to the death of the Prophet.
3. Andrew F. Smith, *The Saintly Scoundrel: The Life and Times of Dr. John Cook Bennett*, 56.
4. Joseph Smith, Letter to John C. Bennett, August 8, 1840, in *History of the Church*, 4:178. See also Andrew F. Ehat and Lyndon W. Cook, eds., *The Words of Joseph Smith: The Contemporary Accounts of the Nauvoo Discourses of the Prophet Joseph Smith*, 416.
5. Joseph Smith's Red Brick Store Daybook, December 8, 1843, account #59; quoted in Richard and Pamela Price, *Joseph Smith Fought Polygamy*, 1:79.

John C. Bennett. Courtesy LDS Church History Library.

in the city as most of the Quorum of the Twelve were away on missions and Sidney Rigdon was ill. Bennett's apparent sincerity and charisma were appealing, and he quickly ingratiated himself with Joseph Smith. Less than a month after his arrival, he spoke at the general conference held October 3–5, 1840.

In late November, Bennett represented the Mormons at the Illinois State Capitol where he successfully lobbied for the passage of the Nauvoo Charter.[6] Thomas Ford, Illinois governor from 1842 to 1846, remembered: "Bennett managed matters well for his constituents. He flattered both sides with the hope of Mormon favor. . . . The vote was taken, the ayes and noes were not called for, no one opposed it, but all were busy and active in hurrying it through."[7] Joseph Smith III recalled, "Much of the good that was injected into the by-laws and ordinances of Nauvoo was partially due to his ability to direct civic affairs."[8] Bennett was rewarded for his efforts at the state capitol; on February 1, 1841, Nauvoo's residents elected him as the city's first mayor.

On January 19th, 1841, Joseph Smith dictated a revelation that contained potent if conditional promises for Bennett:

> Again, let my servant John C. Bennett help you in your labor in sending my word to the kings and people of the earth, and stand by you, even you my servant Joseph Smith, in the hour of affliction; and his reward shall not fail *if* he receive counsel.
>
> And for his love he shall be great, for he shall be mine *if* he do this, saith the Lord. I have seen the work which he hath done, which I accept

---

6. The Nauvoo Charter was similar to those granted to other Illinois cities by the state legislature. The difference was largely in how Nauvoo city leaders interpreted its powers. See James L. Kimball Jr., "The Nauvoo Charter: A Reinterpretation." However, Thomas Gregg wrote in 1880 that the charter seemed to have been "contrived to give the Mormons a system of government so far as possible independent of the rest of the state" by omitting a common provision "guarding against infringement of state or federal law." Thomas Gregg, *History of Hancock County, Illinois*, 274.

7. Thomas Ford, *History of Illinois from Its Commencement as a State in 1818 to 1847*, 182.

8. Mary Audentia Smith Anderson, ed., *The Memoirs of President Joseph Smith (1832–1914)*, 29. This section is reprinted from *Saint's Herald* 82 (January 8, 1935).

if he continue, and will crown him with blessings and great glory. (D&C 124:16–17; emphasis mine)

Authors sometimes imply that, despite Bennett's sincerity up to January 1841, the promises extended in this revelation far out-distanced his inherent goodness and worthiness.[9] However, the promises in the verses are conditional. The three sentences addressing John C. Bennett contain three "ifs" that identify the requirements needed to receive the blessings prophesied.[10] Furthermore, none of the surrounding verses that specifically mention five other men contain a single "if" clause: Robert B. Thompson (vv. 12–14), Hyrum Smith (v. 15), Lyman Wight (vv. 18–19), George Miller (vv. 20–21), and John Snider (v. 22). It is true that later in the revelation, "if" language is employed in addressing three additional individuals who are promised rewards contingent on continuous personal righteousness.[11] But like Bennett, those three men also apostatized: William Law (4 "ifs": vv. 82–90), Sidney Rigdon (4 "ifs": vv. 103–110), and Robert D. Foster (1 "if": vv. 115–116).[12] A review of the entire revelation confirms that the verses containing provisional blessings couched in "if" language—language that demanded persistent compliance—seemed to be prophetic of future noncompliance.

Bennett's Pre-Nauvoo Adulterous Behavior

Despite Bennett's multiple talents and charisma, his pre-Nauvoo behavior revealed moral weakness. Historian Linda King Newell comments: "There is no evidence that Bennett was hampered by either theological or ethical

---

9. See, for example, Gary James Bergera, "John C. Bennett, Joseph Smith, and the Beginnings of Mormon Plural Marriage in Nauvoo," 57–58; Richard S. Van Wagoner, *Sidney Rigdon: A Portrait of Religious Excess*, 281.

10. Bennett's patriarchal blessing given September 21, 1840, by Hyrum Smith also contains four "if" clauses. One "if" statement instructs that "if" Bennett "shouldst step aside from the path of rectitude at any time because of temptation," he would "return to the path from whence thou [Bennett] hast strayed," which apparently did not occur. The other three "ifs" describe conditional blessings. Quoted in John C. Bennett, *The History of the Saints, or an Exposé of Joe Smith and Mormonism*, 42–44.

11. Doctrine and Covenants 124 contains thirty-three "ifs," several of which were addressed to men (Vinson Knight, Amos Davies, George Miller, Lyman Wight, John Snider, and Peter Haws) admonishing them to invest in Nauvoo House stock (vv. 70–71, 74, 111–12) but the wording included no specifications of worthiness.

12. Law and Foster were excommunicated April 18, 1844. Rigdon was excommunicated after Joseph's death. However, he and Joseph Smith endured several conflicts in Nauvoo. One was generated by a letter Bennett wrote to Rigdon on January 10, 1843; Rigdon failed to immediately turn the letter over to the Prophet. See Chapter 21 and *History of the Church*, 5:250–51.

considerations."[13] Within months of Bennett's arrival in Nauvoo, Joseph Smith heard rumors of his tainted past.

By mid-February 1841, the Prophet sent George Miller to McConnelsville, Ohio, one of Bennett's former residences, to investigate.[14] Four weeks later, Miller reported back that Bennett, who had been passing himself off as a bachelor, was already married and that "his poor, but confiding wife, followed him from place to place, with no suspicion of his unfaithfulness to her; at length however, he became so bold in his departures, that it was evident to all around that he was a sore offender, and his wife left him under satisfactory evidence of his adulterous connections; nor was this his only fault; he used her bad otherwise."[15] At one point in their marriage, when Bennett was accused of adultery and breaking up another wedded couple, his wife reportedly "declared that if he succeeded in separating the pair . . . that it would be the seventh family that he had parted during their union."[16] According to Gary Bergera: "Depending on the source, either Bennett left/abandoned Mary [his wife] when she refused to accompany him to Illinois [in 1838] or Mary left him because of his infidelities and/or abuse of her."[17]

Governor Thomas Ford reminisced in 1854: "This Bennett was probably the greatest scamp in the Western country. I have made particular enquiries concerning him, and have traced him in several places in which he had lived, before he joined the Mormons, in Ohio, Indiana, and Illinois, and he was everywhere accounted the same debauched, unprincipled, and profligate character."[18]

Bennett's Immorality in Nauvoo

Once established in the city, Bennett's pre-Nauvoo adulterous behavior resumed. In a late recollection, Lyman O. Littlefield recalled one of Bennett's earliest attempted immoralities in Nauvoo:

> During the winter when a lyceum was in progress [early 1841[19]] in the upper room of Joseph's store, this same [John C.] Bennett became enamored

---

13. Linda King Newell, "Emma Hale Smith and the Polygamy Question." 13 note 18.
14. Andrew C. Skinner, "John C. Bennett: For Prophet or Profit?" 256–63.
15. Joseph Smith, "To the Church of Jesus Christ of Latter Day Saints, and to All the Honorable Part of Community," 839–40.
16. Mary Barker Bennett quoted in John Carter, Letter to Lyman Wight, September 1, 1842, *The Wasp*, 1, no. 24 (October 1, 1842): 1.
17. Bergera, "John C. Bennett, Joseph Smith, and the Beginnings of Mormon Plural Marriage," 53 note 5.
18. Ford, *History of Illinois*, 182.
19. Andrew F. Ehat and Lyndon W. Cook reported that the first Lyceum meeting was on January 5, 1841, and that it met thereafter for several months. Ehat and Cook, *The Words of Joseph Smith*, 82 note 1.

of a lady of good repute and comely mien. The lyceum sessions were held regular each Wednesday evening. The husband of this lady was a member of that institution and a regular attendant of the same. The doctor selected these particular evenings as being propitious for the success of his wicked design and commenced to make calls upon her at such hours. Notwithstanding he was well skilled in the etiquette that belongs to social life and knew how to ape refinement when he chose, yet upon these occasions he was grossly rude and impulsive in his advances. The lady, from the beginning, knowing his influence at that time, dreaded to offend him and tried to argue and reason with him against his unjustifiable course. She also dreaded the consequences in case she informed her husband of the facts. She took this course during two of his visits, but finding her efforts ineffectual, she resolved to detain her husband at home when the next evening for the lyceum should arrive. Her pleadings grew so earnest that she became successful, her husband not suspecting the real cause. He was somewhat surprised, of course, when the great Doctor Bennett called at his humble abode.[20]

Similarly, in 1842 Joseph Smith wrote in scathing terms of Bennett's behavior the previous year, with a different woman:

> He [John C. Bennett] had not been long in Nauvoo before he began to keep company with a young lady, one of our citizens; and she being ignorant of his having a wife living, gave way to his addresses, and became confident, from his behavior towards her, that he intended to marry her; and this he gave her to understand he would do. I, seeing the folly of such an acquaintance, persuaded him to desist; and, on account of his continuing his course, finally threatened to expose him if he did not desist. This, to outward appearance, had the desired effect, and the acquaintance between them was broken off.
>
> But, like one of the most abominable and depraved beings which could possibly exist, he only broke off his publicly wicked actions, to sink deeper into iniquity and hypocrisy.... He accomplished his wicked purposes; he seduced an innocent female by his lying, and subjected her character to public disgrace, should it ever be known."[21]

---

20. Lyman Omer Littlefield, *Reminiscences of Latter-day Saints: Giving an Account of Much Individual Suffering Endured for Religious Conscience*, 158. The time frame Littlefield recalls corroborates that Bennett began his improper advances soon after arriving in Nauvoo. Elements of the story are too ambiguous to allow the woman described to be identified. If Littlefield was referring to Sarah Pratt, whose husband, Orson, did not return from his mission until July 1841, then the episode would have been later that same year.

21. Joseph Smith, "To the Church of Jesus Christ of Latter Day Saints, and to All the Honorable Part of Community," 839–40.

The identity of the dishonored lady is not known.[22] However, it is possible that Vilate Kimball, wife of Heber C. Kimball, was aware of the incident. On March 2, 1841, Joseph Smith wrote her:

> I can in some measure enter into your feelings respecting the occurrence which has lately taken place in the church which is indeed painful to every lover of Truth and Holiness, and probably to none more so than myself. I am indeed sorry that any thing should have caused such a stir in the Church, and bro't disgrance [sic] upon persons who are otherwise respectable. The course I have taken in the matter was such as I felt warranted to take from the testimony which was adduced. Whether they were guilty of crime or not I do not say, but this I must say that their imprudence was carried to an unwarranted extent.
>
> I do not desire that you should turn the young woman out of doors, far be it from me to advise any such course I think it would be well for her to remain with you at least until Bro Kimball comes home, because I think that your advise [sic], may be a blessing to *her*, and your council and advise such as will tend to her future welfare and happiness. I have no doubt but you will act in wisdom in this matter I remain yours in the Gospel.[23]

This letter does not mention Bennett specifically, and it may refer to another episode; however, the alignment of the chronology is suggestive.[24] Joseph noted: "The course I have taken in the matter was such as I felt warranted to take." Even if Bennett was not the culprit, the letter demonstrates the Prophet's willingness to show mercy by not revealing the guilty party's transgression to Vilate and maintaining strict public silence concerning the incident. Reportedly, he used this same approach months later with Bennett's specific sexual misdeeds, a decision he came to deeply regret.

---

22. By quoting the writings of Wilhelm Wyl, RLDS conservatives Richard and Pamela Price theorize that Eliza R. Snow was the seduced woman and that she become pregnant in Nauvoo. Price and Price, *Joseph Smith Fought Polygamy*, 1:77, 84–87; W. Wyl, *Mormon Portraits*, 186–87. They provide no evidence to support this hypothesis and, in fact, existing evidence contradicts it. The account refers to a "young woman," and Eliza Snow was older than Bennett by several months, being thirty-seven at the time. In addition, Eliza's known strong character makes it implausible that she would have been beguiled by Bennett's flattery. Also, there is no evidence Eliza was ever pregnant. (See Chapter 26.)

23. Joseph Smith, Letter to Vilate Kimball, March 2, 1841; emphasis his.

24. Littlefield's account *Reminiscences of Latter-day Saints*, 157–59, discussed in the text, may have referred to the same incident referenced in the letter. Littlefield mentioned John C. Bennett's illicit involvement with a woman during the time of the Nauvoo Lyceum, which began meeting regularly on January 5, 1841, and continued for several months. Ehat and Cook, *The Words of Joseph Smith*, 82 note 1. An alternate interpretation is that Francis Higbee was the actual perpetrator. See also Joseph Smith's testimony in "Municipal Court," *Times and Seasons* 5 (May 15, 1844): 538–40.

Despite this reported undercurrent of licentiousness, Bennett's public stature continued to expand; and on April 8, 1841, he was presented to the conference as an "assistant president, until Pres't. Rigdon's health should be restored."[25] (Rigdon's health improved two months later.[26]) Bennett's surprising advancement can be read in two different ways. Perhaps Bennett's improprieties were less severe or he had promised to reform. More likely, the Prophet recognized certain abilities in Bennett that he saw as beneficial to the Church, so he gave him an office and a variety of essentially non-ecclesiastical duties to perform.

In addition, Bennett's calling as "Assistant President" did not make him part of the formal "First Presidency," which is comprised of "three Presiding High Priests" (D&C 107:22, see also 124:91, 103). However, it did allow him to assist members of the First Presidency if needed. Sidney Rigdon was restored as "prophet, seer, and revelator" by Joseph Smith on June 1, diminishing Bennett's role, whatever it might have been.[27] Historical documents indicate Bennett continued to be respected as a Church leader at public events in the months after Rigdon's restoration, including speaking in the April 1841 and April 1842 conferences. His topics generally included non-religious subjects like medicine, the military, or politics.

Alexander Neibaur recorded on Sunday, April 25: "Showery forenoon; went to the preaching in the open air, a fine spot of land near the temple—a platform for the speakers, seats prepared for the congregation. Br. [John C.] Bennett spoke first in respect to his profession [as a medical doctor], all character [sic] being injured by some of those who professed to be Saints. . . . Elder Joseph [Smith] the Prophet followed in very strong language determined to put down all iniquity."[28]

By July 1841, Joseph Smith's concerns about Bennett were intensified. The Prophet later related:

> Sometime about the early part of July 1841, I received a letter from Elder H[yrum]. Smith and Wm. Law, who were then at Pittsburgh, Penn. This letter was dated June 15th, and contained the particulars of a conversation betwixt them and a respectable gentleman from the neighborhood where Bennett's wife and children resided. He stated to them that it was a

---

25. "Minutes," *Times and Seasons* 2 (April 15, 1841): 387.

26. Untitled notice beginning: "We have to announce that Sidney Rigdon has been ordained a Prophet, Seer, and Revelator," *Times and Seasons* 2 (June 1, 1841): 431; *History of the Church*, 4:364.

27. Untitled notice beginning "We have to announce . . . ," 431; see also *History of the Church*, 4:364.

28. Alexander Neibaur, "Story [Autobiography] of Alexander Neibaur, Lancashire, Old England," 12.

fact that Bennett had a wife and children living, and that she had left him because of his ill treatment towards her. This letter was read to Bennett, which he did not attempt to deny; but candidly acknowledged the fact.[29]

The Prophet immediately reprimanded Bennett. L. D. Wasson, Emma Smith's nephew wrote to Joseph in 1842: "I was reading in your chamber last summer [1841]—yourself and Bennett came into the lower room, and I heard you give J.C. Bennett a tremendous flagellation for practicing iniquity under the base pretence of authority from the heads of the Church—If you recollect I came down just before you were through talking."[30] Rather than change his ways, Bennett responded melodramatically:

> Soon after this information reached our ears [summer 1841], Dr. Bennett made an attempt at suicide, by taking poison; but he being discovered before it had taken effect, and the proper antidotes being administered, he again recovered; but he very much resisted when an attempt was made to save him. The public impression was, that he was so much ashamed of his base and wicked conduct, that he had recourse to the above deed to escape the censures of an indignant community.[31]

Evidently Joseph Smith chose patience and mercy, leaving Church members largely unaware of both Bennett's treachery and his verbal pledges to change his ways. Throughout 1841, Bennett continued to rise in Nauvoo's social ranks but without performing any significant religious duties. Soon he served as a physician to many of its residents, secretary to the Nauvoo Masonic Lodge, Master in Chancery of Hancock County, Major General of the Nauvoo Legion, and Chancellor of the University of the City of Nauvoo (yet to be built). His biographer, Andrew F. Smith, wrote: "While in Nauvoo, Bennett had succeeded beyond his own wildest expectations," but he had mainly reached his apogee by the end of 1841.[32]

Despite the Prophet's severe castigation in the summer, Bennett's inappropriate behavior did not abate. His tactics were, however, modified in the autumn of 1841 due to a discourse delivered by the Prophet on Sunday, November 7. As Wilford Woodruff recorded: "Br Joseph then delivered unto us an Edifying address showing us what temperance faith virtue, charity & truth was he also said *if we did not accuse one another God would not accuse us & if we had no accuser we should enter heaven* he would take us there as his backload if we would not accuse

---

29. Joseph Smith, "To the Church of Jesus Christ of Latter-day Saints, and to All Honorable Part of [sic] Community," 840; *History of the Church*, 5:36–37.

30. Lorenzo D. Wasson, Letter to Joseph and Emma Smith, July 30, 1842.

31. "To the Church of Jesus Christ of Latter-day Saints, and to All Honorable Part of Community," 840; *History of the Church*, 5:36–37.

32. Andrew Smith, *The Saintly Scoundrel*, 78.

him he would not accuse us & if we would throw a cloak of charity over his sins he would over ours for Charity coverd a multitude of sins."[33]

Subsequently, Bennett implemented his own version of Joseph's instructions in continued seductions.[34] Catherine Fuller Warren, a young single woman who was seduced by Bennett's follower, Chauncey Higbee, later affirmed that "Chauncy Higbee taught the same doctrine as was taught by J. C. Bennett."[35] Margaret Jane Nyman, who would marry Steward M. Agan on August 17 the following year,[36] but was unmarried prior to that wedding, also testified that Chauncey approached her saying: "Any respectable female might indulge in sexual intercourse, and there was no sin in it, provided the person so indulging keep the same to herself; for there could be no sin where there was no accuser."[37] The fact that Bennett chose to exploit and distort a public teaching of the Prophet to beguile women raises questions concerning his actual knowledge of Joseph Smith's private teachings concerning eternal and plural marriage.

Bennett's House of Ill Fame

Apparently unbeknownst to many Nauvooans, John C. Bennett had close ties to a particular house of ill repute located on the hill behind the temple. Church member John Taylor (not the apostle), who was ordained a teacher in the Aaronic Priesthood in 1832, reported that part of his duties were to "look after the members of the ward to see that no evil speaking or back, biting, or no iniquity was practiced."[38] Consequently, his (unnamed) teachers' quorum president told him that because of rumors of "Bennetts secret wife system," he was commissioned "to search it out" and report back to the president who

---

33. Ehat and Cook, *The Words of Joseph Smith*, 80. See also *History of the Church*, 4:445; emphasis mine; Scott G. Kenney, ed., *Wilford Woodruff's Journal, 1833–1898*, 2:136.

34. In a singular unverified statement, Sarah Pratt alleged that Joseph Smith told her "God does not care if we have a good time, if only other people do not know it." Quoted in Wyl, *Mormon Portraits*, 62. I have concluded from the evidence available that Sarah and Bennett were sexually involved and that both later lied to conceal their relationship.

35. Catherine Fuller Warren, Statement to the Nauvoo High Council, May 25, 1842 see also John S. Dinger, ed., *The Nauvoo City and High Council Minutes*, 417 note 46.

36. Marriage performed by Thomas Grover. Lyndon W. Cook, comp., *Nauvoo Deaths and Marriages, 1839–1845*, 106. Neither Steward or Margaret attended the Nauvoo Temple in 1845–46.

37. "Testimony of Margaret J. Nyman v. Chauncey L. Higbee, before the High Council of the Church of Jesus Christ of Latter-day Saints, in the City of Nauvoo, May 21, 1842," 657.

38. John Taylor, Deposition, Temple Lot Transcript, Complainant's Testimony, Part 2, pp. 396–97, questions 56–60.

would then report to Hyrum Smith, associate president of the Church.[39] In 1892 he recalled:

> I followed him [John C. Bennett] to that house there in Nauvoo where it was said that this thing,—this secret wife system was practiced, and saw him go into it, but he was pretty cunning and never would go to the house, or enter it until it was dark. He used to go there with the saddle bags on his arm. He had a white linen coat and white pants, and he was said to be a doctor, and he was going around treating people . . .
>
> He said he was a doctor and would go around treating people for one thing and another, and he would go into these houses where the women were, and those women that were in them were suspicious women that did not bear good characters. . . .
>
> Well, I heard about this and that he visited these houses, and so I went around to watch him and see if I could catch him going there and so I got into a crab apple patch . . . as I wanted to see all that was going on. I saw him coming and I watched him, and just before he got to the house, he would look this way and that way and the other way, and the women that were there was watching him, I thought to see what he was doing, but he did not see me and I watched him until I saw him step right into the house.[40]

The Nauvoo City Council on October 23, 1841, discussed the brothel on the hill behind the temple site and ordered this "house on the hill" to be "removed."[41] Mayor Bennett opposed the action.[42] This same John Taylor recounted its razing:

> John C. Bennett . . . built an ill famed house there near the temple, and there was a meeting ground in the oak grove nearby there, and they put up an ill fame house right by there, and after they had put it up, John C. Bennett and the Fosters . . . wrote on it in large letters what it was for,—an ill fame house, and the sign that they put on it proclaimed what it was, and what it was there for, but I don't remember just what the inscription or sign was that they put on it. . . .
>
> Well when we went to meeting we could not get there,—that is, we couldn't get to meeting without passing this house there looking right at it, for it was close to the meeting grounds, and a thousand or two thousand would go there to meeting on a sabbath day, and they didn't feel very good seeing that house there with these great big capital letters right there facing them when they would look at it. Well that house was built right there close

---

39. Ibid., questions 60–63.
40. Ibid., p. 397, questions 64–67.
41. Nauvoo City Council, Minutes, October 23, 1841.
42. Robert D. Foster, Letter to the editor, September 27, 1842, *The Wasp* 1, no. 26 (October 15, 1842): 3, col. 4.

there to the temple and the meeting ground, for it was right on the same street but a little north of the temple . . . .

Well the city council held a counsel over it, and they considered it was a nuisance to the city, and they so declared it to be a nuisance. They considered that house was a nuisance, and the authorities passed an ordinance against it, and notified them to move the nuisance outside of the city limits, and gave them time sufficient to do so. Well they paid no attention to that order for they did not feel inclined to obey it and they did not move it.

They had some furniture in it,—not much,—and the police gathered around and one of the policemen went to go in to move some of the furniture, or some things that were in it out, and John Eagle,—a man by the name of Eagle,—a tall raw boned stout man that weighed over two hundred pounds,—they called him "Bully,["] and he was a bully to look at him,—he hit the policeman and knocked him down, and Joseph Smith took him by here (indicating the seat of his breeches and the nape of his neck),—he took him by the breeches there and here, and he pitched him right out, and [said] "that is the way we do, away down east" said Joseph, and that settled it.

Well they went in then and took the building and put it on rollers, and there was a deep gully there and they pitched the house in it,—they just rolled the house off and tipped it over in this gully shingles and all,—down it all went into that gulley, and that was the end of that transaction. That was the end of that bad house.[43]

The *Times and Seasons* gave this report apparently regarding the destruction of the same building:

It is known to many of our patrons, that a certain young man very injudiciously, and contrary to the remonstrancies [sic] of his friends, and in violation of the ordinances of this city, not long since erected a small building, near the Temple square, avowedly for the purpose of transacting the business of a Grocer. Said building was for a short time occupied for that purpose; but so heavy did the frown of public disapprobation rest upon it, that it was finally vacated, and stood some time, a lonely wreck of folly. In the mean time, the very sanctimonious and extremely unfortunate Mr. Kilbourn of Montrose, threw out to the public, ungentlemanly and slanderous imputations concerning the matter, saying that the Presidency of the church abetted and approbated the concern, &c., and the building having become a monument for every fool to write upon and exhibit his folly, to the annoyance of the citizens, the City Council very judiciously ordered the building removed as a neusance [sic.]. Some opposition to the execution of this order was exhibited, and the authorities manifest a determination to carry out strictly the temperence ordinances of the city, and in this we wish them "God speed."[44]

---

43. Taylor, Deposition, pp. 403–4, question 140.
44. "The Neusance" [sic], *Times and Seasons* 3 (November 15, 1841): 599–600.

Apparently other brothels could be found in the city, and these houses were dealt with later. On May 14, 1842, Joseph recorded: "City council. Advocated strongly the necessity of some active measures being taken to suppress houses & acts of infamy in the city; for the protection of the innocent & virtuous—& good of public morals. Shewing clearly that there were certain characters in the place who were disposed to corrupt the morals & chastity of our citizens & that houses of infamy did exist. Upon which a city or[d]inance was passed to prohibit such things."[45]

Bennett's Excommunication

Bennett's lasciviousness resurfaced early in 1842 but Joseph was still reticent to expose him. Concerning forgiveness, Joseph Smith taught the Relief Society in April 1842: "The sympathies of the heads of the Church have induced them to bear a long time with those who were corrupt until they are obliged to cut them off."[46] His April 29 diary entry records: "[It] was made manifest[,] a conspiracy against the peace of his househould."[47] "J.C.B." is written lightly in the margin by scribe Willard Richards. Precisely what transpired is unknown, but Bennett and/or his followers may have visited Emma, accusing Joseph of "spiritual wifery" to foment her mistrust of her husband. Joseph would have resolutely denied such a charge since he did not consider celestial marriage to be spiritual wifery.

While the Prophet's patience was undoubtedly wearing thin, he still admonished forbearance and forgiveness. The following month he counseled the Relief Society: "[They] are fellow mortals, we loved them once, shall we not encourage them to reformation? We have not yet forgiven them seventy times seven, as our Savior directed; perhaps we have not forgiven them once. There is now a day of salvation to such as repent and reform;—and they who repent not should be cast out from this society; yet we should woo them to return to God, lest they escape not the damnation of hell!"[48]

Ultimately, Joseph Smith regretted the way that he handled John C. Bennett's immoral behavior: "The only sin I ever committed was in exercising sympathy and covering up their [John C. Bennett and others] iniquities, on their solemn promise to reform, and of this I am ashamed, and will never do

---

45. Dean C. Jessee, ed., *The Papers of Joseph Smith: Volume 2, Journal, 1832–1842*, 382; see also *History of the Church*, 5:8.

46. Ehat and Cook, *The Words of Joseph Smith*, 117.

47. Jessee, *Journal, 1832–1842*, 379; Andrew H. Hedges, Alex D. Smith, and Richard Lloyd Anderson, eds., *Journals, Volume 2: December 1841–April 1843*, 53 note 196.

48. Relief Society Minutes, May 26, 1842, 51–52, in Turley, *Selected Collections*, Vol. 1, DVD #19; see also *History of the Church*, 5:18–19.

so again."⁴⁹ William Law wrote: "Joseph thought he was using him [Bennett], and he was using Joseph."⁵⁰ Contrastingly, Law also recalled: "Bennett was a tool of Joseph for a time, but for some cause which I never knew, Joseph cast him off."⁵¹ Law's ignorance regarding Joseph's alienation from Bennett further substantiates that, although both were counselors to Joseph Smith or to the First Presidency, their dealings together were limited.

In 1854, Apostle John Taylor (not the John Taylor quoted above) spoke at the tenth anniversary of the martyrdom:

> About this time John C Bennett commenced some of his operations. He made use of some of those principles to corrupt to destroy not only himself but others. And as it was impossible ~~almost~~ together to come out and teach correct principles before the public in those days, some of those men got an inkling of these things and corrupted themselves—were full of <lasciviousness> and abomination, and corrupted their own bodies—and sought to destroy others. And they succeeded in great measure with many. I could name the names of many: John C Bennett, the two Higbees, and some others I could name [but] do not feel disposed [to do so]. But they had to be handled and brought before the high council and the council had to sit with closed doors because of the corruptions there manifested. It was pretty generally known the course that was pursued. Joseph wished an ~~ordinances~~ ordinance to be introduced there upon adulterous practices. This militated so much against John C. Bennett, he began to go away from that time and to be Joseph's enemy. ~~and~~ He then began to publish and circulate [his letters].⁵²

By late spring of 1842, it was obvious that John C. Bennett was not going to abandon his immoral behavior. Hyrum Smith reported that, when confronted in early May, Bennett "said he had seduced six or seven" women in the city "and said if he was forgiven, he would not be guilty any more."⁵³ The exact sequence of the events surrounding his excommunication is not entirely clear. Joseph Smith and other Church leaders apparently withdrew fellowship from Bennett on May 11, 1842, although I have not been able to locate any

---

49. Manuscript History of the Church, May 8, 1844, in Turley, *Selected Collections*, Vol. 1, DVD #1; see also *History of the Church*, 6:360.

50. William Law, Letter to Dr. W. Wyl, January 7, 1887, quoted in "The Mormons in Nauvoo: Three Letters from William Law on Mormonism, *[Salt Lake] Daily Tribune*, July 3, 1887.

51. William Law, Letter to T. B. H. Stenhouse, November 24, 1871, quoted in T. B. H. Stenhouse, *Rocky Mountain Saints*, 198.

52. LaJean Purcell Carruth, transcriber, "John Taylor's June 27, 1844 Account of the Martyrdom," 43–44.

53. Hyrum Smith's comment at the trial of Francis Higbee, May 6, 1844, quoted in "Municipal Court," *Times and Seasons* 5 (May 15, 1844): 540.

minutes from that meeting and it is not mentioned in Joseph Smith's journal.[54] The notice of excommunication, dated May 11, was published in the June 15 issue of the *Times and Seasons*.[55] Regardless, Bennett's comments as recorded in Joseph's journal on May 19 indicate that, by that date, the Doctor knew he was not in full fellowship. The May 26 entry acknowledges that, previous to that date, Bennett had been excommunicated: "Dr. Bennett was notified the day previous that the first Presidency, Twelve & Bishops had withdrawn fellowship from him."[56]

The precise sequence may not be overly important because it is a matter of record that, on May 17, Bennett signed a public affidavit exonerating Joseph Smith of sexual misbehavior:

> Personally appeared before me, Daniel H. Wells, an Alderman of said city of Nauvoo, John C. Bennett, who being duly sworn according to law, deposeth and saith: that he never was taught any thing in the least contrary to the strictest principles of the Gospel, or of virtue, or of the laws of God, or man, under any circumstances, or upon any occasion either directly or indirectly, in word or deed, by Joseph Smith; and that he never knew the said Smith to countenance any improper conduct whatever, either in public or private; and that he never did teach to me in private that an illegal illicit intercourse with females was, under any circumstances, justifiable, and that I never knew him so to teach others.[57]

Hyrum Smith provided additional details:

> On the seventeenth day of May, 1842 . . . He [John C. Bennett] reached out his hand to Br. Joseph and said, will you forgive me, weeping at the time; he said Br. Joseph, I am guilty, I acknowledge it, and I beg of you not to expose me, for it will ruin me; Joseph replied, Doctor! why are you using my name to carry on your hellish wickedness? Have I ever taught you that fornication and adultery was right, or polygamy or any such practices? He said you never did. Did I ever teach you any thing that was not virtuous—that was iniquitous, either in public or private? He said you never did.

---

54. Hedges, Smith, and Anderson, *Journals, Vol. 2*, 55; see also 63 note 249. It is also absent from Wilford Woodruff's journal. See Scott G. Kenney, ed., *Wilford Woodruff's Journal*, 2:175.

55. "Notice," *Times and Seasons*, 3 (June 15, 1842) 16: 830. It is signed by the First Presidency of Joseph Smith, Hyrum Smith, and William Law, along with nine of the apostles: Brigham Young, Heber C. Kimball, Lyman Wight, William Smith, John E. Page, John Taylor, Wilford Woodruff, George A. Smith, and Willard Richards. Also adding their signatures are Church bishops Newel K. Whitney, Vinson Knight, and George Miller.

56. Hedges, Smith, and Anderson, *Journals, Volume 2*, 63.

57. "To the Church of Jesus Christ of Latter Day Saints, and to All the Honorable Part of Community," 840–41.

Did you ever know anything unvirtuous or unrighteous in my conduct or actions at any time, either in public or in private? he said, I did not.[58]

Two days later on May 19, Bennett resigned as mayor and Joseph Smith, the vice-mayor, was immediately elected mayor by the Nauvoo City Council.[59] The Prophet's diary for that date states:

> Dr John C. Bennet, Ex mayor, was then called upon by the mayor [newly elected Joseph Smith] to state if he knew ought against him,—when Dr. Bennet replied "I know what I am about. & the heads of the church know what they are about. I expect: I have no difficulty with the heads of the church. I publicly avow that any one who has said that I have stated that General Joseph Smith has given me authority to hold illicit intercourse with women is a Liar in the face of God. Those who have said it are damned Liars: They are infernal Liars. He never \either/ in public or private gave me any such authority or license, & any person who states it is a scoundrel & a Liar. . . . I have no difficulty with the heads of the church & intend to continue with you. & hope the time may come when I may be re[s]tored to full confidence. & fellowship. & my former standing in the church, & that my conduct may be such as to warrant my restoration.—& should the time ever come that I may have the opportunity to test my faith it will then be known whether I am a traitor or a true man.[60]

Despite Bennett's feigned contrition, a month later, almost to the day, on June 18, Joseph Smith publicly spoke out against him. Wilford Woodruff reported: "The Citizens of Nauvoo Both Male & female assembled near the Temple for a general meeting many thousands were assembled Joseph the seer arose & spoke upon several subjects Among other subjects he spoke his mind in great plainness concerning the iniquity & wickedness of Gen John Cook Bennet, & exposed him before the public ."[61] In response, Bennett left Nauvoo three days afterwards. A week later on June 27, Bennett wrote to the *Sangamo Journal*, claiming that his affidavit and confessions had been forced from him by threats: "My affidavit as taken before Esq. Wells, and my statements before the City Council, in relation to the holy Joe, were made under DURESSE—my life was threatened unless I submitted to the requisitions of Joe. . . . I could have been murdered and no person would have been the wiser."[62] In response, affidavits from several of the participants were pub-

---

58. "Affidavit of Hyrum Smith," *Times and Seasons* 3 (August 1, 1842): 870–71.

59. Hedges, Smith, and Anderson, *Journals, Vol. 2*, May 19, 1842, 58; John S. Dinger, ed., *The Nauvoo City and High Council Minutes*, 85.

60. Jessee, *Journal, 1832–1842*, 384–85. See also published version: "To the Church of Jesus Christ of Latter Day Saints, and to All the Honorable Part of Community," 841.

61. Ehat and Cook, *The Words of Joseph Smith*, 124–25.

62. John C. Bennett, "For the Sangamo Journal, June 27, 1842," *Sangamo Journal*, July 8, 1842.

lished in an extra of *The Wasp* contradicting Bennett's claims of duress. Hyrum Smith affirmed that, at the time Bennett wrote his confession: "I know he was not under duress at the time for his testimony was given free and voluntarily. . . . I was present with him, and there was no threats used, nor harshness, every thing was as pacific as could be under existing circumstances."[63] William Clayton similarly attested: "Bennett made the affidavit of his own free will, and that no influence whatever from any person was used over said Bennett at the time."[64]

The Prophet immediately attempted damage control at home. A week after Bennett's renunciation, on July 4, 1842, Charles Edward Pancoast went to Nauvoo from St. Louis with two boatloads of excursionists. He and about 200 other Missourians listened to Joseph Smith make a speech at the Independence Day celebration.

> I well remember one of his arguments he [Joseph Smith] intended to confound us with. He said we had accused him of being untrue to his dear wife Eliza [sic], of having a plurality of wives, and of being too familiar with his sisters in the Church. "Now," he said, "All of my female flock are here present and I call upon all or any of them to answer: Is there any truth in those charges? I pause for a reply." And after pausing for a minute and no female deigning to get up and accuse him, he answered himself: "No, not one! There is the answer."[65]

Bennett's Letters to the *Sangamo Journal*

Had John C. Bennett quietly departed from Nauvoo, leaving the flurry of accusations to fade over the passage of time, the remainder of Joseph Smith's life might have been dramatically altered. However, the prideful Bennett was unwilling to endure such public humiliation and instead looked for revenge. In addition, he was intelligent and gifted in many areas, with established ties to publishers and politicians in the East and West. Months later he penned: "He [Joseph Smith] has awakened the wrong passenger . . . and must suffer."[66] John C. Bennett commanded a formidable armada of personal resources and was willing to employ them in combating his new enemy: Joseph Smith.[67]

---

63. *Affidavits and Certificates, Disproving the Statements and Affidavits Contained in John C. Bennett's Letters.*

64. Ibid.

65. Charles Edward Pancoast, *A Quaker Forty-Niner: The Adventures of Charles Edward Pancoast on the American Frontier*, 52.

66. John C. Bennett, Letter to Sidney Rigdon and Orson Pratt, January 10, 1842 [sic; should be 1843].

67. Fawn M. Brodie, *No Man Knows My History: The Life of Joseph Smith, the Mormon Prophet*, 317 note.

His first onslaught consisted of six letters to the *Sangamo Journal* in Springfield, Illinois, penned between July 8 and August 19. His first letter made multiple defamatory claims about Joseph Smith's morality: "Joseph Smith, the great Mormon seducer, one who has seduced not only hundreds of single and married females, but more than the great Solomon... the PROPHET'S SECRET WIVES. Hundreds of cases can be instanced."[68] As mentioned in Chapter 14, he also named several individuals, inviting them to assist him. "[I] call upon Nancy Rigdon . . . Miss Martha Brotherton . . . [and] Miss Mitchell"[69] to assist him.[70] The editor of the *Sangamo Journal*, Simeon Francis, expanded Bennett's request the following week in an editorial note accompanying Bennett's second letter, published July 15:

> A sense of duty to the community in which we live, impels us to call upon Messrs, ORSON PRATT, SIDNEY RIGDON, GEORGE W. ROBINSON, WILLIAM MARKS, and FRANCIS M. HIGBEE, not to disappoint public expectation at this eventful crisis, but to come out like honest and pure men, and expose the corruptions of the imposter. . . . With the same purpose we would also implore Messrs. CHAUNCY L. HIGBEE, HENREY MARKS, MRS. SARAH M. PRATT, MISS NANCY RIGDON, and MISS MITCHELL, all of Nauvoo, and Rev. SAMUEL JAMES, and Capt. JOHN F. OLNEY, of La Harpe; and the Messrs. KILBOURNS of Montrose, Iowa; to come out with published statements.[71]

In Bennett's July 2 letter (published July 15), he described his own version of several damaging stories involving Sarah Pratt and Nancy Rigdon that had occurred months before.[72] He also included an affidavit from Melissa Schindle:

> In the fall of 1841, she was staying one night with the widow [Catherine] Fuller, who has recently been married to a Mr. Warren, in the city of Nauvoo, and that Joseph Smith came into the room where she was

---

68. Bennett, "For the Sangamo Journal, June 27, 1842."

69. Pamela Mitchell Michael, who lived with Orson and Marinda Hyde in 1842, signed an affidavit, July 25, stating: "Inasmuch as J. C. Bennett has referred the people to me for testimony against Pres. Joseph, Smith, I take this opportunity to state before the public that I know nothing derogatory to his character, either as a christian, [sic] or a moral man. Mr. Bennett made use of my name without my knowledge or consent." Pamela M. Michael, "Certificate of Miss Pamela M. Michael," *Times and Seasons* 3, no. 19 (August 1, 1842): 874–75.

70. Bennett, "For the Sangamo Journal, June 27, 1842"; "Bennett's Second and Third Letters," *Sangamo Journal*, July 15, 1842.

71. Ibid. Typographical variations in original.

72. Bennett portrays himself as protecting Nancy from being "ensnared by the *Cyprian Saints* . . . taken in the net of the *chambered Sisters of Charity*... [and avoiding] the poisoned arrows of the *Consecratees of the Cloister*." Bennett, *The History of the Saints*, 241. Bennett's description of polygamy in Nauvoo is unsupported by any other source and is contradicted by all other available evidence, suggesting that he was fictionalizing his assertions.

sleeping about 10 o'clock at night, and after making a few remarks came to her bedside, and asked her if he could have the privilege of sleeping with her. She immediately replied no. He, on the receipt of the above answer told her it was the will of the Lord that he should have illicit intercourse with her, and that he never proceeded to do any thing of that kind with any woman without first having the will of the Lord on the subject; and further he told her that if she would consent to let him have such intercourse with her, she could make his house her home as long as she wished to do so, and that she should never want for anything it was in his power to assist her to but she would not consent to it. He then told her that if she would let him sleep with her that night he would give her five dollars but she refused all his propositions. He then told her that she must never tell of his propositions to her, for he had ALL influence in that place, and if she told he would ruin her character, and she would be under the necessity of leaving. He then went to an adjoining bed where the Widow [Fuller] was sleeping got into bed with her and laid there until about 1 o'clock, when he got up, bid them good night, and left them, and further this deponent saith not.

MELISSA (her X mark) SCHINDLE.[73]

Schindle's signing an "X" indicates her illiteracy and that she needed assistance from another individual in composing the original text. Bennett's influence in the construction of the affidavit is unclear, but may have been substantial. Certainly he would have been willing to assist and even coach the unschooled Melissa throughout the process.

Two weeks after the affidavit was published, Melissa Schindle's moral character was questioned in Nauvoo's "secular" newspaper, *The Wasp* in a July 27, 1842 "Extra" edition: "Who is Mrs. Schindle? A harlot." At her Church court before the Nauvoo High Council, May 25, 1842, Catherine Fuller testified before the Nauvoo High Council on May 28, 1842 that Bennett told her: "He also was with Mrs Shindle now living beyond Ramus."[74] D. Michael Quinn lists Schindle as one of Bennett's "free-love" companions.[75]

The affidavit describes several implausible events. First, in Nauvoo in 1841, it is unlikely that a man, even Joseph Smith, might have been allowed to wander at ten o'clock at night into a room where women were already in bed sleeping. Second, Schindle's claim that Joseph Smith "told her it was the will of the Lord that he should have illicit intercourse with her" depicts him as an adulterous hypocrite, one who acknowledges from the onset that the re-

---

73. Bennett, "Bennett's Second and Third Letters," July 15, 1842.

74. Catherine Fuller Warren, Statement to the Nauvoo High Council, May 25, 1842; copy of holograph in Valeen Tippetts Avery Collection, MSS 316, Box 24, fd. 14, Merrill-Cazier Library, Utah State University.

75. D. Michael Quinn, The *Mormon Hierarchy: Origins of Power*, 536.

lationship would have been "illicit." Such a depiction of the Prophet contrasts with numerous other public and private evidences from more reliable sources supporting that Joseph Smith taught and practiced a different moral standard. Third, that such hypocrisy would have been unnoticed by others would be surprising. Fourth, another problematic assertion centers on the Prophet's offering Schindle to "make his house her home" if she would acquiesce. That Emma Smith, the Prophet's legal wife, would have tolerated such an arrangement at their Nauvoo Homestead is improbable. Fifth, the offering of money, "five dollars" in exchange for sex describes prostitution, not polygamy or even Bennett's spiritual wifery. In his plural marriage proposals, Joseph never offered material incentives or financial favors to his potential polygamous wives. Plural wife Lucy Walker recalled Joseph telling her as he discussed a plural sealing with her: "I have no flattering words to offer."[76] Sixth, in the affidavit, Schindle declares she refused Joseph Smith's advances and then witnessed sexual relations between him and Catherine Fuller. Fuller herself denied under oath any knowledge of any improper conduct of the Prophet. Questions also arise concerning the possibility that Joseph and widow Fuller might have shared an "adjoining bed" in full view of Schindle. How readily would the couple have engaged in sexual intercourse in that setting with at least one spectator? Seventh, available documents indicate that Joseph Smith used the utmost secrecy and discretion in his associations with his plural wives. But in this account, after the alleged act was done, "he got up, [bade] them good night and left them."

This affidavit may represent an attempt by Bennett to cover up his own immorality by accusing Joseph Smith of the same behavior. Melissa Schindle's checkered past and sexually intimate friendship with Bennett do not enhance her credibility.

Of the individuals invited to join Bennett, Francis Higbee, who was Nancy Rigdon's suitor, also responded to the call. Higbee obtained Joseph Smith's letter to Nancy Rigdon on "happiness" written in April 1842. (See Chapter 17.) Richard Van Wagoner wrote: "Nancy apparently first told her boyfriend Francis Higbee about the prophet's behavior. Higbee, who ultimately obtained the letter, spread the word through his circle of friends, including John C. Bennett, his superior officer in the Nauvoo Legion."[77] Without Nancy's permission, Bennett included the letter in his sixth epistle to the *Sangamo Journal*, published on August 19.[78] (See Table 19.1)

---

76. Affidavit dated December 17, 1902, Journal History, May 1, 1843; Littlefield, *Reminiscences of Latter-day Saints*, 47.

77. Van Wagoner, *Sidney Rigdon*, 296.

78. See reprint in Bennett, *The History of the Saints*, 241–45.

TABLE 19.1
JOHN C. BENNETT LETTERS

Letter Number	Date Published (1842)	Date Written (1842)	Location Written	Polygamy-Related Content	Reprint in *History of the Saints*
1	July 8	June 27	Nauvoo, Illinois	General accusations	No
2	July 15	July 2	Carthage, Illinois	Sarah Pratt account	226–32
				Nancy Rigdon account	241–45
				Bennett reports he saw Joseph Smith with Mrs. Fuller	253
				Melissa Schindle affidavit	253
3		July 4	Carthage, Illinois	*History of the Saints* to be published	No
4	July 22	July 15	St. Louis, Missouri	Reference to letters written from Springfield, Illinois, to Mrs. Emeline White signed "Old White Hat"	232–36
				Martha Brotherton's lengthy account written two days earlier	236–41
5	August 19	July 23	River steamer *Imposter*	[nothing]	No
6		August 3	Erie Canal Boat *Nassau*	"Happiness" letter to Nancy Rigdon	243–45
7[a]	September 2	July 30	Cleveland, Ohio	Reference to "Cloistered, Chambered, and Cyprian maids and maidens!!"	217–18[b]
	Not included			Account of "Widow Miller"	255–56

a. Reprint from *Louisville Journal*.
b. Expanded on pages 218–25.

Bennett Schemes with Martha Brotherton

A few months earlier, Bennett learned of Martha Brotherton's accusations against Brigham Young. Accordingly, days after leaving Nauvoo in July, he traveled to meet her in St. Louis and together they composed an affidavit providing a description of Young's plural marriage proposal to her, sworn before Dubouffay Fremon, justice of the peace for St. Louis County, on July 13, 1842, the very day of his arrival. Andrew F. Smith observed:

> Bennett arrived in St. Louis by July 13. There he visited the editor of the *Daily Missouri Republican*, armed with a letter of introduction from Simeon Francis. On July 14 the *Daily Missouri Republican* announced Bennett's arrival in St. Louis and reported it would publish his disclosures the following day. On July 15 the *Daily Missouri Republican*, diplomatically announced that the article was omitted "for want of room." It made no further mention of Bennett or his disclosures. In fact, Bennett had taken the article to Vespasian Ellis, editor of the *American Bulletin*, who had promptly published it. . . .

While in St. Louis, Bennett met with Martha Brotherton and asked her to write a letter relating her experiences with Smith. Her comprehensive letter was published in the *American Bulletin* on July 16. . . .

Brotherton's letter was among the more damaging accusations made against Joseph Smith. Her allegations were widely accepted by the non-Mormon press, and this acceptance gave credibility to Bennett's other charges. . . . The *Hawk-Eye and Iowa Patriot* stated that Brotherton's letter confirmed "the most important statements of Gen. Bennett. Whatever may be thought of General Bennett as acting the part of Benedict Arnold h[i]s astounding disclosures, may be as valuable to the cause of truth as would have been those of the traitor of the Revolution to the cause of the British. Bennett may be considered a traitor by the Mormon party but his treason may be nevertheless highly beneficial in stopping the progress of one of the most rotten Sects that ever sprung into existence."

Not all St. Louis newspapers were sympathetic to Bennett, however. The editors of the *Missouri Reporter* stated that they had not great confidence in his statements. . . . Had Bennett appeared before the public under more favorable circumstances, the editors said they "might have been induced to give some credit to his pretended disclosures."[79]

Some of the details included in Brotherton's account seem accurate and were quoted in Chapter 17. However, a number of Brotherton's statements are better explained as the direct influence of John C. Bennett.[80] Although it is true that Brotherton and Bennett apparently did not know each other in Nauvoo, Martha did not produce the affidavit until Bennett personally appeared in St. Louis and asked her to write it. Furthermore, to assume that Bennett did not influence the text is to ignore three themes that appear in the Brotherton document and in Bennett's other creations, but which are not found in accounts from other Nauvoo polygamy participants.

For example, the affidavit claimed that Brigham Young stated: "If there is any sin in it [polygamy], I will answer for it." As discussed above, Bennett used this same line in his efforts to seduce women. Catherine Fuller Warren recalled Bennett's assurances as he attempted to seduce her: "He said there should be no sin upon me. If there was any sin it should come upon himself."[81] In contrast, no Nauvoo polygamists reported similar talk from Joseph Smith

---

79. Smith, *The Saintly Scoundrel*, 105–6.

80. Gary James Bergera wrote concerning the affidavit: "Her [Martha Brotherton's] experience did not involve Bennett and her account is free of Bennett's possible contamination." Bergera, "John C. Bennett, Joseph Smith, and the Beginnings of Mormon Plural Marriage," 78. Bergera's assessment does not seem to be supported by the available evidence.

81. Catherine Fuller Warren, Testimony before the Nauvoo High Council, May 25, 1842; "Affidavit of Hyrum Smith," 870. Terminal punctuation and initial capitals added.

or any other Church leaders, including Brigham Young.[82] On the contrary, the Prophet's teachings about celestial marriage stressed that lawful plural marriages were not sinful (D&C 132:41–44, 61–63).

In addition, another Bennettesque reference found in the Brotherton-Bennett affidavit states that at one point, Brigham said: "I will have a kiss, any how."[83] This description of a kiss taken from an unwilling woman appears in two additional Bennett accounts. In his version of Joseph Smith's courtship of Nancy Rigdon, Bennett wrote: "He [Joseph Smith] then attempted to kiss her, and desired her to kiss him."[84] Bennett is the only person to make this report. Similarly, when writing of the Prophet and Sarah Pratt, Bennett also asserted that Joseph Smith "stealthily approached and kissed" her.[85] Neither woman ever corroborated these claims, although Sarah Pratt had many opportunities to repeat Bennett's accusation, especially when interviewed by Wilhelm Wyl in 1886.[86]

In fact, available documents confirm that, in contrast to Bennett's charges, Joseph Smith did not engage in any form of premarital physical affection. When Emily Partridge was giving testimony in the Temple Lot case, the attorney asked if, during their year-long courtship: Did Joseph Smith ever "lay his hand on your shoulder?" or "put his arm around you?" or "offer to take your hand then?" Emily Partridge testified: "He never did for he was not that kind of a man. He was a gentleman in every way and did not indulge in liberties like that. . . . not before we was [sic] married."[87]

---

82. In general conference on October 8, 1854, Brigham Young offered to accept the sin of plural marriage, if any existed, but not the sin of fornication: "If there are any of my friends who do not belong to the Church here, I want to tell you one thing. I will take all the sin there is before God and angels in men having one wife, two wives, ten, or fifty wives, that will use them well, upon my own shoulders, if they will acknowledge them, support them, raise children by them and bring them up as well as they know how. I say I will take all the sins there is in this, of the whole of the Latter-day Saints, and place them with one sin of you poor devils who when you were young men courted that poor innocent girl and made her believe you would marry her, then got her in the family way and left her to the wide world." Richard S. Van Wagoner, ed., *The Complete Discourses of Brigham Young*, 2:853–54. Bennett, in contrast, was proposing to accept the sin of fornication.

83. Bennett, *The History of the Saints*, 238.

84. Ibid., 243.

85. Ibid., 231. Concerning Sarah Pratt's relationship with Bennett, Stephen Goddard later testified: "She could let a certain man smack upon her mouth and face half a dozen times or more in my house without making up the first wry face." Stephen H. Goddard, Letter to Orson Pratt, July 23, 1842, published in *Affidavits and Certificates, Disproving the Statements and Affidavits Contained in John C. Bennett's Letters*.

86. See the numerous comments by Sarah Pratt's ("Mrs. P.") in Wyl, *Mormon Portraits*, 10, 16–17, 22–23, 27–28, 33–34, 41–42, 53–56, 59–63, 72–73, and 89–90.

87. Emily Partridge, Deposition, Temple Lot Transcript, Respondent's Testimony, Part 3, pp. 357–58, questions 148–54, 179–85. Emily also testified that she did not have sexual

The Brotherton-Bennett affidavit also stated that Brigham "unlocked the door, and took the key, and locked me up alone. He was absent about ten minutes." This locked-door detail has received some attention by antagonistic writers who interpret it as an attempt to imprison Martha. Another interpretation is that Brigham was trying to prevent anyone from wandering into Joseph's office asking questions. Certainly he realized that, if Martha were to call for help, someone in the lower level or outside of the building would have instantly come to investigate.

Martha Brotherton's affidavit was published in the *Sangamo Journal* on July 22, 1842, and reprinted widely in eastern papers. Church leaders in Nauvoo rebutted Martha's claims. A month later, when it became obvious that interest in Bennett's charges remained high, Brigham published an affidavit on August 25, 1842, containing a carefully worded denial: "I do hereby testify that the affidavit of Miss Brotherton that is going the rounds in the politics and religious papers, is a base falsehood, with regard to any private intercourse or unlawful conduct or conversation with me."[88] This defense is technically true. Because of Joseph's presence, Young's conversation with Brotherton was not "private," at least not completely; and because the plural marriage never took place, no "unlawful conduct" occurred. Admittedly, however, the public at large would probably not have recognized how narrowly Brigham Young was using these terms. Such verbal hairsplitting was commonly employed by pluralists attempting to conceal polygamous interactions in Nauvoo and later in Utah without actually prevaricating.

Bennett's allegations spread far, even to England. Parley P. Pratt, editor of the *Millennial Star*, the Church's English periodical, wrote, also in August but before Brigham Young had issued his denial: "For the information of those who may be assailed by those foolish tales about the two wives, we would say that no such principle ever existed among the Latter-day Saints, and never will; this is well known to all who are acquainted with our books and actions, the Book of Mormon, Doctrine and Covenants; and also our periodicals are very strict and explicit on that subject."[89] Undoubtedly he spoke sincerely. It is clear he did not learn of the official restoration of plural marriage until his return to the states the next year.

The *Ontario Messenger*, published in Canandaigua, New York, on August 3, reported: "The Western papers, St. Louis and Illinois, abound in statements and counter statements, from the Mormon Prophet Joe Smith, and Gen. John C. Bennett, lately one of his disciples and followers, but expelled from the 'fellowship of the saints' for alleged misconduct. These revelations, if the half are true, convict both parties of the grossest immoralities; and serve to confirm the general impression that the association is little else than a compound of bigotry and knavery."[90]

---

relations with Joseph Smith prior to their sealing. Ibid., Part 3, p. 371, questions 481–84.
88. *Affidavits and Certificates, Disproving the Statements and Affidavits Contained in John C. Bennett's Letters.*
89. Parley P. Pratt, "Apostasy," 74.
90. "The Mormons," *Ontario Messenger* (Canandaigua, N.Y.), August 3, 1842, in

By August 11, Bennett was in New York where he gave a series of lectures. The editor of the *New York Sun* was happy "to see the General so much engaged in exposing this abominable delusion, and bid him go on with his 'labors of love' with all our heart." However, the editor believed Bennett was "just about as big a rogue as Joe."[91]

Joseph Smith Counterattacks

Joseph Smith tried to neutralize John C. Bennett's charges in several ways including plain denials.[92] Bennett's immoralities were viewed as very different from restored plural marriage. Joseph also sent missionaries out specifically to counteract Bennett's claims against the Church. Henry William Bigler recalled: "In the month of August [1842] at a special conference, a goodly number of elders were called to go on missions and to rebuke John Bennett's lies, among the number I was called."[93]

In addition, the Prophet commissioned the publication of *AFFIDAVITS AND CERTIFICATES, Disproving the Statements and Affidavits Contained in John C. Bennett's Letters* (August 31, 1842). This single double-sided sheet contained thirteen affidavits and other communications designed to undermine Bennett's credibility. Two of the affidavits were from Stephen and Zeruiah Goddard and dealt with Bennett's claims concerning Sarah Pratt:

> July 23, 1842.
> BR. ORSON PRATT, Sir:—Considering it a duty upon me I now communicate unto you some things relative to Dr. Bennett and your wife that came under the observation of myself and wife, which I think would be satisfactory to the mind of any man could he but realize the conduct of those two individuals while under my notice. I would have been glad to have kept forever in silence if it could have been so and been just. I took your wife into my house because she was destitute of a house, Oct. 6, 1840, and from the first night, until the last, with the exception of one night it being nearly a month, the Dr. was there as sure as the night came, and generally two or three times a day—for the first two or three nights he left about 9 o'clock—after that he remained later, sometimes till after midnight; what their conversation was I could not tell, as they sat close together, he leaning on her lap, whispering continually or talking very low—we generally went to bed and had one or two naps before he left. After being at my house nearly a month she was furnished with a house by Dr. Foster, which she lived in until sometime about the first of June, when she was turned out of

---

Journal History, August 3, 1842; in Turley, *Selected Collections*, Vol. 2, DVD #1.

91. Quoted in Smith, *The Saintly Scoundrel*, 116.

92. According to Thomas Gregg, *The Prophet of Palmyra*, 228, "Some of these denials are carefully worded, and when closely examined are found to be partly denial and partly evasion."

93. Henry William Bigler, Journal Excerpts, 11.

the house and came to my house again, and the Dr. came as before. One night they took their chairs out of doors and remained there as we supposed until 12 o'clock or after; at another time they went over to the house where you now live and come back after dark, or about that time. We went over several times late in the evening while she lived in the house of Dr. Foster, and were most sure to find Dr. Bennett and your wife together, as it were, man and wife. Two or three times we found little Orson [born July 11, 1837] lying on the floor and the bed apparently reserved for the Dr. and herself—she observing that since a certain time he [three-year-old Orson] had rather sleep on the floor than with her. . . .

There are many more things which she has stated herself to my wife, which would go to show more strongly the feelings, connexion, and the conduct of the two individuals. I shall not testify of these things at present for certain reasons, but can let you know them if you feel disposed to hear them. . . .

        Your Friend,
        STEPHEN H. GODDARD.

I certify that the above statement of my husband is true according to the best of my knowledge.

        ZERUIAH N. GODDARD.
        Sworn to before me July 23d 1842.
        GEO. W. HARRIS.
        Alderman of the City of Nauvoo.[94]

Years later Sarah attempted to discredit the Goddards by claiming that they had been pressured to sign affidavits that were already written. Sarah quoted Mrs. Goddard as saying: "Hyrum Smith came to our house with the affidavits all written out, and forced us to sign them."[95] However, an examination of the letter and affidavit shows that they contained specific details that Hyrum could not have known, including that Bennett stayed until 9 o'clock on multiple visits and remained until midnight at later rendezvous. Such details make it unlikely that anyone but the Goddards themselves could have written them. Most likely Sarah was trying to neutralize damaging evidence that exposed her infidelity with Bennett.

Richard S. Van Wagoner discounted the accuracy of Goddards' claims against Sarah: "The Goddard story had serious problems that even Sarah did not point out. Bennett had been appointed 4 October 1840 to work with Smith on drafting the Nauvoo Charter. On this same day he was also selected as a delegate to lobby for passage of the bill through the state legislature at Springfield, nearly one hundred miles distant. That Bennett could draft the complicated documents, make the necessary trips to Springfield, and be with Sarah Pratt every night except one during a one-month period seems improbable."[96]

---

94. Goddard, Letter to Orson Pratt, July 23, 1842.
95. Sarah Pratt, quoted in Wyl, *Mormon Portraits*, 62–63.
96. Richard S. Van Wagoner, *Mormon Polygamy: A History*, 38 note 12. According to

In fact, Bennett was not sent to Springfield until the end of November.[97] Both the Prophet and Bennett were commissioned to write the document, and both later claimed credit for its creation.[98] Robert B. Flanders wrote: "Smith and Bennett had already been at work on the charter and probably had it completed before the [October 4, 1840] conference met."[99] James L. Kimball Jr. agreed: "The speed with which the committee worked strongly suggests a prior agreement as to the contents of the document."[100]

Larry Foster observed: "The city charter granted to the Nauvoo Mormons actually was very similar to those granted other Illinois cities of the period.[101] Edwin Brown Firmage and Richard Collin Mangrum concurred: "The Charter was obviously modeled after the city charter of Springfield, which the legislature had passed earlier in 1840."[102] It therefore seems unlikely it was created from scratch. In looking at Bennett's personal circumstances during October of 1840, it does not appear that he was then constantly journeying to Springfield or completely preoccupied as Van Wagoner wrote.

Also during the turbulent month of August 1842, Sidney Rigdon addressed the commotion that included Nancy's forced involvement in a letter to *The Wasp*, Nauvoo's secular newspaper, that was reprinted in the *Sangamo Journal*:

> Nauvoo, Aug. 27th, 1842.
> Editor of the *Wasp*.
> Dear Sir: I am fully authorized by my daughter, Nancy, to say to the public through the medium of your paper, that the letter which has appeared in the *Sangamo Journal*, making part of General Bennett's letters to said paper, purporting to have been written by Mr. Joseph Smith to her, was unauthorized by her, and that she never said to Gen. Bennett or any other person, that said letter was written by said Mr. Smith, nor in his hand writing, but by another person, and in another person's hand writing. She further wishes me to say, that she never at any time authorized Gen. Bennett to use her name

---

Gary James Bergera, *Conflict in the Quorum: Orson Pratt, Brigham Young, Joseph Smith*, 31, "As historian Richard Van Wagoner has shown, these allegations are demonstrably false." In fact, it could be argued that Van Wagoner's logic and claims are subject to important limitations and insufficiencies.

97. Andrew Smith, *The Saintly Scoundrel*, 59.
98. James L. Kimball Jr., "A Wall to Defend Zion: The Nauvoo Charter," 492.
99. Robert Bruce Flanders, *Nauvoo: Kingdom on the Mississippi*, 96.
100. Kimball, "A Wall to Defend Zion," 492.
101. William Lawrence Foster, "Between Two Worlds: The Origins of Shaker Celibacy, Onedia Community Complex Marriage, and Mormon Polygamy," 221 note 1. See also Kimball, "The Nauvoo Charter: A Reinterpretation," 70; Edwin Brown Firmage and Richard Collin Mangrum, *Zion in the Courts: A Legal History of the Church of Jesus Christ of Latter-day Saints, 1830–1900*, 84–87.
102. Firmage and Mangrum, *Zion in the Courts*, 85.

in the public papers, as he has done, which has been greatly to the wounding of her feelings, and she considers that the obtruding of her name before the public in the manner in which it has been done, to say the best of it, is a flagrant violation of the rules of gallantry, and cannot avoid to insult her feelings, which she wishes the public to know. I would further state that Mr. Smith denied to me the authorship of that letter.

SIDNEY RIGDON[103]

Rigdon's comment on the penmanship of the letter is correct. Even though the original has not survived, Rigdon would have been familiar with Joseph's hand and thus correctly noted that someone other than Joseph Smith had actually written it down. However, it is unlikely that the refutation successfully deflected attention away from the probability that the Prophet dictated it. In addition, Rigdon spoke at a Sunday meeting of the Saints. *The Times and Seasons*, the Church's official periodical, reported:

> He [Sidney Rigdon] was not upon the stand to renounce his faith in Mormonism, as had been variously stated by enemies and licentious presses, but appeared to bear his testimony of its truth, and add another to the many miraculous evidences of the power of God. Neither did he rise to deliver any regular discourse, but to unfold unto the audience a scene of deep interest, which had occurred in his own family.
>
> He had witnessed many instances of the power of God, in this church, but never before had he seen the dead raised: yet, this was a thing that had actually taken place in his own family: his daughter Eliza was dead;—the doctor told him that she was gone, when, after a certain length of time she rose up in the bed and spoke in a very powerful tone to the following effect, in a supernatural manner:—and said to the family that she was going to leave them, being impressed with the idea herself, that she had only come back to deliver her message, and then depart again:—saying the Lord had said to her the very words she should relate,—and so particular was she in her relation, that she would not suffer any person to leave out a word, or add one.
>
> She called the family around her and bade them all farewell, with a composure and calmness that defies all description:—still impressed with the idea that she was to go back. Up to the time of her death, she expressed a great unwillingness to die, but after her return, she expressed equally as strong a desire to go back. She said to her elder sister, Nancy, it is in your heart to deny this work, and if you do, the Lord says it will be the damnation of your soul. . . . And concerning Dr. Bennett, that he was a wicked man, and that the Lord would tread him under his feet. Such is a small portion of what she related.
>
> Elder Rigdon observed, that there had been many idle tales and reports abroad concerning him, stating that he had denied the faith, but he would take

---

103. Sidney Rigdon, Letter to the editor, August 27, 1842, "Editor of the Wasp," *The Wasp*, September 3, 1842, 4. It was reprinted in the *Sangamo Journal*, September 16, 1842.

the opportunity to state that his faith was and had been unshaken in the truth. It has also been rumored that I believe that Joseph Smith is a fallen prophet: In regard to this, I unequivocally state, that I never thought so—but declare that I know he is a prophet of the Lord, called and chosen in this last dispensation, to roll on the kingdom of God for the last time."[104]

After the initial wave of propaganda from the Bennett defamatory machine had passed, Joseph Smith wrote in his diary on September 8, 1842: "I was his [John C. Bennett's] friend. I am yet his friend, as I feel myself bound to be a friend to all the sons of Adam; whether they are just or unjust, they have a degree of my compassion and sympathy. If he is my enemy, it is his own fault; and the responsibility rests upon his own head."[105]

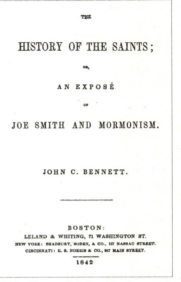

Title Page of John C. Bennett's *The History of the Saints*.

The History of the Saints

In late October 1842, Bennett fired his next round by publishing an exposé titled *The History of the Saints: Or an Exposé of Joe Smith and Mormonism*.[106] His biographer, Andrew F. Smith, assessed: "Although the book was almost 350 pages, four-fifths consisted of material previously written. This included Bennett's previously published [newspaper] articles, personal letters and testimonials. Bennett's major contributions were to organize and determine the contents and to promote and advertise the book."[107]

Bennett's depiction of the practice and teachings of polygamy in Nauvoo were remarkable, even extravagant, and its weaknesses were not lost even on later anti-Mormon authors. T. B. H. Stenhouse, a lapsed Mormon, cautioned in 1873: "There is no doubt, much truth in Bennett's book . . . but no statement that he makes can be received with confidence."[108] Ann Eliza Webb Young wrote in her own 1876

---

104. "Elder Rigdon etc.," *Times and Seasons* 3 (September 15, 1842): 922; see also Jessee, *Journal, 1832–1842*, 419.

105. Jessee, *Journal, 1832–1842*, 463.

106. The first advertisement for sales occurred in the *Sangamo Journal*, November 11, 1842.

107. Andrew Smith, *The Saintly Scoundrel*, 123.

108. Stenhouse, *The Rocky Mountain Saints*, 184 note 2. See also Harry M. Beardsley, *Joseph Smith and His Mormon Empire*, 247.

exposé: "It is probable that the book would have had a much wider influence had not Bennett's character been so well known. He was a notorious profligate, and was pronounced by Gentiles who had known him before he embraced Mormonism to be 'the greatest villain unhung.'"[109] Illinois historian Theodore Calvin Pease concurred: "Undoubtedly Bennett was able to tell many things regarding the aims, methods, and morals of the Mormon leaders; but his exposures appear unreliable."[110] Fawn Brodie admitted: "To any discerning reader Bennett revealed himself in his own book to be a base and ignoble opportunist."[111] Most authors depict Bennett as a reprobate. Wilhelm Wyl recorded: "'All decent people in Nauvoo,' says Mr. K.,[112] 'regarded Bennett as a perfect scoundrel' . . . Mr. Webb says: 'he was a very small, villainous-looking man. . . . Ambition and women filled his soul.' 'He was full of low cunning and licentiousness,' says Mrs. [Sarah] Pratt."[113]

CONSEQUENCES OF JOHN C. BENNETT'S APOSTASY

Several important consequences resulted from John C. Bennett's apostasy. First, he had influenced a small group of individuals, facilitating their sexual misconduct through his teachings. Most of these men and women were called before the Nauvoo High Council for Church discipline. They included some believing and sincere people, most of whom sought to repent and be forgiven. Second, Bennett's charges in print created a rapidly spreading public nightmare for Church leaders to counteract. It appears that Bennett was the first person to ever publish accusations that Joseph Smith was either a womanizer or polygamist (and most readers would not have distinguished between the two anyway). His earliest allegations in the *Sangamo Journal* were reprinted in other venues throughout the East, culminating in his October *History of the Saints*.

His accusations incited a vigorous reaction from Joseph Smith and priesthood authorities, tying up valuable Church resources for a time. Richard Van Wagoner noted: "To the church's advantage, Bennett dramatically overstated his case in white-washing his own behavior, making it possible to discredit him in the eyes of the Saints and effectively equating his name with licentiousness and betrayal."[114]

---

109. Ann Eliza Webb Young, *Wife Number 19, or, The Story of a Life in Bondage, Being a Complete Exposé of Mormonism, and Revealing Sorrows, Sacrifices, and Sufferings of Women in Polygamy*, 74.

110. Theodore Calvin Pease, *The Frontier State 1818–1848*, 346.

111. Brodie, *No Man Knows My History*, 317.

112. Wyl does not identify many of the people he quotes, which complicates the process of validating his quotations and statements. Wyl reported that he interviewed "some eighty… men and women," but as a rule would abbreviate the names to conceal the interviewee's identity. Wyl, *Mormon Portraits*, 10.

113. Ibid., 133.

114. Van Wagoner, *Sidney Rigdon*, 302.

TABLE 19.2
CHRONOLOGY OF JOHN C. BENNETT'S MORMON-RELATED LIFE

Year	Month	Event in John C. Bennett's Life
1832		Meets Joseph Smith and Sidney Rigdon.
1835		Attends Church services at Kirtland
1840	July	Writes flattering letters to Joseph Smith.
	August	Joseph replies: "Let all that will, come, and partake of the poverty of Nauvoo freely."
	September	Arrives in Nauvoo—boards with the Smith family.
	October	Participates in October general conference.
	December	Facilitates passage of the Nauvoo Charter through Illinois State General Assembly.
1841	February	Is elected Mayor of Nauvoo.
		Joseph seeks information on Bennett's past.
	March	Joseph learns that Bennett was "an imposter" and had abandoned his wife and children. Joseph chooses to handle information privately. Joseph pens a letter to Vilate Kimball about an unidentified seducer in Nauvoo that may have been Bennett.
	April	Bennett is sustained as "assistant" to the First Presidency until Sidney Rigdon's health improves two months later.
	May	Bennett moves out of the Smith home. His domicile during the remainder of his stay in Nauvoo is not precisely known.
	June	Sidney Rigdon's health restored, begins serving again in First Presidency.
	July	Bennett is confronted with his sordid past and attempts suicide.
		Joseph "flagellates" Bennett for his illicit behaviors.
1842	May 11	Bennett is accused of seducing several women and, according to published documents, was excommunicated, but available journals do not corroborate a disciplinary meeting that day.
	May 17	Bennett signs a public affidavit exonerating Joseph Smith of sexual misbehavior and later claims it was made under duress.
	May 19	Bennett resigns as mayor.
	May 26	Bennett is informed of his excommunication.
	June 18	Joseph Smith publicly speaks of the "wickedness of Gen John Cook Bennett."
	June 27	Bennett writes his first of several letters to the *Sangamo Journal*.
	August 31	The *Wasp* publishes an extra containing "affidavits and certificates" designed to disprove Bennett's statements.
	October	Bennett publishes his exposé: *The History of the Saints*
	Fall	Bennett lectures against Joseph Smith.
1844	June	Joseph Smith is martyred.
	July	Bennett returns to Nauvoo and briefly joins with Sidney Rigdon.
1846	July	Joins James J. Strang's group.
1847	Spring	Excommunicated from Strang's group.
1850		Publishes very successful book on domestic fowl.
1853		Moves to Iowa.
1867		Dies at Des Moines.

Third, the secret expansion of celestial plural marriage in Nauvoo was slowed. Evidence suggests that there were no additional plural marriages during the remainder of 1842 after August.[115] A fourth observation is that Bennett's charges preconditioned skeptics and anti-Mormons throughout the area to believe reports of sexual impropriety leveled at Joseph Smith. Two years later, when William Law came out with accusations of adultery, they were only too ready to accept them as true and to take action on them. (See Chapter 31.) Prior to the accusations in Bennett's writings, only one charge of indecency had been published, an implausible second-hand allegation of an attempted seduction occurring in the late 1820s.[116] Had Law's allegations been the first reports against the Prophet regarding polygamy or extramarital sexual behavior, the uproar might have been diminished from its beginning, perhaps never crescendoing to the fatal climax.

Summary

In review, relatively few Church members were duped by Bennett's teachings. While many of them may have wondered about the whispered rumors, the vast majority disbelieved his published claims. Instead, they generally embraced the statements crafted by Church leaders that truthfully denied Bennett's spiritual wife teachings, without hinting at the possible appropriateness of celestial plural marriage.[117]

In spite of his problematic personality, John C. Bennett's journey through Mormonism impacted Joseph Smith and Nauvoo in far-reaching and significant ways. Masonic historian Mervin B. Hogan lamented: "It is a great pity that John Cook Bennett couldn't consistently and honestly direct his inherited talent and ability to positive and constructive ends. Due to his defective character, he almost certainly threw away a rare opportunity for achievement, recognition, and possible greatness in the founding of the State of Utah and the future development, growth and recognition of the Mormon Church."[118]

---

115. The exact date of Reynolds Cahoon's plural marriage is unknown. Family traditions date it to "1841–1842." However, 1841 is very unlikely; 1842 or 1843 would be more consistent with events transpiring in Nauvoo. See Gary James Bergera, "Identifying the Earliest Mormon Polygamists, 1841–1844," 6.

116. "Mormonism," *Susquehanna Register, and Northern Pennsylvanian*, May 1, 1834. See Chapter 2.

117. Larry Foster, "Between Two Worlds: The Origins of Shaker Celibacy, Onedia Community Complex Marriage, and Mormon Polygamy, 204, observes that the term "spiritual wifery," was used in some parts of the country in the 1820s as "a catchall suggesting rationalized infidelity."

118. Mervin B. Hogan, *John Cook Bennett: Unprincipled, Profligate, Cowan* [sic], 98.

Chapter 20

John C. Bennett: Polygamy Confidant or Sexual Opportunist?

During the past decades, numerous authors, from Fawn Brodie to George D. Smith, have composed their reconstructions of Nauvoo polygamy, taking the position that John C. Bennett was a personal confidant of Joseph Smith and probably had a firsthand knowledge of plural marriage from the Prophet himself.[1] This chapter will examine this possibility by analyzing both supportive and contradictory evidence.

Traditional Interpretation: Bennett Was Joseph Smith's Polygamy Confidant

It appears that the earliest observer to assert that Bennett was Joseph Smith's confidant was Oliver Olney, who penned in a quasi-journal-notebook on June 18, 1842, "If Bennett had not moved quite so fast, all would have been well, now as I look at things with them."[2] Oliver had been excommu-

---

1. See Fawn M. Brodie, *No Man Knows My History: The Life of Joseph Smith, the Mormon Prophet*, 309–16; Linda King Newell and Valeen Tippetts Avery, *Mormon Enigma: Emma Hale Smith*, 111; Gary James Bergera, "John C. Bennett, Joseph Smith, and the Beginnings of Mormon Plural Marriage in Nauvoo," 58; Harry M. Beardsley, *Joseph Smith and His Mormon Empire*, 247; William D. Morain, *The Sword of Laban: Joseph Smith Jr. and the Dissociated Mind*, 188; Rodger I. Anderson, *Joseph Smith's New York Reputation Reexamined*, 12; Richard S. Van Wagoner, "Sarah M. Pratt: The Shaping of an Apostate," 71–72; Gregory A. Prince, *Power from On High*, 134. George D. Smith, *Nauvoo Polygamy: ". . . but we called it celestial marriage,"* 65, 67, 70.

2. Oliver Olney, "Journal notes, poetry, etc.," Olney Papers, item 8, June 18, 1842. On April 8, 1842, he recorded: "And some of the twelve are trying to be very intimate with females. But if it was so, I thought as they had wives." At that time, in addition to Joseph Smith, only Apostle Heber C. Kimball had married polygamously. Brigham Young was the only other apostle to marry plurally in 1842. It seems that many of Olney's assertions are in error. Nevertheless, he manifested a precocious understanding of several secular and religious developments in Nauvoo, such as Joseph Smith's 1842

nicated three months earlier on March 17, 1842, thus distancing him from the Church hierarchy during Bennett's fall from grace, but his views might have been shared by others in Nauvoo.[3] In 1873, T. B. H. Stenhouse, a British convert who was baptized in 1845, likewise reported: "Many even of the 'good Mormons' have always believed that Joseph taught Bennett of the proposed introduction of polygamy, but that Bennett ran ahead of his teacher, and introduced free-loveism in its broadest sense."[4] In Brodie's influential biography, she described Bennett: "For a year and a half he [John C. Bennett] was Joseph's most intimate friend."[5]

According to Robert Bruce Flanders in his landmark 1965 publication, *Nauvoo, Kingdom on the Mississippi*, "Bennett, a promiscuous and lascivious man, stumbled onto a developing religious principle which he apparently distorted to aid and justify himself in his amours.... Just who took the first step [Joseph Smith or John C. Bennett], or when, is impossible to determine from reliable sources."[6] David E. Miller and Della S. Miller concluded that Bennett "joined the church and soon won the complete confidence of the prophet."[7]

More recently, Larry Foster wrote that Joseph had taken John C. Bennett "into his full confidence."[8] Richard S. Van Wagoner concurred: "He [Bennett] was clearly in a privileged position to witness Smith's involvement in polygamy."[9] Todd Compton also agreed: "Bennett is not always reliable, but

---

plan to remove the Saints to the Rocky Mountains.

3. "Try the Spirits," *Times and Seasons* 3 (April 1, 1842): 747–48.

4. T. B. H. Stenhouse, *The Rocky Mountain Saints*, 184. See biographical information in Linda Wilcox DeSimone, ed., *Fanny Stenhouse: Exposé of Polygamy, A Lady's Life among the Mormons*, 10–12.

5. Brodie, *No Man Knows My History*, 309.

6. Robert Bruce Flanders, *Nauvoo: Kingdom on the Mississippi*. 267; see also John Henry Evans, *Joseph Smith: An American Prophet*, 272.

7. David E. Miller and Della S. Miller, *Nauvoo: The City of Joseph*, 3rd ed., 142.

8. Larry Foster, "Between Two Worlds: The Origins of Shaker Celibacy, Oneida Community Complex Marriage, and Mormon Polygamy," 271 note 1. Foster also gave this interesting analysis in *Religion and Sexuality: Three American Communal Experiments of the Nineteenth Century*, 171: "Bennett's indiscretions and excesses threatened the legitimate development of polygamy.... Joseph Smith was faced with a dilemma in trying to deal with Bennett. The man knew too much to be summarily thrown out, yet his indiscretions were so great that if he were not thrown out the lid would blow off eventually anyway. Bennett never understood what Joseph Smith was really trying to do. His account [of polygamy] is like the reflection in a fun-house mirror, grotesquely elongated or distorted in different directions, although the original object reflected did in fact exist." In contrast, as I interpret the evidence, Joseph Smith never taught Bennett the principle of polygamy and he surmised the Prophet's dealings only through rumors.

9. Richard S. Van Wagoner, *Mormon Polygamy: A History*, 23. Richard Van Wagoner, *Sidney Rigdon: A Portrait of Religious Excess*, 298, also stated: "Much of what Bennett wrote

he did have early first-hand knowledge of the Mormon leader's polygamous activities."[10] Gary Bergera reflected this same perspective:

> He [Bennett] probably knew more about the origins of plural marriage in Nauvoo than any other person besides Smith himself.[11]

The thirty-seven-year old Bennett had been privy to Smith's April 1841 plural marriage and was conversant with his controversial teachings. Consequently, he believed he too was authorized, whether or not Smith conveyed such an impression, to initiate himself and others into the prophet's new order. Smith worried that the enthusiasm with which Bennett embraced the celestial doctrine, and especially his introduction of it to others without Smith's permission, failed to emphasize sufficiently the religious aspects of his revelation.[12]

In 2008, George D. Smith in *Nauvoo Polygamy: ". . . but we called it celestial marriage* repeatedly affirmed this view: "One of the instrumental people in the inauguration of plural marriage was John Bennett, who in 1841 functioned as perhaps Joseph Smith's closest confidant. . . . Much of what he reported can be confirmed by other eyewitness accounts." "Bennett was well positioned to know all about any behind-the-scenes transactions." "About that time [September 1840 to July 1842], Smith was courting several women, all while Bennett was still a guest in the Smith home and otherwise accompanied the prophet's every step."[13]

Examining the Evidence

Several pieces of evidence are often cited to support John C. Bennett as a polygamy insider. The most obvious is that he himself made the claim, both directly and indirectly. In his second letter to *Sangamo Journal*, he allegedly quoted Joseph Smith saying: "It is known that you [Bennett] are well acquainted with all my private acts, better than any other man, and it is in your power to save

---

about Mormonism's inner circles was factual. As a member of the First Presidency, he was clearly in a privileged position to witness much of Joseph's personal behavior." He cites no evidence to support these assumptions.

10. Todd Compton, *In Sacred Loneliness: The Plural Wives of Joseph Smith*, 239.

11. Bergera, "John C. Bennett, Joseph Smith, and the Beginnings of Mormon Plural Marriage," 52. See also Bergera, *Conflict in the Quorum: Orson Pratt, Brigham Young, Joseph Smith*, 16.

12. Gary James Bergera, "'Illicit Intercourse': Plural Marriage, and the Nauvoo Stake High Council, 1840–1844," 65.

13. George Smith, *Nauvoo Polygamy*, 65, 67, 70. See also George D. Smith, "The Summer of 1842: Joseph Smith's Relationships with the 12 Wives He Married after His First Wife, Emma," 12; and his "The Forgotten Story of Nauvoo Celestial Marriage," 138–39. Although Bennett was certainly in the Smith household at the invitation of Joseph Smith, he was a boarder, not a guest.

or damn me."[14] In several other published documents Bennett also declared himself conversant with the Prophet's private plural marriage teachings.[15]

Possibly the most convincing observation supporting the possibility that John Bennett was a close friend and even polygamy confidant of the Prophet is that, after his arrival in Nauvoo in the September of 1840, he boarded with the Smith family for three dollars a week for the next thirty-nine weeks.[16] That he and Joseph experienced many personal—but not necessarily private—conversations at this time is likely, given the small size of the Smith home. The Homestead then consisted of three rooms, a living room area, a back kitchen, and a single room upstairs.[17] How Bennett and the family arranged themselves to share that small space is unknown, but such close quarters would have easily allowed multiple exchanges and sharing of lives and ideas. Naturally, Bennett would have accompanied Joseph outdoors to do the daily chores of milking, chopping wood, and caring for the animals. It is certain that they did *not* discuss polygamy in Emma's presence, since the available evidence supports that she learned of Joseph's plural marriages only in 1843. (See Chapters 24–27.)

Another useful observation is that, at the same time the Prophet introduced plural marriage by being sealed to Louisa Beaman, Bennett was engaged in extra-legal sexual relations. As discussed in the previous chapter, I believe Bennett was the seducer mentioned in Joseph Smith's March 2, 1841, letter to Vilate Kimball.[18] Catherine Fuller Warren testified he propositioned her in June of that year (see below).[19] Lorenzo D. Wasson, Emma Smith's nephew, recalled that, in the summer of 1841, the Prophet castigated Bennett for his immorality.[20] These documents suggest that if Bennett's pre-Nauvoo lasciviousness subsided after joining the Latter-day Saints, it was not for very long.

Authors often observe the chronological parallel between the Prophet's introduction of plural marriage and Bennett's lasciviousness and assume that the Bennett became aware that Joseph Smith was teaching polygamy in some form. However, writers seldom account for the fact that Bennett had been

---

14. John C. Bennett, "Bennett's Second and Third Letters," *Sangamo Journal*, July 15, 1842.

15. John C. Bennett, *The History of the Saints: Or an Exposé of Joe Smith and Mormonism*, 217–53.

16. "Joseph Smith's Red Brick Store Daybook," December 8, 1843, account number 59; quoted in Richard Price and Pamela Price, *Joseph Smith Fought Polygamy*, 1:79.

17. Recent research suggests that the western two-level portion of the Homestead may have been completed during Joseph Smith's lifetime rather than after his death. Lachlan MacKay, Conversation with Brian Hales, September 24, 2011. If so, the Smith quarters may not have been as cramped as described.

18. Joseph Smith, Letter to Vilate Kimball, March 2, 1841; emphasis his.

19. Catherine Fuller Warren, Statement before the Nauvoo High Council, May 25, 1842. Catherine Fuller married William Warren on April 27, 1842.

20. L. D. Wasson, Letter to Joseph and Emma Smith, July 30, 1842.

accused of sexual impropriety before arriving in Nauvoo.[21] His reputation included previous marital infidelity.[22] Accordingly, another possible interpretation is that, rather than learning of Joseph Smith's teachings regarding plural marriage and perverting them, his behavior among the Mormons may have simply represented a continuation of his previous immoral activities. In this scenario, he would have opportunistically engaged in sexual relations with a Mormon woman who succumbed to his blandishments; but when he eventually heard rumors of polygamy, probably in the spring of 1842, he exploited them to his advantage, mostly in his writings later that year. It does not appear that he needed encouragement or theological justifications from Joseph Smith to continue his sexual self-indulgence.

A fourth observation supporting Bennett as a polygamy confidant arises from his meteoric rise in both Church leadership and local politics. On April 8, 1841, he was presented as an "assistant president, until Pres't. Rigdon's health should be restored,"[23] which occurred two months later.[24] This advancement supports a close relationship between the Prophet and Bennett, at least at that time. It is also surprising if, as recounted in 1842, Joseph had learned of his pre-Nauvoo immoralities just weeks before. Regardless, the scant records of ecclesiastical meetings and functions during 1841 fail to show that Bennett was involved in any meaningful way. Joseph Smith kept no diaries between October 15, 1839, and December 13, 1841, so journal data from most of 1841 when Bennett's popularity among the Latter-day Saints increased, is unavailable.[25] Wilford Woodruff arrived in Nauvoo October 6, 1841, and mentions Bennett only once during the next nine months—an entry written February 18, 1842 in conjunction with business transacted at a Nauvoo City Council meeting.[26] As discussed in Chapter 9, seven members of the Quorum of the Twelve Apostles, Brigham Young, Heber C. Kimball, John Taylor, Orson

---

21. [Correspondence], *The Wasp* 1, no. 24 (October 1, 1842): 1 col. 2; W. P. Rowell, in *Affidavits and Certificates, Disproving the Statements and Affidavits Contained in John C. Bennett's Letters, Nauvoo*; Price and Price, *Joseph Smith Fought Polygamy*, 1:63–73.

22. Joseph Smith, "To the Church of Jesus Christ of Latter Day Saints, and to All the Honorable Part of Community," *Times and Seasons* 3 (July 1, 1842): 839–40.

23. "Minutes," *Times and Seasons* 2 (April 15, 1841): 387.

24. Untitled notice beginning, "We have to announce that Sidney Rigdon has been ordained a Prophet, Seer, and Revelator," *Times and Seasons* 2 (June 1, 1841): 431; *History of the Church*, 4:364.

25. See discussion in Andrew H. Hedges, Alex D. Smith, and Richard Lloyd Anderson, eds., *Journals, Volume 2: December 1841–April 1843*, xiii–xxi; and Brian C. Hales, "Review of Andrew H. Hedges, Alex D. Smith, and Richard Lloyd Anderson, eds., *Journals, Volume 2: December 1841–April 1843*," 236–54.

26. Scott G. Kenney, ed., *Wilford Woodruff's Journal*, 2:235; see also *History of the Church*, 2:154.

Pratt, George A. Smith, Wilford Woodruff, and Willard Richards, returned from England in the summer and fall of 1841.[27] They all left recollections that Joseph Smith taught them of plural marriage soon after their arrival and none mentions Bennett as participating in those discussions. In light of his eventual apostasy, they may not have felt inclined to recall his involvement, although some reference, even in derision, might be expected.

Bennett's apparent lack of participation is more readily documented in Joseph Smith's journal entries between December 13, 1841, and the summer of 1842 when Bennett left Nauvoo. Apparently, he was not then invited to the private meetings of Church leaders where expanding spiritual doctrines were explained. Joseph's journals mention Bennett only five times prior to his resignation as mayor:

January 18	"...Debated, in the evening, with they the Mayor"
January 25	"...in the evening debated with J. C. Bennet"
February 13	"Council with Mayor, H[yrum] Smith,[28] the Patriarch, Recorder..."
March 9	"Examining copy for the Times & Season presented by [John] Taylor & Bennet"
March 11	"...the Mayer issued his warrant..."
May 19	"Mayor John C. Bennet[t] having resigned his office . . . "[29]

In contrast, other Church leaders are mentioned many times during that span with eighteen references to Brigham Young, fifteen to Heber C. Kimball, fourteen to Willard Richards, eight to John Taylor, seven to Hyrum Smith and Wilford Woodruff, five to Newel K. Whitney, and three to Orson Pratt and William Law.[30] These observations suggest that if Bennett had ever been a personal confidant of the Prophet, his involvement ended prior to December of 1841, or that such interactions were not visible to Joseph's scribes or corroborated in his journal.

Bennett spoke in the April conferences of 1841 and 1842, and performed a few civil marriages in his role as mayor. However, he did not speak at the October 1841 conference; Van Wagoner assumes that he was in Springfield, but I have found no corroborating evidence, and the legislative session did

---

27. See Elden Jay Watson, ed., *Manuscript History of Brigham Young, 1801–1844*, August 16, October, 30, 31, November 28, 30, December 11, 12, 19, 26, 27, 1841; January 2, 17, 28, 29, 30, 31, March 1, 9, April 6, 12, 1842.

28. This would not have been an occasion to discuss plural marriage because Hyrum Smith did not learn of the doctrine until May 26, 1843. See George D. Smith, ed. *An Intimate Chronicle: The Journals of William Clayton*, 106.

29. Andrew H. Hedges, Alex D. Smith, and Richard Lloyd Anderson, eds., *Journals, Volume 2: December 1841–April 1843*, 18, 30, 42, 43, 58.

30. Ibid., 10–74.

John C. Bennett: Polygamy Confidant or Sexual Opportunist? 553

not begin that early. Furthermore, Bennett did not receive sealing authority nor was he invited to solemnize any eternal marriages. During that eighteen-month period before Bennett's excommunication, Joseph was sealed to perhaps eleven women, but all available evidence demonstrates that Bennett was not involved in any of them, either as officiator or as witness.

A review of the *Times and Seasons* shows numerous references to First Presidency members Joseph Smith, Sidney Rigdon, and William Law, and also to Associate President Hyrum Smith. All of them were identified by the title of "president," but Bennett, despite his impressive title as "assistant to the First Presidency" never was called "president" in the newspaper or any other source I have seen.[31] Instead, Bennett's titles are "doctor," "general," "mayor," and "chancellor."[32] These observations may be why biographer Andrew F. Smith concluded: "Despite the importance of his position, Bennett appears to have officiated at few public religious activities. He occasionally preached, and as mayor of Nauvoo he performed a few [civil] marriage ceremonies. He did serve as president pro tem in a special conference held on April 6, 1842, but otherwise he played little role in church conferences."[33]

A valid question is whether Joseph Smith could have prevented John C. Bennett, his "assistant president" from learning about his plural marriage activities during this time. The answer appears to be an unqualified "yes." The historical record indicates that the Prophet successfully kept his own brother, Associate Church President and Church Patriarch Hyrum Smith, unaware of the principle until May of 1843, nearly a full year after Bennett's excommunication, even though Hyrum was in Nauvoo during the entire time period.[34] Similarly, William Law, who was appointed as second counselor in the First Presidency on January 19, 1841 (D&C 124:126), over two months prior to Bennett's calling, reported not learning about plural marriage until 1843.[35] Both of these men held higher callings than John C. Bennett. It is unknown when and to what extent Sidney Rigdon, Joseph's first counselor, learned about polygamy, but he undoubtedly became aware of its restoration during the aftermath of Joseph's plural proposal to his daughter Nancy on April 9, 1842. (See Chapter 17.). Sidney Rigdon's immediate and indignant

---

31. John C. Bennett was identified as "Gen. Bennett Pres't. pro tem." at the April 6, 1842, "Special Conference" with "Pres't William Law" and "Pres't. H. Smith." "Conference Minutes," *Times and Seasons* 3 (April 15, 1842): 761.

32. Computerized search for the respective titles in *Times and Seasons*.

33. Andrew F. Smith, *The Saintly Scoundrel: The Life and Times of Dr. John Cook Bennett*, 62.

34. George D, Smith, ed., *An Intimate Chronicle: The Journals of William Clayton*, 106, May 26, 1843. See also Andrew F. Ehat, "Joseph Smith's Introduction of Temple Ordinances and the Mormon Succession Question," 56–60.

35. William Law, Affidavit, July 17, 1885, quoted in Charles A. Shook, *The True Origin of Mormon Polygamy*, 126.

rejection of the principle (which may be equally well explained as protectiveness of his daughter) apparently prompted Joseph to withhold doctrinal details and understandings, even while he labored until their personal relationship was patched up. In light of these three examples—Hyrum Smith, William Law, and Sidney Rigdon—assumptions that being a counselor to the First Presidency gave Bennett insider information seems unjustified. Based on these same three examples, if Joseph Smith wished to keep Bennett uninformed about the restoration of plural marriage, he could have successfully done so.

Five Plural Wives Identified Correctly

Perhaps the only solid evidence that John C. Bennett possessed some insider knowledge about polygamy appears in his *History of the Saints*, printed in late October or early November of 1842. In it, he reveals the identities of five of Joseph Smith's plural wives. These names raise two questions: (1) How did he know about these five but not the other approximately eleven women to whom Joseph had been sealed by that point;[36] and (2) Why did their names not appear in any of the seven letters he wrote to the *Sangamo Journal* between June and August? As discussed in Chapter 12, a letter to the *Pittsburgh Morning Chronicle* published July 29, 1842, refers to several sexual partners of Joseph Smith as "Mrs._____."[37] The dating of the letter and the information implied suggests that Bennett knew their identities at that time but chose not to disclose them.

In *History of the Saints*, Bennett wrote:

> I will semi-state two or more cases, among the vast number, where Joe Smith was privately married to his spiritual wives—in the case of Mrs. A**** S****, by Apostle Brigham Young; and in that of Miss L***** B*****, by Elder Joseph Bates Noble. Then there are the cases of Mrs. B****, Mrs. D*****, Mrs. S*******, Mrs. G*****, Miss B***** etc. etc.[38]

In this paragraph, Bennett correctly identified Brigham Young and Joseph Bates Noble as officiators in their respective cases. He provided no sealing dates, and it is not clear why he presented the names in this order.

Bennett mentions seven women without divulging their names, but only five have been verified. The firm identifications are: Mrs. A**** S****

---

36. Compton, *In Sacred Loneliness*, 4–6.
37. John C. Bennett, "Bennett's Affidavit," *Pittsburgh Morning Chronicle*, July 29, 1842; see also George D. Smith, "The Forgotten Story of Nauvoo Celestial Marriage," 139–40 (see also 160 note 101) mistakenly writes that the names of the women were included "both in a letter to the *Sangamo Journal* of July 15, 1842, ... and in his exposé *History of the Saints*."
38. Bennett, *The History of the Saints*, 256.

(Agnes Coolbrith Smith, sealed January 6, 1842), Miss L***** B***** (Louisa Beaman, sealed April 5, 1841), Mrs. B**** (Presendia Huntington Buell, sealed December 11, 1841), Mrs. D***** (most probably Elizabeth Davis Durfee), and Mrs. S******* (Patty Bartlett Sessions, sealed March 9, 1842).[39] He also lists a Mrs. G***** and a Miss B*****, whose identities have not been confirmed. (See discussion below.)

For the purposes of the discussion in this chapter, the key question is whether Bennett learned about these women from Joseph Smith or from some other source. According to my evaluation of the evidence, both circumstantial and direct, I conclude that Bennett's source was not Joseph Smith. Other scholars differ. For example, concerning Bennett's identification of Louisa Beaman (L***** B*****), Gary James Bergera hypothesizes: "Given their friendship, for Smith not to have told Bennett of his ideas and of his marriage to Louisa Beaman (and others) seems unthinkable. Though exactly when these conversations took place is uncertain. Smith no doubt introduced the topic gingerly, then in great detail."[40] However, I find "friendship" alone to be an unpersuasive argument.

Bennett's flow of information appears to have stopped after March 9, 1842, the latest sealing date of the plural wives who can be identified. Joseph's next plural nuptial—to Marinda Johnson Hyde—occurred in April 1842, and Bennett does not include her.[41] Otherwise, it appears Bennett missed only two of the Prophet's pre-March 9, 1842 sealings.[42] Absent from Bennett's list is the "late February" sealing to Mary Elizabeth Rollins Lightner. Another omission is that of Zina Huntington Jacobs, sealed to Joseph on October 27, 1841, although Bennett lists her sister Presendia, sealed to Joseph two months later.[43] He also does not include Sylvia Sessions Lyon, whom many authors list as sealed to Joseph Smith on February 8, 1842, although this date is unreliable so her absence is not surprising. (See Chapter 13.) Bennett also fails to include the other three Nauvoo men (Heber C. Kimball, Brigham Young, and Vinson Knight) who married their first plural wives before the publication of his book.

---

39. Ibid., 256.

40. Bergera, "John C. Bennett, Joseph Smith, and the Beginnings of Mormon Plural Marriage," 63–64.

41. See the final entry (July 14, 1843) in Joseph Smith's journal. Richard E. Turley Jr., ed., *Selected Collections from the Archives of the Church of Jesus Christ of Latter-day Saints*, Vol. 1, DVD #20; see also Scott H. Faulring, ed., *An American Prophet's Record: The Diaries and Journals of Joseph Smith*, 396.

42. Compton, *In Sacred Loneliness*, 4, dates Elizabeth Davis Durfee's sealing to the Prophet as "< 29 June 1842." No precise sealing date is available. Assuming that "Mrs. D*****" is Durfee and that my hypothesis is correct, the sealing could be dated several months earlier.

43. John C. Bennett performed the civil wedding for Zina Huntington and Henry Jacobs on March 7, 1841. Lyndon W. Cook, comp., *Nauvoo Deaths and Marriages, 1839–1845*, 92.

In short, his information was spotty and incomplete. Presumably, if Joseph had been sharing details about his plural unions, Bennett's information would have more complete. How, then, did he learn about these five (seven) women?

While it is impossible to indisputably identify the actual source of Bennett's knowledge of Joseph Smith's plural wives, a possible informant is Nancy Rigdon. According to George W. Robinson, husband of Nancy's sister Athalia, at some point prior to August 29, 1842, Nancy Rigdon was "sick and Dr. John C. Bennett was the attending physician."[44] Bennett had also received a copy (by way of Francis and Chauncey Higbee) prior to August 3, of the "happiness" letter that the Prophet dictated to her. (See Chapter 17.)[45] Joseph proposed plural marriage to Nancy on April 9 and may have told her of a few of his previous sealings to convince her that the practice was a legitimate restoration of the Old Testament practice. If so, Nancy would not have been privy to sealings occurring after that date, none of which Bennett lists.

Regarding the mysterious Mrs. G***** and Miss B*****, Fawn Brodie asserts that Mrs. G***** was Sally Ann Fuller Gulley, claiming: "The Nauvoo Temple Record states that on January 29, 1846, she [Sally Ann Fuller] was sealed to Joseph Smith Jr., 'for eternity' and to [Samuel] Gulley 'for time.'"[46] In fact, the Nauvoo Temple record contains no such entry.[47] Sally Ann Fuller did not marry Samuel Gully (as a polygamous wife) until January 29, 1847, in Winter Quarters.[48] In addition to misstating the source of her information, Brodie apparently misspelled the true surname "Gully" as "Gulley," to make it comply with the number of asterisks in Bennett's book.[49] Regardless of Brodie's misstatements, Bennett would have known Sally Ann Fuller as "Miss

---

44. George W. Robinson, "Certificate," in Bennett, *The History of the Saints*, 252.

45. Bennett, *The History of the Saints*, 245. The letter was included in his August 3 letter to the *Sangamo Journal* published August 19.

46. Brodie, *No Man Knows My History*, 469.

47. See Sealings in Pre-Endowment House Ordinances, CR 334 13, LDS Church History Library vault. See also Lisle G Brown, *Nauvoo Sealings, Adoptions, and Anointings: A Comprehensive Register of Persons Receiving LDS Temple Ordinances, 1841–1846*, 107, 120, 379; Thomas Milton Tinney, *The Royal Family of the Prophet Joseph Smith Jr.*, 41; Devery S. Anderson and Gary James Bergera, eds., *The Nauvoo Endowment Companies: 1845–1846: A Documentary History*, 525–26.

48. Tinney, *The Royal Family of the Prophet Joseph Smith, Jr.*, 114. Gully died in 1849, and Sally Ann married Elijah Knapp Fuller on September 8, 1850.

49. Some entries in historical documents record Samuel's surname as "Gulley," but official records spell it "Gully." If Bennett had only heard the name and not seen it written, he might have been referring to Sarah's sister Ovanda; but as noted in the text, no documentation I know of associates Ovanda with Joseph Smith. Sarah and Ovanda were no known relation to Catherine Fuller Warren, who was drawn into Bennett's immoral activities.

John C. Bennett: Polygamy Confidant or Sexual Opportunist? 557

Fuller" or "Miss F*****," not as "Mrs. G*****" during his stay in Nauvoo.[50] Samuel Gully had been sealed to Ovanda Fuller, Sally Ann's sister, a year earlier on January 17th, 1846, in the Nauvoo temple. So Ovanda could not be the mysterious Mrs. G*****.[51]

Another possibility is Samuel Gully's first wife, Jane Jones Frilick (sometimes Frylick) Gully, whom he married October 9, 1833 and with whom he had three children.[52] She would have been known as "Mrs. Gully" or "Mrs. Gulley" in Nauvoo. Jane Gully was not sealed to Samuel Gully in the Nauvoo Temple.[53] However, after his 1849 death, she was sealed to Benjamin Freeman Bird in the Salt Lake City Endowment House on February 27, 1852 by Heber C. Kimball.[54] Her willingness to be sealed for time and eternity to Bird argues against a Nauvoo plural sealing to the Prophet. No other evidence has been found connecting Joseph Smith to Jane Jones Frilick (Frylick) Gully Bird.

Brodie also speculates that Miss B***** might have been "Sarah Bapson."[55] I have found no contemporary documentation that a woman named Sarah Bapson lived in Nauvoo in the 1840s. Sarah *Rapson* (b. 1793) married Stephen Poulterer in 1817, but she would have been known in Nauvoo as "Mrs. Sarah Poulterer." She is also apparently documented under the names of "Sarah

---

50. Although lacking an asterisk, another possibility is "Mrs. Granger," Sarah Stiles who married Carlos Granger on May 31, 1813. Sarah joined the Church; her husband never did but remained friendly to the Church and its leaders. In 1840, Carlos wrote: "I am not nor never have been a member of the church of Jesus Christ of Latter day saints called Mormons." Clark V. Johnson, ed., *Mormon Redress Petitions: Documents of the 1833–1838 Missouri Conflict*, 452–53. While hiding from lawmen attempting to arrest him on charges stemming from Missouri Governor Boggs's near-fatal shooting, Joseph hid at their home. On August 17, 1842, fearing his retreat had been discovered and "it was no longer safe for him to remain at brother [Edward] Sayers . . . [Joseph] went to Carlos Grangers." Hedges, Smith, and Anderson, *Journals, Volume 2: December 1841–April 1843*, 96. Whether Joseph would have approached Sarah Stiles Granger, particularly in 1841 or early 1842, for an "eternity only" sealing as he did other women married to nonmembers, is unknown but possible. See also [Oliver Olney?], uncatalogued manuscript, Western Americana MSS at Beinecke Library, Yale, folder: "Nauvoo Female Society," transcription by D. Michael Quinn, Michael Quinn Papers. In "Topic—Polygamy, Joseph Smith's," the entry mentions a "Mrs Granger" as a plural wife of Joseph Smith.

51. Brown, *Nauvoo Sealings, Adoptions, and Anointings*, 120.

52. James B. Gully, born "ABT 1836," Martha Gully born December 15, 1851, and Harriet Gully born April 30, 1840.

53. Brown, *Nauvoo Sealings, Adoptions, and Anointings*, 120.

54. Endowment House Records, LDS Family History Library, Special Collections, February 27, 1852, record 338, microfilm 0,183,393.

55. Brodie, *No Man Knows My History*, 469.

Davis,"[56] "Sarah Royson,"[57] "Sarah Rapsin,"[58] and "Sarah Poulter,"[59] none of which correlate to "Miss B*****."

Despite intensive research by several investigators, no plausible identities for Bennett's "Mrs. G*****" and "Miss B*****" have been identified. In summary, as matters currently stand, John C. Bennett correctly identified five plural wives while two additional names (presented as initials followed by asterisks) remain unverified and may been speculations by Bennett or his informant.

Plural Marriage Verses Spiritual Wifery

After leaving Nauvoo in the summer of 1842, Bennett wrote letters and a book outlining his version of Joseph Smith's polygamy in Nauvoo. Today, many descriptions of early polygamy are available from participants enabling researchers to form a clearer picture of what happened, at least through the eyes of the men and women authorized by the Prophet to practice plural marriage. Contrasting these accounts to Bennett's descriptions reveals multiple significant differences. The two elements in common are that (1) both demanded secrecy, and (2) both authorized sexual relations with partners other than a legal spouse.

Joseph Smith's plurality demanded obedience to the law of chastity of all participants, monogamous or polygamous.[60] He also described plural marriage as "the new and everlasting covenant of marriage" and as an "order of the priesthood." He taught that it was a restoration of Old Testament plural marriage like that practiced by Abraham and Jacob. The Prophet also related that he had been commanded by a sword-wielding angel to engage in the practice. (See Chapter 8.) In Joseph's teachings, marriage ceremonies were always necessary, otherwise the relationship constituted adultery (D&C 132:41–42, 63). Those sealings, whether monogamous or polygamous, required that the officiator possessed special priesthood power, bestowed on him at the sole discretion of the "one" man who held the sealing keys—keys that were received through ordination:

---

56. Susan Easton Black and Harvey Bischoff Black, *Annotated Record of the Baptism for the Dead, 1840–1845, Nauvoo, Hancock County, Illinois*, 5:2948–49.

57. "Sarah Royson," *LDS Vital Records Library*.

58. Tinney, *The Royal Family of the Prophet Joseph Smith Jr.*, 48(A).

59. Ibid., 247, records a "Sarah Rapson Poulter." See also Family Group record for a Sarah Davis who married a Thomas Arnold Poulter in 1814.

60. In April 1842 Joseph Smith introduced the temple endowment ceremony, which required strict vows of chastity. See Dean C. Jessee, ed. *The Papers of Joseph Smith: Volume 2, Journal, 1832–1842*, 380–81; *History of the Church*, 5:2. See also Catherine Lewis, *Narrative of Some of the Proceedings of the Mormons; Giving an Account of their Iniquities*, 10; James E. Talmage, *The House of the Lord*, 84.

> All covenants, contracts, bonds, obligations, oaths, vows, performances, connections, associations, or expectations, that are not made and entered into and sealed by the Holy Spirit of promise, *of him who is anointed*, both as well for time and for all eternity, and that too most holy, by revelation and commandment through the medium of *mine anointed, whom I have appointed* on the earth to hold this power (and I have appointed unto my servant Joseph to hold this power in the last days, and there is *never but one on the earth at a time on whom this power and the keys of this priesthood are conferred*), are of no efficacy, virtue, or force in and after the resurrection from the dead; for all contracts that are not made unto this end have an end when men are dead. (D&C 132:7; emphasis mine)

Marriages performed without his authority are "not valid":

> And again, verily I say unto you, if a man marry a wife, and make a covenant with her for time and for all eternity, if that covenant is not by me or by my word, which is my law, and is not sealed by the Holy Spirit of promise, *through him whom I have anointed and appointed unto this power*, then it is not valid neither of force when they are out of the world, because they are not joined by me, saith the Lord, neither by my word; when they are out of the world it cannot be received there, because the angels and the gods are appointed there, by whom they cannot pass; they cannot, therefore, inherit my glory; for my house is a house of order, saith the Lord God. (D&C 132:18; emphasis mine)

Even correct ceremonial language and complete sincerity on the part of the participants did not authorize such unions if the officiator lacked proper priesthood authority.

Joseph Smith's polygamy created genuine husband-wife relationships that were designed to endure (D&C 132:19–20). Both companions accepted specific obligations to the union and to any future children. The husband was responsible for helping with the plural wife's daily maintenance (consistent with D&C 83:2). No plural wife was more important than the other, although the first wife was permitted to participate through the "law of Sarah."[61]

---

61. Joseph Smith did not elaborate, but Orson Pratt gave this instruction concerning the "law of Sarah": "When a man who has a wife, teaches her the law of God, as revealed to the ancient patriarchs, and as manifested by new revelation, and she refuses to give her consent for him to marry another according to that law, then, it becomes necessary, for her to state before the President the reasons why she withholds her consent; if her reasons are sufficient and justifiable and the husband is found in the fault, or in transgression, then, he is not permitted to take any step in regard to obtaining another. But if the wife can show no good reason why she refuses to comply with the law which was given unto Sarah of old, then it is lawful for her husband, if permitted by revelation through the prophet, to be married to others without her consent, and he will be justified, and she will be condemned, because she did not give

Bennett's Personal Spiritual Wifery: Seductions and Sexual Relations

Bennett's label for Joseph Smith's polygamy teachings and practices was "spiritual wifery," a term that had been used in religious contexts in previous centuries, but which was first introduced into the Mormon community by Bennett so far as records indicate.[62] Importantly, there is no evidence that Joseph Smith ever used that precise term in any setting. However, on October 15, 1843, he cautioned his listeners to "stop this spinning street yarn and talking about spiritual wives."[63] Months later on May 26, 1844, he commented: "This spiritual wifeism! Why, a man dares not speak or wink, for fear of being accused of this."[64] The revelation on celestial and plural marriage, dictated by Joseph Smith does not use "spiritual" or "wifery." Equally importantly, Bennett did not use synonyms or equivalent terms like "everlasting wifery," "celestial wifery," "eternal wifery," or "spiritual marriage." Bennett's terminology was straightforward; "spiritual wifery" created "spiritual wives" who could have sex with men to whom they were not married as long as they kept the union a secret. Spiritual wifehood was not part of a meaningful marriage after the liaison unless the couple decided to recreate their secret sexual union at some future time. In essence, Bennett promoted one-night-stands and labeled them "spiritual wifery."

Between May 21 and 28, 1842, the Nauvoo High Council met several times to investigate reports of adulteries instigated by Bennett and his followers.[65] It does not appear that Bennett himself was the focus of the inquiries, since he had been disciplined days before. Instead, the council sought

---

them unto him, as Sarah gave Hagar to Abraham, and as Rachel and Leah gave Bilhah and Zilpah to their husband, Jacob." Orson Pratt, "Celestial Marriage," *The Seer* 1. no. 3 (March, 1853): 41.

62. The term "spiritual wifery" was first used in America by the religionists in and near the Blackstone Valley of Rhode Island and Massachusetts in the 1740s. See William G. McLoughlin, "Free Love, Immortalism, and Perfectionism in Cumberland, Rhode Island, 1748–1768," 67–85; see also John L. Brooke, *The Refiner's Fire: The Making of Mormon Cosmology, 1644–1844*, 56; Larry [W. Lawrence] Foster, "Between Two Worlds: The Origins of Shaker Celibacy, Onedia Community Complex Marriage, and Mormon Polygamy," 204.

63. Andrew F. Ehat and Lyndon W. Cook, eds., *The Words of Joseph Smith: The Contemporary Accounts of the Nauvoo Discourses of the Prophet Joseph Smith*, 257; recorded by Willard Richards in Joseph Smith's diary, October 15, 1843.

64. Ibid., 377; reported by Thomas Bullock, May 26, 1844.

65. Nauvoo High Council, Minutes, May 21–28, 1842, LDS Church History library; photocopy of holograph in Valeen Tippetts Avery Collection MSS 316, Box 24, fd. 14, Merrill-Cazier Library; also John S. Dinger, ed., *The Nauvoo City and High Council Minutes*, 413–19.

to identify and address iniquities that he may have supported through his teachings and example. Among the women called to testify were Catherine Fuller Warren, Mary Hardman, Melinda Lewis, Caroline Butler, Matilda Nyman, Margaret Nyman, Polly Mecham, Polly Masheres, Melinda Lewis, and Maria Champlin. Besides naming Bennett, the witnesses incriminated other men and women including Justus Morse, Mrs. Schindle, Mrs. Barriss, George W. Thatcher, Lyman O. Littlefield, Joel S. Miles, Mrs. Alfred Brown, J. B. Backenstos, and Alexander McRay.

During the proceedings, Sarah Miller testified against Chauncey Higbee, who had seduced her. Regarding Bennett, she quoted Higbee saying, "That it [their sexual relations] would never be known. I told him that it might be told in bringing forth [pregnancy]. Chauncey said there was no Danger <& that> Dr Bennt understood it & would come & take it away if there was any thing."[66] The next day, Catherine Fuller Warren affirmed:

> Nearly a year ago I became acquainted with John C. Bennett, after visiting twice and on the third time he proposed unlawful intercourse, being about one week after first acquaintance. He said he wished his desires granted I told him it was contrary to my feelings he answered there was others in higher standing than I was who would conduct in that way, and there was not harm in it. He said there should be no sin upon me if there was any sin it should come upon himself. . . . John C. Bennett was the first man that seduced me—no man ever made the attempt before him.[67]

In addition, Fuller mentioned a "Mrs Brown" as another possible Bennett conquest saying she witnessed "Dr. J. C. Bennett and Mrs [Alfred] Brown sitting very close together."[68] She also attested that Bennett told her, "He also was with Mrs Shindle now living beyond Ramus. and also with the two Miss Nymans."[69] Both Matilda and Margaret Nyman verified this in their testimonies before the Council.[70]

Matilda Nyman also reported: "Widow Fuller is guilty of the same[.] Dr Bennet was with her… Saw Bennet in the act with Sis Fuller."[71] She added: "Chauncey Higbee taught the same doctrine as was taught by Bennett."[72] Concerning the daughter of a "Mr. Gee," Matilda affirmed: " Mr Gee lived

---

66. Sarah Miller, Testimony before the Nauvoo High Council, May 24, 1842.
67. Catherine Fuller Warren, Statement before the Nauvoo High Council, May 25, 1842.
68. Ibid.
69. Ibid.
70. Matilda Nyman, "Testimony against Chauncey L. Higbee before the Nauvoo High Council, May 21, 1842.
71. Ibid.
72. Ibid.

above our house Bennt called almost every Day. Mr Gee would send his little Girl away till Bennt left."[73]

The testimonies support that Bennett had made the rounds with a number of Nauvoo women, interposing the line, "Such intercourse might be freely indulged in, and was no Sin, that any respectable female Might indulge in Sexual intercourse and there was no sin in it, provided the person so indulging, keep the same to herself, for there could be no Sin when there was no accuser."[74] This teaching had spread to others who used it to justify illicit sexual relations.

John C. Bennett's Later Description of Nauvoo Polygamy

Unlike Joseph Smith, Bennett did not describe Nauvoo polygamy as originating from the teachings of a divine messenger. Neither did he implement any references to the plural marriage of biblical patriarchs. His portrayal of Nauvoo polygamy, as described in his letters and *History of the Saints*, divided participating women into three different "orders": "Cyprian," "Chambered," and "Cloistered."[75] (See Table 20.1.)

Bennett's language ("Cyprian," "Chambered," "Cloistered," "Seraglio," "Abbess," etc.) has no counterpart in Mormon documents and was apparently borrowed straight from scandal-tinged depictions of exposés of Catholic monastic orders and exotic descriptions of Muslim harems. Bennett's descriptions of the "Cyprian," "Chambered," and "Cloistered" women mentioned a marriage ceremony only for some of the "Consecratees of the Cloister" in the third level. Regardless, even those women could be thereafter sexually involved with non-husbands. Women in the other two categories apparently needed no marriage ceremony. "Cyprian" means "prostitute," suggesting that women at this level could be sexually available to any number of men. Further, the connotations of promiscuity are confusing when applied, as Bennett did, to Joseph Smith's system of plural *marriage*.[76]

---

73. Ibid.

74. Ibid.

75. Bennett, *The History of the Saints*, 220–25. Larry Foster, *Religion and Sexuality*, 173, suggested one possible parallel between Bennett's descriptions of polygamy in Nauvoo and Joseph Smith's teachings on plural marriage: "Thus, 'wives and concubines' could well correspond to Bennett's two upper levels of plural wives." There is no evidence of women being designated as "concubines" or of "concubines" being married in Nauvoo. Nor is there any form of official sanction of concubinage in the Church before or after Joseph Smith's death.

76. "Cyprian" does not appear in Noah Webster, *An American Dictionary of the English Language; Exhibiting the Origin, Orthography, Pronunciation, and Definitions of Words*, 3rd ed., 1830. A modern dictionary defines it as "prostitute." *American Heritage Dictionary*, 3rd. ed., digital version.

TABLE 20.1
JOHN C. BENNETT'S DESCRIPTION OF NAUVOO POLYGAMY

Designation	Veil Color	Characteristics
Cyprian Saints	White	"The members of the Female Relief Society, who are ever upon the watch for victims, have the power, when they know, or even suspect, that any Mormon female has, however, slightly, lapsed from the straight path of virtue. . . . She is immediately, by the council, pronounced a Cyprian, and is excluded from any further connection with the Relief Society. . . . [H]er name and failing are stealthily promulgated among the *trustworthy* members of the Church at whose command she is, for licentious purposes, forever after." Bennett, *History of the Saints*, 220.
Chambered Sisters of Charity	Green	"This order comprises that class of females who indulge their sensual propensities, without restraint, whether married or single, by the express permission of the Prophet. . . . [They] are much more numerous than the *Cyprian Saints*. This results naturally from the greater respectability of their order." 221–22.
Consecratees of the Cloister or Cloistered Saints	Black	"This degree is composed of females whether married or unmarried, who, by an express grant and gift of God, through his Prophet the Holy Joe, are set apart and consecrated to the use and benefit of particular individuals as *secret, spiritual wives*. . . . When an Apostle, High Priest, Elder, or Scribe, conceives an affection for a female, and he has satisfactorily ascertained that she experiences a mutual flame, he communicates confidentially to the Prophet his *affaire du Coeur* and requests him to inquire of the Lord." 223.

It is true that Bennett spoke of "wifery"; however, there is no record that he performed a "spiritual wife" ceremony or any other kind of rite to create a polygamous marriage relationship. Admittedly the records are skimpy, but none of the women sexually involved with him or his followers reported any mention of a ceremony. It seems likely that victims of his seduction like Catherine Fuller Warren would have described such a ceremony as part of explaining why she succumbed to his enticements. Instead, she forthrightly labeled Bennett's activities as "unlawful intercourse."[77] It seems that Bennett's "spiritual wives" were "wives" primarily in the sense that they had shared a bed with a man.[78] "Spiritual wifery" did not obligate the participants to ac-

---

77. Catherine Fuller Warren, Testimony before the Nauvoo High Council, May 25, 1842.

78. Charles V. Dyer, undated letter to *The Wasp* beginning "It will be seen by this…", 1, no. 15 (July 23, 1842): 2, also accused John C. Bennett of "buggery" or homosexual activity. However, Andrew F. Smith, *The Saintly Scoundrel*, 112, observed: "No support for this charge was offered, and perhaps it was made in the heat of battle." D. Michael

cept familial responsibilities. Jacob Backenstos, who also had intercourse with Catherine Fuller (before she married William Warren), paid her two dollars, although this exchange seems to be more like a client's fee to a prostitute than a husband's supplying his wife's material needs.[79]

Gary James Bergera wrote: "Smith required a marriage/sealing ceremony be performed with his permission by an authorized priesthood holder prior to sexual contact; Bennett believed that worthy couples, married or not, could engage freely in sexual activity provided they keep their conduct a secret."[80] There is no evidence that Bennett required his followers to maintain a standard of worthiness or what such a standard would have been.

Also, John C. Bennett's "spiritual wifery" allowed a woman to be sexually active with more than one man during the same time period, creating a "polyandrous" wifery situation. The revelation that became Doctrine and Covenants 132 condemned such arrangements (D&C 132:42, 63).

Examining Bennett's charges as published in *History of the Saints* reveals several factual errors. He refers to Emma Smith as: "Lady Abbess of the Seraglio, or 'Mother of the Maids,'" implying that she was an active participant in the debaucheries he described.[81] However, Emma did not accept plural marriage until 1843 and was not a participant at any level—probably was not even aware of the official practice—during Bennett's stay in Nauvoo. (See Chapter 24.)

Bennett discusses three levels of polygamous women implying numerous participants. According to Bennett, "The members of the Female Relief Society . . . are ever watchful for victims" who become the Cyprian Saints.[82] The Chambered Sisters of Charity are reportedly "at the service of each and all of the Apostles, High Priests, and Elders of Israel."[83] The Consecratees of the Cloister are "the most honorable among the daughters of Jacob. Their spiritual husbands are altogether from the most eminent members of the Mormon Church."[84] Most readers would conclude that participation by Nauvoo men and women was fairly broad as of July 1842 when he left the city. However, in reality,

---

Quinn apparently accepted the charge. D. Michael Quinn, *Same-Sex Dynamics among Nineteenth-Century Americans: A Mormon Example*, 266–68.

79. Catherine Fuller Warren testified: "J. B. Backenstos has also been at my house . . . gave me two dollars." Catherine Fuller Warren, Statement before the Nauvoo High Council, May 25, 1842.

80. Bergera, "'Illicit Intercourse,' 65–66. I have been unable to find any manuscript documentation for the assertion that Bennett required some level of "worthiness" prior to sexual activity.

81. Bennett, *The History of the Saints*, 227.

82. Ibid., 220.

83. Ibid., 222.

84. Ibid., 223.

TABLE 20.2
DIFFERENCES BETWEEN JOSEPH SMITH'S PLURAL MARRIAGE
AND JOHN C. BENNETT'S SPIRITUAL WIFERY

	Joseph Smith	John C. Bennett
Name(s) of Relationship	New and Everlasting Covenant of Marriage or Order of the Priesthood	Spiritual Wifery
Restoration of Old Testament polygamy?	Yes	No
Angel with a sword commanding?	Yes	No
Ceremony required?	Yes	No
Priesthood authority required?	Yes	No
Worthiness required?	Yes	No
Husband-wife marriage relationship established?	Yes	No
Eternal relationship formed?	Yes	No
"No sin where there was no accuser" doctrine?	No	Yes
Polyandrous sexual relations permitted?	No	Yes
Need to keep relationship completely secret?	No	Yes
Three orders of polygamous wives?	No	Yes

only three men besides Joseph[85] had entered plural marriage, and Joseph had been sealed to perhaps a dozen women, most of whom were "eternity only" sealings which, I have concluded, did not involve sexual relations on earth. (See Chapters 14–16.) Thus, by May 1842, a maximum of four men and thirteen women may have been involved in eternal plural marriages authorized by the Prophet, with conjugal relations occurring in perhaps four or five of the relationships. In contrast, Bennett reportedly admitted that, "he had seduced six or seven" women in the city.[86] So together, he and followers had probably seduced more women in the name of "spiritual wifery" than Joseph Smith had sealed in "time and eternity" plural marriages by that time.[87]

---

85. Besides Joseph Smith, these earliest pluralists were Heber C. Kimball, Brigham Young, and Vinson Knight (who died July 31, 1842). These three men were sealed to only one plural wife at this point. Brent J. Belnap, "Life Story of Martha McBride Knight Smith Kimball." See also Bergera, "Identifying the Earliest Mormon Polygamists, 1841–1844," 14.

86. Hyrum Smith's comment at the trial of Francis Higbee, May 6, 1844 in "Municipal Court," *Times and Seasons* 5 (May 15, 1844): 540.

87. Fuller Warren, Statement before the Nauvoo High Council, May 25, 1842; see also affidavits quoted in "History of Joseph Smith," *Millennial Star* 23 (October 12, 1861): 658.

Despite Bennett's detailed descriptions concerning Nauvoo polygamy, there is no evidence that any of it was grounded in fact. No other contemporary documents except for his own letters and book refer to his three-level Cyprian/Chambered/Cloistered wives. In his own "spiritual wifery" practices, the only requirement to authorize sexual relations between consenting partners was keeping them secret.

Bennett's 1843 Ignorance of Eternal Marriage

Bennett's biographer, Andrew F. Smith, acknowledged the disconnect between the teachings of Joseph Smith and those of John C. Bennett: "No primary evidence has been presented indicating that Bennett was officially involved in the evolving practice of polygamy at Nauvoo. . . . No evidence indicates that Bennett's extramarital relationships were sanctioned by Joseph Smith."[88] An important clue to Bennett's genuine proximity to Joseph Smith's secret plural marriage teachings is found in Bennett's October 28, 1843, letter written to the *Hawk Eye* (Burlington, Iowa) newspaper:

> According to promise, I now address you a few lines in relation to the new doctrine of "MARRYING FOR ETERNITY," lately gotten up by the Holy Joe . . . for the benefit of his flock. Joe says that as "they neither marry, nor are given in marriage; but are as the angels which are in Heaven," *in eternity*, it has been revealed to him that there will be no harmony in heaven unless the *Saints* select their companions and marry IN TIME, FOR ETERNITY!!! They must marry *in time* so as to begin to form that sincere attachment and unsophisticated affection which it is so necessary to consummate *in eternity* in order to the peace of Heaven. So Joe Smith has lately been married to his present wife Emma, *for eternity* as well as *for time*. . . . "This '*marrying for eternity*' is not the '*Spiritual Wife doctrine*' noticed in my Expose [*The History of the Saints*], but is an entirely new doctrine established by special Revelation. The "SPIRITUAL WIVES,' *for time!* And the 'CELESTIAL WIVES,' *for eternity!*"[89]

Here Bennett differentiates between "this 'marrying for eternity'" and the "Spiritual Wife doctrine" he had written about in his book. He calls it "an entirely new doctrine established by special Revelation." In other words, eternal marriage was "an entirely new doctrine" to Bennett. Since Bennett is not always reliable in his claims, he may have sensationalized his declared ignorance for effect and simply did not wish to admit his prior knowledge. However, in his six letters published in the *Sangamo Journal* in the summer of 1842 and in his 344-page *History of the Saints* (printed in late October or early

---

88. Andrew F. Smith, "John Cook Bennett's Nauvoo," 114–15.
89. John C. Bennett, "Letter from General Bennett," October 28, 1843, *Hawk Eye* (Burlington, Iowa), December 7, 1843, 1; emphasis and typographical variations in original.

November), Bennett does not describe or even allude to eternal marriage.[90] For example, he published a text purporting to be the plural marriage ceremony, a ceremony he claimed he learned from Joseph Smith:

> I now anoint you with holy, consecrated oil, in the name of Jesus Christ, and by the authority of the holy priesthood, that you may be fully and unreservedly consecrated to each other, and to the services of God, and that with affection and fidelity you may nourish and cherish each other, so long as you shall continue faithful and true in the fellowship of the Saints; and I now pronounce upon you the blessings of Jacob, whom God honored and protected in the enjoyment of like special favors; and may the peace of Heaven, which passeth all understanding, rest upon you in time and in eternity![91]

Bennett's version of the Prophet's marriage ceremony is unique in several ways. It refers to plural marriage as a "favor," a term that Joseph Smith did not use to refer to plural marriage in any available document.[92] It also describes anointing with consecrated oil, which was not a part of the sealing ordinance. Bennett's inclusion of consecrated oil may reflect rumors he had heard regarding the temple rituals experienced by those in the Quorum of the Anointed.[93] He was never invited to join this quorum or attend its meetings.[94]

---

90. The sole exception may be the Martha Brotherton affidavit, in which she quotes Brigham Young as saying: "If you will have me in this world, I will have you in that which is to come." Quoted in Bennett, *The History of the Saints*, 238.

91. Ibid., 224. Foster, *Religion and Sexuality*, 172, comments: "This statement is essentially identical to—though slightly more detailed than—the one suggested as a model in a recently published revelation dated July 27, 1842." He is referring to Joseph Smith, Revelation for Newel K. Whitney, July 27, 1842; but that revelation contains numerous dissimilarities, does not mention the word "favor," and specifies that the marriage would persist "through [o]ut all eternity." Quoted in H. Michael Marquardt, *The Joseph Smith Revelations: Text and Commentary*, 315–16.

92. George D. Smith argues that Joseph Smith used "favor" as a synonym for "plural marriage." George D. Smith, "Nauvoo Roots of Mormon Polygamy, 1841–46: A Preliminary Demographic Report," 10, and his *Nauvoo Polygamy*, xiii, xv, 45, 47, 217, 241, 244, 245, 410, 453, 473, etc., where it even appears in one of his chapter titles (241). Except for Bennett's use, only one secondhand reference supports the possibility that Joseph Smith used "favor" to refer to plural marriage. On March 7, 1843, William Clayton recorded: "Elder Brigham Young called me on one side and said he wants to give me some instructions on the priesthood the first opportunity. He said the prophet had told him to do so and give me a favor which I have long desired." George D. Smith, *An Intimate Chronicle*, 94. Whether Joseph specifically used the words "give [him] a favor," or simply directed Brigham to help Clayton, is unclear.

93. George W. Robinson wrote concerning the endowment ceremony of which he was not a participant: "After they are initiated into the lodge, they have oil poured on them..." George W. Robinson, Letter to John C. Bennett, August 8, 1842, reproduced in Bennett, *The History of the Saints*, 247–48.

94. The first endowment meeting occurred on May 1, 1842. Devery S. Anderson and

Perhaps the most instructive detail is Bennett's use of the words, "time and eternity." In Bennett's ceremonial prayer, the *marriage* is not sealed for "time and eternity." Instead, it applies to a completely different blessing: that the "peace of Heaven" should "rest upon you in time and eternity." Joseph Smith's sealing ordinances do not refer to the "peace of Heaven," but marriage covenants are sealed "for time and eternity" (D&C 132:18). It appears that Bennett heard about "time and eternity," but didn't know how it actually fit into the ceremony.

It might be argued that the inclusion of "time and eternity" in a marriage ceremony implies that the marriage would be for eternity. However, Bennett's version, invoking peace on the participants, does not inherently require eternal matrimony. A common Christian belief was that marriage was dissolved at death, but this dissolution would not preclude heaven's peace from continuing with the two single individuals in the next life. Again, surviving records are skimpy, and only one ceremonial sealing ceremony uniting Joseph to any of his plural wives has been documented—his union with Sarah Ann Whitney. It stated that they would be together "so long as you both shall live" and "also through out all eternity."[95] But if Bennett had been privately taught by Joseph Smith about plural marriage, it seems he would also have been correctly instructed regarding how to perform the ordinance. However, his writings and behaviors indicate that this was knowledge he did not possess.

Bennett continued that, after this so-called marriage ceremony, the couple "consider themselves as united in spiritual marriage, the duties and privileges of which are in *no particular different from those of any other marriage covenant.*"[96] In Joseph Smith's plural marriages, the covenants were eternal, which made them different from Christian marriage covenants.

As reviewed above, Joseph Smith taught that marriage relationships could be everlasting as early as the mid-1830s.[97] On September 16, 1835, W.

Gary James Bergera, eds., *Joseph Smith's Quorum of the Anointed, 1842–1845: A Documentary History*, 1. As discussed in the text, whatever ecclesiastical involvement Bennett may have experienced in 1841, if any, had ended by the time Joseph Smith began his personal journal on December 13. Hence, it is not surprising that he was not invited to participate in the highly secret and sacred endowment ceremony first presented months later. On June 26, the quorum of the anointed met and specifically "united in Solemn prayer that God would . . . deliver his anointed, his people from all the evil designs" of several individuals and groups including John C. Bennett. Ibid., 10.

95. Joseph Smith, Revelation for Newel K. Whitney, July 27, 1842, quoted in Marquardt, *The Joseph Smith Revelations*, 315–16; see also Revelations in Addition to Those Found in the LDS Edition of the D&C.

96. Bennett, *The History of the Saints*, 224; emphasis mine.

97. W. W. Phelps, Letter to Sally Phelps, May 26, 1835, Journal History, photo reproduction of typescript in Turley, *Selected Collections*, Vol. 2, DVD #1. See also Bruce

W. Phelps in Kirtland wrote to his wife, Sally, in Missouri: "Brother Joseph has preached some of his greatest sermons. . . . You will be mine in this world and in the world to come."[98] Parley P. Pratt recorded that the Prophet's private teachings to him in Philadelphia in 1840 included eternal, but not plural marriage, that "the wife of my bosom was an immortal, eternal companion."[99] Joseph taught of other eternal ordinances in Nauvoo in the early 1840s, such as baptism for the dead.[100] On August 15, 1840, he instructed: "People could now act for their friends who had departed this life, and . . . the plan of salvation was calculated to save all who were willing to obey the requirement of the law of God."[101] Bathsheba Smith claimed that the first time she heard of a new marriage doctrine was "in 1843. . . . I heard of being married for eternity before that time, but that had nothing to do with plurality of wives at all."[102]

Importantly, available evidence indicates that Joseph Smith never taught about polygamy, except in the context that those unions could be eternal.[103] Mary Ann West, who became William Smith's plural wife in the fall of 1843, the ceremony performed by Brigham Young, recalled the Prophet telling her "that God had given him a revelation, that a man was entitled to more wives than one. . . . He said that there was power on earth to seal wives in plural marriage. . . . He said it was for time and eternity, and not until death, as we were generally married,—it was for eternity."[104] William Clayton remembered that Joseph taught of celestial marriage, "to myself and others. . . . From him I learned that the *doctrine of plural and celestial marriage* is the most holy and important doctrine ever revealed to man on the earth, and that without obedience to that principle

---

Van Orden, "Writing to Zion: The William W. Phelps Kirtland Letters (1835–1836)," 550; M. Guy Bishop, "Eternal Marriage in Early Mormon Marital Beliefs," 78.

98. W. W. Phelps, Letter to Sally Phelps, September 16, 1835; Van Orden, "Writing to Zion," 564.

99. Parley P. Pratt Jr., ed., *Autobiography of Parley Parker Pratt, One of the Twelve Apostles of the Church of Jesus Christ of Latter-day Saints*, 1972 ed., 297–98.

100. Alexander L. Baugh, "'For This Ordinance Belongeth to My House': The Practice of Baptism for the Dead outside the Nauvoo Temple," 47–58.

101. Simon Baker, Journal History, August 15, 1840; photo reproduction in Turley, *Selected Collections*, Vol. 2, DVD #1.

102. Bathsheba Smith, Deposition, Temple Lot Transcript, Respondent's Testimony, Part 3, p. 295, questions 67–71.

103. For example, the Revelation for Newel K. Whitney, July 27, 1842, provided the word-for-word ceremony he used to seal his daughter, Sarah Ann, to the Prophet. It specifies that the marriage is "as long as you both shall live" and "also throughout all eternity" or for "time and eternity." Quoted in Marquardt, *The Joseph Smith Revelations*, 315–16; see also Revelations in Addition to Those Found in the LDS Edition of the D&C.

104. Mary Ann West, Deposition, Temple Lot Transcript, Respondent's Testimony, Part 3, p. 504, questions 269–78.

no man can ever attain to the fullness of exaltation in celestial glory."[105] Yet Bennett clearly had another understanding when he stated that "Spiritual Wives ... [are] for time! And the 'Celestial Wives' [are] for eternity!"[106]

Joseph Bates Noble affirmed that the sealing he performed uniting Joseph Smith and Louisa Beaman on April 5, 1841, was "according to the order of Celestial Marriage," which meant it would exist in the celestial world.[107] Ironically, Bennett correctly identified Louisa as one of the Prophet's plural wives but was apparently unaware that it was a celestial (eternal) union.

Bennett was surrounded by clues but failed to read them correctly. His *History of the Saints* contains seven references to "eternity," yet never in a context describing the duration of sealed marriage.[108] It also contains a quotation, reportedly from Sarah Pratt, mentioning the "everlasting covenant of our heavenly Father."[109] In addition, he published the Martha Brotherton affidavit quoting Brigham Young saying: "[I] will take you straight to the celestial kingdom; and if you will have me in this world, I will have you in that which is to come." Her affidavit also quotes Joseph Smith declaring: "I have the keys of the kingdom, and whatever I bind on earth is bound in heaven."[110] Also, Bennett referred to the "blessings of Jacob" as polygamy but evidently did not realize that the "blessings of Abraham" brought a "continuation of the seeds" (D&C 132:19–20), the zenith blessing in Joseph Smith's eternal marriage revelation. Bennett wrote about Abraham, but not in the context of eternal progeny.[111] He apparently was familiar with the term "time and eternity" but not its application to matrimony.

Given these many hints, it seems curious that Bennett lived for more than twenty months in Nauvoo but remained oblivious to Joseph Smith's secret teachings about eternal marriage. Equally remarkable is the fact that Bennett's creativity and deductive reasoning were insufficient to put the puzzle pieces together. Doubtless Bennett would have posed as an insider if it brought him such advantages as facilitating potential sexual conquests or, later, vilifying his enemy Joseph Smith.

In short, writers who take the position that Bennett was one of Joseph Smith's polygamy confidants and thereby take his statements at face value are giving him a privileged status that is not based on any credible evidence.

---

105. Andrew Jenson, "Plural Marriage," 226, emphasis mine; see also George Smith, *An Intimate Chronicle*, 559.
106. Bennett, "Letter from General Bennett," October 28, 1843, 1; emphasis removed.
107. Joseph B. Noble, Affidavit, Joseph F. Smith, Affidavit Books, 1:3.
108. Bennett, *The History of the Saints*, 43, 131, 154, 172, 224, 244, 320.
109. Ibid., 229.
110. Ibid., 238–39.
111. Ibid., 42, 43, 59, 114, 131, 147, 154, 238.

Although not all of Bennett's statements are inaccurate, the things he recounted correctly could have come from individuals other than Joseph Smith. In addition, Bennett's assertions would all benefit from verification from other sources before they can confidently be included in any historical reconstruction of Nauvoo polygamy. Available documents support that Bennett never learned about eternal marriage from Joseph Smith, even though four men (including Joseph) and approximately sixteen women were then practicing plural marriage and an estimated two dozen had learned about the principle from Joseph himself by the time Bennett's book was published.

Accordingly, Bennett's reports of personal conversations with Joseph Smith regarding plural marriage must be dealt with cautiously, seeking a second reliable witness wherever possible. Included are comments about Sarah Pratt: "Joe Smith told me, *confidentially*, during the absence of her husband, that he intended to make Mrs. [Sarah] Pratt one of his *spiritual wives*, one of the *Cloistered Saints*, for the Lord had given her to him as a special favor for his faithfulness and zeal; and, as I had influence with her, he desired me to assist him in the consummation of his hellish purposes."[112] Similarly, Bennett claimed that Joseph bribed him to further his courtship of Nancy Rigdon: "Knowing that I had much influence with Mr. Rigdon's family, Joe Smith said to me, one day last summer [1841], when riding together over the lawn in Nauvoo, "If you will assist me in procuring Nancy [Rigdon] as one of my spiritual wives, I will give you five hundred dollars, or the best lot on Main Street.""[113]

Bennett's letters and *History of the Saints* allege that he witnessed kisses or conjugal visits between Joseph Smith and specific women (wives or non-wives), but such allegations are contradicted by the reports of plural wives that there were no acts of physical affection from Joseph during the "courtship" period. These descriptions are easily explained as Bennett's attempt to invent details that would position himself as an insider. Even more improbable are Bennett claims that Joseph Smith attempted to kiss Sarah Pratt, afterwards saying: "I did not desire to kiss her; *Bennett made me do it!*"[114] If the Prophet did not share a new but non-controversial teaching like eternal marriage with Bennett, how likely is it that he would have permitted Bennett to witness such actions as those described here and even positioned himself as under Bennett's influence in taking such actions?

It appears Bennett was positioned to hear rumors: rumors about polygamy, rumors about "time and eternity," rumors about consecrated oil, and

---

112. Ibid., 228; emphasis Bennett's. See also Bennett, "Bennett's Second and Third Letters."

113. Bennett, *The History of the Saints*, 241; see also Bennett, Letter to the *Sangamo Journal*, July 2, 1842.

114. Bennett, *The History of the Saints*, 231; emphasis Bennett's. See also Bennett, "Bennett's Second and Third Letters."

rumors about the identities of plural wives. John Taylor (not the apostle) recalled that John C. Bennett's knowledge of plural marriage in Nauvoo came from "an inkling" rather than from personal instruction from the Prophet.[115] However, his backhanded confession that he never learned about eternal marriage in Nauvoo and his descriptions of Joseph Smith's plural marriage teachings undermine his claims as Joseph's confidant where polygamy was concerned.

Nauvooans on Bennett's "Spiritual Wifery"

Concerning Bennett's "spiritual wifery" ideas, William Law affirmed in his July 1842 affidavit published in the *Wasp*: "J. C. Bennett declared to me before God that Joseph Smith had never taught him such doctrines, and that he never told anyone that he (Joseph Smith) had taught any such things, and that anyone who said so told base lies; nevertheless, he said he had done wrong, that he would not deny, but he would deny that he had used Joseph Smith's name to accomplish his designs on any one; stating that he had no need of that, for that he could succeed without telling them that Joseph approbated such conduct."[116] William Law would split from Joseph Smith two years later (see Chapter 31), but in his recollections did not paint Bennett as a participant in First Presidency business during 1841 or as a confidant of Joseph Smith at any time.[117]

Parley P. Pratt, who had not been in Nauvoo during all of Bennett's twenty-month sojourn in the city, challenged Bennett's claims in an undated discourse, a "fragment" of which was published in the July 1, 1845, *Millennial Star*:

> Beware of seducing spirits, and doctrines of devils, as first introduced by John C. Bennett, under the name of 'Spiritual Wife' doctrine.... It is but another name for whoredom, wicked and unlawful connexion, and every kind of confusion, corruption, and abominations...
>
> As to sealings, and covenants, to secure the union of parents, children, and companions in the world to come, or in the resurrection; it is a true doctrine, and as holy and pure as the throne of God, having emanated from his own bosom. Its laws are strict, and it admits of no confusion, unlawful connexion, or unvirtuous liberties. It is calculated to exalt society to the highest degree of happiness, union, purity, fidelity, virtue, confidence, and love, in this world and in that which is to come.[118]

---

115. Taylor, "Sermon in Honor of the Martyrdom," June 27, 1854.

116. William Law, Affidavit, July 20, 1842, in *Wasp*, Extra, July 27, 1842.

117. See William Law, Letter to Dr. W. Wyl, January 7, 1887, quoted in "The Mormons in Nauvoo: Three Letters from William Law on Mormonism, *[Salt Lake] Daily Tribune*, July 3, 1887. William Law, Letter to T. B. H. Stenhouse, November 24, 1871, quoted in T. B. H. Stenhouse, *Rocky Mountain Saints*, 198.

118. Parley P. Pratt, "Fragment of an Address by P. P. Pratt," *Millennial Star* 6, no. 2 (July 1, 1845): 22. Pratt was in the United States when this "fragment" appeared; I have

President Wilford Woodruff, whose Nauvoo residence overlapped Bennett's from October 1841 until Bennett left, recalled fifty years later in 1892 when he was providing testimony under adversarial questioning in the Temple Lot Case: "[The] spiritual wives business . . . was got up by Bennett, and it was nothing that was acknowledged by Joseph Smith at all, or by the church. That was an invention of Bennett's that was not acknowledged or countenanced by either the Church or Joseph Smith."[119] Woodruff's recollection might reflect a revisionist interpretation embraced by the Saints of that time, but it could also represent an accurate assessment of what actually happened, which correlates precisely with my own conclusions.

Also in 1892, giving testimony in the same case, Cyrus Wheelock, who testified that he lived in Nauvoo at the time of the Bennett scandal gave this assessment of those days:

> John C. Bennett got up a company,—a secret combination, the purpose of which was to form a society altogether different to the purpose of that revelation [D&C 132]. His system was a scheme somewhat similar to a public seraglio. It was got up for the purpose of cultivating the baser passions in human nature and these men were sworn not to reveal their system, and it was given out secretly by Bennett that Joseph Smith had told him he could get up such a society or system, and finally it came to Joseph's ears, and Bennett was excommunicated.[120]

Summary

The evidence and observations presented in this chapter support that the traditional belief that John C. Bennett's licentiousness was simply a variation on Joseph Smith's plural marriage teachings should be rescrutinized. A more likely interpretation is that Bennett was an adulterer prior to arriving in Nauvoo and simply continued his lascivious activity, eventually hearing rumors of polygamy that he implemented into his seduction techniques.

It appears that the Prophet learned of Bennett's improprieties early and tried to rehabilitate his talented friend. Joseph later expressed regret for extending mercy as he patiently dealt with the mayor's immoral behaviors.

Bennett first admitted that Joseph Smith never taught him about plural marriage, claiming to William Law that he could accomplish his seductions without using Joseph's name. But after he had left Nauvoo, Bennett sensation-

---

been unable to locate the entire discourse.

119. Wilford Woodruff, Deposition, Temple Lot Transcript, Respondent's Testimony, Part 3, p. 57, question 551.

120. Cyrus Wheelock, Deposition, Temple Lot Transcript, Respondent's Testimony, Part 3, p. 534, question 45.

ally announced the eternal marriage was not the same as plural marriage, thus casting doubt on the Prophet as the source of any information Bennett might have had about the new and everlasting covenant of marriage, including polygamy. Church President Joseph F. Smith, who was born in 1838, wrote this summary in 1903, a time when the Church was under heavy pressure because of the Reed Smoot hearings to prove that it was stepping away from polygamy (announced in 1890). This statement, which had the obvious motive of defending the Church against charges of hypocrisy, appeared in *The Arena*, a monthly magazine published in Boston:

> During the period immediately preceding the assassination of Joseph and Hyrum Smith, what was known as "spiritual wifeism" was secretly taught by pretended latter-day Saints, who subsequently apostatized and became the bitterest and most unscrupulous enemies of the "Mormons." Among them was the notorious John C. Bennett, who led away several foolish men and women by his wiles. It was that false and vicious doctrine that was denied by affidavit and by official declaration as being sanctioned by the church. The principle of celestial and plural marriage, as made known in the revelation of 1843, is not to be confounded with Bennett's system of lust.[121]

An examination of the non-traditional marriage systems reportedly present in Nauvoo in 1842 reveals three forms. First, a few individuals had entered into secret plural marriages authorized by Joseph Smith. Second, a dozen or so individuals were personally involved in unstructured seductions and adulteries, with Bennett leading the way. Third, months after leaving Nauvoo, Bennett wrote of a triple-echelon system of cyprian, chambered, and cloistered sisters who could experience sexual relations with men without the preliminary performance of a marriage ceremony. The historical record fails to document even a single case of this third dynamic, which appears to have been a fictional construct described by Bennett to sell his book, *History of the Saints*. Despite the vast differences between these three processes, all were labeled "spiritual wifery" by onlookers, a name that persists to this day, usually without any attempt to distinguish the actual details of the association being referenced.

A closer look at both Bennett's immoral behaviors and the Prophet's restoration of polygamous marriage supports the conclusion that the two processes ran a parallel course that never truly intersected.

---

121. Joseph F. Smith, "The Mormonism of To-day," 450.

Chapter 21

John C. Bennett, Sarah Pratt, and Orson Pratt

Both Orson and Sarah Pratt became entangled in dramatic events initiated by John C. Bennett. At the heart of the controversy was Sarah's involvement with Bennett and/or Joseph Smith. Born on February 5, 1817, Sarah Marinda Bates accepted the Restoration, was baptized on June 18, 1835, fell in love with one of her missionaries, twenty-four-year-old Apostle Orson Pratt, and married him the next year.[1] By the early 1840s, Sarah was living alone in Nauvoo while Orson, by then an apostle, served a mission from August 1839 to July 1841 to the British Isles. Two contradictory stories regarding Sarah Pratt in 1840 and 1841 before Orson's return are chronicled in the historical record.

---

1. While serving as a missionary, Orson Pratt recorded that Sarah M. Bates (his own future wife) had received a polygamous proposal from a Church member who was excommunicated for the attempt: "The 10th Elder Luke Johnson who had been labouring a few weeks in those parts came to Bro Bates'. We held a meeting about 3 miles distant in afternoon. In the evening Elders Johnson & Dutcher & myself & Bro. Bates come together in order to deal with Elder Blakesly who was also present who was guilty of some verry improper conduct towards \one of the/ Sisters Sally M. Bates such as telling her that she had won his affections & that he loved her as much as he did his own wife; requesting her [to] break her engagements with me \a young man with whom she had had some acquaintance/ & remain single saying that he did not think that his own wife would live a great while—those the above I learned from \the/ Sister's [illegible name] own mouth who felt much disgusted at his conduct & desired that he should be dealt with. Elder Blakesly did not deny the above but at first said his motives were pure but afterwards after [sic] acknowledged that he had done very wrong Sister [written over Sally] we told him that his conduct had been such that we considered him unworthy to hold a license for a period of time & that it was necessary for him to make his acknowledgments to Sally \we &[?] the/ family \he had offended/ & also to the church & some individuals who did not belong to the church who resided in Mexico [Jefferson County, New York] at which place he had not been sufficiently reserve[d] in his conduct towards \the/ Sister [illegible] \mentioned/ ( ) & in other branches where his conduct had not been such as becomes an Elder he agreed to do as was required & the same evening made his confessions to the [name erased] family \whom he had offended/ we took his license from him until he should \make/ satisfaction among the different Branches of the church where he had offended and also until he should be sufficiently chastened." Orson Pratt, Journal, June 10, 1836; terminal punctuation and initial capitals added.

Story One: Joseph Smith Attempts to Make Sarah Pratt a "Spiritual Wife"

In a letter published in the *Sangamo Journal* on July 15, 1842, John C. Bennett alleged that Joseph Smith had surreptitiously requested Bennett's assistance in securing Sarah Pratt as a "Spiritual Wife":

> Joe Smith stated to me at an early day in the history of that city, that he intended to make that amiable and accomplished lady one of his *spiritual wives*, for the Lord had given her to him, and he requested me to assist him in consummating his hellish purposes, but I told him that I would not do it—that she had been much neglected and abused by the church during the absence of her husband in Europe, and that if the Lord had given her to him he must attend to it himself. I will do it, said he, for there is no harm in it if her husband should never find it out. I called upon Mrs. Pratt and told that Joe contemplated an attack on her virtue, *in the name of the Lord*, and that she must prepare to repulse him in so infamous an assault. . . . Accordingly in a few days Joe proposed to me to go. . . . We then proceeded to the house where Mrs. Pratt resided, and Joe commenced discourse as follows: "Sister Pratt, the Lord has given you to me as one of my spiritual wives. I have the blessings of Jacob granted me, as he granted holy men of old, and I have long looked upon you with favor, and hope you will not deny me." She replied: "I care not for the blessings of Jacob, and I believe in no such revelations, neither will I consent under any circumstances. I have one good husband, and that is enough for me." . . . Three times afterwards he tried to convince Mrs. Pratt of the propriety of his doctrine, and she at last told him: "Joseph, if you ever attempt any thing of the kind with me again, I will tell Mr. Pratt on his return home. I will certainly do it."[2]

An 1884 document purportedly associated with Sarah Pratt (misidentified throughout the document as "Hyde," no doubt because both apostles were named "Orson") recounts:

> As the wife of Orson ~~Hyde~~ \Pratt/ the Apostle, Mrs. ~~Hyde~~ \Pratt/ was very familiar with the workings of Mormonism for many years. Mrs Emma Smith and Mrs Heber C. Kimball were among her most intimate friends; specially intimate as she was left without any relative but her infant son while her husband was off on his missions to England. . . .
>
> In Joseph Smith she had implicit confidence. ~~in.~~ She accepted his inspired revelations; her husband had written many at his dictation. He appeared much interested in her affairs and brought Dr. John C. Bennett once

---

2. John C. Bennett, "Bennett's Second and Third Letters," *Sangamo Journal*, July 15, 1842; italics in original. He reprinted an edited version in *The History of the Saints: Or an Exposé of Joe Smith and Mormonism*, 228–31.

or twice with him when he called: At first his calls were made upon her in her home where she was living with another family; then when she moved into a little house by herself his attentions became more frequent. He told her at one time that his wife Emma had become jealous of her; she at once called upon Emma and assured her of the folly of such an idea; she told her that she was thoroughly bound up in her husband, Mr. Hyde [sic], and had no thought for any one else. At one of his calls with Dr. Bennet, Joseph told Mrs. Hyde [sic] that there was something he wanted to say to her but dare not for fear she would lose respect for him. That seemed impossible to her, ~~but~~ \as/ she told him; he however postponed the announcement. . . .

Sometime after this Joseph called again and said that now he should tell her what he meant to have told her before. He said ~~it~~ that he knew she must be lonely now that her husband was away, and that it was not at all necessary that it should be so. She needed the company of some man, and he would stay with her when ~~the~~ she wished it; that there was no sin in it as long as she kept it to herself; that the sin was wholly in making it known ~~to~~ herself ~~or~~ to her husband or any one else. She replied to Joseph's proposal most indignantly; she told him she loved her husband most devotedly, and upbraided him \sharply/ for what he had suggested. He replied that if she told of it he had it in his power to ruin her character. From that time she discontinued her habit of going to his house to sew, and asked Emma Smith to send the work to her instead.

After he had left her ~~she~~ Mrs. Hyde [sic] was in \great/ distress of mind. Here she was ~~friendless and~~ alone scarcely more than twenty years of age, with one who was almost as a god to her counselling her in this way. . . . There was nothing said then as to Celestial Marriage or revelation.

One day Dr. Bennet, who knew of Smith's proposal to Mrs. Pratt and its rejection, and who in consequence confided to her some of Smith's iniquities, one day ~~he~~ called upon her, and told her that a revelation was to be made five days later, to Joseph Smith, authorizing polygamy; that Smith had been so general in his attentions ~~that~~ to the women that he was obliged to shield himself by these means.[3]

The author of this document is unknown; but it seems unlikely that Sarah was closely involved with its composition, if she was associated with it at all. The writer mistakenly substitutes the surname "Hyde" for "Pratt" in six different places, three times correcting it and three times not. It is an error Pratt herself would not have made and would have quickly rectified in the document if she had been given the opportunity. In addition, it contains numerous unsubstantiated claims and factual errors. I have found no documentation corroborating that Sarah Pratt was an "intimate friend" of "Mrs. Emma Smith and Mrs. Heber C. Kimball," nor have I found any evidence that Joseph Smith

---

3. [Anon.] "Workings of Mormonism Related by Mrs. Orson Pratt," 1–3.

paid "frequent" visits to Sarah Pratt's home. Also undocumented is Emma's alleged jealousy of Sarah, any teaching by Joseph Smith that adultery was not sinful if kept secret, or that Sarah Pratt was in the "habit of going to his [Joseph Smith's] house to sew." At the time, the Smiths lived in the Homestead, a small three-room dwelling with one room upstairs. It would have been crowded to have a sewing woman present on a daily basis. Chronologically the discussion that a "revelation was to be made five days later" is problematic. The alleged interaction between Joseph and Sarah occurred prior to July of 1841, but the revelation of celestial marriage (now D&C 132) was not written until two years later. Despite these numerous problems, Gary Bergera characterizes Bennett's account as "accurate in many details."[4]

In 1886, Sarah was quoted by anti-Mormon Wilhelm Ritter von Wymetal, writing under the pseudonym of Wilhelm Wyl, who said she told him this version of the events:

> When my husband went to England as a missionary, he got the promise from Joseph that I should receive provisions from the tithing-house.[5] Shortly afterward Joseph made his propositions to me and they enraged me so that I refused to accept any help from the tithing-house or from the bishop. Having been always very clever and very busy with my needle, I began to take in sewing for the support of myself and children, and succeeded soon in making myself independent. When Bennett came to Nauvoo, Joseph brought him to my house, stating that Bennett wanted some sewing done, and that I should do it for the doctor. I assented and Bennett gave me a great deal of work to do. He knew that Joseph had his plans set on me; Joseph made no secret of them before Bennett, and went so far in his impudence as to make propositions to me in the presence of Bennett, his bosom friend. Bennett, who was of a sarcastic turn of mind, used to come and tell me about Joseph to tease and irritate me.[6]

These three reports are not corroborated by other witnesses other than the two participants, John C. Bennett and Sarah Bates Pratt, but are generally consistent with each other and claim, among other things, that Joseph Smith sought an illicit relationship with Sarah.

---

4. Gary James Bergera, "John C. Bennett, Joseph Smith, and the Beginnings of Mormon Plural Marriage in Nauvoo," 60 note 50; see also Bergera, *Conflict in the Quorum: Orson Pratt, Brigham Young, Joseph Smith*, 16.

5. The Twelve Apostles left for England on April 26, 1839, from Far West, Missouri (D&C 118:5). At that time, there was no tithing office in the Church and the city of Nauvoo had yet to be chosen as the next gathering place.

6. W. Wyl [pseud. of Wilhelm Ritter von Wymetal], *Mormon Portraits, or the Truth about Mormon Leaders from 1830 to 1886, Joseph Smith the Prophet, His Family and His Friends: A Study Based on Fact and Documents*, 61.

Story Two: John C. Bennett and Sarah Pratt Were Sexually Involved

Accounts from several other witnesses describe a very different situation concerning Sarah Pratt and John C. Bennett in 1840 and early 1841. As quoted in Chapter 19, Nauvoo resident and Church member Stephen Goddard signed an affidavit stating that, on October 6, 1840, "from the first night, until the last, with the exception of one night it being nearly a month, the Dr. was there as sure as the night came, and generally two or three times a day—for the first two or three nights he left about 9 o'clock—after that he remained later, sometimes till after midnight."[7] He also claimed that Sarah later moved into a separate house where she and Bennett were seen there "together, as it were, man and wife."[8]

Goddard's wife, Zeruiah, not only made an affidavit confirming her husband's statement, but swore out her own affidavit on August 28, 1842:

> Dr. Bennett came to my house one night about 12 o'clock, and sat on or beside the bed where Mrs. Pratt was and cursed and swore very profanely at her; she told me next day that the Dr. was quick tempered and was mad at her, but gave no other reason. I concluded from circumstances that she had promised to meet him somewhere and had disappointed him; on another night I remonstrated with the Dr. and asked him what Orson Pratt would think, if he should know that you were so fond of his wife, and holding her hand so much; the Dr. replied that he could pull the wool over Orson's eyes. . . .
>
> My husband and I were frequently at Mrs. Pratt's and stayed till after 10 o'clock in the night, and Dr. Bennett still remained there with her and her little child alone at that late hour.
>
> On one occasion I came suddenly into the room where Mrs. Pratt and the Dr. were; she was lying on the bed and the Dr. was taking his hands out of her bosom; he was in the habit of sitting on the bed where Mrs. Pratt was lying, and lying down over her.
>
> I would further state that from my own observation, I am satisfied that their conduct was anything but virtuous, and I know Mrs. Pratt is not a woman of truth, and I believe the statements which Dr. Bennett made concerning Joseph Smith are false, and fabricated for the purpose of covering his own iniquities, and enabling him to practice his base designs on the innocent.[9]

---

7. Stephen H. Goddard, Letter to Orson Pratt, July 23, 1842, in *Affidavits and Certificates, Disproving the Statements and Affidavits Contained in John C. Bennett's Letters*. His wife, Zeruiah, in the immediately following paragraph, certified the accuracy of her husband's statement, and George W. Harris, a city alderman, certified their affidavits.

8. Ibid.

9. Ibid. She also subscribed to this affidavit before George W. Harris, a Nauvoo alderman.

On July 28, 1842, J. B. Backenstos, the non-Mormon sheriff of Hancock County, signed the following affidavit:

> Personally appeared before me Ebenezer Robinson an acting Justice of the Peace, in and for said county, J. B. Backenstos, who being duly sworn according to law, deposeth and saith, that some time during last winter, he accused Doctor John C. Bennett, with having an illicit intercourse with Mrs. Orson Pratt, and some others, when said Bennett replied that she made a first rate go, and from personal observations I should have taken said Doctor Bennett and Mrs. Pratt as man and wife, had I not known to the contrary, and further this deponent saith not.[10]

Richard Van Wagoner discounts this affidavit: "Backenstos's statement may be dismissed as slander—during the winter mentioned, Orson was in Nauvoo, and Sarah sick and pregnant with their daughter Celestia Larissa."[11] In fact, Backenstos did not date his accusation more precisely than "last winter" (1841–42), which accused Bennett of a previous sexual involvement (date unspecified) with Sarah Pratt. What prevented Backenstos from making the accusation closer to the alleged moral transgression? Backenstos, as one of Bennett's former followers, was clearly positioned to have had such a conversation with the Doctor.[12]

Ebenezer Robinson reported in 1890: "In the spring of 1841 Dr. Bennett had a small neat house built for Elder Orson Pratt's family [Sarah and one male child] and commenced boarding with them. Elder Pratt was absent on a mission to England."[13] John D. Lee recalled: "[John C. Bennett] became intimate with Orson Pratt's wife, while Pratt was on a mission. That he built her a fine frame house, and lodged with her, and used her as his wife."[14]

Mary Ettie V. Coray Smith, a sometimes confused informant, related:

> Orson Pratt, then, as now [1858], one of the "Twelve," was sent by Joseph Smith on a mission to England. During his absence, his first (*i.e.* his lawful) wife, Sarah, occupied a house owned by John C. Bennett, a man of some note, and at that time, quartermaster-general of the Nauvoo Legion. Sarah was an educated woman, of fine accomplishments, and attracted the attention of the Prophet Joseph, who called upon her one day, and alleged he found John C. Bennett in bed with her. As we lived

---

10. "Affidavit of J. B. Backenstos," in ibid.

11. Richard S. Van Wagoner, *Mormon Polygamy: A History*, 34.

12. Catherine Fuller Warren named Backenstos and several others of Bennett's followers in her testimony before the Nauvoo High Council, May 25, 1842, admitting that Backenstos had paid her two dollars for sex.

13. Ebenezer Robinson, "Items of Personal History," *The Return*, 1, no. 11 (November 1890): 362.

14. John D. Lee, *Mormonism Unveiled*, 148.

but across the street from her house we heard the whole uproar. Sarah ordered the Prophet out of the house, and the Prophet used obscene language to her.[15]

Other witnesses provided similar testimony that a relationship existed between John C. Bennett and Sarah Pratt that exceeded the bounds of propriety. After reviewing the available evidence, historian D. Michael Quinn concluded it to be a sexual relationship or even a marriage by referring to her as "Sarah M. Bates (Pratt, Bennett, Pratt)."[16]

Orson Pratt's "Mind Temporarily Gave Way"

Returning from England on July 19, 1841, Orson Pratt apparently heard little concerning Sarah's alleged extramarital involvement with Joseph Smith or John C. Bennett or he was unimpressed by the accusations.[17] It is not clear whether Joseph Smith personally introduced him to the principle of plural marriage, as he had done with Brigham Young, Heber C. Kimball, John Taylor, and other apostles—indeed, almost as soon as they arrived.[18] Biographer Breck England wrote: "If he [Orson Pratt] did hear it [plural marriage] that summer, his reaction is unknown. He was not at that time required to enter the plural marriage covenant."[19] Joseph Smith may have chosen to deal with Orson Pratt differently than with the other members of the Quorum of the Twelve.

The first signal of Orson Pratt's discontent occurred on May 11, 1842, ten months after his return from England, when his signature was not included on a document withdrawing fellowship from General John C. Bennett that was signed by all other members of the Twelve who were present in Nauvoo.[20] The absence of Orson's name is conspicuous, but the precise reason is not known. The schism apparently continued to widen in ensuing weeks, though no contemporary details are available. On July 5, William M. Allred, the husband of Sarah Pratt's sister, Orissa,[21] wrote to John C. Bennett stating: "Mr.

---

15. Nelson Winch Green, ed., *Fifteen Years among the Mormons: Being the Narrative of Mrs. Mary Ettie V. Smith*, 31.

16. D. Michael Quinn, *The Mormon Hierarchy: Origins of Power*, 503, 536.

17. Elden J. Watson, ed., *The Orson Pratt Journals*, 143–77. .

18. According to Bergera, *Conflict in the Quorum*, 15, "Nor did Pratt reveal the extent of his own knowledge, if any, of 'the new and everlasting covenant' of marriage before mid-1842."

19. Breck England, *The Life and Thought of Orson Pratt*, 77.

20. "Notice," *Times and Seasons*, June 15, 1842, 830.

21. Born December 24, 1819, near Nashville, Tennessee, William Moore Allred was baptized in 1832 and married Sarah Pratt's sister, Orissa Bates, January 9, 1842.

Pratt would write, but he is *afraid to*. He wishes to be *perfectly still*, until your second letter comes out—then you may hear."[22]

John C. Bennett's story of Joseph Smith seeking Sarah as a spiritual wife was published in the July 15 issue of the *Sangamo Journal*.[23] Unsurprisingly, Bennett painted himself as a noble and virtuous gentleman. Sarah apparently sided with Bennett, thus creating a profoundly distressing situation for Orson. Joseph Smith's diary for that day notes:

> This A.M. early a report was in circulation that O.P. [Orson Pratt] was missing. A letter of his writing was found directed to his wife stating to the effect that he was going away. Soon as this was known Joseph summoned the principal men of the city and workmen on the Temple to meet at the Temple Grove where he ordered them to proceed immediately throughout the city in search of him lest he should have laid violent hands on himself. After considerable search had been made, but to no effect a meeting was called at the Grove where Joseph stated before the public a general outline of J.C. Bennetts conduct and especially with regard to sis P [Sarah Pratt] . . . O. P. [Orson Pratt] returned at night. He was seen about 2 miles this side Warsaw, set on a log. He says he has concluded to do right.[24]

In 1890, Ebenezer Robinson recalled: "Under these circumstances his [Orson's] mind temporarily gave way, and he wandered away, no one knew where. . . . He was found some five miles below Nauvoo, sitting on a rock on the bank of the Mississippi river."[25] The explanation of temporary insanity, while extreme, would not be required to explain the intense emotional dilemma of a young husband and devoted apostle who found himself in a situation where he had to confront apparently irreconcilable contradictions; it would be natural for Orson to seek solitude in which to appraise the information and try to come to emotional terms with it. At some point, apparently during that agonizing day, Orson captured his turmoil in poignant prose:

> I am a ruined man! My future prospects are blasted! The testimony upon both sides seems to be equal: The one in direct contradiction to the other—how to decide I know not neither does it matter for let it be either way my temporal happiness is gone in this world if the testimonies of my wife and others are true then I have been deceived for twelve years past—

---

22. William M. Allred, Letter to John C. Bennett, July 5, 1842; printed in Bennett, *The History of the Saints*, 46; emphasis Allred's.

23. John C. Bennett, "Bennett's Second and Third Letters," *Sangamo Journal*, July 15, 1842; also printed in Bennett, *The History of the Saints*, 226–32.

24. Dean C. Jessee, ed., *The Papers of Joseph Smith: Vol. 2, Journal, 1832–1842*, 398–99.

25. Ebenezer Robinson, "Items of Personal History of the Editor—Including Some Items of Church History Not Generally Known," *The Return* 2, no. 11 (November 1890): 363. See also *History of the Church*, 5:60–61.

my hopes are blasted and gone as it were in a moment—my long toils and labors have been in vain. If on the other hand the other testimonies are true then my family are ruined forever. Where then is my hope in this world? It is gone—gone not to be recovered!! Oh God, why is it thus with me! My sorrows are greater than I can bear! Where I am henceforth it matters not.[26]

Two days later on July 17, the day after Orson's safe return, Brigham Young wrote to Orson's brother, Parley, who was still in England on his mission: "Br Orson Pratt is in trubble in consequence of his wife, his feelings are so rought up that he dos not know whether his wife is wrong, or whether Josephs testimony and others are wrong and due Ly and he decived for 12 years or not; he is all but crazy about matters, you may ask what the matter is concirning Sister P.—it is enoph, and doct. J. C. Bennett could tell all about it if he himself & hir- - - - - "[27]

Just five days later on July 22, Wilson Law presented a resolution attempting to suppress Bennett's influence at a public meeting. Whatever Orson meant, by the report that he had resolved to "do right," it apparently did not mean that he fully accepted Joseph Smith's account. The *Times and Seasons* description of the meeting, published on August 1, reported:

> At a meeting of the citizens of the city of Nauvoo held in said city at the meeting ground [near the temple site], July 22d 1842. . . . The meeting was called to order by the chairman, who stated the object of the meeting to be to obtain an expression of the public mind in reference to the reports gone abroad, calumniating the character of Pres. Joseph Smith. Gen. Wilson Law then rose and presented the following resolution.
>
> (Resolved) That, having heard that John C. Bennett was circulating many base falsehoods respecting a number of the citizens of Nauvoo, and especially against our worthy and respected Mayor, Joseph Smith, we do hereby manifest to the world that so far as we are acquainted with Joseph Smith we know him to be a good, moral, virtuous, peaceable and patriotic man, and a firm supporter of law, justice and equal rights; that he at all times upholds and keeps inviolate the constitution of this State and of the United States.
>
> A vote was then called and the resolution adopted by a large concourse of citizens, numbering somewhere about a thousand men. Two or three, voted in the negative.

---

26. Orson Pratt, Letter, addressee unnamed, n.d., ca. July 15–19, 1842. Bergera, *Conflict in the Quorum*, 23 note 52, clarifies: "This document, apparently in Pratt's hand, is in the uncatalogued Orson Pratt Papers, LDS Church Archives. It has been in the possession of the LDS Church History Department since at least the early 1970s when historian D. Michael Quinn examined it." Although this document is restricted, I received permission to view it on microfilm.

27. Brigham Young, Letter to Parley P. Pratt, Nauvoo, July 17, 1842.

Elder Orson Pratt then rose and spoke at some length in explanation of his negative vote. Pres. Joseph Smith spoke in reply

Question to Elder Pratt, "Have you personally a knowledge of any immoral act in me toward the female sex, or in any other way?" Answer, by Elder O. Pratt, "Personally, toward the female sex, I have not."

Elder O. Pratt responded at some length.[28]

Church leaders sought to assist their troubled apostle-colleague during the ensuing weeks. Brigham Young recorded on August 8, 1842: "Assisted by Elders H. C. Kimball and Geo. A. Smith, I spent several days laboring with Elder Orson Pratt, whose mind became so darkened by the influence and statements of his wife, that he came out in rebellion against Joseph, refusing to believe his testimony or obey his counsel. He said he would believe his wife in preference to the Prophet. Joseph told him if he did believe his wife and follow her suggestions, he would go to hell."[29] Apostle John Taylor similarly recalled: "When I saw that he was very severely tried, as I had always held pleasant relations with him, I took every pains that I possibly could to explain the situation of things, to remove his doubts, and to satisfy his feelings, but without avail. At one time I talked with him for nearly two hours, to prevent, if possible, his apostasy or departure from the church. But he was very sorely tried, and was very self-willed and stubborn in his feelings, and would not yield. His feelings were bitter towards the Prophet Joseph Smith and others."[30]

Caught between two stories, one from his wife whom he loved and the other from his Prophet, to whom he had been unquestionably devoted for twelve years, Orson wavered between the two, unable to find a resolution that honored both. After a month of turmoil, he apparently took enough of a stand in accepting Sarah's story that both were excommunicated on August 20, 1842, he for "insubordination," and she for "adultery."[31] Apparently this

---

28. "John C. Bennett," *Times and Seasons* 3 (August 1, 1842): 869. The Prophet's diary for July 22 records: "A.M. at the stand conflicting with O.P. and correcting the public mind with regard to reports put in circulation by Bennett & others." In Jessee, *The Papers of Joseph Smith: Volume 2, Journal, 1832–1842*, 400.

29. Elden Jay Watson, ed., *Manuscript History of Brigham Young, 1801–1844*, 120–21.

30. G. Homer Durham, comp. and ed., *The Gospel Kingdom: Selections from the Writings and Discourses of John Taylor*, 193.

31. Richard S. Van Wagoner and Steven C. Walker, *A Book of Mormons*, 212. I have been unable to find primary historical documentation of the Church disciplinary action against Sarah Pratt that Van Wagoner and Walker describe. Michael Marquardt explained: "As far as I know there is no actual record that Sarah Pratt was excommunicated. She was rebaptized, along with Orson Pratt and Lydia Granger on January 20, 1843. It is possible that there were no minutes taken of the meeting when Orson Pratt was cut off from the church by three members of the Quorum of the Twelve. Willard Richards was out of town and would not have recorded the meeting."

punishment and signal of separation from Orson's identity community had so sharp an effect on his mind that, the very next day, Orson swerved back to allegiance to the Prophet. Joseph Smith's diary noted on August 21: "Orson Pratt has also signified his intention of coming out in defence of the truth and go to preaching."[32] He did not immediately depart on a mission, but his announcement indicates the depths of his turmoil.

Rumors concerning Orson Pratt's possible collaboration with John C. Bennett prompted Orson to publish a letter in *The Wasp*, then being published in Nauvoo by William Smith, on September 3, 1842: "I hereby certify, that I have not been absent from Nauvoo during twenty four hours, at any one time, since I returned from my English Mission, which was upwards of one year ago. Neither have I renounced the Church of Jesus Christ of Latter Day Saints, but believe that its doctrine, which has been extensively published in both America and Europe, is pure and according to the scriptures of eternal truth, and merits the candid investigation of all lovers of righteousness."[33]

Furthermore, in addition to making a strong declaration of faith, Orson continued by distancing himself completely from Bennett saying: "We have never at any time written any letter or letters to Dr. J. C. Bennett, on any subject whatever. Neither are we 'preparing to leave and expose Mormonism' but intend to make NAUVOO OUR RESIDENCE AND MORMONISM OUR MOTTO."[34] No contemporary record of Sarah's reaction to these turbulent events is known. However, the fact that she did not leave Orson, the Church, or Nauvoo must be interpreted as a statement of continued loyalty, even though her personal and marital history would continue to prove complicated in the following years.

Sorting through the Conflicting Claims

Gary James Bergera observed that Bennett's "mixture of fact and fantasy makes it difficult to know when he is telling the truth."[35] As discussed in the last chapter, I find it unlikely that Bennett learned about eternal marriage in Nauvoo, thus lessening the likelihood that the Prophet would have divulged to Bennett secret plans to marry Sarah polygamously or to get her as a "spiritual

---

Email to Brian Hales, October 3, 2008. Bergera, *Conflict in the Quorum*, 27, notes that Orson Pratt was "cut off from the church. . . . Surprisingly, no mention is made of any action against Sarah."

32. Jessee, *The Papers of Joseph Smith—Journal, 1832–1842*, 2:421.

33. Orson Pratt, "For the Wasp," *The Wasp* 1, no. 20 (September 3, 1842): 4.

34. Ibid.; emphasis Pratt's. By "we," Orson was using a common nineteenth-century authorial device, which should not necessarily be read as speaking for Sarah as well.

35. Gary James Bergera, "'Illicit Intercourse': Plural Marriage, and the Nauvoo Stake High Council, 1840–1844," 70 note 55. See also Andrew F. Smith, *The Saintly Scoundrel: The Life and Times of Dr. John Cook Bennett*, 80–83.

wife" (a term Joseph Smith never used when referring to his plural spouses), even assuming that Joseph had such intentions.

Larry Foster has suggested the possibility that it was Sarah who made advances to Joseph Smith: "Allegations that Smith asked married women to become his wives may be instances of what might be called the 'Potiphar's wife syndrome,' in which women to whom Smith refused his attentions alleged that he had attempted to seduce them."[36]

In Salt Lake City, Joseph Smith III visited Sarah Pratt in 1876 when she was fifty-nine and had been separated from Orson, who by then had ten plural wives, for thirteen years. He recorded yet another version of uncertain accuracy due either to Sarah's willingness to prevaricate, her reshaping of her experience to a version that exonerated her, or to Joseph's rosy recollection of problematic testimony or a combination:[37]

> She [Sarah Pratt] told me to proceed [with the interview] and the following conversation took place.
> "Did you know my father in Nauvoo?"
> "Yes, I knew him well."
> Were you acquainted with his general deportment in society, especially towards women?"
> "Yes."
> "Did you ever know him to be guilty of any impropriety in speech or conduct towards women in society or elsewhere?"
> "No sir, never. Your father was always a gentleman, and I never heard any language from him or saw any conduct of his that was not proper and respectful."
> "Did he ever visit you or at your house?"
> "He did."
> Did he ever at such times or at any other time or place make improper overtures to you, or proposals of an improper nature—begging your pardon for the apparent indelicacy of the question?"
> To this Mrs. Pratt replied, quietly but firmly, "No, Joseph; your father never said an improper word to me in his life. He knew better."
> "Sister Pratt, it has been frequently told that he behaved improperly in your presence, and I have been told that I dare not come to you and ask you

---

36. Larry Foster, "Between Two Worlds: The Origins of Shaker Celibacy, Oneida Community Complex Marriage, and Mormon Polygamy," 254. This view is supported by two accounts: Alexander Neibaur, Diary, May 24, 1844, and Bathsheba Smith, Deposition, Temple Lot Transcript, Respondent's Testimony, Part 3, p. 318, questions 564–77.

37. See, for example, Sarah Pratt's inaccurate claims in Wyl, *Mormon Portraits*, 54. For a contrasting account from Joseph Smith III and Malissia Lott concerning their October 20, 1885 visit, see Compton, *In Sacred Loneliness*, 593–95.

about your relations with him, for fear you would tell me things which would be unwelcome to me."

"You need have no such fear," she repeated. "Your father was never guilty of an action or proposal of any improper nature in my house, towards me, or in my presence, at any time or place. There is no truth in the reports that have been circulated about him in this regard. He was always the Christian gentleman, and a noble man."

That I thanked Mrs. Pratt very warmly for her testimony in these matters my readers may be very sure.[38]

The scenario is further complicated by the possibility that the Prophet may, in fact, have discussed the possibility of an "eternity only" sealing with Sarah. Interviewed in Salt Lake City by Wilhelm Wyl in 1886, she reportedly told Wyl that Joseph "made his propositions to me and they enraged me."[39] In a meeting of the Twelve Apostles on January 20, 1843, Joseph Smith told Orson that Sarah "lied about me." The Prophet continued: "I never made the offer which she said I did."[40] What would he have meant by "offer"? Scanty documentation of Joseph's other plural relationships establishes that at least some of his proposals during that period to legally married women were for "eternity only." Thus, he may, in fact, have had such a discussion with Sarah, which she either misunderstood or sensationalized, especially if she was, in fact, improperly involved with Bennett and was attempting to deflect attention from that relationship.

Orson and Sarah Pratt Are Rebaptized

On January 10, 1843, a little over two months after John C. Bennett published his book, he continued his hostilities with the Prophet by sending a letter addressed to both Sidney Rigdon and Orson Pratt that obviously assumed they were disillusioned with Joseph and would assist him in his attacks.[41] Bennett wrote:

> Dear Friends:—It is a long time since I have written you, and I should now much desire to see you; but I leave tonight for Missouri, to meet the

---

38. Mary Audentia Smith Anderson, ed., *The Memoirs of President Joseph Smith (1832–1914)*, 33–34.
39. Wyl, *Mormon Portraits*, 61.
40. Minutes of the Quorum of the Twelve, January 20, 1843. See also Richard S. Van Wagoner, "Sarah M. Pratt: The Shaping of an Apostate," 80. Reportedly visitors heard Joseph Smith refer to Sarah Pratt on July 14, 1842, as a "[Whore] from her mother's breast." John C. Bennett, "A Rumor—Holy Joe Demanded," *Sangamo Journal*, July 29, 1842.
41. See discussion in Watson, *The Orson Pratt Journals*, 177–88.

messenger charged with the arrest of Joseph Smith, Hyrum Smith, Lyman Wight and others, for murder, burglary, treason, etc., etc., who will be demanded in a few days on new indictments, found by the grand Jury of a called court, on the original evidence and in relation to which a *nolle prosequi* was entered by the district attorney. New proceedings have been gotten up on the old charges and no habeus corpus can then save them. We shall try Smith on the Boggs case[42] when we get him into Missouri. The war goes bravely on; and, although Smith thinks he is now safe, the enemy is near, even at the door. He is a murderer, and must suffer the penalty of the law....

P.S. Will Mr. Rigdon please hand this letter to Mr. Pratt after reading.[43]

Sidney Rigdon received the letter first; and rather than warning Joseph Smith of the grand jury and the "new proceedings," he gave the letter to Orson who immediately informed the Prophet. Orson's behavior signaled a change of heart, confirming his loyalty to Joseph. Both he and Sarah were rebaptized on January 20.[44] The Prophet then rather ambiguously counseled Orson: "I will not advise you to break up your family—unless it were asked of me. Then I would council [sic] you to get a bill from your wife and marry a virtuous woman."[45] Obviously, the Prophet did not hold Sarah Pratt and her morals in high esteem in 1842.

In May 1843, Orson wrote to his friend John Van Cott saying: "J. C. Bennett has published lies concerning myself & family & the people with which I am connected. His book I have read with the greatest disgust[.] No candid honest man can or will believe it. He has disgraced himself in [the] eyes of all civilized society who will dispise his very name."[46] In 1878, when Orson had married ten plural wives and had been separated from Sarah for fifteen years, he co-authored a report with Joseph F. Smith in which he recalled "his own trial in regard to this matter in Nauvoo, and said it was because he got his information from a wicked source, from those disaffected, but as soon as he learned the truth he was satisfied."[47] Although he speaks in generalities here, obviously by the "wicked source," he meant Sarah herself.

---

42. Morris A. Thurston, "The Boggs Shooting and Attempted Extradition: Joseph Smith's Most Famous Case," 5–56.

43. John C. Bennett, Letter to Sidney Rigdon and Orson Pratt, erroneously dated January 10, 1842—likely one year later; typescript in Journal History, misfiled under January 10, 1842. See also *History of the Church*, 5:250–51.

44. Scott H. Faulring, ed., *An American Prophet's Record: The Diaries and Journals of Joseph Smith*, 294–95.

45. Minutes of the Quorum of the Twelve, January 20, 1843, See also Van Wagoner, "Sarah M. Pratt," 80.

46. Parley P. Pratt, Letter to John Van Cott (his cousin), May 7, 1843, with a postscript by Orson Pratt.

47. Joseph F. Smith and Orson Pratt, "Report of Elders Orson Pratt and Joseph F.

In late 1845, more than a year after the Prophet's death, Sidney Rigdon reported that in Nauvoo three years earlier: "Pratt resented the insult offered his wife, and on the public stand, called Smith a liar, and said he knew him [Smith] to be a liar."[48] Orson repudiated this 1842 statement and told Rigdon: "He said that he had got a bad spirit when he said so, and that he had repented of it. Thus literally telling the people that all Smith said about his wife was true."[49]

In the spring of 1848, Sarah, Orson's legal wife, accompanied her husband when he was called to preside over the European Mission; they returned in July 1849. Other than this time together, Orson served alone on numerous other missions until 1868. Men typically did not take their plural wives with them on missionary assignments because the woman would not be recognized by local law enforcement as a legal spouse and could expose the man to bigamy or adultery charges. Sarah lived alone in Salt Lake City in a home arranged for by Orson; how she managed financially is not clear, and Orson was never in comfortable circumstances; but she presumably received some support from him. In 1874, she was excommunicated for "apostasy." The following year, she was called as a witness before the U.S. House of Representatives Committee on Elections to testify regarding polygamy charges against Apostle George Q. Cannon, elected delegate from the Territory of Utah. She began by assuring her audience that Cannon had three wives. When questioned about her own beliefs, she responded: "I have not been a believer in the Mormon doctrines for thirty years and am now considered an apostate, I believe."[50]

1886 Accusations of Sarah Pratt

On May 21, 1886, as already noted, Wyl interviewed Sarah, publishing her alleged comments in his book, *Mormon Portraits*.[51] Her recollections, partially quoted and partially paraphrased by Wyl, are still of interest to researchers today, but many statements are inaccurate or exaggerated. For example, Sarah Pratt alleged: "Next door to my house was a house of bad reputation. One single woman lived there, not very attractive. She used to be visited by people from Carthage whenever they came to Nauvoo. Joseph used to come on horseback, ride up to the house and tie his horse to a tree, many of which

---

Smith," 788.

48. Sidney Rigdon, "Tour East," *Messenger and Advocate of the Church of Christ* 2, no. 2 (December 1845): 1.

49. Ibid.

50. "Delegate Cannon's Case," *Salt Lake Herald*, Journal History, January 22, 1875, in Richard E. Turley Jr., *Selected Collections from the Archives of the Church of Jesus Christ of Latter-day Saints*, Vol. 2, DVD #6.

51. Wyl, *Mormon Portraits*, 10.

stood before the house. Then he would enter the house of the woman from the back. I have seen him do this repeatedly."[52]

Sarah's report (as filtered through Wyl) is intriguing in several respects. First is Joseph Smith's odd mixture of shamelessness and openness. It seems contradictory that he would openly "ride up to the house [of bad reputation] and tie his horse to a tree," since Joseph's horse was known to many Church members and leaving it in plain sight would have sent a message to all passersby that he was inside the house. Equally puzzlingly is Sarah's statement that he would walk around the house to enter by the back door. Either he should have concealed his horse *and* his entrance or neither. Further, Joseph took well-documented pains to maintain extreme secrecy in dealing with his genuine plural wives.

That the Prophet would need to ride his horse to the house is also puzzling. Sarah's house was not far distant from Joseph Smith's.[53] At that time, traveling by horseback required the rider to take the horse from the stable and saddle it before riding. Unless he was planning to run several errands, such an action would have been an opportunity for Emma, one of the children, a boarder, or a passing member to inquire where he was going, thus requiring him to invent an errand. If his only errand was to visit the woman of unsavory reputation, such elaborate preparations seem counterintuitive.

It is also surprising that Sarah Pratt was the only witness to Joseph's behavior, at least part of which (the ride) was undeniably public and even though he allegedly did this "repeatedly." Almost any Church member might have seen such unconcealed activities and mentioned it, even innocently, given the intense interest in Joseph's whereabouts and behavior. If the woman's unsavory reputation was known, then such a mention would have started a rumor that would not have been easy to stifle. Believers would have been disillusioned at Joseph's double standard and enemies would have undoubtedly exploited the reports in many ways.

Wyl also quotes Sarah Pratt saying: "Elizabeth Ann Whitney, the second 'lady,' [of the Relief Society], had been seduced by Joseph."[54] Sarah Pratt is the only person to make such an allegation. No other historical accounts,

---

52. Ibid., 60.

53. Records show that Orson Pratt owned several properties in Nauvoo (Nauvoo block 135, lot 4, Kimball survey, block 13, lot 4, Wells survey block 8, lot 1 and block 9, lot 2; available at http://earlylds.com/index.html, accessed July 30, 2009). Sarah roomed with other families as well in the 1840–41 period. I have not identified the precise house "next door" to Sarah's house. However, it could be argued that, in light of Nauvoo's small geographic size (the lower section was less than a mile square and the upper section was perhaps a third that size) a horse might not have been required to traverse the entire width or length.

54. Wyl, *Mormon Portraits*, 90.

anti-Mormon or otherwise, repeat this allegation, nor has my research found any sexual or polygamous connection between the Prophet and Elizabeth. That Pratt would have been privy to such information is less likely; she was never admitted as a member of the Nauvoo Relief Society, probably due to concerns about her character.[55] As discussed in Chapter 18, Elizabeth Ann Whitney and her husband, Bishop Newel K. Whitney, accepted the principle of plural marriage in the summer of 1842 when both experienced a vision confirming the correctness of plural marriage: "We were seemingly wrapt in a heavenly vision, a halo of light encircled us, and we were convinced in our own minds that God heard and approved our prayers and intercedings before Him. Our hearts were comforted."[56] They consented to the sealing of their daughter, Sarah Ann, to Joseph Smith; and three days later, Elizabeth and Newel were sealed for time and eternity by the Prophet.

In addition, Elizabeth Whitney appears to have retained her belief in Joseph Smith as a Prophet throughout her life. In 1879, she recounted: "He [Joseph Smith] prophesied to me that I should have another daughter [besides Sarah Ann], who would be a strength and support to me to soothe my declining years."[57] This prophecy was probably dictated near the date of Sarah Ann's sealing to the Prophet on July 27, 1842. "In January, 1844," Elizabeth Ann notes, "my youngest daughter was born. She was the first child born heir to the Holy Priesthood, and in the New and Everlasting Covenant in this dispensation."[58]

Wyl recorded another quotation reportedly from Sarah Pratt:

> "I have told you that the prophet Joseph used to frequent houses of ill-fame. Mrs. White,[59] a very pretty and attractive woman, once confessed to me that she made a business of it to be hospitable to the captains of the Mississippi steamboats. She told me that Joseph had made her acquaintance very soon after his arrival in Nauvoo, and that he had visited her dozens of times."[60]

---

55. Maurine C. Ward, "'This Institution Is a Good One': The Female Relief Society of Nauvoo, 17 March 1842 to 16 March 1844," 172.

56. Elizabeth Ann Whitney, "A Leaf from an Autobiography," *Woman's Exponent* 7 (December 15, 1878): 105; see also Carol Cornwall Madsen, ed., *In Their Own Words: Women and the Story of Nauvoo*, 201–2.

57. Elizabeth Ann Whitney, "A Leaf from an Autobiography," *Woman's Exponent*, 7, no. 18 (February 15, 1879): 191.

58. Ibid.

59. This may be a reference to Emeline White who, John C. Bennett said, received a letter from "Old White Hat," apparently a reference to Joseph Smith. See Bennett, "Gen. Bennett's 4th Letter," *Sangamo Journal*, July 22, 1842, and his *The History of the Saints: Or an Exposé of Joe Smith and Mormonism*, 235.

60. Wyl, *Mormon Portraits*, 60.

This is a second account from Sarah Pratt, albeit, secondhand, accusing Joseph Smith of frequenting a house of ill repute. Her informant, "Mrs. White," made no secret to Sarah that she was the proprietor of a house of prostitution. Wyl lists White's father as Davison Hibard, a general in the Nauvoo Legion, which is incorrect.[61] Like Sarah Pratt's other accusations, plausibility problems accompany the allegation that Joseph Smith frequented a house of prostitution "repeatedly" or "dozens of times" without anyone else, anti-Mormon or Latter-day Saint, ever noticing and making the charge. Regardless, from the 1820s forward, Joseph Smith was being watched by critics eager to discredit him. Church members were likewise scrutinizing his behavior, seeking inspiration in his words and deed but also, for the same reason, supersensitive to possible hypocrisy or transgression. Joseph Smith rarely, if ever, traveled alone. It seems unlikely that he might have engaged even once in the conduct asserted by Wyl/Pratt without drawing attention to himself. Although it is true that he frequently moved about Nauvoo, including occasionally visiting plural wives, accompanied by one of his clerks or by his diarist, William Clayton, these men accepted those relationships as genuine, though secret, marriages, not as visits to a prostitute.

On March 31, 1886, Sarah Pratt had signed a statement affirming: "This certifys that I was well acquainted with the Mormon Leaders and Church in general, and know that the principle [sic] statements in John Bennetts Book on Mormonism are true."[62] This statement would either validate the truthfulness of *The History of the Saints* or diminish Sarah's credibility as a reliable witness. Living in Salt Lake City as she did, she could not have expected her statement to be widely regarded as truthful, nor was it. Church leaders denounced Wyl's book, although they did not single out Sarah beyond her excommunication. Of the six children she and Orson had together, only one remained active in the Church, an obvious indication that her disillusionment was passed on as skepticism to the next generation.[63]

Summary

John C. Bennett's ability to generate confusion and strife was illustrated in his interactions with Sarah Pratt. Bennett said Joseph sought Sarah as a spiritual wife, while Sarah accused the Prophet of making an indecent proposal or even a seduction attempt. In response, Joseph and several other witnesses accused Bennett and Sarah of adultery during Orson's absence on a mission.

---

61. Ibid., 285, 301. See Hamilton Gardner, "The Nauvoo Legion, 1840–1845—A Unique Military Organization," 181–97.

62. Sarah Pratt, Statement, March 31, 1886.

63. Van Wagoner, "Sarah M. Pratt," 90 note 5.

After a surprisingly long period of quiescence, Orson reacted with emotional turmoil, rejecting Joseph Smith's description of the events, which led to the Pratts' excommunications. Within a few months, however, Orson and Sarah were rebaptized. Orson became a staunch defender of the principle of plural marriage and of Joseph Smith's prophetic role. Years later, Sarah left the Church for the second and last time.

Chapter 22

Post-Bennett Resurgence

During the last five months of 1842, apparently no new polygamous marriages were performed in the Church. The next known plural marriages followed in February 1843. However, this hiatus did not necessarily represent a contraction or retreat in the spread of the doctrine. The practice was nearly two years old; and while only four men (Joseph Smith, Brigham Young, Heber C. Kimball, and Vinson Knight had married plurally, additional Latter-day Saints were embracing it as quickly as the Prophet was willing to teach them about it. Importantly, it had endured a brutal assault from John C. Bennett, who accused Joseph Smith and other Church members of sexual improprieties. In all, the Church emerged perhaps better than might have been expected. Bennett had been revealed as a renegade, and the restored practice remained largely secret from both members and nonmembers.

One 1844 writer characterized the Bennett scandal: "He went forth, and wrote, and spoke, and made affidavits to the most pernicious and revolting practices, and the most startling crimes, and he found plenty of listeners who were ready to grasp anything that would militate against the Mormons."[1] Nevertheless, it appears that most individuals, especially the Latter-day Saints, were willing to regard Bennett's allegations as fantastic and viewed the other rumors with skepticism.

The Peace Maker

Several writers have suggested that in the fall of 1842 Joseph Smith commissioned Udney Hay Jacob, a sixty-one-year-old non-Mormon living near Nauvoo, to write a pamphlet as a trial balloon to broach the topic of polygamy.[2] Born in 1781, Jacob fancied himself a preacher and expounder of scripture.[3]

---

1. G. W. Westbrook, quoted in James H. Hunt, *Mormonism Embracing the Origin, Rise and Progress of the Sect*, Appendix, 13–14.
2. See Harry M. Beardsley, *Joseph Smith and His Mormon Empire*, 269; Richard S. Van Wagoner, *Mormon Polygamy: A History*, 50–51; B. Carmon Hardy, *Solemn Covenant: The Mormon Polygamous Passage*, 7–8, 366–67; John L. Brooke, *The Refiner's Fire: The Making of Mormon Cosmology, 1644–1844*, 265; William D. Morain, *The Sword of Laban: Joseph Smith Jr. and the Dissociated Mind*, 190; B. Carmon Hardy, "Polygamy, Mormonism, and Me," 95.
3. Some writers have mistakenly referred to him as "Jacobs." Udney Hay Jacob

On March 3, 1840, he wrote a letter to Latter-day Saint Oliver Granger but obviously, from the salutation, hoped it would reach a wider audience: "Brethren, my hearts desire and prayer to God is that you might be saved from the bitterness and false wrath created in you by sorcery. For I bear you record that you have a zeal of God, but not according to knowledge."[4]

Apparently Jacob had been welcomed, to some extent, into Nauvoo society because, at the end of October 1842, he contracted with the Church-owned printing press to publish his thirty-seven-page booklet, *The Peace Maker*.[5] The title page lists Joseph Smith as the "Printer." Two months after its publication, on January 1, 1843, Nauvoo resident and excommunicated Mormon, Oliver Olney, recorded a prose journal entry:

> Is well known by many
> That a plurality of wives was the theme
> One year ago they in it commenced to move
> That some few added to their spouses some few
> That now stands as brides to privileged ones,
> Yet in toto they have denied the fact
> That they have ever harbored such a thought
> But to my surprise what has come to view
> But a pamphlet printed by Joseph Smith
> Yet it stands in the name of a Jacobs. . . .
> Its tenor is reasoning from the scriptures
> By picking passages to encourage polygamy
> From Genesis to Revelations[.][6]

Other Nauvooans also believed that Joseph Smith was responsible. John D. Lee wrote in 1877:

> Joseph, the Prophet, set a man by the name of Sidney Hay Jacobs [sic], to select from the Old Bible such scriptures as pertained to polygamy, or celestial marriage, and to write it in pamphlet form, and to advocate that doctrine. This he did as a feeler among the people, to pave the way for celestial marriage. This, like all other notions, met with opposition, while a few favored it. The excitement among the people became so great that the subject was laid before the Prophet. . . . Joseph saw that it would break up the

---

was born to Richard Jacob and Elizabeth Kellogg Jacob on April 24, 1781, and later married Elizabeth Hubbard (FamilySearch.org).

4. Udney Hay Jacob, Letter to O. Granger, March 3, 1840.

5. Udney Hay Jacob, *An Extract, from a Manuscript Entitled The Peace Maker, or the Doctrines of the Millennium: Being a Treatise on Religion and Jurisprudence. Or a New System of Religion and Politicks* (hereafter cited as *The Peace Maker*).

6. Oliver Olney, Journal, January 1, 1843; see also Oliver H. Olney, *The Absurdities of Mormonism Portrayed*, 10–11.

Post-Bennett Resurgence

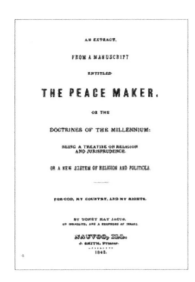

Title page of *The Peace Maker* reads: An extract from a manuscript entitled the peace maker, or the doctrines of the millennium; being a treatise on religion and jurisprudence. Or a new system of religion and politicks. For God, my country and my rights. By Udney Hay Jacob, an Israelite, and a shepherd of Israel, Nauvoo, Ill., J. Smith, printer, 1842. Capitalization removed.

Church, should he sanction it, so he denounced the pamphlet through the *Wasp* [sic—should be *Times and Seasons*],[7] a newspaper published at Nauvoo by E. Robinson, as a bundle of nonsense and trash. He said if he had known its contents he would never have permitted it to be published. . . . He dared not proclaim it publicly, so it was taught confidentially to such as were strong enough in the faith to take another step.[8]

Larry Foster, in "A Little-Known Defense of Polygamy from the Mormon Press in 1842," referred to Jacob's pamphlet as "the only explicit defense of polygamy ever printed under the auspices of the main body of the Mormon Church prior to 1852."[9]

Notwithstanding these assessments, several pieces of evidence indicate that Joseph Smith was not involved with its publication.[10] In 1850, Eli B.

---

7. "Notice," *Times and Seasons* 4 (December 1, 1842): 32.

8. John D. Lee, *Mormonism Unveiled, or, The Life and Confessions of the Late Mormon Bishop, John D. Lee*, 146. Oliver Olney, *The Absurdities of Mormonism Portrayed: A Brief Sketch*, 10, described it as "a pamphlet said to be written by a man by the name of Jacobs but published by Joseph Smith Editor[.] We find if the pamphlet was not written by the authorities of the Church, it by them was revised in Jacobs name."

9. Larry Foster, "A Little-Known Defense of Polygamy from the Mormon Press in 1842," 23; see also his *Religion and Sexuality: Three American Communal Experiments of the Nineteenth Century*, 174; *Women, Family, and Utopia: Communal Experiments of the Shakers, the Oneida Community, and the Mormons*, 273 note 19.

10. Concerning the possibility that Joseph Smith may have authored the booklet, historian Kenneth W. Godfrey reported: "It seems safe to conclude that Jacob, not Joseph Smith, wrote *The Peace Maker*. . . . [It] should [not] be viewed as binding upon

Kelsey, a Mormon elder then on a mission in the British Isles, provided this summary to the *Millennial Star*:

> I am desirous that no honest-hearted man or woman should be deceived with regard to the origin of this book [*The Peace Maker*], and thus be led to associate the name of Joseph Smith with such a nonsensical medley of stuff as it contains. . . .
>
> Sometime previous to the year 1842, Mr. Smith established a printing office in the city of Nauvoo, for the purpose of printing the various publications of the church and executing job work for the convenience of the public. He placed a foreman over it to take charge of the printing department, and although the business was done in his name, it was frequently the case that he was not inside the office once in a month. A Mr. Udney H. Jacobs, not a member of the church, who lived a short distance from Nauvoo, came to the office and wished the foreman to print several hundred copies of a work, entitled the *Peace Maker*, written by himself. The foreman did so, and of course attached Mr. Smith's name as printer, who was entirely ignorant of the matter until he saw the work in print, with his name attached.[11]

Udney Jacob did not reside in Nauvoo, but in Pilot Grove, Illinois, some sixteen miles to the east. It appears that he never met the Prophet. Ronald O. Barney, a descendant, explained: "In Udney's 6 January 1844 letter to Joseph Smith, whom Jacob states that he had never met, Jacob, while announcing that he had been by this time baptized a Mormon, quizzed Smith about several theological particulars without once mentioning his pamphlet, its implications, or any prior association. . . . Also Udney Jacob's March 1851 letter to Brigham Young contains language clearly indicating that his production of *The Peacemaker* was not with church approval, much less collaboration."[12]

Perhaps the most convincing observation that the Prophet was not involved with *The Peace Maker* is found in the text itself.[13] The pamphlet's full title is: "An Extract from a Manuscript Entitled the Peace Maker or the Doctrines of the Millennium being a Treatise on Religion and Jurisprudence or a New

---

members of The Church of Jesus Christ of Latter-day Saints. [It was], in fact, written by a nonmember of the Church." Kenneth W. Godfrey, "A New Look at the Alleged Little Known Discourse by Joseph Smith," 53.

11. Eli B. Kelsey, "A Base Calumny Refuted," 92. See also Richard and Pamela Price, "How *The Peace Maker* Has Been Wrongly Used to Promote a False Theory," 26. The Prices' treatise of *The Peace Maker* incident is the best currently available.

12. Ronald O. Barney, *The Mormon Vanguard Brigade of 1847: Norton Jacob's Record*, 21 note 18. See also Kenneth W. Godfrey, "Causes of Mormon-Non-Mormon Conflict in Hancock County, Illinois, 1839–1846," 97.

13. Williard Griffith believed that "Parley Pratt was the prime originator of the system of polygamy" and that he wrote the "book called 'Father Jacobs,'" which is likely *The Peace Maker*. Griffith, Deposition, Temple Lot Transcript, Part 4, p. 40, questions 121, 123.

System of Religion and Politicks." The extract deals specifically with marriage and gender relationships, blaming many of the world's problems upon female defiance of God's laws and illicit sexual relations. Apparently Jacob believed that adherence to his ideas would bring peace—hence the name. Importantly, it discusses polygamy on only three out of thirty-seven pages, with brief references to it in two other places.[14] Rather than justifying and defending the practice of plural marriage, as several authors have asserted, it appears that Jacob simply cited the practice of Old Testament polygamy as one more evidence that women should be subordinate to men.

The Peace Maker is not a gentle defense of the correctness of plural marriage in Old Testament times. Instead, Jacob uses a sledgehammer approach that could have had little effect other than to alienate its readers, especially women, concerning the practice of polygamy: "A man cannot be put lawfully under the law of marriage to the woman; she is his property in marriage."[15] "Many husbands, are induced by the unnatural and intolerable nature of female tyranny and usurpation."[16] Other parts of Jacob's narrative are also deeply misogynistic:

> The idea of a woman taking a man to be her husband is not found in the word of God. But the man marries the woman; and the woman is given in marriage. She is therefore the property of the husband in marriage. But the husband is not the property of the wife in any sense of the word . . . . The woman has no power to divorce the man. How can property divorce its owner? . . . Putting the man under the woman, would degrade his mind and that of his posterity in many cases wretchedly; and produce imbecility of mind, disorder and confusion there, like intoxicating wine; and render them finally their passive slaves. . . . In ninety-nine instances out of a hundred no doubt, where the woman is naturally of a mild and submissive make, families live in peace.[17]

Importantly, *The Peace Maker* says nothing regarding the possibility that marriage (including plural marriage) could be eternal.[18] Joseph Smith always taught eternal marriage in conjunction with plural marriage and sometimes did not mention polygamy at all.[19] For him, eternal sealings were far more

---

14. Jacob, *The Peace Maker*, 29–31, 17, 36. Richard S. Van Wagoner, *Mormon Polygamy: A History*. 50, assesses: "*The Peace Maker*, a thirty-seven-page-booklet, skillfully articulated scriptural and theological justifications for polygamy." I submit an alternate view in the text.
15. Jacob, *The Peace Maker*, 29–30.
16. Ibid., 5.
17. Ibid., 16–18, 25.
18. The word "eternity" is used twice (ibid., 11, 19) and "eternal" twice (ibid., 10, 21).
19. For example, according to Parley P. Pratt, Joseph Smith instructed him in January 1840 in Philadelphia about eternal marriage without mentioning plural marriage. Parley P. Pratt Jr., ed., *Autobiography of Parley Parker Pratt, One of the Twelve Apostles of the Church of Jesus Christ of Latter-day Saints*, 259–60.

important than plurality. (See Volume 3, Chapter 10.) If the Prophet intended Udney Jacob's writings to serve as a sort of litmus test regarding polygamy, introducing it as a restoration of Old Testament polygamy with an emphasis on the possibility of eternal unions would have been a much more logical starting point and would have been much more enticing to the general readership. Notwithstanding, Udney says nothing concerning eternal matrimony. For him, marriage ended at death.[20]

Significantly, Jacob made two extravagant claims regarding his own importance that cast doubt on his mental balance: "It is written in Malachi 4:5–6: Behold I will send you Elijah the Prophet. . . . The author of this work professes to be the teacher here foretold."[21] He also interpreted Isaiah 66:7–8: "Before she travailed, (that is before Zion travailed) she brought forth: before her pain came she was delivered of a man child (even the author of this book)."[22] It seems improbable that Joseph Smith would have endorsed statements that so clearly conflicted with his own revelations, denied the priesthood line of authority, or supported a publication containing them.[23]

Understandably, Church sisters in Nauvoo were disturbed by the prolix and domineering message and brought it to the Prophet's attention shortly after its publication in November. In response, he wrote in the *Times and Seasons*: "There was a book printed at my office, a short time since, written by Udney H. Jacob, on marriage, without my knowledge; and had I been apprised of it, I should not have printed it; not that I am opposed to any man enjoying his privileges; but I do not wish to have my name associated with the author[']s, in such an unmeaning rigmarole of nonsense, folly, and trash."[24]

Udney H. Jacob was baptized into the Church in 1843, but apparently struggled in his faith. His son, Norton Jacob, then thirty-nine, recalled his father's vacillations in his diary on November 1, 1845: "My father, Udney H. Jacob, came to my house from Pilot Grove and in the evening he said he now fully believed this work, viz. Mormonism, to be true. Indeed he now knew it to be the work of God foretold by the prophets. But when he was baptized two years ago, he did not know it to be true. I was much rejoiced to hear this and it was soon arranged that he should be re-baptized on the morrow. There had been some difficulty in the Branch in Pilot Grove which had caused him to request his name to be taken

---

20. Jacob, *The Peace Maker*, 23: "If thus they are wedded together, no power but death can righteously part them."

21. Ibid., 2 (preface).

22. Ibid., 26.

23. Joseph Smith and Oliver Cowdery had already witnessed the return of Elijah in the Kirtland Temple on April 3, 1836 (D&C 110:13–16). See Chapter 8.

24. "Notice," *Times and Seasons* 4 (December 1, 1842): 32.

from the record. All was now right."²⁵ Udney was ordained a high priest in 1846, traveled with the Saints to Utah, and died in Salt Lake City in 1860.²⁶

Joseph Cautiously Teaches Others

While Joseph Smith denied any association with *The Peace Maker*, he nevertheless continued to secretly teach others the principle of celestial marriage. It appears that the Prophet wanted the faithful Saints to learn about eternal and plural marriage as soon as they were ready. Mary Ann Barzee Boice recalled that Nancy Ann Boice Gilbert, the sister of her husband, John, and Nancy Ann's husband, Truman Gilbert, "lived in a log house which had two rooms she often talked to me about the Prophet and Women coming there and holding counsel in that room."²⁷

Joseph Smith was naturally concerned about his personal safety, requesting his plural wives and others who knew of his private involvement to maintain complete silence. He did not, however, require them to take vows of silence as part of the teaching process. In 1892 when Lucy Walker was being deposed as part of the Temple Lot case, her interlocutor asked: "Did you agree with Joseph Smith when he was teaching you this principle, that you would guard it as a secret?" She answered: "I entered into no such agreement. There was no such an arrangement."²⁸ Then she lamented: "He would have revealed it himself, had he lived, in his own good time, and then there could be no dispute about it, but he did not have the opportunity unfortunately."²⁹

Cyrus Wheelock (1813–94) who was a close friend of Joseph Smith in Nauvoo, recalled that he first learned the principle of plural marriage from Joseph at Noble's home in 1841.³⁰ He reported that such teachings were subsequently shared with others on a "rainy and chilly" day in a forest setting about a mile west of Montrose, Iowa; Joseph taught a small group of men regarding plural marriage:

> Joseph had to be on the run to keep out of the way of his enemies, and some times he would go out in the country to one of our neighbors,

---

25. Norton Jacob, Journal, November 1, 1845, typescript, p. 18.
26. Ibid., 27.
27. John Boice and Mary Ann Barzee Boice, "Record, 1884–85," 178–79. Nauvoo land records show that Truman Gilbert owned several plots in Nauvoo, Block 21, Lot 1; Block 144 part as tenant; Block 157; Block 135, Lot 2; and Block 75, Lot 1. Nauvoo Land and Records Office, P.O. Box 215, Nauvoo, IL, 62354. Which of these, if any, might have been the lot where the described two-room cabin was built is unknown.
28. Lucy Walker Smith Kimball, Deposition, Temple Lot Transcript, Respondent's Testimony, Part 3, p. 481, questions 729–31.
29. Ibid.
30. Cyrus Wheelock, Deposition, Temple Lot Transcript, Respondent's Testimony, Part 3, p. 538, question 78.

for he felt that he could trust anyone that lived in the woods or forest down the river, and we would go out in the timber to talk under the trees about the principles of the church, amongst other principles that of baptism for the dead was discussed and the building of the temple and all those things together. It was at this time, amongst others, that he taught us the principle of plural marriage, but his teaching was not specially directed to me, but to all who were in the company. We talked about it as we might here or any brother qualified and having authority to do so will discuss principles when he gets along with his brethren in friendly and confidential discourse.[31]

The time it was taught to me in Nauvoo, it was not supposed to be practiced as a principle,—that is, publicly like our proceedings in the temple for the dead. It was not taught or practiced openly, but it was given to me and I understood it as a crude principle that would be fully and openly revealed to the Church when the proper time came for it to be revealed.[32]

Despite his early introduction to plural marriage, Wheelock did not become a polygamist until 1853 in Utah.

Reports of spiritual experiences often supplemented the processes through which individuals accepted the teachings regarding plurality.[33] Jane Snyder Richards, the legal wife of future apostle Franklin D. Richards, reported such a manifestation, writing in third person: "A few months previous to her marriage [which occurred in December 1842] the idea of more than one [marriage] was \generally/ spoken of, tho the practice of polygamy was of later growth. It was repugnant to her ideas of virtue and it was not until she saw Joseph Smith in a vision who told her in time all would be explained, that she was satisfied to abide by Mormon teachings whatever they were."[34]

---

31. Ibid., p. 539, question 80. See also questions 107, 136, 139, 142.

32. Ibid., p. 563, question 371. Wheelock does not identify any of the other men present in this small group.

33. Reports of angelic visitors continued as Latter-day Saints were introduced to plural marriage in Utah. Mary Isabella Hales Horne had the following experience in 1857: "While her husband was on exploring expedition . . . in the winter of 1857, while she was praying to the Lord a heavenly messenger suddenly appeared at her bed side. He was clad in white with a girdle. He exerted [such] an influence upon her as he talked that she should never forget. He told her that she should have to pass thro' severe afflictions and trials, but to 'bear it all patiently, for it will exalt you, and you will shine brightly in the kingdom of God.' The house was filled with the holy influence left behind him." Mrs. Joseph Horne [Mary Isabella Hales Horne], "Migration and Settlement of the Latter Day Saints, Salt Lake City, 1884," 33–34. Mary Isabella still struggled with the practice of polygamy, but this memory sustained her.

34. Jane Snyder Richards, "The Inner Facts of Social Life in Utah by Mrs. F. D. Richards, San Francisco, 1880," 1.

Nauvoo Temple carpenter David Moore was troubled when he learned about plural marriage during the fall of 1842.[35] Fifty years later in his autobiography, he recorded his own experience:

> During this fall [of 1842] and the beginning of winter, the order of celestial marriage began to be talked of as existing in the Church. I must confess that my mind was somewhat troubled on the subject, until I had the following dream. I dreamed that my sister Hannah was dead in the spirit, took a chair and set down in front of my bed and said to me, "David, your mind is troubled in respect to the order of Marriage which you do not understand at the present, but where I am we understand all about it, its all right, and when the right time comes I want you to remember me."[36]

Moore also related his conversation with a woman member of the Church who had reluctantly married polygamously:

> About this time a Widow Johnson[37] was living with Chas A. Chase. She had come with the Vermont Camp. She was much troubled about the order of marriage which was now almost the general topic. I used to take pleasure in talking to her on the subject and see her rage and scold about the system. One time I was talking to her when I asked her if she wanted me to prophesy on her head. She said she did not care whether I did or not, I then told her that twelve months would not pass over her head before she would be sealed to some man that had another wife. She was angry with me for saying so, but before six months had passed away she was sealed to Reynolds Cahoon, but I had no opportunity of laughing at her for so doing for she seemed quite shy every time I met her after.
>
> During the winter private meetings were held all over the city in which much good instruction was given on the subject of the Plan of Redemption. Often the sealing covenant was touched upon but never plainly preached.[38]

These accounts provide a rich view of the feelings and reactions of Church members who confronted the practice with hesitancy, if not repulsion. Any allegation that the Latter-day Saints embraced polygamy for licentious reasons is undercut by the narratives and recollections of the participants themselves.

---

35. "Demise of Bishop David Moore," *Deseret Evening News*, January 29, 1901, 7.

36. David Moore, "Compiled Writings of David Moore," 19–20.

37. Lucina Roberts Johnson married Peter Johnson on November 24, 1824. The couple had six children before Peter died in 1838. Lucina married Reynolds Cahoon in 1842, exact date unavailable.

38. Ibid.

Church Discipline for Sexual Immorality and Unauthorized Polygamy

Even as the number of pluralists secretly increased, Church leaders continually disciplined freelance polygamy, unauthorized marriages, adultery, or fornication. Joseph taught that he controlled the authority, or keys, to plurality and that marriages performed without it were not valid and had no efficacy after death (D&C 132:18). His approval was indispensable: "[There is] no salvation between the two lids of the bible without a legal administrator," he taught.[39] Joseph Smith taught that due to the angelic ordinations he had received in the Kirtland Temple, he was that "legal administrator" (D&C 110:11–16).

As plural marriage was being secretly promoted by the Prophet, the Nauvoo High Council was very active in disfellowshipping or excommunicating Church members who were involved in any sort of sexual indiscretion.[40] With respect to the moral conduct in Nauvoo, it appears that a number of women were seduced by conniving men. Despite the embarrassing circumstances, those victims subsequently swore out affidavits with details outlining their misconduct.[41] Consequently, several males were accused of "unchaste and unvirtuous conduct" with various females.[42]

Between February of 1841 and April of 1844, the Nauvoo High Council records show that twenty-nine separate cases were brought up for Church discipline for alleged sexual misconduct, comprising about a third of the total cases considered by the council during that time.[43] None of the offenders claimed that their licentiousness was in any way related to Joseph Smith's plu-

---

39. Andrew F. Ehat and Lyndon W. Cook, eds., *The Words of Joseph Smith: The Contemporary Accounts of the Nauvoo Discourses of the Prophet Joseph Smith*, 235.

40. Danel W. Bachman, "A Study of the Mormon Practice of Plural Marriage before the Death of Joseph Smith," 129–33; Gary James Bergera, "'Illicit Intercourse,' Plural Marriage, and the Nauvoo Stake High Council, 1840–1844," 64; Scott G. Kenney, ed., *Wilford Woodruff's Journal: 1833–1898*, 2:177, May 29, 1842.

41. "History of Joseph Smith," *Millennial Star* 23 (October 12, 1861): 657–59. See also Bergera, "'Illicit Intercourse,'" 68–71. Catherine Fuller Warren testified: "I had an unlawful connection with Chauncey L. Higbee. Chauncey Higbee taught the same doctrine as was taught by J.C. Bennett, and that Joseph Smith taught and practiced those things; but he stated that he did not have it from Joseph, but he had his information from Dr. John C. Bennett. He, Chauncey L. Higbee, has gained his object about five or six times. Chauncey L. Higbee also made propositions to keep me with food, if I would submit to his desires." Catherine Fuller Warren, "Testimony before Nauvoo High Council," *Millennial Star* 23 (October 12, 1861): 657–58.

42. "Municipal Court," *Times and Seasons* 5 (May 15, 1844): 538–40.

43. See also Bergera, "Illicit Intercourse," 64.

ral marriage teachings. Most, it seems, were unaware of the secret doctrine then expanding among the Latter-day Saints.

Two of the cases involved men who married a second wife without divorcing their first. On January 21, 1843, the high council reviewed a bigamous marriage between John Thorp and Sarah Miller. Thorp was already married to Charity Arms, from whom he had separated, but not divorced. He refused to be present at the high council court for fear of being arrested for bigamy.[44] The two were disfellowshipped. A second case involved Jordan P. Hendrickson who "married a second woman when his first wife was living" for which he was excommunicated.[45]

Just previous to that time (December 1842), four men, including Joseph Smith, had entered into plural relationships. The contrast between these four and the two bigamy cases underscores the crucial factor of authority. Joseph Smith, who reported receiving sealing authority from the prophet Elijah in 1836, had authorized the plural unions, and they were sealed by properly delegated priesthood power. Two other factors were also relevant. The high councilors were not formally advised of the principle of plurality until July 1843. Finally, with the probable exception of Emma Smith, the first wives of the three men accepted these plural marriages.

Some writers have failed to acknowledge these differences, grouping all plural marriages together, irrespective of the authority solemnizing them.[46] However, the second distinction, the need for Joseph Smith's authorization, was considered paramount, being rigidly observed in Nauvoo. LDS theology holds that the senior apostle, who rises to that position through the date of his ordination as a member of the Quorum of the Twelve, becomes the only man authorized to exercise all priesthood keys upon the death of the previous presiding apostle (D&C 132:7). Utah Saints believe that Brigham Young, John Taylor, Wilford Woodruff, and Lorenzo Snow served as the presiding apostle and key holder in their respective times, administering sealing ordinances throughout the remainder of the nineteenth century.[47]

The importance of having proper authorization before entering a plural marriage was emphasized three years after the Prophet's death. In 1847, long-time devoted member W. W. Phelps served a mission to the eastern states. In St. Louis, he married three wives polygamously, with his mission companion,

---

44. Collier, *The Nauvoo High Council Minute Books*, 83.

45. Ibid., 104.

46. Gary James Bergera, "Buckeye's Laments: Two Early Insider Exposés of Mormon Polygamy and Their Authorship," 383 note 1. Carmon Hardy seems to take this approach in tabulating plural marriages after 1890. Hardy, *Solemn Covenant*, 394 (entire nonpaginated table). He gives little attention to the question of whether the Church president authorized these post-1890 Manifesto plural marriages.

47. Brian C. Hales, *Modern Polygamy and Mormon Fundamentalism: The Generations after the Manifesto*, 9–11, 29–36, 43–45, 59–65.

TABLE 22.1
INDIVIDUALS TRIED BY THE NAUVOO HIGH COUNCIL,
1841–44, FOR SEXUAL INDISCRETIONS[a]

	Individual	Charge	Date	Outcome
	1841			
1.	Theodore Turley	Sleeping with two females; kissing females	Feb. 6	Sustained—fellowship retained after repentance
	Unnamed	Crime or imprudence with an unmarried woman	March 2	Joseph Smith dealt with episode privately
	1842			
2.	Jesse Turpin	Adultery	April 22	Fellowship withdrawn
3.	Chancy L. Higbee	Unchaste conduct	May 20	Expelled from the Church
4	Catherine Fuller Warren	Unchaste behavior	May 25	Restored to fellowship
5.	Lyman Littlefield	Unvirtuous conduct	May 27	Disfellowshipped
6.	Darwin Chase	Unvirtuous conduct	May 27	Restored to fellowship
7.	Joel S. Miles	Unvirtuous conduct	May 27	Disfellowshipped
8.	Justice Morse	Unvirtuous conduct	May 28	Disfellowshipped
9.	Amanda Smith	Insinuating adultery	June 10	Sustained but fellowship retained after repentance
10.	Gustavus Hills	Illicit intercourse	Sept. 3	Disfellowshipped
	1843			
11.	Enoch King	Adultery	Jan. 21	Acquitted
12.	Mary Eggleston	Adultery	Jan. 21	Acquitted
13	John Thorp	Adultery	Jan. 21	Cut off from the Church
14	Sarah Miller	Adultery	Jan. 21	Cut off from the Church
15.	Thomas Prouse	Adultery	Jan. 21	Disfellowship
16.	Charity Thorp	Adultery	Jan. 21	Disfellowship
17.	John Blazard	Adultery	Jan. 28	Cut off
18.	Mrs. Pool	Adultery	Jan. 28	Cut off
19.	James Reed	Adultery	Jan. 28	Held in fellowship
20.	Mary Powell	Adultery	Jan. 28	Held in fellowship
21	John Wells Taylor	Adultery	Jan. 28	Expelled from Church
22.	Mary Cook	Adultery	Jan. 28	Expelled from Church

a. Fred C. Collier, *The Nauvoo High Council Minute Books of the Church of Jesus Christ of Latter Day Saints*, 29–30, 50, 56–60, 65–67, 80–85, 87–88, 90, 98, 104–05, 111–12, 116–17, 121–25, 127, 136–38.

	Individual	Charge	Date	Outcome
23.	Job Green	Attempt to go to bed two young females	March 4	Not sustained
24.	Jordan P. Hendrixson	Adultery	April 1	Not sustained
25.	Elizabeth Rowe	Adultery	July 22	Fellowship withdrawn
26.	George J. Adams	Adultery	Sept. 1	Not sustained
27.	Quartus S. Sparks	Impregnating a woman	Nov. 18	Fellowship withdrawn
28.	Harrison Sagers	Seducing a young girl	Nov. 25	Not sustained
1844				
29.	Harrison Sagers	"Spiritual wives"	April 13	Not sustained

Henry B. Jacobs, performing the marriages. These men did not first obtain permission from President Young. When Phelps returned to Winter Quarters, Iowa, with the three women where he rejoined his legal wife, Sally, Brigham Young heard the story and addressed Phelps directly: "You have been living in adultery—[N]o man can have the 2nd woman unless he ha[s] the consent of the man who holds the sealing power...." He also remarked to the council: "[I]f bro Phelps had told us last Spring that he was going to bring a girl—I wo[ul]d. have given her to you & [would have been] glad to do it."[48] Hosea Stout, an attorney and police officer who was present, journalized on December 5:

> Went to a council today which had been called to investigate the cases of H[enry]. B. Jacobs and W. N. Phelps [sic] while they were East on a mission.
>
> It appeared that Phelps had while East Last summer got some new ideas into three young women & they had consented to become his wives & got Jacobs to marry them to him in St Louis and he lived with them as such all the way to this place. After a long and tedious hearing of the matter which was altogether their own admissions, President Young decided that Phelps had committed addultery every time that he had laid with one of them & that Jacobs should be silenced for the part he had taken in marrying them.[49]

Notes on a meeting of the Quorum of the Twelve about this same episode read:

> G[eorge]. A. Smith feels stung at the conduct of the Old Judge (Phelps) he who has been so much in Council—
>
> H[eber].C.K[imball]. If he will go & do what he was told to do—it will do, or it must be made public—he is no better than any of the 12 nor so

---

48. *Minutes of the Apostles of The Church of Jesus Christ of Latter-day Saints, 1835–1893*, 130, November 30, 1847.

49. Juanita Brooks, ed., *On the Mormon Frontier: The Diary of Hosea Stout, 1844–1861*, 1:289.

good. There has been mercy shewn him. cut him off baptize him & again ordain him.

O. H. [Orson Hyde:] I Wo\d/ not let him have his women.

H C K. If you rip them up you will destroy them.

A[masa]. Lyman: I move that W. W. Phelps be cut off from the Church for—misconduct—violating the Laws of the Priesthood—in taking ~~women~~ women that do not belong to him & committing adultery with them"—H. C. Kimball second[ed] —All hands up.[50]

Phelps was excommunicated on December 6, 1847, but was rebaptized two days later after acknowledging his misunderstanding. Brigham Young also reprimanded Henry Jacobs: "Never let bro: Henry go a preaching again until he knows better."[51] That same year another Church member, Milo Andrus, was also excommunicated for marrying a plural wife without authorization.[52]

Nauvoo Saints Recall Their Introductions to Plural Marriage

The historical record contains several recollections written by different individuals who recalled their personal introductions to the principle of plural marriage. William Clayton left a detailed affidavit concerning his introduction to polygamy by the Prophet:

> I was employed as a clerk in President Joseph Smith's office. . . . I was necessarily thrown constantly into the company of President Smith, having to attend to his public and private business, receiving and recording tithings and donations, attending to land, and other matters of business. . . .
>
> During this period the Prophet Joseph frequently visited my house in my company, and became well acquainted with my wife Ruth, to whom I had been married five years. One day in the month of February 1843, date not remembered, the Prophet invited me to walk with him. During our walk, he said he had learned that there was a sister back in England to whom I was very much attached.[53] I replied there was, but nothing farther than an attachment such as a brother and sister in the church might rightfully entertain for each other. He then said, "Why don't you send for her?" I replied, "in the first place, I have no authority to send for her, and if I had, I have not the means to pay expenses." To this he answered, "I give you authority to send for her, and I will furnish you the means," which he did. This was the first time the

---

50. *Minutes of the Apostles of The Church of Jesus Christ of Latter-day Saints, 1835–1893*, 141–42, December 6, 1847.

51. Ibid., 130, November 30, 1847.

52. Kenney, *Wilford Woodruff's Journal, 1833–1898*, 3:299, December 6, 1847.

53. George D. Smith, ed., *An Intimate Chronicle: The Journals of William Clayton*, 94–95 note 4, theorized that the woman was Sarah Crooks.

Prophet Joseph talked with me on the subject of plural marriage. He informed me that the doctrine and principle was right in the sight of our Heavenly Father, and that it was a doctrine which pertained to Celestial order and glory. After giving me lengthy instructions and information concerning the doctrine of celestial or plural marriage, he concluded his remarks by the words, "It is your privilege to have all the wives you want."

After this introduction, our conversations on the subject of plural marriage were very frequent, and he appeared to take particular pains to inform and instruct me in respect to the principle. He also informed me that he had other wives *living*, besides his first wife Emma, and in particular gave me to understand that Eliza R. Snow, Louisa Beman, Desdamona C. Fullmer, and others were his lawful wives in the sight of Heaven.

William Clayton. Courtesy of LDS Church History Library.

On the 27th of April 1843 the Prophet Joseph Smith married to me Margaret Moon, for time and eternity, at the residence of Elder Heber C. Kimball; and on the 22nd of July 1843, he married to me, according to the order of the church, my first wife Ruth.

On the 1st day of May, 1843, I officiated in the office of an Elder by marrying Lucy Walker to the Prophet Joseph Smith, at his own residence.

During this period the Prophet Joseph took several other wives. Amongst the number I well remember Eliza Partridge, Emily Partridge, Sarah Ann Whitney, Helen Kimball and Flora Woodworth. These all, he acknowledged to me, were his lawful, wedded wives, according to the celestial order. His wife Emma was cognizant of the fact of some, if not all, of these being his wives, and she generally treated them very kindly. . . .

During the last year of his life we were scarcely ever together, alone, but he was talking on the subject, and explaining that doctrine and principles connected with it. He appeared to enjoy great liberty and freedom in his teachings, and also to find great relief in having a few to whom he could unbosom his feelings on that great and glorious subject. From him I learned that the doctrine of plural and celestial marriage is the most holy and important doctrine ever revealed to man on the earth, and that without obedience to that principle no man can ever attain to the fullness of exaltation in Celestial glory.[54]

---

54. William Clayton, Affidavit, February 16, 1874.

Clayton's recollection paints Joseph Smith as discreet but eager to share, not only teachings about plural marriage, but also the much broader theology of "celestial marriage" and the "doctrines and principles connected with it."

Church missionary and future apostle (ordained in 1849) Erastus Snow left two accounts regarding his experience at this same time:

Apostle Erastus Snow. Courtesy LDS Church History Library.

> [About April 1843] I had a very enjoyable visit for about a month with the Prophet and my kindred and brethren. It was during this visit that the Prophet told me what the Lord had revealed to him touching upon baptism for the dead and marriage for eternity, and requiring his chosen and proved servants to take unto themselves wives, and introduced several of those who had been sealed to himself and others of the first elders of the Church. Foremost among the former was my wife's sister Louisa, whose integrity, devotion, and purity of soul were known to all her acquaintances.[55]

In the afternoon of a conference of St. George Stake on June 17, 1883, Snow explained:

> In April 1843 I went to Nauvoo [where] I learned definitely what I had but heard rumored [.] At that time the Prophet Joseph personally taught me the doctrine on the banks of the Mississippi—and showed me several of those who had been seald to him. . . .
>
> I know that I went to the Prophet Joseph Smith and he approved my receiving in this Holy Covenant my wife Minerva, my second wife who is with me here to day—and that he sent his Brother Hyrum to perform the ceremony by which we became husband & wife.[56]

One listener further recorded: "The Prophet Joseph had said to him [Erastus] 'That the law of the Lord concerning these things was exceedingly strict—and many of the Elders would do things because they saw him do them—but many by this means would fall.' He had seen the fulfillment of this in too many instances."[57]

---

55. Franklin R. Snow, "Autobiography of Erastus Snow," 109.
56. Erastus Snow, Address, Sunday, June 17, 1883, 2 p.m., St. George Utah Stake [Conference].
57. Ibid.

Joseph Smith also taught the principle of plural marriage to Mary Ann Price at Orson Hyde's home, but she was initially repelled:

> On the return of Orson Hyde from his mission [December 7, 1842] to Palestine he carried letters of introduction to me and invited me to visit his wife [Marinda Johnson Hyde]. I was there met by Joseph Smith, the Prophet, who, after an interesting conversation introduced the subject of plural marriage and endeavoured to teach me that principle. I resisted it with every argument I could command for, with my tradition, it was most repulsive to my feelings and rendered me very unhappy as I could not reconcile it with the purity of the gospel of Christ.
>
> Mr. Hyde took me home in a carriage and asked me what I thought of it and if I would consent to enter his family? I replied that I could not think of it for a moment.
>
> Thus it rested for awhile and Mr. Hyde married another young lady. In the mean time I was trying to learn the character of the leading men, for I sincerely hoped they were men of God. But, in my mind, plurality of wives [was] a serious question.
>
> I soon learned to my satisfaction, that Mr. Orson Hyde was a conscientious, upright and noble man and became his third wife. Mrs. Hyde had two sweet little girls and I soon learned to love them and their dear mother who in the spring of 1842 [sic—should be 1843] received me into her house as her husband's wife. [I was] \sealed to him by Joseph the Prophet in her presence/ . . .
>
> I will here state that since my first trial in receiving the principle of plural or celestial marriage I have never doubted this being the work of God and *know* that it is the most "glorious dispensation of the fullness of times" destined to usher in the Millennium, when peace shall reign on the earth.[58]

Benjamin F. Johnson wrote two accounts of his introduction to plural marriage in the spring of 1843 by the Prophet:

> On the first day of April A.D. (1843,) eighteen hundred and forty-three, President Joseph Smith, Orson Hyde, and William Clayton and others came from Nauvoo to my residence in Macedonia or Ramus in Hancock Co. Illinois, and were joyfully welcomed by myself and family as our guests.
>
> On the following morning, Sunday April second, President Smith took me by the arm for a walk, leading the way to a secluded spot within an adjacent grove, where to my great surprise, he commenced to open up to me the principle of plural or celestial marriage, but I was more astonished by his asking for my sister Almera to be his wife.
>
> I sincerely believed him to a prophet of God, and I loved him as such, and also for the many evidences of his kindness to me, yet such was the force

---

58. Mary Ann Price Hyde, "Statement, 1880," 2–4.

of my education, and the scorn that I felt towards anything un-virtuous that under the first impulse of my feelings, I looked him calmly, but firmly in the face and told him that, "I had always believed him to be a good man, and wished to believe it still, and would try to;"— and that, "I would take for him a message to my sister, and if the doctrine was true, all would be well, but if I should afterwards learn that it was offered to insult or prostitute my sister I would take his life." With a smile he replied "Benjamin, you will never see that day, but you shall live to <u>know</u> that it is true, and rejoice in it."

He wished me to see my sister and talk to her,—I told him, I did not know what I could say to convince her, he replied, "when you open your mouth, you shall be able to comprehend, and you shall not want for evidence nor words." . . . I called my sister to [a] private audience and with fear and trembling, and feelings that I cannot express commenced to open the Subject to her, when, just as he had promised, the light of the Lord Shone upon my understanding and my tongue was loosed and <u>I</u> at least was convinced of the truth of what I was attempting to teach.

My sister received my testimony, and in a short time afterwards consented to become the wife of President Smith.

Subsequent to this I took her to the City of Nauvoo, where she was married or Sealed for time and eternity to President Joseph Smith, by his brother Hyrum, in the presence of myself, and Louisa Beaman who told me She had also been Sealed or married to the Prophet Joseph.[59]

Benjamin's second account adds some details to the first account:

About the first of April, 1843, the Prophet with some of the Twelve and others came to Macedonia to hold a meeting, which was to convene in a large cabinet shop owned by Brother Joseph E. [Johnson] and myself, and as usual he put up at my house. Early on Sunday morning he said, "Come Brother Bennie, let us have a walk." I took his arm and he led the way into a by-place in the edge of the woods surrounded by tall brush and trees. Here, as we sat down upon a log he began to tell me that the Lord had revealed to him that plural or patriarchal marriage was according to His law; and that the Lord had not only revealed it to him but had commanded him to obey it; that he was required to take other wives; and that he wanted my Sister Almera for one of them, and wished me to see and talk to her upon the subject. If a thunderbolt had fallen at my feet I could hardly have been more shocked or amazed. He saw the struggle in my mind and went on to explain. But the shock was too great for me to comprehend anything, and in almost an agony of feeling I looked him squarely in the eye, and said, while my heart gushed up before him, "Brother Joseph, this is all new to me; it may all be true—you know, but I do not. To my education it is all wrong, but I am going, with the help of the Lord to do just what you say, with this promise to you—that if ever I know you

---

59. Benjamin F. Johnson, Affidavit, March 4, 1870, Joseph Smith, Affidavit Books, 2:3–6.

Post-Bennett Resurgence

do this to degrade my sister I will kill you, as the Lord lives." He looked at me, oh, so calmly, and said, "Brother Benjamin, you will never see that day, but you shall see the day you will know it is true, and you will fulfill the law and greatly rejoice in it." And he said, "At this morning's meeting, I will preach you a sermon that no one but you will understand. And furthermore, I will promise you that when you open your mouth to your sister, it shall be filled."[60]

Benjamin F. Johnson. Courtesy of Greg Kofford Books.

Evidence indicates that the careful spread of the teachings of plural marriage was largely kept secret except among selected Church members. On March 26, 1843, non-Mormon Charlotte Haven wrote to her family: "I have read their holy books, and when I have occasionally attended a meeting, I have taken in all I could."[61] However, she never alluded to anything that could be constructed as plural marriage, suggesting that the teaching was then not widely known.

Lorenzo Snow Embraces Plural Marriage

During 1842–43 while serving a mission in England, future apostle (ordained in 1849) and Church president (1898–1901), Lorenzo Snow reported receiving personal revelation that prepared him to more easily accept the principle:

> It was revealed to me [Lorenzo Snow] before the Prophet Joseph Smith explained it to me. I had been on a mission to England between two and three years and before I left England I was perfectly satisfied in regard to something connected with plural marriage. When I returned to Nauvoo with my company of about 250, it was made manifest to me in reference to the truth of this principle.[62]
>
> The Spiritual wife doctrine came upon me abroad in such a manner I never forget—one blood particular things belong to. after all we r of blood & one flesh all the nations of the earth—Joseph said I command you to go

---

60. Benjamin F. Johnson, *My Life's Review*, 94–95. Benjamin spells his sister's name as both "Almera" and "Almira." I use "Almera" except in quotations.
61. Charlotte Haven, "A Girl's Letters from Nauvoo," 626–27.
62. Lorenzo Snow, "Discourse, May 8, 1899," 548.

& get another wife. I felt as if the grave was better for me than anything—but I was so filled with the Holy Ghost that my wife & Bro: Kimballs wife would upbraid me for highness in those days.[63]

These feelings apparently dovetailed with some rumors of the practice of plural marriage that reached Lorenzo in England from Nauvoo.[64] Upon returning to Nauvoo in April 1843, Lorenzo heard reports about the restoration of plural marriage:

> There was a man by the name of Sherwood,[65] an intimate friend of mine, and he was a great friend to Joseph Smith,—an intimate friend to him in Kirtland, and there I became acquainted with this man Sherwood. . . . Well, I had only returned to Nauvoo [from England] a few days,—two or three, maybe four or five days, and I called on this gentleman Mr. Sherwood, and had quite a chat with him, and he asked me to step out to one side and he said . . . to me, "Lorenzo," calling me by my name,—he called me by my given name, and he said "Lorenzo, I want to tell you something to prepare your mind." He said, "I have no right to tell you this, but I will do it to prepare your mind," and then he went on and explained these principles to me.[66]

Lorenzo Snow. Courtesy LDS Church History Library.

---

63. Salt Lake Stake, High Council Minutes, 1847–1904, February 16, 1849 (Meeting of First Presidency, Twelve, and Seventies).

64. Heber J. Grant, Diary for April 1, 1896, records: "Pres[iden]t Lorenzo Snow stated that he was in England with Bro[ther] Pratt when reports came from Nauvoo to the effect that the doctrine of plural marriage was being taught. Upon his return to Nauvoo in the spring of 1843 he had a long talk with the Prophet Joseph Smith, who fully explained to him the doctrine of plural marriage, and stated that an angel with a drawn sword had visited him and commanded him to go into this principle, and President Smith told Bro[ther] Snow to enter into plural marriage. Pres[iden]t Snow said that the principle was just as true today as it ever was, and bore his testimony to the effect that it will again be practiced by this people."

65. This is undoubtedly Henry Garlie Sherwood, baptized in 1832 and appointed Nauvoo city marshal on February 1841. He was well known to Joseph Smith, being mentioned in D&C 124:81, 132. On another occasion Lorenzo Snow mentioned "Elder Sherwood" as "one of the right hand men of the Prophet." Snow, quoted in "The Grand Destiny of Man," *Deseret News*, July 20, 1901, 22. Sherwood was also a member of the Nauvoo High Council. Collier, *The Nauvoo High Council Minute Books*, 51.

66. Lorenzo Snow, Deposition, Temple Lot Transcript, Respondent's Testimony, Part 3, p. 115, questions 102–5.

Lorenzo's recollection continued: A few days later Joseph Smith "told me the principle of plural marriage for time and eternity was a revelation from God and he was commanded to put it into practice."[67] Lorenzo left several accounts of his experience, each providing different details:

> In the month of April 1843 I returned from my European Mission. A few days after my arrival at Nauvoo, when at President Joseph Smith's house, he said he wished to have some private talk with me, and requested me to walk out with him; It was toward evening, we walked a little distance and sat down on a large log that lay near the bank of the river; he there and then explained to me the doctrine of plurality of wives. He said that the Lord had revealed it unto him, and commanded him to have women sealed to him as wives, that he foresaw the trouble that would follow, and sought to turn away from the commandment, that an angel from heaven appeared before him with a drawn sword, threatening him with destruction unless he went forward and obeyed the commandment.[68]
>
> I was at Joseph Smith's one afternoon on a visit, and after conversing upon different subjects he asked me to walk out with him, as he wished to speak to me privately. We went down to the banks of the Mississippi river and sat down on a log that lay there in the sand. Then and there he explained to me the principle of plural marriage most perfectly and clearly; he told me in regard to the angel coming to him and making this principle known to him, and what would follow if he did not practice it.[69]
>
> At the interview on the bank of the Mississippi, in which the Prophet Joseph explained the doctrine of Celestial Marriage, I felt very humble and in my simplicity besought him earnestly to correct me and set me right if, at any time, he should see me indulging any principle or practice that might tend to lead astray, into forbidden paths; to which he replied, "Brother Lorenzo, the principles of honesty and integrity are founded within you and you will never be guilty of any serious error or wrong, to lead you from the path of duty. The Lord will open your way to receive and obey the law of Celestial marriage. . . .
>
> There is one singular feature in it relating to plural marriage. In regard to that doctrine, allow me first to say I have a knowledge of it as a principle, revealed from God, belonging to the religion we have espoused. I was personally acquainted with Joseph Smith, the Prophet, during twelve or fourteen years, by whom I was first taught this doctrine, and knew him to be a man of truth and honor. But then, I am not dependent on his word for my knowledge of plural marriage; the Lord gave me a divine testimony confirming His teachings, which no man can give nor take away.[70]

---

67. Ibid., p. 114, question 87.
68. Lorenzo Snow, Affidavit, August 28, 1869.
69. Lorenzo Snow, "Discourse, May 8, 1899," 548.
70. Lorenzo Snow, in Eliza R. Snow, *Biography and Family Record of Lorenzo Snow*, 70, 405.

Joseph Smith also told Lorenzo, "that my sister Eliza R. Snow had been sealed to him as his wife for time and eternity. He told me that the Lord would open the way, and I should have women sealed to me as wives. This conversation was prolonged, I think one hour or more, in which he told me many important things."[71] Eliza R. Snow had been concerned how her brother would react to the teaching and her plural marriage:

> While my brother was absent on this, his first mission to Europe [1841–1843], changes had taken place with me, one of eternal import, of which I supposed him to be entirely ignorant. The Prophet Joseph had taught me the principle of plural, or celestial marriage, and I was married to him for time and eternity. In consequence of the ignorance of most of the Saints, as well as people of the world, on this subject, it was not mentioned only privately between the few whose minds were enlightened on the subject.
>
> Not knowing how my brother would receive it, I did not feel at liberty, and did not wish to assume the responsibility of instructing him in the principle of plural marriage, and either maintained silence, or, to his indirect questioning, gave evasive answers, until I was forced, by his cool and distant manner, to feel that he was growing jealous of my sisterly confidence—that I could not confide in his brotherly integrity. I could not endure this—something must be done. I informed my husband of the situation, and requested him to open the subject to my brother. A favorable opportunity soon presented, and, seated together on the lone bank of the Mississippi river, they had a most interesting conversation. The Prophet afterwards told me that he found that my brother's mind had been previously enlightened on the subject in question, and was ready to receive whatever the spirit of revelation from God should impart. That Comforter which Jesus said should "lead into all truth," had penetrated his understanding, and while in England had given him an intimation of what at that time was, to many, a secret. This was the result of living near the Lord, and holding communion with Him.[72]

Parley P. Pratt and Mary Ann Frost Stearns Pratt

While several members of the Quorum of the Twelve returned to America from their missions in Great Britain in the summer of 1841, Parley P. Pratt, his wife, Mary Ann Frost Stearns Pratt, and her sister, Olive Frost, remained behind. His responsibilities ended in late 1842; and on April 12, 1843, they arrived in Nauvoo with a group of English Saints. Mary Ann Stearns Winters, who was the daughter of Mary Ann Frost Stearns and her first husband, Nathan Stearns (d. 1833), recounted their reunion with the Prophet:

---

71. Lorenzo Snow, Affidavit, August 28, 1869.
72. Eliza R. Snow, *Biography and Family Record of Lorenzo Snow*, 68–69.

Parley Parker Pratt. Courtesy LDS Church History Library.

Mary Ann Frost Stearns Pratt. Courtesy International Society of the Daughters of Utah Pioneers.

Brother Joseph came on the boat and into the cabin where our family were. After cordial greetings, he took a seat and taking the little boys, Parley and Nathan, [Parley's sons by his first wife, Thankful, and his second wife, Mary Ann] upon his knees, seemed much affected, Brother Pratt remarking, "We took away three children and have brought back five." Then Brother Joseph said, "Well, well, Brother Parley, you have returned bringing your sheaves with you," the tears streaming down his face. Brother Pratt, seeing the general emotion this caused, said, in a tender jesting fashion, "Why, Brother Smith, if you feel so bad about our coming home, I guess we will have to go back again," tears of joy filling his own eyes. This broke the spell—smiles returned, and joy unbounded filled every heart.[73]

Less than a month after their arrival, Joseph Smith introduced Parley to the principle of plural marriage that had been presented to the other returning apostle-missionaries in 1841. Joseph invited the Pratts and Olive to join a hundred other Saints on a steamer cruise up the Mississippi. Winters's account continues: "On the [ninth of May] 1843,[74] there was an excursion, on the little *Maid of Iowa*, up to Burlington, Iowa, and my father and mother and Aunt

---

73. Mary Ann Stearns Winters, "Mothers in Israel: Returning from England," 577.
74. The original date is given as the "fourth of July," which is incorrect.

Olive went on the pleasure trip. Mother and Aunt Olive were dressed alike and were standing a little distance off, when Brother Joseph said to Brother Parley, 'It is the will of the Lord that those two sisters should never be parted' (meaning that they should both belong to one man)."[75]

It was clear to Mary Ann Winters in retrospect, probably as her mother later told her the story, that the Prophet was subtly referring to the principle of plural marriage; however, it is also possible that Joseph was suggesting to Parley that he should marry Olive, his sister-in-law, since he was already legally married to her sister, Mary Ann. This possibility does not seem likely, however; within weeks, Joseph instructed Parley that Elizabeth Brotherton should become his first plural wife.

A second possibility posits a test for Parley and Mary Ann—that Joseph was hinting that he wished Parley to give him Mary Ann as a plural wife. Such a test would have been similar to that experienced by John Taylor, Heber C. Kimball, and perhaps other apostles. At some unknown date, Joseph Smith was sealed to Olive Frost.[76] If he had already married her or if he had made it known to Parley that he intended to do so, then the Prophet would have, in effect, been telling Parley that he wanted to also be sealed to Mary Ann. Probably Parley was unaware of the "tests" of his fellow apostles and would likely have taken Joseph's words to mean that Joseph was asking Parley to give him Mary Ann as a plural wife. Daughter Mary Ann Winters wrote: "I heard Brother Pratt tell it [this conversation] on his return home, and my mother also told me about it, and remembered it all her life, and frequently spoke about it."[77] Mary Ann may have immediately understood that Joseph Smith wanted her to be sealed to him.

The incompleteness of the historical record prevents a clear reconstruction of the events. However, the Prophet's instructions to Parley concerning plural marriage were apparently not completed on that date nor by June 13, when the Smith family started north to visit Emma's sister in Dixon, Illinois. Impatient to learn more, Parley and Mary Ann asked Hyrum Smith, who had accepted plural marriage in May (see Chapter 24), to seal them for "time and all eternity." Whether Mary Ann or Parley was the primary mover is unclear

---

75. Winters, "Returning from England," 580–81.

76. Mary Ann Frost's biographer, Jayne Winters Fife, hypothesizes: "It is probable that their marriage for time and eternity took place on or near September 17th, the date that she received her Patriarchal Blessing from Hyrum Smith, in which she was promised that she 'shall be blessed in the Covenant with Abraham Isaac and Jacob'." Fife, "Letters from My Husband Parley P. Pratt." This date corresponds to the second period of Emma's acceptance of plural marriage and is a possibility. See Chapter 24.

77. Winters, "Returning from England," 580–81.

from available records. Regardless, on June 23, Hyrum did so.[78] However, this action countered Joseph Smith's plan. According to Andrew Ehat:

> Hyrum's zealousness [in promoting eternal marriage] soon led to some difficulties that would underscore the exclusive authority only his brother, the Prophet, held. Two years before his [May 1843] conversion, Hyrum was appointed by revelation as a prophet, seer, and revelator to the Church. And so he could "act in concert" with Joseph in all the affairs of the church, this revelation nominated him Assistant President of the Church in the place of the fallen Oliver Cowdery. Additionally, Hyrum was promised in this revelation that he would "hold the sealing blessings of [the] church, even the Holy Spirit of promise, whereby [one may be] sealed up unto the day of redemption, that [one] may not fall." When Hyrum became Joseph's chief representative in teaching and administering eternal and plural marriage he assumed because of these earlier appointments that he had the authority to perform these ordinances independent of consultation with Joseph.[79]

Two days later, the Saints in Nauvoo learned that Joseph had been arrested by Missouri law officers who were hurrying him back to that state for indictment. The next few days were a flurry of alarms, quasi-military, and legal maneuverings that resulted in Joseph's release and return to Nauvoo. During his absence, Parley and Mary Ann approached Vilate Kimball for counsel some time prior to July 27. Vilate reported in a letter to her husband, Apostle Heber C. Kimball, the next day:

> I have had a visit from brother Parley and his wife, they are truly converted it appears that J[oseph] has taught him some principles and told him his privilege, and even appointed one for him. I dare not tell you who it is [Elizabeth Brotherton], you would be astonished and I guess some tried. She has been to me for council. I told her I did not wish to advise in such matters. Sister [Mary Ann] Pratt has been rageing against these things. She told me herself that the devil had been in her until within a few days past. She said the Lord had shown her it was all right. She wants Parley to go ahead, says she will do all in her power to help him; they are so ingagued I fear they will run to[o] fast. They ask me many questions on principle. I told them I did not know much and I rather they would go to those that had authority to teach

---

78. Belinda Marden Pratt, Diary, March 11, 1850; Parley P. Pratt, "Family Record of Parley Parker Pratt," March 11, 1850.

79. Andrew F. Ehat, "Joseph Smith's Introduction of Temple Ordinances and the Mormon Succession Question," 66–71; bracketed text Ehat's, internal endnote references removed. See also Elizabeth Brotherton Pratt, Affidavit, August 2, 1869, Joseph F. Smith, Affidavit Books, 1:62; Mary Ann [Frost] Pratt, Affidavit, September 3, 1869, Joseph F. Smith, Affidavit Books, 2:38, affirms Mary Ann's sealing to Parley; Mary Ann [Frost] Pratt, Affidavit, September 3, 1869, Joseph F. Smith, Affidavit Books, 2:40, affirms that she witnessed Elizabeth's sealing to Parley. Both sealings occurred July 24, 1843.

Parley said he and Joseph were interrupted before he got what instruction he wanted, and now he did not know when he should have an opportunity. He seemed unwilling to wait, I told him these were sacred things and he better not make a move until he got more instruction.[80]

Returning to Nauvoo on June 30, Joseph Smith soon learned that Hyrum had sealed Parley and Mary Ann for eternity. The Prophet rebuked his brother and cancelled the sealing because Hyrum was not authorized to exercise that authority without Joseph's permission. Brigham Young referred to the incident in an 1845 letter to Joseph's only surviving brother, William B. Smith:

Joseph said that the sealing power is always vested in one man, and that there never was, nor never would be but one man on the earth at a time to hold the—sealing power—keys of the sealing power in the church, that all sealings must be performed by the man holding the keys or by his dictation, and that man is the president of the church.

Hyrum held the patriarchal office legitimately. . . . Hyrum was counseller . . . but the sealing power was not in Hyrum, legitimately, neither did he act on the sealing principle only as he was dictated by Joseph in every case [sic] This was proven, for Hyrum did in one case [sic] undertake to seal without counsel, & Joseph told him if he did not stop it he would go to hell and all those he sealed with him.[81]

Undoubtedly Joseph Smith was concerned that anyone, even his own brother, would presume to seal without his authorization (D&C 132:7). It is also possible that the Prophet detected an attempt by Parley and/or Mary Ann to evade an Abrahamic-level test that other of the apostles had confronted.[82] Possibly Joseph Smith was testing Parley by hinting that he wanted to be sealed to Mary Ann (as occurred with John and Leonora Taylor and Heber and Vilate Kimball). Presumably if they had relented, Joseph would have sealed Parley and Mary Ann in an eternal marriage (as he did with the Kimballs and Taylors), rather than marrying her himself. However, unaware of the test they were enduring, the two Pratts may have sought to circumvent the possibility of being

---

80. Vilate Kimball, Letter to Heber C. Kimball, June 27–29, 1843; also partly quoted in Helen Mar Kimball Whitney, "Scenes and Incidents at Nauvoo," *Woman's Exponent* 11 (September 15, 1882): 58.

81. Brigham Young, Letter to William Smith, August 10, 1845; see also William Smith, Letter to Brigham Young, August 27, 1844.

82. In council with Wilford Woodruff, George Q. Cannon, Brigham Young Jr., John Henry Smith, John W. Taylor, and George F. Gibbs, on June 25, 1896, Franklin D. Richards referred to "trials or tests to which Prests. B. Young & Jno. Taylor were put by Prest. Joseph the Prophet in Nauvoo, as the plurality & Eternity of the M. Covenant was being revealed. [A]lso what Emma was commanded to abstain from, and O. Hyde's trial also." Franklin D. Richards, Diary, June 25, 1896.

separated by obtaining an eternal sealing from Hyrum.

Whatever the intentions and feelings of the participants, a few weeks later on July 24 at Brigham Young's home, Hyrum Smith, (with Joseph's approval) sealed Parley P. Pratt to his deceased wife, Thankful Halsey, with Mary Ann standing proxy. Joseph had chosen Elizabeth Brotherton, not Olive Frost, as a plural wife for Parley. The Pratts had become acquainted with Elizabeth in Manchester, England, the year before; and the Brotherton family had immigrated to Nauvoo where Elizabeth's younger sister, Martha, was affronted by being invited into plural marriage by Brigham Young. (See Chapter 17.) The Prophet also sealed Mary Ann and Elizabeth Brotherton to Parley in separate ceremonies.[83]

Mary Ann Frost Stearns Pratt in later life. Courtesy of Jayne Winters Fife.

In 1869, Mary Ann testified that her sealing to Parley was for "time and eternity," but questions concerning it have been raised.[84] Wilford Woodruff recorded the following entry (strike-overs his) dating it "Jan 21st 1844":

> Joseph said Concerning Parley P Pratt that He had no wife sealed to him for Eternity and asked if their was any harm for him to have another wife for time & Eternity as He would want a wife in the Resurrection or els his glory would be Cliped. Many arguments He used upon this subject which were rational & consistant. Br Joseph said now what will we do with Elder P P Pratt? He has no wife sealed to him for Eternity. He has one living wife but she had a former Husband and did not wish to be sealed to Parly for Eternity. Now is it not right for Parley to have another wife that can [ ]?[85]

In fact, at the time Woodruff made this entry, Parley had been sealed to two wives, independent of the status of his sealing to Mary Ann Frost (his

---

83. Mary Ann [Frost Stearns] Pratt, Affidavit, September 3, 1869, in Joseph F. Smith, Affidavit Books, 2:38, 3:38, attest to her sealing to Parley P. Pratt. She made two additional affidavits attesting to Elizabeth Brotherton's sealing to Parley P. Pratt," Joseph F. Smith, Affidavit Books, 2:40, 3:40. See also Winters, "Mothers in Israel: Autobiographical Sketch of Mary Ann Stearns Winters," 643.

84. Mary Ann [Frost Stearns] Pratt, "Affidavit," September 3, 1869, Joseph F. Smith, Affidavit Books, 2:38, 3:38, affirms her sealing to Parley P. Pratt.

85. Scott G. Kenny, ed., *Wilford Woodruff's Journal, 1833–1898*, 2:340, January 21 1844.

deceased spouse, Thankful, and his plural wife Elizabeth Brotherton). Joseph Smith was not present that day, and Woodruff may have marked out the quotation purportedly from Joseph because he later learned it was inaccurate. Or possibly other undefined factors prompted the self-censorship.

Several authors have written that Mary Ann Frost was sealed to Joseph Smith.[86] Mary Ann Frost Stearns Pratt's biographer, Jayne Winters Fife, believes that such a sealing is unlikely for two reasons.[87] First, proponents list July 24, 1843, as the date of Mary Ann's sealing to the Prophet but without citing any evidence.[88] In 1869, as noted, Mary Ann signed an affidavit saying she was sealed to Parley P. Pratt on July 24, 1843—not Joseph Smith.[89] Second, Fife writes:

> On Feb 6, 1846, Mary, who had not been resealed in the [Nauvoo] temple to Parley because of their estrangement over his secret plural wives, asked him to allow her to be sealed "over the Altar in the Temple before it would be closed." He "told her it was her privilege to make a choice, and that she could be sealed to anyone she chose. She replied that he would be her choice but she wanted to know the mind and will of the Lord." At the temple, they consulted with Brigham Young, who understood their current situation and advised that Mary be sealed to Joseph for eternity. Parley remained responsible for her for time.[90]

Throughout her life, Mary Ann struggled mightily with plural marriage, and her relationship with Parley also suffered. In 1850, Parley recounted an embittered version of their relationship problems:

> Mary Ann Frost who was sealed to Parley P. Pratt for time and all eternity at the house of Hyram Smith and by his hand in Nauvoo, June 23, 1843. Afterward alienated from her husband and taught by all manner of falsehoods to destroy his influence and character. But repenting of these things and confessing them before President B. Young in the temple

---

86. George D. Smith, *Nauvoo Polygamy: ". . . but we called it celestial marriage,"* 207–9; Fawn M. Brodie, *No Man Knows My History: The Life of Joseph Smith, the Mormon Prophet*, 484; Gary James Bergera, "Identifying the Earliest Mormon Polygamists, 1841–1844," 67; Lyndon W. Cook, ed., *Nauvoo Marriages, Proxy Sealing, 1843–1846*, 12, 17; Lisle G Brown, *Nauvoo Sealings, Adoptions, and Anointings: A Comprehensive Register of Persons Receiving LDS Temple Ordinances, 1841–1846*, 285.

87. Jayne Winters Fife, "Letters from My Husband Parley P. Pratt," forthcoming.

88. George Smith, *Nauvoo Polygamy*, 206–9; Brodie, *No Man Knows My History*, 484; Cook, *Nauvoo Marriages, Proxy Sealing 1843–1846*, 12, 17; Brown, *Nauvoo Sealings, Adoptions, and Anointings*, 285.

89. Mary Ann [Frost Stearns] Pratt, Affidavit," September 3, 1869, in Joseph F. Smith, Affidavit Books, 2:38, 3:38.

90. Jayne Winters Fife, email to Brian Hales, June 5, 2009. She is quoting John Taylor, Letter to Moroni L. Pratt, October 29, 1886, First Presidency Letterpress Copybook, LDS Church History Library, restricted.

at Nauvoo and solemnly covenanting to take back her words of falsehood wherever they had been spoken she was frankly forgiven by her husband and was by mutual consent of parties and by the advice of President Young sealed to Joseph Smith (the deceased President of the Church) for eternity and to her former husband for time, as proxy. This ordinance took place about the eighth [sic—should be the sixth] of Feby 1846 by the hand of B. Young in the temple at Nauvoo.[91]

The absence of adequate documentation prevents a full evaluation of the interactions among the Prophet, Parley P. Pratt, and Mary Ann Frost. However, the known evidence is not sufficient to identify her as a plural wife of Joseph Smith during his lifetime.

Summary

Late 1842 represented a brief hiatus in the growth of plural marriage in Nauvoo due to the influence of John C. *Bennett's* writings including his *History of the Saints* published in late October. However, early in 1843 the Prophet once again promoted the expansion of polygamy by sharing his teachings with other men, seven of whom married plural wives.[92] Allegations that Udney Jacob's *The Peace Maker* was commissioned by Joseph Smith appear to be unfounded. A review of the interactions between Parley P. Pratt, Mary Ann Frost Pratt, and Joseph Smith is difficult due to a lack of available documentation. However, it appears the Prophet may have may have been testing Parley's convictions as he had with John Taylor and Heber C. Kimball.

---

91. Belinda Marden Pratt, Diary, March 11, 1850.

92. Included were Willard Richards, William D. Huntington, Orson Hyde, Lorenzo Dow Young, Joseph Bates Noble, William Clayton, and Benjamin F. Johnson. See Chapter 29.

Also by Brian C. Hales

Modern Polygamy and Mormon Fundamentalism: The Generations after the Manifesto

Paperback, ISBN: 978-1-58958-109-8

Winner of the John Whitmer Historical Association's Smith-Pettit Best Book Award

This fascinating study seeks to trace the historical tapestry that is early Mormon polygamy, details the official discontinuation of the practice by the Church, and, for the first time, describes the many zeal-driven organizations that arose in the wake of that decision. Among the polygamous groups discussed are the LeBaronites, whose "blood atonement" killings sent fear throughout Mormon communities in the late seventies and the eighties; the FLDS Church, which made news recently over its construction of a compound and temple in Texas (Warren Jeffs, the leader of that church, is now standing trial on two felony counts after his being profiled on America's Most Wanted resulted in his capture); and the Allred and Kingston groups, two major factions with substantial membership statistics both in and out of the United States. All these fascinating histories, along with those of the smaller independent groups, are examined and explained in a way that all can appreciate.

Praise for *Modern Polygamy and Mormon Fundamentalism*:

"This book is the most thorough and comprehensive study written on the sugbject to date, providing readers with a clear, candid, and broad sweeping overview of the history, teachings, and practices of modern fundamentalist groups."
—Alexander L. Baugh, Associate Professor of Church History and Doctrine, Brigham Young University

Made in the USA
Las Vegas, NV
20 March 2025